PRODUCTION & OPERATIONS MANAGEMENT

AUTHOR

Dr. Navin Kumar Dev

Asst. Professor

Dayalbagh Educational Institute

Uttar Pradesh - 282005

REVIEWER

Prabhas Bhardwaj

Professor,

Mechanical Engineering Deptt.,

IIT (BHU) VARANASI,

Varanasi-221005, UP, India

All India Council for Technical Education

Nelson Mandela Marg, Vasant Kunj, New Delhi, India

Dear Readers,

To prevent the piracy, this book is secured with HIGH SECURITY HOLOGRAM on the front title cover. In case you don't find the hologram on the front cover title, please write us to at contact@khannabooks.com or whatsapp us at +91-99109 09320 and avail special gift voucher for yourself.

Specimen of Hologram on front Cover title:

Moreover, there is a SPECIAL DISCOUNT COUPON for you with EVERY HOLOGRAM.

How to avail this SPECIAL DISCOUNT:

Step 1: Scratch the hologram

Step 2: Under the scratch area, your "coupon code" is available

Step 3: Logon to www.khannabooks.com

Step 4: Use your "coupon code" in the shopping cart and get your copy at a special discount

Step 5: Enjoy your reading!

ISBN: 978-93-5538-458-4

Book Code: UG489EN

Production & Operations Management

by Dr. Navin Kumar Dev

First Edition: 2026

Originally Published by:

All India Council for Technical Education, Ministry of Education, GOI

Exclusively Published & Distributed by:

Khanna Book Publishing Co. (P) Ltd.

4C/4344, Ansari Road, Daryaganj,
New Delhi (INDIA)

Visit us at: **www.khannabooks.com**

Write us at: **contact@khannabooks.com**

To view complete list of books,
Please scan the QR Code:

Printed in Bharat.

प्रो. टी. जी. सीताराम
अध्यक्ष
Prof. T. G. Sitharam
Chairman

अखिल भारतीय तकनीकी शिक्षा परिषद्
(भारत सरकार का एक सांविधिक निकाय)
(शिक्षा मंत्रालय, भारत सरकार)
नेल्सन मंडेला मार्ग, वसंत कुंज, नई दिल्ली–110070
दूरभाष : 011–26131498
ई–मेल : chairman@aicte-india.org

ALL INDIA COUNCIL FOR TECHNICAL EDUCATION
(A STATUTORY BODY OF THE GOVT. OF INDIA)
(Ministry of Education, Govt. of India)
Nelson Mandela Marg, Vasant Kunj, New Delhi-110070
Phone : 011-26131498
E-mail : chairman@aicte-india.org

FOREWORD

Engineers are the backbone of any modern society. They are the ones responsible for the marvels as well as the improved quality of life across the world. Engineers have driven humanity towards greater heights in a more evolved and unprecedented manner.

The All India Council for Technical Education (AICTE), have spared no efforts towards the strengthening of the technical education in the country. AICTE is always committed towards promoting quality Technical Education to make India a modern developed nation emphasizing on the overall welfare of mankind.

An array of initiatives has been taken by AICTE in last decade which have been accelerated now by the National Education Policy (NEP) 2020. The implementation of NEP under the visionary leadership of Hon'ble Prime Minister of India envisages the provision for education in regional languages to all, thereby ensuring that every graduate becomes competent enough and is in a position to contribute towards the national growth and development through innovation & entrepreneurship.

One of the spheres where AICTE had been relentlessly working since past couple of years is providing high quality original technical contents at Under Graduate & Diploma level prepared and translated by eminent educators in various Indian languages to its aspirants. For students pursuing 2nd year of their Engineering education, AICTE has identified 87 books, which shall be translated into 12 Indian languages - Hindi, Tamil, Gujarati, Odia, Bengali, Kannada, Urdu, Punjabi, Telugu, Marathi, Assamese & Malayalam. In addition to the English medium, books in different Indian Languages are going to support the students to understand the concepts in their respective mother tongue.

On behalf of AICTE, I express sincere gratitude to all distinguished authors, reviewers and translators from the renowned institutions of high repute for their admirable contribution in a record span of time.

AICTE is confident that these outcomes based original contents shall help aspirants to master the subject with comprehension and greater ease.

T. G. Sitharam

(Prof. T. G. Sitharam)

ACKNOWLEDGEMENT

I bow low and dedicate this book to Most Revered Param Guru Huzur *Dr. M. B. Lal Sahab*, the August founder of Dayalbagh Educational Institute, Dayalbagh. I also express my deepest and infinite gratitude to Most Revered *Prof. Prem Saran Satsangi Sahab*, Chairman Advisory Committee on Education, Dayalbagh, for His paternal guidance, incessant encouragement, and unbounded grace bestowed on me which has crowned my humble efforts with success throughout my life.

I am grateful to the authorities of AICTE, particularly Prof. T. G. Sitharam, Chairman; Dr. Abhay Jere, Vice-Chairman; Prof. Rajive Kumar, Member-Secretary, and Dr. Sunil Luthra, Director, Training and Learning Bureau for their planning to publish the book on Production & Operations Management for UG Degree Course in Mechanical Engineering.

I sincerely acknowledge the valuable contributions of the reviewer of the book Prof. Prabhas Bhardwaj, Professor, Department of Mechanical Engineering, IIT Banaras Hindu University, India, for making it students' friendly and giving a better shape in an artistic manner. In fact, he guided from the very beginning as a Reviewer of this book on Production and Operations Management, providing many important suggestions wherever required and also giving his critical comments throughout. This book is an outcome of various suggestions of AICTE members, experts, and authors who shared their opinion and thought to further develop the education on Production and Operations Management in our country. Acknowledgements are due to the contributors and different workers in this field whose published books, review articles, papers, photographs, footnotes, references and other valuable information enriched us at the time of writing the book.

Last but not the least, I wish to thank my wife Shalini, without whose constant support, encouragement and unbounded patience this book would never have been possible. Thanks also to my daughters Aishna and Neshtha, and my granddaughter Aarya, my symbols of love and innocence. The constant help and advice of my parents will of course always be remembered.

Dr. Navin K. Dev

PREFACE

Welcome to the world of Production & Operations Management! This book includes the topics recommended by AICTE, in a very systematic and orderly manner serves as your comprehensive guide to understanding the principles, concepts, and applications of Production and Operations Management. Whether you are a student embarking on a journey of learning or a professional seeking to refresh your knowledge, this book is designed to provide you with a solid foundation in this fascinating field.

In today's rapidly evolving business environment, understanding the interplay between manufacturing processes, project management, and operational strategies is crucial for achieving success. This book provides a comprehensive guide to the concepts, technologies, and techniques necessary to navigate the complexities of modern production systems, project management, and operational efficiency. It begins by exploring the managerial decisions made at each stage of the production life cycle, focusing on how decisions impact both product quality and cost efficiency. It then delves into the critical role of production systems, including the advanced capabilities of CNC (Computer Numerical Control) technology, which has revolutionized mass production by enabling precision and scalability. This section also examines the tooling necessary for CNC machines and outlines the roles of supervisors and managers in optimizing these systems for maximum productivity.

The book then shifts to project management fundamentals, providing readers with a thorough understanding of the project life cycle, from the initial request for proposals to the establishment of a project team and the definition of scope and terms of reference. A key component of successful project management is the ability to create a detailed work breakdown structure and manage risks effectively. The concepts of project scheduling, including key techniques like the Critical Path Method (CPM) and Program Evaluation and Review Technique (PERT), are explored in-depth, offering readers practical strategies to optimize time-cost tradeoffs and culminate in a strategic plan for project closure.

Next, the book addresses production planning, starting with an exploration of external and internal factors that influence production planning decisions. Key topics such as aggregate planning techniques, master scheduling, and Material Requirements Planning (MRP) are discussed, alongside strategies for applying production planning techniques and assessing their impact on overall operational performance. The role of inventory management is also covered extensively, including the identification of different inventory types, the application of Economic Order Quantity (EOQ), and strategies for production quantity models and information-based ordering decisions.

The principles of Just-In-Time (JIT) manufacturing are explored, detailing its modules, the pull system, and the Kanban system, with an emphasis on vendor relationships and challenges in JIT implementation. The book also discusses the evolution of supply chain management (SCM), its objectives, and how companies can mitigate the bullwhip effect and implement sustainable practices. Forecasting plays a vital role in operational efficiency, and this book offers insights into both qualitative and quantitative forecasting methods, helping readers refine their ability to predict demand and improve supply chain responsiveness.

Further, the book examines facility layout and material handling systems, highlighting the importance of selecting appropriate equipment and optimizing layouts to improve workflow. The integration of lean principles and green manufacturing practices is also discussed, showcasing how organizations can adopt sustainable practices while reducing waste and improving performance metrics. Quality management is another critical focus, with a detailed exploration of Total Quality Management (TQM), including key quality gurus' contributions, the PDSA cycle, and the costs of quality.

The final sections of the book explore the cutting-edge technologies that are shaping the future of manufacturing, such as Industry 4.0, smart manufacturing systems, additive manufacturing, and the applications of AI and machine learning in operations. The book also touches on human resource management principles, team dynamics, and navigating flexible work arrangements. It offers valuable insights into logistics, with a deep dive into transportation models, linear programming applications, and network theory, helping readers develop analytical skills essential for solving real-world operational problems.

Overall, this book is designed to equip students, professionals, and managers with the knowledge and tools necessary to understand and implement modern manufacturing and management strategies, enabling them to succeed in an increasingly complex and competitive landscape. We would like to express our gratitude to the countless researchers, educators, and engineers who have contributed to the field of Production and Opeations Management over the years. Their collective efforts have paved the way for the advancements we witness today. We hope that this book will serve as a tribute to their contributions and inspire you to further explore the exciting possibilities of Production and Operations Management.

We sincerely hope that this book will be a valuable resource in your journey of learning and discovery. We invite you to immerse yourself in the world of Production and Operations Mangement and embark on an adventure that will empower you to shape the future.

Happy reading! Happy Learning!

Dr. Navin K. Dev

OUTCOME BASED EDUCATION

For the implementation of an outcome based education the first requirement is to develop an outcome based curriculum and incorporate an outcome based assessment in the education system. By going through outcome based assessments evaluators will be able to evaluate whether the students have achieved the outlined standard, specific, and measurable outcomes. With the proper incorporation of outcome based education there will be a definite commitment to achieve a minimum standard for all learners without giving up at any level. At the end of the programme running with the aid of outcome based education, a student will be able to arrive at the following outcomes:

PO1. Engineering knowledge: Apply the knowledge of mathematics, science, engineering fundamentals, and an engineering specialization to the solution of complex engineering problems.

PO2. Problem analysis: Identify, formulate, review research literature, and analyze complex engineering problems reaching substantiated conclusions using first principles of mathematics, natural sciences, and engineering sciences.

PO3. Design / development of solutions: Design solutions for complex engineering problems and design system components or processes that meet the specified needs with appropriate consideration for the public health and safety, and the cultural, societal, and environmental considerations.

PO4. Conduct investigations of complex problems: Use research-based knowledge and research methods including design of experiments, analysis and interpretation of data, and synthesis of the information to provide valid conclusions.

PO5. Modern tool usage: Create, select, and apply appropriate techniques, resources, and modern engineering and IT tools including prediction and modeling to complex engineering activities with an understanding of the limitations.

PO6. The engineer and society: Apply reasoning informed by the contextual knowledge to assess societal, health, safety, legal and cultural issues and the consequent responsibilities relevant to the professional engineering practice.

PO7. Environment and sustainability: Understand the impact of the professional engineering solutions in societal and environmental contexts, and demonstrate the knowledge of, and need for sustainable development.

PO8. Ethics: Apply ethical principles and commit to professional ethics and responsibilities and norms of the engineering practice.

PO9. Individual and team work: Function effectively as an individual, and as a member or leader in diverse teams, and in multidisciplinary settings.

PO10. Communication: Communicate effectively on complex engineering activities with the engineering community and with society at large, such as, being able to comprehend and write effective reports and design documentation, make effective presentations, and give and receive clear instructions.

PO11. Project management and finance: Demonstrate knowledge and understanding of the engineering and management principles and apply these to one's own work, as a member and leader in a team, to manage projects and in multidisciplinary environments.

PO12. Life-long learning: Recognize the need for, and have the preparation and ability to engage in independent and life-long learning in the broadest context of technological change.

COURSE OUTCOMES

After completion of the course the students will be able to:

CO-1: Students will develop a thorough understanding to make informed managerial decisions across the production life cycle, and understand CNC technology's role in mass production. It also covers CNC equipment, tooling, and the essential roles of supervisors and managers in optimizing production processes.

CO-2: Students will gain expertise in production planning techniques, aggregate planning, and project scheduling methodologies such as the Critical Path Method (CPM) and Program Evaluation and Review Technique (PERT), enabling them to optimize efficiency.

CO-3: Learners will acquire the skills necessary to evaluate supply chain dynamics, mitigate the bullwhip effect, and implement effective inventory management systems, including Just-In-Time (JIT) methodologies and Material Requirement Planning (MRP).

CO-4: Students will apply lean manufacturing principles, Total Quality Management (TQM) practices, and analyze their impact on operational performance and sustainability, preparing them to implement improvements in manufacturing processes.

CO-5: Learners will understand the implications of Industry 4.0 technologies, including AI, blockchain, and smart manufacturing systems, and assess their impact on modern operations management.

CO-6: Students will develop analytical capabilities in linear programming, transportation models, queuing theory, and network model, enabling them to formulate and solve complex operational problems effectively.

Course Outcomes	Expected Mapping with Programme Outcomes (1- Weak Correlation; 2- Medium correlation; 3- Strong Correlation)											
	PO-1	PO-2	PO-3	PO-4	PO-5	PO-6	PO-7	PO-8	PO-9	PO-10	PO-11	PO-12
CO-1	2	2	2	2	1	2	2	1	2	2	2	1
CO-2	3	3	2	2	2	2	2	2	2	3	3	2
CO-3	3	3	2	3	2	2	3	2	3	3	3	2
CO-4	3	2	3	2	2	2	3	3	2	3	3	2
CO-5	2	3	3	3	3	3	3	2	3	3	3	2
CO-6	3	3	3	3	3	3	2	2	3	3	3	3

GUIDELINES FOR TEACHERS

To implement Outcome Based Education (OBE) knowledge level and skill set of the students should be enhanced. Teachers should take a major responsibility for the proper implementation of OBE. Some of the responsibilities (not limited to) for the teachers in OBE system may be as follows:

- Within reasonable constraint, they should manoeuvre time to the best advantage of all students.
- They should assess the students only upon certain defined criterion without considering any other potential ineligibility to discriminate them.
- They should try to grow the learning abilities of the students to a certain level before they leave the institute.
- They should try to ensure that all the students are equipped with the quality knowledge as well as competence after they finish their education.
- They should always encourage the students to develop their ultimate performance capabilities.
- They should facilitate and encourage group work and team work to consolidate newer approach.
- They should follow Blooms taxonomy in every part of the assessment.

Bloom's Taxonomy

Level	Teacher should Check	Student should be able to	Possible Mode of Assessment
Create	Students ability to create	Design or Create	Mini project
Evaluate	Students ability to justify	Argue or Defend	Assignment
Analyse	Students ability to distinguish	Differentiate or Distinguish	Project/Lab Methodology
Apply	Students ability to use information	Operate or Demonstrate	Technical Presentation/ Demonstration
Understand	Students ability to explain the ideas	Explain or Classify	Presentation/Seminar
Remember	Students ability to recall (or remember)	Define or Recall	Quiz

GUIDELINES FOR STUDENTS

Students should take equal responsibility for implementing the OBE. Some of the responsibilities (not limited to) for the students in OBE system are as follows:

- Students should be well aware of each UO before the start of a unit in each and every course.
- Students should be well aware of each CO before the start of the course.
- Students should be well aware of each PO before the start of the programme.
- Students should think critically and reasonably with proper reflection and action.
- Learning of the students should be connected and integrated with practical and real life consequences.
- Students should be well aware of their competency at every level of OBE.

ABBREVIATIONS AND SYMBOLS

List of Abbreviations

Abbreviations	Full Form
CO	Course outcome
PO	Programme outcome
UO	Unit outcome
CNC	Computer Numerical Control
CAD	Computer-Aided Design
CAM	Computer Aided Manufacturing
HMLV	High-Mix Low-Volume
RFP	Request for Proposal
WBS	Work Breakdown Structure
PMI	Project Management Institute
DPR	Detailed Project Report
AHP	Analytic Hierarchy Process
RBS	Risk Breakdown Structure
PND	Project Network Diagram
CPM	Critical Path Method
PERT	Program Evaluation and Review Technique
AOA	Activity-on-Arrow
AON	Activity-on-Node
PPC	Production Planning and Control
MTS	Make-to-Stock
ATS	Assemble-to-Stock
BTO	Build-to-Order
MTO	Make-to-Order
ERP	Enterprise Resource Planning
MRP	Material Requirement Planning
BOM	Bill of Materials
FCFS	First come First Served

Abbreviations	Full Form
SPT	Shortest Processing Time
EDD	Earliest Due Date
CR	Critical Ratio
S/O	Slack per Operation (S/O)
MPS	Master Production Schedule
ATP	Available-to-Promise
EOQ	Economic Order Quantity
WIP	Work in Process
POS	Point-of-Sale
JIT	Just-in-Time
ROP	Reorder Point
FBD	Family-Based Dispatching
VCM	Virtual Cellular Manufacturing
ICT	Information and Communication Technology
VMI	Vendor-Managed Inventory
CONWIP	CONstant Work in Process
SCM	Supply Chain Management
CRP	Continuous Inventory Review Policy
EDI	Electronic Data Interchange
3PL	Third-Party Logistics
CODP	Customer Order Decoupling Point
WMS	Warehouse Management System
FMCG	Fast-moving Consumer Goods
WCED	World Commission on Environment and Development
TBL	Triple Bottom Line
SSCM	Sustainable Supply Chain Management
GSCM	Green Supply Chain Management
GPS	Global Positioning System
RFID	Radio Frequency Identification
GT	Group Technology

Abbreviations	Full Form
PFA	Production Flow Analysis
FMS	Flexible Manufacturing System
AGV	Automated Guided Vehicles
AS/RS	Automated Storage and Retrieval System
LGV	Laser Guided Vehicle
LiDAR	Light Detection and Ranging
VSM	Value Stream Mapping
PDCA	Plan-Do-Check-Act
SMED	Single Minute Exchange of Die
DfE	Design for Environment
LCA	Life Cycle Assessment
MTBF	Mean Time Between Failures
MTTR	Mean Time To Repair
FMEA	Failure Mode and Effects Analysis
TQM	Total Quality Management
IoT	Internet of Things
CPS	Cyber-Physical Systems
AI	Artificial Intelligence
CPPS	Cyber-Physical Production Systems
WSN	Wireless Sensor Networks
DNN	Deep Neural Networks
HMI	Human Machine Interface
CSaaS	Control System as a Service
AM	Additive Manufacturing
ML	Machine Learning
HRM	Human Resource Management
LP	Linear Programming
MODI	Modified Distribution
AP	Assignment Problem
TSP	Traveling Salesman Problem

List of Symbols

Symbols	Description
ES	Earliest Start
EF	Earliest Finish
LS	Latest Start
LF	Latest Finish
t_m	Most Likely Duration
t_o	Most Optimistic Duration
t_p	Most Pessimistic Duration
σ^2	Variance
TE	Expected Duration Times
σ	Standard Deviation
z	Number of standard deviations away from the mean for a specific confidence level
C_c	Carrying Cost
C_o	Ordering Cost
D	Annual Demand
Q	Order size
p	Daily Production rate
d	Daily Demand rate
P	Price of item per unit
LT	Lead Time
R	Reorder point
S	Safety Stock Level
σ_{dLT}	Lead time demand standard deviation
σ_d	Standard deviation of demand
σ_{LT}	Standard deviation of lead time
C_s	Shortage cost
C_e	Excess cost
MA	Simple Moving Average
WMA	Weighted Moving Average
W_i	Weight for period i
F_t	Forecast of current period
α	Weighting factor

Symbols	Description
TAF	Trend adjusted forecast
β	Smoothing constant for trend
MSE	Mean Squared Error
MAD	Mean Absolute Deviation
MAPE	Mean Absolute Percent Error
TS	Tracking Signal
e_t	Error in time t
RSFE	Running sum of forecast errors
C_a	Actual Cycle time
C_d	Desired Cycle time
E	Efficiency of assembly line
N	Number of workstations
R_s	Reliability of the system
C_p	Capability Ratio
C_{pk}	Capability Index
USL	Upper specification limit
LSL	Lower specification limit
$S_1, S_2, \ldots S_n$	Slack variables
M/M/1:∞/FIFO	Poisson arrival/Exponential service/Single-server: Infinite population/First-in-first-out
M/M/1:N/FIFO	Poisson arrival/Exponential service/Single-server: Finite population/First-in-first-out
M/M/C:∞/FIFO	Poisson arrival/Exponential service/Multiple-server: Infinite population/First-in-first-out
λ	Arrival rate
μ	Service rate
P_n	Probability of customer in the system $n = 0,1, \ldots n$
U	Utilization factor
L_q	Average number of customers in the queue
W	Waiting time in the system
W_q	Waiting time in queue
W_b	Expected time in queue for busy system

LIST OF FIGURES

Unit 1

Unit 2

Unit 3

Unit 4

Unit 5

Unit 6

Unit 7

Unit 8

Unit 9

Unit 10

Unit 11

Unit 12

Unit 13

Unit 14

Unit 15

Unit 19

Unit 20

LIST OF TABLES

CONTENTS

UNIT 1

INTRODUCTION TO PRODUCTION AND OPERATIONS MANAGEMENT

UNIT SPECIFICS

This unit elaborately discusses the following topics:

- Managerial decisions across the production life cycle
- Types of production system
- CNC Production equipments
- CNC in mass production
- Tooling for CNC machines
- Role of production supervisor and production manager

The topics' state-of-the-art are covered in order to increase understanding of how the topics are applied in actual manufacturing systems and to spark additional interest and innovation. There are several multiple-choice questions and short- and long-answer questions that are divided into two groups based on Bloom's taxonomy's lower and higher orders. The unit includes a list of references and recommended readings for the purpose of gaining additional knowledge. It's crucial to remember that certain parts feature QR codes that can be scanned to obtain pertinent supporting material on a variety of interesting subjects.

A supplemental section ("Along the..."), carefully designed for the book's user's advantage, has been included following the unit's related topic based on the content. This material mostly focuses on the fascinating facts about the subject matter covered in the contemporary intriguing industrial setting, which adds to the topic's interest.

RATIONALE

This unit provides a comprehensive exploration of essential concepts in modern manufacturing management. Understanding managerial decisions across the production life cycle is crucial for optimizing product development and market readiness. By examining different types of production systems, readers gain insights into selecting the most effective approach for specific manufacturing needs. The unit further highlights the significance of CNC production equipment and its transformative role in mass production, emphasizing enhanced precision and efficiency. Additionally, an in-depth look at tooling for CNC machines underscores its critical influence on production quality. Finally, clarifying the roles of production supervisors and managers ensures that readers appreciate the importance of leadership and team dynamics in achieving operational success. Collectively, these topics provide a foundational framework for effective production management in today's technologically advanced landscape.

UNIT OUTCOMES

List of outcomes of this unit is as follows:

U1-UO1 – Understand Managerial Decisions at each stage of the production life cycle

U1-UO2 – Identify Production Systems

U1-UO3 – Describe CNC Equipment

U1-UO4 – Role of CNC technology in mass production

U1-UO5 – Explore Tooling for CNC Machines

U1-UO6 – Define Roles of Supervisors and Managers

UNIT-1 Outcomes	EXPECTED MAPPING WITH COURSE OUTCOMES (*1-Weak Correlation; 2-Medium Correlation; 3-Strong Correlation*)					
	CO-1	**CO-2**	**CO-3**	**CO-4**	**CO-5**	**CO-6**
U1-UO1	3	2	2	2	2	2
U1-UO2	3	2	2	2	3	2
U1-UO3	3	1	-	-	2	-
U1-UO4	3	2	3	3	3	1
U1-UO5	3	-	1	2	2	1
U1-UO6	3	1	-	1	1	-

1.1 INTRODUCTION

Technology is becoming an essential component of production management in the contemporary business world. Traditional production techniques have been completely transformed by automation, data analytics, and artificial intelligence. This has made it possible to make decisions more quickly, with greater precision, and with less human error. To have a competitive edge, production managers must be aware of these technical developments and successfully incorporate them. Production management arranges a sophisticated management of resources, procedures, and strategies from the time an idea is conceived until the time the finished product is released onto the market.

As the foundation of manufacturing, production management encompasses the coordination of resources, procedures, and tactics to realize a product. It involves a complex interaction between action and vision, integrating strategic planning, effective resource management, accurate coordination, and a dedication to quality. Maximizing effectiveness and minimizing expenses is a primary goal of production management. This calls for a keen observation for finding production process bottlenecks and optimizing workflows. Production managers work to shorten lead times, get rid of inefficient procedures, and eventually improve the overall effeciency and effectiveness of the production cycle.

We define Production system as:

The arrangement made up of resources like facilities, machinery, and equipment that use technology and processes to convert resources into valuable output.

In other words, we can think of it as a mechanism that can satisfy market demand by converting inputs into outputs. It is primarily concerned with the operations/production function's system component. It consists of the three important parts (Fig. 1.1):

1. Input: Labor, Capital, Machines, Equipment, and Tools
2. Process of Conversion
3. Output: Goods and Services

Production is the process of converting multiple inputs into one output, or the product. A system is a collection of interconnected elements that functions as a whole. Production systems are used by businesses to meet the needs of their intended market. But throughout time, the needs of the clients continue to change. As a result, the production's requirements likewise alter in tandem.

Fig. 1.1 System approach of production

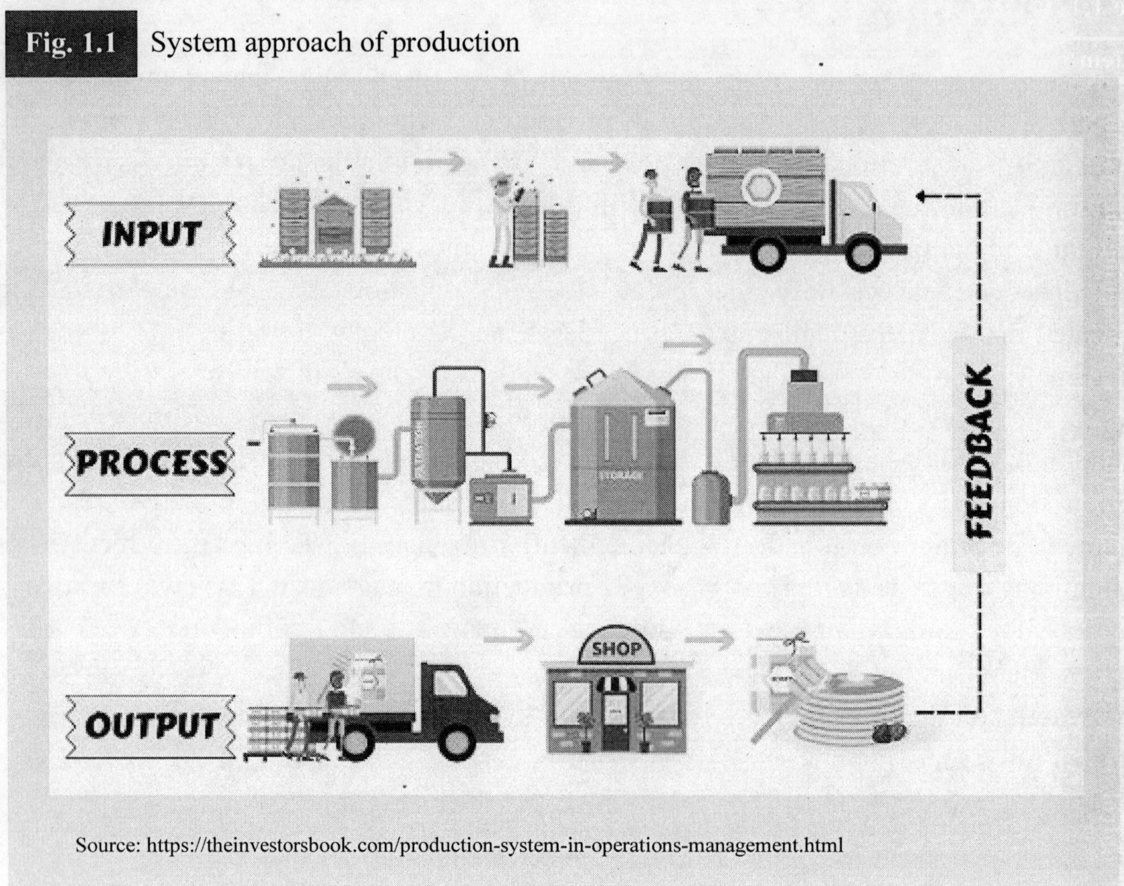

Source: https://theinvestorsbook.com/production-system-in-operations-management.html

These days, a lot of businesses prioritize customer satisfaction and continuous improvement. It is necessary to keep looking for ways to make the production system better. To do this, one must have a thorough awareness of the most recent advancements in production system management. The company's current priorities include consumer satisfaction with regard to availability, variety, and performance, in addition to profitability. The companies need to take some crucial decisions concerning production are: (i) Designing the system, (ii) Operations, and (iii) Planning and control. These are elaborated in Table 1.1 according to different phases.

Table 1.1 Making managerial decisions across the production life cycle

System	Stage	Decision-Making
Designing the system	Conception of the system	• Identification of goals • Identification of product and services
	Design of the product and selection of the process	• Product specifications • Technology to be used
	Design of the operation	• Facility location • Facility layout • Maintenance policies • Quality assurance
Operation	System's action plans	• Formulation of Job assignment for each worker • Process planning of each part • Calculation of wages of workers
	Initiating the system	• Operations starting • Duration to reach desired output
Planning and control	The steady-state system	• How to operate the system • Methods for enhancing the system • How to handle issues related to operations
	Revision of the system	Revision of system in view of changes in: • New technology • Newer method of manufacturing/services • New product variants • Innovation • Environmental issues
	The system's termination	• How to terminate the system (closed-loop or an open system) • Policy of salvaging of resources.

1.2 TYPES OF PRODUCTION SYSTEM

The manufacturing process differs between factories and between products. However, the volume of manufacturing is one of the most crucial factors. Fig. 1.2 presents a classification of the most prevalent types of production systems.

Fig. 1.2 Production systems

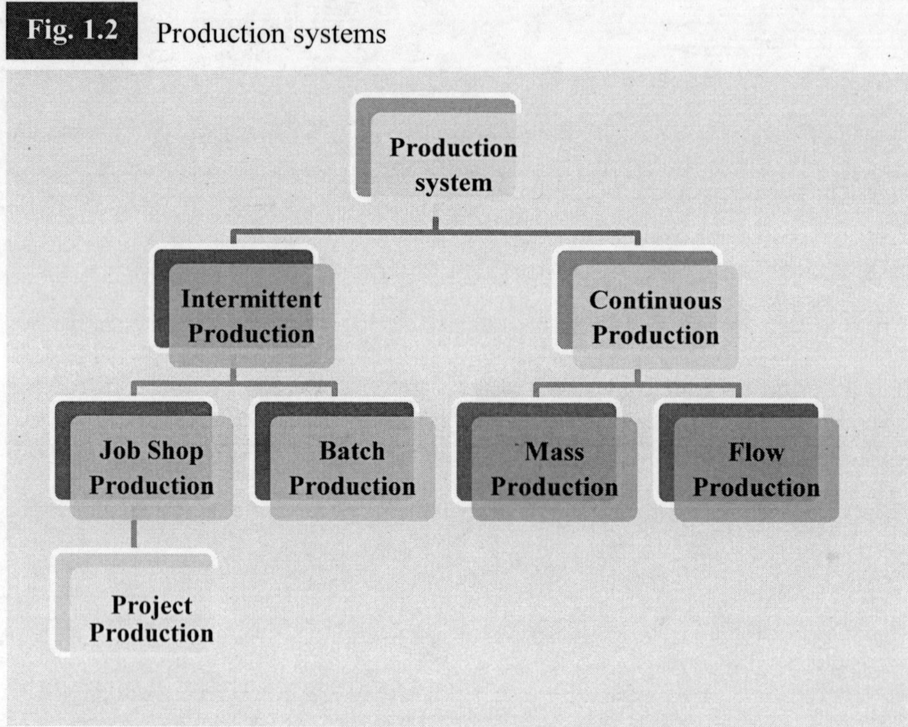

Project Production – Project production is a common use of civil engineering projects in the construction and military industries. This involves the undertaking of a vast and difficult manufacturing task. Instead of being done in a factory, work is typically done at the location. Every resource, including labor, materials, and tools, arrived at the location. One instance of project production is the ship-building industry. It is advised that this type of manufacturing system use a fixed position plant layout (see Unit 10 for fixed position layout).

Job-shop Production – Job-shop manufacture things that are customized. Production of one or few items happens here. Additionally, it is done according to the user's specifications completely and within the allotted budget and time frame. The low production volume and non-standardized parts of the job-shop production system is its defining feature.

One form of intermittent production is job-shop production, in which the flow of production is irregular or sporadic. It denotes erratic start and stop times for the production process. In this instance, manufacturing is done "make-to-order," or in response to consumer orders. The manufacturer can therefore alter their goods in accordance with the orders that they receive. Depending on the order received, the jobs and route are modified each time. Consequently, general-purpose production equipment needs to be installed by the producer.

It has following characteristics:

i. Commonly used to meet a particular customer need.
ii. Production lot size is generally small.
iii. Product variety is generally very high.
iv. Production equipments are mostly general-purpose and flexible to meet specific customer order, which varies from time to time.
v. Highly skilled labour is needed to handle the equipments, as variety and product range are very high.

Advantages of Job-shop production are:

(a) A wide range of products can be made available to clients.
(b) As compared to other systems, the workers have higher skill levels.
(c) Simplicity in management as a result of few labor and resources.
(d) Process flexibility and innovative approaches to produce distinctive results.
(e) By concentrating on each product, you can use all of your resources to fulfill orders in an efficient manner.

Disadvantages of Job-shop production are:

(a) The orientation of products produced in a job shop could differ. This indicates that there is a greater chance of backtracking because things will proceed to the subsequent step differently and might even return to the same workstation many times.
(b) A considerable lead time for the system.
(c) Many job shop manufacturers understand that orders can be inconsistent and irregular, which frequently results in a backlog. It's possible that you'll receive a large volume of orders one day and very few the next, so you'll need to adjust your timetable frequently to accommodate orders.

ALONG THE JOB SHOP PRODUCTION

Customers at Framed by Karl for Eyeglasses can personalize their own glasses. Because job shops have a distinct layout, producers are able to customize each specific item. The consumer selects their own unique glasses from a selection of standard frames. Additionally, customers can choose the specific kind of wood they wish to have at this point. In order to start production, the business will get the customer's dimensions for the item's blueprint. In addition to many options, clients have the option to select hinges at the time of order placement.

The raw materials are prepared from the company's inventory after the order is placed. The material is then cut to fit the specifications of the customer's request. A worker meticulously shapes the material into the required shape. This particular workstation will be used only for this stage of the production process. Workstations are split in manufacturing job shops to prevent waste and backlogs.

The product is varnished after the frame is prepared. In order to keep the wood from warping, a single layer of varnish will be applied and then removed after 30 minutes. This procedure is repeated numerous times over the course of several days. Multiple iterations of a procedure are common in the manufacturing of products in job shops.

Before being finished, the frames will go through one more round of polishing. After the object has gone through the necessary job shop production processes, the finishing touches are applied.

This rigorous method of working enables total customization of an order for a client. The product can be moved to the next step more readily when the workstations are arranged in this manner. Personalized items, however, guarantee that the things will not be sent in the same order.

Batch production – Batch production works well for medium-sized quantities of similar products. The production order is repeated on a regular basis. Given that over 75% of parts produced globally are produced in batches of 50 or fewer, the significance of batch production in the contemporary manufacturing environment can be clearly understood. If an organization is involved in the manufacturing of a product mix, producers may choose to alter the specifications from one batch of products to the next, therefore each batch may differ.

The features of batch production include the following:

1. Usually used to fulfill recurring orders from customers.
2. Medium-sized production lots are done in batches. This might occur even in the face of the customer's continuous demand because part variety is also medium and switching between parts is crucial.
3. Adequate for a moderate range of products.
4. Although general-purpose, production equipment is appropriate for larger production volumes.
5. To shorten setup times and enhance output, specialized jigs and fixtures can be employed.
6. In batch manufacturing, labor skill levels should be somewhat higher, however they might be lower than in a job shop. This is because there isn't as much variance and variety.

Advantages of batch production include:

i. It is possible to do quality checks at each stage of the production cycle. Additionally, equipment can be inspected in between batches to make sure there are no issues with performance. It is not feasible to provide this level of versatility using other methods.

ii. Purchasing supplies in large quantities as opposed to lesser amounts is also less expensive. A larger order will probably result in a better value from suppliers if you're ready for a larger batch.

iii. There will be less waste if a producer produces a product in smaller batches rather than in one big batch in the event that one of the batches contains defective goods.

iv. Batch production allows for item tweaking from one production cycle to the next, in the event of a new industry trend or a wave of seasonal demand (rather than having an unmodified item for a long period of time).

Disadvantages of batch production include:

i. When producing in batches, there will be higher storage expenses (relative to a smaller operation) due to higher work-in-process inventory. Furthermore, in the event of an error, the entire batch could be lost.

ii. Increased lead time as a result of setup changes.

Mass Production – Businesses use it to perform extremely large-scale production without compromising on quality. It entails the production of individual components, sometimes referred to as assemblies. In this instance, the businesses use a make-to-stock (i.e., based on the forecasted demand – not on the realization of actual demand of the customer) business plan. Continuous production of identical parts is a good fit for mass production. The rate of production is typically very high. It is distinguished by the subsequent traits:

1. Especially appropriate for products in great demand.
2. There is continuous manufacturing and a very large production lot size.
3. There is extremely little variation in the products, possibly one of its types.
4. The economies of scale principle are applied in large-scale production. It is sought to strike the ideal balance between manual labor and machinery. To maximize production, standardization, specialization, and division of labor are combined. Cost is reduced as a result.
5. There is extremely little variety in the products, possibly one of its types.
6. It can be necessary to have specialized tools and equipment.
7. Due to the requirement for repetitive work on the same equipment, workers' skill levels may be somewhat low.
8. The entire plant is set up to handle a select few unique product variations.

9. Because specialized machinery and specific purpose operations are required, a larger investment in machinery is required.

Advantages of mass production include:

i. Bulk manufacturing lowers expenses while also raising overall productivity. A Central Chinese iPhone factory reportedly produces an astounding 500,000 devices every day, according to the New York Times. The iPhone is put together in 400 steps at a speed of 350 units per minute.

ii. Mass production offers the clear benefit of quicker delivery for a product with high demand. Customer waiting times will decrease as a direct result of this.

iii. The firms are able to operate at a low profit margin because to bulk production. This aids businesses in surviving in cutthroat marketplaces.

Disadavantages of mass production include:

i. Establishing a bulk manufacturing facility is costly, particularly the startup costs. The cost of personnel, equipment, and land is in the millions. As a result, relatively few businesses can afford to produce on a huge scale. Therefore, most startups that wish to produce in large quantities are at a disadvantage.

ii. In essence, mass production equals mass uniformity. Therefore, it is challenging to make changes beyond minor adjustments. In a world that is changing quickly, consumer perception is also shifting quickly, which puts bulk manufacturing enterprises at a disadvantage. They have less adaptability. Making significant adjustments to a product will be simpler for smaller production units.

iii. Large production runs the risk of producing a huge loss if there isn't a correspondingly large demand. Another major barrier to large-scale production is what's known as inventory building. Consequently, bulk manufacturing firms are more vulnerable to shifts in consumer preferences and tastes.

ALONG THE MASS PRODUCTION

Henry Ford, the US industrialist, is well-known for creating the assembly line (in picture). Henry Ford founded the Ford Motor Company quite rapidly. He was able to bring cost-effectiveness, division of labor, and volume production together in 1913.

Source: https://www.sciencephoto.com/media/999334/view/interior-of-the-ford-works-trafford-park-manchester

A century later, the assembly line is still widely used with just little modifications. The sheer number is amazing; contemporary assembly lines produce an astounding 10,000 units per month instead of just 100 – 200. A large number of workers and equipment are needed for assembly line manufacturing.

Production on the enormous manufacturing line is measured in units per hour. Measuring the time spent by each worker was a critical step in large-scale production throughout the industrial revolution. At these stages of the workflow, improvements are made. The goal is to guarantee economical, intelligent work.

In mass production, assembly line synchronization is the greatest issue. It involves numerous moving pieces, with each employee performing a particular task in synchrony with another. One malfunction will cause the entire assembly to stall. Therefore, there is very little margin of error. There are set goals for assembly lines for each day, week, and month. Maintaining the assembly requires controlling the supply chain, inventory, expenses, and quality assurance.

Flow production – Continuous production is an alternative term for flow production. On an assembly line, it makes it possible to build a product in multiple stages.

It is characterized by the constant flow of goods through the manufacturing process. In this production method, large quantities of the same commodities are manufactured continually. On a flow production assembly line, a high degree of automation is frequently possible. A bottling plant (in picture) is one of the examples. The other flow production industries include: food processing industry, oil refinery, drug and pharmaceutical unit, etc.

This kind of mass production is unique in that it produces continuously. In contrast to discrete components production systems, there is a continuous flow of output. A continuous monitoring system is typically included in this production. Typically, all of these controls are computer-controlled and automated.

Advantages of flow production include:

i. Economies of scale are possible because the cost per unit will be minimal.
ii. Time and money are saved by automated assembly lines.
iii. Quality control systems can be incorporated into the process at every stage.
iv. Reduced amount of waste.
v. Workers with a semi-skill can be employed.
vi. It is simpler to forecast and control production times and costs because the process is continuous and does not experience delays or interruptions.
vii. Low work-in-process inventory.

Disadvantages of flow production include:

i. Adjusting the production rates to meet changing customer demand may be challenging because flow manufacturing is designed for continuous output.
ii. Ignorance of maintenance might halt output and cause disruptions in the process. A preventative maintenance schedule is essential to minimizing downtime and guaranteeing optimal performance from processes and equipment.

ALONG THE CONTINUOUS PRODUCTION

Heinz has been producing sauces, condiments, and other food items continuously for a long time. The massive international corporation Heinz was established in America in 1869. It has adapted to the times and now produces a large portion of its goods in large quantities using automated technologies.

Novartis claims that manufacturing times for drugs might be reduced by 90% with continuous production techniques. Also, they claim that it might result in a 50% decrease in the cost of producing pharmaceuticals. The multinational pharmaceutical company inaugurated its first continuous-flow production plant in Switzerland in 2017.

ArcelorMittal produces steel through continuous production. Before being cooled, the production process forces liquid steel through a mold. It begins as a solid steel slab that is then cut to length to create the final product.

Coca-Cola, a titan of the beverage sector, produces billions of drinks monthly with efficiency thanks to continuous production methods. Since its founding in 1886, the company has grown to offer a wider range of beverages, such as teas, juices, and water, in addition to its signature Coca-Cola beverage. Currently, two billion of its beverages are consumed globally each day.

ExxonMobil produces chemicals, gas, and refines petroleum using cutting-edge processing methods. ExxonMobil claims that these procedures are best practices and provide clients with greater outcomes. Among the biggest chemical firms in the world is ExxonMobil.

When making its ice cream, **Ben & Jerry's** use both batch and continuous production techniques. Founded in Vermont, the company provides tours of its first facility, which was constructed in 1985 and currently produces about 350,000 pints of ice cream daily.

1.2.1 COMPARISON BETWEEN INTERMITTENT AND CONTINUOUS PRODUCTION

The differences between intermittent and continuous production processes are seen in the following table:

	BASIS	INTERMITTENT PRODUCTION SYSTEM	CONTINUOUS PRODUCTION SYSTEM
1.	Flexibility	More flexibility	Less flexibility
2.	Lead time	Due to the frequent setup changes, there is a longer lead time.	Here, lead time is shorter and once set, adjustments are not necessary.
3.	Wastage	Increased waste production occurs.	Decreased production of waste.
4.	Product variety	Product variety is high	Identical product
5.	Cost per product unit	The high price is a result of the customization.	Because of mass production and standardization, costs are minimal.
6.	Company strength	Capability and range	Product and specialization
7.	Inventory		
(a)	Raw material	As required	Highly planned
(b)	Work-in-process	High due to possible backtracking and different cycle time of the processes involved.	Very low due to streamlined process and balanced cycle time.

(c)	Finished goods	Low, because batch sizes are manufactured in smaller quantities to meet need.	High, given that a large number of products are created.
8.	Level of automation	Low, because the relevant processes are not streamlined.	High because of the streamlined procedure.
9.	Scheduling	Difficult	Easy
10.	Inspection	Individual (off the line)	On-line inspection
11.	Focus	Product focussed	Process focussed
12.	Setups	High setup time	Setup required only at initial stage
13.	Effect of ignorance of maintenance	Low effect	Severe effect
14.	Economy of scale	None	High
15.	Tools, jigs and fixtures	General purpose	Specially designed
16.	Suitability	General purpose workshop	Flow process system

1.3 PRODUCTION EQUIPMENTS

The process of choosing production equipment for a specific component involves a number of criteria. The choice of machine tool is determined by a multitude of criteria. For example, the dimensions and strength of the machine, the necessary feeds, speeds, and the maximum depth of cut that the machine can achieve. These elements will ultimately affect the production equipment's feasibility in terms of batch size and production rate. We shall limit our discussion in this unit to the kind of production system indicated in Section 1.2.

The tooling for the process selection must be chosen once the equipment decision has been made. In manufacturing, the term "tooling" encompasses not only cutting tools but also workholders, jigs, and fixtures in its widest definition. The most important component of the machining system, choosing the right cutting tools for the job at hand, is essential to a successful machining process. Workpiece material, cut type, component shape, batch size, machine tool characteristics, cutting tool materials, tool holding, and quality/capability needs are a few of the variables to take into account while choosing the right tooling.

1.3.1 CNC MILLING MACHINE FOR BATCH PRODUCTION

Modern computer numerical control (CNC) technology is combined with the flexibility inherent in small-batch outputs in CNC milling (in picture) for small-batch production. It responds to the growing demand for tailored, specialist solutions across a range of industries. It's also not just about fulfilling expectations; it's about reaching perfection without sacrificing efficiency or quickness. Businesses may achieve this balance with accurate operations and quick production cycles using CNC milling for small batches.

https://www.alamy.com/stock-photo/cnc-machine-and-modern.html?sortBy=relevant

By using computer programming to control machine equipment, CNC milling ensures that every product is made to exact specifications. Small-batch CNC milling is especially useful for tasks requiring a high degree of precision and customization. The processing stages on CNC milling machine include:

1. Design and planning are the cornerstones of any CNC milling job. This is where the created and imagined product for manufacturing is done. The milling machine can then comprehend this design once it has been converted into a digital format. A thorough 3-dimensional model of the product is usually produced using CAD (Computer-Aided Design) software.

2. Materials ranging from metals to plastics can be selected based on the requirements and specifications of the product. After that, the chosen material is ready for milling to make sure its dimensions are correct.

3. The process by which a raw material is turned into a product is the central stage. After everything is ready, the milling process starts. The raw material is first cut, drilled, and shaped by the CNC machine under the direction of the G-code. The CNC machine's precision allows for the great accuracy of even the most complex designs.

The demand for produced parts has seen significant advances and shifts in the manufacturing industry. These days, the demand for production has changed to "made-to-order" and "on-demand" manufacturing, including batch order and High-Mix Low-Volume (HMLV) manufacturing. While batch orders entail recurrent production orders of 1 or 10 pieces up to 500 or 1,000 parts, low levels of stock (from one piece up to a maximum of 50 components) are sought in HMLV manufacturing. Let's examine in more detail the main applications for small-batch CNC milling.

(i) **Rapid protyping** – The capacity to quickly turn concepts into prototypes is invaluable in this era of rapid technology innovation and competitive marketplaces. Using CNC milling for rapid prototyping is essential for entrepreneurs and innovators. Making a model is only one aspect of prototyping; other tasks include determining the viability of the idea, identifying its advantages and disadvantages, and iteratively improving it. This procedure is accelerated by CNC machining. CNC milling creates prototypes quickly and precisely in contrast to older processes, which can be labor- and time-intensive. This allows for quicker design iterations and modifications.

(ii) **Customized products** – The market for personalized goods is expanding as people value uniqueness more and more. Customized products hold a special position in the market, whether it's a piece of jewelry with a customized story or a particular part made for an unusual industrial purpose. With its accuracy and adaptability, CNC milling is the perfect solution for these requirements. Manufacturers can meet unique customer needs without incurring the costs of bulk production by producing in small quantities.

(iii) **Replacement parts** – Reproducing parts is essential because machinery often outlasts the availability of its components. Finding new components can be difficult, particularly for businesses that depend on outdated equipment for which parts are no longer mass-produced or for customers who own antique things. One option is CNC milling. CNC milling guarantees that machines and treasured things acquire a fresh lease of life by reproducing components with high accuracy even if they are no longer accessible on the market.

ALONG THE HIGH-MIX LOW-VOLUME CNC MACHINE

With mostly exclusive CNC machining centers and a small number of CNC turning centers, an aerospace and semiconductor part manufacturer in Singapore operates a very profitable part manufacturing business. Two shifts of ten hours each are used for the production.

Challenge for the company – Hiring and keeping skilled CNC machine operators is a challenge in Singapore. The CEO/Managing Director found this particularly annoying, especially considering the surge in demand from his clients for semiconductor-machined parts. The manufacturer made the decision to purchase an automatic workpiece changer and CNC machining center in order to overcome his difficulties. For High Mix–Low Volume (HMLV) production and other flexible manufacturing requirements, this kind of setup is perfect.

The manufacturer may now run 20 pieces of the same design or 20 completely different parts in a single setting thanks to this innovative setup. Additionally, he has the ability to virtually work the CNC machine tools around-the-clock, greatly boosting output, and earnings. But that's not all. While the CNC machining center automatically creates the necessary parts, his machine operator can work on other machines in parallel. Due to the shortage of operators, it not only filled in the remaining four hours of the day but also removed the need for any more downtime. The company's profits and productivity both rose as a result of this new configuration. The manufacturer may now filter this part with priority into the automated system anytime his customer needs parts completed quickly, significantly reducing his response time for urgent orders.

There are other CNC machines for batch production, viz′, Lathe machine, Grinding machines, Drilling machines, and others. Some of the advanced manufacturing CNC machines include: Water jet cutting, Laser cutting, and others. The reader can scan the QR code for further reading on CNC Lathe machine and CNC Laser cutting machine.

SCAM ME
for
CNC Lathe machine

SCAN ME
For
CNC Laser cutting machine

1.3.2 CNC IN MASS PRODUCTION

CNC machining is one of the most widely used automation processes when it comes to producing large quantities of high-quality parts and products for a variety of industries, such as the robotics, aerospace, and medical sectors. This approach involves the use of robotics in conjunction with CNC machining to create robotic components. CNC robotics machining is the practice of using robotic arms to carry out machining tasks using CNC. Metals, polymers, and composites are just a few of the materials that can be machined using this procedure. There are various varieties of CNC robotics machining, and each has pros and cons of its own. Three types of CNC robotics machining are most commonly used:

1. **Spindle-based machining** – The robot arm is fixed on a spindle in this kind of machining, allowing you to control the machine tool with it. Although spindle-based machining is more costly than other forms of CNC robotics machining, it is typically more accurate.

Source: https://www.istockphoto.com/photo/the-milling-spindle-attached-with-the-robotics-arm-finishing-cut-the-aluminium-gm1222800615-358947083

2. **Gantry-based machining** – The robot arm is positioned on a gantry in this sort of machining, which is a kind of structure that supports the arm and permits linear movement. Although less expensive than spindle-based machining, gantry-based machining is less accurate.

Source: https://howtorobot.com/expert-insight/gantry-robot

3. **Cartesian-based machining** – The robot's arm is positioned on a cartesian coordinate system in this kind of machining, enabling three-dimensional mobility. The most adaptable method is cartesian-based machining, which can produce parts with intricate shapes.

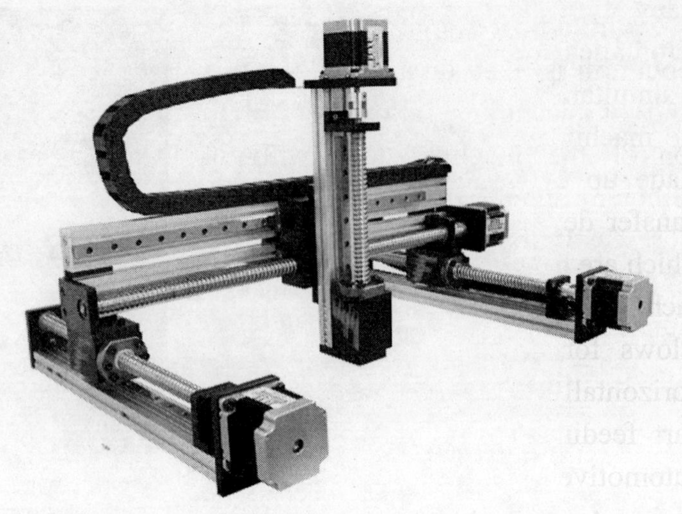

Source: https://fuyumotion.en.made-in-china.com/product/xdEQmpblRnWq/China-Multi-Axis-Industrial-Cartesian-Robot-Arm-Linear-Motion-System.html

4. **CNC Transfer machines** – Transfer machines are multi-station machines used for many types of machining operations in the metalworking industry. Workpieces are automatically indexed from station to station as they are fed into the system. The workpiece is simultaneously subjected to a separate operation at each station, and when it emerges from the machine, it may be partially or fully completed. Typical transfer machine systems are made up of a number of sequential mechanical parts, including work, indexing tables, transfer devices, and cutting heads. A circular or linear path is used to index workpieces, which are held in place by fixed or movable fixtures. Throughout a cycle, parts move through each work station where they receive particular machining processes. The indexing table allows for both continuous and sporadic movement and can turn either vertically or horizontally. Transfer machines boost output when paired with an automated transfer line for part feeding.

Mass manufacture of metal parts for a range of industries, including the automotive and industrial machinery sectors, is one use for transfer machines. Discrete component production can be done with special systems.

5. **Types of transfer machines** – Transfer machines are multi-station machines used for many types of machining operations in the metalworking industry. Workpieces are automatically indexed from station to station as they are fed into the system. The workpiece is simultaneously subjected to a separate operation at each station, and when it emerges from the machine, it may be partially or fully completed. Typical transfer machine systems are made up of a number of sequential mechanical parts, including work, indexing tables, transfer devices, and cutting heads. A circular or linear path is used to index workpieces, which are held in place by fixed or movable fixtures. Throughout a cycle, parts move through each work station where they receive particular machining processes. The indexing table allows for both continuous and sporadic movement and can turn either vertically or horizontally. Transfer machines boost output when paired with an automated transfer line for part feeding. Mass manufacture of metal parts for a range of industries, including the automotive and industrial machinery sectors, is one use for transfer machines. There are three basic categories of transfer machines:

(a) **Rotary transfer machine** – One type of CNC machine tool used to machine metal parts is the rotary transfer machine. Turning, milling, drilling, gear cutting, broaching, slotting, tumbling, honing, grinding, and assembling are all processing stages that can be finished in one go. The workpiece is mounted onto a rotatable indexing table and is machined in both horizontal and vertical directions by up to 20 process stations, each of which has three or more tools.

SCAN ME
for
Functioning of Rotory transfer machine

(b) **In-line or Linear transfer machines** – On a production line, linear transfer enables extremely accurate part movement. This indexed kinematics machine is made up of a chain conveyor in the shape of a hippodrome that moves the parts on pallets connected by a mechanical chain. The design of the pallets and chain permits a high level of accuracy in the arrangement of the components at the different work stations. Either mechanical or electronic cams drive every movement in unison.

A mechanical indexer equipped with a global cam and mechanical cams guarantee the movement of the work stations in a mechanical linear transfer.

SCAN ME
for
Linear transfer machine

A fully synchronous mechanical transmission is powered by a single motor. Every cycle, the movements are precisely the same as before. The workstations and chain movements are mostly guaranteed by brushless motor technology when using an electronic linear transfer. A brushless motor with precisely controlled position and speed can, in fact, replace each cam. Securing precise synchronization between all motor motions is made possible with the help of an axis controller. A very high degree of precision and operating reliability is provided by this electronic cam linear transfer technology.

(c) **Trunnion transfer machines** – The trunnion is a horizontal shaft around which parts are indexed. The components' rotating motion is comparable to that of a Ferris wheel. Each index can deliver a finished product since cutting tools engage the parts at their designated positions simultaneously. The machine's size determines the number of machining units.

SCAN ME
for
Trunnion transfer machines

The ability of CNC-enabled trunnions to modify their tooling eliminates the requirement for related labor and tooling, as well as secondary procedures. More recent trunnion transfer devices have the ability to process a workpiece axially at both ends. They can be set up with additional tooling units, either angular or vertical, so that during the machining process they make five-sided contact with the part.

In order to make sure the expense is justified, the predicted yield must be examined, with the cost per transfer machine operating at $1,000,000 or more. When producing one million parts or more, transfer machine tool integration was previously taken into consideration. Modern sophisticated material handling technologies, computer-aided vision systems, and other advances are integrated into advanced machining machines. With a minimum of 200,000 units, these instruments can produce significantly smaller volumes while maintaining control over production time and cost. These systems can be specially designed for a given application; they are not a one-size-fits-all solution. They can also operate continuously, which increases return on investment compared to similar devices or procedures. One crucial factor to take into account is a transfer machine's customizing choices.

1.4 TOOLING FOR CNC MACHINE TOOLS

Cutting tools for machining operations are the main focus of the tooling selection. This is because machining accounts for the great majority of secondary processing. We shall, however, limit our consideration of tooling to modern CNC machining technologies in this unit.

Three primary material types are available for cutting tools: ceramic, tungsten carbide, and high-speed steel. Tungsten carbide is utilized on high-silicon aluminums, steels, stainless steels, and exotic metals, whereas high-speed steel is typically employed on aluminum and other nonferrous alloys. Ceramic inserts are applied to unusual metals and strong steels. For numerous CNC applications, inserted carbide tooling is increasingly being chosen. It is imperative to provide careful consideration to the selection and use of equipment, including work holding devices, cutting tools, and tool holders, in order to fully utilize CNC machines. CNC machines require tools that can be swiftly changed to minimize non-cutting time, can be preset and reset externally, have a high degree of interchangeability, are very stiff, and boost reliability. The cutting tools can be categorized based on the material, construction, and setup of the tool:

Based on the Cutting Tool Setup

(a) **Preset tools** – Preset tools are those that have been set up beforehand in special holders, away from the machine tool or offline. The axial and radial positions of the tool tip on the tool holder are preset using a presetting device. After completing this, the tool holder can be installed on the machine to generate a known dimension. There are devices that can be preset to different levels of sophistication, such as optical projectors. The modern CNC machines' tool length and tool diameter correction features have diminished the significance of presetting. When the tool is inserted in the spindle, its actual dimensions must be known since the CNC part program, which is essentially the coordinates through which the cutting tool tip moves, generates the actual geometry.

Throughout the CNC machining process, particular attention must be paid to the tool's interaction to the tool retaining mechanism. The tool tip is the real point that needs to be programmed in a CNC component program, but the axes will be moving in relation to a known location in the spindle, for example, the spindle center in the case of machining centres. Therefore, it becomes essential to determine the exact amount by

SCAN ME
for

Tool Offset Determination in CNC Machines

which the tool tip deviates from the spindle's gauge point. It is possible to rapidly and simply maintain accuracy in the range of ±0.2 microns.

(b) **Qualified tools** – The cutting edge of qualified tools is precisely positioned within close tolerances in relation to a designated datum on the tool holder or slide because they are made to fit into a certain spot on the machine. These instruments' cutting edges or tips are held at a constant distance from the holder's reference surface, with a tolerance of ±0.05 mm. Because presetting is not necessary, there is minimal investment. Programming is simple because the tool's control dimensions are nominal and fixed. We do not need to measure each of these instruments separately. The qualified tool with holder displayed in the picture.

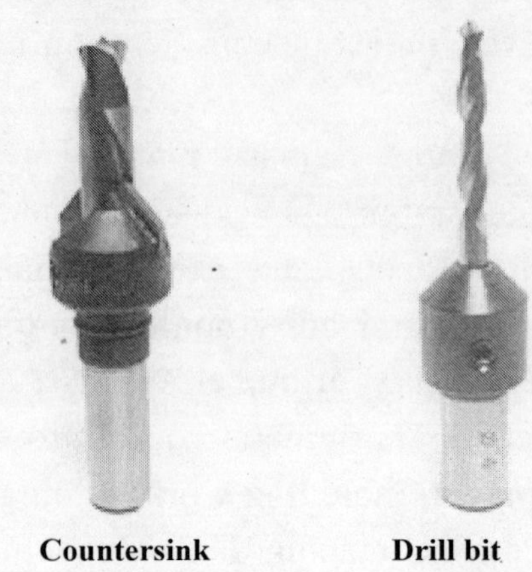

Countersink **Drill bit**

Source: http://ecoursesonline.iasri.res.in/mod/page/view.php?id=2790

The following requirements are met by the qualified cutting tools:

i. There is no need to measure each tool separately.
ii. There's no presetting gadget in use.
iii. The known and fixed dimensions of the tool holder.
iv. The setup time is shortened.
v. The tool's control dimensions are fixed and nominal.
vi. Tighter control over resharpening tools like reamers and drills.
vii. Cutter, such as teamers or end mills, for improved size control.
viii. The gadget has chip-breaking capabilities built in.
ix. Enhanced patterns.

(c) **Semi-qualified tools** – Tools that are classified as semi-qualified have movable buttons or screws on the tool shank that enable the dimensions to be changed to meet machining specifications (Fig. 1.3). To achieve precise dimensioning, these machines require routine calibration and maintenance.

By scanning the provided QR code, users can access the additional cutting tools used on CNC machines, which are based on (i) construction and (ii) material.

SCAN ME
for
CNC Cutting tools

Fig. 1.3 Semi-qualified tool

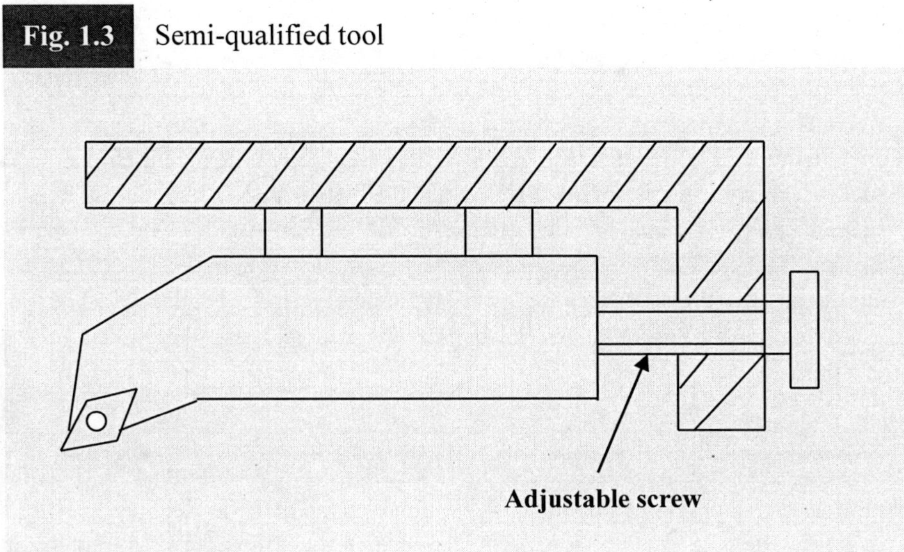

ALONG THE HIGHER LEVEL AUTOMATION

CNC machines have always included automation as a crucial component, and future developments will offer even more sophisticated automation features. Cobots, or collaborative robots, will operate side by side with human operators to complete repetitive jobs, freeing up humans to concentrate on more intricate and imaginative elements of manufacturing. This partnership will result in lower labor expenses, better safety, and more production.

By simplifying processes, automation can increase efficiency in a sector where production orders frequently have lower batch sizes. Reductions in production cycles, lower labor costs, and improved capacity can result from this. Additionally, as automation requires less power than human operators to operate a CNC machine, it can aid in reducing energy consumption. This can have a big effect on the carbon footprint and overall energy efficiency of a facility. Automation can also help a factory maintain a constant level of output and avoid having too much downtime. For instance, automation can continue where it left off in terms of design fidelity even in the event of an operator's illness or a machine malfunction. Automation also has the ability to store designs for later usage. This implies that the business may carry on manufacturing the same goods without any problems even in the event that one employee leaves. By eliminating the need for repetitive, laborious physical chores that might irritate workers and cause tiredness, this can also raise staff morale.

Artificial Intelligence Integration

CNC machine technology is going to be significantly shaped by artificial intelligence (AI). Artificial intelligence (AI) algorithms and machine learning capabilities will make these devices smarter and more flexible. They will be able to make real-time modifications, examine enormous volumes of data, and optimize machining procedures for optimal performance. Predictive maintenance will be possible with AI integration, decreasing downtime and increasing production efficiency. It is incredible how CNC machines may be used in conjunction with artificial intelligence. These robots can help boost efficiency, cut costs, and raise output by doing a range of jobs that were previously completed by people. They may also function as a kind of helper for human workers, assisting them in finishing jobs more quickly and precisely. Faster and more dependable production machines are essential for companies that require short turnaround times. To ensure that they can fulfill production schedules, experts are devoting a great deal of effort to improving the reliability of CNC machines. They are accomplishing this, among other things, by adding 3D CAD viewers to their common machine platforms. This helps technicians troubleshoot any issues that may arise by enabling them to see how their work is progressing. It can also save expenses by lowering the need to recruit additional staff to supervise the procedure. This implies that greater funds can be allocated to other crucial areas like production scheduling, process integration, and training.

Internet of Things (IoT) integration

CNC machines are among the many industries that are being revolutionized by the Internet of Things (IoT). By enabling real-time monitoring and data interchange, IoT integration will facilitate production analytics and offer insightful information about machine performance and maintenance requirements. Remote diagnostics, predictive maintenance plans, and increased operational efficiency are all made possible by this connectivity.

Improved Accuracy and Precision

Further improvements in accuracy are anticipated from CNC machines as the market for high-precision components grows. Technological developments in sensor and feedback systems will allow machines to monitor and precisely alter machining parameters. Tighter tolerances, complicated geometries, and elaborate designs will all be possible with this increased accuracy.

Flexibility and Customization

Unprecedented degrees of customisation and flexibility will be available with CNC machines in the future. From workspace configuration to incorporating specialized tools to accommodating varying material qualities, manufacturers will have the ability to customize the machines to meet their unique needs. Thanks to this personalization, producers will be able to streamline their workflow and quickly adapt to shifting consumer needs.

1.5 ROLE OF PRODUCTION SUPERVISOR

A production supervisor's duties and responsibilities include making ensuring that teams fulfill goals and produce goods that meet customer specifications and quality standards. They are primarily responsible for the following duties:

1. **Controlling the production process**: From obtaining raw materials to producing final goods, a production supervisor is in charge of every facet of the production process. Planning

and organizing production schedules and workflows, making sure the production team fulfills all goals within financial restrictions, and wise resource allocation are all part of this.

2. **Maintaining Quality Assurance**: To ensure that manufactured goods satisfy client demands and quality standards, they install and maintain quality control systems. This entails carrying out audits and inspections, analyzing production data, and putting remedial measures in place as needed to preserve quality standards.

3. **Managing safety and health issues**: To guarantee team member safety and legal compliance, the production supervisor puts into practice efficient health and safety protocols. To ensure that team members are aware of safety procedures and protocols, this entails carrying out routine safety inspections, spotting and addressing possible hazards, and creating safety training programs.

4. **Directing and fostering the production group**: They are in charge of the team by inspiring and motivating others to work productively. This entails defining high performance expectations, giving team members precise instructions and feedback, determining what training is needed, and creating training schedules to aid in team members' growth.

5. **Making decisions and resolving issues**: To reach production goals, the production supervisor recognizes problems and creates workable solutions. This calls for both analytical and creative thinking in order to pinpoint the underlying causes of challenges and provide workable solutions that deal with them.

In addition to the above a production supervisor is expected to have following skills.

1. **Technical expertise** – A production supervisor needs to have a thorough technical understanding of manufacturing procedures, tools, and technologies in order to ensure that the manufactured goods fulfill customer specifications and quality standards. Understanding technical drawings, specs, and blueprints is part of this. In addition, he needs to be knowledgeable with various kinds of gear and equipment and have the capacity to diagnose technical issues throughout production.

2. **Production planning** – The act of figuring out how to optimally distribute resources and assign deadlines in order to meet production objectives is known as production planning. A production supervisor can maximize the utilization of labor, equipment, and materials while making sure deadlines and quality requirements are fulfilled by carefully creating production schedules. Good production planning helps departments make better decisions and coordinate their efforts, which eventually leads to higher customer satisfaction and a more competitive business.

3. **Enhancement of the process** – Finding and putting into practice methods to increase the efficacy and efficiency of manufacturing processes is known as process improvement. This ability is necessary for production supervisors to analyze their current workflows, pinpoint areas for development, and put new ideas into action that boost output while cutting expenses.

4. **Managing the inventory** – Production supervisor may better organize, monitor, and manage the stock of raw materials and completed goods with the use of inventory management. With the use of this ability, he can guarantee that the production process functions efficiently and that supply and demand are balanced to perfection. Efficient inventory control minimizes waste, lowers expenses, and boosts overall production efficiency.

5. **Managing the time** – A production supervisor who manages their time well can prioritize activities, establish objectives, and distribute resources efficiently. He may optimize work processes, minimize downtime, and maintain a consistent workflow by managing his time well, which will increase production, lower expenses, and improve performance all around. Additionally, it facilitates his ability to interact with team members more effectively and resolve any obstacles or hold-ups, which eventually guarantees on-time delivery.

1.6 ROLE OF PRODUCTION MANAGER

A production manager is in charge of making sure that manufacturing product production begins and ends on schedule, within budget, and without delay. They organize, coordinate, plan, and schedule various production schedules and tasks. The production manager makes sure every product satisfies the necessary requirements of quality. These managers improve an organization's manufacturing and production through a variety of strategies and tactics.

A production manager is in charge of the following in addition to supervising the manufacturing process and organizing production-related activities and operations:

- Putting together a manufacturing schedule.
- Choosing, looking for, and fixing equipment.
- Establishing benchmarks for quality.
- Ensuring economical production and a cost-effective production method.
- Discussing with clients about their expected budgets.
- Ensure that machinery and equipment follow health and safety procedures.
- Managing group members while optimizing effectiveness.
- Cutting costs throughout all product categories.

- Keeping the level of product quality that management has specified.
- Working together as a team to establish and assess production targets.
- Figuring out how to increase the effectiveness of production.
- Encouraging, assisting, and directing colleagues.

In addition to the above, the production manager should have following skills.

1. **Communication** – To effectively explain corporate objectives and aims to their team, a production manager needs to possess strong communication skills. They can convey their thoughts to management or the employees on their production line using written or verbal communication abilities. They might also generate production reports using their written communication abilities.

2. **Resolving issues** – Businesses frequently rely on production managers to resolve issues in the production process or to replace malfunctioning equipment. To identify a solution, these specialists need to have exceptional problem-solving abilities. Maintaining the production schedule on time can be aided by finding solutions to production-related issues.

3. **Leadership** – Encouraging team members to increase production efficiency is one of a production manager's responsibilities. Strong leadership abilities are needed for this. A manager can gain the trust of their team members by demonstrating strong leadership skills. This helps to enhance the entire production process and is essential to finishing projects on schedule and under budget.

4. **Technical proficiency** – To evaluate and enhance the entire functionality of the manufacturing process, production managers frequently employ technical expertise. For a production manager to succeed in their job, they must be able to operate various industrial equipments. Furthermore, it would be advantageous for this position if you could pick up new technical skills and technologies.

5. **Teamwork** – In a manufacturing setting, production managers frequently have to coordinate and work with team members to complete a task. Working well in a team is a desirable quality for this position. A competent production manager sets priorities for their jobs and makes sure that everyone in the team does the same and works effectively.

6. **Organizing abilities** – Production managers frequently have strict timelines to meet. They need to be very well-organized in order to achieve the deadlines and objectives. They need to be very good at multitasking in order to succeed in their role since they supervise numerous manufacturing processes. Additionally, a production manager with great organizational abilities may finish a work without overlooking any important elements.

7. **Critical thinking abilities** – To find opportunities for improvement, production managers frequently evaluate the production statistics and reports. This contributes to increasing the effectiveness and quality of the production process. These experts examine each stage of complicated production processes to identify problems and identify opportunities for improvement.

8. **Competency with manufacturing norms** – A production manager must be knowledgeable about various manufacturing standards, regardless of the industry in which they operate, in order to meet customer demands for product quality. A production manager also develops and puts into practice performance metrics to guarantee necessary production standards. This necessitates a solid understanding of the manufacturing standards associated with the specific industry they operate in.

UNIT SUMMARY

- ***Managerial Decisions in Production Life Cycle*** – Discusses strategic planning, process selection, quality assurance, and operational control.
- ***Types of Production Systems*** – Covers job-shop, batch, mass, and flow production, highlighting their advantages, disadvantages, and applications.
- ***CNC Production Equipment*** – Explains the role of Computer Numerical Control (CNC) machines in modern manufacturing, including small-batch CNC milling and CNC in mass production.
- ***Tooling for CNC Machines*** – Discusses the selection and use of cutting tools, work holders, jigs, and fixtures.
- ***Roles of Production Supervisor & Production Manager*** – Highlights their responsibilities, skills, and impact on efficiency, quality control, and team management.

EXERCISES

MULTIPLE CHOICE QUESTIONS

1.1 Which stage of the production life cycle involves determining the optimal production process and technology to be used?

(a) Design phase	(b) Planning phase
(c) Execution phase	(d) Monitoring phase

1.2 Which managerial decision is crucial during the controlling phase of the production life cycle?

(a) Implementing cost-cutting measures	(b) Identifying and resolving bottlenecks
(c) Developing new product features	(d) Expanding market reach

1.3 Which type of production system is characterized by producing customized products in small quantities?

(a) Intermittent production	(b) Continuous production
(c) Job shop production	(d) Batch production

1.4 Which production system involves producing a specific quantity of products before switching to a different product?

(a) Intermittent production	(b) Continuous production
(c) Job shop production	(d) Batch production

1.5 Which of the following is a key advantage of continuous production over intermittent production?

(a) Higher flexibility in production scheduling	(b) Lower setup costs
(c) Higher production efficiency	(d) Reduced risk of machine breakdowns

1.6 Which type of production system is best suited for producing customized products with varying specifications?

(a) Intermittent production	(b) Continuous production
(c) Batch production	(d) Mass production

1.7 What is a common challenge faced in intermittent production that is not typically encountered in continuous production?

(a) High setup costs	(b) Limited product variety
(c) Difficulty in maintaining consistent quality	(d) Inefficient use of resources

1.8 In batch production, how does the use of CNC machines benefit the manufacturing process?

(a) Reducing setup times between batches	(b) Increasing labor costs
(c) Decreasing machine precision	(d) Slowing down production speed

1.9 How does a CNC transfer machine differ from a traditional machining center?

(a) CNC transfer machines are more versatile	(b) CNC transfer machines require less operator intervention
(c) CNC transfer machines are less accurate	(d) CNC transfer machines are slower in production

1.10 How does CNC technology contribute to reducing production lead times in mass production?

(a) By eliminating the need for quality	(b) By automating the production process
(c) By increasing the number of manual laborers required	(d) By decreasing the use of raw materials

1.11 Which type of tool is commonly used in CNC machining to remove material from a workpiece?

(a) End mill	(b) Drill bit
(c) Lathe tool	(d) Saw blade

1.12 Which type of tool material is known for its high hardness and wear resistance in CNC tooling?

(a) High Speed Steel (HSS)	(b) Carbide
(c) Ceramics	(d) Cobalt

1.13 How are CNC tools qualified for use in machining operations?

(a) By visually inspecting the tools	(b) By running test cuts and measuring performance
(c) By checking the tool material	(d) By adjusting tool settings

1.14 Which position is responsible for overseeing day-to-day operations on the production floor?

(a) Production supervisor	(b) Production manager
(c) Quality control inspector	(d) Human resources manager

1.15 Which of the following is a key duty of a production manager?

(a) Training new employees	(b) Planning the production
(c) Handling customer complaints	(d) Evaluating the production statistics and reports

Answers of Multiple Choice Questions

1.1 (a), 1.2 (b), 1.3 (c), 1.4 (d), 1.5 (c), 1.6 (a), 1.7 (a), 1.8 (a), 1.9 (b), 1.10 (b), 1.11 (a), 1.12 (b), 1.13 (b), 1.14 (a), 1.15 (d)

SHORT AND LONG ANSWER TYPE QUESTIONS

Category I

1.1 How does the choice of production process impact overall efficiency and cost-effectiveness?

1.2 What role does demand forecasting play in production decision-making?

1.3 How can technology and automation influence production decisions?

1.4 Explain the characteristics of a production system where products are manufactured in small quantities at irregular intervals.

1.5 What are the key features of a job-shop production system, and how does it compare to mass production in terms of customization and flexibility?

1.6 How does batch production differ from flow production in terms of production scheduling and inventory management?

1.7 Elaborate the benefits of mass production in terms of economies of scale and cost efficiency compared to other production systems.

1.8 How does CNC technology improve efficiency in batch production processes?

1.9 Explain the main differences between spindle-based machining and other CNC machining methods.

1.10 Elaborate on the key features of transfer machining systems and their impact on efficiency in mass production.

1.11 How do transfer machines facilitate the seamless transfer of workpieces between different machining operations?

1.12 How does the selection of appropriate tooling impact the quality of machined parts?

1.13 What is the purpose of preset tools in CNC machining?

1.14 How does a production supervisor contribute to ensuring quality control and adherence to production standards?

1.15 What strategies can a production supervisor implement to optimize production efficiency and meet production targets?

1.16 How does a production manager collaborate with other departments to ensure seamless coordination and communication in the production process?

Category II

1.17 How do factors such as market demand, production costs, and resource availability influence decision-making processes in production planning?

1.18 Can you elaborate on the importance of considering technological advancements and industry trends when making strategic decisions about production methods and processes?

1.19 In what ways do quality control standards and regulatory requirements impact decision-making in production management?

1.20 Discuss the role of risk assessment, contingency planning, and continuous improvement initiatives in shaping decisions concerning production strategies and resource allocation?

1.21 In what ways can companies optimize their production processes to effectively balance the benefits and limitations of intermittent production?

1.22 In what ways can continuous production systems be customized and optimized to meet the specific needs and requirements of different industries and products?

1.23 In what ways do job-shop production facilities optimize resource utilization and minimize idle time through strategic layout design and workflow management?

1.24 In what ways can companies optimize their batch production processes to maximize productivity and minimize lead times?

1.25 How do CNC machine tools enhance the precision and repeatability of parts in batch production processes?

1.26 In what ways can CNC transfer machine tools be customized or adapted to accommodate varying workpiece sizes, shapes, and material specifications in a mass production environment?

1.27 Company XYZ is a medium-sized manufacturing company that produces electronic devices. The company has been experiencing a surge in demand for their products due to a recent increase in consumer interest. As a result, the management team is faced with crucial decisions concerning production to meet the growing demand.

The company currently operates with a single production facility that is running at full capacity. The management team is considering two options to address the increased demand:

Option 1: Expand the existing production facility to increase capacity. This would involve investing in new equipment, hiring additional staff, and potentially renovating the current facility to accommodate the expansion.

Option 2: Outsource a portion of the production to a third-party manufacturer. This would allow the company to quickly scale up production without the need for significant upfront investment in infrastructure and resources.

As the newly appointed production manager, you have been tasked with analyzing the two options and presenting a recommendation to the executive team. Your analysis should consider factors such as cost, lead time, quality control, scalability, and potential risks associated with each option.

Based on your analysis, make a recommendation on which option Company XYZ should pursue to effectively manage the increased demand for their products while ensuring long-term sustainability and profitability.

REFERENCES AND SUGGESTED READINGS

1. Amstead, B.H., Ostwald, P.F. and Begeman, M.L. *Manufacturing Processes*, 8th Edition, Wiley, 1987.
2. Chang, T.C. and Wysk, R.A. *An Introduction to Automated Processes Planning Systems*, Prentice-Hall, 1985.
3. Evans, J.R. *Applied Production and Operations Management*, 4th Edition, West, 1999.
4. Goetsch, D.L. *Modern Manufacturing Processes*, Delmar, 1991.

5. Gosling, J., and Naim, M. M. The Influence of Production Life Cycle on Decision-Making in Operations Management. *International Journal of Production Economics*, Vol. 133(2), 463-472, 2011.
6. Groover, M. P. *Automation, Production Systems, and Computer-Integrated Manufacturing*, 4th Edition, Pearson, 2015.
7. Halevi, G. and Weill, R.D. *Principles of Process Planning – A Logical Approach*, Chapman & Hall, 1995.
8. Jain, R. K., and Sharma, M. K. *Advanced Manufacturing Technology*, 1st Edition, Tata McGraw-Hill, 2013.
9. Krajewski, L. J., Ritzman, L. P., and Malhotra, M. K. *Operations Management: Processes and Supply Chains*, 11th Edition, Pearson, 2018.
10. Meyers, F. E., and Hoh, J. H. *CNC Machining Handbook: Building, Programming, and Implementation*, 1st Edition, McGraw-Hill, 2012.
11. Nanfari, F., Uccello, T. and Murphy, D. *The CNC Workbook*, Addison-Wesley, 1995.
12. Palaniappan, S., and Srinivasan, V. Advances in CNC Production Systems. *Journal of Manufacturing Science and Engineering*, Vol. 128(1), 123-132, 2006.
13. Rosen, D. W., and Bohn, M. S. Application of Computer Numerical Control (CNC) in Mass Production. *International Journal of Advanced Manufacturing Technology*, Vol. 38(5-6), 446-457, 2008.
14. Scallan, P. *Process Planning: The Design / Manufacture Interface*, Butterworth-Heinemann, 2003.
15. Shao, Y., and Kuo, Y. Design and Optimization of CNC Machine Tool Tooling Systems. *International Journal of Machine Tools and Manufacture*, Vol. 64, 1-11, 2013.
16. Singh, R. K., and Singh, M. K. A Comparative Study of Different Types of Production Systems. *International Journal of Advanced Manufacturing Technology*, Vol. 43(5-6), 504-510, 2009.
17. Tansel, I., and Ozdemir, R. *CNC Tooling and Machining*, 2nd Edition, CRC Press, 2013.
18. Wang, X., and Lee, K. The Role of Production Managers in Lean Manufacturing Environments. *International Journal of Production Research*, Vol. 53(22), 6884-6896, 2015.

UNIT **2**

PROJECT MANAGEMENT

UNIT SPECIFICS

This unit elaborately discusses the following topics:

- What is a project
- Stages of Project life cycle
- Request for proposal
- Establishing a project team
- Defining scope and terms of reference
- Work breakdown structure
- Risk management

The topics' comprehension and ramifications for fostering additional interest and inventiveness are covered, along with the preliminary needs for project development. In order to help the reader grasp the concepts more thoroughly, the unit includes a list of references and recommended readings in addition to a significant number of multiple-choice questions and short and long answer questions classified into two categories based on the lower and higher order of Bloom's taxonomy. It is significant to note that the technique (AHP) QR code is provided for the purpose of providing further information on the practical element of rating alternative projects. This code can be scanned to obtain pertinent supporting information.

RATIONALE

This unit provides a comprehensive overview of fundamental concepts essential for successful project management. It begins by defining what constitutes a project, emphasizing its unique characteristics and objectives. The stages of the project life cycle are explored to illustrate the systematic progression from initiation to closure. The unit highlights the importance of a Request for Proposal (RFP) as a tool for soliciting bids and fostering competition. Establishing a project team is discussed as a critical step in ensuring diverse expertise and effective collaboration. Additionally, the significance of defining the project scope and terms of reference is examined to set clear boundaries and expectations. The Work Breakdown Structure (WBS) is introduced as a method for organizing tasks and deliverables, while risk management is emphasized as a vital practice for identifying, assessing, and mitigating potential challenges throughout the project's duration. Together, these elements provide a structured framework for managing projects efficiently and effectively.

UNIT OUTCOMES

List of outcomes of this unit is as follows:

U2-UO1 – Understanding project

U2-UO2 – Project life cycle

U2-UO3 – Request for proposal

U2-UO4 – Establishing a project team

U2-UO5 – Defining scope and terms of reference

U2-UO6 – Work breakdown structure and risk management

UNIT-2 Outcomes	EXPECTED MAPPING WITH COURSE OUTCOMES (*1-Weak Correlation; 2-Medium Correlation; 3-Strong Correlation*)					
	CO-1	CO-2	CO-3	CO-4	CO-5	CO-6
U2-UO1	2	3	2	2	1	1
U2-UO2	3	3	2	3	2	2
U2-UO3	1	2	1	1	2	1
U2-UO4	3	3	2	3	2	1
U2-UO5	1	3	2	2	2	1
U2-UO6	3	3	2	3	2	1

2.1 INTRODUCTION

From creating the great pyramids to finding a treatment for tuberculosis to landing a man on the moon, all of humanity's greatest achievements started out as projects.

Experts and business executives have declared that project management is essential to long-term, steady economic growth. The creation of new goods and services, continual innovation, and raising output and quality standards all contribute to the creation of new jobs and a competitive edge. This is the project management domain. Project management gives individuals a strong toolkit that enhances their capacity to organize, carry out, and oversee tasks in order to meet predetermined corporate goals. However, project management is a result-driven management approach that emphasizes fostering cooperative relationships across a wide range of stakeholders. It is not simply a collection of tools.

The project approach has long been the standard method of conducting business in the construction sector, large consulting businesses, and the U.S. Department of Defense contracts. Project management is now used in every field of employment. Project teams work on anything from information system upgrades to hospital reorganizations to port extensions these days. They are exploring the furthest regions of space, researching sustainable energy sources, and building fuel-efficient cars of the future. In the electronics business, where young professionals are the new folk heroes due to their tireless efforts producing a steady stream of new hardware and software products, project management has a particularly significant impact.

Project management is not just used in the business world. Moreover, project management can be used to carry out charitable work and address social issues. Modern project management skills and techniques would be beneficial in endeavors like organizing a community effort to renovate a public playground, planning a strategy to reduce crime and drug abuse within a city, or providing emergency aid to areas affected by natural disasters.

2.2 WHAT IS A PROJECT?

What is the commonality among the following headlines?

- Millions watch the opening ceremony of the Cricket World Cup.

- The city's internet cable is about to launch.
- Hospital reacts to newly formed medical camps
- Samsung releases a new smartphone.
- The city is given stimulus money to expand its Metro-rail system initiatives.

Each of these occurrences is a project.

According to the Project Management Institute (PMI), a project is defined as follows:

A **project** is a temporary endeavour undertaken to create a unique product, service, or result.

A project's main objective, like that of other organizational efforts, is to meet the needs of the client. The features of a project help set it apart from other organizational endeavors beyond these essential similarities. An initiative should have the following main characteristics:

1. A predetermined goal.
2. A predetermined lifespan having a start and finish.
3. Usually the participation of numerous divisions and experts.
4. Usually, undertaking an action that has never been taken before.
5. Precise deadlines, expenses, and performance standards.

First of all, projects have a clearly stated goal, such as building a Mall Retail Complex by January 1st or launching a new mobile phone version as soon as feasible. In the day-to-day operations of a firm, where employees execute repetitive tasks every day, this singular purpose is frequently absent.

Second, unlike regular occupations, which have ongoing responsibilities and duties, projects have a definite endpoint since they have a specified aim. Instead of sticking with one employment, people frequently switch between projects. Following their assistance with the installation of new equipment, an engineer can be tasked with creating a plan for the erection of equipment for a different client.

Third, a range of specialists are usually needed to work together on projects, unlike a lot of organizational work that is divided up based on functional expertise. Upon completion of a project, professionals in various fields such as engineering, finance, marketing, or quality control collaborate closely under the direction of a project manager, rather than operating independently in separate offices under differing managers.

A project's nonroutine and distinctive aspects make up its fourth attribute. Of course, breaking new ground in technology and resolving unsolvable issues is necessary to achieve unprecedented feats, like developing an autonomous vehicle or setting foot on the moon's

South Pole. Conversely, even simple construction projects including pre-existing routines and procedures need to be customized to some extent in order to make them distinct.

Ultimately, initiatives are bound by precise schedule, cost, and performance limitations. Tasks are assessed based on their completion, expense, and duration. There is a greater level of accountability imposed by these triple limits than in most other positions. These three also draw attention to a key role of project management, which is to balance performance, cost, and time trade-offs in order to satisfy clients.

Projects, however, should not be mistaken with regular work. A project isn't just regular, monotonous labor! Daily labor usually involves repeating the same or similar tasks, whereas a project is completed once, creating a new product or service in its wake. For example, although taking notes in class is routine work, writing a term paper is a project; similarly, while answering requests from the supply chain is routine work, creating a supply chain network system is a project. Understanding the differences is crucial since, all too frequently; resources are expended on routine tasks that don't support long-term organizational strategies that call for innovative new products.

2.3 THE PROJECT LIFE CYCLE

As we've previously discussed, a project is an endeavor in which humans, machines, and other resources are combined to achieve a certain goal. A variety of instances of initiatives at the individual, community, organizational, national, and international levels have also been examined. These projects go through comparable stages as they develop from conception to completion, despite their differences. Therefore, as indicated below, we can discuss the project life cycle and identify its key stages:

- Selection of a project
- Project planning
- Project implementation
- Project completion and audit

2.3.1 SELECTION OF PROJECT

One of the most important decisions made by an organization's top management is choosing a new project. The necessity for the new project may stem from the desire to provide a new product that will put the company in a more favorable financial position, to defend against competition by building cutting-edge service facilities, or to implement e-commerce in order to attract online clients. It is generally true that selecting the right initiatives at the right time is critical to an organization's growth and success. Three main tasks comprise project selection: project identification, project appraisal, and project selection.

Project identification

The process of identifying a project involves looking at potential new possibilities and environmental hazards and producing workable solutions that the organization can use. This is accomplished via the company's think tank coming up with fresh concepts. When conducting this assignment in a group, brainstorming is a highly useful method. The process of brainstorming can be organized so that the coordinator asks each group member for an idea in turn, records the concept, then moves on to the next person. At any point, if a person has nothing to offer, all he has to do is say "pass" to move on to the next person in line. This procedure keeps going until the required number of ideas are generated (a brainstorming session usually yields between 20 – 30 ideas). The process is changed in the alternative brainstorming method, known as unstructured brainstorming, such that it starts with the person who comes up with the first idea and moves on to the person who is willing to come up with the next, and so on. The procedure keeps going till the necessary amount of ideas are produced. While a few vocal members may control an unstructured brainstorming session, structured brainstorming guarantees the participation of all members.

The coordinator should inform the participants of the exercise's goal prior to starting it, assuring them that the thoughts produced will remain private and won't be utilized by the business for any kind of subjective assessment.

During project selection the top management has to

- Be open to fresh, innovative concepts
- Possess an idea for future expansion
- Remember your long-term goals
- Create a SWOT map by arranging your internal strengths and weaknesses alongside external opportunities and threats
- Determine the worthiness of a project proposal by assessing the project's technical and financial viability

Project appraisal

All projects must be evaluated from multiple angles prior to implementation. This assessment takes into account the following types of appraisal and is typically more stringent than the project concept screening that occurs following brainstorming during the project identification phase. In this phase a detailed project report (DPR) is formed. A DPR serves as both a blueprint for the project's implementation and ultimate operation and a comprehensive, final appraisal report. It includes information on the fundamental program, roles and duties, all of the tasks that must be completed, the materials needed, potential hazards, and suggested precautions against them. DPR touches on all aspects of a project, including:

- Market appraisal
- Financial appraisal
- Technical appraisal
- Sustainability appraisal

Market appraisal – The DPR's section on marketing planning needs to include:

- Aggregate future deamand
- Market share
- Current and future competition
- Location and accessibility of consumers
- Technological scenario/obsolescence
- Possible pricing options

Financial appraisal – A very thorough estimate of the expected expenses and income over the project's anticipated lifespan is included in the DPR. In terms of cash flow, investments, and other factors, a financial appraisal is performed to verify the project's viability. This makes it possible to determine whether or not the project one wants to work on will benefit them financially. The project's financial appraisal aids in your comprehension of the details surrounding the project's finances, including its cash flow and investments. A project's DPR provide financial components encompass the following crucial elements:

- Cash flows over time
- Profitability
- Break even point to decide the volume at which the project should operate
- Net present value
- Internal rate of return
- Payback period
- Risk

Technical appraisal – Before financing any project, a technical appraisal is conducted to help understand the three main issues: whether the project was adequately conceived, engineered, and followed established standards. For the project, the DPR must take into account the sources and necessity of any specialized technical know-how. A technical collaboration agreement with an organization that has significant expertise using the same technology and is able to share its knowledge with others may be required for a number of current technology initiatives. While such a cooperating organization might exist domestically, one must typically search overseas for a technological partner. The following essential components are included in DPR for a project's technical appraisal:

- Engineering and technology aspects
- Locations
- Size
- Layout
- Production process
- Storage and material handling
- Facilities and equipment for packaging and distribution

Sustainability appraisal – The project's potential socio-economic and environmental effects are considered in the sustainability assessment. The DPR ought to suggest certain control methods and wastewater treatment plants in order to get the environment back to allowable levels. For instance, plans can call for the development of chemical treatment facilities to remove harmful substances from fluids before disposal, electrostatic precipitators to capture dust particles, and plants to produce beneficial byproducts, among other things. The sustainability assessment of DPR for a project includes the following crucial elements:

- Benefits and costs (in shadow prices)[1]
- Distribution of income in society
- Level of saving and investment
- Self-sufficiency, employment, and social order
- Environmental damage
- Restoration measures

---

[1] Benefits are visible through shadow prices; following model optimization, the dual prices derived from each equation indicate the number of units by which the objective function improves with a one-unit change in this resource. Shadow pricing are used in economic analyses of large-scale projects, such as building a large ship or anything similar.

Project selection

The process of assessing suggested projects or groupings of projects and selecting which ones to implement in order to meet the goals of the parent organization is known as project selection. Any aspect of the company's operations where decisions between conflicting options must be made can use this same methodical approach. For instance, a TV station can choose which of several syndicated comedies to rerun in its 6:30 p.m. weekly time slot; a construction company can choose the best subset of a large group of potential projects on which to bid; a hospital can find the best combination of psychiatric, orthopedic, obstetric, other services. Every project will have unique expenses, advantages, and threats. These are rarely known for sure. It is challenging to choose just one project from a set when there are such discrepancies. Selecting a portfolio, which consists of several projects, is much more difficult. When choosing a project, are significant decisions able to be made rationally? Do they ever rethink their decision once it has been made, and if so, how? These inquiries highlight the requirement for efficient selection models. With the use of the models, we are able to virtually completely eliminate reality from an issue, enabling us to handle only the pertinent elements of the "real" scenario. Modeling the problem is the process of removing undesirable facts from the core of an issue.

These models can be applied, within reason, to boost earnings, choose investments among scarce capital resources, or strengthen an organization's position in the marketplace. The organization's limited resources can be allocated and reallocated with their help since they can be utilized for both initial and continuous evaluation.

Finally, project selection is based on a number of criteria for which a detailed a prison and evaluation has been carried out for the entire candidate project proposals. Some important criteria that are relevant in project evaluation are given below:

1. *Practicality* – The model should accurately depict the decision-making environment of the company, particularly the various goals that the company and its management have, keeping in mind that it is hard to compare several projects side by side in the absence of a consistent measuring method. Along with reflecting project technical and market risks, the model should also account for the firm's actual limitations in terms of facilities, capital, personnel, and other resources. These aspects include performance, cost, time, client rejection, and execution.
2. *Proficiency* – In order to handle the various time periods, internal and external project circumstances (such as strikes or changes in interest rates), and other pertinent aspects, the model should be sufficiently advanced.

3. *Adaptability* – Within the spectrum of scenarios that the organization may encounter, the model ought to produce reliable findings. Changes in the firm's environment, such as new technical developments that affect risk levels, changes in tax laws, and most importantly, changes in organizational goals, should be simple to adapt to.
4. *Simple to apply* – The model must to be reasonably practical, quick to implement, and simple to use and comprehend. It shouldn't call for specialized interpretation, hard-to-get data, a surplus of staff, or nonexistent equipment.
5. *Expenses* – The expenditures of collecting data and modeling should be minimal in comparison to the project's total cost and its possible advantages. Every expense, including those related to managing the data and executing the model, needs to be taken into account.
6. *Digitalization* – Gathering, storing, and sharing data in a computer database should be simple and convenient. Standard computer programs that are widely available should also make it easy to manipulate data in the model.

Project selection models can be broadly classified into two categories: numerical and non-numeric. Both are frequently utilized. A lot of organizations utilize models that combine the two or both at the same time. As the name suggests, non-numerical models do not accept numerical inputs. Numerical models do, however the measurement criteria may be objective or subjective. It's crucial to keep in mind that a project's attributes could be quantified, and that subjective measurements aren't always less accurate or valuable than objective ones. The two crucial details that are important to remember are:

- Decisions are made by humans, not by models. The decision belongs to the manager and not the model. The manager can assign a model to help with the decision-making process, but the manager cannot abandon their duty.
- No matter how complex they are, all models only capture a portion of the reality they are supposed to depict. We can never fully represent reality in any model; it is simply too complex. No model, therefore, can produce an ideal outcome unless it operates inside a potentially insufficient context.

We provide here one possible numeric model within the two fundamental categories of selection models: nonnumeric and numeric. In the numeric category, Multi-criteria decision making (MCDM) techniques can be used to rank and choose the winning project proposal because project decision-making is a multi-criteria problem, involving a number of in commensurate, open, intangible criteria with varying degrees of importance for each candidate project. Here we explain a generalized model of MCDM.

We can give weights to the criterion when we have N distinct projects that need to be assessed based on M various standards. All project options are also assessed according to every criterion. With each entry R_{ij} representing the ith project's score on the jth evaluation criterion, this evaluation yields an $N \times M$ matrix. Each matrix entry is multiplied by the matching criterion weight W_j to arrive at the ultimate score. Figure 2.1 illustrates a multi-criteria assessment framework. The proposal that receives the highest rating is chosen. Many multi-criteria decision-making approaches can be used for this, including ELECTRE (Elimination and Choice Translating Reality), AHP (Analytic Hierarchy Process), WPM (Weighted Product Method), TOPSIS (Technique for Order of Preference by Similarity to Ideal Solution), and SAW (Simple Additive Weighting). The feasibility assessment, which took into account each of these factors before project adoption, served as the basis for the ultimate project selection.

Fig. 2.1 A framework for multi-criteria evaluation of projects

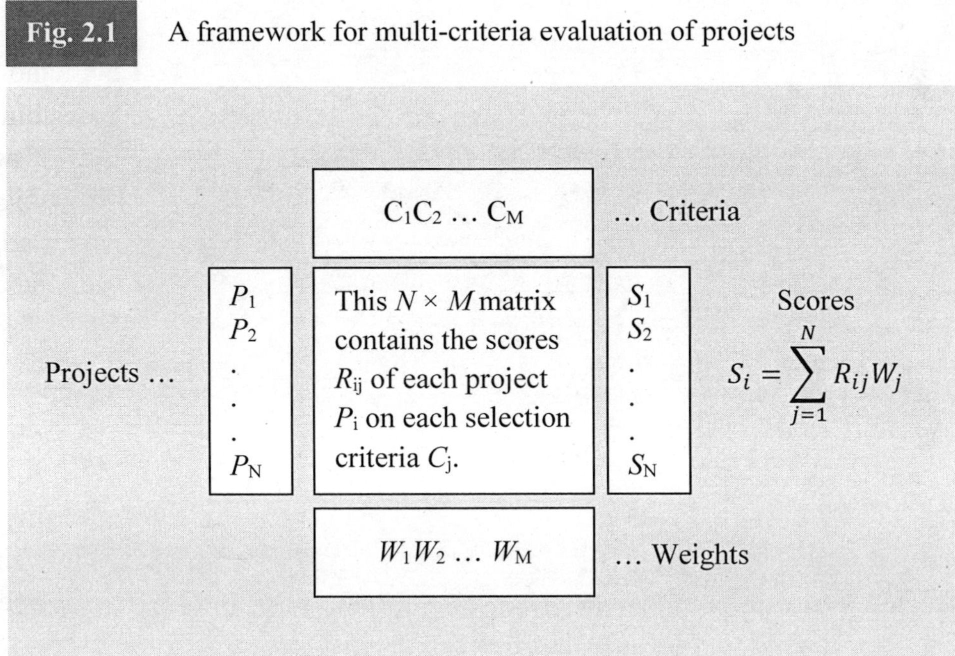

S-curve pattern of life cycle

In order to reach the project goal, a project goes through different phases which are also exhibited as a "stretched-S" pattern of slow-rapid-slow advancement (Fig. 2.2). This phenomenon is evident to everyone who has watched a house or building being constructed.

It mostly results from the shifting amounts of resources used at different periods of the life cycle. Plotting project effort against time, with time divided into the various project stages, Fig. 2.3 displays the effort, typically expressed in person-hours or resources used per unit of time (or the number of people working on the project). When developing the project concept and putting it through the project selection procedures, there is minimal work involved in the beginning. (In a later section, we shall contend that putting in more work at the beginning of a project's life cycle increases the likelihood of success.) In Fig. 2.2 for life-cycle progress curve and in Fig. 2.3 for effort curve typically exhibit a strong association, as work typically leads to corresponding progress; however this isn't always the case. Additionally, the progress curve won't typically be symmetrical because the effort curve is typically nonsymmetrical as well.

Fig. 2.2 The common Stretched-S project life cycle

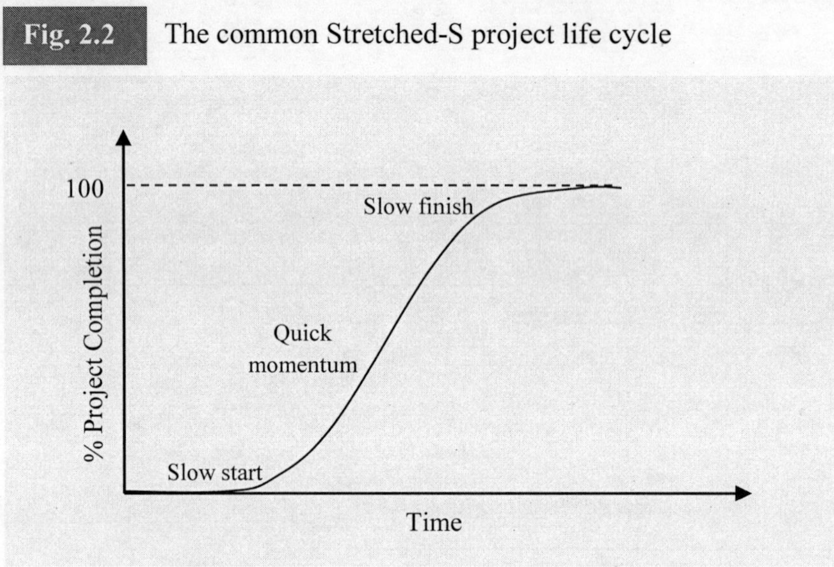

As the project moves forward and the actual work begin, there is an increase in activity. As the project draws to an end, this peaks and then starts to decline, eventually coming to an end when the evaluation is finished and the project is closed. Although the level of effort rises and falls during every project, no specific pattern appears to characterize all of them, and there is no reason why the project's final slowdown to reflect its initial increase. As illustrated in Fig. 2.3, some initiatives come to an end without being pulled out. Some, on the other hand, might finish "not with a bang but a whimper," progressively slowing down until it's almost surprising to learn that project activity has stopped. In certain instances, the effort might never reach zero since the project team – or at the very least, a cadre group – might be retained for the next project that fits the bill. Then, the new enterprise will emerge from the ashes of the old, resembling a phoenix.

Major considerations during the course of a project are the ever-present objectives of achieving scope, schedule, and cost. Before the project's life cycle began, scope was often considered to be more important. The planners' attention is now focused on identifying the precise techniques needed to accomplish the project's scope objectives. Because they include the application of a science or art, we refer to these techniques as the project's technology.

Fig. 2.3 The distribution of project effort

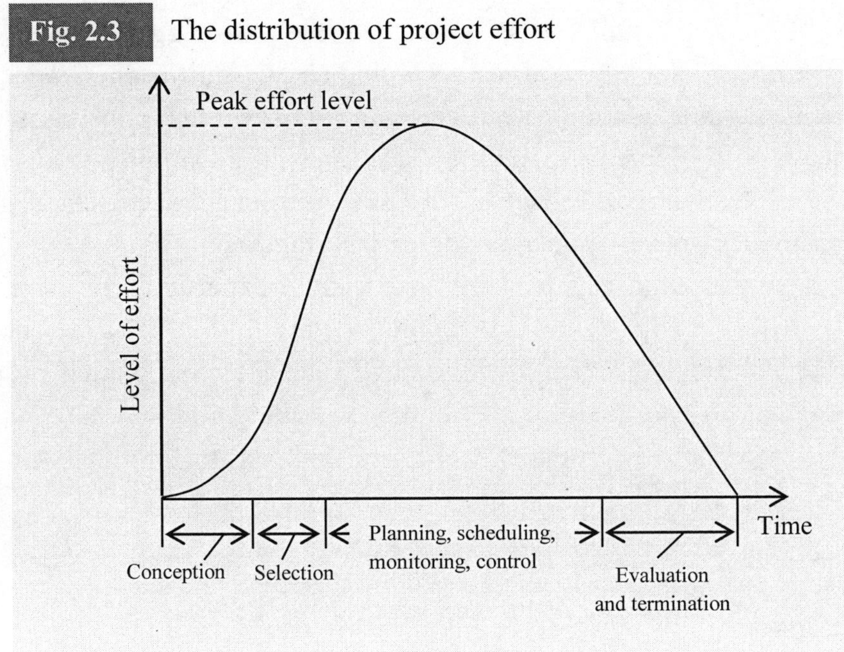

After resolving the primary "how" issues, project managers may become focused on expanding the scope, frequently above and beyond what was initially specified. This quest for greater scope increases expenses and causes scheduling delays.

Project schedule design and cost estimation occur concurrently with the definition of the project's technology. Cost was seen to be the most important factor during high activity periods, and schedule became the most important factor during the final stages when the client wanted delivery, much as scope was assumed to take precedence over schedule and cost early in the life cycle. As it happens, this common knowledge is false. According to recent studies, cost is not as significant as scope and schedule at any point.

Contrary to popular belief, many projects have a life cycle that differs significantly from the S-shaped shown in Fig. 2.2. Recall that "percent project completion" is displayed as a function of "time" in figure 2.2. If we substitute "resources" for the horizontal axis, the life-cycle function remains substantially the same. The life cycle essentially illustrates what an economist could refer to as "return on input," or the amount of project completion attributable to resource and time inputs. For certain projects, the S-shaped return curve accurately depicts reality; yet, for other projects, it is incredibly deceptive.

A new technological installation with several components, each of which produced distinct incremental benefits, could represent a particular kind of life-cycle curve. In these situations, companies would rather install the parts that provide "the biggest bang for the buck" first. As a result, the life-cycle curve that results would show significant advancement at first, slightly less the next, and continuously decreasing as the remaining parts were installed, essentially concave with "decreasing return to scale," as the economist would put it. Furthermore, there may even be an "inverse S-curve" that shows rapid advancement at first, a slowdown in the middle, and then speeding up again in the last stages.

The example of baking a cake can be used to illustrate a particularly significant alternate life cycle shape. After combining the ingredients, we are told to bake the cake for 35 minutes at 350 degrees Fahrenheit. When will we have cake after the baking process? Expert bakers are aware that in the final few minutes of baking, the mixture quickly transforms from "goop" – a technical term that cooks and bakers are familiar with – to "cake." This process' life cycle resembles the stretched-J curve depicted in Fig. 2.4.

Fig. 2.4 The stretched-J project life cycle

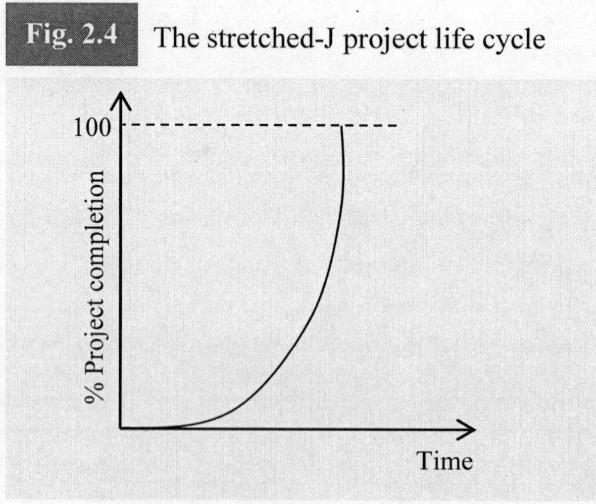

Many real projects, such as those involving computer software, chemistry, and chemical engineering, have a life cycle that is comparable to these. This life cycle is typically associated with projects whose output is made up of multiple subunits that, taken as a whole, are relatively helpful but have little utility on their own. This life-cycle curve would also be typical for projects in which an output undergoes a quick chemical reaction that turns it from goop to cake – a usable product.

2.3.1.1 REQUEST FOR PROPOSAL (RFP)

A request for proposals (RFP) for the project or portions of the project must usually be developed by the customer or project manager when the organization picks a project.

Data input from all parties involved in the activities included in the RFP will be needed by the project manager. An announcement of the RFP will be made to outside vendors and contractors who have sufficient experience to carry out the project. For instance, government projects often include advertisements asking for outside contractors to submit "requests for proposals" for the construction of roads, buildings, airports, military hardware, and spacecraft. In a similar vein, companies use RFPs to request quotes for tasks including creating a clean room, creating a new manufacturing procedure, providing software for insurance invoicing, and surveying the market. All of these examples show how specifications and features have to be provided in sufficient depth to provide contractors a precise idea of the finished product that will satisfy the needs of the client. To facilitate a straightforward evaluation of the various contractor responses, the RFP typically includes an intended format for the contractor's bid proposal. Though most of us associate RFPs with hiring outside contractors, some organizations utilize them internally, meaning they send out an RFP to different divisions or departments.

It is crucial that the RFP's content be included. In actuality, the most frequent mistake is to submit an RFP with insufficient information. This lack of information frequently leads to disagreements, miscommunications, legal disputes between the owner and contractor, and unsatisfied customers. Although each RFP is unique, we will provide a quick overview of the RFP's development below.

1. **An overview of the demands and action requests** – First, some background data and a concise overview of the project's final output are given. For example, through simulated war games, the defense navy of one nation found that its big battleships

from the past are too susceptible to contemporary weapons. They also discover that the Navy's current responsibilities involve supporting ground forces and conducting peacekeeping missions, both of which need being closer to shore. As a result, the Navy modernizes ships for near-shore operations. From among the responses to its request for proposals, the Navy would select a more advanced vessel that satisfies every need for a ship.

2. **A statement of work (SOW) that outlines the main deliverables and their scope** – For instance, if the project calls for conducting a market research study, the main outputs can include designing, gathering, and analyzing data, and offering suggestions by a specific date at a cost that won't go over a predetermined limit.
3. **Assignments, features, and deliverable requirements** – In order to validate contractor bid proposals and subsequently use them for control, this stage needs to be extremely thorough. Physical characteristics including size, quantity, materials, speed, and color are covered by typical standards. For instance, a detailed specification for hardware, software, and training may be part of an IT project. If tasks are known, they can be included to finish deliverables.
4. **Accountabilities: supplier and client** – When the contractor performs the project, it is well known that if the obligations for both parties are not clearly stated, there will be major issues. Who pays for what, for instance? (Will the contractor have to cover the cost of office space if they are going to be on site?) What are the contractor's limitations and exclusions? (For instance, who will provide the testing apparatus?) Which communication strategy will the owner and contractor follow? What procedure will be followed if it becomes essential to escalate a problem? How will advancement be assessed? Clear responsibilities now will prevent a lot of unanticipated issues later.
5. **Timeline for the project** – Creating a "hard" timeline that can be utilized for monitoring and controlling progress is the focus of this step. Owners are typically rather particular about the project timeline being met. Time-to-market is a significant "hot button" that affects market share, expenses, and profits in the current corporate environment. What, who, and when should all be specified in the schedule.
6. **Prices and the timeline for the payments** – The RFP must specify exactly how, when, and how the process of figuring out the price and terms of progress payments will be carried out.
7. **Kinds of agreements** – In essence, there are two kinds of contracts: cost-plus and fixed-price. Fixed-price agreements fix a price or lump sum up front, which doesn't

alter as long as the terms governing the agreement's scope stay the same. This kind is favored for clearly defined projects with low risk and predictable expenses. When predicting costs, the contractor must be careful because underestimating will result in lower profits for the contractor. Under cost-plus agreements, the contractor receives payment for all or a portion of the costs spent in carrying out the contract. The charge is usually negotiated in advance and is expressed as a percentage of the overall expenses. Cost-plus agreements typically include "time and materials" in addition to a profit factor. Both kinds of contracts may contain reward provisions for exceeding expectations in terms of both cost and schedule, or in certain situations, penalties for failure to meet project completion deadlines.

8. **Personnel and experience** – The contractor's capacity to carry out the project can require specialized knowledge; this expertise should be mentioned together with a guarantee that the team will be available for the project.
9. **Standards of evaluation** – The project contract's evaluation and awarding criteria must to be clearly defined. Methodology, pricing, timeline, and experience are a few examples of selection factors that are commonly used; in certain situations, these criteria are weighted. A well-written request for proposals (RFP) will give contractors enough direction to draft a proposal that distinctly addresses the needs of the customer and the project.

2.4 PROJECT PLANNING

A project enters the phase of detailed planning once it has been approved following all statutory, financial, and other appraisals. During this phase, the work breakdown structure is developed, roles for various tasks are decided upon, a schedule for completing various tasks is prepared, the resource requirements – including labor, equipment, materials, and money – are determined, and appropriate provisioning for the key resources is made to enable implementation. The project manager and his team can use their experience and knowledge to help establish a realistic project plan during the active phase of project management, known as project planning. Numerous networking strategies, analyses, simulations, and analytical models can offer extremely helpful hints to address some of the common issues that a project manager might be dealing with at this point. The planning stage involves a number of key actions, some of which are covered here.

2.4.1 ESTABLISHING A PROJECT TEAM HEADED BY A LEADER

Generally speaking, choosing a project leader who will oversee the entire endeavor is the most crucial first step in guaranteeing the project's success. The project manager needs to be an informed, seasoned professional with people-management abilities. Choosing individuals with the appropriate abilities and dedication, he would assemble a team based on the requirements of the project. The degree to which this diverse mix of individuals works together as an inspiring team under the direction of the project manager will determine how successful the project is, by far. In addition to the requisite number of systems developers, engineers, testers, clerks, and the like, the following essential team members may be required. In a variety of initiatives, people would have different titles, but they would still play comparable roles.

Systems developer – In addition to functional analysis, specifications, drawings, cost estimates, and documentation, the systems architect manages the fundamental product design and development.

Engineer for development – In addition to unit testing, manufacturing engineering, code design and production, production scheduling, and other production duties, this engineer's job is to efficiently produce the product or process that the project engineer has created.

Engineer for testing – After the engineering is finished, this person is in charge of the product's installation, testing, and support.

Administrator of contracts – The administrator oversees all official documentation, including monitoring standard compliance (including quality and dependability), billing, customer (engineering) modifications, inquiries, grievances, legal issues, expenses, and negotiations of other issues pertaining to the contract approving the project. The contract administrator frequently performs the roles of archivist and project historian.

Project controller – The controller maintains daily records of capital equipment status, labor charges, project supplies, and cost variations. In addition, the controller communicates often with the project management and the company controller and submits reports on a regular basis. The controller can take on the role of historian in place of the administrator.

Manager of support services – This individual oversees purchasing, contract negotiations, data processing, subcontractors, product support, and general management support duties.

It is crucial that the project controller and the systems developer answer directly to the project management out of all these key project personnel. This makes it easier to maintain control over the project's two primary objectives: budget and technical performance.

Project managers use a projection of staffing requirements for the project's duration to staff the project. A few unique charts are used to help with this. In order to ascertain the precise nature of the tasks necessary to finish the project, a work breakdown structure (WBS) must first be created.

2.4.2 DEFINING SCOPE AND TERMS OF REFERENCE

The project's terms of reference and goals must be directly linked to the organization's overarching mission, objectives, and strategy; this may be seen in the project portfolio process, for example. Senior management should spell out the project's objectives, its scope, and how the project's anticipated outcomes will support the organization's objectives in the project overview. Project planning (and subsequent progress) can quickly go wrong in the absence of a clear beginning.

Since the project may involve a large number of people and agencies with competing interests, it is important to keep the goals and terms of reference clear to all members of the project team in order to prevent any disputes or tensions from arising as the project moves forward. In a new project, the terms of reference and scope are frequently extremely loosely stated. The project team would be wise to develop a precise scope through mutual discussion in such circumstances. The partners would benefit from the exercise by having a clear understanding of their responsibilities within the project and how they depend on everyone else.

2.4.3 WORK BREAKDOWN STRUCTURE (WBS)

To facilitate efficient planning and execution, the project has been logically divided into smaller, more manageable segments. People or groups can then be given individual accountability for their respective portions of the job. Building the work breakdown structure can be done in a variety of ways. As an example, a functional categorization system might be used, wherein project components such as design, planning, procurement, erection, and commissioning are categorized. Alternative approaches include discussing the propulsion system, ballistic shell, payload, and launching platform in the context of a missile development project.

WBS is used to find useful work packages to use as planning and progress tracking units for projects. Every station should have about the same cycle time, just like in an assembly line. Similar to this, the work packages ought to be manageable in terms of length and structure.

Fig. 2.5 Work breakdown structure

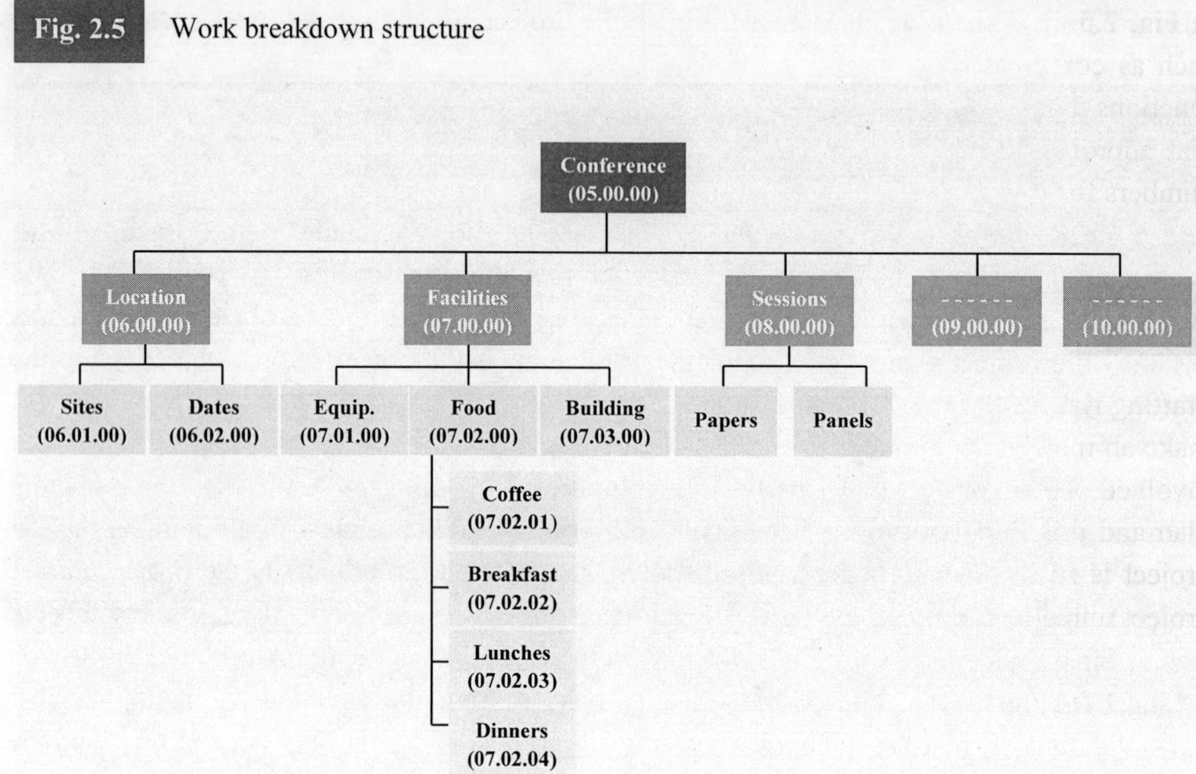

All of the activities should be listed in the approximate sequence that they will happen. This is the 1st level. At this level, anywhere from 2 to 20 activities might be considered suitable. (These boundaries are not inherently sanctified. The smallest number of related items that can be arranged and planned with ease at a particular level of aggregation is 2, while the maximum is approximately 20). Divide the level 1 items into 2 to 20 tasks. It's level 2. Divide each level 2 task into two to twenty smaller tasks in the same manner. It's level 3 here. Continue in this manner until the specific activities at a level – typically the level of each worker – are so well understood that further work breakdown is not necessary. The "hierarchical planning process" is demonstrated by this. The most fundamental level (Level 1) and perhaps even the subsequent level will be produced by the project management. The creation of extra levels will be left to the people or teams in charge of completing the work, unless the project is extremely small.

The WBS is essentially a condensed version of the project plan that is task-oriented. It frequently displays the organizational components of a project broken out into work packages, subtasks, and other hierarchical units of tasks. A conference's WBS looks like this in Fig. 2.5. The facilities staff's food group is in charge of providing meals and beverages, such as coffee breaks and water pitchers in conference rooms.There are five distinct food functions displayed, all of which are probably subdivided into more specific duties.To ensure that appropriate charges are made for each activity completed on the project, the account numbers for each task are displayed in this instance.

2.4.4 RISK MANAGEMENT PLANNING

Starting risk management at an early stage of a project is never too soon. It is impossible to make an informed judgment on which projects to choose without being aware of the dangers involved. Thus, prior to the project being formally chosen for support, the risk management plan and preliminary risk identification need to be completed. Thus, as soon as a possible project is recognized, the risk management group needs to be established. We will discuss project implementation and project completion ini the next unit.

2.4.4.1 RISK IDENTIFICATION

Initially, project risk is ill-defined, with a predominant emphasis on externalities like the status of technology in project-relevant domains, business conditions in related industries, and so on. When faced with external hazards, the typical course of action is to monitor relevant environments and calculate the project's probability of survival under different scenarios. Risks related to project technology, schedule, budget, and resource allocation won't start to materialize until the project is in the planning stages.

Fig. 2.6 Graph of risk events

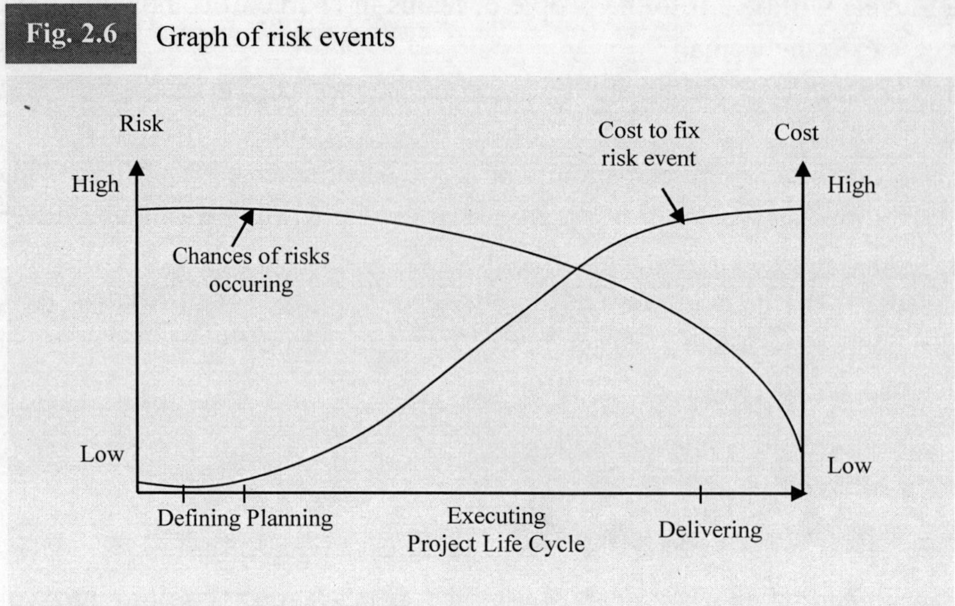

A graphic representation of the risk management dilemma is shown in Fig. 2.6. Early in a project, there is a greater probability of a risk event occurring (such as an error in cost, schedule, or design technology). At this point, there is the most ambiguity and a lot of unresolved questions. Risk decreases when the project moves closer to completion and the answers to important questions, concerning feasibility of technology, timeline, etc. are resolved. For instance, the risk event of a design problem developing after a prototype has a bigger financial or time impact than if the flaw was found in the project's planning stages.

Work breakdown structures (WBSs) and risk breakdown structures (RBSs) are used by organizations to assist management teams in identifying and eventually analyzing hazards. An example of an RBS in general is shown in Fig. 2.7. Rather to concentrating on a particular area of the project or network, the initial focus should be on risks that have the potential to impact the entire undertaking. The team may recognize the prospect of project budget cuts after the project has commenced as a serious risk event, for instance, as a result of the funding conversation. Similarly, in talking about the market, the group might include reacting to rivals' new product releases as a risk event.

Fig. 2.7 The risk breakdown structure (RBS)

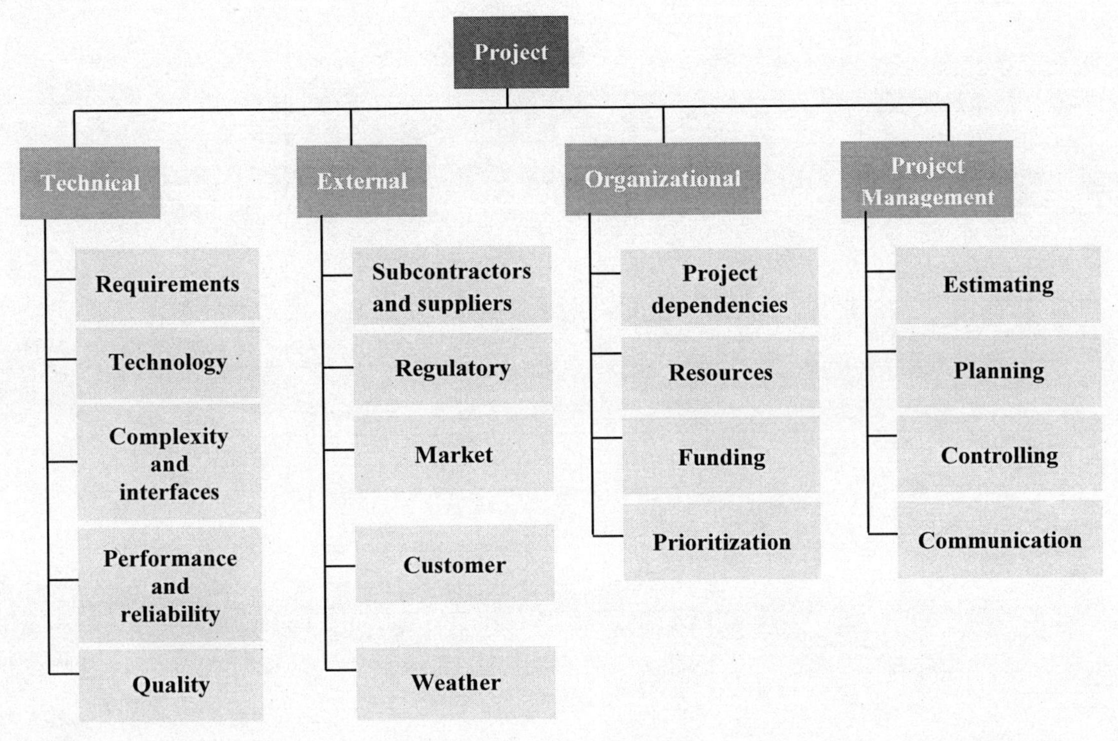

2.4.4.2 RISK ASSESSMENT

In order to focus attention on the most critical risks, the risk identified in the previous phase must be prioritized using *qualitative risk analysis*. This technique may be used quickly, easily, and flexible to both opportunities and dangers due to its qualitative nature. An objective (or subjective, if available) evaluation of the risk's likelihood of happening is required; this estimate could come from a Delphi process carried out with a group of subject-matter experts. The probability values don't have to be exact; in fact, they may just be "low," "medium," or "high," or even just a rank on a scale of 1 to 5.

Fig. 2.8 Risk Matrix

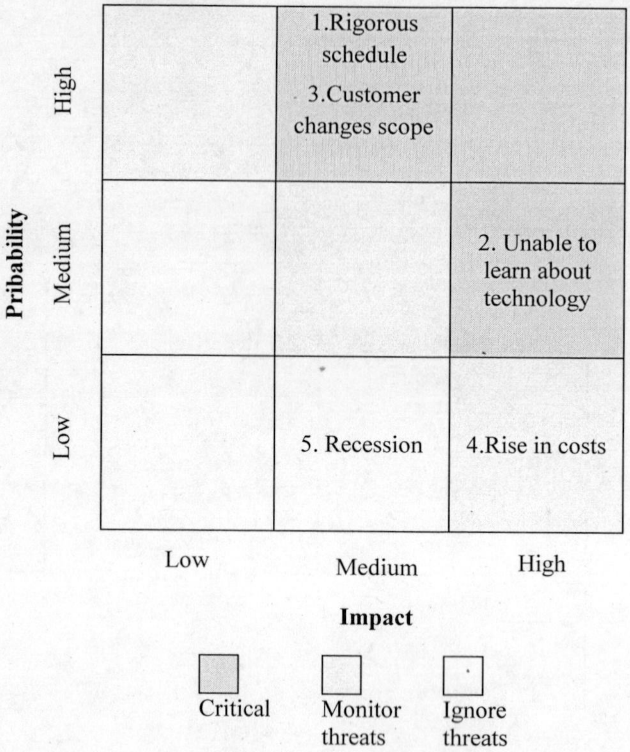

Pribability \ Impact	Low	Medium	High
High		1.Rigorous schedule 3.Customer changes scope	
Medium			2. Unable to learn about technology
Low		5. Recession	4.Rise in costs

Critical | Monitor threats | Ignore threats

After determining the likelihood and impact levels, a Risk Matrix can be created, as shown in figure 2.8. The most basic variant is seen above, with nine cells representing the "low, medium, and high" categories. A 1 to 5 range would have 25 cells to take into account, and a percentage of a 100 range could be divided into as many relevant cells as possible. For example, Figure 2.8 illustrates that threats with a high value on one measure and a medium or high value on the other are considered "critical"; in this instance, this means that the threat is high probability – medium impact, high on each, and medium probability – high impact. Similar categories apply to the other cells; in this case, we employed only three symmetrical categories: "critical," "monitor," and "ignore." Nonetheless, using four categories – or even just two – for some threats would be appropriate, and each threat's cells might be assigned a separate category. On the other hand, one matrix can be used to show the distribution of all threats if the risk matrix cell categories appear appropriate for all threats. This is what we have done in Fig. 2.8 by listing the five threats, for instance, in their respective cells.

Sometimes, once the major risks facing a project have been determined by the qualitative risk analysis, a quantitative risk analysis is carried out. If the data are available, it is usually more exact and more precise. Here, we cover three methods: An extra process element, decision tree analysis utilizing expected monetary values, and simulation are all included in the more rigorous Failure Mode and Effect Analysis (FMEA) method of analyzing the risk matrix.

FMEA involves using a scoring methodology. It is simple, widely employed, especially in engineering, and can be applied to risk with ease by following the six steps.

1. Enumerate the potential reasons why a project could fail.
2. Assess the impact severity (*S*) of every kind of failure using a 10-point rating system, where "1" represents "no effect", and 10 represents "extremely severe."
3. Determine the probability (*P*) that each cause of failure will occur using a 10-point scale, where "1" represents "remote" and 10 represents "almost certain."
4. Calculate the probability that a failure connected to each cause won't be detected (*D*). On a 10-point scale, "1" indicates that detectability with standard monitoring/control systems is almost assured, and "10" indicates that failure will most likely not be discovered in time to prevent or mitigate it.
5. Find the Risk Priority Number (RPN), where $RPN = S \times P \times D$.
6. With a noticeably high RPN, think about methods to lower the *S*, *P*, and *D* for every cause of failure.

UNIT SUMMARY

- ***What is a Project?*** – Defines a project as a temporary endeavor with a unique objective, a defined timeline, and performance constraints.
- ***Project Life Cycle*** – Describes the four main stages of a project: Selection (identifying, evaluating, and choosing a project), Planning (defining scope, work breakdown, and resource allocation), Implementation (executing and managing resources), and Completion and Audit (evaluating outcomes and closing the project).
- ***Request for Proposal*** (RFP) – Explains how organizations solicit bids from vendors and contractors for project execution.
- ***Establishing a Project Team*** – Covers team composition, leadership roles, and the importance of collaboration.
- ***Defining Scope and Terms of Reference*** – Highlights the need to clearly define project objectives, deliverables, and boundaries.

- ***Work Breakdown Structure*** (WBS) – Introduces WBS as a method to break down a project into smaller, manageable tasks.
- ***Risk Management*** – Explains risk identification, assessment, and mitigation strategies to handle uncertainties.

EXERCISES

MULTIPLE CHOICE QUESTIONS

2.1 Why is it important to conduct a feasibility study during project identification?

(a) To determine project objectives	(b) To assess the project's technical and financial viability
(c) To allocate project resources	(d) To define project scope

2.2 What is the purpose of a detailed project report in market appraisal for project selection?

(a) To assess the technical feasibility of the project	(b) To evaluate the financial viability of the project
(c) To analyze the market potential and demand for the project	(d) All of the above

2.3 Which of the following is NOT typically included in a detailed project report for market appraisal?

(a) SWOT analysis	(b) Comprtitor analysis
(c) Marketing strategy	(d) Employee training manuals

2.4 How does a detailed project report (DPR) help in project selection?

(a) By providing information on project team members	(b) By outlining the project timeline and milestones
(c) By identifying potential risks and uncertainties	(d) By listing the company's competitors

2.5 What financial metrics are commonly used in the financial appraisal section of a DPR?

(a) Net Present Value (NPV) and Internal Rate of Return (IRR)	(b) Customer satisfaction and brand loyalty
(c) Employee turnover rate and absenteeism	(d) Market share and revenue growth

2.6 What role does the detailed project report play in the decision-making process for project selection?

(a) It provides a summary of the project's financial risks	(b) It helps stakeholders understand the project's technical requirements
(c) It outlines the project's advertising campaign	(d) It determines the project's location

2.7 How can socio-economic and environmental appraisals in a detailed project report contribute to long-term sustainability goals?

(a) By prioritizing short-term gains over long-term impacts	(b) By incorporating community feedback and addressing social inequalities
(c) By disregarding environmental regulations	(d) By focusing solely on financial returns

2.8 Which methodological approach is commonly used to integrate socio-economic and environmental considerations in a detailed project report?

(a) Linear programming	(b) Multi-criteria decision making
(c) Simple random sampling	(d) Qualitative research methods

2.9 In the context of the S-pattern project life cycle, how does the maturity phase differ from the growth phase?

(a) Maturity phase focuses on innovation, while growth phase focuses on expansion	(b) Maturity phase involves cost reduction, while growth phase involves resource allocation
(c) Maturity phase emphasizes stability, while growth phase emphasizes rapid development	(d) Maturity phase prioritizes risk management, while growth phase prioritizes stakeholder engagement

2.10 In the context of the Stretched-J curve, which project is most likely to experience initial high costs followed by a period of negative returns before eventual profitability?

(a) Building a new shopping mall	(b) Launching a new software product
(c) Establishing a renewable energy plant	(d) Organizing a music festival

2.11 How can project managers use the project effort curve to optimize resource allocation in the project life cycle?

(a) By allocating more resources during the decline phase	(b) By reducing resources during the growth phase

(c) By aligning resource allocation with peak effort requirements	(d) By maintaining a constant level of resources throughout the project

2.12 Which of the following is NOT typically included in a request for proposal (RFP) in project management?

(a) Project objectives and scope	(b) Budget allocation details
(c) Evaluation criteria for vendor selection	(d) Legal terms and conditions

2.13 How does an RFP differ from a request for quotation (RFQ) in project management?

(a) RFP focuses on technical specifications, while RFQ focuses on pricing	(b) RFP is issued by vendors, while RFQ is issued by project managers
(c) RFP is a legally binding document, while RFQ is not	(d) RFP is used for small projects, while RFQ is used for large projects

2.14 Which of the following best describes the purpose of a work breakdown structure (WBS) in project management?

(a) To allocate resources efficiently	(b) To define project objectives
(c) To identify project risks	(d) To schedule project activities

2.15 How does a work breakdown structure (WBS) help in project planning and execution?

(a) By defining project scope and objectives	(b) By assigning responsibilities to team members
(c) By estimating project costs and timelines	(d) By monitoring project progress and performance

2.16 Which of the following is an example of a technical risk that may be identified during risk management planning?

(a) Changes in government regulations	(b) Supplier bankruptcy
(c) Technology obsolescence	(d) Inaccurate cost estimation

2.17 What is the purpose of risk assessment in project risk management planning?

(a) To eliminate all project risks	(b) To transfer all risks to external parties
(c) To identify, analyze, and prioritize risks to develop effective risk response strategies	(d) To ignore risks and proceed with the project as planned

Answers of Multiple Choice Questions

2.1 (b), 2.2 (d), 2.3 (d), 2.4 (c), 2.5 (a), 2.6 (b), 2.7 (b), 2.8 (b), 2.9 (c), 2.10 (a), 2.11 (c), 2.12 (b), 2.13 (a), 2.14 (a), 2.15 (c), 2.16 (c), 2.17 (c)

SHORT AND LONG ANSWER TYPE QUESTIONS

Category I

2.1 What are the benefits of conducting a SWOT analysis during the project identification phase?

2.2 How does the market appraisal component of the project selection process consider factors such as consumer behavior, market segmentation, and demand forecasting to inform strategic planning and project implementation?

2.3 What key financial metrics and indicators are considered in the financial appraisal process within project selection, and how do these metrics influence decision-making regarding project investment and resource allocation?

2.4 In what ways does the detailed project report for technical appraisal address issues related to technology readiness, infrastructure requirements, and technical risks to ensure the successful development and deployment of the project?

2.5 In what ways does the detailed project report on socio-economic and environmental appraisal analyze the environmental implications and sustainability considerations of a project, including resource use, waste management, and carbon footprint?

2.6 How does the S-curve model in project management illustrate the different phases of a project's life cycle, and what factors influence the timing and shape of each curve segment?

2.7 How can project managers use the project effort curve to identify potential bottlenecks and areas for improvement in project execution?

2.8 What role does the work breakdown structure (WBS) play in defining project scope and ensuring project deliverables are clearly defined?

2.9 What role does effective leadership play in creating a high-performing project team?

2.10 What potential factors should be considered when identifying risks in a project management plan?

2.11 What strategies can be implemented to continuously monitor and update risk assessments throughout the lifecycle of a project in order to mitigate potential risks?

Category II

2.12 How can organizations effectively prioritize and rank potential projects based on their strategic alignment, resource requirements, and expected benefits during the project identification and appraisal stages?

2.13 How does the concept of the Stretched S-curve in project management relate to the Project Effort Curve, and how can an understanding of these models help project managers optimize resource allocation, manage project timelines, and mitigate potential risks throughout the project lifecycle?

2.14 How can the development and evaluation of a comprehensive Request for Proposal (RFP) in project management ensure that project requirements are clearly defined, stakeholders' expectations are aligned, and potential vendors are effectively assessed based on their capabilities, experience, and proposed solutions, ultimately leading to the successful selection and execution of the project?

2.15 How can a systematic and thorough approach to project risk identification and risk assessment in project management planning help project teams proactively identify, analyze, and prioritize potential risks, develop effective risk response strategies, and ultimately enhance project success by minimizing the impact of uncertainties and unforeseen events throughout the project lifecycle?

Numerical Problem

2.16 A company is considering three potential projects to invest in: Project A, Project B, and Project C. The company needs to prioritize these projects based on criteria such as profitability, feasibility, and strategic alignment. The decision-makers have assigned weights to each criterion as follows:

- Profitability: 40%
- Feasibility: 30%
- Strategic Alignment: 30%

They have also evaluated each project's performance against these criteria and assigned scores on a scale of 1 to 9, with 1 being the least favorable and 9 being the most favorable. The scores for each project are as follows:

Project A:
- Profitability: 7
- Feasibility: 8
- Strategic Alignment: 6

Project B:
- Profitability: 6
- Feasibility: 7
- Strategic Alignment: 8

Project C:
- Profitability: 8
- Feasibility: 6
- Strategic Alignment: 7

Using the AHP (Analytic Hierarchy Process) method, calculate the overall priority or ranking of the three projects based on the weighted scores for each criterion.

SCAN ME
for
AHP

Note: The AHP method analysis can be studied by the reader by scanning the QR code.

REFERENCES AND SUGGESTED READINGS

1. Adams, J.R. and Barndt, S.E. Behavorial Implications of the Project Life Cycle, in Cleland, D.I. and King, W.R., Edition, *Project Management Handbook*. New York: Van Nostrand Reinhold, 1983.
2. Baker, B.N., Murphy, P.C., and Fisher, D. Factors Affecting Project Success, in Cleland, D.I. and King, W.R., Edition, *Project Management Handbook*, New York: Van Nostrand Reinhold, 778 – 801, 1983.
3. Chapman, C., and Ward, S. *Project Risk Management*: *Processes, Techniques and Insights*, 2nd Edition, Wiley, 2011.
4. Dewhurst, H.D. *Project Teams*: *What Have We Learned*? PM Network, 1998.
5. Duncan, W. R. A Guide to the Project Management Body of Knowledge. *Project Management Journal*, Vol. 27(2), 29-35, 1996.
6. Gray, C.F., Larson, E.W. and Desai, G.V. *Project Management*: *The Managerial Process*, 6th Edition, McGraw Hill Education (India), 2014.
7. Hillson, D., and Murray-Webster, R. (2017). *Understanding and Managing Risk Attitude*, 2nd Edition, Routledge, 2017.
8. Hubbard, D.G. Work Structuring, in Dinsmore, P.C., Edition, *The AMA Handbook of Project Management*, New York: AMACOM, 1993.
9. Kloppenborg, T. J. *Project Management*: *A Systems Approach to Planning, Scheduling, and Controlling*, 12th Edition, Pearson, 2019.
10. Meredith, J. R., and Mantel, S. J. *Project Management*: *A Managerial Approach*, 9th Edition, Wiley, 2017.
11. Project Management Institute (PMI). *A Guide to the Project Management Body of Knowledge* (PMBOK Guide), 6th Edition, Project Management Institute, 2017.
12. Sarker, S., and Sarker, S. Exploring Agility in Distributed Information Systems Development Teams. *Information Systems Research*, Vol. 20(3), 442-460, 2009.

13. Schwalbe, K. *Information Technology Project Management*, 8th Edition, Cengage Learning, 2015.

14. Shenhar, A. J., and Dvir, D. Project Success: A Multidimensional Strategic Concept. *Long Range Planning*, Vol. 40(4), 399-414, 2007.

15. Thamhain, H.J. and Wilemon, D.L. Conflict Management in Project Life Cycles. *Sloan Management Review*, Summer, 1975.

16. Ward, S., and Chapman, C. Transforming Project Risk Management into Project Uncertainty Management. *International Journal of Project Management*, Vol. 21(2), 97-105, 2003.

17. Wysocki, R. K. *Effective Project Management*: Traditional, Agile, Extreme, 7th Edition, Wiley, 2014.

UNIT 3

PROJECT SCHEDULING AND CLOSURE

UNIT SPECIFICS

This unit elaborately discusses the following topics:

- Fundamental ideas behind project scheduling
- Key scheduling terminology
- Network development
- Estimates of deterministic time (Critical Path Method)
- Estimates of probabilistic time (Program Evaluation and Review Technique)
- Time-cost tradeoff (crashing)
- Deliverables for project closure.

The topics' real-world applications are examined in order to foster greater creativity and curiosity as well as enhance problem-solving skills. The unit includes assignments through a number of numerical problems, a list of references, and suggested readings in addition to a large number of multiple-choice questions and questions with short and long answer types marked in two categories following lower and higher order of Bloom's taxonomy. These can be completed for practice.

RATIONALE

This unit centers on the essential role of project scheduling in effective project management. Understanding the fundamental ideas behind scheduling equips project managers with the tools to allocate resources efficiently and meet deadlines. Familiarity with key scheduling terminology ensures clear communication among stakeholders, while network development provides a visual representation of task dependencies, enhancing planning accuracy. The unit explores both deterministic time estimates through the Critical Path Method (CPM), which identifies critical tasks that determine project duration, and probabilistic time estimates using the Program Evaluation and Review Technique (PERT), which helps manage uncertainty and risk. Additionally, the discussion on time-cost tradeoffs (crashing) enables managers to make informed decisions when balancing project timelines and budgets. Ultimately, mastering these concepts leads to the successful delivery of project outcomes and the achievement of deliverables necessary for project closure, ensuring that projects meet their goals and stakeholder expectations.

UNIT OUTCOMES

List of outcomes of this unit is as follows:

U3-UO1: Understanding Project Scheduling Fundamentals

U3-UO2: Key terminology in Project Scheduling

U3-UO3: Developing a Project Scheduling Network

U3-UO4: Applying the Critical Path Method (CPM)

U3-UO5: Utilizing the Program Evaluation and Review Technique (PERT)

U3-UO6: Implementing Time-Cost Tradeoff Strategies and culminating in a strategic plan for project closure

UNIT-3 Outcomes	EXPECTED MAPPING WITH COURSE OUTCOMES (*1-Weak Correlation; 2-Medium Correlation; 3-Strong Correlation)*					
	CO-1	**CO-2**	**CO-3**	**CO-4**	**CO-5**	**CO-6**
U3-UO1	1	3	2	2	1	2
U3-UO2	1	3	2	2	1	1
U3-UO3	2	3	1	2	1	2
U3-UO4	2	3	1	2	2	3
U3-UO5	2	3	1	2	1	1
U3-UO6	3	3	1	2	1	2

3.1 INTRODUCTION

The process of converting a project's work breakdown structure (WBS) into an operating schedule is called scheduling. As such, it forms the cornerstone for tracking and managing project activities and, when combined with the plan and budget, is perhaps the most important instrument for project management. Because projects lack the continuity of continuing operations and frequently offer far more complex coordination challenges, the scheduling function is more crucial in a project setting than it would be in an ongoing one. In fact, project timing is so crucial that clients occasionally want a precise timeline. One of the most important tools in establishing the project's monitoring and control systems is a well-crafted, comprehensive schedule.

There is no requirement for the same level of detail when scheduling project tasks. There might actually be multiple schedules (the master timetable, the calendar for development and testing, and the schedule for assembly, for instance). The previously established WBS that will cover the work package is usually the basis for these schedules. Listing every work package is not always required, though. The ones that require the most attention in order to keep proper control over the project can be the primary emphasis. These kinds of products are typically costly, challenging, or have a short completion timeline.

The fundamental idea behind all scheduling systems is to create a network of linkages between events and activities that visually represents the order in which tasks in a project are completed. Then, jobs that must come first or come after others are recognized with precision, both in terms of timing and functionality. An effective tool for project planning and management, this kind of network offers the following advantages:

- It is a dependable framework for planning, scheduling, monitoring, and managing the project.
- It demonstrates how all tasks, work packages, and work elements are interdependent.
- It indicates the times at which particular people and materials must be accessible to work on a particular project.
- It helps to make sure that departments and functions are properly communicating with one another.
- It establishes the anticipated date of project completion.
- It pinpoints so-called key tasks that, if postponed, will also extend the project's timeline for completion.

- It also indicates which tasks have slack and may be postponed for predetermined amounts of time without incurring penalties, as well as which resources can be borrowed for a short time without risk.
- It establishes when tasks can be begun, or when they must be started in order for the project to stay on time.
- It demonstrates which tasks need to be scheduled in order to prevent conflicts with resources or time.
- Additionally, it shows which jobs can – or need to – be completed concurrently in order to meet the project's deadline.
- Since task dependencies are made obvious, it resolves certain interpersonal disputes.
- The data utilised could enable an approximation of the likelihood of project completion by different deadlines, or the date that corresponds to a specific a priori probability.

3.2 KEY SCHEDULING TERMINOLOGY

A lot of technical terminology are used frequently in project scheduling, thus they require definitions. They frequently use the Project Management Institute's Body of Knowledge as the source for their definitions. Here is a list of some of the themes that you will encounter frequently during this unit. Several of these terms are ones you have already encountered in earlier units.

Scope – The work and outputs of a project or a project component are referred to as its scope. By listing all of the tasks completed, the materials used, and the final goods produced – including quality standards – the scope is completely defined.

Work Breakdown Structure (WBS) – An organized, defined, and visually represented "family tree" of tasks that outlines all the work that needs to be done to complete a project in order to meet its goals. A more thorough definition of the project goal is represented by each declining level.

Work package – An item of work completed during a project that is listed as a deliverable at the bottom of the work breakdown structure. A projected cost and duration are typically included in a work package. Task and activity are other general names for project work.

Project network diagram (PND) – Any diagram that shows the projects' actions in a logical order.

Path – A series of tasks specified by the project's network logic.

Early start date (ES) – The earliest date, contingent upon network logic and any schedule constraints, on which the outstanding portions of an activity (or project) can begin. Early start dates are subject to change as the project develops and the project plan is adjusted.

Late start date (LS) – The latest date on which an activity can start without causing a delay in a designated milestone, typically the project completion date.

Forward pass – Network computations that establish each activity's earliest start and earliest finish time (date). It is ascertained by proceeding through every action within the network.

Backward pass – Late finish timings (dates) are calculated for all unfinished network activities by going backwards and going through each activity one by one.

Event – A point in time when something is either started or finished. Events are frequently used in conjunction with AOA (activity on arrow) networks; they don't use any resources and don't have a completion period.

Node – A junction point connected to some or all other points of a network by dependency lines, or routes, are one of the defining points of the network.

Predecessors – Those activities that need to be finished before a subsequent network activity can begin.

Successors – Tasks that need the completion of earlier tasks before they can begin. These jobs come after the earlier, predecessor ones.

Merge activity – An activity that has two or more immediate predecessors or tasks that flow into it. Locating merge activity in the network can be achieved by doing a forward pass.

Burst activity –An activity that has two or more tasks that flow directly from it. Locating burst activity requires making a backward pass over the network.

Float – The duration of a delay in an activity from its initial start date that won't affect the project's completion date. As the project develops and the project plan is modified, the mathematical calculation known as "float" may also alter. It is also known as path float, slack, and total float. The difference between the early start date (ES) and the late start date (LS) are commonly referred to as float.

Critical path – It is the longest path through the project network. Depending on when tasks are finished ahead of time or behind plan, the critical route may occasionally alter. Project float is lowest for tasks on the critical route.

Critical path method – An approach to network analysis that identifies the path or sequence of activities with the least degree of scheduling flexibility (float) will probably dictate when the project can be finished. It entails figuring out the start and end dates of each task early (ahead scheduling) and late (reverse scheduling). This method operates under the implicit assumption that all resources needed at any given time will be available.

Resource-limited schedule – A project schedule with start and end dates that correspond to anticipated resource availability. There should always be a resource constraint on the ultimate project timeline.

Program Evaluation and Review Technique (PERT) – An event- and probability-based network analysis system that is typically employed in projects with ill-defined activities and durations. In extensive programs involving multiple organizations in widely different locations, PERT is frequently employed.

When building activity networks, Activity-on-Arrow (AOA) and Activity-on-Node (AON) logic are the two most popular approaches. The task, or activity, is represented by the arrow in the AOA method, and the node denotes a connection between events that implies the conclusion of one activity and the possibility of beginning the next. The node in the AON approach stands for an activity, and the path arrows show the logical order in which the node moves through the network. Although AOA methodologies were most popular several decades ago and are still utilized to some level in the construction sector, AON methodology is now heavily emphasized due to the rapid expansion of computer-based scheduling applications.

3.3 NETWORK DEVELOPMENT

In order to schedule projects as effectively as possible, network diagramming is a logical, sequential procedure that calls for you to think about the sequence in which activities should take place. PERT and CPM are the two main techniques used to create activity networks. The U.S. Navy, Booz-Allen Hamilton, and Lockheed Corporation worked together to develop PERT, or the Program Evaluation and Review Technique, in the late 1950s in order to create the Polaris missile program. PERT originated from probability analysis and was initially utilized in research and development (R&D), an area where estimating activity time can be challenging. Critical Path Method, or CPM, was independently developed by DuPont, Inc. concurrently with PERT. According to CPM, durations are more predictable, meaning they can be assigned to activities with more confidence because they are simpler to determine. Furthermore, the purpose of CPM was to improve the relationship between (and consequently, regulate) the time and expenses of project activities, especially the time/cost trade-offs that result in impulsive judgments (accelerating the project).

When creating the network diagram, there are a few basic guidelines that you should familiarize yourself with before building an activity network. Understanding the logic of activity networks is greatly aided by these guidelines.

1. Before building the network, some order must be determined for the precedence of the activities. That is, every activity, including those that come before and those that come after, ought to make sense in relation to one another.
2. Network diagrams often have a left-to-right flow.
3. Before any related activity can start, all previous ones must be finished.
4. On networks, arrows show logic flow and precedence. Arrows can cross over one another, but whenever feasible, try to keep this effect as little as possible for the sake of clarity.
5. Every activity ought to have a special code, letter, number, etc. attached to it. These identifiers should be larger than the identifiers of previous activities and should occur in ascending order for simplicity's sake.
6. It is not allowed to loop through activities, or recycle through them.
7. Even in situations when there are numerous alternative start points, it is customary to begin a project from a single beginning node, while this is not necessary. Typically, a single node point serves as the project end indicator.

By keeping these basic guidelines in mind, you may start to understand some of the fundamental concepts of constructing a network diagram. Keep in mind that the AON technique views each activity as a node within the network. Arrows are solely used to show how the project's activities run sequentially from the beginning to the end.

3.3.1 SERIAL ACTIVITIES

Activities that proceed sequentially from one to the next are called serial activities. Based on the reasoning presented in Figure 3.1, we are unable to start working on Activity B until Activity A is finished. Activity B and A must be completed before starting Activity C. The simplest activity networks are serial ones since they simply establish connections between sequential activities. Serial networks are a suitable depiction of project activity in many circumstances.

Fig. 3.1 Activities in series

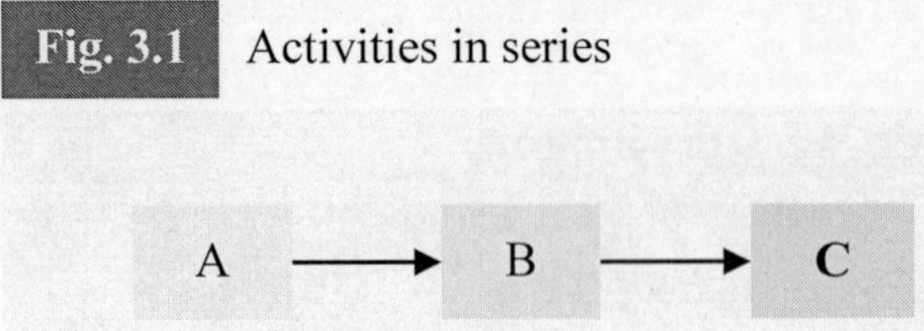

According to network logic:

- Activity A is a starting activity, or it can start right away.
- Activity A must be finished before starting Activity B.
- Before activity C may start, activity A and B must be finished.

3.3.2 CONCURRENT ACTIVITIES

It is often possible to start working on multiple tasks at once, provided we have the resources necessary for both. An illustration of how concurrent or parallel project paths are shown in an activity network may be found in Figure 3.2. Concurrent activities are those that can be completed while working on a project; these activities are referred to as parallel project activity paths since they are built through the network.

Fig. 3.2 Concurrent activities

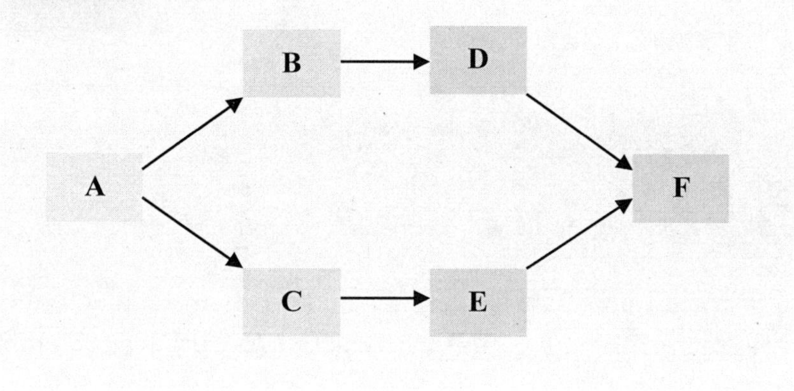

According to network logic:

- After activity A is finished, you can start activities B and C.
- Activity D can start independently of activity C and after activity B is finished.
- Activity E can start independently of activity B and after activity C is finished.
- After both activities D and E are finished, activity F can start.

3.3.3 MERGE ACTIVITIES

Activities involving mergers have two or more direct antecedents. A partial network diagram that illustrates the graphic expression of merge activities is presented in Figure 3.3. Merge activities are frequently crucial intersections, locations where two or more concurrent project pathways meet within the network as a whole.

According to network logic:
Only when activities A, B, and C have been finished can activity D start.

Fig. 3.3 Merge activities

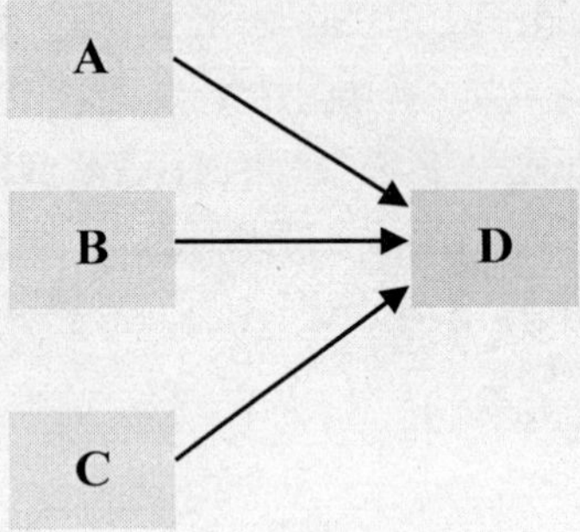

3.3.4 BURST ACTIVITIES

Activities that have two or more immediate successors are known as burst activities. A burst activity network is shown graphically in Fig. 3.4, where activities B, C, and D are planned to happen after activity A is finished.

Fig. 3.4 Burst activities

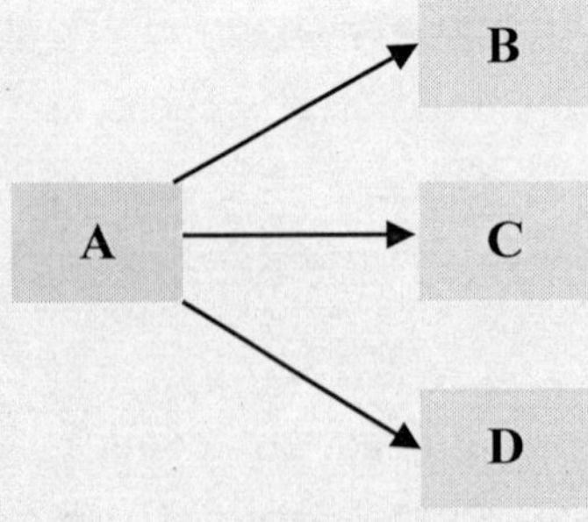

According to network logic:
Activity A must be finished before moving on to activities B, C, and D.

Example 3.1

Now let's start building a simple activity network. Eight tasks and their antecedents in a basic sample project are listed in table below. After identifying the actions required to complete the project, it's critical to start connecting those tasks to one another. Essentially, we are appending a project timeline to the project tasks found in the Work Breakdown Structure.

Activity	Description	Predecessor
A	Signing of a contract	None
B	Design of questionnaires	A
C	ID of the target market	A
D	Sample of the survey	B, C
E	Create a preentation	B
F	Examine the outcome	D
G	Study of demographics	C
H	Presentation to the customer	E, F, G

The process of building a network can start as soon as the network activity table is created and the predecessors are located. The initial activity (A), which is located far to the left of our figure and is the starting point in the network, has no predecessors. Next, activities A is identified as the predecessor by both activities B and C. The completed activity network is displayed in Fig. 3.5. Remember from previously that this network has one point at the beginning (activity A) and one point at the end (activity H). Activity D, which involves the merging of activities B and C at this node, and activity H, which involves the merging of activities E, F, and G at this node, are the merge activities linked to this network. There are three burst activities: A, B, and C.

Fig. 3.5 Complete activity network/precedence diagram for project

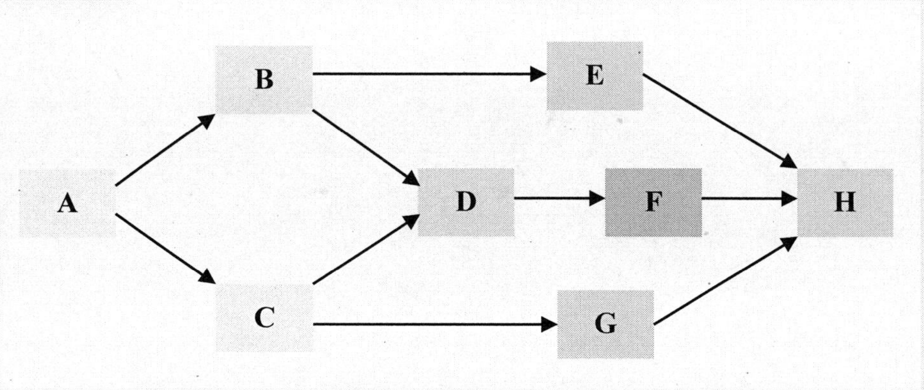

Remember that actions that have two or more immediate successors in the network are referred to as burst activities. Tasks B and C are the successors of activity A, tasks D and E are the activities that follow it, and tasks D and G are the tasks that follow activity C.

3.4 ESTIMATES OF DETERMINISTIC TIME

We refer to time estimations as deterministic if we have a high degree of confidence that the actual times won't deviate greatly from the estimates. The analysis of networks with deterministic time estimates is covered in this section. This section discusses probabilistic times in more detail later on. One can comprehend the nature of network analysis for deterministic time estimations by considering the following example.

Example 3.2

Fig. 3.6 Project network/precedence diagram

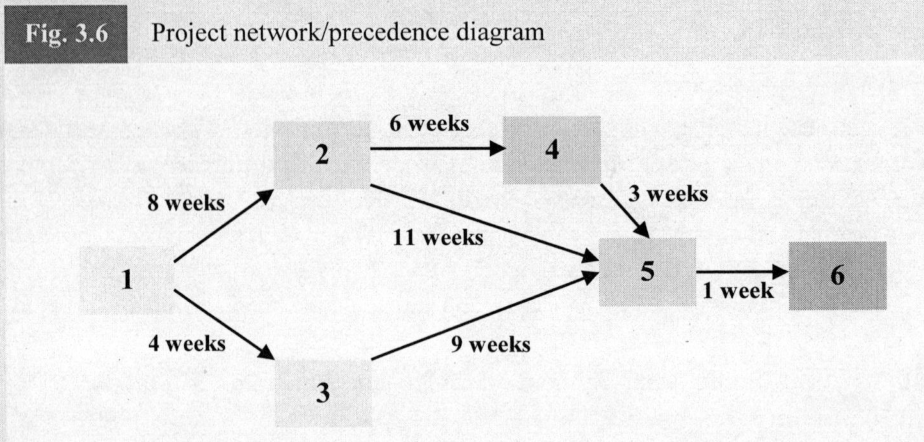

Given the above network diagram of a project in Fig. 3.6, determine:

(a) The length of each path
(b) The critical path
(c) The expected length of the project
(d) Amount of slack time for each path

Solution

(a) The path lengths are 18 weeks, 20 weeks, and 14 weeks, as indicated in the following table.
(b) The critical path is 1 – 2 – 5 – 6, as it is the longest path (20 weeks).
(c) The project's expected duration, or 20 weeks, is the same as the critical path's length.

(d) As seen in the table's final column, we determine each path's slack by deducting its length from the critical path's length.

Path	Length (weeks)	Slack
1 – 2 – 4 – 5 – 6	8 + 6 + 3 + 1 = 18	20 – 18 = 2
1 – 2 – 5 – 6	8 + 11 + 1 = 20*	20 – 20 = 0
1 – 3 – 5 – 6	4 + 9 + 1 = 14	20 – 14 = 6

* Critical path length

The earliest start (ES) and earliest finish (EF) for the forward pass, and the latest start (LS) and latest finish (LF) for the backward pass, are the four pieces of information regarding the network activities used by the CPM algorithm, also known as deterministic time estimates.

- If all actions before it begin as early as possible, ES is the earliest time an activity can begin.
- The earliest time that the activity can end is EF.
- LS is the latest time an activity can begin without causing the project to be delayed.
- The last time an activity can be completed without causing a delay in the project is known as LF.

After determining these values, one can use them to ascertain:

1. Project duration anticipated.
2. Slack time.
3. The critical path.

Using Fig. 3.6, the subsequent examples show how to compute such values using the precedence diagram.

Example 3.3

Determine the earliest starting and earliest finishing times for every task in the Fig. 3.6 diagram.

First, put brackets at each starting activity's two ends.

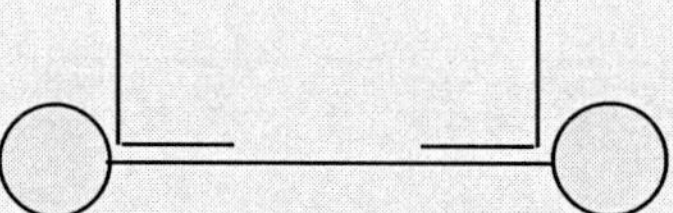

The earliest starting time (ES) and earliest finish time (EF) for each activity are calculated and entered into the brackets as follows:

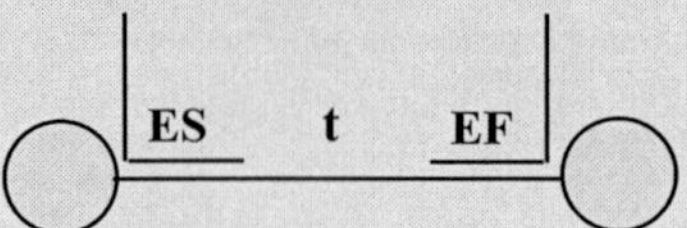

Proceed to the right side of the priority diagram after starting at the left side for each activity. EF can be calculated by adding the activity time, t, to ES once ES has been established for each activity: ES + t = EF. Here is the precedence diagram shown in Fig. 3.7 that results from entering all of the ES and EF values:

Fig. 3.7 Precedence diagram of forward pass

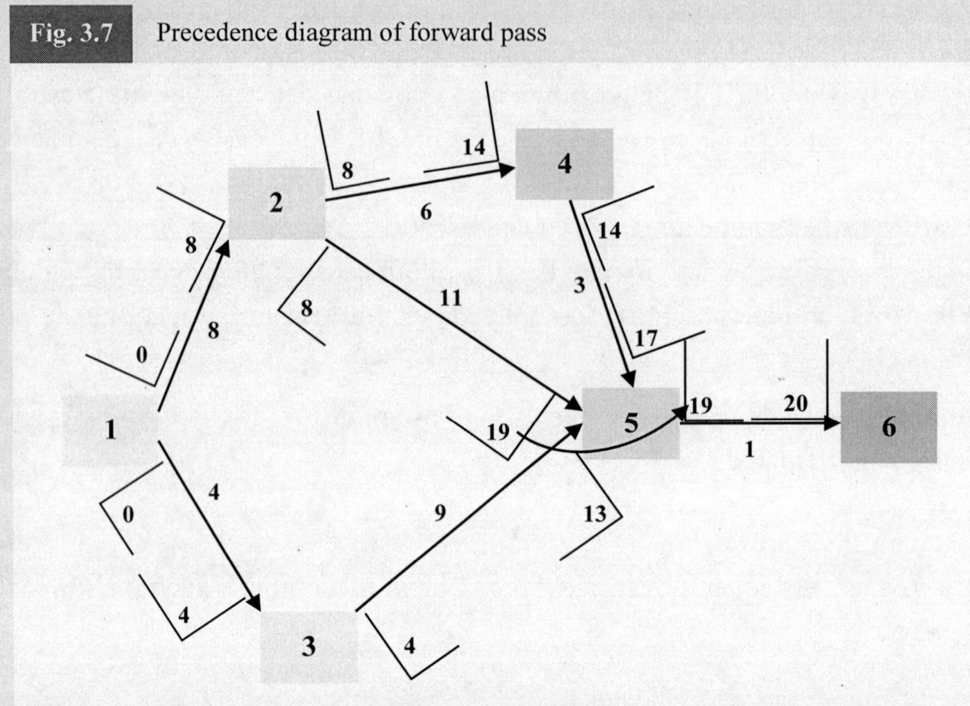

Computing LS and LF times

Two rules help in the computation of the most recent start and finish times:

1. Each activity's latest starting time is equal to its latest finishing time minus the amount of time it is predicted to take:

LS = LF – t

2. When an arrow leaves a node, the LF of all arrows entering that node matches the LS of the leaving arrow. The smallest LS of the leaving arrows for a node with multiple leaving arrows is equal to the LF for arrows entering that node.

LS and LF times must be found by making a "backward pass" around the network. As a result, we have to start at the last activity's EF and utilize that time as the last activity's LF. The latest activity's LS is then calculated by deducting its expected duration from its LF.
The LS and LF times need to be added to the diagram's brackets.

LS LF
ES t EF

After all the values have been inserted in accordance with the specified algorithm, Fig. 3.8 shows the final backward pass precedence diagram.

Fig. 3.8 Precedence diagram of backward pass

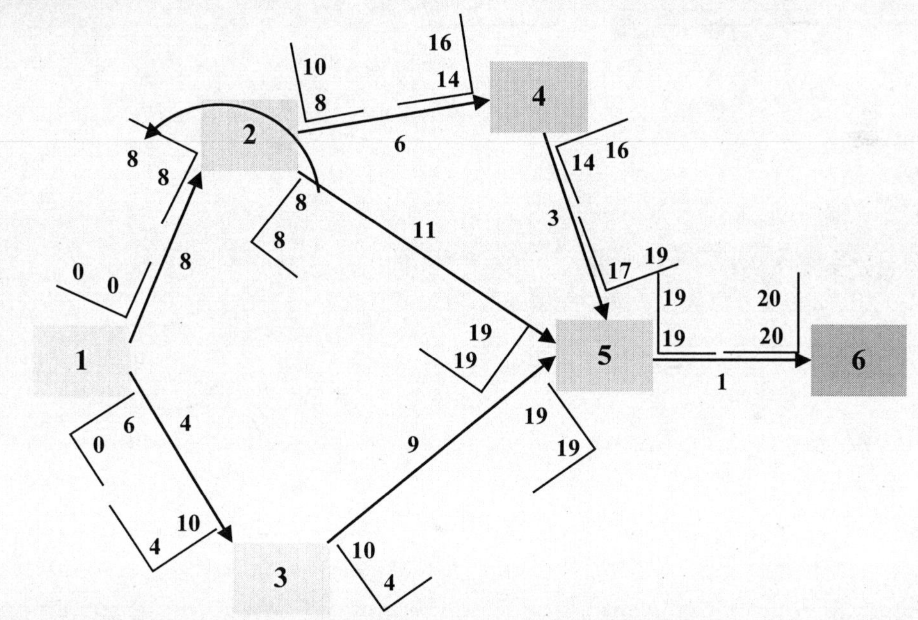

Computing Slack Times
There are two methods to calculate the slack time:

Slack = LS – ES or LF – EF

Using this computational approach, the activities with zero slack time indicate the critical path. As a result, Table 3.1 shows that tasks 1 – 2, 2 – 5, and 5 – 6 are all critical, which is consistent with the outcomes of the intuitive method used in the previous example.

Managers can plan the distribution of limited resources and focus control efforts on the activities that could most likely cause the project to be delayed by knowing when slack times occur. It is crucial to understand that the activity slack times in this context are predicated on the idea that every action on the same path will begin at the earliest opportunity and won't take longer than anticipated. Moreover, this will be the entire slack accessible to both if two activities have the same slack (two weeks), are on the same path (activities 2 – 4 and 4 – 5 in the preceding example), and both. The tasks have essentially shared slack. As a result, if the first action uses up all of the slack, there won't be any more or much less slack left for any subsequent activities that follow along the same path.

Table 3.1 Slack activities

Activity	LS	ES	Slack (LS – ES)
1 – 2	0	0	0
1 – 3	6	0	6
2 – 4	10	8	2
2 – 5	8	8	0
3 – 5	10	4	6
4 – 5	16	14	2
5 – 6	19	19	0

3.5 ESTIMATES OF PROBABILISTIC TIME

Estimating the duration of each project step is the next stage in creating the network. First and foremost, keep in mind that these estimations are predicated on the assumption of standard operating procedures during regular business or working hours. Second, activity durations are usually a little hazy, even though variables like prior experience or familiarity with the task will affect how accurate these estimates are. Thirdly, job estimates can range in duration from a few hours for brief tasks to days or weeks for more extensive ones.

We must take into consideration the fundamentals of probability distributions in order to comprehend how to apply mathematical reasoning to calculate expected activity durations. According to probability, one can rarely predict with certainty how long an activity will take; instead, one must sample a range of likelihoods, or probabilities, that the event will occur. From 0 (no probability) to 1 (full probability), these likelihoods are expressed. Three values must be determined in order to obtain a fair probability estimate for the duration of any activity: (1) the *most likely* duration of the activity; (2) the *most pessimistic* duration of the activity; and (3) the *most optimistic* duration of the activity. The amount of time needed to finish an activity is calculated as the most likely duration, given that the activity develops as planned. The anticipated amount of time required to develop the activity on the presumption that everything would go wrong is known as the pessimistic duration. Ultimately, an optimistic timeframe is calculated based on the supposition that the development process will run incredibly smoothly.

Both symmetric (the normal distribution) and asymmetric (the beta distribution) probability distributions can be used for these time estimates. The chance of an event occurring in the most likely amount of time is implied by a normal distribution, which is centered on the distribution mean (Fig. 3.9). Pessimistic and optimistic values, which are calculated from either extreme of the distribution at 99% confidence level, will cancel each other out, leaving the mean value as the anticipated length of the activity.

It is quite uncommon to find examples of optimistic and pessimistic durations that are symmetrical about the mean in real life. It is more typical in project management to encounter symmetrical probability distributions, or "beta distributions." We may acknowledge that some events are less likely to happen than others based on the asymmetry of the probability distribution. Furthermore, an activity's optimistic time may be one standard deviation from the mean, whereas its pessimistic time may be three or four standard deviations from the mean.

Fig. 3.9 Symmetrical (Normal) Distribution

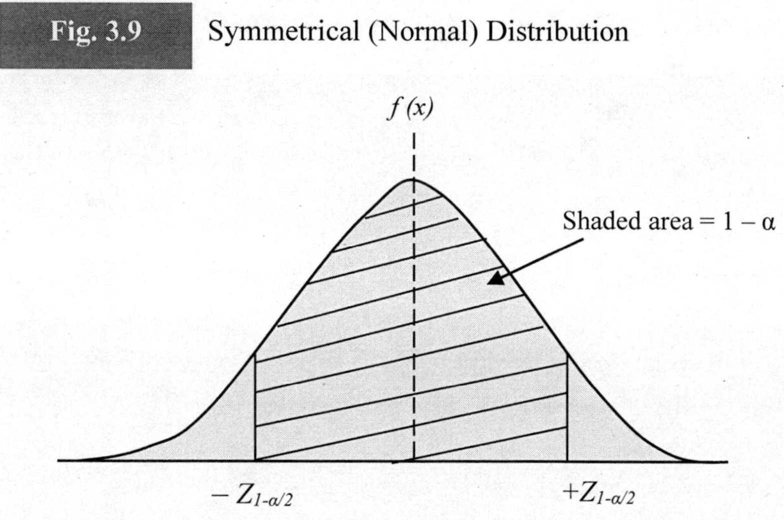

In essence, the optimistic and pessimistic numbers represent the distribution range's top and bottom boundaries. The beta distribution is shown in Fig. 3.10, where the values for the most likely duration (m), most optimistic duration (a), and most pessimistic duration (b) are indicated.

Fig. 3.10 Asymmetrical (Beta) distribution

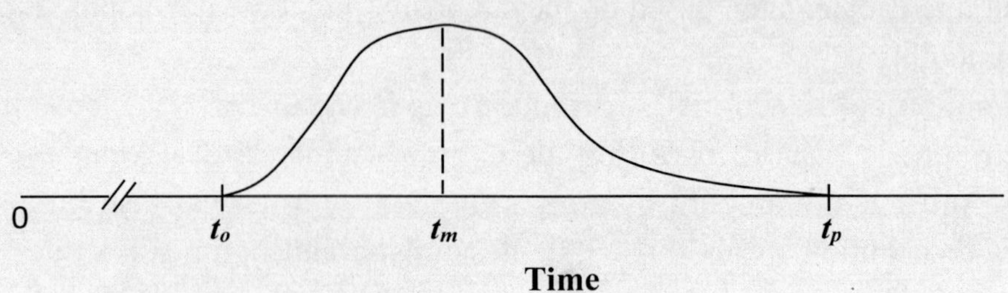

The values of t_m, t_a, and t_p are converted into estimates of the expected time (TE) and variance (σ^2) of the activity's duration using two assumptions. One crucial presumption is that the task's standard deviation, or *s*, will equal one-sixth of the range for realistically achievable time requirements. The following formula provides the variance for an activity duration estimate:

$$\sigma^2 = \left[\frac{1}{6}(t_p - t_o)\right]^2$$

This assumption is justified by the knowledge that observations must be within three standard deviations of the mean in either direction in order to produce a probability distribution with a 99% confidence interval. Therefore, 99.7% of the potential activity duration options fall within a six standard deviation tail to tail spread in the probability distribution.

The second assumption relates to the probability distribution's structure since optimistic and pessimistic periods are not symmetrical about the mean. Once more, the distribution of potential alternate expected duration times (TE) for predicting activities is better represented by the beta, or asymmetrical, distribution. According to the beta distribution, the following computation should be used to determine TE:

$$\text{TE} = \frac{(t_o + 4t_m + t_p)}{6}$$

where

TE = estimated time for activity

t_o = most optimistic time frame for finishing the task

t_m = the activity's most likely completion time, the distribution's mode
t_p = most pessimistic estimate for finishing the task

This computation uses the weighted arithmatic mean of the mode and midrange as the midpoint between the optimistic and pessimistic values. This represents two-thirds of the total weighting for the estimated time (TE). The purpose of the additional weighting is to emphasize how predicted values, irrespective of the length of the optimistic and pessimistic tails (total distribution standard deviation), cluster around the distribution mean.

The amount of uncertainty surrounding the duration of an activity is reflected in the variance's size; the higher the variance, the higher the uncertainty.

Finding the predicted time for each path's standard deviation is also a desired step. This can be accomplished by adding up all of the activity variations on a path, then calculating the square root of that total; that is,

$$\sigma_{path} = \sqrt{\sum \text{(variances of activities on path)}}$$

The expected times of all the events on a path are added up to determine the path's expected time.

Example 3.4

With three time estimates for each task, the network diagram for the project is displayed in Fig. 3.11. Weekly activity times are used. Take the following action:
(a) Determine the expected duration of each path and the expected time for each activity.
(b) Determine the critical path.
(c) Determine the variance of every path and activity.

Solution
A manager can create probabilistic estimates of the project completion time by knowing the expected path timings and their standard deviation. Examples of these estimates include:

- The likelihood that the project will be finished by the deadline.
- The likelihood that the project will take longer to complete than expected.
- These approximations can be obtained from the likelihood that different routes will be finished within the given time frame.

Fig. 3.11 Network diagram for probabilistic time estimate

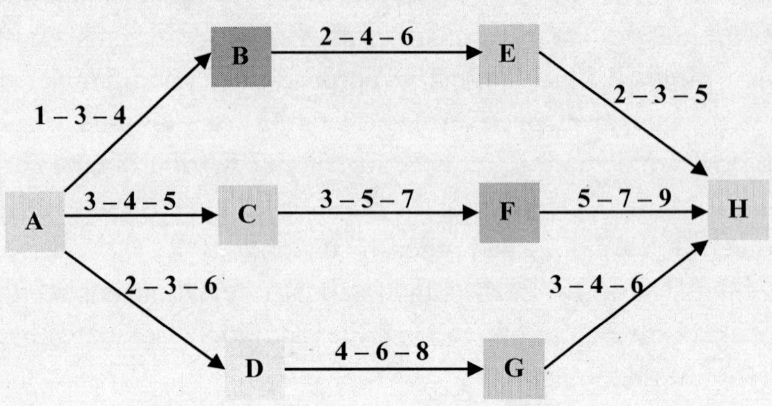

		Times				
Path	**Activity**	t_o	t_m	t_p	$t_e = t_o + 4t_m + t_p / 6$	**Path Total**
A – B – E – H	A – B	1	3	4	2.83	10.00
	B – E	2	4	6	4.00	
	E – H	2	3	5	3.17	
A – C – F – H	A – C	3	4	5	4.00	16.00
	C – F	3	5	7	5.00	
	F – H	5	7	9	7.00	
A – D – G – H	A – D	2	3	6	3.33	13.50
	D – G	4	6	8	6.00	
	G – H	3	4	6	4.17	

The critical path is the one with the longest expected duration. The critical path is path A – C – F – H since it has the largest path total.

		Times					
Path	**Activity**	t_o	t_m	t_p	σ^2	σ^2 **path**	σ **path**
A – B – E – H	A – B	1	3	4	9/36	34/36 = 0.94	0.97
	B – E	2	4	6	16/36		
	E – H	2	3	5	9/36		
A – C – F – H	A – C	3	4	5	4/36	36/36 = 1.00	1.00
	C – F	3	5	7	16/36		
	F – H	5	7	9	16/36		
A – D – G – H	A – D	2	3	6	16/36	41/36 = 1.14	1.07
	D – G	4	6	8	16/36		
	G – H	3	4	6	9/36		

3.5.1 DETERMINING PATH PROBABILITIES

The following formula can be used to calculate the likelihood that a particular path will be finished in a certain amount of time:

$$z = \frac{\text{Specified time-Path mean}}{\text{Path standard deviation}}$$

The resultant value of *z* shows how many standard deviations of the path the given time deviates from the expected path duration. (A negative value of z means that the given time was reached sooner than the anticipated travel time.) After determining the value of *z*, the Normal Probability Distribution table can be used to predict the likelihood that the path will be finished by the deadline. As illustrated in Fig. 3.12, take note that the probability equals the area under the normal curve to the left of *z*.

Fig. 3.12 Path probability under the normal curve

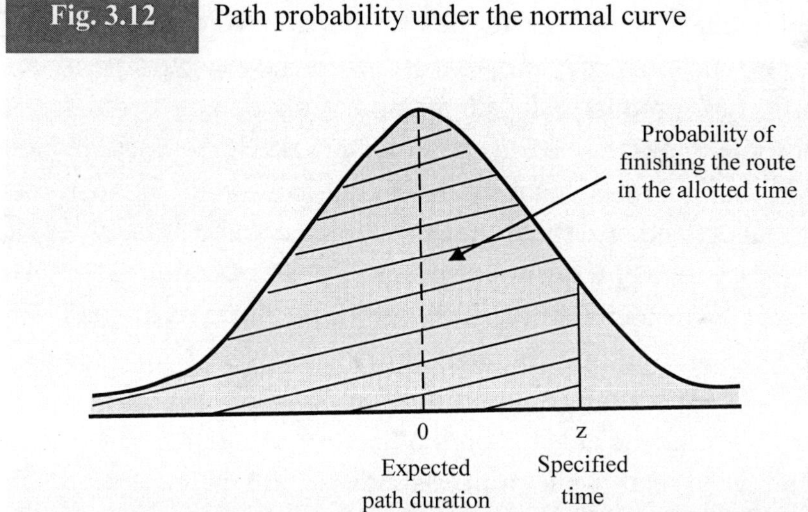

The use of a normal distribution is justified by the fact that, regardless of the distribution of the individual variables, the sum of random variables (activity times) tends to be regularly distributed. The more random variables there are, the better the normal tendency is. However, the normal approximation offers an acceptable approximation to the real distribution even when the number of items being summed is rather small. With the data from Example 3.4, we are able to respond to the following question:

- What is the probability that the project will be finished in the allotted 17 weeks?

You must first calculate the value of z in order to determine the probability that the project will be finished in 17 days.

$$z = \frac{17 - 16}{1.00} = +1.00$$

Given that the critical path takes for 16 weeks, 16 is used as the path mean value for z in the formula above. If you look at the normal distribution table with $z = +1.00$, you can see that 0.8413 is the area under the curve to the left of z. Therefore, there is an 84.13 percent probability that the project will be completed within 17 weeks of beginning.

3.6 TIME-COST TRADE-OFFS: CRASHING

Project activity time estimates are typically calculated for a specific resource level. It is frequently possible to shorten a project's duration by adding more resources. The motivation behind project shortening may stem from attempts to avoid late fees, to capitalize on financial rewards for timely or early project competitiveness, or to free up resources for use on other projects. A new product's development and shortening could result in a strategic advantage: entering the market ahead of the competitors. Sometimes, though, the desire to abbreviate a project's duration is just an attempt to cut back on the indirect costs of managing the project, like labor and personal expenses, supervision, facilities and equipment expenditures, and other costs. Frequently, managers possess certain alternatives that enable them to abbreviate or expedite specific tasks. Using more money, supporting more employees or more effective equipment, and easing some work requirements are some of the most obvious solutions. Therefore, in order to accelerate a project and save indirect project costs, a project manager may be able to shorten the project by raising direct charges. Finding actions that will lower the total of the project's indirect and direct expenses is the aim of the time-cost tradeoff evaluation process.

A management requires specific information in order to rationally decide which activities, if any, should crash and how much crashing is desirable:

1. Estimates of regular and crash times for every task.
2. For every task, regular and crash cost estimates are provided.
3. A list of tasks that are on the critical path.

Because cutting noncritical activities would not affect the overall project duration, activities on the critical path are prospective candidates for crashing. Economically speaking, activities ought to be crashed in accordance with their crashing costs, starting with the ones that have the lowest crash costs. Furthermore, crashing ought to go on as long as the advantages of crashing outweigh the costs. These advantages could be in the form of savings on indirect project expenses, government contract incentive payments for early project completion, or both. The fundamental link between indirect, direct, and total project expenses resulting from crashing is shown in Fig. 3.13. Generally speaking, crashing works like this:

1. Find out how much each activity will cost and when it will be regular and crash.
2. Calculate all pathways' lengths and slack times for paths.
3. Ascertain which critical activities are involved.
4. Crash critical activities in the order that costs rise, provided that benefits do not outweigh costs. Because of the possibility that two or more paths will become critical as the initial critical path gets shorter, it will be necessary to simultaneously shorten two or more paths in order to make further improvements. An action that is on two or more of the critical paths may in some circumstances be more cost-effective to abbreviate. This holds true if the cost of crashing a combined activity is lower than the total cost of crashing each individual activity on its own path.

Fig. 3.13 Crashing costs curves

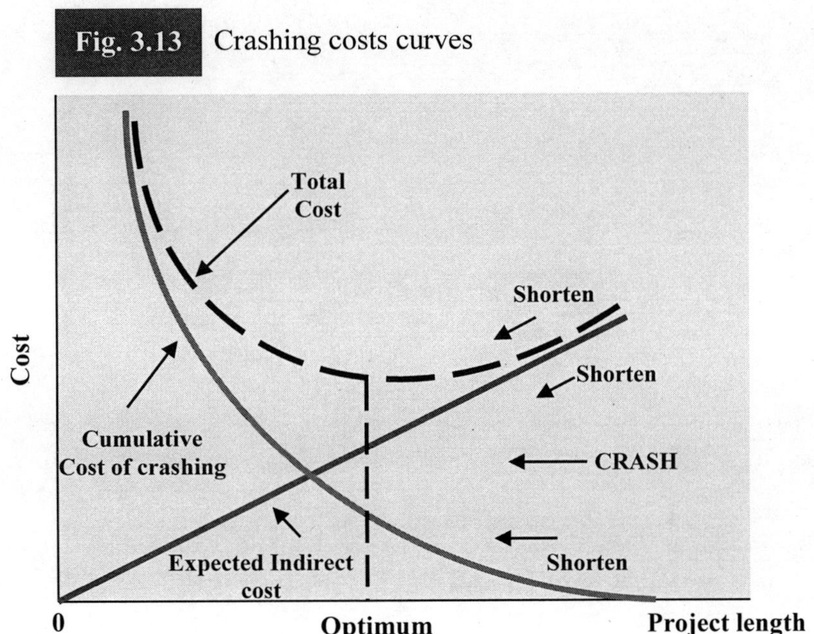

Example 3.5

Using the information in following table and AOA network, develop the optimal time-cost solution. Indirect project costs are $1,000 per day.

Activity	Normal time	Crash time	Cost per day to crash
a	6	6	–
b	10	8	$500
c	5	4	300
d	4	1	700
e	9	7	600
f	2	1	800

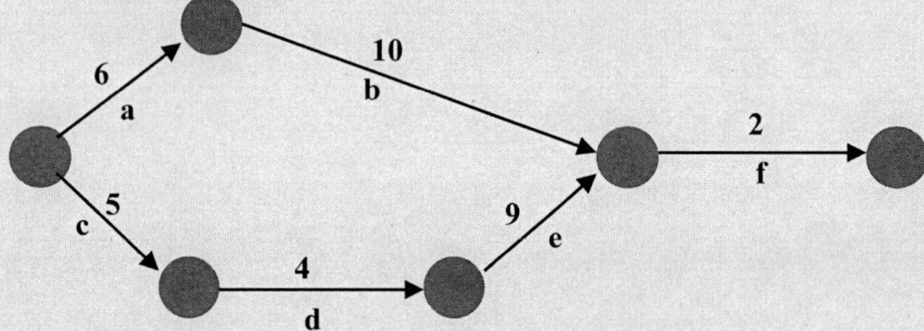

Solution

(a) Ascertain which tasks are on the critical path, how long it is, and how long the alternate path is:

Path	Length
a – b – f	18
c – d – e – f	20 (critical path)

(b) Determine the number of days that each key path activity can be crashed by ranking them according to lowest crashing cost.

Activity	Cost per day to crash	Available days
c	$300	1
e	600	2
d	700	3
f	800	1

(c) Start cutting the project down, one day at a time, and assess which path is critical after every reduction. (After a while, the length of the shorter critical path might be equaled by another path.) Consequently:

1. Reduce activity 'c' by one day, at a $300 expense. The critical path is now 19 days long.
2. It is no longer possible to abbreviate activity 'c'. Reduce activity 'e' by one day at a $600 expense. It is now 18 days, the same as the length of path a – b – f, for the length of path c – d – e – f.
3. Since both paths are now critical, more advancement will require that both paths be shortened.

The expenses associated with the remaining crashing activities are:

Path	Activity	Crash cost per day
a – b – f	a	No reduction possible
	b	$500
	f	800
c – d – e – f	c	No further reduction possible
	d	$700
	e	600
	f	800

Given that it has the largest crashing cost, it would appear at first that crashing 'f' would not be beneficial. But since 'f' is on both paths, cutting 'f' by one day would add one day to the length of both paths and, consequently, the project, at a cost of $800. Reducing the least costly activity on each path by $500 for 'b' and $600 for 'e' would result in a total cost of $1,100. Cut 'f' short by one day as a result. There are presently 17 days left in the project.

4. It is not possible to make any more improvements at this time. The expenses to crash 'b' and 'e' are $500 and $600, respectively, totaling $1,100. This would be more than the daily indirect project costs of $1,000.
5. The following is a summary of the crashing sequence:

	Length after crashing n days:			
Path	n = 0	1	2	3
a – b – f	18	18	18	17
c – d – e – f	20	19	18	17
Activity crashed		c	e	f
Cost		$300	$600	$800

3.7 PROJECT CLOSURE

Completing a project involves an enormous amount of work. The project manager used to be in charge of seeing that all tasks and unfinished business were finished and approved, especially for smaller projects. This is no longer accurate. The project manager, project teams, project office, oversight review committee, and an independent retrospective facilitator are all responsible for completing closing responsibilities in today's project-driven organizations with multiple projects ongoing at the same time. Numerous duties are concurrent, overlap, and necessitate coordination and collaboration from all of these entities. The following is a description of the three main deliverables for project closure:

1. Project wrap-up: Making sure the customer has approved and accepted the project is the main wrap-up responsibility. Closing accounts, paying bills, reassigning personnel and equipment, looking for new job possibilities for project staff, closing facilities, and writing the final report are some more wrap-up tasks. A lot of people use checklists to make sure things don't go missed. In many organizations, the project office works in tandem with the project manager to complete the majority of the closure duties. One project office employee is often tasked with preparing the final report after gathering feedback from all stakeholders. These closure tasks are left to the project manager and team in smaller organizations and projects.
2. Performance and project management evaluation: Performance of the project manager, the team, and individual team members are all included. External input might be provided by vendors and customers. An assessment of the main participants yields valuable insights for the future.
3. Retrospectives: The goal of retrospectives on lessons gained is to enhance performance on ongoing and upcoming initiatives. The majority of retrospectives conducted nowadays are overseen by a third-party facilitator. A significant portion of the closure report, which will include lessons learned, is also contributed by the facilitator. The team should participate in these post-project reviews in order to identify any gaps or unresolved concerns.

3.7.1 CLOSURE ACTIVITES

Carrying out the closure procedure entails a number of wrap-up tasks. With expertise, many organizations create long lists of projects to close. They make sure nothing is missed and are really beneficial. Putting closedown into action entails the following six main tasks:

1. Getting the customer to accept the delivery.
2. Turning off resources and allocating them to other use.
3. Reassigning members of the project team.
4. Close accounts and verify that all debts have been settled.

5. Giving the client the completed project.
6. Finishing the report.

Handling the specifics of finishing a project might be frightening. There are check lists for over 100 final tasks in certain organizations! The facilities, teams, employees, customers, vendors, and the project itself are all covered in these checklists for closure details.

OBTAINING CUSTOMER ACCEPTANCE

If only getting the customer's approval could be as simple as announcing, "Hey, we're done!" and having them say, "Ok, great!" A few months later, the client can come back and express dissatisfaction, claiming that something went missing or that the results fell short of the company's expectations. That is the risk associated with this cordial but unlikely conversation. Obtaining formal acceptance from the client and other stakeholders that the project is finished is the best method to end it and ensure that it stays closed.

Customer acceptance is rarely a yes or no decision for most initiatives. Deliverables and success criteria that you outlined in the project plan no longer serve as guidelines for the project team; instead, they become benchmarks that the project customer uses to assess the project's completion.

Since deliverables are typically tangible, clients may confirm whether or not they received them. If the deliberable is, for instance, a recommendation for the health insurance provider that your business will work with, you just need to make it and call it a day. On the other hand, acceptance tests are necessary for success criteria and must be passed. Consider the following scenario: you recently finished a software project, and more than 99.99 percent system availability is one of the acceptance requirements. Establishing a realistic test environment, figuring out the precise measurement procedure, putting the system through a period of testing using test cases, and processing the resulting data to compute availability are all necessary to ascertain whether the system satisfies this requirement. In the event that the system fails the test, the project reverts to the execution phase, when issues are fixed and another test is conducted.

Project planners frequently collaborate with the customer to create procedures for acceptance tests. Tests are outlined in these procedures for each feature or specification that the project is expected to provide. Each feature that is successfully shown is approved by the customer when you and they conduct the acceptance tests during the closure phase.

TRANSITIONING RESOURCES

After your project is over, the people and tools you assigned to it go on to something else. It may not seem like your job to plan what resources do once they leave your employ, but it's in everyone's best interest to do so. You may make sure that your team members complete the task they are assigned to complete for your project by collaborating with them and their managers to design their assignments. In addition, you become respected as a person who is detail-oriented and attentive of others by both the people and their bosses. Additionally, you could gain favor with the functional supervisors who are scheduling the team members for their upcoming tasks.

Knowing how much and for how long you will require the resources can help you plan the resource transition. Managers of those employees will value knowing when their staff members are available if resources are returned to their functional groups. This way, they may schedule extra work without worrying about overworking or benching their employees.

Since assignments typically overlap, it's crucial to know if resources can begin working on something else while clearing up their responsibilities for you. Since assignments don't always need the same amount of effort or time to complete, it's typical for people to begin working more on a new project as their progress on an old one gradually declines. Knowing when they'll be finished is helpful to contractors and consultants since it allows them to start scheduling new work without worrying about missing deadlines, needing to reschedule a client, or managing two full-time contracts at once.

ACCOUNTS CLOSURE

The primary purpose of releasing a formal project closure statement is to prohibit extra expenditures related to the primary project cost accounts. This is especially crucial to prevent the project's hard-earned earnings from being undermined by sneaky timesheet bookings made only because the account is still open. It is common knowledge that timesheets may be abused when it comes to recording hours worked. Unscrupulous employees sometimes try to 'lose' unaccounted for or wasted time by assigning it to big projects in the hopes that no one would notice. Although this danger can be reduced with good supervision, it is more efficient to tell the computer to reject any future timesheet entries made against the project number.

In order to collect a few tale-end costs, company accountants could want to keep a project account active for their own purposes after the project's official conclusion date. Even though reservations for additional man-hours are prohibited beyond the closing date, there are typically things like unpaid invoices from suppliers and subcontractors that need to be paid for. These can keep coming in for several months after a big job is finished. These costs can be substantial, but they shouldn't have a substantial impact on the estimated profit because, barring a lack of oversight over day labor and subcontracts, these should have been recognized and recorded in the accounts at the time the purchase orders or subcontracts were awarded.

HANDING OVER THE PROJECT

Even after projects conclude, they usually leave some residue behind. Regardless of the nature of the project – a backyard makeover that the homeowner will manage, a product that the sales team must now market or a service that the technicians must install and maintain – someone else must be aware of your work and its current state. For instance, as-built drawings, which document the construction process regardless of the architect's original design, are usually turned over at the end of a construction project. As-built plans may display a power line that was moved due to a loose rock or a modified frame detail. Alternatively, information from a software development project is transferred to the group responsible for maintaining the application when it is put into use at customers' locations.

The project determines what information you transfer. A few things you may wish to give the team taking over are as follows:

- Where the project documentation are stored in case the team need further information.
- The reports on closeout.
- The status of any unfinished jobs and the reasons behind their non-completion.
- Unresolved problems.
- Test outcomes.
- As-built drawings, product documentation, and final specifications.

THE FINAL REPORT

Effective project management systems possess an organizational process asset and a memory. The Project Final Report is a crucial component of this memory. The final report represents the project's history rather than an additional evaluation, though it can be used as an input for one or for postproject control.

The following is a list of topics that ought to be included in the final report. It helps to take into account the locations of the source materials while thinking about these factors. The project master plan, which comprises the charter, the WBS, all budgets, schedules, change orders, and updates of the aforementioned, contains the majority of the necessary information. The necessary input data is included in all project audits and assessments in addition to the master plan. Nearly all other requirements for the final report are reflective, drawing from the opinions of the project management team and other stakeholders.

1. **Project performance**: One of the report's main components is a comparison between the project's goals (the project proposal) and its actual results (the terminal evaluation). This comparison could be rather detailed and ought to account for all notable real departures from the plan. Finally, a conversation about earned value may

be beneficial. The final report can represent the project management's best assessment of the reasons behind the successes and failures because it is not a formal review. After this comparison, a list of suggestions for upcoming initiatives addressing related or comparable technological issues should be made.

2. **Administrative performance**: Typically, a project's substantive aspects receive a lot of attention, but its administrative aspects are frequently disregarded until issues arise. Additionally, practically everyone has a strong inclination to see "pencil pushers" with reluctant tolerance, at best. Technical issues cannot be resolved by project management, although it can facilitate the adoption of useful technology or obstruct it. Reviewing administrative procedures and highlighting those that performed exceptionally well or poorly is a good idea. Reporting the reasons why a particular practice was successful or unsuccessful is crucial, whenever it is feasible. Knowing why certain things work well in an organization's environment and others don't is essential to avoiding bad management and implementing excellent practices. The recommendations that follow the discussion are based on this.
3. **Organizational structure**: Every organizational structure utilized for a project has a special set of benefits and drawbacks. An analysis of how the structure helped or hindered the project's progress should be included in the final report. A recommendation for a shift to a different basic organisational form or a modification to the established form of project organisation should be made if it seems like it could be beneficial for project management. It goes without saying that proposals need to be supported by thorough justifications and explanations.
4. **Project and administrative teams**: When a high degree of interpersonal connection and cooperation is needed, people who are competent and likeable as individuals occasionally perform poorly as team members. A senior personnel officer of the parent organization may receive a private section of the final report suggesting that these persons not be assigned to any future projects. In a similar vein, the project management may suggest that people or teams that demonstrated exceptional teamwork be retained for next projects or reallocated to the company's regular operations.
5. **Project management techniques**: Since the project's result is largely dependent on how well the forecasting, planning, budgeting, scheduling, resource allocation, risk management, and control are managed, care must be taken to ensure that these activities were completed. It is necessary to suggest better practices if the estimates, finances, and timelines were not at least somewhat correct. A close examination of the methods for planning, controlling, and managing risk is also necessary.

Proposals for altering present practice must to be included and justified for every topic addressed in the final report. The probable changes and their applicability should be recorded as much as feasible. Remarks and suggestions regarding those project elements that performed exceptionally well are sometimes disregarded, yet they are just as significant. Project teams, managers, and most projects themselves create informal protocols that facilitate scheduling, expedite budget preparation, enhance forecasting, and other related tasks. Such knowledge is best stored in the final report. Upon reporting, the approaches can be put to the test and, if found to be generally beneficial, added to the list of approved project management techniques by the parent organization.

UNIT SUMMARY

- ***Project Scheduling Fundamentals*** – Discusses the importance of scheduling in project management, converting the Work Breakdown Structure (WBS) into an actionable schedule.
- ***Key Scheduling Terminology*** – Defines important concepts like critical path, float, forward and backward pass, early/late start, and finish dates.
- ***Network Development*** – Explores how Project Network Diagrams (PND) visualize task dependencies, including serial, concurrent, merge, and burst activities.
- ***Critical Path Method*** (CPM) – Describes deterministic time estimation to find the longest path of dependent activities, ensuring project completion on time.
- ***Program Evaluation and Review Technique*** (PERT) – Introduces probabilistic time estimation to manage uncertainty, using optimistic, pessimistic, and most likely time estimates.
- ***Time-Cost Tradeoff*** (Crashing) – Discusses how to shorten project duration by adding resources, balancing costs and deadlines.
- ***Project Closure*** – Covers the final phase, ensuring: Customer acceptance, Resource reallocation, Final report documentation, and Lessons learned for future projects.

EXERCISES

MULTIPLE CHOICE QUESTIONS

3.1 What is the fundamental idea behind project scheduling in project management?

(a) Identifying project risks	(b) Allocating resources efficiently
(c) Setting project objectives	(d) Monitoring project progress

3.2 In project management, what is the primary purpose of creating a project schedule?

(a) Tracking project expenses	(b) Communicating project timelines
(c) Resolving project conflicts	(d) Evaluating project performance

3.3 What does the term "PERT" stand for in project scheduling?

(a) Project Evaluation and Review Technique	(b) Project Execution and Resource Tracking
(c) Project Estimation and Risk Tracking	(d) Project Efficiency and Resource Testing

3.4 Which of the following is NOT a critical step in building a network diagram in project scheduling?

(a) Identifying project activities	(b) Determining activity durations
(c) Assigning resources to activities	(d) Defining dependencies between activities

3.5 What is the purpose of defining dependencies between activities in a network diagram?

(a) To allocate resources efficiently	(b) To determine the critical path
(c) To identify project milestones	(d) To estimate project costs

3.6 What is the significance of the critical path in a network diagram?

(a) It represents the shortest path through the project	(b) It indicates the sequence of activities that must be completed on time to prevent project delays
(c) It shows the activities with the highest resource requirements	(d) It determines the total project duration

3.7 In project scheduling, which term refers to activities that can be performed simultaneously without any dependencies between them?

(a) Serial activities	(b) Concurrent activities
(c) Critical activities	(d) Lag activities

3.8 In project scheduling, what is the term used to describe the minimum amount of time required to complete a series of dependent activities?

(a) Total Float	(b) Free Float
(c) Lead Time	(d) Slack Time

3.9 Which of the following scheduling terms refers to a group of activities that are combined into a single activity to simplify the project schedule?

(a) Merge activities	(b) Burst activities
(c) Critical path activities	(d) Float activities

3.10 Burst activities in project scheduling are used to:

(a) Accelerate the completion of critical path activities	(b) Break down complex tasks into smaller, manageable components
(c) Identify potential risks and uncertainties in the project plan	(d) Allocate resources based on project priorities

3.11 Which of the following statements about the Critical Path Method (CPM) is true?

(a) CPM is a deterministic model that assumes fixed activity durations.	(b) CPM is a probabilistic model that accounts for uncertainty in activity durations.
(c) CPM is primarily used for resource leveling in project management.	(d) CPM does not consider dependencies between project activities.

3.12 What is the purpose of calculating the Total Float in CPM analysis?

(a) To determine the earliest possible start time for an activity.	(b) To identify the activities those are critical for project completion.
(c) To calculate the difference between the Early Start and Late Start times.	(d) To measure the flexibility in the start and finish times of non-critical activities.

3.13 What is the purpose of using the Backward Pass calculation in CPM analysis?

(a) To determine the latest possible start and finish times for each activity.	(b) To identify the critical activities that must be completed on time.
(c) To calculate the difference between the Late Start and Early Start times.	(d) To optimize the resource allocation for project activities.

3.14 What is the formula used to calculate the Expected Time (TE) in PERT analysis?

(a) TE = (Optimistic Time + 4 x Most Likely Time + Pessimistic Time) / 6	(b) TE = (Optimistic Time + 3 x Most Likely Time + Pessimistic Time) / 5
(c) TE = (Optimistic Time + 2 x Most Likely Time + Pessimistic Time) / 4	(d) TE = (Optimistic Time + Most Likely Time + Pessimistic Time) / 3

3.15 In PERT analysis, what does the term "Standard Deviation" represents?

(a) The difference between the Optimistic and Pessimistic Time estimates	(b) The variability or uncertainty associated with the activity duration
(c) The average time taken to complete an activity	(d) The total float available for an activity

3.16 What is the primary objective of crashing in project management?

(a) Minimizing project costs	(b) Maximizing project scope
(c) Optimizing project quality	(d) Accelerating project schedule

3.17 What is the main risk associated with crashing a project schedule?

(a) Increased project scope	(b) Decreased project budget
(c) Compromised project quality	(d) Delayed project completion

3.18 What is the primary purpose of conducting a project closure meeting?

(a) To celebrate the successful completion of the project	(b) To hand over project deliverables to the client
(c) To review the project's performance and document lessons learned	(d) To assign new tasks to team members for future projects

3.19 Which of the following is NOT a common task during the closure phase of a project?

(a) Releasing project resources	(b) Conducting a risk assessment
(c) Obtaining sign-off from stakeholders	(d) Celebrating project success with the team

3.20 What is the primary purpose of a final project report in project management?

(a) To document the initial project plan	(b) To provide a summary of project progress and outcomes

(c) To outline future project ideas	(d) To request additional project funding

3.21 Which of the following is NOT typically included in a final project report?

(a) Project objectives and scope	(b) Budget allocation for future projects
(c) Project timeline and milestones	(d) Lessons learned and recommendations for future projects

Answers of Multiple Choice Questions
3.1 (b), 3.2 (b), 3.3 (a), 3.4 (c), 3.5 (b), 3.6 (b), 3.7 (b), 3.8 (a), 3.9 (a), 3.10 (b), 3.11 (a), 3.12 (d), 3.13 (a), 3.14 (a), 3.15 (b), 3.16 (d), 3.17 (c), 3.18 (c), 3.19 (b), 3.20 (b), 3.21 (b)

SHORT AND LONG ANSWER TYPE QUESTIONS

Category I

3.1 Define project scheduling and explain its importance in project management.

3.2 Describe briefly (i) project network diagram, (ii) Early start date, (iii) backward pass, (iv) float, (v) critical path, (vi) program evaluation and review technique.

3.3 How does resource leveling impact project scheduling and resource allocation?

3.4 What is the purpose of network development in project scheduling?

3.5 What is the significance of identifying dependencies between activities in network development for project scheduling?

3.6 How does a project manager determine the critical path in network development for project scheduling?

3.7 What role does network development play in resource allocation and time management in project scheduling?

3.8 Explain the concept of a dummy activity in network development in project scheduling.

3.9 How does the network development technique assist project managers in managing project risks?

3.10 Describe the difference between a merge activity and a burst activity in the context of activity networks.

3.11 Explain how the concept of "free float" differs from "total float" in activity networks and its significance in project scheduling.

3.12 Explain the role of dependencies in developing an activity network for project scheduling and provide examples of different types of dependencies.

3.13 Explain the concept of serial activities in project scheduling and provide an example.

3.14 Describe merge activities in an activity network and give a real-world scenario.

Category II

3.15 Explain the importance of project scheduling in the context of project management. Discuss how effective scheduling contributes to project success, considering various stakeholders and project constraints.

3.16 Discuss the role and significance of activity definition in project scheduling networks. How does effective activity definition contribute to project clarity, resource allocation, and risk management?

3.17 Analyze the role of dummy activities in project networks. Explain when and why dummy activities are used, and discuss their impact on project scheduling accuracy and complexity. Provide examples to illustrate their application in real-world projects.

3.18 Describe the concept of milestones in project network scheduling. How do milestones differ from regular activities, and what role do they play in monitoring project progress, identifying critical paths, and communicating project milestones to stakeholders?

3.19 Evaluate the role of leads and lags in project network scheduling. Explain how leads and lags influence task sequencing, project duration, and critical path analysis. Provide examples to illustrate their application in optimizing project schedules.

3.20 Compare and contrast the advantages and limitations of activity-on-node (AON) and activity-on-arrow (AOA) network diagrams in project scheduling. Provide examples to illustrate their respective applications and suitability for different project types.

3.21 Discuss the significance of critical paths in project networks. How does identifying and managing critical paths contribute to project scheduling, resource allocation, and risk management? Provide real-world examples to illustrate their impact.

NUMERICAL PROBLEMS

3.1 Given the following activities for a construction project with their durations and predecessors, calculate the earliest start (ES), earliest finish (EF), latest start (LS), latest finish (LF), and float (slack) for each activity. Identify the critical path.

Activity	Duration (Days)	Predecessor
A	5	–
B	7	A
C	3	A
D	6	B,C
E	4	D
F	2	C
G	5	D,F
H	3	E,G

3.2 For a software development project, the following activities and their estimated durations are given. Calculate the total project duration and identify the critical path.

Activity	Duration (Days)	Predecessor
A	2	–
B	3	A
C	4	A
D	2	B,C
E	1	C
F	3	D,E
G	2	F
H	1	F
I	2	G,H

3.3 Consider the AOA project network below. Calculate the total float (slack) for each activity and identify all critical activities.

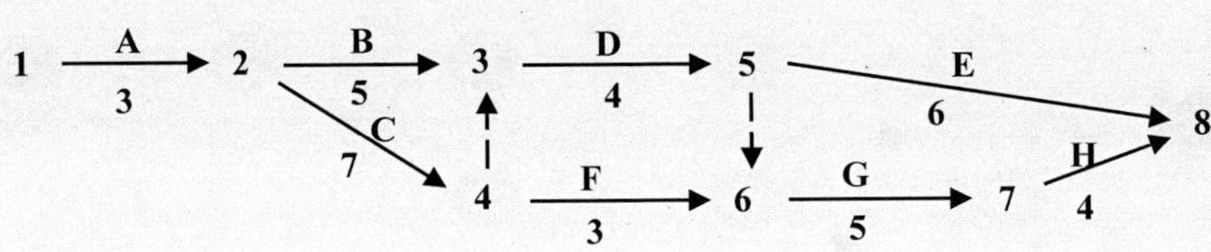

3.4 Consider a project for which the time estimates are given in the table below. Construct the PERT network. What is the critical path? Find the probability of completing the project before 23 days.

Activity	Estimated times (days)		
	Most Optimistic (t_o)	Most Likely (t_m)	Most Pessimistic (t_p)
1 – 2	2	5	8
1 – 3	1	4	7
2 – 3	0	0	0
2 – 4	2	4	6
2 – 6	5	7	12
3 – 4	3	5	10
3 – 5	3	6	9
4 – 5	4	6	10
4 – 6	2	5	8
5 – 6	2	6	6

3.5 A new automated banking system is going to be installed by a bank. The following activities, their relative priorities, and estimated times for each activity has been identified by bank management in order to complete the project:

Activity	Description	Activity Predecessor	Time Estimates (Weeks)		
			Most Optimistic (t_o)	Most Likely (t_m)	Most Pessimistic (t_p)
A	Position hiring	–	5	8	17
B	Development of the system	–	3	12	15
C	System education	A	4	7	10
D	Equipment instruction	A	5	8	23
E	Manually testing the system	B,C	1	1	1
F	Initial system switchover	B,C	1	4	13
G	Employee-computer	D,E	3	6	9

	interface				
H	Modification to equipment	D,E	1	2.5	7
I	Testing of equipment	H	1	1	1
J	Installation and troubleshooting of systems	F,G	2	2	2
K	Changeover of equipment	G,I	5	8	11

Establish the project's projected completion time and standard deviation, the earliest and latest activity times, and the likelihood that it will be finished in less than 40 weeks.

3.6 Project crash data and the information needed to build a project network are shown in the following table:

Activity	Activity Predecessor	Activity Time (Weeks)		Activity Cost ($)	
		Normal	Crash	Normal	Crash
A	–	16	8	2000	4400
B	–	14	9	1000	1800
C	A	8	6	500	700
D	A	5	4	600	1300
E	B	4	2	1500	3000
F	B	6	4	800	1600
G	C	10	7	3000	4500
H	D,E	15	10	5000	8000

Build the project's network, and then crash it as much as possible.

REFERENCES AND SUGGESTED READINGS

1. Barker, J. R. *Project Management: A Practical Guide for Beginners*. Sage Publications, 2008.

2. Burman, P.J. *Precedence Networks for Project Planning and Control*. New York: McGraw-Hill, 1972.

3. Gray, C.F., Larson, E.W. and Desai, G.V. *Project Management: The Managerial Process*, 6th Edition, New York: Irwin/McGraw-Hill, 2017.

4. Kerzner, H. *Project Management: A Systems Approach to Planning, Scheduling, and Controlling*, 12th Edition, Wiley, 2017.

5. Levy F., Thompson, G. and Wiest, J. *The ABC's of the Critical Path Method.* Harward Business Review, Vol. 41(5), 1963.

6. Madhavi, R., and Ahuja, I. Optimizing Project Schedules Using PERT and CPM: A Comparative Study. *International Journal of Project Management*, Vol. 30(6), 713-721, 2012.

7. Mantel, S. J., Meredith, J. R., Shafer, S. M., and Sutton, M. M. *Project Management in Practice*, 7th Edition, Wiley, 2018.

8. Martinich, J.S. *Production and Operations Management*: *An Applied Modern Approach*. John Wiley & Sons, Wiley-India, 1997.

9. Moder, J., Phillips, C.R. and Davis, E.W. *Project Management with CPM and PERT and Precedence Diagramming*, 3rd Edition, New York: Van Nostrand Reinhold, 1983.

10. Morris, P. W. G., and Hough, G. H. The Anatomy of Major Projects: A Study of the Reality of Project Management. *International Journal of Project Management*, Vol. 5(1), 44-54, 1987.

11. Patanakul, P., and Milosevic, D. Defining the Criteria for Successful Project Scheduling: A Case Study Using PERT. *Project Management Journal*, Vol. 40(1), 78-86, 2009.

12. Ritzman, L.P. and Krajewski, L.J. *Operations Management*: *Strategy and Analysis*, 5th Edition, Pearson, 1998.

13. Tharp, G. D. Using CPM and PERT in Project Scheduling. *Journal of Construction Engineering and Management*, Vol. 141(5), 04015015, 2015.

14. Wiest, J.D. and Levy F.K. *A Management Guide to PERT/CPM*, 2nd Edition, Upper SaddleRiver, NJ: Prentice Hall, 1977.

15. Wysocki, R.K. *Effective Project Management*: *Traditional, Adaptive, Extreme*, 4th Edition, New York: Wiley, 2007.

UNIT 4

PRODUCTION PLANNING AND CONTROL

UNIT SPECIFICS

This unit elaborately discusses the following topics:

- Role of production planning
- Characteristics of external factors effecting production planning like make-to-stock, build-to-order, etc.
- Characteristics of internal factors affecting production panning like customer adjustment strategies, demand chase strategy, level capacity strategy, and mixed strategy
- Steps of production planning and control including Routing, scheduling, tracking, loading, sequencing, and Dispatching

The topics' real-world applications are examined in order to foster greater creativity and curiosity as well as enhance problem-solving skills. The unit includes assignments through a number of numerical problems, a list of references, and suggested readings in addition to a large number of multiple-choice questions and questions with short and long answer types marked in two categories following lower and higher order of Bloom's taxonomy. These can be completed for practice.

Based on the content, an additional section ("Along the...") has been added after the unit's related topic. It has been thoughtfully created for the benefit of the book's reader. This content primarily concentrates on the amazing information about the issue addressed in the contemporary, fascinating industrial context, which heightens interest in the subject.

RATIONALE

This unit on production planning lies in its critical role in enhancing operational efficiency and responsiveness in manufacturing environments. By identifying key factors that influence production planning, both external and internal, students gain a comprehensive understanding of the complexities involved in aligning production processes with market demands. Analyzing external characteristics, such as make-to-stock and build-to-order strategies, alongside evaluating internal approaches like demand chase and mixed strategies, equip learners with the analytical tools necessary for effective decision-making. Furthermore, outlining the essential steps of production planning – from routing to dispatching – provides a structured framework for implementation. Applying these techniques in practical scenarios fosters critical thinking, while assessing the impact of various strategies enables students to appreciate the broader implications on organizational performance, ultimately preparing them for real-world challenges in the field.

UNIT OUTCOMES

List of outcomes of this unit is as follows:

U4-UO1: Defining role of production planning

U4-UO2: Analyze External Characteristics affecting production planning

U4-UO3: Evaluate internal strategies for production planning

U4-UO4: Outline production planning steps

U4-UO5: Apply Planning Techniques

U4-UO6: Assess Impact of Strategies

UNIT-4 Outcomes	EXPECTED MAPPING WITH COURSE OUTCOMES (*1-Weak Correlation; 2-Medium Correlation; 3-Strong Correlation*)					
	CO-1	CO-2	CO-3	CO-4	CO-5	CO-6
U4-UO1	3	3	2	3	2	3
U4-UO2	2	3	3	3	2	2
U4-UO3	2	3	3	3	2	2
U4-UO4	2	3	3	3	2	2
U4-UO5	3	3	3	3	3	3
U4-UO6	2	3	3	3	3	3

4.1 INTRODUCTION

Production planning and control (PPC) is the process of efficiently managing and optimizing the production activities within an organization. It involves the coordination of various tasks, resources, and processes to meet customer demand while minimizing costs and maximizing productivity.

Early 19th-century production planning served as the model for modern production planning. It came about as a result of a demand for data on internal control planning. Internal administrative frameworks were necessary for organizations such as railroads, textile mills, and other enterprises to manage the various procedures required in delivering their core product or service on a big scale. First production schedules were straightforward. Relatively small factories produced a small number of goods in big quantities. Technical experts in their domain oversaw all scheduling and planning, which occasionally amounted to nothing more than a list of production orders together with the completion date.

Manufacturers have been trying to enhance their operations over the years by controlling their inventory, boosting production, and making the most use of their resources. These are a few of the largest issues that manufacturers deal with. Numerous strategies have surfaced as means of enabling industrial processes to enhance their overall productivity. One such strategy is production planning and control, or PPC, a word that refers to the two crucial aspects of manufacturing, planning, and control. The actions required prior to the start of production, such as capacity planning, operations scheduling, and materials planning, are handled by the production planning section. By ensuring that the production team is meeting its goals and keeping to the schedule, the production control section keeps an eye on the actual manufacturing process. All things considered, production planning and control can significantly impact production through cost minimization, waste reduction, and schedule optimization.

Although the book primarily focuses on manufacturing, service businesses can also benefit from the principles of manufacturing in many situations. Of course, service organizations are those whose main products are services to individuals rather than manufactured items. Examples of "production" outputs that are services include banking, insurance, haircutting, accountancy, and legal services. Although there are undoubtedly some significant distinctions between a production and service setting, these distinctions also influence the degree of formality and methodology used when applying these principles, although the general ideas are frequently still applicable. The planning and control technique used by the service organization is somewhat more challenging to manage for at least four main reasons. These four concerns typically have the biggest impact on how planning and control strategies are created for service organizations:

i. **Time**: There is frequently not much time in service companies between the moment a demand is identified and the anticipated delivery of a process outcome. When customers approach some service establishments, they anticipate receiving their orders almost immediately. Service providers frequently make some effort to regulate this, particularly if their capacity to provide the service is highly expensive or fixed. Some service organizations try to manage the demand for process output through the use of appointments and reservations.

ii. **Customer interaction**: The fact that the client is frequently far more involved in the design of the "product" or output of the experience in a service setting is related to the time issue. Furthermore, the person providing the service is frequently the contact point. In this sense, a service provider might be considered a sales representative as well as an operations representative.

iii. **Quality**: The fact that a large portion of quality in service firms may be intangible and hence more challenging to quantify is a crucial aspect of quality in these organizations.

iv. **Inventory**: Organizations that provide "pure" services, that is, those whose production consists almost entirely of non-physical goods, frequently cannot afford to inventory their output. For example, it is difficult to inventory a sauna bathing. Given that they are frequently under pressure to reduce inventory, many in the manufacturing industry may find it surprising that inventory is viewed as a luxury. However, from the standpoint of factory planning, inventory is actually best understood as "stored capacity." Essentially, inventory, especially finished goods, can be thought of as the organization's use of its capacity before the actual demand for its output is realized. In this case, it will enable the company to apply the output processes a little more smoothly, increasing their efficiency and frequently their effectiveness.

The following are some advantages of production planning and control:

By properly scheduling the machine items, it assures optimal utilization of production capacity and minimizes both idle time and overuse.

It guarantees that inventory levels are consistently maintained at optimal levels, meaning that neither overstocking nor understocking occurs.

Additionally, it makes sure that production time is maintained at its best, which lengthens the turnover time.

Because it ignores every facet of the production process, the final product's quality is consistently upheld.

4.2 PRODUCTION PLANNING

The process of production planning is organizing and building out what has to be done in order to produce goods or services in the required quantity and on right time. The process of determining the measures to be performed in the future, such as what needs to be done, how much needs to be done, and when it should be done, is known as production planning. Since this planning relates to the future, it is predicated on forecasts derived from historical data as well as certain conjecture. Production planning aims to maximize efficiency and effectiveness in the areas, viz, labor capabilities, raw material optimization, resource management, and production capacity management to efficiently satisfy market demand. To guarantee efficient execution, every plan must be reviewed through control. That is, the process of production planning and subsequently the control function should be concurrently performed on a regular basis. A production schedule that specifies the kinds of products, their quantities, and their schedules for manufacturing are the end result of production planning. In order to prevent excess or insufficient inventory, maintain a balance between supply and demand, and optimize the use of company resources, production planning is essential. Companies can increase customer satisfaction by producing timely, demand-driven products, mitigating production costs, and improve operational efficiency with effective production planning. A company plans their production considering external and internal factors that constitutes an industry environment. Fig. 4.1 shows internal and external factors affecting production planning.

Fig. 4.1 Internal and external factors governing production planning

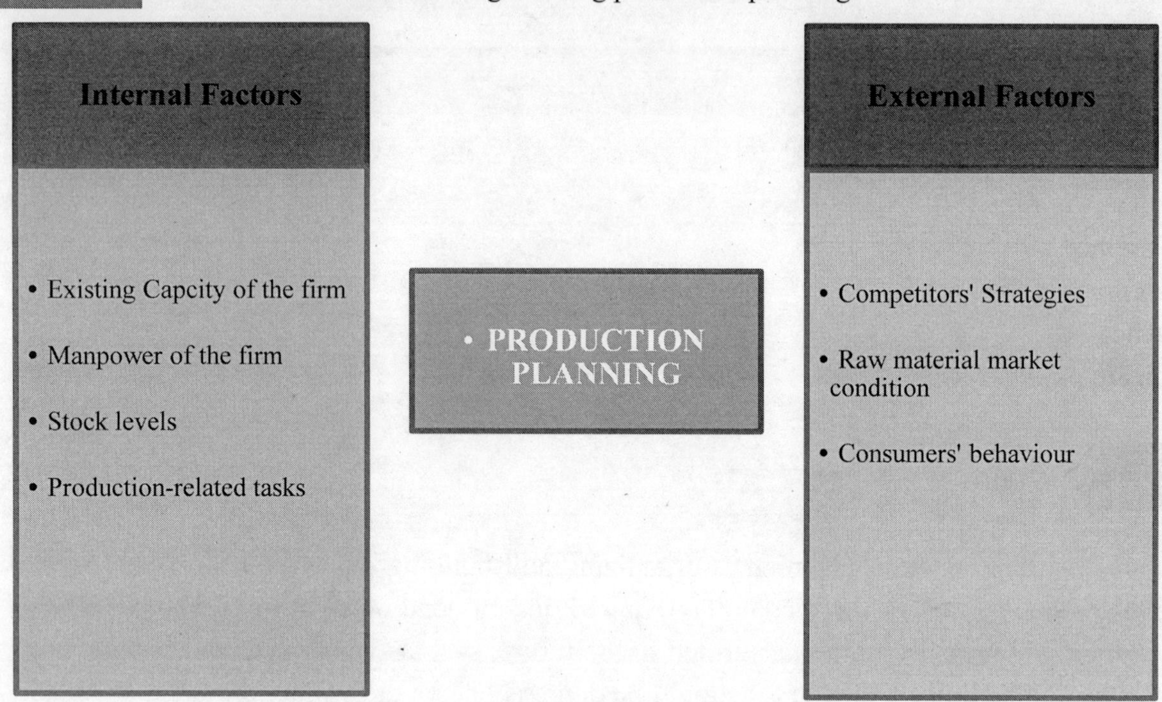

4.2.1 PRODUCTION PLANNING FROM EXTERNAL FACTORS PERSPECTVE

In general, external environment is outside the control of the company's decision makers, but in some companies, demand for the product can be managed through close cooperation between marketing and operations by promotional activities, for instance, using models like Bass model in which the consumer behaviour can be studied through key performance indicators like service rates and can be identified from the rate of innovation and immitation of a product (Dev et al., 2020).

For companies dealing with cyclical swings in demand, complementary items could be an effective alternate. When there is less demand for the primary product, complementary items might help the manufacturing system run more smoothly. For example, a company that sells refrigerators and finds great demand in the summer but weak demand in the winter can develop heater-related components like thermostats, which are also in high demand during the winter. But even so, there are limits to how much demand can be controlled depending upon the trade-off between promotional costs and managing the cost involving internal factors, viz, capacity, manpower expenditure, and other production related tasks. The new approach to facilitate adaptation of these internal factors due to change in external factors is termed as *flexibility* of the firm.

Customer design influence is a topic that is sometimes addressed as part of the company's core strategy and other times as a response to market forces. For example, a lot of cars are bought from a dealer's lot as finished items since the buyers don't want to wait for an automobile to be built with the exact features they want. The degree of consumer influence or *consumer behaviour* can generally be characterized by the following categories, which are presented here in increasing order of flexibility.

4.2.1.1 MAKE-TO-STOCK (MTS)

These are products that are fully produced into their final shape and stocked as finished goods. In the early stages of product design, the entire consumer base may have some effect on the final design, but once the product is made, a buyer essentially has only one choice: to buy or not to buy. Further, these buying habits can affect general modifications in product design, but typically not for a specific client. These things are widely available and may be obtained in almost every retail store. Examples include office supplies, apparel, hardware, groceries, and so forth.

4.2.1.2 ASSEMBLE-TO-STOCK (ATS)

This combines multiple component parts into a finished product, which is then stocked in inventory to satisfy customer demand. Examples are watches, tools, appliances.

4.2.1.3 ASSEMBLE-TO-ORDER (ATO) or BUILD-TO-ORDER (BTO)

Since customers can choose from a variety of pre-designed subassemblies, the customer has more design control in this scenario. Subsequently, the manufacturer will integrate these choices into the ultimate product for the client. Similar to the MTS, each client can only choose from the available options; but, the entire customer base has the ability to impact the final products and option designs. Two excellent examples of these kinds of goods are cars and computers. For instance, when a consumer gets a car from a dealer, they frequently have a wide range of alternatives when it comes to colors, body types, engines, transmissions, and other "pure" features like cruise control. Because the packaging is customer-specified, this method is frequently referred to as "*package-to-order*" in some industries. Products like baking goods (flour, baking soda, etc.) and morning cereals don't change; instead, they can be packaged in a variety of ways and quantities to suit the needs of the consumer.

ALONG THE BUILD-TO-ORDER APPROACH

Dell computers demonstrated that the most lucrative business model in the PC sector is internet-based mass customisation, which is based on a BTO scenario. Dell's online computer builder allowed consumers to create their own PCs, generating a 160% return on investment. After that, the manufacturing department sent these PCs, giving them a five-day lead time.

Automakers such as ***Renault*** and ***Volvo*** have already initiated BTO initiatives to curtail expensive incentives and inventory levels. Renault's "Project Nouvelle Distribution" is the most well-known of them, with the goal of creating a BTO car in 14 days from purchase to delivery. Volvo was the first company to implement this strategy, aiming to achieve 100% "customer-based" production and cutting order-to-delivery times from six weeks to 28 days in the early 1990s and then to 14 days in 1995. *Ford* and *Volkswagen* offer comparable 14 or 15 day automobile plans. *BMW* is even aiming for a lead time of 10 days from order to delivery.

4.2.1.4 MAKE-TO-ORDER

In this setting, the client can select the precise layout of the finished good or service, provided standard components and raw materials are used. A bakery or specialized furniture maker could serve as examples. For instance, a customer in a furniture shop can request that a certain type of sofa be made for the home. They may be restricted to specific sofa size, type of wood, and other factors, but they have a wide range of design options for the sofa. But there's a distinction between build-to-order (BTO) and MTO.

In comparison to MTO, lead times are shorter in BTO. Regarding BTO, the parts and components are prepared for assembly, that is, similar to ATO. Mass customization is the result of a significant paradigm shift brought about by the BTO concept. With the success of its implementation in Compaq, BMW, and Dell Computers, BTO has gained popularity as an operation pattern. Several sectors are currently implementing the BTO approach in order to achieve mass customization. It has been noted that with the current paradigm change to reverse logistics, manufacturers and merchants who use BTO policies have far lower return rates; roughly half of what the sector as a whole experiences.

ALONG THE ASSEMBLE-TO-ORDER APPROACH: VIRTUAL BUILD-TO-ORDER

A new order fulfillment technique called *Virtual Build-to-order* (VBTO) uses integrated information systems to improve the fulfillment process. The main novelty of VBTO systems is their ability to make all unsold products in the production process available to all customers. A customer in a VBTO system may be satisfied by a BTO product, a product that is in the pipeline, or a product that is in stock. The pipeline is usually unreachable, and a customer might be satisfied with a product that is manufactured to order or one that is available in stock. According to information provided by the automotive industry, customers are likely to find a vehicle with the color and options they most desire if they are connected to the vast, albeit dispersed, array of vehicles already in existence, including vehicles on dealer's lots, in transit, on assembly lines, and scheduled for production, either online or in dealer showrooms. The VBTO method is being used by big automakers. In the basic VBTO system, the terms "finished stock" and "pipeline" refer to the order in which the goods are being created or will be manufactured. There are three ways to satisfy a customer: either a product from stock is supplied, or a product in the pipeline is assigned to the customer, or a product is made to become BTO (at which point it enters the start of the pipeline). Fig. 4.2 shows that three segments of the system are visible.

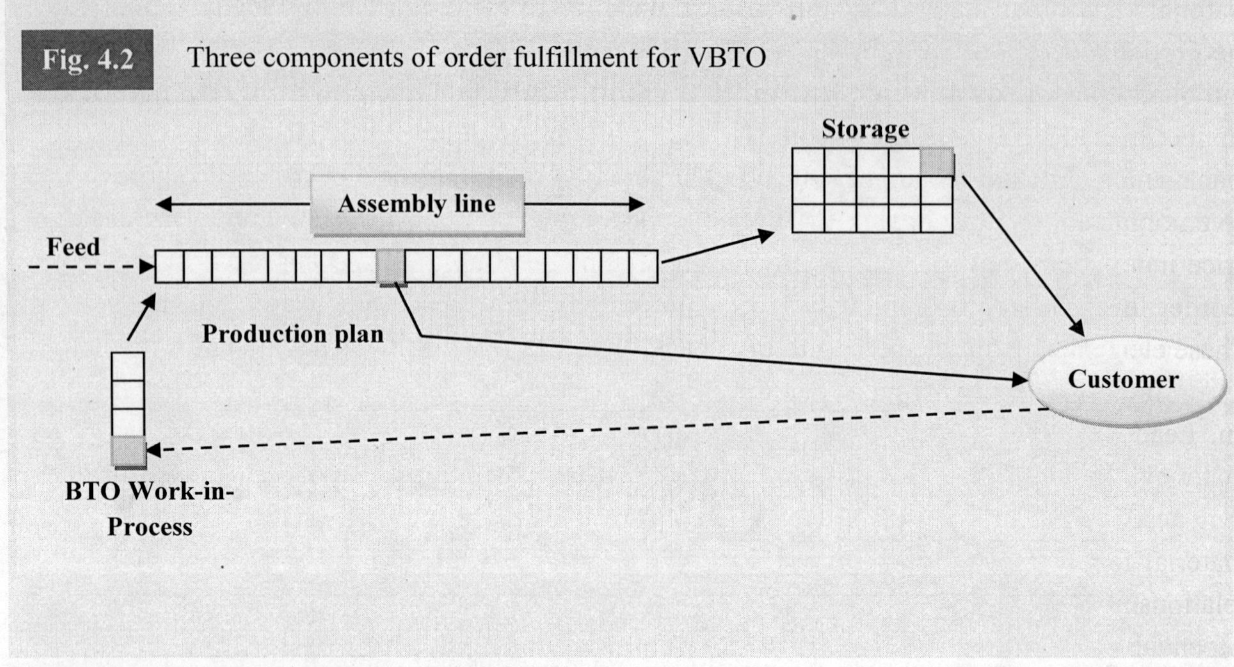

Fig. 4.2 Three components of order fulfillment for VBTO

4.2.1.5 ENGINEER-TO-ORDER (ETO)

In this case, the client has virtually total control over how the good or service is designed. Frequently, they are not even restricted to using ordinary parts or raw materials; instead, they can request that the manufacturer creates something "from scratch." Customers do colloborate and support the manufacturing staff. This aids them in achieving the desired outcome during ETO. Moreover, ETO is frequently utilized in the production of unique and complex goods. ETO goods are now found in practically every industry. Essentially, the need for customized or ETO products are rising. For example, equipment for commercial HVAC (Heating, Ventilation and Air Conditioning), boilers in the power plants, commercial cranes, aerospace manufacturing, security, and defense industry, energy sector, and many others.

4.2.1.6 RAW MATERIAL AVAILABILITY

Production planning may also be impacted by the availability of raw materials. Production capacity may be impacted by limited availability or unforeseen supply chain problems, which may result in delays or higher expenses. It is impossible to overstate the significance of raw materials for the smooth operation of a manufacturing organization, as their availability in the proper number and quality will define, to a reasonable degree, the availability, quality, and quantity of the final product. Any manufacturing company's total performance depends on its ability to manage raw materials. The raw material condition in terms of efficient management and good planning impacts the activity level, turn-over, and final profit in a given organization, in addition to demand and other factors like rival actions and the general price index. In any industrial setting, determining the minimum and maximum stock levels, reorder level, and economic order quantity (EOQ) is crucial for raw material management. These elements of inventory control are discussed ahead in the section on inventory control.

For streamline raw material availability, lead time is a very important factor to focus on. Lead times are the durations required for suppliers to deliver completed items or raw materials. Short lead times may cause shortages in inventories or higher expenses, whereas long lead times may cause manufacturing delays. For streamlining the availability of raw material forecasting based inventory control should be closely monitored. Building trusting relationships with suppliers is crucial at this point to make sure the supply chain is dependable. Companies work together with their suppliers to arrange delivery times, settle disputes over costs, and uphold uniform quality requirements.

Having a strong manufacturing ERP* (Enterprise Resource Planning) software or Material requirement Planning (MRP discussed ahead in detail) system integrated into the company will assist guarantee that you always have the necessary raw materials on hand. This implies that stockouts or delayed supply orders will never force you to halt manufacturing. That means:

- It is advised that manufacturing companies always ascertain the bare minimum of inventory to maintain. This is done to prevent stock-outs or unexpected shortages. Other ills like lost production time, low capacity utilization, and failure to reach production goals would disappear along with stock-outs.
- That manufacturing companies prepare and plan for the delivery of raw materials and other inventory so that there is no delay between the time of demand and the time of supply. This will stop production activities from being interrupted, and as a result, issues with low capacity utilization and failure to reach production goals will be resolved.

---

* ERP software makes it simple to build and maintain a production plan. Before making a production plan, you would need the goods, bill of materials, routings, client orders, and material requests available.

- It is important to identify and record the time of need for any slow-moving inventory items to make sure that maintenance on them is stopped right away. To recover the capital locked up in them, all outdated objects had to be sold. Recognizing changes in business and technology settings could help eliminate the purchase of outdated goods. A precise determination of the maximum stock level could prevent overstocking. Following advice on overstocking, slow-moving inventory, and obsolete goods will guarantee that funds that could be utilized as working capital are freed up. Manufacturing companies' liquidity positions will improve as a result.
- The issue of not being able to employ inventory models will be significantly resolved by using electronic data processing devices (e.g. ERP). The main obstacle to shop staff using models is their ignorance of the usage of quantitative values to generate information.

4.2.2 PRODUCTION PLANNING FROM INTERNAL FACTORS PERSPECTIVE

4.2.2.1 CAPACITY ADJUSTING STRATEGIES

We saw in the previous discussion how the design of planning and control approaches can be influenced by the business environment, often known as the external environment. Regarding the analysis of the internal procedures used to provide the client with goods and services, there are a number of other matters that need to be resolved. Fundamentally, there are three approaches to production planning internal to the industry from the capacity adjusting perspective (i) demand chase strategy, (ii) level capacity strategy, and (iii) combination strategy. Trade-offs between the capacity of machine, size of the workforce, work hours, inventory, and backlogs are part of these techniques. We briefly discuss these strategies here and would be further discussed in detail in the section on "Aggregated Planning" ahead.

4.2.2.2 DEMAND CHASE STRATEGY

It is a manufacturing strategy involving adjusting output to suit variations in consumer demand. Utilizing a chase production strategy might help to schedule output and prevent stock-outs. The fundamental concept is to monitor consumer demand and make enough goods to satisfy it while maintaining inventory. It is most appropriate for companies whose demand varies significantly. Seasonal variables may be responsible for this, such as a company that sells hot soups in the winter and ice cream cones in the summer. Other factors may also be at play, such as a company that manufactures customized goods or competes in a very competitive market. There are a few simple steps to implementing the Chase Production Strategy shown in Fig. 4.3.

i) Determine production levels: The amount of goods to be manufactured must be determined in advance. Based on your anticipated sales and the quantity of goods you must maintain in stock, this number should be determined.

ii) Calculate customer demand: Estimate the demand for the product once ideal production volume is established. Monitor the quantity of produce and the time that your customers purchase from you. You can use this information to plan your output ahead of time.

iii) Produce enough products: Make enough goods to satisfy consumer demand and allow for inventory.

iv) Adjust production: Adapt your output to the needs of your customers. Increase production in response to rising demand. Lower production if demand declines.

Fig. 4.3 Steps of demand chase strategy

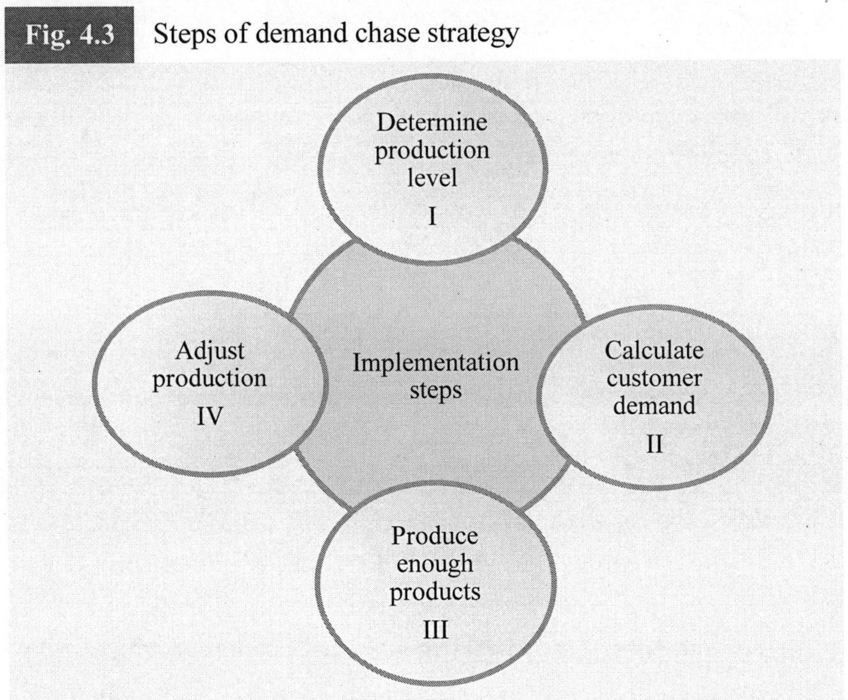

This method, from the standpoint of the workforce, entails recruiting and laying off workers in response to fluctuations in demand. Having a pool of readily trained laborers on hand to draw from as volume rises is essential to the success of this method. Clearly, there are motivational effects. Workers may feel forced to slow down when order backlogs are small because they fear being laid off as soon as current orders are finished. The alternate approach for having different productivity levels is overtime/slack time. A more practical method of adjusting capacity to meet demand is to use overtime/slack hours.

Overtime can occasionally lead to decreased output, worse quality, more accidents, and higher payroll expenses. Conversely, idle or slack time leads to less productive utilization of fixed assets, such as machinery. Slack time programs can be started by creating new demand for goods or services that need the same manufacturing processes in order to use the spare capacity, especially in cases when the business policy prohibits layoffs. Examples of demand chase strategy are:

- Second-tier suppliers for manufactured products. Customers two or more layers down the supply chain frequently generate demand for these products, making it challenging, if not impossible, to change demand. A provider of automotive light bulbs, for instance, responds to demand from automakers, who in turn respond to auto buyers. The demand for cars itself is largely independent of the light bulb maker.
- Service sectors where it is challenging to forecast and change demand. Several instances include:
    - Grocery stores and banks, where customers' needs are frequently not met until they walk in and express them.
    - Expert tax accounting services, who have limited opportunity to change the demand pattern, are forced to try to provide the majority of their services during tax "season".
    - Electric utility companies are among the "process" sectors.

4.2.2.3 LEVEL CAPACITY STRATEGY

When a company employs a level capacity approach, it will produce regardless of the level of demand at a steady rate. In companies that produce to stock, this means that during periods of low demand, finished goods inventory levels will rise, and during periods of high demand, they will fall. Backlogs, lost sales, and carrying cost are the key performance indicators of this strategy. Stable work schedules are advantageous to employees, but they may come at the expense of higher inventory expenses and possibly lower customer service standards. The potential for things that are inventoried to become outdated is another issue.

The alternate approach to exploit backorders entails transferring demand to other periods, ideally to the periods in which demand is lower. Backorders enable demand to fluctuate over time, particularly to times when it can be met while maintaining the regular production rate for that time or to a time when demand is lower, provided that the customer agrees to the postponed delivery dates. It entails scheduling production hours, acquiring additional human resources when needed, and managing inventories to maximize production efficiency.

Another approach to overcome the problems viz, backorders, inventory related issues, and workers layoff is "Subcontracting", i.e. outsourcing all or some portion of the production periodically. However, subcontracting necessitates analyzing supply sources, increase in potential cost, output control, schedule, and even quality concerns. It requires a long term relationship with outsourced suppliers for fulfilling the demand in sudden surge-in-demand situations. This strategy is more prevalent and undoubtedly more desirable in settings where changing resources is costly or complex. This is also typically how "lean production" environments operate. Examples of level capacity strategy include:

- Lodging and aviation. The resources (rooms and seats, respectively) in both situations are expensive and challenging to change in quantity. Further, appointments are utilized to change demand patterns under a different name, reservations. Furthermore, price tactics (such as weekend rates and super-saver tickets) are employed to modify demand patterns in order to bring the demand closer to the availability of resources. This also has a large number of eateries and vehicle repair shops.

- Professionals like physicians and dentists. Appointments are typically used by professional services to adjust and smooth demand patterns around the availability of the rather costly and challenging-to-alter resource; the doctors and dentists themselves that they represent.

- Similar features can be found in some manufacturing processes. Certain chemical processes cannot be slowed down or accelerated, and they also cannot be switched off without costly and time-consuming restart procedures. Manufacturing certain glass items in big quantities is one example. It might be necessary to run the glass furnace constantly because stopping it down would require cleaning the entire furnace and restarting it. The capacity to stockpile the output rather than adjusting demand is the one "luxury" that manufacturing processes have over the two earlier examples.

4.2.2.4 MIXED STRATEGY

This strategy is by far the most popular one. As the name suggests businesses that employ this strategy would "mix and match," adjusting resources and demand to optimize performance according to predetermined standards, such as profit, inventory investment, and human impact.

Fig. 4.4 Comparison of Basic and Mixed strategy

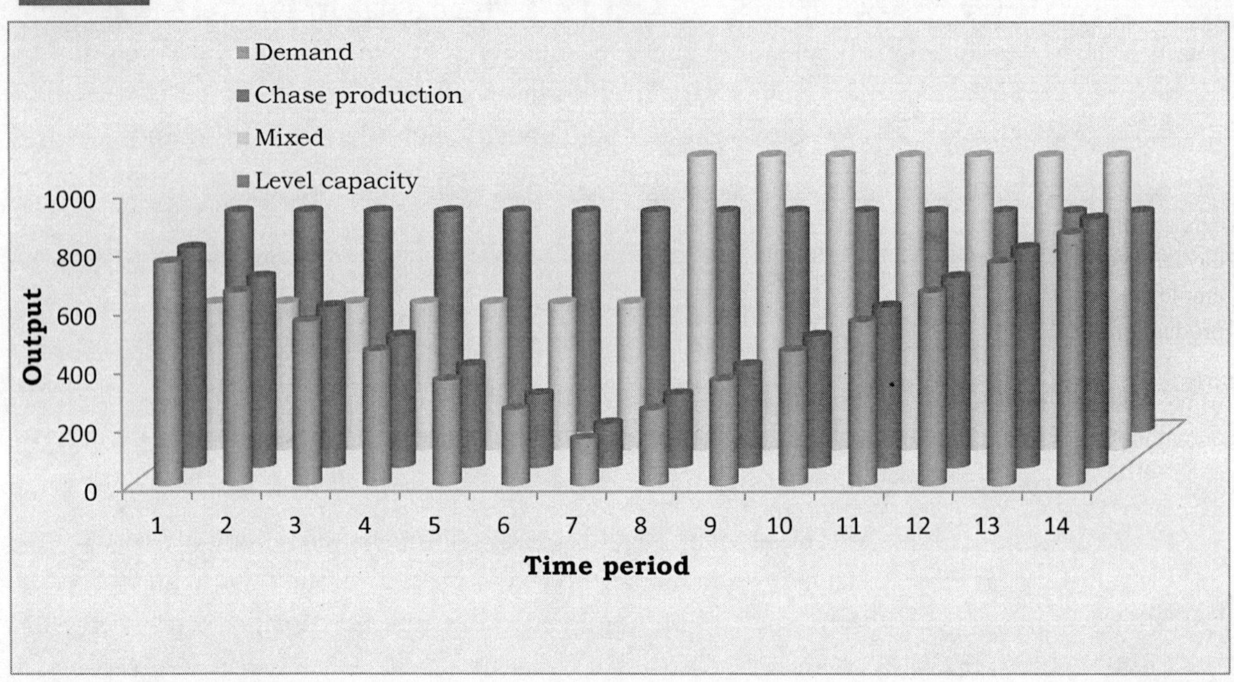

In Fig. 4.4, take note of the fact that level capacity, that is, production is significantly higher than demand at time period 7. At that stage, the fastest pace of inventory buildup is occurring. Though not as much as with the level method, the mixed strategy line still displays an inventory building. Demand is close to both the level capacity and the mixed approach's production rate by the time point 14 is achieved. At that moment, the inventory that was generated during the period of low demand will be utilized quite quickly. Compared to the level capacity method, significantly fewer inventories would have been created with the mixed approach. Because of this, they must boost the mixed approach's manufacturing rate to avoid running out of inventory. Remember that there might be an endless number of mixes of production rates and timing adjustments for those rates; the mixed strategy shown in the diagram is just one of them.

Discussion: A simple example

To illustrate a simple spreadsheet approach for each of these methods, let us examine a simple planning problem:

A car company has a demand forecast for all its cars for the next 6 months. The forecast is:

Month	Demand
January	250
February	300
March	420
April	560
May	610
June	580

At the moment, ten personnel are allocated to the production line, and between them, they can produce about 15 cars a month. In this straightforward example, we'll suppose that there is exactly the same number of production days in every month. At a $400 per worker hiring and training expense, they can increase their workforce. Each employee will incur $1,000 in unemployment benefits if they fire any employees. The normal cost of production for each car is $300, which includes labor, material, and overhead.

They can use overtime to make cars, but each worker can only produce an additional three cars per month using overtime, and each car produced in overtime adds $60 to labor costs. The monthly cost for each automobile in inventory at the end of the month will be $6 if they maintain any cars on hand. If the company can't fulfill market demand, the consumer will probably find another supplier, costing them $120 in earnings. They identify this loss of earnings as a stockout cost (selling price less standard cost). There aren't any cars in stock right now.

Using this simple data, the following tables will illustrate planning approaches using chase demand, level capacity, and a mixed strategy.

Chase demand To accommodate every demand in this case, we shall employ a minimal amount of workers. Inventory will not be permitted, and if needed, overtime can be used in place of hiring a new employee who might add inventory. Production of overtime will be restricted to 15 cars per month, as it is more advantageous to hire another worker at that point. By dividing the demand by 15 (the regular production per worker per month), one can determine the required workforce. For instance, in January, 16.67 is obtained by dividing the demand of 250 by 15. This suggests that 16 workers are required, resulting in a regular production of 240, with the remaining 10 to be produced on overtime. $832,100 is the amount for hire/fire, standard production costs, and overtime.

Month	Demand	Workers	Reg. Prod.	OT Prod.	Hire & Fire	H/F cost ($)	Reg. Cost ($)	OT Cost ($)
Jan	250	16	240	10	+6	2400	75,000	600
Feb	300	20	300	0	+4	1600	90,000	0
Mar	420	28	420	0	+8	3200	126,000	0
Apr	560	37	555	5	+9	3600	`168,000	300
May	610	40	600	10	+3	1200	183,000	600
Jun	580	38	570	10	-2	2000	174,000	600
Total						**14,000**	**816,000**	**2,100**

Level Capacity We aim to maintain a level workforce for the full six months using this plan. The average demand is approximately 453 cars when we split the overall demand (2720 units) over the course of 6 months by 6. By setting the production level at 450 (thirty workers), we guarantee that we will roughly match the average demand, even if it is inevitable that shortages or inventories will arise because every month is different. We shall maintain a steady, level production pace while allowing for inventory or shortage scenarios. We must remember to include the $8,000 one-time recruiting cost of the extra 20 employees at the end.

Over the course of 6 months, this overall cost, which includes production, inventory, shortages, and the one-time hiring cost, is $828,260, or $3,840 less than the chase demand strategy. On the down side, though, 20 buyers in June did not receive the car they had desired. Keep in mind that only columns with pertinent activity are included in order to conserve space. For instance, we might have included a column for hire/fire costs, but because January was the only action, we decided to include that expense at the end.

Month	Demand	Production	Inventory	Shortage	Reg. Prod. Cost ($)	Inventory Cost ($)	Shortage Cost ($)
Jan	250	450	200	0	135,000	1200	0
Feb	300	450	350	0	135,000	2100	0
Mar	420	450	380	0	135,000	2280	0
Apr	560	450	270	0	135,000	1620	0
May	610	450	110	0	135,000	660	0
Jun	580	450	0	20	135,000	0	2,400
Total					**810,000**	**7,860**	**2,400**

Mixed strategy As previously stated, the "mixed strategy" category encompasses a wide range of strategies. We'll only use one example. Starting with 25 employees, we have the manpower to handle early-year demand and create some inventory in this option. We will use the inventory and begin authorizing overtime as demand increases. We will eventually need to hire more staff in order to satisfy demand. The 25 workers will only be allowed to create 75 extra cars on overtime, and this may not be sufficient for some months due to a 3-car limit per worker per month on overtime. But adding the bare minimum of employees will be policy.

Month	Demand	Reg. Prod.	Inv.	OT Prod.	# Wkrs	H/F	Reg. Cost ($)	H/F Cost ($)	Inv. Cost ($)	OT Cost ($)
Jan	250	375	125	0	25	+15	112,500	6,000	750	0
Feb	300	375	200	0	25		112,500		1,200	0
Mar	420	375	155	0	25		112,500		930	0
Apr	560	375	0	30	25		121,500		0	1,800
May	610	510	0	100	34	+9	183,000	3,600	0	6,000
Jun	580	495	0	85	33	-1	174,000	1,000	0	5,100
Total							**816,000**	**10,600**	**2,880**	**12,900**

Even with overtime, we were unable to meet demand by the time May arrived. With 25 workers, we could only create 450 units (each person can produce 18–15 in regular time and 3 in overtime) once the inventory was depleted in April. It was decided to bring on 9 workers. Keep in mind that they wish to reduce the overall workforce. We took the May demand of 610 and split it by 18 to get 33.9, which is the number of workers. That suggests that 34 workers might meet demand by putting nearly all of the approved overtime to use. June's demand, which is 580 divided by 18, equals 32.2, indicating that they can fulfill demand with one fewer worker while still requiring most of them to put in extra time. Although this approach has the highest total cost ($842,380) of the three, it has the benefit of meeting all demand and causing the least amount of interruption to new hires. There may be considerably less expensive options available.

ALONG THE CAPACITY PLANNING

The **Manchester City** football club's stadium, originally intended to hold 80,000 spectators, was intended to serve as the focal point of Manchester's 1996 Olympic bid. After Atlanta was chosen to host the games, the City of Manchester turned its attention to their successful bid to host the 2002 Commonwealth Games. This was reduced to a stadium with 60,000 seats for the Commonwealth Games. The proposal was again altered to allow for the stadium's potential use as Manchester City's new home field in place of Moss Side's Main Road Stadium, but the Council's primary concern was that the stadium should have a sustainable future. According to the revised design, the Games' capacity was 38,000 in 2002 and increased to 48,000 in 2003 after the Manchester City football club took over.

Four months before the games, the stadium's construction, which employed 3,000 people for just over two years, was turned over to the organizers. The City of Manchester and British competitors both experienced tremendous success from the Commonwealth Games. But when the bulldozers arrived, a few hours after the closing ceremony, nobody seemed to care.

The central pitch was reduced, a third level of seating was constructed, and the track was taken out. The football team paid the £30 million pounds for the conversion. Prominent athletes strongly opposed this plan, arguing that a sizable athletics stadium should remain. But the stadiums from the Olympics in Sydney and

Atlanta were converted into baseball and rugby fields, respectively. With 60,000 seats, the Manchester Stadium is one of the biggest outdoor concert venues in Europe when it comes to performance space. An application to increase the capacity to 60,000 football supporters was approved in 2010. The Manchester Commonwealth stadium featured two levels of seating in 2002, but once it was transformed into a football field, it added three levels. A bus service is available for concerts and special events, and there are two rail stations within a half-hour's walk of the stadium. There are 2,000 parking spots at the stadium itself and an additional 8,000 spaces nearby. During the football season, the stadium is used twice a week and can accommodate weddings, conferences, and big sporting events.

4.3 STEPS OF PRODUCTION PLANNING

The main steps of production planning include:

4.3.1 PREPARATION

The first step is to build the foundation for everything that comes after by setting the groundwork. This involves letting the right persons know when new production runs are scheduled. Give them the details of the order amount and the deadline. Finding the correct materials (and the right amounts) from suppliers to finish the customer order in full is another aspect of preparation. Before beginning a manufacturing run, machinery should be inspected to make sure everything is in good operating order.

4.3.2 ROUTING

The process of choosing the order of operations and the path (route) of work is known as routing. Prior to routing, consider the following factors:

a) Product quantity and quality.
b) The personnel, equipment, supplies, etc. to be employed.
c) The kind, quantity, and order of manufacturing processes; and
d) The location of production.

Understanding Routing Operations in Production Processes

The order and actions involved in creating a product are determined by routing operations and sequences, which are crucial components of manufacturing processes. They offer a thorough roadmap that illustrates how raw materials pass through different workstations and are transformed into final goods.

Routing operations – The discrete jobs or activities that must be completed at every workstation during the production process are referred to as routing operations. Cutting, machining, assembly, painting, testing, and packing are a few examples of these procedures. Every operation has particular needs, including the equipment and tools necessary, the operators' level of expertise, and the amount of time needed to finish the job.

Bill of Materials (BOM) – Because it contains a list of all the components, subassemblies, and raw materials needed for every operation, the Bill of Materials (BOM) is a crucial part of routing. In order to prevent material shortages and production delays, the BOM makes sure that the necessary materials are accessible at the right workstation.

Lead Times – Lead times, or the amount of time it takes to finish an activity once it is started, are also related to routing operations. Lead times are essential for scheduling manufacturing and fulfilling delivery dates to customers.

Sequence of operations – Routing describes the sequence in which various processes should be carried out to convert raw resources into final goods. It guarantees that every step is completed in the right order, avoiding mistakes and holding up the production process.

Workstation Allocation – The workstations or machines where each operation should be performed are specified by routing. By ensuring that the appropriate tools and resources are accessible at every turn, this allocation maximizes the use of both manpower and machinery.

Resource Planning – Careful resource planning is needed for manufacturing routing, including determining the necessary equipment, supplies, and labor. Routing makes sure that the resources are available at every stage, which reduces downtime and maintains production efficiency. Resource planning also includes the decisions like make or buys, i.e., the parts and components are to be made in-house or bought from the outside supplier.

Time Estimation – Routing enables firms to effectively plan and schedule production activities by providing time estimates for each operation. It assists in establishing reasonable production schedules and fulfilling customer orders.

Quality Control – Inspections and quality control checks are part of the routing process at different production stages. Manufacturers may ensure that only high-quality items reach customers by identifying and correcting faults early in the process by integrating quality checks into the routing.

Cost Optimization – Manufacturers can find ways to optimize their processes and cut costs by using routing. Routing helps the production process optimize costs by reducing waste and simplifying procedures.

Flexibility and Adaptability – The production process can be flexible and adaptable with appropriate routing. It allows producers to adapt to unforeseen circumstances or shifts in demand by rearranging production schedules, allocating resources, and changing operational procedures.

Standardization – Routing guarantees uniformity in manufacturing processes by giving standardized instructions for every task. Standardization lowers variances in the finished product and produces products of consistent quality.

Continuous Improvement – Initiatives for continual improvement are built on routing. Manufacturers can optimize the manufacturing process by employing data-driven decision-making to discover bottlenecks or inefficiencies by evaluating the performance of individual operations.

PREPARATION OF ROUTE SHEETS

The operations required to process the product are determined by the routing choice and are enumerated in the correct sequence on the route sheet. Fig. 4.5 displays the route sheet. Using the route sheet technique, a flowchart that aids in visualizing operations that might be combined, streamlined, or removed can be created. Additionally, it might be useful in altering the order of processes.

To put it briefly, routing chooses "What," "How much," "With which," "How," and "Where" to generate. The type of production determines the complexity of routing. It is automatic in continuous production, meaning it is very straightforward. It is, nevertheless, extremely complicated in a job sequence. Routing is impacted by human interaction. It should therefore be aware of human requirements, wants, and expectations. It is also impacted by the equipment's features, plant structure, etc.

Finding (fixing) the most efficient and cost-effective order of activities and making sure the factory follows it are the primary goals of routing. Routing provides a very methodical way to turn raw resources into final products. It results in productive and easy work. It results in the best possible use of available resources, including labor, equipment, materials, etc. It results in labor division. It guarantees a nonstop, uninterrupted flow of materials. Time and space are saved. The production engineers and foremen find their jobs easier as a result. It has a significant impact on the installed machinery and building architecture of the factory. Routing is therefore a crucial phase in production planning. It is frequently employed in discrete manufacturing industries where goods are produced in individual batches or units, such as the automotive, aerospace, electronics, and equipment industries.

Fig. 4.5 Route sheet

ROUTE SHEET									
						Order No.			
Name of the part/Component						Specifications			
Component No.						Materials			
Drawing No.						Scrap Allowance			
S.No.	Deptt. No.	Operation No.	Operation	Specifications		Manpower Required	Time per Piece	Due Dates	
				Machine	Tools, Jigs & Fixtures			Start	End

4.3.3 SCHEDULING

Scheduling in an organization refers to deciding when to employ particular resources inside that organization. It has to do with how infrastructure, machinery, and human activity are used. All organizations, regardless of the type of work they do, schedule. Manufacturers, for instance, have to plan their output, which entails creating timetables for their staff, machinery, purchasing, maintenance, and other requirements. Admissions, surgeries, nursing assignments, and support services including meal preparation, security, maintenance, and cleaning must all be scheduled by hospitals. Classrooms, teachers, and students all need to be scheduled by educational institutions. Additionally, appointments are needed for auto repair businesses, dentists, doctors, lawyers, and hair salons. Scheduling decisions have a limited breadth and latitude because they must be made within the limitations imposed by numerous other previous decisions to scheduling like, system capacity, choice of equipment, personnel selection and training, and product and service design. Generally speaking, scheduling aims to minimize client waiting times, inventory, and processing times while achieving trade-offs between competing goals, such as effective staff, equipment, and facility use.

Task scheduling is mostly influenced by the amount of output produced by the system. Approaches needed for high-volume systems differ significantly from those needed for job shops, and additional approaches are needed for project scheduling. We will discuss scheduling for low-volume (job shop) systems, intermediate-volume systems, and high-volume systems in this chapter. We have already discussed project scheduling previously in Unit 3.

SCHEDULING IN FLOW SYSTEM

Standardized tools and processes that perform exact or very similar actions on customers or goods as they move through the system define flow systems. A smooth rate of flow of customers or items through the system is the aim in order to maximize the use of manpower and equipment. Flow systems are commonly referred to as *high-volume systems*. Toys, appliances, radios, TVs, audio equipment, cars, and personal computers are a few examples of high-volume products. Examples of process industries include mining, waste treatment, fertilizer manufacture, sugar, and petroleum refining. Mass vaccination campaigns, news broadcasts, and cafeteria queues are a few examples of services. Many of the loading and sequence choices are made during the system's design because of how extremely repetitious these systems are. Since every item follows essentially the same sequence of activities, the division of labor, the use of dedicated material-handling equipment, the layout of equipment, and the use of highly specialized tools and equipment are all intended to improve the flow of work through the system. *Line balancing* which involves assigning the necessary tasks to workstations in a way that satisfies technical (sequencing) requirements and is balanced with respect to equal work durations among stations is a significant component in the design of flow systems. Systems that are highly balanced maximize the use of both humans and equipment while producing at the highest potential pace. Chapter on plant layout discusses line balance.

The possible dissatisfaction of employees due to the specialization of job duties in flow systems must be taken into account by designers when setting up these systems; high work rates are sometimes attained by breaking the work up into a number of relatively basic tasks that are given to various workers. The tasks are typically monotonous, and they may lead to weariness, absenteeism, turnover, and other issues that impede production and disturb the orderly flow of work. Despite the inherent scheduling characteristics of flow systems, certain scheduling issues still exist. One is because most flow systems have to handle a range of sizes and types; very few are exclusively focused on single good or service. An automaker will therefore put together a wide variety of car combinations: two-door and four-door versions; some with and without air conditioning; premium and standard trim; CD players; tinted glass; and so forth. Toy, appliance, and electronics manufacturers can all agree on this. Every modification necessitates scheduling slightly changed parts, material, and processing requirements into the line. A supervisor is responsible for coordinating the work and material flow to ensure seamless operation of the line. This necessitates planning the acquisitions as well as the inputs, processing, and outputs. Achieving a steady flow and preventing an excessive accumulation of inventory are both crucial. Again, the inventory requirements for each size or model variant will likely vary slightly, necessitating the need for extra scheduling efforts.

Potential system disturbances that produce less than expected production are one cause for scheduling concern. These may be brought up by accidentss, absences, low supplies, and malfunctioning equipment. Since flow systems are made to function at a specific rate, it is typically not feasible to increase the output rate in practice to make up for these factors. Rather, tactics like overtime or subcontracting are frequently needed; however it's not always possible to subcontract on short notice. Partially finished work can occasionally be completed off the line.

Even if they are not as serious, scheduling issues might also arise in the opposite scenario. This occurs when the intended output is lower than the typical rate. However, it is typically essential to operate the system at the regular rate, but for fewer hours, rather than lowering the succeeding rate of output. A production line might, for example, momentarily run seven hours a day rather than eight. For processing and handling, high-volume systems typically need automated or specialized equipment. Furthermore, a high, consistent output is how they function best. As a result, the following elements frequently impact how successful a system like this is:

1. *Product design and process*: Here, achieving a smooth system flow is just as critical as cost and manufacturability.
2. *Preventive maintenance*: Maintaining equipment in good working order helps reduce malfunctions that could impede job flow.
3. *Prompt fixing when malfunctions arise*: Both professionals and supplies of essential replacement parts may be needed for this.
4. *Ideal mixes of products*: The best combinations of inputs can be found using methods like linear programming to get desired results at the lowest possible cost. This is especially true when it comes to the production of diet items, animal feed, and fertilizers.
5. *Reduction of issues with quality*: Issues with quality have the potential to cause significant disruptions, necessitating shutdowns while issues are set. Furthermore, in

addition to production loss, there is a waste of labor, material, time, and other resources involved when output does not satisfy quality standards.

6. *Timeliness and dependability of suppliers*: Supply shortages are a clear cause of disruption and should be prevented. However, hoarding resources as a solution could result in exorbitant carrying costs. It is helpful to reduce wait times for supplies, create dependable supply schedules, and carefully project needs.

SCHEDULING IN INTERMITTENT SYSTEM

Intermittent systems produce at an output that lies between high volume systems and job shop systems that are created to order; these systems are referred to as *intermediate volume systems*. Similar to high-volume systems, intermediate-volume systems typically produce standard outputs when it comes to production. Instead of being produced to order, the products may be offered for purchase if manufacturing is involved. However, in many cases, the volume of output is not enough to sustain continuous manufacturing. Instead, processing these items intermittently is more economical.

As a result, jobs at intermediate-volume work center facilities change periodically. The run sizes are comparatively larger than at a job shop. Products manufactured in these systems include baked goods, paint, cosmetics, and canned goods. The run size of jobs, the timing of jobs, and the order in which jobs should be processed are the three fundamental problems with these systems. Sometimes, the run size problem can be solved by applying a model, such the economic run size model covered in chapter on Inventory Management. The runsize that would save the most money on setup and inventory is

$$Q_O = \sqrt{\frac{2DS}{H}}\sqrt{\frac{p}{p-u}} \qquad \text{... (4.1)}$$

The setup cost could be a crucial factor. One factor that could affect setup costs is the sequence in which operations are completed; jobs that are similar to one another can require less setup variation between them. To cut down on the amount of setups required, tasks at a print shop could be arranged according to the color of the ink. By taking processing sequence into consideration, this offers up the option of lowering setup cost and time. Additionally, it increases the complexity of sequencing and necessitates evaluating task setup costs for each sequence combination.

In a similar spirit, businesses are attempting to shorten setup times in order to minimize downtime for equipment replacement. Offline configurations, snap-on components, modular setups, and adaptable equipment that can accommodate a range of processing needs are examples of tactics.

The fact that usage is not always as seamless as the model assumes presents another challenge. Certain products have a tendency to run out more quickly than anticipated and require replacement sooner. Furthermore, scheduling production to coincide with ideal run intervals is not always feasible due to the need to process different items.

Utilizing a master schedule created from customer orders and demand projections as the foundation for production is another often employed strategy. The number and anticipated time of tasks for components would then be ascertained by companies involved in assembly activities using an MRP (material requirement planning) approach (explained ahead in Unit 7). After comparing anticipated needs with anticipated capacity, the manager would use that data to create a workable schedule. Businesses that produce processed goods instead of assembled goods, such as food products like canned goods and beverages; magazines; paints and cleaning supplies, would take a slightly different approach; the time-phasing data from MRP would not play a significant role.

SCHEDULING IN JOB SHOP SYSTEMS

Job shop system are the *low-volume systems*, have characteristics that differ significantly from high and intermediate-volume systems. Since products are created to order, orders typically vary greatly in terms of the materials used, the processing time, the processing sequence, and the setups involved. Owing to these factors, job-shop scheduling is typically somewhat intricate. This is made worse by the fact that solid timetables cannot be established before the project orders are received. For schedulers, job-shop processing raises two fundamental questions: how to divide the workload among work centers and which job processing order to employ.

4.3.4 TRACKING

In a job shop setting, where jobs travel through various routes within the shop, visit numerous machine centers, and compete for comparable resources. Tracking a job's status is not always simple. It is reasonably simple to watch the queue that the jobs join when they are first released to the shop and estimate when their preliminary activities might be finished. It gets harder to follow the job through the system, though, as it gets further along or the shop gets more conjested. A job's progress can be hampered by a number of factors, including setup needs, equipment malfunctions, quality issues, and competition for resources, which can lead to lengthy queues.

The tracking procedure has been simplified by bar code technology and RFID (Radio frequency identification) tags, which eliminate most of the tediousness and mistakes associated with typing information on a computer keyboard. In its most basic form, the worker uses a wand to read the bar code that is affixed to the work at the start and finish of each workday. In other instances, the pallet or container that transports the goods from one work center to another has an RFID tag fastened to it. As it comes into and goes out of the work area, the tag is instantly read. Similar records can be kept for the amount of time an employee spends on each task, the outcomes of quality assurance or inspections, and the use of resources.

The data collected at each work center needs to be accurate, current, and available to operations staff in order for it to be useful. Production control's monitoring function collects this data and uses it to create a variety of reports that managers and employees can access. Progress reports can be created to display the state of certain jobs, the accessibility, or use of particular resources, and the productivity of specific employees or work centers. To draw attention to shortcomings in certain areas, such as scrap, rework, shortages, expected delays, and unfulfilled orders, exception reports may be created. The jobs that have the highest priority and need to be completed right away are listed on the hot list. A well-managed facility will generate more progress reports than exception reports. The Gantt chart and the input/output control chart are two examples of progress reports that are discussed in the following sections.

GANTT CHARTS

Gantt charts are visual aids that are used for many scheduling-related tasks. Henry Gantt, who invented the use of charts for industrial scheduling, is the source of their name. Gantt charts are used to map out or plan work tasks. They can also be used to track an assignment's progress in relation to the plan. Gantt charts are used to arrange and make clear how resources are actually or intended to be used within a given time frame. Generally, resources that need to be scheduled are listed vertically, and a time scale is displayed horizontally as shown in Fig. 4.6.

Fig. 4.6 A Gantt Chart

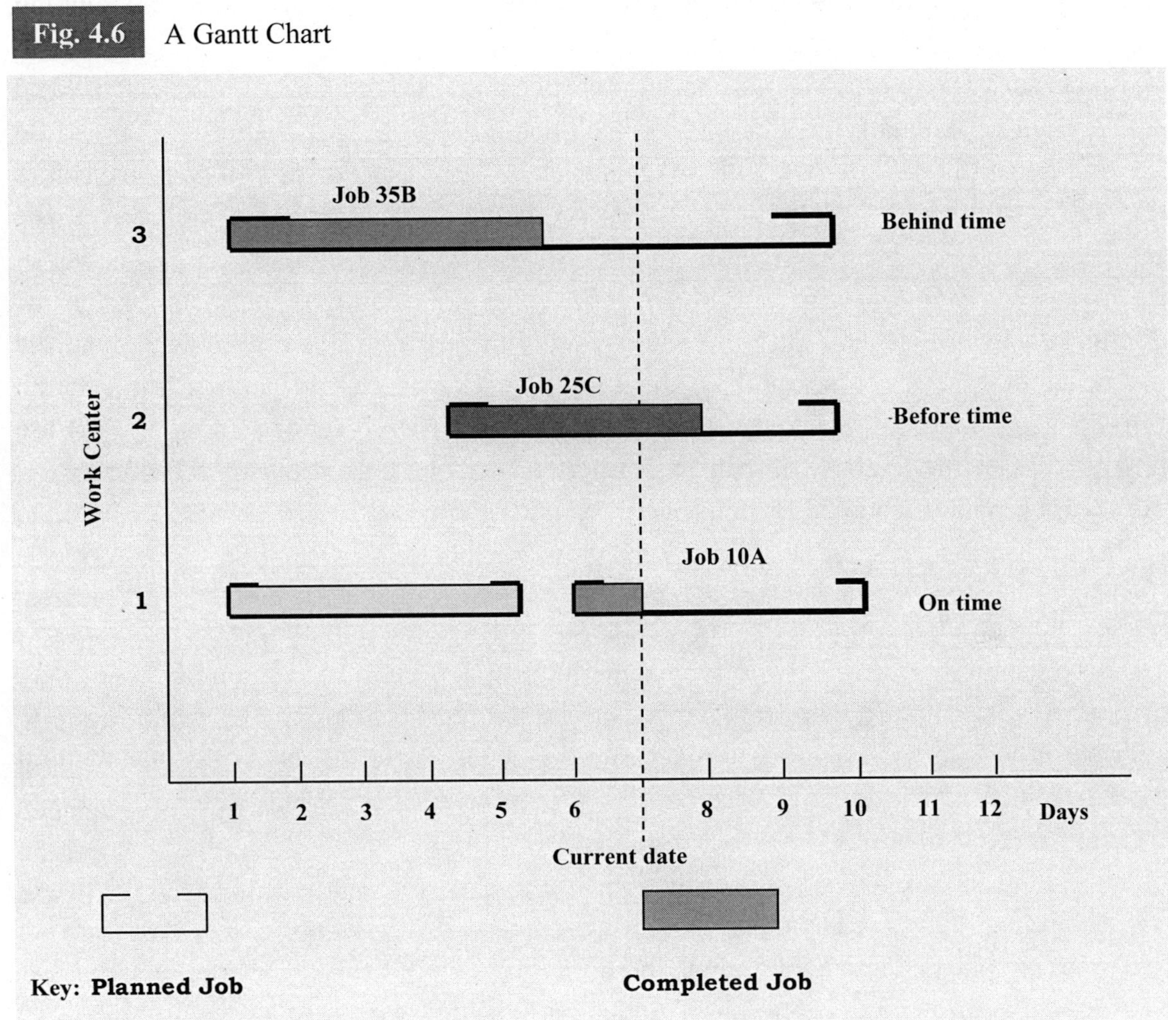

The chart's body displays how the resources are used. The charts can be used by managers to build a trial-and-error plan and obtain a sense of what various arrangements might entail. Therefore, if an operation takes longer than anticipated, a tentative operation schedule may show that not enough time has been allocated for it and can be adjusted accordingly. It would be less common to schedule two distinct classes in the same room at the same time if the chart was used for classroom scheduling. The dashed line in Fig. 4.6, which shows the current date, crosses over the work schedules for jobs 10A, 25C, and 35B. Because the bar tracking work 10A's completion precisely matches the line for the current date, it is easy to tell from the chart that it is completed precisely on time. Job 35B is running behind time, and job 25C is ahead of time.

Since the early 1900s, Gantt charts have been in use and are still widely utilized today. They can be manually created and updated or digitally. Large scheduling boards (the size of multiple bulletin boards) with magnetic strips, pegs, or thread of various colors marking job schedules and progress for everyone to view make up some facilities' Gantt charts.

Forward scheduling and *backward scheduling* are the two main approaches of scheduling. Backward scheduling refers to scheduling backward from a deadline, and forward scheduling refers to scheduling ahead of time from a certain point in time. If the question is: "How long will it take to complete this job?" forward scheduling is used. If the question is: "When the latest a job can be started and still be completed by the due date?" then backward scheduling would be employed.

INPUT/OUTPUT CONTROL

The input and output from every work center are tracked by input/output (I/O) control. Before this kind of research, it was typical to look at a work center's output alone and compare what was produced there to what was scheduled in the shop schedule. In a job shop setting where the output of various work centers is interconnected, applying that method could lead to incorrect inferences regarding the root cause of an issue. The issues at the current work center as well as the issues at the earlier work centers that supplied the current work center could be the source of a reduction in output at one stage in the manufacturing process. Consequently, in order to determine the exact cause of an issue, it is necessary to compare both the planned and actual input and output of a work center. Calculations are used to determine the differences between intended and actual values, and their cumulative impacts are examined. We keep an eye on the resulting backlog or waiting line of work to be finished to make sure it stays within a reasonable bound.

A work center's input rate can only be managed during a job's beginning operations. Because most jobs must pass through the initial work centers before further activities can be completed, they are frequently referred to as gateway work centers. Since downstream work centers' input to subsequent operations is dependent on how well the rest of the shop is running – that is, where queues are building and how smoothly jobs are moving through the system – it is challenging to control. By regulating the feeding work centers' output rates, it is possible to reduce the difference between the intended and actual input for downstream work centers. The best way to demonstrate the use of input/output reports is through an example.

The data required to govern the flow of work to and from a network of work centers is provided via input/output control. A work center that is processing all of the work that is available to it will not produce more if its capacity is increased. Finding the problem's origin is necessary. Backlogs, or excessive lines, are one indication that bottlenecks are present. Work centers experiencing bottlenecks can be relieved by addressing the issue generating the backlog, reducing input into the work center, or adjusting the work center's capacity. A work center experiencing a bottleneck cannot have its output increased by increasing its intake. It will just lead to more system congestion and lengthier work-in-process waits.

Example: Input/Output planning

Input/output planning has started for Perfect Products industry's work centers. The intended inputs and outputs for work center 2 are listed below.

a. At the end of period 4, what backlog will there be if production goes according to plan?
b. How much output can be anticipated from work center 2 if the actual input values for periods 1 through 4 are, respectively, 55, 55, 60, and 60, and the output values cannot be greater than 70?
c. Does Work Center 2's production have a problem?

Input/Output Report for Work Center 2						
Period		1	2	3	4	Total
Planned input		60	60	65	65	250
Actual input						0
Deviation						0
Planned output		70	70	70	70	280
Actual output						0
Deviation						0
Backlog	30					

Solution

a.

Input/Output Report for Work Center 2						
Period		**1**	**2**	**3**	**4**	**Total**
Planned input		60	60	65	65	250
Actual input						0

Deviation						0
Planned output		70	70	70	70	280
Actual output						0
Deviation						0
Backlog	30	20	10	5	0	

By period 4, if all goes according to plan, there will be no backlog.

b.

Input/Output Report for Work Center 2						
Period		**1**	**2**	**3**	**4**	**Total**
Planned input		60	60	65	65	250
Actual input		55	55	60	60	230
Deviation		-5	-5	-5	-5	-20
Planned output		70	70	70	70	280
Actual output		70	70	60	60	260
Deviation		0	0	-10	-10	-20
Backlog	30	15	0	0	0	

Although the backlog is cleared faster due to the decreased input, overall production cannot stay up with the schedule.

Work center 2 has only generated 260 units as opposed to 280, however it seems that the process feeding work center 2 is the source of the issue. Observe that the input and output values exhibit identical deviations from the planned values.

4.3.5 LOADING

Loading is the process of assigning production resources to particular manufacturing processes and products in a production planning and control system. Loading seeks to guarantee that manufacturing processes are running as efficiently as possible by utilizing the right mix of resources. A manufacturing environment has a finite supply of workforce, machinery, and other resources. The availability of these resources must be considered by production planning when assigning them to particular processes. A resource's excess or deficiency can cause production delays and inefficiencies.

An evaluation of the available production resources precedes the loading process. A production schedule that specifies which procedures will be carried out when is then created using the information provided. A loading plan is then established using the production schedule, allocating particular resources to each activity. Production can start as soon as the loading plan is finalized. The loading plan is kept an eye on and modified as needed to make sure production is proceeding as planned. The loading plan might be modified if more details regarding the production resources are obtained.

The work center load is the estimated total time needed to do all of the jobs at a certain work center. A common way to assess load is in time units, such as work hours. Prior to look into the techniques for loading, it is useful to comprehend two essentially distinct methods for managing a load.

INFINITE LOADING

This method loads jobs into a work center based on consumer demand and when they need to be completed, independent of load level relative to capacity. In a way, the workload is arranged as though the work center has an almost infinite capacity, which is obviously not rational. Managing the load is the main problem with infinite loading. For instance, in the period with higher demand than capacity, the manager will most likely need to take some action, like setting up overtime, to temporarily raise the capacity.

FINITE LOADING

This method, as its name suggests, assumes that the work center has a known, quantifiable, limited capacity. For a certain amount of time, the work center operates as full as possible; once that time looks to have reached its limit, the work is pushed to the following time period. There is no doubt that this finite loading strategy smooths the load and reduces excess costs from overtime and other expediting operations, but there is also no doubt that it has a drawback. In particular, customer due dates may suffer if the load is moved to a later time frame when the capacity is achieved. In other sense, even while it would be beneficial for the facility's stability, it might seriously weaken customer service. Despite this, it is often utilized, particularly in businesses where it is prohibitively expensive or impractical to expand short-term capacity. A relative graph of capacity of machine versus infinite and finite loading appears like as shown in Fig. 4.7.

Before using this system, it is also necessary to understand a few presumptions. When loading, there is an underlying presumption that both the capacity and the job processing time are known and precise. However, both of those metrics are based on work standards that are not only somewhat arbitrary when they are first created but also evolve over time as a result of continous improvements. Consequently, there are two methods to load a work centre.

Fig. 4.7 Infinite loading, Finite loading, and Machine capacity

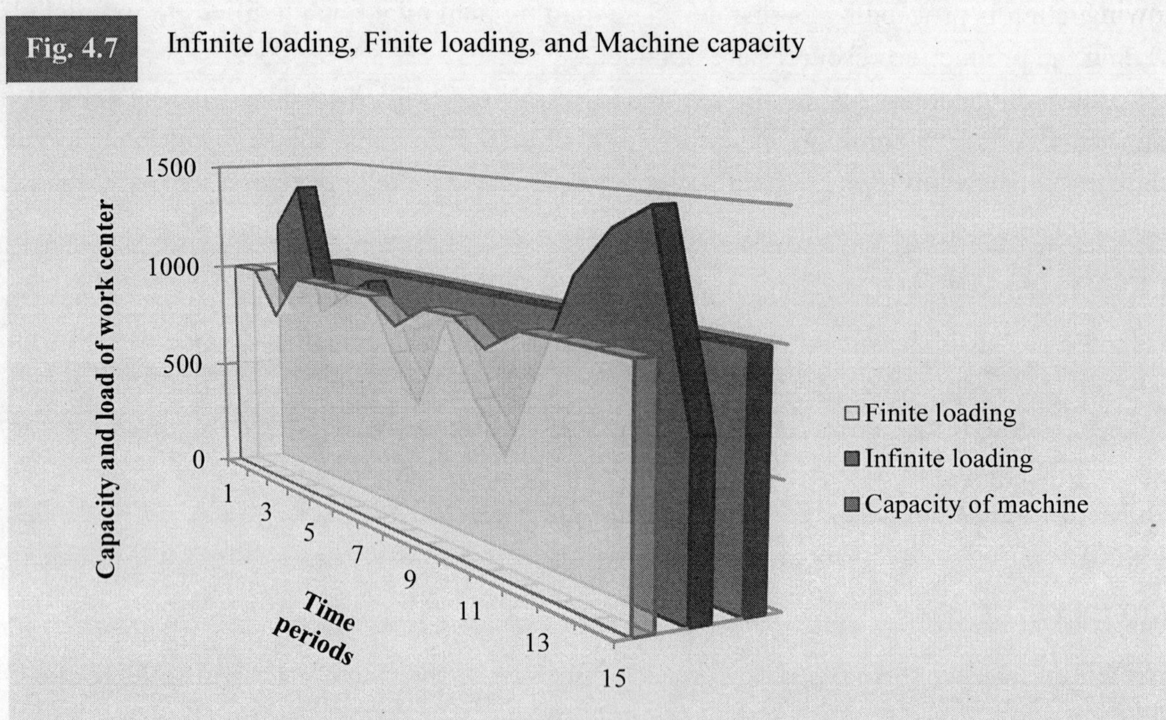

Vertical loading – Using various priority rules (described ahead in Sequencing), work center is chosen, and jobs are loaded into it one by one. The work center is the main emphasis, and each job is loaded one at a time, work center by work center.

Horizontal loading – Using this method, the highest priority jobs are loaded, one by one, into each work center that will be needed. Work center by work center, the following job is then loaded, and so on. The aforementioned finite scheduling systems most frequently employ this technique. Here, the job is the main emphasis, chosen and loaded work center by work center.

4.3.6 JOB ASSIGNMENT

The *assignment technique* is a specific linear programming (see the Unit on linear programming) solution process that can be used to determine which task to assign to a machine or which worker. The process generates an *opportunity cost matrix* given a table of tasks and resources, then chooses the optimal assignment by weighing trade-offs between options. Each employee or machine may be given a single task using this method. The following is a summary of the minimization problem procedure:

1. To perform *row reduction*, take the smallest value in each row and subtract it from all the other row values.
2. To perform *column reductions*, take each column's minimal value and subtract it from the values of the other columns.
3. The *opportunity cost matrix* is the table that results. In the matrix, cross out every zero by using the fewest possible horizontal or vertical lines.
4. An ideal solution has been found and assignments can be made to the locations where the zeros appear in the matrix if the number of lines in the matrix equals the number of rows. If not, *modify the matrix* by adding the same amount to each cell where two lines intersect and removing the least uncrossed value from all other uncrossed values. The matrix's other values don't change at all.
5. Steps 3 and 4 should be repeated until an optimal answer is found.

Smaller assignment tasks are typically completed by hand, like the one in the example below. Excel's Solver can be used to solve more complex problems. Increasing revenue or satisfying customers may also be the focus of an assignment problem. Each entry in the first matrix should be deducted from the greatest matrix value when solving a maximizing problem by hand. This should be done before moving on to a minimization problem.

Example: Assignment Work at Starhealth

Starhealth Inc. has four health projects that need to be finished, and its four personnel have varied levels of project development experience in the health sector. Below are each employee's estimated processing time (in hours) for each project. An hour of development work costs $100 on average. To minimize costs, give each employee a project to work on.

Initial matrix	Project 1	Project 2	Project 3	Project 4
Carl	12	7	8	12
John	10	4	8	10
Wright	11	12	7	8
Mike	13	9	6	14

1. **Row reduction** Sort each row's assignments into the best one. Each row's smallest value is subtracted from all other row values. The amount that emerges is the opportunity cost of putting an employee on the project. Project 2, for instance, would be Carl's ideal assignment. Its value in the ensuing matrix is therefore 0. Carl would need an extra hour to finish project 3 and five extra hours (12 – 7) to finish projects 1 or 4, respectively.

Row Reduction	Project 1	Project 2	Project 3	Project 4
Carl	5	0	1	5
John	6	0	4	6
Wright	4	5	0	1
Mike	7	3	0	8

2. **Column reduction** See which assignment in each column is the best. Each column's smallest value should be subtracted from all other values in the column. With Wright leading the project, for instance, project 1 can be finished the quickest and has no opportunity cost. Mike's assignment to project 1 has an opportunity cost of 3 since it would take 3 more hours of processing.

Column Reduction	Project 1	Project 2	Project 3	Project 4
Carl	1	0	1	4
John	2	0	4	5
Wright	0	5	0	0
Mike	3	3	0	7

3. **Search for distinctive tasks** Cover all zeros in the matrix as you examine it. Keep in mind that each individual can only be allocated to one project, and there can only be one leader for each project. When project 2 works best for Carl and John, there is an issue. Mike and Wright would benefit most from project 3. The optimal assignments are indicated by highlighting in different color in the rows and columns of the following matrix. "Covering all zeros" (with white font) is the term used for this. A modification to the matrix is required if there are fewer highlighted lines (three in this casse) than rows (four).

First Assignment	Project 1	Project 2	Project 3	Project 4
Carl	1	0	1	4
John	2	0	4	5
Wright	0	5	0	0
Mike	3	3	0	7

4. **Modify the matrix** Determine the least value among the entries that are not covered as highlighted (one in this case). Add that amount to the entries where the highted rows cross after subtracting it from any other non-highlighted entries. The values of Wright's projects 2 and 3 (i.e., enteries 5 and 0) have been added to the intersection point values below, which are the results of subtracting 1 from the non-highlighted entries.

Adjusted Matrix	Project 1	Project 2	Project 3	Project 4
Carl	0	0	1	3
John	1	0	4	4
Wright	0	6	1	0
Mike	2	3	0	6

5. **Search for distinctive tasks** As you study the matrix, once more cover all zeros. There are four rows and four highlighted lines, as we can see. We thereby arrive at the best possible outcome. Now place each employee on

the most suitable project that is available. Project 1 is Carl's appointed task (bold zero). Because John can only be assigned to project 2 with least value zero, it should be noted that Carl cannot be allocated to project 2, even with zero entry. Projects 4 and 3 are allocated to Wright and Mike, respectively.

6. **Determine performance** To figure out how long it will take the assigned staff to complete each project, see the original assignment matrix. The project will cost (12 + 4 + 8 + 6) × \$100 = \$3,000 to finish at an hourly rate of \$100.

4.3.7 SEQUENCING

The sequence in which the jobs waiting at a particular work center are to be processed is not indicated by loading choices aforementioned, even though they do specify the machines or work centers that will be used to handle particular works. The goal of sequencing is to establish the order in which jobs are processed. The order in which jobs are processed at different work centers and at individual workstations within the work centers is determined by sequencing decisions.

Sequencing has no special challenges provided work centers are not overly loaded and if each batch of jobs requires the same amount of processing time. However, the order of processing can be crucial for heavily loaded work centers, particularly when reasonably long processing time jobs are involved. This is because it can affect both the amount of idle time at the work centers and the costs associated with works waiting for processing. We will look at a few job sequencing strategies in this section.

Under heavily loaded work centers scenario, there will usually be a queue of jobs waiting processing. *Priority rules* are straightforward heuristics that determine the order in which tasks will be completed. Although many more complex rules have been created for certain uses (many machines, for instance), the chapter is confined to cover a few basic priority rules. Table 4.1 contains a list of some of the most accepted ones. The principles are based on the general supposition that processing sequence do not built on task setup time or cost.

Shortest processing time (SPT) has the benefit of finishing several tasks rapidly. The drawback of this rule is that the regulation does not specify when the customer needs the order. This rule will usually cause the big projects to be left until the very end, which will lead to repeated delays. In settings where huge jobs frequently represent a large and valuable customer, that is not a good situation.

Table 4.1 Common priority rules

Priority rules	Description
First come first served (FCFS)	Jobs are processed in the order that they come at a machine or work center.
Shortest processing time (SPT)	At a machine or work center, jobs are processed based on processing time, jobs with the least processing time jobs are handled first.
Earliest Due Date (EDD)	Work is processed in accordance with due dates, starting with the earliest date.
Critical Ratio (CR)	Jobs are completed in accordance with the shortest ratio of processing time left to the remaining time until the deadline.
Slack per operation (S/O)	Jobs are handled based on average slack time, which is calculated by subtracting the remaining processing time from the due date. Calculate by dividing the total number of operations (including the current one) by the slack time.

Due dates and job processing periods are crucial pieces of information when applying these criteria. Processing and setup times are typically included in job time. Reduced setup times may result from jobs requiring similar settings, given the sequencing rule accounts for this. Due dates can be the outcome of managerial choices, material requirement planning (MRP) processing, or delivery schedules that customers were promised. To provide context for sequencing decisions, they must be kept up to date and are susceptible to change. It should be noted that all regulations have due dates, with the exception of S/O (Slack per Operation) and CR (Critical Ratio), which are for the operation that is going to be completed. S/O and CR deadlines are usually final dates for orders rather than departmental deadlines that are in between.

Discussion: A simple example

The following table lists the processing times (including setup times) and deadline dates for six jobs that are pending processing at a work center. For every rule, find the job sequence, average flow time, average days late, and average number of jobs in the work center.

a. FCFS
b. SPT
c. EDD
d. CR

Assume that the jobs are arriving in the order shown in table below

Job	Processing Time (Days)	Due Date (Days)
A	3	8
B	9	17
C	5	5
D	11	18
E	6	15
F	13	19

Solution

(a) The A-B-C-D-E-F ***FCFS*** sequence is straightforward. The effectiveness metrics are as follows (see table):

Job Sequence	Processing Time (1)	Flow Time (2)	Due Date (3)	Tardiness (Days Late) (2)- (3) (0 if negative)
A	3	3	8	0
B	9	12	17	0
C	5	17	5	12
D	11	28	18	10
E	6	34	15	19
F	13	47	19	28
TOTAL	47	141		69

1. Average Flow Time = 141/6 = 23.5 days
2. Average Tardiness = 69/6 = 11.5 days
3. Makespan = 47 days
4. Average No. of jobs at the work center = 141/47 = 3

The average amount of time each job spends at the work center is determined by adding up all of the processing times and dividing the result by the total number of jobs handled. This is indicated by the flow time column which indicates the cumulative processing times. Likewise, by adding up all of the flow times and dividing by the overall processing time, you can determine the average number of jobs at the center.

(b) The job sequence, according to the ***shortest processing time*** **(SPT)** *rule*, is A-C-E-B-D-F (refer to the following table). The final numbers for the three effectiveness metrics are:

Job Sequence	Processing Time (1)	Flow Time (2)	Due Date (3)	Tardiness (Days Late) (2)- (3) (0 if negative)
A	3	3	8	0
C	5	8	5	3
E	6	14	15	0
B	9	23	17	6

D	11	34	18	16
F	13	47	19	28
TOTAL	47	129		53

Average Flow Time = 129/6 = 21.5 days
Average Tardiness = 53/6 = 8.83 days
Makespan = 47 days
Average No. of jobs at the work center = 129/47 = 2.74 ~ 3 jobs

(c) The job sequence is C-A-E-B-D-F based on the selection criterion of ***earliest due date*** **(EDD)**. The effectiveness metrics are as follows (see table):

Job Sequence	Processing Time (1)	Flow Time (2)	Due Date (3)	Tardiness (Days Late) (2)- (3) (0 if negative)
C	5	5	5	0
A	3	8	8	0
E	6	14	15	0
B	9	23	17	6
D	11	34	18	16
F	13	47	19	28
TOTAL	47	131		50

Average Flow Time = 131/6 = 21.83 days
Average Tardiness = 50/6 = 8.33 days
Makespan = 47 days
Average No. of jobs at the work center = 131/47 = 2.78 ~ 3 jobs

(d) Applying the ***critical ratio*** **(CR)** method, we determine the least ratio:

Job Sequence	Processing Time	Flow Time	Due Date	Critical Ratio	Tardiness
C	5	5	5	= 1.0	0
F	13	18	19	= 1.4 (=19/13)	0
D	11	29	18	= 1.6	11
B	9	38	17	= 1.8	21
E	6	44	15	= 2.5	29
A	3	47	8	= 2.6	39
TOTAL	47	181			100

Average Flow Time = 181/6 = 30.16 days
Average Tardiness = 100/6 = 16.6 days
Makespan = 47 days
Average No. of jobs at the work center = 181/47 = 3.8 ~ 4 jobs

In this example, the SPT rule performed slightly worse on average tardiness than the EDD rule and was the best according to two efficacy criteria. In every case, the CR rule was the worst. SPT, however, consistently outperforms other methods when it comes to reducing flow time.

The FCFS rule's main drawback is that lengthy tasks often cause other jobs to get delayed. Workstations downstream will have longer machine idle times if a procedure involves multiple machines. However, the FCFS rule is by far the most important priority rule for service systems where customers are directly involved. This is mostly due to its intrinsic fairness, but it is also a result of the inability to get accurate processing time estimates for individual operations.

Lower in-process inventories may arise from the SPT rule since it consistently yields the lowest (i.e., optimal) average flow time. Additionally, it frequently yields the lowest (ideal) average tardiness, which can lead to higher standards of customer service. Lastly, there is typically less traffic in the work area because there are always fewer jobs on average at the work center. Additionally, SPT reduces downstream idle time. However, since SPT does not include due dates, managers may choose not to use it because due dates are frequently at the top of their minds.

A significant drawback of the SPT rule is that it frequently causes lengthy jobs to wait, possibly for extended periods of time, especially when new and shorter jobs are added to the system on a frequent basis. In an attempt to prevent this, several changes may be made. As an illustration, any jobs that are left automatically advance to the front of the queue after a predetermined amount of waiting. The abbreviated SPT rule is what is meant by this.

Due dates are specifically addressed by the EDD rule, which typically reduces tardiness. Its primary drawback, despite its obvious appeal, is that processing time is not taken into consideration. One potential outcome could be that some jobs end up taking a very lengthy period, which would increase both shop congestion and in-process inventories.

Example of S/O rule The following jobs should be scheduled using the ***slack per operation*** **(S/O)** rule. Keep in mind that processing time includes the amount of time left over for the current and next operation. You also need to know how many operations are left, including the one you are currently performing.

Job	Remaining Processing time	Due Date	Remaining number of operations
A	4	14	3
B	16	32	6
C	8	8	5
D	20	34	2
E	10	30	4
F	18	30	2

Solution: Calculate the difference between each operation's processing time and due date. Sort the operations in order of low to high after dividing the total by the number of operations left. This produces the following job sequence:

Job	(1) Remaining Processing Time	(2) Due Date	(3) Slack (2) – (1)	(4) Remaining No. of Operations	(5) Ratio (3)/(4)	(6) Rank
A	4	14	10	3	3.33	3
B	16	32	16	6	2.67	2
C	8	8	0	5	0	1
D	20	34	14	2	7.00	6
E	10	30	20	4	5.00	4
F	18	30	12	2	6.00	5

The given order is C-B-A-E-F-D (see column 6).

It is crucial to reassess the sequence following each operation since, according to the S/O rule, the assigned work sequence could alter after any particular operation. It should be noted that any of the preceding priority criteria might be applied in this case, station by station; the S/O technique just includes downstream information when arriving at a work sequence.

In actuality, there are numerous priority rules available for job sequencing, and depending on the situation, a different rule might yield better outcomes. By looking at a few principles, we hope to shed light on the nature of sequencing rules. A special-purpose algorithm that may be used to arrange a set of jobs that need to be completed at the same two machines or work centers is covered in the following section.

4.3.7.1 **TWO WORK CENTERS SEQUENCING**

Managers can apply *Johnson's rule* to reduce the amount of time it takes to process a batch of jobs on two machines or at two consecutive work centers (also known as a two-machine flow shop). The overall amount of idle time at the work centers is also reduced. Some requirements need to be met for the technique to function, including:

1. Every job at every work center needs to have a known and consistent amount of time for setup and processing.
2. The work sequence and the job times must not be related.
3. Every job needs to adhere to the same two-step procedure.
4. Priorities for jobs cannot be used.
5. Before moving on to the second work center, a job must finish all of its units at the first work center.

These steps must be taken in order to determine the ideal sequence:

1. At each work center, make a list of the jobs and their times.
2. Choose the task requiring the least amount of time. Schedule the job at the first work center if it will take the least amount of time; if it will take longer at the second work center, schedule it last. Break ties at random.
3. Discard the job and its duration from consideration.

4. Proceed to the middle of the sequence by repeating steps 2 and 3 until all jobs have been scheduled.

Example: Discussion on Johnson's rule

A flow shop with two machines is to process a set of six jobs. Washing is the first process, and colouring is the second. Establish a workflow for this set of tasks that will minimize the overall completion time. The following are the processing times:

PROCESSING TIMES (HOURS)		
JOB	WORK CENTER 1	WORK CENTER 2
A	5	5
B	4	3
C	8	9
D	2	7
E	6	8
F	12	15

a. The job with the least processing time should be chosen. It's task D, and it will take two hours.

b. Job D should be scheduled first because it is at the first work center. Remove job D for further consideration.

c. The next shortest time is for Job B. As it is located at the second work center, give it priority over job B and schedule it last. Right now, we have

1st	2nd	3rd	4th	5th	6th
D					B

d. Notably, Job A has the same processing time at each work center; after removing D and B, there is a tie for the shortest remaining time. Consequently, it doesn't matter if we locate in the begining or at the end of the sequence at that point. Say it is positioned at the very end in an arbitrary manner. Right now, we have

1st	2nd	3rd	4th	5th	6th
D				A	B

e. For job E at work center 1, the least amount of time left is six hours. As a result, place that work after job D and towards the beginning of the sequence. Consequently,

1st	2nd	3rd	4th	5th	6th
D	E			A	B

f. Out of the two occupations that remain, Job C has the least time. Put it third in the sequence since it is for the first work center. When the last job, F, is assigned to the fourth position, the outcome is

1st	2nd	3rd	4th	5th	6th
D	E	C	F	A	B

g. Making a chart is one method of figuring out the work centers' throughput and idle times.

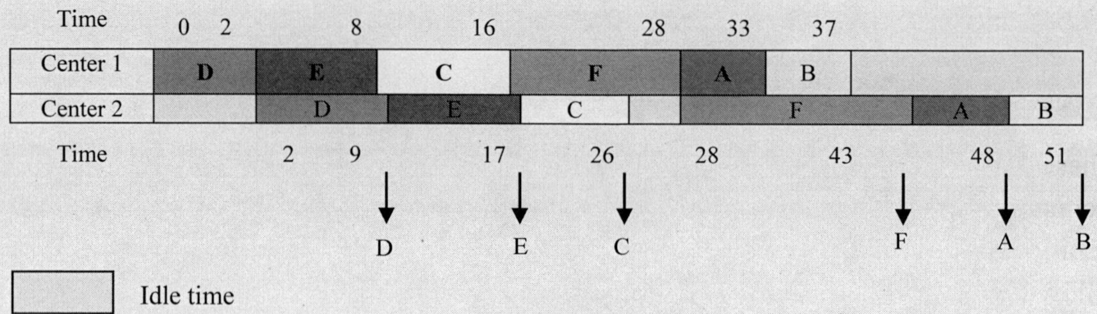

It will therefore take 51 hours to do the group of tasks. In addition to waiting two hours for job C to be completed, the second work center will also wait two hours for its first job. Center 1 will take 37 hours to complete. Naturally, idle time at the start or finish of the sequence can be utilized for other tasks, maintenance, or setup/teardown procedures.

ALONG THE ADVANCE PLANNING AND SCHEDULING SYSTEMS

Numerous techniques, such as mathematical programming, network analysis, simulation, constrained-based programming, genetic algorithms, neural networks, and expert systems, are employed by finite scheduling systems to create their schedules. A significant amount of effort is spent integrating the unique qualities and requirements of the production system into the database and knowledge base of the scheduling software, since the scheduling system, not the human scheduler, makes the majority of the decisions. Advanced Planning and Scheduling (APS) is one of the most reputable software programs. The Advanced Planner and Optimizer (APO) solution from SAP is an add-on for the ERP system. Additionally, these technologies facilitate cooperative scheduling and planning with trading partners.

Case example

Leading provider of transportation solutions, Siemens Mobility, was facing challenges in accelerating the throughput time of their 32-step railcar body surface treatments. They were having trouble with supplies that were delayed and production difficulties.With the integration of Advanced Planning and Scheduling with their ERP system, Siemens Mobility is now able to plan capacity for all of their manufacturing resources more quickly, accurately, and thoroughly.

All of the production resources that are available have been effectively scheduled, and any modifications or malfunctions are immediately notified and taken into consideration during the scheduling process. They have delivered the solution to every workstation in the surface coating area and updated work plans using a generated template.

Siemens Mobility has been able to cut lead times by 10% and the percentage of non-value-added activity by up to 60% since APS was implemented. Their non-conformance expenses have decreased due to more accurate timetables. Siemens has synchronized process and drying times with throughput data. They estimate a two-year payback period, and the superior source data generated will allow for increased efficiency and productivity in subsequent projects. They therefore intend to employ the program in other areas of the company, such as their body shop.

4.3.8 DISPATCHING

This phase is known as action, doing, or implementation. It follows scheduling and routing. Dispatching denotes the beginning of the production process. It gives the required authorization to get the job started. Route sheets and schedule sheets serve as its foundation. The following are included in dispatching:

a) The supply of supplies, equipment, fixtures, and other items required for real manufacturing.
b) Orders, guidelines, blueprints, etc. are issued to get the process started.
c) Keeping accurate records of when each task is started and finished on schedule.
d) Shifting work between processes in accordance with the timetable.
e) Beginning the process of control.
f) Tracking how long machines are idle.

There are two types of dispatching: centralized and decentralized. A centralized authority issues instruction directly under centralized dispatching, whereas under decentralized dispatching, the relevant department issues orders.

4.3.9 FOLLOW-UP

The final phase in the planning and control of manufacturing is called follow-up or expediting. It is a mechanism of control. It is focused on the results evaluation. In the production process, follow-up identifies and eliminates flaws, delays, restrictions, bottlenecks, loopholes, etc. It calculates the difference between the expected and actual performances. It keeps accurate records of all labor, delays, and obstructions. In the future, these records are utilized to manage output. In the event that production declines despite appropriate routing and scheduling, additional action is required. Production disruptions can occur from strikes, absenteeism, power outages, equipment failures, and shortages of commodities. Follow-up eliminates these obstacles and enables a seamless production.

UNIT SUMMARY

- ***Role of Production Planning*** – Explains how PPC helps in managing production activities, minimizing costs, and maximizing productivity.
- ***External Factors Affecting Production Planning*** – Discusses demand-driven approaches like Make-to-Stock (MTS), Build-to-Order (BTO), and Engineer-to-Order (ETO).
- ***Internal Factors in Production Planning*** – Covers strategies like Demand Chase, Level Capacity, and Mixed Strategy to balance supply and demand efficiently.
- ***Steps in Production Planning and Control*** – Describes the essential steps: Routing (determining the production path), Scheduling (setting timelines for tasks), Tracking (monitoring progress using tools like Gantt Charts), Loading (assigning work to resources), and Sequencing (determining job priority).
- ***Real-World Applications*** – Examines case studies, numerical problems, and assignments to enhance problem-solving skills.

EXERCISES

MULTIPLE CHOICE QUESTIONS

4.1 What is the primary objective of Production Planning and Control (PPC) systems in manufacturing?

(a) Minimize raw material costs through bulk purchasing.	(b) Maximize machine utilization to reduce production cycle times.
(c) Ensure efficient use of resources to meet production schedules.	(d) Reduce lead times by increasing buffer stocks at key stages.

4.2 What distinguishes production planning from production control within the broader scope of PPC?

(a) Production planning focuses on long-term capacity planning, while production control focuses on real-time monitoring and adjustment.	(b) Production planning is concerned with material procurement, while production control deals with quality assurance.

(c) Production planning emphasizes workforce scheduling, while production control manages inventory levels.	(d) Production planning determines product design specifications, while production control oversees production line layout.

4.3 Why is effective coordination between production planning and control crucial in modern manufacturing environments?

(a) To minimize overhead costs associated with production inefficiencies.	(b) To maximize the utilization of automated production technologies.
(c) To mitigate risks associated with volatile market demands.	(d) To streamline communication between different departments.

4.4 Which of the following factors is NOT typically considered during the production planning phase?

(a) Availability of raw materials and components.	(b) Employee training and development programs.
(c) Production capacity and constraints.	(d) Lead times for manufacturing processes.

4.5 What role does forecasting play in production planning and control?

(a) Forecasting helps in predicting changes in regulatory compliance requirements.	(b) Forecasting guide decisions related to outsourcing non-core manufacturing activities.
(c) Forecasting assists in estimating future demand for products and services.	(d) Forecasting determines the optimal layout of manufacturing facilities.

4.6 In a Make-to-Stock (MTS) production strategy, which of the following statements accurately describes the primary characteristic?

(a) Products are manufactured based on specific customer orders received in advance.	(b) Inventory levels are maintained based on anticipated customer demand forecasts.
(c) Production schedules are adjusted dynamically in response to real-time market fluctuations.	(d) Finished goods are customized to meet unique customer specifications.

4.7 Which of the following factors is a primary advantage of adopting the Make-to-Stock (MTS) strategy in manufacturing?

(a) Prompt availability of product in inventory is ensured.	(b) Increased flexibility to accommodate customized product requests.

(c) Enhanced control over production lead times and cycle times.	(d) Minimized dependency on accurate demand forecasting.

4.8 Which of the following challenges is typically associated with implementing a Make-to-Stock (MTS) strategy?

(a) High variability in customer preferences and requirements.	(b) Difficulty in maintaining consistent quality standards across customized products.
(c) Limited flexibility in responding to sudden changes in market demand.	(d) Increased lead times due to frequent setup and changeover processes.

4.9 In a Make-to-Order (MTO) production strategy, which of the following statements accurately describes the primary characteristic?

(a) Products are manufactured in large batches to optimize production efficiency.	(b) Finished goods are customized based on specific customer orders received.
(c) Inventory levels are maintained based on anticipated customer demand forecasts.	(d) Production schedules are adjusted dynamically in response to real-time market fluctuations.

4.10 What is the primary risk associated with inadequate raw material availability in production planning?

(a) Increased lead times for production processes.	(b) Overproduction and excess inventory.
(c) Higher labor costs due to overtime work.	(d) Reduced production cycle times.

4.11 Which of the following is a primary advantage of adopting the demand chase strategy?

(a) Reduced setup costs and production changeovers.	(b) Enhanced flexibility to respond quickly to market changes.
(c) Increased economies of scale through batch processing.	(d) Minimized dependency on accurate demand forecasting.

4.12 Which production planning and control (PPC) technique is most aligned with supporting the demand chase strategy?

(a) Material Requirements Planning (MRP)	(b) Economic Order Quantity (EOQ) model
(c) Theory of Constraints (TOC)	(d) Just-in-Time (JIT) manufacturing principles

4.13 What challenge is commonly associated with implementing the demand chase strategy?

(a) Difficulty in optimizing production efficiency due to frequent setup changes.	(b) Increased risk of overproduction and excess inventory.
(c) Limited ability to leverage economies of scale in production.	(d) Higher costs associated with maintaining buffer stocks.

4.14 What is the primary goal of level capacity strategy in production planning?

(a) To maintain a consistent production output over time	(b) To adjust production levels based on demand fluctuations
(c) To maximize production efficiency through flexible capacity	(d) To minimize production costs by varying capacity levels

4.15 What is a key advantage of using a level capacity strategy in production planning?

(a) Reduced inventory holding costs	(b) Increased flexibility to meet demand fluctuations
(c) Improved production efficiency	(d) Lower setup costs for production runs

4.16 When is a mixed strategy most commonly used in production planning?

(a) When demand is highly variable	(b) When demand is stable and predictable
(c) When production costs are the primary concern	(d) When there is a need to maximize production efficiency

4.17 What is the primary goal of loading in production planning?

(a) To assign work to specific work centers or machines	(b) To determine the optimal sequence of production tasks
(c) To estimate the total production time for a given order	(d) To calculate the total cost of production for a specific product

4.18 What is the purpose of scheduling in production planning?

(a) To ensure timely delivery of products to customers	(b) To minimize production costs
(c) To maximize employee productivity	(d) To determine the optimal production sequence

4.19 How does loading differ from scheduling in production planning?

(a) Loading focuses on assigning work to specific resources, while scheduling determines the order of production tasks.	(b) Loading is concerned with machine availability, while scheduling considers employee availability.

(c) Loading is a long-term planning activity, while scheduling is a short-term planning activity.	(d) Loading is more strategic, while scheduling is more tactical in nature.

4.20 In a flow system, scheduling is typically focused on optimizing:

(a) Machine utilization	(b) Job priorities
(c) Setup times	(d) Material handling

4.21 Job shop systems are characterized by:

(a) High levels of automation	(b) Low customization of products
(c) Flexibility in processing a variety of different products	(d) Continuous flow of products through workstations

4.22 Which of the following is NOT a common feature of a Gantt chart?

(a) Resource allocation	(b) Task dependencies
(c) Sales forecasting	(d) Timeline visualization

4.23 What is the purpose of using sequencing rules in production planning?

(a) To increase setup times	(b) To decrease production efficiency
(c) To improve scheduling decisions	(d) To ignore due dates for jobs

4.24 How does the Critical Ratio (CR) sequencing rule differ from other sequencing rules in production planning?

(a) It prioritizes jobs based on their due dates	(b) It considers both due dates and processing times
(c) It ignores due dates and processing times	(d) It focuses solely on minimizing setup times

4.25 What is the main benefit of using Johnson's rule in production planning?

(a) Increased production costs	(b) Reduced machine utilization
(c) Improved production efficiency	(d) Higher inventory holding costs

Answers of Multiple Choice Questions

4.1 (c), 4.2 (a), 4.3 (c), 4.4 (b), 4.5 (c), 4.6 (b), 4.7 (a), 4.8 (c), 4.9 (b), 4.10 (a), 4.11 (b), 4.12 (a), 4.13 (a), 4.14 (a), 4.15 (a), 4.16 (a), 4.17 (a), 4.18 (a), 4.19 (a), 4.20 (a), 4.21 (c), 4.22 (c), 4.23 (c), 4.24 (b), 4.25 (c)

SHORT AND LONG ANSWER TYPE QUESTIONS

Category I

4.1 What is production planning?

4.2 Why is production control important in manufacturing?

4.3 What role does forecasting play in production planning and control?

4.4 How does make-to-order production differ from make-to-stock production?

4.5 What is the key advantage of an assemble-to-order production strategy?

4.6 How does make-to-order production impact lead times compared to make-to-stock production?

4.7 In what type of industry is assemble-to-order production commonly used?

4.8 Explain how the availability of raw materials can affect production planning decisions.

4.9 How does the demand chase strategy differ from the level capacity strategy in production planning?

4.10 What are the key advantages of using a mixed strategy in production planning?

4.11 In what type of industry or market environment is the level capacity strategy most commonly used in production planning?

4.12 How can a company effectively transition between different production planning strategies, such as from a chase demand strategy to a mixed strategy?

4.13 What are the key benefits of a flow scheduling system?

4.14 How does intermittent scheduling differ from job shop scheduling?

4.15 What is the benefit of using a Gantt chart in project management?

4.16 How does effective input/output control contribute to streamlined production processes?

Category II

4.17 Compare and contrast the make-to-stock, assemble-to-order, make-to-order, and engineer-to-order strategies in production planning. Analyze the strategic implications, operational considerations, and suitability of each approach across different manufacturing environments and industries. Provide specific examples to illustrate how companies leverage these strategies to optimize inventory management, enhance customer satisfaction, and achieve competitive advantage in their respective markets.

4.18 Compare and contrast the chase demand strategy, level capacity strategy, and mixed strategy in production planning. Analyze the strategic considerations, benefits, and challenges associated with each approach, emphasizing their application across diverse manufacturing industries. Provide detailed examples to illustrate how companies effectively deploy these strategies to optimize production efficiency, manage costs, and meet customer demand fluctuations.

4.19 Compare and contrast the flow scheduling system, intermittent scheduling system, and job shop scheduling system in production planning. Analyze the strategic advantages and limitations of each approach, considering their application in different manufacturing environments and their impact on operational efficiency, flexibility, and responsiveness to customer demands. Provide detailed examples from industry sectors to support your analysis.

4.20 In production planning, discuss the strategic implications of adopting finite and infinite loading techniques. Analyze how each approach influences resource allocation, scheduling precision, and the ability to meet customer demands. Provide specific examples from manufacturing sectors to illustrate your arguments.

4.21 What role does sequencing play in optimizing production efficiency? How does Johnson's rule contribute to optimizing job sequencing in production planning?

NUMERICAL PROBLEMS

4.1 The Kwality Company has three plants across the globe where they produce a range of candies. The demand for its brand of chocolate candies has a very seasonal pattern, with peaks in the winter due to the holidays and Christmas Day and falls in the summer because people are controlling their weight and the chocolate tends melt. Determine whether it would be more cost-effective to (a) level production or (b) chase demand to fulfill the demand for chocolate candy given the following costs and quarterly sales forecasts:

Quarter	Sales forecast (lbs)
Spring	80,000
Summer	50,000
Fall	120,000
Winter	150,000

Hiring cost = \$100 per worker
Layoff cost = \$500 per worker
Inventory carrying cost = \$0.50 per pound pre quarter
Production per employee = 1000 pounds per quarter
Beginning workforce = 100 workers

4.2 In the fall and winter, momos are a popular culinary item; in the spring and summer, they are merely average. Which production planning strategy is appropriate for Momos can be determined using the following demand predictions and costs:

a. Level production for the full year.
b. Produce each month in order to meet demand. Adjust staffing levels to accommodate variations in demand.
c. Maintain the present level of labor force. Add more by working extra and hiring contractors as needed.

Month	Demand forecast
March	2000
April	1000
May	1000
June	1000
July	1000
August	1500
September	2500

October	3000
November	9000
December	7000
January	4000
February	3000

Overtime capacity per month	Regular production
Subcontracting capacity per month	Unlimited
Regular production cost	$30 per pallet
Overtime production cost	$40 per pallet
Subcontracting cost	$50 per pallet
Holding cost	$2 per pallet
Beginning workforce	10 workers
Production rate	200 pallets per worker per month
Hiring cost	$5000 per worker
Layoff cost	$8000 per worker

4.3 Determine the work backlog for each period using the information on planned and actual inputs and outputs for a service center. Work totaling 12 hours is the starting backlog. The numbers displayed represent typical labor hours.

		Period				
		1	2	3	4	5
Input	Planned	24	24	24	24	20
	Actual	25	27	20	22	24
Output	Planned	24	24	24	24	23
	Actual	24	22	23	24	24

4.4 A company needs to assign 4 workers (W1, W2, W3, W4) to 4 tasks (T1, T2, T3, T4) based on their efficiency for each task. The table below shows the time (in hours) each worker takes to complete each task:

Worker \ Task	T1	T2	T3	T4
W1	9	2	7	8
W2	6	4	3	7
W3	5	8	1	8
W4	7	6	9	4

Determine the optimal assignment of workers to tasks to minimize the total time required to complete all tasks using Hungarian method.

4.5 As of Monday at 9 a.m., the orders to be processed at a machine shop are displayed in the table below. There are several procedures that must be followed for each work. Processing times are in days. The order of arrival for jobs is listed.

(a) Apply each of these rules to ascertain the processing sequence: (i) FCFS, (ii) SPT, (iii) DD, (iv) CR, and (v) S/O.

(b) Determine each rule's efficacy using the following metrics: (i) The average number of jobs in the system, (ii) the average number of jobs at the work center, (iii) the average completion time, (iv) the average tardiness, and (v) the average number of jobs overall.

Job	Processing Time (days)	Due Date (days)	Remaining Number of Operations
A	8	20	2
B	10	18	4
C	5	25	5
D	11	17	3
E	9	35	4

4.6 Consider a factory with 6 jobs (Job 1 through Job 6) that need to be processed on two machines (Machine A and Machine B). The processing times (in hours) for each job on each machine are given as follows:

Job	Machine A	Machine B
1	4	7
2	3	9
3	8	6
4	5	4
5	6	5
6	7	3

Use Johnson's rule to determine the optimal sequence for minimizing makespan (total completion time).

REFERENCES AND SUGGESTED READINGS

1. Axsäter, S. Inventory Control in a Production Planning and Control System. *International Journal of Production Economics*, Vol. 100(2), 231-239, 2006.
2. Dev, N.K., Shankar, R., Dey, P.K., and Gunasekaran, A. Holonic Supply Chain:. A Study from Family-Based Manufacturing Perspective. Computers and Industrial Engineering, Vol. 78, 1-11, 2014.
3. Dev, N. K., Shankar, R., and Swami, S. Diffusion of Green Products in Industry 4.0: Reverse Logistics Issues during Design of Inventory and Production Planning System. *International Journal of Production Economics*, 223, 107519, 2020.
4. **Heizer, J., Render, B., and Munson, C.** *Operations Management: Sustainability and Supply Chain Management*, 12th Edition, Pearson, 2017.
5. Jain, P. K., and Sharma, R. K. *Production Planning and Control: Principles and Techniques*. Khanna Publishers, 2015.
6. Krajewski, L. J., Ritzman, L. P., and Malhotra, M. K. *Operations Management: Processes and Supply Chains*, 11th Edition, Pearson, 2018.
7. Kuo, R. J., and Chen, L. S. A Hybrid Decision Model for Production Planning and Control. *Expert Systems with Applications*, Vol. 38(3), 1634-1644, 2011.
8. Li, W., and Xu, H. Optimization of Production Planning and Scheduling in a Multi-Product, Multi-Stage Production System. *Computers & Industrial Engineering*, Vol. 85, 248-261, 2015.
9. Mollenkopf, D. A., and Closs, D. J. The Role of Production Planning and Control in Logistics. *International Journal of Physical Distribution & Logistics Management*, Vol. 35(7), 441-457, 2005.
10. Panneerselvam, R. *Production and Operations Management*, 2nd Edition, Prentice Hall India, 2012.

11. Rezaei, J., and Ortt, R. J. A Literature Review on Production Planning and Control: Challenges and Perspectives. *Computers & Industrial Engineering*, Vol. 98, 246-259, 2016.

12. Slack, N., Chambers, S., and Johnston, R. *Operations Management*, 6th Edition, Pearson Education, 2010.

13. Stevenson, W. J. Production and Operations Management: The Challenge of New Product Development. *Production and Operations Management*, Vol. 18(1), 1-12, 2009.

14. Tersine, R. J. *Principles of Inventory and Materials Management*, 6th Edition, Pearson Education, 2006.

15. Vollmann, T. E., Berry, W. L., and Whybark, D. C. *Manufacturing Planning and Control for Supply Chain Management*, McGraw-Hill Education, 2005.

16. Williamson, J., and Berman, O. *Production Planning and Control: A Guide for the Manufacturing Manager*. Routledge, 2013.

UNIT **5**

AGGREGATE & RESOURCE PLANNING

UNIT SPECIFICS

This unit elaborately discusses the following topics:

- Aggregarte planning technique
- Disaggregating the aggregate plan
- Master scheduling
- Material requirement planning
- Master production schedule
- Structure for material requirement planning
- Rules for lot sizing in MRP system

Examined the topics' with practical applications to improve problem-solving abilities and encourage increased creativity and curiosity. In addition to a significant number of multiple-choice questions and questions with short and long answer types indicated in two groups according to lower and higher order of Bloom's taxonomy, the unit offers assignments through a number of numerical problems, a list of references, and suggested reads. Reader can practice by completing these.

RATIONALE

In this unit, we explore essential methodologies and frameworks within the realm of aggregate planning, focusing on the cut and try technique that facilitates effective decision-making. We delve into the process of disaggregating the aggregate plan to create detailed schedules, emphasizing the importance of master scheduling and its role in aligning production with demand. The discussion extends to material requirement planning (MRP), highlighting the structure necessary for successful implementation. Additionally, we address the master production schedule and its significance in coordinating resources efficiently. Finally, we outline key rules for lot sizing in MRP systems, ensuring optimal inventory management and operational effectiveness. Together, these elements provide a comprehensive understanding of how to integrate planning and scheduling to meet organizational goals.

UNIT OUTCOMES

List of outcomes of this unit is as follows:

U5-UO1: Understanding Aggregate Planning Techniques

U5-UO2: Disaggregation Skills

U5-UO3: Master Scheduling Proficiency

U5-UO4: Material Requirement Planning (MRP) Insights

U5-UO5: Master Production Schedule Development

U5-UO6: Lot Sizing Rules Application

UNIT-5 Outcomes	EXPECTED MAPPING WITH COURSE OUTCOMES (*1-Weak Correlation; 2-Medium Correlation; 3-Strong Correlation*)					
	CO-1	CO-2	CO-3	CO-4	CO-5	CO-6
U5-UO1	2	3	3	2	2	3
U5-UO2	2	3	3	2	3	3
U5-UO3	3	3	3	3	2	2
U5-UO4	2	2	3	3	3	2
U5-UO5	2	3	3	2	3	2
U5-UO6	2	2	3	3	2	3

5.1 INTRODUCTION

The planning horizon discussed in Unit 4 including machine loading, job assignment, job sequencing, work schedules are under short-term planning decisions. Short-term capacity decisions must be made within the parameters defined by intermediate decisions, which are related to overall levels of employment, output, and inventories. Coordination of the intermediate plans of several organizational activities, including marketing, operations, and finance, is a major goal of business planning. Engineering and materials management are also included in coordinating in manufacturing organizations. As a result, collaboration amongst all of these functional areas is required to create the aggregate plan.

Aggregate planning is an intermediate-range capacity planning within the production planning spectrum. It usually spans a time horizon of 2 to 12 months, though in certain businesses it may go up to 18 months. It is especially helpful for companies whose capacity or demand fluctuates due to seasonality or other factors. A production plan that efficiently uses the organization's resources to meet anticipated demand is the aim of aggregate planning. Decisions about output rates, employment levels and fluctuations, inventory levels and fluctuations, back orders, and subcontracting must be made by planners. We already discussed how aggregate planning is performed under pure strategies involving demand and capacity in Unit 4. We now discuss various other techniques for aggregate planning presented with some examples of cost evaluation of alternative plans.

5.2 CUT-AND-TRY TECHNIQUE

Businesses frequently create aggregate plans using graphic approaches and basic cut-and-try charting. A "cut-and-try" strategy is estimating the costs of multiple production planning options and choosing the most cost-effective one. Complex spreadsheets are created to help in the decision-making process. These spreadsheets frequently integrate advanced techniques like simulation and linear programming. In the following we demonstrate a spreadsheet approach to evaluate four strategies for meeting demand for the Precision Product Company.

Example 5.1

Production is typically planned for the entire year by a company with significant seasonal variance in order to account for demand fluctuations throughout the busiest and slowest months. However, we can use a shorter horizon to demonstrate the general idea. Let's say we want to schedule the manufacturing facility of Precision Products Company for the following six months in terms of production. We are provided with the subsequent details:

Days of work and Demand							
	Jan.	Feb.	Mar.	Apr.	May	Jun.	TOTAL
Demand forecast projections	1,600	1,300	800	1,000	1,500	1,700	7,900
Days of operation	25	16	24	18	25	17	125
Costs							
Materials	$220/unit						
Inventory carrying costs	$2.50/unit/month						
Stockout's marginal cost	$4.00/unit/month						
Marginal cost of outsourcing	$20/unit ($240 subcontracting cost less $220 material saving)						
Cost of hiring and training	$100/worker						
Expense of Layoffs	$150/worker						
Hours of labor required	5/unit						
Total cost of straight time (first eight hours each day)	$20/hour						
Cost of working overtime	$30/hour						
Inventory							
Beginning Inventory	600 units						
Safety stock	25% of month demand						

There are 600 units of inventory at the start of the first period. The Precision Products Company has concluded that a safety stock, or buffer stock, should be produced to lessen the likelihood of backorders because the demand estimate is not flawless. Assume for the purposes of this example that the safety stock ought to equal 25% of the demand estimate for the current period. By making this assumption, the planner avoids financial penalties for maintaining the buffer.

It is frequently helpful to translate demand forecasts into production requirements that take safety stock estimations into consideration before looking into alternative production plans.

Take note of the requirements in Table 1 of this example, which implicitly assume that the safety stock is never really used and that each month's closing inventory equals the safety stock. For instance, at the end of January, the inventory is equal to the January safety stock of 400, which is 25% of the January demand of 1600. Demand plus safety stock less starting inventory equals the production need for January (1600 + 400 - 600 = 1400). We now have to come up with different production schedules for Precision Products Company. We look into four different plans using the spreadsheet in an effort to determine which has the lowest overall cost.

Plan 1. Produce with a normal eight-hour workday and according to precise monthly production requirements by adjusting the labor size.

Plan 2. Over the following six months, produce enough to meet the anticipated average demand while keeping a steady workforce. The average daily workforce necessary over the horizon is used to compute this constant workforce size. Multiply the overall production requirements by the amount of time needed for each item. Next, divide the result by the whole amount of time one employee works throughout the course of the project [(7,900 units × 5 hours per unit) ÷ (125 days × 8 hours per day) = 40 workers]. Shortages are covered by backorders from the following month's manufacturing, allowing inventory to build up. Demand is backordered when beginning inventory levels are negative. You'll see that in order to fulfill anticipated demand, we used our safety supply in January, February, March, and June of this plan.

Plan 3. Produce with a consistent workforce on schedule in order to fulfill the April minimum estimated demand. To fulfill extra output requirements, subcontract. Finding the lowest monthly production requirement and calculating the number of workers required for that month (1,050 units × 5 hours per unit) ÷ (18 days × 8 hours per day) = 36 workers) yields the required number of workers, which is then subcontracted to cover any monthly difference between requirements and production.

Plan 4. For the first two months, only produce enough to meet demand with a constant workforce on a regular schedule. To satisfy the higher output requirements, work overtime. For this plan, the objective is to complete June with an ending inventory that is as near to the June safety stock as feasible.

Table 5.1: Requirements for Aggregate Production Planning

Requirements for Planning Aggregate Production						
	Jan.	Feb.	Mar.	Apr.	May	June
Beginning Inventory	600	400	325	200	250	375
Demand forecast	1,600	1,300	800	1,000	1,500	1,700
Safety Stock (0.25 × Demand forecast)	400	325	200	250	375	425
Production requirement (Demand forecast + safety stock – Beginning inventory)	1,400	1,225	675	1,050	1,625	1,750
Ending inventory (Beginning inventory + Production requirement – Demand forecast)	400	325	200	250	375	425

The cost of each plan must then be determined. This calls for the set of easy computations displayed in Tables 5.2 through Table 5.5. Keep in mind that each plan has a different set of headings since every problem is unique and needs its own set of facts and computations.

Tabulating, graphing, and comparing the costs of each plan is the last stage. Table 5.6 shows that Plan 3 – the use of subcontractors – produced the lowest cost.

Table 5.2

Four Production Plans' Costs							
1st Production Plan: Precise Manufacturing; Varying Manpower							
	Jan.	Feb.	Mar.	Apr.	May	June	Total
Production requirements (based on table 1)	1,400	1,225	675	1,050	1,625	1,750	
Required production hours (Production requirements × 5hr/unit)	7,000	6,125	3,375	5,250	8,125	8,750	
Working days/month	25	16	24	18	25	17	
Hours per month per worker (working days × 8 hrs/day)	200	128	192	144	200	136	

Workers required (Required prod. hrs./hours per month per worker)	35	48	18	36	41	64	
Hired new workers (presuming initial workforce is equivalent to first-month labor requirement of 35)	0	13	0	18	5	23	
Cost of hiring (New workers hired × $100	$0	$1,300	$0	$1,800	$500	$2,300	$5,900
Workers layoffs	0	0	30	0	0	0	
Cost of layoffs (Workers layoffs × $150)	$0	$0	$4,500	$0	$0	$0	$4,500
Instantaneous- time cost (Required production hrs. × $20) ($)	140,000	122,500	67,500	105,000	162,500	175,000	772,500
							Total cost ($) 782,900

Table 5.3

2nd Production Plan: Workforce constant; Adjusting Stock and Backorder as Required							
	Jan.	Feb.	Mar.	Apr.	May	June	Total
Starting inventory	600	560	258	956	1,079	1,139	
Working days/month	25	16	24	18	25	17	
Available production hrs. (Working days per month × 8 hr/day × 39 workers)*	7,800	4,992	7,488	5,616	7,800	5,304	
Actual production (production hrs. available / 5hr/unit	1,560	998	1,498	1,123	1,560	1,061	
Demand forecast (From Table 1)	1,600	1,300	800	1,000	1,500	1,700	
Finishing inventory (Starting inventory + Actual production – demand forecast)	560	258	956	1,079	1,139	500	
Cost of Backorders (Units short × $4) ($)	0	0	0	0	0	0	
Safety stock (From Table 1)	400	325	200	250	375	425	
Units excess (Finishing inventory – safety stock) *only if positive amount*	160	0	756	829	764	75	

*(Sum of production requirement in Table 5.1 × 5 hr/unit)/(Sum of production hrs. avaialble × 8 hr/day) = (7725 × 5)/(125 × 8)=39

Cost of inventory (Units excess × $2.50) ($)	400	0	1,890	2,073	1,910	188	6,461
Instantaneous-time cost (Available production hrs. × $20) ($)	156,000	99,840	149,760	112,320	156,000	106,080	780,000
							Total cost ($) 786,461

Table 5.4

3rd Production Plan: Consistent Low Workforce; Subcontract							
	Jan.	Feb.	Mar.	Apr.	May	June	Total
Production required (from Table 1)	1,400	1,225	675	1,050	1,625	1,750	
Days of working per month	25	16	24	18	25	17	
Available production hrs. (working days × 8 hrs./day × 18)*	3,600	2,304	3,456	2,592	3,600	2,448	
Production Actual (Available production hrs. / 5 hr. per unit)	720	461	691	518	720	490	
Subcontracted units (Production required – Production Actual) *zero if negative*	680	764	0	532	905	1260	
Subcontracted cost (Units subcontracted × $20) ($)	13,600	15,280	0	10,640	18,100	25,200	82,620
Instantaneous-time cost (Available production hrs. × $20)	72,000	46,080	69,120	51,840	72,000	48,960	360,000
							Total cost ($) 442,620

Table 5.5

4th Production Plan: Consistent Workers' Overtime							
	Jan.	Feb.	Mar.	Apr.	May	June	Total
Starting inventory	600	400	0	544	552	452	
Days of working per month	25	16	24	18	25	17	
Available production hrs. (Days of working	7,000	4,480	6,720	5,040	7,000	4,760	

* Minimum production requirement, in this example, March has minimum of 675 units. Number of workers for March is (675 × 5)/(24 × 8) = 18

× 8 hr/day × 35 workers)[$]							
Regular shift work output (Available production hrs./ 5 hr. per unit)	1,400	896	1,344	1,008	1,400	952	
Demand forecast (From Table 1)	1,600	1,300	800	1,000	1,500	1,700	
Units at hand prior to overtime (Starting inventory + Regular shift work output – Demand Forecast)	400	-4	544	552	452	-296	
Units overtime	0	4	0	0	0	296	
Cost of overtime (Units overtime × 5hr./unit × $30/hr.) ($)	0	600	0	0	0	44,400	45,000
Safety stock (From Table 1)	400	325	200	250	375	425	
Excess units (Units at hand prior to overtime – Safety stock) *only if positive*	0	0	344	302	77	0	
Cost of inventory (Excess units × $2.50) ($)	0	0	860	755	193	0	1,808
Instantaneous-time cost (Available production hrs. × $20)	140,000	89,600	134,400	20,160	140,000	95,200	619,360
							Total cost ($) 666,168

In this case, take note of another assumption we have made. No hiring or layoff expenses apply, thus the plan can begin with any number of employees. Typically, this is the case since an aggregate strategy can be initiated by utilizing current staff members. In practice, though, the assumption might be altered by the presence of current employees who are transferable from other departments within the company.

Table 5.6

Comparison of Four Plans				
Costs ($)	**Plan 1: Precise Manufacturing; Varying Manpower**	**Plan 2: Workforce constant; Adjusting Stock and Backorder**	**Plan 3: Consistent Low Workforce; Subcontract**	**Plan 4: Consistent Workers' Overtime**
Hired new workers	5,900	0	0	0
Layoff	4,500	0	0	0
Inventory excess	0	6,461	0	1,808

[$] Workers ascertained by experimentation. For an explanation, see the text.

Backorder	0	0	0	0
Subcontract	0	0	82,620	0
Overtime	0	0	0	45,000
Instantaneous-time	772,500	780,000	360,000	619,360
Total	782,900	786,461	442,620	666,168

These four plans – the first three of which were straightforward pure strategies – all concentrated on a single expense. Of course, there are a plenty of additional workable strategies, some of which would include overtime, subcontracting, and labor modifications. In reality, the ultimate strategy would be determined by looking into a range of options and projecting the future longer than the six-month planning horizon that we have employed.

Remember that a "cut-and-try" strategy does not ensure that the least expensive solution will be found. Spreadsheet applications, like Microsoft Excel, on the other hand, have made "what-if" analysis more sophisticated by enabling quick and easy cost estimations. More advanced programs, like "Linear Programming," can provide far superior results without requiring the user to step in, unlike the cut-and-try approach.

5.3 DISAGGREGATING THE AGGREGATE PLAN

The aggregate plan must be broken down in order for the production plan to be converted into terms that are relevant for production. To ascertain labor requirements (skills, workforce size), resources, and inventory needs, this entails breaking down the aggregate plan into discrete product requirements. It is easier to do intermediate planning when you use aggregate units. Nevertheless, in order to execute the production plan, those aggregate units must be broken down into units of the real goods or services that will be produced or provided. An automaker might, for instance, have a combined plan that specifies 200 bikes in January, 300 in February, and 400 in March. That company might manufacture 250, 350, and 100 cc bikes. There would be some variations in the materials, parts, and processes that each type requires, even if all the motorcycles most likely have some of the same parts and require some comparable or same activities for manufacturing and assembly. Therefore, before actually buying the necessary materials and parts, scheduling operations, and calculating inventory requirements, the 200, 300, and 400 aggregate bikes that are to be manufactured during those three months must be translated into exact numbers of bikes of each type.

A master schedule that details the amount and timing of particular end items for a specified horizon – typically spanning six to eight weeks ahead – is produced by breaking down the aggregate plan. A master schedule displays the anticipated output for individual items as well as the manufacturing schedule, as opposed to a set of products as a whole. Important information for both production and marketing is included in the master schedule. It shows the dates on which orders are planned for manufacture and shipping after they are finished. Following the development of a tentative master schedule, a planner can perform rough-cut capacity planning to ensure that there are no evident capacity restrictions and to assess the viability of a proposed master schedule in relation to available capacities. This entails assessing workers, vendors, production and warehousing facility capacities, and other factors to make sure there are no glaring shortcomings that would make the master schedule unfeasible. Short-term planning is therefore based on the master schedule. Note that the master schedule only covers a fraction of the time covered by the aggregate plan, which is, let's say, 12 months. Stated differently, the overall strategy is broken down into segments, or stages, which could last anything from a few weeks to two or three months. Furthermore, even though the master schedule spans two or three months, it may be revised once a month. For example, at the end of January, the bike master schedule would likely be revised to reflect any changes to the scheduled output for February and March as well as any new information regarding the projected output for April.

Table 5.7 provides an illustration of the aggregate plan's disaggregation principle. To effectively illustrate the idea of disaggregation, the illustration makes the following basic assumption: The aggregate and disaggregated unit totals are same. That isn't always the case in practice. Consequently, it could take a lot of work to breakdown the aggregate plan. The aggregate plan is broken down by units in Table 5.7. Showing the breakdown in percentages for various products or product groups, however, might also be helpful.

Table 5.7 Disaggregating the Aggregate Plan

Aggregate Plan		Jan.	Feb.	Mar.
	Monthly Planned Output*	200	300	400

* Aggregate units

Master Schedule	**Monthly Planned Output***	Jan.	Feb.	Mar.
	100 cc bike	100	100	100
	250 cc bike	75	150	200
	350 cc bike	25	50	100
	Total	200	300	400

* Actual Units

5.4 MASTER SCHEDULING

A master schedule does not depict planned production; instead, it provides information on the amount and timing (i.e., delivery times) for a certain product or collection of items. For example, a master schedule can specify that 50 bikes of 100cc must be delivered by May 1. However, there might be 200 bikes in product inventory; therefore there might not be a need for production. Or it might need to be produced: To reach the required delivery amount, 10 more bikes would be required if there were 40 bikes in the product inventory. Alternatively, it can include producing 50 or more bikes: Sometimes it makes more sense to create in bulk rather than in smaller quantities, storing the excess in product inventory until needed. Therefore, if more bikes were required (say, 50 bikes), a run of 70 bikes would be produced because the production lot size might be 70 motorcycles.

The *master production schedule* (MPS), which takes into consideration the targeted delivery quantity and time as well as available inventory, shows the amount and timing of planned output. One of the main results of the master scheduling process is the master production schedule, as shown in Fig. 5.1.

Fig. 5.1 Master Scheduling Process

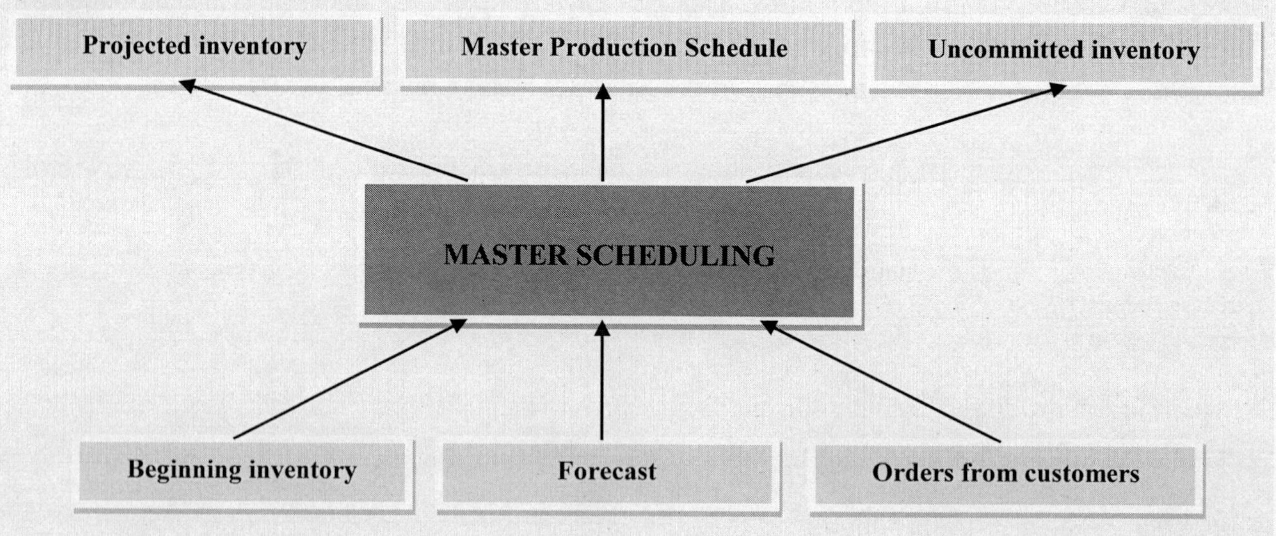

The beginning inventory, or the actual amount on hand from the previous period, projections for each period of the schedule, and client orders, or quantities previously committed to customers, are the three inputs that make up the master schedule.

This data is used by the master scheduling process to calculate the projected inventory, master production schedule, and the consequent uncommitted inventory, also known as available-to-promise (ATP) inventory, period by period. Marketing is able to provide clients with reasonable guarantees regarding the delivery of new orders when they are aware of the uncommitted inventory.

Projected onhand inventory is first calculated in advance of the master scheduling procedure. This indicates when more manufacturing, or inventory, will be required. Consider the example below.

Example 5.2: Calculating the expected on-hand inventory and the MPS

An industrial motor manufacturer would like to set up a master production schedule for the months of August and September. Marketing predicts that there will be a need for 80 motors in August and 120 in September. As shown in Table 5.8, these have been equally dispersed over the four weeks of each month: 20 per week in August and 30 per week in September.

Now, assume that there are customer orders that have been committed (booked) and need to be filled, and that there are now 74 motors in inventory (i.e., beginning inventory is 74 motors). The beginning inventory, the forecast, and the booked or committed client orders are the three main inputs used in the master scheduling process. Three quantities need to be determined with this information: the uncommitted (ATP) inventory, the master production schedule, and the anticipated on-hand inventory. The first stage is to figure up the expected inventory on hand, one week at a time, until it gets below a certain amount. The given limit in this instance will be zero. We shall so keep going till the anticipated on-hand inventory turns negative.

The following formula is used to get the anticipated on-hand inventory:

Projected on-hand inventory = previous week's inventory – current week's requirements, where the current week's requirements being the greater of the forecast and committed customer orders.

Projected on-hand inventory for the first week is equal to the beginning inventory less the greater of the forecast and customer orders. The customer orders amount is used since the customer orders (33) exceed the forecast (30). Consequently, we get for the first week:

Projected inventory on hand: 74 – 23 = 51

Production will be required to replenish inventories when the expected on-hand inventory turns negative. Therefore, planned production will be needed if the expected on-hand inventory is negative. Assume that 70 motors are created in a production lot (chapter on Inventory Management includes a description of how lot size is determined); meaning that 70 motors will be produced anytime manufacturing is required. Because of this, the 4th week's negative predicted on-hand inventory will need the manufacturing of 70 motors, which will satisfy the anticipated 19 motor shortfall and leave 51 (i.e., 70 – 19 = 51) motors for future demand. For the duration of the schedule, these computations are made. A new production lot of 70 motors is added to the schedule each time the planned inventory falls short of what is needed. The results are shown in Table 5.8.

The master schedule and the anticipated on-hand inventory for each week of the program are the end products. The master schedule can now include these (see Table 5.8).

The amount of inventory that is uncommitted and hence available to promise can now be ascertained. In reality, there are several approaches. The method we will use is a "look-ahead" process: Orders from customers that are sum booked week by week, up to and excluding the week when an MPS amount is due. For instance, this process yields 73 in the first week by adding customer orders from weeks 23, 30 and 20. To determine the amount that can be promised in the first week, this sum is deducted from the starting inventory of 74 motors plus the MPS (zero in this case). Thus,

$$74 + 0 - (23 + 30 + 20) = 1$$

It should be noted that the ATP quantity is only determined for the first week and any subsequent weeks if an MPS quantity is present. Therefore, it is computed for weeks 1, 4, and 6.

With the exception of the first week, the computation does not include the beginning inventory; instead, the look-ahead quantity (ATP) is deducted from the MPS quantity.

As a result, for week 4, the ATP is 70 - 15 = 55 and the promised amounts are 10 + 5 = 15.

ATP in week 6 is equal to 70 – 40 = 30 and the promised amounts are 20 + 10 + 10 = 40.

The schedule would be modified to reflect any new orders that were scheduled, and the ATP amounts would be adjusted accordingly. Marketing can use the ATP quantities to give customers reasonable delivery dates.

Table 5.8

	August				September			
74	1	2	3	4	5	6	7	8
Forecast	20	20	20	20	30	30	30	30
Customer orders (commited)	23	30	20	10	5	20	10	10
Projected on-hand inventory	51	21	1	51	21	61	31	1
MPS				70		70		
Available-to-promise inventory (uncommited)	1			55		30		

5.5 MATERIAL REQUIREMENT PLANNING

A computer-based information system called **Material Requirement Planning (MRP)** is used to manage the ordering and scheduling of dependent-demand inventories, such as raw materials, component parts, and subassemblies. The difference between dependent and independent demand is discussed in Unit on Inventory Management. Working backward from the deadline, a production plan for a given quantity of completed goods is converted into requirements for raw materials and component parts. Lead times and other details are used to determine when and how much to order. Therefore, in order to arrange ordering, fabrication, and assembly for the timely completion of end items while maintaining reasonable inventory levels, needs for lower-level components are generated based on requirements for end items. These requirements are then broken down by planning periods, such as weeks. Material requirement planning is an approach to scheduling as much as inventory control, and it is both a philosophy and a practice.

Two issues have always afflicted the ordering and scheduling of assembled products. The first was the enormous job of creating schedules, managing changes to orders and schedules, and keeping track of a lot of parts and components. The other was the inability to distinguish between dependent and independent demand. Assembled products were handled far too frequently using methods intended for independent-demand commodities, leading to enormous stocks. For manufacturers, this meant that scheduling and inventory planning posed significant challenges.

Manufacturers started approaching the independent- and dependent-demand product categories differently in the 1970s as they realized how important it was to distinguish between them. With the use of methods like MRP, many businesses have now shifted a large portion of the load of maintaining records and figuring out material requirements to computers.

An MRP schedule starts with a finished goods schedule, which is then translated into a schedule of needs for the subassemblies, component parts, and raw materials required manufacturing the finished goods within the allotted time. MRP is therefore intended to respond to three queries: *what* is required? *How much* is required? and *When* is it required?

In companies where several items are produced in batches utilizing the same productive machinery, MRP is not useful. Industries that operate on Assemble-to-stock, Assemble-to-order, and Engineer-to-order greatly benefit from MRP. In the Make-to-stock and Process industries, the estimated return on investment using MRP is moderate. In industries where make-to-order policies are used, the MRP system's benefits are rather low. Unit 4 covered the aforementioned categories of industries.

Every production system has resource and capacity limitations. The master scheduler has an extremely difficult task ahead of them. While the aggregate plan offers a broad overview of processes, the master scheduler is responsible for defining the precise output that is expected. The sales department (meet customer deadlines), finance (minimize inventory), management (maximize productivity and customer service, minimize resource needs), and manufacturing (have level schedules and minimize setup time) are just a few of the functional areas that put pressure on these decision-makers.

To determine an acceptable, realistic schedule to be released to the shop, trial master production schedules are run through the MRP program, which is discussed in the next section. In order to ensure that resources are available and completion times are realistic, the resulting planned-order releases, or the full production schedule, are examined. Once the necessary materials, parts, and components from lower levels are identified, which looks to be a workable master schedule may end up requiring too many resources. In the typical scenario where this occurs, the master production schedule is adjusted to reflect these constraints, and the MRP program is then executed once more.

Let's understand the concept of MRP with an example. Let's now look at how one of the component elements, the car wheels, is used. Although there might be some need for wheels on their own, it is obvious that the need to manufacture and maintain supplies of finished cars drives practically all of the demand for wheels. The link between the demand for wheels and the car reorder point is depicted in Fig. 5.2.

Fig. 5.2 Reorder of cars affecting demand for wheels

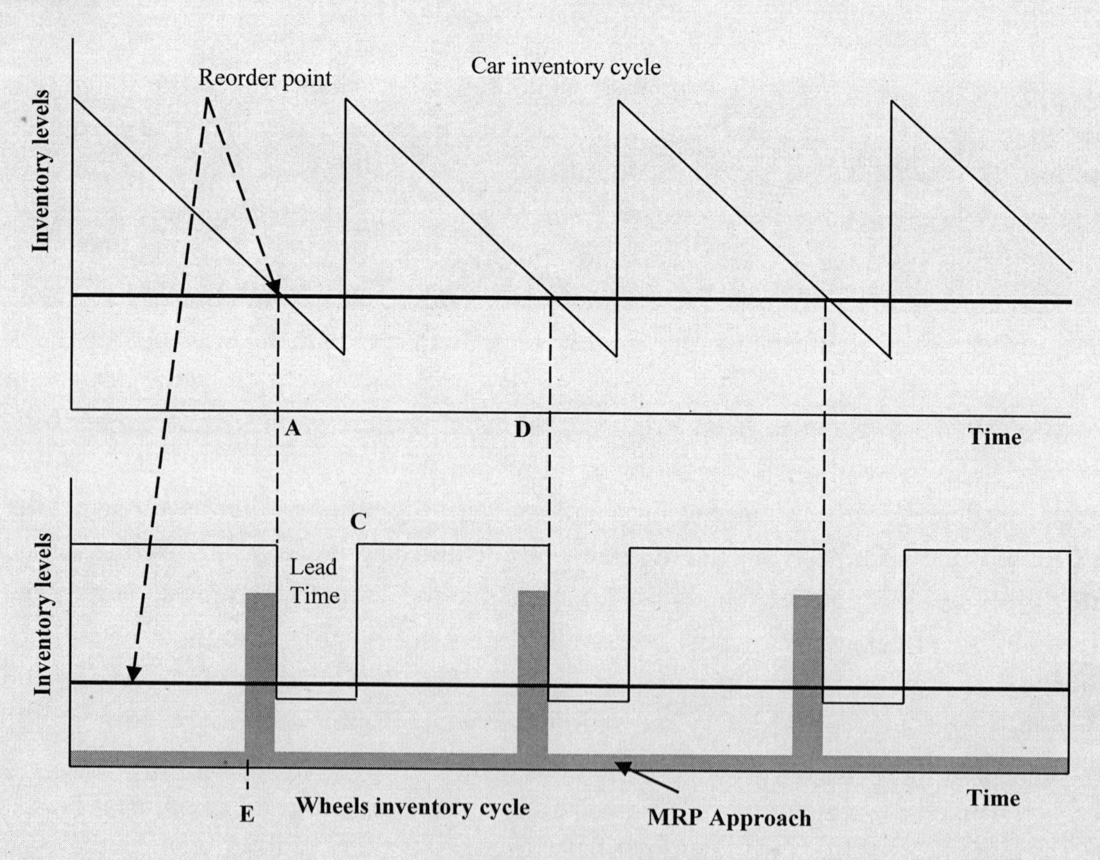

As seen in Fig. 5.2, the factory receives an order to supply the completed automobiles when the cars (A) reach the reorder point. The diagram's bottom section displays the demand for the wheels. There is no need for the wheels at time zero. Since the sole reason for the wheels in this figure is the necessity to construct the vehicles, there is no demand to make finished cars – only inventory can be sold. Until the ordering point (A) for the cars is reached, this demand remains zero (displaying as a flat demand line). There is a need to produce a fresh batch of finished cars at that moment of ordering. Wheels are in high demand right now. There is an almost immediate need for 400 wheels, for instance, if the order is to supply 100 cars. This demand is represented in the diagram as a vertical decrease in wheels quantity.

An order to restock the wheels is generated because the inventory has now dropped below the point of reorder. At point C, new wheels have been added after the lead time has passed. Point D on the diagram represents the request to construct and refill the supply of finished cars, after which the inventory will remain steady until demand spikes again. The primary cause of this "lumpy" demand for the dependent demand inventory items is batch lot sizes, and Fig. 5.2 makes it evident why this is undesirable.

The fundamental idea behind the MRP approach is this: if we can project requirements, we should be able to estimate or compute the time at which the finished cars' reorder point will occur given our understanding of the starting inventory. Because of this, we ought to be able to maintain a minimal supply of wheels until we absolutely require them for assembling the subsequent set of vehicles. The scenario is depicted in shaded area of Fig. 5.2.

The wheel inventory is quite low as shown in Fig. 5.2 (indicated by the darker shaded area of the curve). Since we now have a prediction of the date and quantity of the reorder point, we can build up the supply of wheels just prior to their demand, as represented as point E. That stock runs out extremely fast. It is evident that the cost of the darker shaded area above is substantially lower than that of the previous method. The master production schedule (MPS) projects the timing and quantity of final goods (cars), which is the goal and underlying principle of MRP.

5.6 MASTER PRODUCTION SCHEDULE

The master production schedule (MPS), commonly referred to as the master schedule, outlines the final goods or end items that a company must generate, together with the quantity and timing of production. To recapitulate the planning process, product groupings are specified in the aggregate operations plan. It doesn't list specific products. The master production schedule is the following stage of planning. An MPS, a time-phased plan, can span several months to cover the full creation of the things it contains, and it is typically indicated in days or weeks. *Cumulative lead time* is the overall amount of time needed to create a product.

The MRP process is driven by the MPS. Before the MRP system can produce production schedules for the sub-assemblies and component items, it must first obtain the schedule of final goods from the master schedule. A sample MPS made up of four end products made by a bike gear box manufacturer is displayed in Table 5.9.

Regarding the quantities listed in the MPS, a few points should be addressed.

1. *The quantity figures show production rather than demand*

As demonstrated in previously, demand and production do not always have to coincide. The master production schedule is filtered down by the strategy choices established during the aggregate planning phase. Chase demand, level capacity, and batching are common strategies (covered in Unit 4).

2. *The quantity figures could be a mix of projected demand and consumer orders*

While some of the MPS's estimates are forecasts, some have been proven. It is to be assumed that the amounts in the more recent time periods are more fixed, while the amounts projected further into the future might require multiple revisions before to the deadline. Certain companies establish a time fence, after which further modifications to the master schedule are prohibited. This contributes to the production environment's stabilization.

A feature called available to promise is employed by certain companies for master scheduled items. This feature shows the discrepancy between the number of units that firm customer requests and the number of units that are currently included in the master schedule. Let's take an example where the master schedule shows that 100 units of part A will be produced the next week. The sales team has an additional 45 parts A "available to promise" for delivery that week if customer orders now show that just 55 have actually been sold. This can be an effective tool for arranging manufacturing and sales tasks.

3. *The quantity figures indicate what must be produced, not what is feasible to create*

The MPS is derived from the aggregate plan, therefore its requirements are presumably achievable. However, the MPS's viability cannot be assured until the MRP system takes the time and specific resource needs into account. Because of this, the MRP system is frequently used to simulate production in order to ensure that the MPS is possible or that a specific order can be finished by a given deadline.

4. *The quantity figures show final goods, which might or might not be completed goods*

The type of production system can influence the master scheduling level. The MPS in make-to-stock businesses is made up of completed goods. When it comes to assemble-to-order businesses, the MPS typically stands for multiple subassemblies or modules. The master schedule in make-to-order businesses may include service parts, difficult-to-find materials, and essential components. For the final product or the customer order, separate final assembly schedules are then used.

The MPS is obtained from the aggregate plan, as was previously mentioned. For instance, the total amount of wheel rims of the Suzuki Swift car is planning to create over the course of the upcoming month or quarter may be specified in the car's aggregate plan. The MPS goes the next step down and identifies the particular model of the wheel rim. The MPS would specify every wheel rim that Suzuki Company sold. Additionally, the MPS specifies how often and when each of these wheel rims is needed on a period-by-period (typically weekly) basis. Subsequently, the MRP program, which computes and plans the necessary raw materials, components, and supplies to fabricate the wheel rims as per the MPS, completes the disaggregation process.

The aggregate plan for the total number of wheel rims planned per month is displayed in the upper part of Table 5.9. An MPS detailing the precise kind of wheel rim and the weekly production number is displayed in the lower section. For instance, a total of 1000 wheel rims are planned for the first month: 500 for the "PHANTOM Anthracite" model, 300 for the "FD-05 Black Machined" model, and 200 for the "YS5 Hyper Black" model. The MRP program, which creates comprehensive schedules indicating when tires, hubs, and bearings are required to complete a wheel for a Suzuki Swift automobile, is the next step below (not shown).

Table 5.9 The Aggregate Plan and the Master Production Schedule for Wheel Rims

Aggregate Production Plann for Wheel Rims		
Month	1	2
Wheel rim production	1000	900

Wheel Rim models	MPS for Suzuki Swift car's wheel rims							
	Week							
	1	2	3	4	5	6	7	8
PHANTOM Anthracite	250			250		200	400	
FD-05 Black Machined		150	150		100		100	
YS5 Hyper Black			200			50		50

5.7 STRUCTURE FOR MATERIAL REQUIREMENT PLANNING

Fig. 5.3 An overview of a typical MRP system program's inputs and outputs

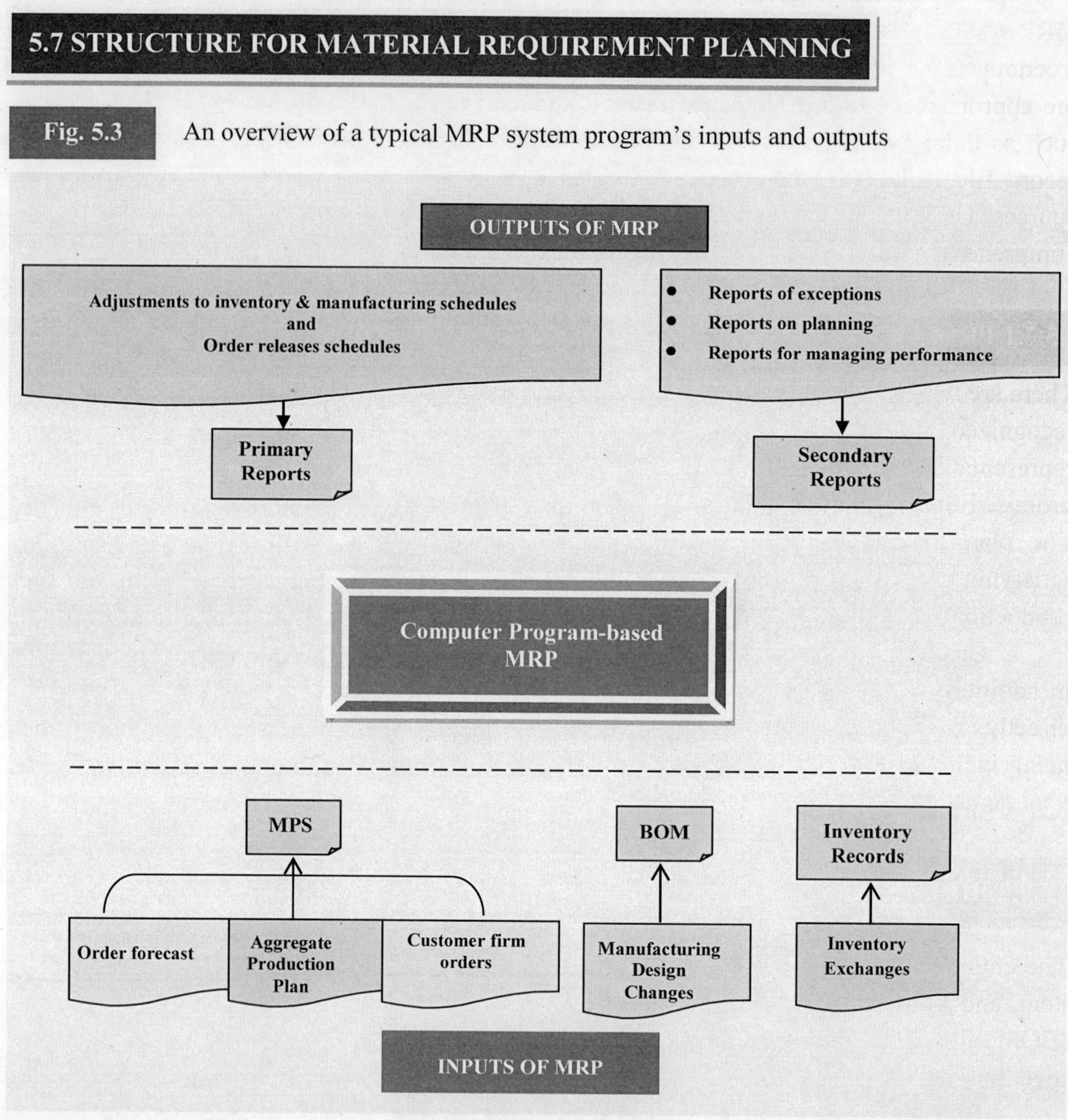

The material requirement planning portion of the manufacturing activities most closely interacts with the master schedule, bill of materials file, inventory records file, and output reports as shown in Fig. 5.3.

The parts that follow go into detail about each aspect of Fig. 5.3, but in general, the MRP system functions as follows: The MPS specifies how many goods must be produced in a certain amount of time. The precise materials required to create each product, together with the appropriate amounts of each, are listed in a bill-of-materials (BOM) file. Information such as the quantity of product units on hand and in stock can be found in the inventory record file. The MPS, BOM file, and inventory records file serve as the program's data sources. Using this information, the MRP program expands the production schedule into a comprehensive order scheduling plan that covers the whole manufacturing process.

5.7.1 PRODUCT DEMAND

There are two main sources of product demand for finished goods. The first group consists of recognized clients who have placed particular orders, like those produced by sales representatives or through cross-departmental transactions. Usually, delivery dates are promised for these items. These orders are simple to add up; there is no forecasting involved. The plan for aggregate production is the second source. The company's approach to satisfying demand going forward is reflected in the overall plan. The comprehensive master production schedule is used to carry out the plan.

Customers order specific parts and components as spares or for servicing and repairs in addition to the finished goods that they require. These requirements are typically input directly, at the appropriate levels, into the material requirement planning program rather than being included in the master production schedule. In other words, they are included in the total demand for that element or part.

5.7.2 BILL-OF-MATERIALS (BOM)

The entire product description, a list of the materials and components, the quantity of each item, and the order in which the product is made are all contained in the *bill-of-materials* (BOM) file. One of the three primary inputs into the MRP program is this BOM file. The inventory records file and the master production schedule are the other two.

Because it illustrates the assembly process of a product, the BOM file is sometimes referred to as the product structure file or product tree. It includes the data needed to identify each item as well as the amount used in each unit of the object it is a part of. Take the product "Motorcycle engine" assembly as an example. For instance, an engine unit has two "cam shafts" and four "cylinders." Every cylinder block has a single "crank shaft."

Moreover, there are four "pistons" and four "connecting rods" on each crank shaft. Three "piston rings" are installed in each piston; however the connecting rod is made up of one "gudgeon pin," one "small-end bearing," one "big-end bearing," and one "bolt." There are four "valves" and four "rocker arms" connected to each cam shaft. Fig. 5.4 depicts the engine's bill-of-materials structure.

Fig. 5.4 BOM (Product Structure Tree) for a motorcycle engine

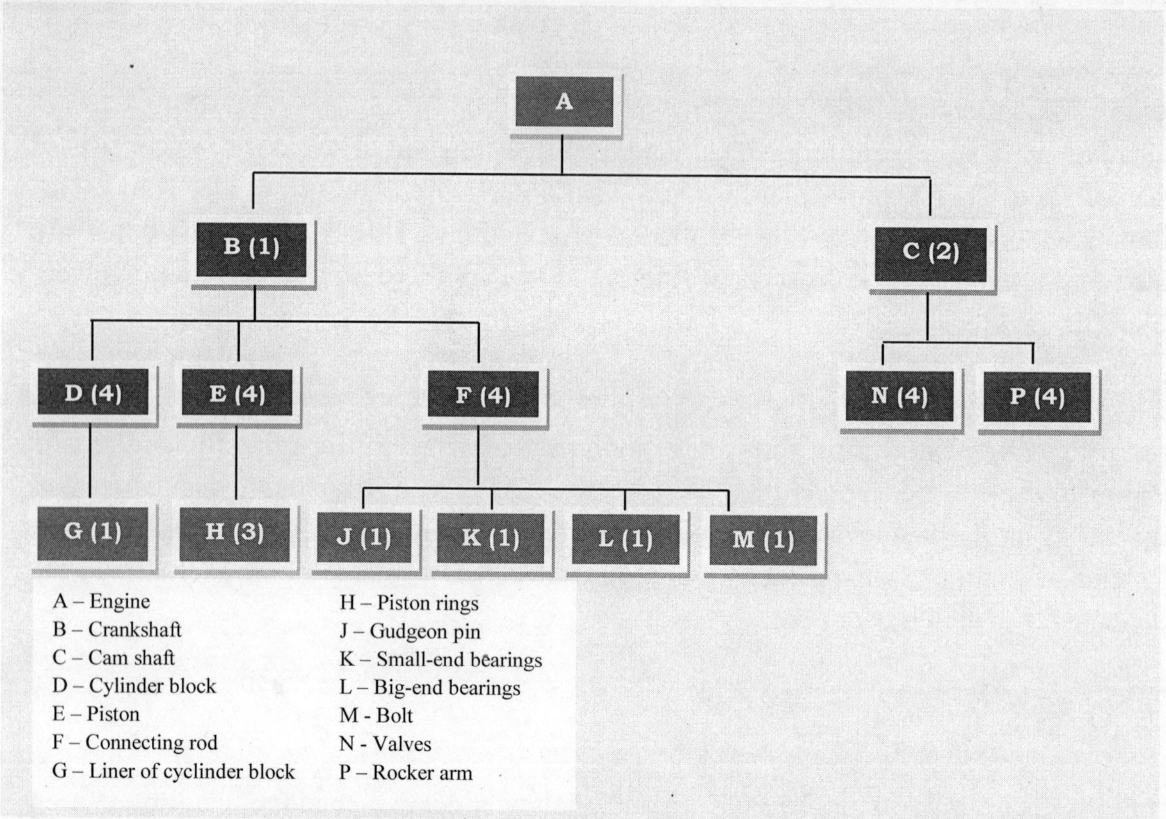

Parts are frequently listed using an indented structure in bill-of-material files. Because each indentation denotes an item's component, it is easy to identify each piece and the way it is put together. The ease of relating the two comparisons is demonstrated by comparing the indented elements in Table 5.10 with the item structure in Fig. 5.4. But from the standpoint of computer programs, it is exceedingly inefficient to store items in indented parts lists. Each item must be enlarged (often referred to as an "MRP explosion") and summed in order to determine the quantity required at the lower levels.

Data about parts can be stored more effectively by using straightforward single-level lists. In other words, every item and component is shown with simply its parent and the quantity of units required for each parent unit displayed. Because it only includes each assembly once, duplication is avoided. The single-level components list and the indented part list for the motor cycle engine are displayed in Table 5.10.

When a product is made in large subassemblies or modules that are then assembled into the finished product with options chosen by the customer, a *modular bill of materials* are appropriate. Using this method, a major option or module rather than a completed product is the end item in the master production schedule. As a result, the MRP system requires fewer bills of material to be input, maintained, and processed. Scheduling events when identical subassemblies show up in various end items is also beneficial. For instance, a car manufacturer can meet the demands of their customers by combining electrical circuits, engines, and transmissions in different ways. It is easier to forecast the consumption of various modules and to schedule and control work when using a modular bill-of-materials. The ability to lower the overall inventory investment is another advantage of adopting modular bills. This is known as standardization of items, where the same item is utilized in multiple goods.

Table 5.10 Parts list presented with indentation and single-level list

Indented Parts List				**Single-Level Parts List**	
A				A	
	B(1)				B(1)
		D(4)			C(2)
			G(1)	B	
		E(4)			D(4)
			H(3)		E(4)
		F(4)			F(4)
			J(1)	C	
			K(1)		N(4)
			L(1)		P(4)
			M(1)	D	
	C(2)				G(1)
		N(4)		E	
		P(4)			H(3)
				F	
					J(1)
					K(1)
					L(1)
					M(1)

Phantom bills are used for transient subassemblies that are used up quickly in the next manufacturing stage and are never stored. Orders for these items will not be released since they have a zero lead time and a unique code. As businesses embrace lean manufacturing (described in Unit 12) and Just-in-Time (JIT) (described in Unit 7) ideas that expedite items through the manufacturing and assembly process, phantom invoices are becoming more prevalent. For instance, the mattresses needed for four-wheelers are purchased right before the anticipated start of the assembly line.

Small, loose components like bolts, nuts, and fasteners are grouped together under one pseudo-item number by **K-bills** or a kit number. In this manner, rather than processing requirements for each individual item, needs are processed only once (for the group). K-bills save the paperwork, processing time, and storage space needed to generate orders for low-cost, small itcms that arc typically ordered in bulk but seldom.

5.7.3 LOW-LEVEL CODING

It is simple to calculate the total number of parts and materials required for a product if all identical pieces appear at the same level for every final product. Take a look at Product X in Fig. 5.5A.

Fig. 5.5A BOM for item X

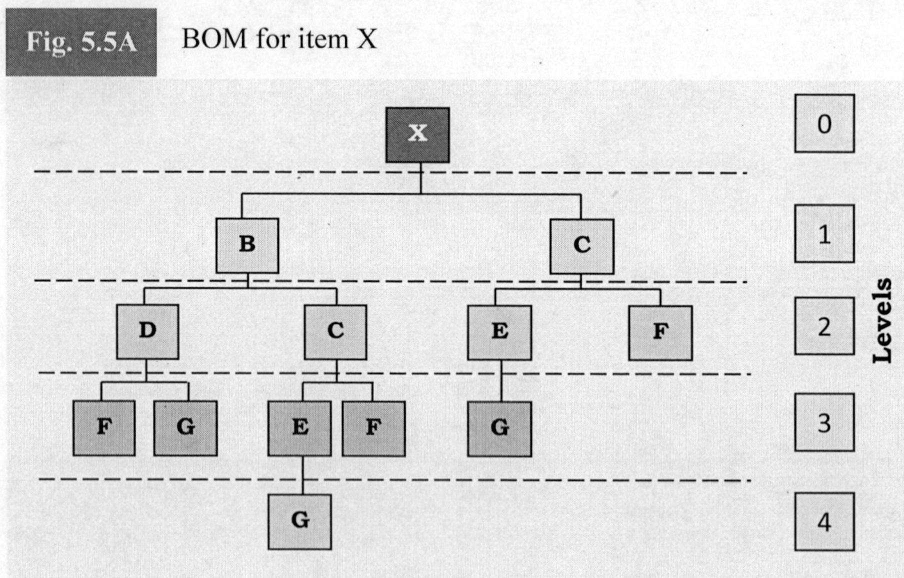

Fig. 5.5B BOM with low-level coding

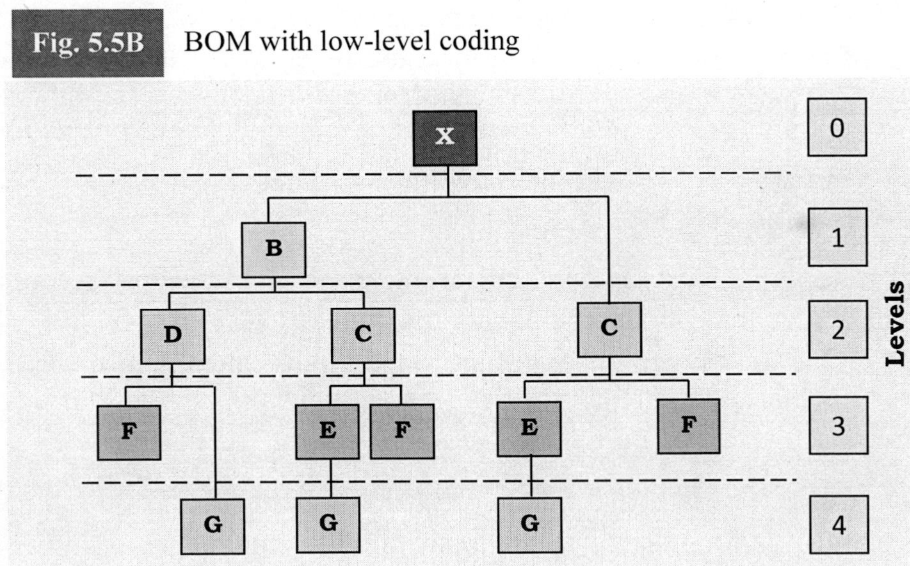

Take note of the fact that, for instance, item C appears as an input to X as well as an input to B. To bring all Cs to the same level, item C must be lowered to level 2 (Fig. 5.5B). The computer can quickly scan each level and determine the total number of units needed for each item if all identical things are arranged at the same level.

5.7.4 ITEM MASTER RECORD FILE

Every item that is created, ordered, or inventoried in the system has a great deal of information about it in the item master file, also known as the **inventory records file**. The MRP program retrieves the record's status section based on predetermined time intervals, more commonly referred to as time buckets. As the program runs, these records are accessed as needed.

As we shall see, the MRP algorithm analyzes the requirements level by level as it works its way down from the top of the product structure. On occasion, nevertheless, it is preferable to pinpoint the parent item that resulted in the material requirements. For instance, we would be interested in knowing which subassemblies are causing us to need a part that we have ordered from a supplier. An attached record file may be created independently or as a component of the inventory record file using the MRP application. By retracing a material requirement up through the product hierarchy and identifying each parent item that generated the demand, the requirements from the attached files help us better understand our product.

Posting inventory transactions as they happen keeps the inventory status file updated. These adjustments are brought about by stock receipts and payments, lost scrap, incorrect parts, canceled orders, and other factors.

5.7.5 COMPUTER PROGRAM MRP

Utilizing data from the master schedule, bill-of-materials, and inventory records, the MRP program runs. The requirements for component items are determined by working down from the top level of the BOM using the requirements from parent items. Orders that are anticipated for receipt in the future are taken into consideration, as are current on-hand balances.

An overview of the MRP explosion process is shown below:

1. The master schedule contains the requirements for level 0 items, sometimes known as end items. The MRP program refers to these criteria as **gross requirements**. The gross needs are usually planned in time intervals of one week.

2. The program then determines the **net requirements** by combining the schedule of orders that will be received in the future with the existing on-hand balance. Net requirements are the quantities that will be required, on a weekly basis, in the future in addition to what is now on-hand, or committed to by an order that has already been released and scheduled.

3. The program determines when orders must be received in order to achieve these needs based on net requirements. This can be as easy as arranging orders to arrive in accordance with the precise net requirements, or it can be more difficult and include combining requirements for several periods of time. **Planned-order receipts** are these scheduled dates for orders to arrive.

4. The next stage is to determine a timeline for when orders are actually released, as each order usually has a lead time. This is accomplished by offsetting the planned-order receipts by the necessary lead time. We call this schedule the **planned-order release.**

5. The program advances to level 1 items once all level 0 items have been processed through these four processes.

6. The planned-order release schedule for each level 1 item's parents is used to compute the gross requirements for each level 1 item. The gross requirements must also account for any additional independent demand.
7. Steps 2 through 4 of the calculation process are used to determine net requirements, planned-order receipts, and planned-order releases once the gross requirements have been established.
8. Then, for every level in the bill-of-materials, this procedure is repeated.

As you will see in the next example, the method for performing these computations is far less complicated than the description. The explosion calculations are usually carried out once a week or anytime the master schedule is modified. The ability to create instantaneous schedules, or net change schedules, is available in certain MRP packages. Because net change systems are activity driven, whenever a transaction is completed that affects an item, requirements and schedules are updated. The system can display the precise state of any item it manages in real time.

5.8 AN MRP EXAMPLE

Danfoss Inc. manufactures a variety of thermostats that are used to regulate temperature in different sorts of refigerators. Apart from the thermostats included within the refrigerated sections, the assemblies are marketed individually for replacement parts and maintenance needs. Determining the production plan to identify each item, the time frame for which it is required, and the proper quantities is the challenge facing the MRP system. After then, the schedule is examined for viability and adjusted as needed.

5.8.1 CREATING A MASTER PRODUCTION SCHEDULE

Assume that the quantities needed to meet both known and random requests for the thermostat and component requirements shown in Table 5.11A must be available during the first week of the month. This assumption makes sense since, in our case, management would rather make thermostats in a single batch once a month than several batches spread out over the course of the month.

The trial master schedule that we employ in these circumstances is displayed in Table 5.11B, where demand for Months 4, 5, and 6 is indicated as Weeks 13, 17, and 21 or in the first week of each month. To keep things brief, we will deal with demand until Week 21. We should review the schedule we create to ensure that resources, capacity, and other requirements are met before making revisions and rerunning it. Nevertheless, after the conclusion of this single schedule, we shall stop with our example.

Table 5.11A Future specifications derived from particular customer orders and projections for thermostats A and B and subassembly Y

	Thermostat A		**Thermostat B**		**Subassembly Y**	
Month	**Confirmed**	**Forecast**	**Confirmed**	**Forecast**	**Confirmed**	**Forecast**
4	950	200	375	50	175	70
5	550	200	250	50	225	70
6	350	200	450	50	325	70

Table 5.11B A master schedule that complies with the demands outlined in Table 5.11A

	Week								
Items	**13**	**14**	**15**	**16**	**17**	**18**	**19**	**20**	**21**
Thermostat A	1,150				750				550
Thermostat B	425				300				500
Subassembly Y	245				295				395

5.8.2 PRODUCT STRUCTURE: BILL-OF-MATERIALS

Thermostats A and B's product structure is depicted in Fig. 5.6 in the conventional manner utilizing low-level coding, where each item is positioned at the lowest level in the hierarchy of the structure. Various sensors, including part E, and a common defrost subassembly Y make up thermostats A and B. We will only be concentrating on part E, the sensor, in order to keep things straightforward.

It is evident from the product structure that subassembly Y – which is utilized in both types of thermostats A and B – uses part E, or the sensor. Part E (sensor) is an auxiliary component required for thermostat A. When a Y is formed, the number 2 in parenthesis next to E denotes that two Es are needed for each Y. The real manufacturing process of the thermostats is shown by the product structure and the indented parts list in Table 5.12a. Subassembly Y is created first, and they may be kept in stock. Thermostats A and B are assembled together in the last step, and for thermostat A, a sensor is a separate part E.

Fig. 5.6 Thermostats A and B's product structure

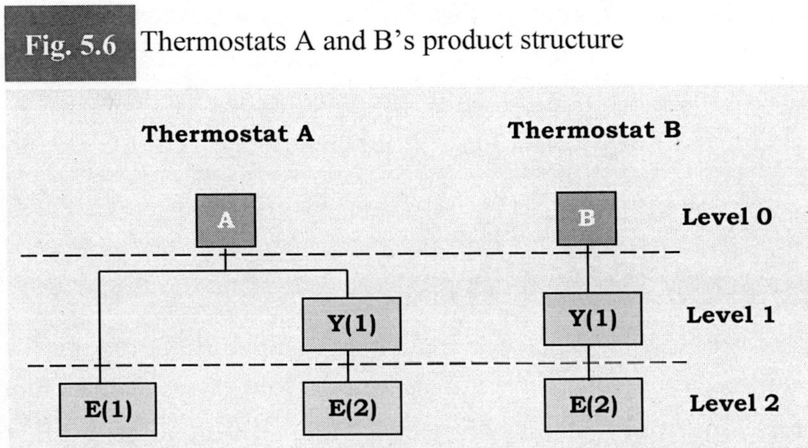

Table 5.12 Thermostat A and B's indented components list, with the amount of parts needed for each parent unit indicated in parenthesis

Thermostat A	Thermostat B
A	B
E(1)	
Y(1)	Y(1)
E(2)	E(2)

5.8.3 INVENTORY DOCUMENTATION

The on-hand inventory at the beginning of the program run, safety stock requirements, and the current status of orders that have already been released are among the inventory pertinent record data (see Table 5.13a).

Table 5.13a Data on lead times and the quantity of items on-hand would be displayed on the inventory record file

Item	On-hand Inventory	Lead Time (Weeks)	Safety Stock	On-Order
A	50	2	0	
B	60	2	0	10 (Week 9)
Y	40	1	5	
E	200	1	20	100 (Week 8)

Safety stock is the bare minimum of inventory that we should always have on hand for each item. For subassembly Y, for instance, we never want the inventory to go below 5 pieces. Additionally, we note that at the start of week 9, we are expecting to receive an order for 10 units of Thermostat B. At the start of week 8, there will be another order for 100 units of part E, which is the sensor.

5.8.4 CONDUCTING THE MRP ESTIMATES

The following parameters are now in place for the MRP computations to run: The master production schedule includes the end-item requirements, along with information on the relevant product structure, inventory status, and lead times. Level after level, the MRP computations (often called an explosion) are performed in conjunction with inventory and master schedule data.

The specifics of these estimates can be seen in Table 5.13b. The reasoning is explained in full in the analysis that follows. The issue of satisfying the gross requirements for 1,150 units of Thermostat A, 425 units of Thermostat B, and 245 units of sensor E in week 13 will be the exclusive focus of our investigation.

Table 5.13b MRP schedule for the production of thermostats

		Week					
Item		**8**	**9**	**10**	**11**	**12**	**13**
A							
LT = 2 weeks	Gross requirements						1,150
On-hand = 50	Scheduled receipts						
Safety stock = 0	Projected available balance	50	50	50	50	50	0
Order qty. = lot-for-lot	Net requirements						1,100
	Planned-order receipts						1,100
	Planned-order release				1,100		
B							
LT = 2 weeks	Gross requirements						425
On-hand = 60	Scheduled receipts						
Safety stock = 0	Projected available balance	60	70 (=60+10)	70	70	70	0
Order qty. = lot-for-lot	Net requirements						355
On order = 10 (week 9)	Planned-order receipts						355
	Planned-order release				355		
Assembly Y							
LT = 1 weeks	Gross requirements				1455 (=1100+355)		

On-hand = 40	Scheduled receipts						
Safety stock = 5	Projected available balance	35	35	35	580	580	580
Order qty. = 2,000	Net requirements				1420		
	Planned-order receipts				2,000		
	Planned-order release			2,000			
E							
LT = 1 weeks	Gross requirements			4,000	1,100		245
On-hand = 200	Scheduled receipts						
Safety stock = 20	Projected available balance	280 (=180+100)	280	1,280 (=5,000-3,720)	180	180	4,935
Order qty. = 5,000	Net requirements			3,720 (=4,000-280)			65
On order = 100 (week 8)	Planned-order receipts			5,000			5,000
	Planned-order release		5,000			5,000	

For every item that the system manages, an MRP record is maintained. Data on *net requirements*, *planned-order releases*, *scheduled receipts*, *projected available balance*, *gross requirements*, and *planned-order receipts* are all included in the record. Gross requirements represent the entire quantity needed for a specific item. Both external customer demand and demand determined by production requirements may be the source of these requirements. Orders that have already been released and are expected to arrive as of the start of the period are represented by planned receipts.

What was a "planned" order before the event becomes a *scheduled receipt* after the paperwork related to that order is released. The amount of inventory anticipated at the end of a period is known as the *projected available balance*. One way to compute this is as follows:

$$\begin{matrix}Projected \\ available \\ balance_{\ t}\end{matrix} = \begin{matrix}Projected \\ available \\ balance_{\ t-1}\end{matrix} - \begin{matrix}Gross \\ requirements_t\end{matrix} + \begin{matrix}Scheduled \\ receipts_{\ t}\end{matrix} + \begin{matrix}Planned \\ order \\ receipts_t\end{matrix}$$

One thing that must be taken into account is the original estimated available balance. The on-hand balance must be decreased by the safety stock in the event that it is required. Therefore, on-hand minus the safety stock equals the expected available balance for Period 0.

The amount required when the planned receipts for a period plus the estimated available balance are insufficient to satisfy the gross requirement is known as the net requirement. The planned-order receipt represents the quantity of an order needed to satisfy a net requirement within the given time frame. The planned-order release, in the end, is the planned-order receipt compensated by the lead time.

The estimated available balance, starting with Thermostat A, is 50 units, and there won't be any net requirements until week 13. To meet the 1,150 units of demand created by the order booked through the master schedule in week 13, extra 1,100 units are required. Since the order quantity is marked "lot-for-lot," we are able to place an order for the precise amount required to satisfy net criteria. As a result, an order is scheduled to be received for 1,100 units at the start of week 13. This order needs to be released at the start of week 11 because of the two-week lead period.

While 10 units order is expected to be delivered in period 9, Thermostat B is comparable to A. By the conclusion of week 9, we anticipate having 70 units ready. In week 13, there is a net requirement of 355 extra units to fulfill the gross requirement of 425 units. An order for 355 units is placed to satisfy this demand, and they must be released at the start of week 11.

The assembly utilized in Thermostats A and B is item C. Additional C's are only required when manufacturing A or B. According to our investigation of A, a 1,100 unit order is scheduled for release in week 11. In week 11, an order for 355 B's will also be released, making 1,455 units of C required. The projected available balance is equal to 40 units on hand less the previously mentioned safety stock of 5 units, or 35 units. The net requirement for week 11 is 1,420 units. A 2,000 unit order quantity is specified in the order policy for C, hence week 11 is set aside for the order receipt of 2,000 units. The one-week lead period means that this order must be released in week 10. Should this order be processed in the future, the projected available balance for weeks 11, 12, and 13 is 580 units.

There are three distinct sources of demand for item E, the sensor. Week 10's demand stems from the need to place E's in subassembly Y. In this instance, 4,000 units, or two Es, are required for every Y. For the order of 1,100 A's that are supposed to be released in week eleven, 1,100 E's are required in the eleventh week. In week 13, an additional 245 units are required to fulfill the autonomous demand as per the master schedule. The anticipated available balance is 280 units at the end of week 8 (200 units on hand plus the 100 units that are expected to be received minus the 20 units of safety stock), and 280 units in week 9. We anticipate receiving an order for 5,000 units (the order quantity) because there will be a net requirement for an extra 3,720 units in week 10. As a result, since 1,100 are needed to meet demand, the anticipated balance for week 11 is 180. By week twelve, 180 units should be ready. Week 13 will see the receipt of an additional 5,000 units due to the demand for 245 in that week, with a net requirement of 65 units.

5.8.5 RULES FOR LOT SIZING IN MRP SYSTEMS

The timing and magnitude of order amounts are established by a lot-sizing rule. Before planned receipts and planned order releases can be calculated, each item needs to have a lot-sizing rule attached to it. The number of setups needed and the expenses associated with keeping inventory for each item are determined by the lot-sizing criteria chosen, which makes them crucial. Lot-for-lot (L4L), economic order quantity (EOQ), least total cost (LTC), and least unit cost (LUC) are the three lot-sizing rules that we provide. Options for calculating lot sizes based on some of the more widely used methods are available in many MRP systems. The complexity of implementing MRP schedules in a plant grows with the usage of lot-sizing strategies. The inventory created by the bigger lot sizes needs to be held in an effort to save setup costs, which complicates plant logistics significantly.

5.8.5.1 LOT-FOR-LOT (L4L)

The most popular method is lot-for-lot (L4L). It precisely matches the net requirements when setting scheduled orders. Every week, it yields precisely what is required, with no extra produced for later times. It does not account for setup costs or capacity constraints and instead reduces carrying expenses.

The lot-by-lot computations are displayed in Table 5.15. Column 2 lists the net requirements. There won't be any inventory left at the end since lot-for-lot logic predicts that the production amount (column 3) will precisely equal the needed quantity (column 2). There is no holding cost if there is no inventory left over for the following week (column 5). But lot-for-lot necessitates a weekly setup fee (column 6). It should be noted that weekly setup fees apply because this is a work center where a range of tasks are completed. This is not an instance where the work center is dedicated to a single product and, when not working on that product, just idles (which would yield a single step). Lot-for-lot incurs significant setup fees.

The net requirements for eight scheduling weeks are displayed in the Table 5.14 for MRP lot-sizing problem that follows:

Table 5.14 Net requirements for MRP lot-sizing problem

Cost per item	$20.00
Order or setup cost	$50.00
Inventory carrying cost/week	0.2%

Weekly net requirements							
1	**2**	**3**	**4**	**5**	**6**	**7**	**8**
40	50	60	50	85	95	50	65

5.8.5.2 ECONOMIC ORDER QUANTITY

The EOQ model, which specifically balances setup and holding costs, is covered in Unit 6. Either a relatively steady demand or a safety stock that is maintained to offset demand variability is required in an EOQ model. An estimate of the whole yearly demand, the setup or order cost, and the holding cost are used in the EOQ model. A system with discrete time periods, like MRP, was not intended for EOQ model. When using lot-sizing procedures for MRP, it is assumed that part requirements are met at the beginning of the period. Then, unlike in the case of the EOQ model, holding costs are only applied to the period's ending inventory rather than the average inventory. Parts are assumed to be used constantly during the period by EOQ. Not every time do the lot sizes produced by the EOQ model encompass all of the periods. The needs for 6.4 periods, for instance, may be provided by the EOQ. The EOQ is computed as follows using the same data as in the lot-for-lot example:

$$\text{Annual demand based on the 8 weeks} = D = \frac{495}{8} \times 52 = 3{,}217.5 \text{ units}$$

$$\text{Annual carrying cost} = C_c = 0.2\% \times 20 \times 52 = \$2.08 \text{ per unit}$$

$$\text{Setup cost} = S = \$50 \text{ (given)}$$

$$EOQ = \sqrt{\frac{2DC_o}{C_c}}$$

$$= \sqrt{\frac{2(3217.5)(\$50)}{\$2.08}} = 393 \text{ units}$$

The MRP schedule with an EOQ of 393 units is displayed in Table 5.16. The requirements for weeks 1 through 6 and a portion of week 7 can be satisfied with the EOQ lot size from week 1. Then, in week 7, an additional EOQ lot is scheduled to fulfill the prerequisites for weeks 7 and 8. You'll see that the EOQ plan leaves some inventory for week 9 (=291 units) at the conclusion of week 8.

Table 5.15 MRP schedule lot-by-lot run size

(1)	(2)	(3)	(4)	(5)	(6)	(7)
Weeks	**Net Requirements**	**Production Qty.**	**Ending Inventory**	**Carrying Cost**	**Setup Cost**	**Total Cost (Cumulative)**
1	40	40	0	$0.00	$50.00	$50.00
2	50	50	0	0.00	50.00	100.00
3	60	60	0	0.00	50.00	150.00
4	50	50	0	0.00	50.00	200.00
5	85	85	0	0.00	50.00	250.00
6	95	95	0	0.00	50.00	300.00
7	50	50	0	0.00	50.00	350.00
8	65	65	0	0.00	50.00	400.00

Table 5.16 MRP schedule EOQ run size

(1)	(2)	(3)	(4)	(5)	(6)	(7)
Weeks	**Net Requirements**	**Production Qty.**	**Ending Inventory**	**Carrying Cost**	**Setup Cost**	**Total Cost (Cumulative)**
1	40	393	353	$14.12	$50.00	$64.12
2	50	0	303	12.12	0.00	76.24
3	60	0	243	9.72	0.00	85.96
4	50	0	193	6.52	0.00	92.48
5	85	0	108	4.32	0.00	96.80
6	95	0	13	0.52	0.00	97.32
7	50	393	356	14.24	50.00	161.56
8	65	0	291	11.64	0.00	173.20

5.8.5.3 LEAST TOTAL COST

A dynamic lot-sizing methodology called the least total cost method (LTC) compares the setup (or ordering) and carrying costs for different lot sizes to determine the order quantity. It then chooses the lot where these costs are mainly almost equal.

The least cost lot size results are displayed in Table 5.17A. Comparing order costs and carrying costs over a range of weeks is how least total cost lot sizes are calculated. Costs are compared, for instance, when production occurs in week 1 to meet requirements for week 1, when production occurs in week 1 to cover weeks 1 and 2, when production occurs in week 1 to cover weeks 1, 2, and 3, and so forth. For instance, the computation for the order placed in week 1 covering weeks 1, 2, and 3 comprises a single ordering cost of \$50 in addition to the costs associated with carrying 50 units for one week (50 × \$20 × 0.2% × 1 = \$2.00) and 60 units for two weeks (60 × \$20 × 0.2% × 2 = \$4.80). The lot size where the ordering and carrying costs are roughly equal is the one that should be chosen. The optimal lot size in Table 8 is 380 because \$45.40 and \$50 ordering and carrying costs are closer than \$57.40 and \$50 (\$4.60 versus \$7.40). This lot size satisfies week 1 through week 6 requirements. The lot size only includes whole numbers of periods, in contrast to EOQ.

We are currently in week 7, and our challenge is figuring out how many weeks into the future we can supply from here, based on the decision made in week 1 to place an order to cover 6 weeks. According to Table 8, ordering and carrying costs are most similar when it comes to the amount needed to meet the requirements for Weeks 7 and 8. Here, you'll see that carrying and ordering costs are far apart. This is due to the fact that our sample only covers week 8. The lot size scheduled for week 7 would probably extend past week 8 if the planning horizon were longer. This brings up one of LTC's and LUC's (addressed next) limitations. The length of the planning horizon affects both strategies. The final run size and overall cost are displayed in Table 5.17B.

Table 5.17A Run Size for Least Total Cost in an MRP Schedule

Weeks	Quantity Ordered	Carrying Cost (\$)	Ordering Cost (\$)	Total Cost (\$)
1	40	0.00	50.00	50.00
1 – 2	90	2.00	50.00	52.00
1 – 3	150	6.80 (=2.0+4.8)	50.00	56.80
1 – 4	200	12.80 (=6.80+6)	50.00	62.80
1 – 5	285	26.40 (=12.8+13.6)	50.00	76.40
1 – 6	**380**	45.40 (=26.4+19)	50.00	**95.40** 1st order

				(lowest overall cost)
1 – 7	430	57.40 (=45.4+12)	50.00	107.40
1 – 8	495	75.60 (57.4+18.2)	50.00	125.60
7	50	0.00	50.00	50.00
7 – 8	115	2.60	50.00	52.60 2nd order (Lowest overall cost)

Table 5.17B Final run size for Least Total Cost

(1)	(2)	(3)	(4)	(5)	(6)	(7)
Weeks	**Net Requirements**	**Production Qty.**	**Ending Inventory**	**Carrying Cost**	**Setup Cost**	**Total Cost (Cumulative)**
1	40	380	340	$13.60	$50	$63.6
2	50	0	290	11.60	0.00	75.2
3	60	0	230	9.20	0.00	84.4
4	50	0	180	7.20	0.00	91.6
5	85	0	95	3.80	0.00	95.4
6	95	0	0	0.00	0.00	95.4
7	50	115	65	2.6	50.00	171.40
8	65	0	0	0	0	171.40

5.8.5.4 LEAST UNIT COST

The least unit cost approach is a dynamic lot-sizing strategy that determines the lot size with the lowest unit cost by adding ordering and inventory carrying costs for each trial lot size, dividing by the number of units in each lot size, and then choosing that lot size.

Table 5.18A Run size for Least Unit Cost

Weeks	Quantity Ordered	Carrying Cost ($)	Ordering Cost ($)	Total Cost ($)	Unit Cost ($)
1	40	0.00	50.00	50.00	1.2500
1 – 2	90	2.00	50.00	52.00	0.5777
1 – 3	150	6.80	50.00	56.80	0.3786
1 – 4	200	12.80	50.00	62.80	0.3140

1 – 5	285	26.40	50.00	76.40	0.2680
1 – 6	380	45.40	50.00	95.40	0.2510
1 – 7	**430**	57.40	50.00	107.40	**0.2497** 1st order (Lowest unit cost)
1 – 8	495	75.60	50.00	125.60	0.2537
8	**65**	0.00	50.00	50.00	**0.7692** 2nd order (unit cost of last period)

Table 5.18B Final Run size for Least Unit Cost

(1)	(2)	(3)	(4)	(5)	(6)	(7)
Weeks	**Net Requirements**	**Production Qty.**	**Ending Inventory**	**Carrying Cost**	**Setup Cost**	**Total Cost (Cumulative)**
1	40	430	390	$15.60	$50.00	$65.60
2	50	0	340	13.60	0.00	79.20
3	60	0	280	11.20	0.00	90.40
4	50	0	230	9.20	0.00	99.60
5	85	0	145	5.80	0.00	105.40
6	95	0	50	2.00	0.00	107.40
7	50	0	0	0	0	107.40
8	65	65	0	0	50.00	157.40

To meet the needs of weeks 1 through 8, the unit cost for the ordering lots is calculated in Table 5.18A. The quantity of 430 that was ordered in week one was adequate to cover weeks one through seven, which is when the minimum occurred. If the planning horizon had been longer than eight weeks, the lot size plan for week 8 would have been extended. The run size and total cost with the lowest unit cost are shown in Table 5.18B. Observe that the production amount in week 8 is the same as net requirements because the planning horizon terminates at that point. Similar to the lot-for-lot rule, this operates. There isn't any ending inventory, but this week's manufacturing amount will require a $50 setup fee, making the total cost $157.40.

Based on the analysis shown above, we can calculate the following total costs: $400 for the eight weeks under the lot-for-lot (L4L) rule; $173.20 for the EOQ rule; $171.40 for the least total cost (LTC) rule; and $157.40 for the least unit cost (LUC) rule. With a unit cost of $157.40, the lowest cost was achieved. The lowest cost might change if there were more than eight weeks. The least unit cost method has the advantage of being a more thorough analysis, as it accounts for ordering or setup expenses that may vary as order size grows.

UNIT SUMMARY

- ***Aggregate Planning Techniques*** – Introduction to the cut-and-try method, which evaluates various production strategies using spreadsheets and cost analysis.
- ***Disaggregating the Aggregate Plan*** – The process of breaking down aggregate production into detailed master schedules for specific products and components.
- ***Master Scheduling*** – The Master Production Schedule (MPS) defines what is produced, in what quantity, and at what time.
- ***Material Requirements Planning*** (MRP) – A computerized system that determines raw material needs based on MPS, ensuring timely procurement and inventory control.
- ***Lot Sizing in MRP Systems*** – Rules for determining optimal order sizes, including Lot-for-Lot (L4L), Economic Order Quantity (EOQ), Least Total Cost (LTC), and Least Unit Cost (LUC).

EXERCISES

MULTIPLE CHOICE QUESTIONS

5.1 Aggregate planning primarily focuses on:

(a) Detailed scheduling of individual operations.	(b) Long-term capacity planning to meet demand.
(c) Day-to-day allocation of resources.	(d) Managing inventory levels in real-time.

5.2 Disaggregate planning is concerned with:

(a) Allocating resources within specific departments.	(b) Balancing production across different product lines.
(c) Detailed scheduling of production activities.	(d) Adjusting capacity to meet seasonal demand.

5.3 Which of the following is a key objective of aggregate planning?

(a) Minimizing setup costs.	(b) Maximizing inventory levels.
(c) Matching production capacity with demand.	(d) Minimizing lead times.

5.4 Disaggregate planning is essential for:

(a) Determining optimal production batch sizes.	(b) Optimizing inventory holding costs.
(c) Adjusting workforce levels over the long term.	(d) Scheduling day-to-day production operations.

5.5 Which of the following is NOT a strategy used in aggregate planning?

(a) Hiring and firing workers	(b) Overtime and undertime
(c) Level production	(d) Individual product scheduling

5.6 Which of the following documents serves as the output of the master scheduling process?

(a) Bill of Materials (BOM)	(b) Work Breakdown Structure (WBS)
(c) Master Production Schedule (MPS)	(d) Production Order

5.7 What role does the master schedule play in production planning and control?

(a) It details the sequence of operations for each production run.	(b) It determines the optimal batch size for manufacturing.
(c) It coordinates production activities to meet demand over a specific time horizon.	(d) It specifies the number of units to be produced daily

5.8 Which of the following best describes the relationship between master scheduling and aggregate planning?

(a) Master scheduling focuses on short-term detailed planning, whereas aggregate planning is more long-term and strategic.	(b) Aggregate planning is concerned with balancing demand and capacity, while master scheduling deals with resource allocation.
(c) Master scheduling determines overall production goals, while aggregate planning specifies daily production targets.	(d) Aggregate planning encompasses all aspects of production scheduling, while master scheduling focuses solely on inventory management.

5.9 What is the primary purpose of a Bill of Materials (BOM) in manufacturing and production?

(a) To document financial transactions related to raw materials.	(b) To list the tools and equipment required for assembly.
(c) To specify the quantity and description of components needed for production.	(d) To schedule production timelines and delivery dates.

5.10 In a manufacturing BOM, what does the term "phantom item" refer to?

(a) A material that appears in the BOM but is not used in the final product.	(b) An item that only exists in the imagination of the production team.
(c) A component that is critical for assembly but not readily available.	(d) A placeholder for materials that are yet to be sourced.

5.11 How does a Bill of Materials (BOM) contribute to effective inventory management?

(a) By detailing the cost of each material used.	(b) By indicating the supplier for each component.
(c) By providing a checklist for quality control.	(d) By specifying the amount of each component needed for production.

5.12 Which lot-sizing rule aims to minimize the holding costs associated with excess inventory?

(a) Economic Order Quantity (EOQ)	(b) Least Unit Cost (LUC)
(c) Lot-for-Lot (L4L)	(d) Fixed Order Quantity (FOQ)

5.13 The Economic Order Quantity (EOQ) formula balances which two types of costs?

(a) Ordering costs and carrying costs	(b) Holding costs and shortage costs
(c) Fixed costs and variable costs	(d) Purchase costs and transportation costs

5.14 What does the Least Unit Cost (LUC) lot-sizing rule prioritize?

(a) Minimizing setup costs per order.	(b) Maximizing the order quantity to benefit from volume discounts.
(c) Minimizing holding costs for inventory.	(d) Balancing safety stock levels with demand variability.

Answers of Multiple Choice Questions

5.1 (b), 5.2 (c), 5.3 (c), 5.4 (d), 5.5 (d), 5.6 (c), 5.7 (c), 5.8 (a), 5.9 (c), 5.10 (a), 5.11 (d), 5.12 (c), 5.13 (a), 5.14 (a)

SHORT AND LONG ANSWER TYPE QUESTIONS

Category I

5.1 Why is aggregate planning important for organizations?

5.2 What are the key strategies used in aggregate planning?

5.3 How does disaggregate planning differ from aggregate planning?

5.4 What are some challenges associated with aggregate planning?

5.5 How does disaggregate planning contribute to operational efficiency?

5.6 What are the key components of master scheduling?

5.7 How does Master Production Scheduling interact with other planning processes?

5.8 What are some challenges associated with Master Production Scheduling?

5.9 What are the key objectives of Material Requirements Planning?

5.10 How does Material Requirements Planning benefit manufacturing operations?

5.11 How does MRP help in determining the quantity and timing of materials needed for production?

5.12 What are the primary purposes of a Bill of Materials?

5.13 How does a Bill of Materials support production planning?

5.14 How does a Bill of Materials help in managing inventory levels?

5.15 How can MRP software help streamline the material planning process for a company?

5.16 How is low-level coding implemented in MRP systems?

5.17 What is the Economic Order Quantity (EOQ) rule?

5.18 How does the Least Total Cost (LTC) rule work?

5.19 How does the Lot-for-Lot (L4L) rule differ from other lot sizing rules?

5.20 What is the significance of choosing the right lot sizing rule in MRP systems?

Category II

5.21 How can organizations effectively implement aggregate planning to achieve strategic objectives?

5.22 How does aggregate planning differ from detailed scheduling and operational planning?

5.23 How can organizations effectively manage capacity constraints when disaggregating aggregate plans? Discuss strategies and techniques that can be employed to optimize resource utilization and mitigate capacity bottlenecks.

5.24 Define master scheduling and discuss its significance in production planning and control. How does master scheduling integrate with other planning activities within the manufacturing environment?

5.25 Explain the role of ERP (enterprise resource planning) systems in supporting master scheduling processes. How do ERP systems enhance the accuracy and efficiency of master scheduling activities in manufacturing organizations?

5.26 In a complex manufacturing system, how does the bill-of-material (BOM) serve as a foundational document for production planning and control, and what are the key elements that should be included in a detailed BOM to ensure accurate and efficient manufacturing operations?

5.27 Explain the lot-for-lot rule in the context of inventory management and production planning. Provide detailed examples to illustrate scenarios where the lot-for-lot rule is most appropriate. Analyze the factors that influence the decision to use the lot-for-lot rule, including cost considerations, demand variability, and production setup times. Evaluate the impact of adopting the lot-for-lot rule on inventory levels, operational efficiency, and supply chain dynamics. Finally, discuss how advancements in technology and data analytics are influencing the application and effectiveness of the lot-for-lot rule in modern manufacturing and distribution environments.

5.28 Explain the concept of the least unit cost lot sizing rule in the context of inventory management, and discuss the factors that influence the determination of the optimal lot size to minimize costs in a manufacturing setting.

NUMERICAL PROBLEMS

5.1 A range of semiconductors made by Precision Semiconductor Company is designed to be installed in different kinds of electronic equipment. The business is attempting to come up with a manufacturing schedule for the upcoming 12 months. The primary requirement for this plan is to maintain a stable level of employment throughout the duration. The company wants to avoid creating any negative sentiment among the local workforce; therefore it is keeping up its R&D efforts to create new applications. For the same reason, even if working a full workweek isn't the most economical option, all employees should do so. For the upcoming 12 months, the forecast is:

MONTH	FORECAST DEMAND	MONTH	FORECAST DEMAND
JAN.	600	JULY	200
FEB.	800	AUG.	200
MAR.	900	SEP.	300
APR.	600	OCT.	700
MAY	400	NOV.	800
JUNE	300	DEC.	900

Each set of chips has a $200 manufacturing cost, which is split equally between labor and materials. The monthly cost of inventory storage is $5. There is a shortage due to a lack of sets, which is anticipated to cost $20 less per unit.

There are 200 units in stock at the start of the planned period. Each device requires ten labor hours. Eight hours make up the workday.

Using a steady workforce, create an aggregate production schedule for the year. Assume 22 working days every month for the sake of simplicity, with the exception of July, when the plant closes for three weeks of vacation, leaving seven working days. Assume that total demand is equal to or greater than total production capacity.

5.2 Create a master schedule using the data below; similar to what is displayed in Table 5.8. In an eight-week schedule, the forecast is 50 units per week. Production must be scheduled in accordance with the MPS rule if there would be a negative projected on-hand inventory otherwise. The following are committed orders from customers:

Week	Customer Orders
1	52
2	35
3	20
4	12

Using a production lot size of 75 units and no beginning inventory, determine the available-to-promise (ATP) quantities for each period.

5.3 Two units of Subassembly B, three units of C, and one unit of D make up Product A. Four units of E and three units of F make up B. Three D units and two H units combine to form C. Two units of G and five units of E combine to form H.

a. Create a basic bill of materials (tree of products).

b. Use low-level coding to build a product structure tree.

c. Make a list of indented components.

d. Calculate how many units of B, C, D, E, F, G, and H are needed in order to make 100 units of A.

5.4 At the start of week six, eighty units of end item E are required. J has been ordered in three boxes (30 units each box), with one box expected to arrive in week three, the other two in week four, and the third in week five. It should be noted that B must be produced in multiples of 120 units, and J must be ordered by the box. Right now, there are 20 units of J and 60 units of B available. For E and B, the lead times are two weeks each, and for J, they are one week.

a. Create a plan for component J's material requirements.
b. Let's say that the required amount of E is reduced from 80 to 70 in week 4. All of the scheduled releases for week three have been carried out. In week six, how many extra Bs and Js will be available?

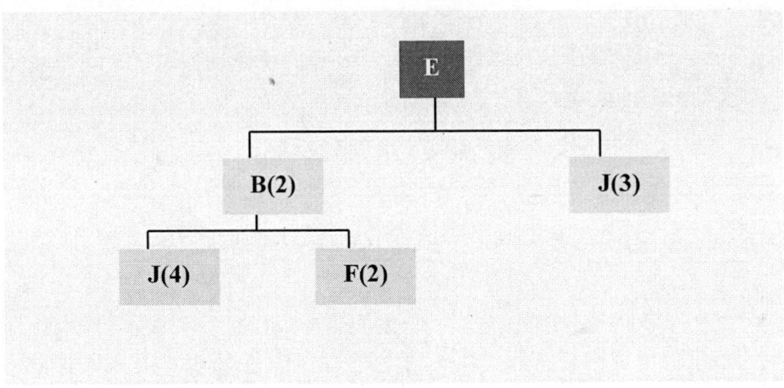

5.5 Imagine that you run a shop that assembles household accessories. A recent order for fifty food processors has reached you; they are scheduled to be sent at the beginning of week eight. Important details about the food processor are as follows:

Item	Lead Time (weeks)	On Hand	Components
Food Processor (S)	2	15	A(2), B(1), C(4)
A	1	10	E(3), D(1)
B	2	5	D(2), F(3)
C	2	65	E(2), D(2)
D	1	20	
E	1	10	
F	2	30	

a. Create an assembly time chart, a master schedule, and a product structure tree.

b. Using lot-for-lot ordering for every item, create the material requirement plan for component E.

5.6 Create a strategy outlining the materials needed for component H. The final product and every component – aside from B – have lead times of one week. Three weeks is the lead time for B. At the beginning of week eight, sixty units of A are required. There are 130 units of E and 15 units of B available right now, while 50 units of H are in production and should be finished by the beginning of week 2. All products will be ordered on a Lot-for-Lot basis.

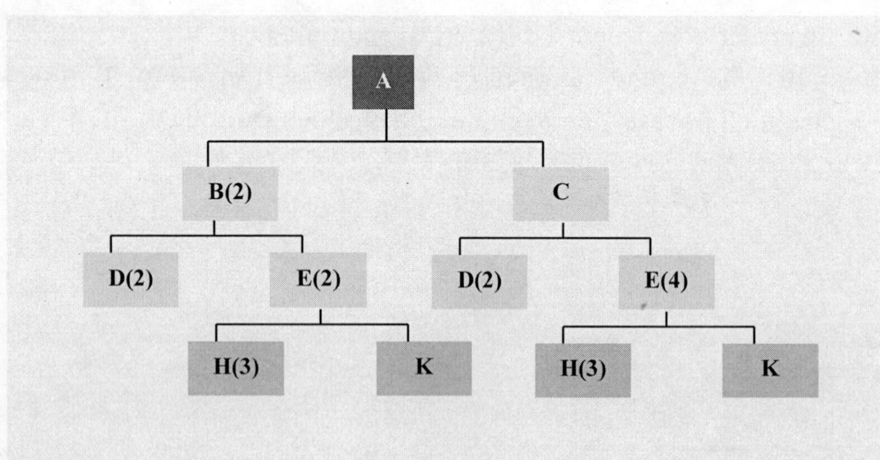

REFERENCES AND SUGGESTED READINGS

1. Chandrasekaran, M., and Vrat, P. A Review of Aggregate Production Planning Models. *International Journal of Production Research*, Vol. 37(10), 2259-2284, 1999.
2. Harris, R. L., and Krajewski, L. J. MRP and Its Role in Production Planning. *Production and Inventory Management Journal*, Vol. 33(4), 12-20, 1992.
3. Heizer, J., Render, B., and Munson, C. *Operations Management: Sustainability and Supply Chain Management*, 12th Edition, Pearson, 2017.
4. Hopp, W. J., and Spearman, M. L. Factory Physics: Foundations of Manufacturing Management. *International Journal of Production Research*, Vol. 38(6), 1297-1305, 2000.
5. Jacobs, F. R., and Berry, W. L. *Manufacturing Planning and Control for Supply Chain Management*, 6th Edition, McGraw-Hill Education, 2014.
6. Krajewski, L. J., Ritzman, L. P., and Malhotra, M. K. *Operations Management: Processes and Supply Chains*, 12th Edition, Pearson, 2018.
7. Li, S., and Liu, F. A Hybrid Approach to Disaggregating the Aggregate Plan in Multi-level Production Systems. *International Journal of Production Economics*, Vol. 106(1), 57-69, 2007.
8. Shah, J. B., and Lee, D. The Impact of Master Production Scheduling on Supply Chain Performance. *International Journal of Production Economics*, Vol. 124(1), 140-151, 2010.
9. Silver, E. A., and Peterson, R. The Theory and Practice of Inventory Management. *Journal of Operations Management*, Vol. 4(4), 254-276, 1985.
10. Singh, P., and Gupta, H. A Review of Aggregate Planning in Manufacturing. *International Journal of Operations & Production Management*, Vol. 26(1), 16-28, 2006.
11. Tersine, R. J., and Hasegawa, H. *Principles of Inventory and Materials Management*, 6th Edition, Prentice-Hall, 2004.

12. Vollmann, T. E., Berry, W. L., and Whybark, D. C. *Manufacturing Planning and Control for Supply Chain Management*, 5th Edition, McGraw-Hill Education, 2004.

13. Westbrook, R., and New, S. Master Production Scheduling in MRP Systems: A Survey of Practices in the Manufacturing Industry. *International Journal of Operations & Production Management*, Vol. 30(3), 294-312, 2010.

14. Wight, O. W. *Manufacturing Planning and Control for Supply Chain Management*, 6th Edition, McGraw-Hill, 2013.

15. Wight, O. W., and Nigam, A. Master Scheduling in MRP and ERP Systems. *International Journal of Production Research*, Vol. 45(7), 1505-1524, 2007.

UNIT 6

INVENTORY MANAGEMENT

UNIT SPECIFICS

This unit elaborately discusses the following topics:

- Types of inventory and their functions
- Purpose of inventory
- Continuous and periodic inventory review system
- Cost of inventory
- System of classification of inventory
- Economic order quantity model
- The model of production quantity
- Quantity discount
- Decision about order timing for fixed-order quantity model (safety stock, service level)
- Decisions about order timing for fixed-time period model (safety stock, service level)
- Single period inventory model

In order to improve problem-solving abilities and encourage increased creativity and curiosity, the topics' practical applications are explored. Along with several multiple-choice questions and questions with short and long answer types categorized into two groups based on lower and higher order of Bloom's taxonomy, the unit also offers assignments through a number of numerical problems, a list of references, and recommended reads. You can practice these by attempting them out. An extra section ("Along the...") has been added following the unit's associated topic in accordance with the content. It has been carefully crafted to help the reader of the book. In order to increase interest in the topic, this content mainly focuses on the incredible facts regarding the problem that is being treated in the modern, intriguing industrial setting.

RATIONALE

This unit provides a comprehensive overview of inventory management, highlighting the various types of inventory and their essential functions within a business. It explores the fundamental purposes of inventory, including meeting customer demand and optimizing production processes. The unit contrasts continuous and periodic inventory review systems, emphasizing their respective cost implications. Key concepts such as inventory classification, economic order quantity (EOQ), and production quantity models are examined to illustrate effective ordering strategies. Additionally, the unit addresses decision-making regarding order timing in both fixed-order and fixed-time models, factoring in safety stock and service levels. Finally, the single-period inventory model is discussed to underscore its relevance in managing perishable goods and seasonal items.

UNIT OUTCOMES

List of outcomes of this unit is as follows:

U6-UO1: Identify and Classify Inventory Types

U6-UO2: Understand Inventory Purposes

U6-UO3: Evaluate Inventory Review Systems

U6-UO4: Analyze Inventory Costs

U6-UO5: Application of EOQ and Production Quantity Models

U6-UO6: Information-based Ordering Decisions

UNIT-6 Outcomes	EXPECTED MAPPING WITH COURSE OUTCOMES (*1-Weak Correlation; 2-Medium Correlation; 3-Strong Correlation*)					
	CO-1	CO-2	CO-3	CO-4	CO-5	CO-6
U6-UO1	2	3	3	2	1	1
U6-UO2	2	2	3	3	2	2
U6-UO3	2	2	3	3	2	2
U6-UO4	1	2	3	3	2	2
U6-UO5	2	3	3	3	2	2
U6-UO6	1	2	3	2	3	2

Most companies' supply chains and overall operations depend on effective inventory management. Effective inventory management is in the best interests of operations, marketing, and finance. Ineffective inventory management reduces customer satisfaction, impairs operations, and raises operational expenses.

While many firms manage their inventories satisfactorily, some have exceptional inventory control. However, an excessive number have inadequate inventory management, which might occasionally be an indication that management does not understand the value of stockpiles. However, the recognition is present most of the time. The knowledge of what must be done and how to achieve it is what is lacking. The ideas that form the basis of effective inventory management are covered in this unit.

The management of acquired parts, retail items, raw materials, and completed things is also covered in this unit. Functions of inventories, prerequisites for efficient inventory management, goals of inventory control, and methods for figuring out what to order and when to order it are among the subjects covered. Analysis of inventories is the main focus.

6.1 INTRODUCTION

Inventory is a company's store of goods maintained on hand to fulfill demand from clients, both internal and external. Almost all kinds of organizations keep some kind of inventory. Every retail item that a department store or grocery store sells has an inventory; a store in a mall has an inventory of various groceries, fruits, vegetables, and other edibles; a bike agency has an inventory of bikes; and a major league cricket team keeps an inventory of the players on its minor league teams. Even a family home keeps supplies including food, clothes, medical equipment, and personal hygiene products on stock.

A finished good that is awaiting retail sale, such as hospital stock medications or packaged frozen food, is how most people think of inventory. Its most significant application is undoubtedly this one. But aside from completed commodities, inventory can also include:

Raw materials, particularly in a manufacturing company – reflect merchandise that has been bought to be used in the business's manufacturing process but hasn't seen any value addition.

Purchased supplies and parts – reflect inventory that has been bought to be used in the business's manufacturing process but hasn't seen any value additions.

Partially finished work in progress (WIP) – indicate merchandise that has undergone some value addition but needs more processing to be finished before it can be used to fulfill client orders.

Finished products – reflect inventory that has undergone all firm processing. With the possible exception of packing, it is typically prepared for usage in meeting client demand.

Tools and equipments – inventory that's kept on hand to help with business and production procedures, but it's rarely sold to customers directly. It consists of office supplies, cutting tools, cleaning supplies, machine oil, spare parts, and so on.

One essential component of business is inventory. They improve consumer happiness in addition to being essential for operations. Take into account the following to have an understanding of the importance of inventories: While the precise percentages and quantities of inventories held by various kinds of businesses vary greatly, a typical business likely invests in inventory to the extent of 30 percent of its current assets and possibly as much as 90 percent of its working capital. Profit after taxes divided by total assets is known as return on investment (ROI), and it is a commonly used metric to assess managerial success. A reduction in inventories can lead to a considerable gain in return on investment, as they may constitute a substantial fraction of total assets.

If one is to truly approach inventory management in a company from the right perspective, two key ideas must be realized. These ideas start with the idea that a large portion of a company's inventory is actually stored capacity. Accordingly, the majority of inventory is an example of how the company uses its ability to produce a good before there is a real need for it. One of the main differences between the planning and control of a manufacturing company and a pure service company is this concept. The typical service provider cannot afford to plan and use capacity before demand for it arises; rather, it must wait to use capacity until demand is generated.

The second idea is that, despite the common assertion that "having too much inventory is one of our problems," inventory is virtually never an issue in any business. Inventory is typically a sign of how the company is operated. Although inventory is frequently blamed for issues, it is actually an indicator rather than the cause of the issue, albeit one that is frequently highly apparent and costly. In order to effectively manage inventory, it is necessary to look at the managerial strategies used in the company that result in the inventory. The chapter devotes at least some of its time to elucidating those relationships and will shed light on strategies for better managing them.

6.2 FUNCTIONS OF INVENTORY

There are several uses for inventories. Among the most crucial are the following:

1. To fulfill expected demand.

2. To make easier the demands of production.
3. To separate the production-distribution system's components.
4. To prevent stockouts.
5. To benefit from order cycles.
6. To benefit from bulk discounts or as a hedge against price hikes.
7. To allow for operations.

Let's examine each of these in turn.

To fulfill expected demand

A mechanic requesting a tool from a tool crib, a retail client buying new furniture, or a manufacturing operation can all be considered customers. Because these stocks are kept to meet predicted (i.e., average) demand, they are known as anticipation stocks. When classifying inventory according to the source of demand, there are basically two methods:

- ***Independent demand inventory*** – This kind of inventory usually has demand coming from sources outside the organization, usually from a third-party customer. It is considered independent because, for the most part, demand for it is unaffected by any firm internal activities. These goods are frequently the final products of manufacture, frequently a "sellable" finished good.
- ***Dependent demand inventory*** – The determination of how much of a given commodity to manufacture when is the primary internal choice that determines the source of dependent demand inventory. It should be noted that while some may believe that this is still dependent on customers, many businesses actually have the freedom to choose to create at rates and periods that range greatly from those of the external customer demand. This brings up the idea of inventory as capacity that has been stored.

A comparison could make the differences more clear. Assume the business produces cars. There is an independent demand for the completed cars from outside suppliers. However, the internal choice of how many cars to produce and when to make them determines the demand for the seats, wheels, and lights, etc.

For production planning and control, the difference between independent and dependent inventory is crucial. The methods and tools used to design and manage independent inventory differ greatly from those used to manage dependent inventory, and this leads to frequently highly disparate systems. Even the strategy used to meet each type's requirement varies. Forecasting independent demand is typically followed by sales order entry. On the other hand, dependent demand can be determined using a schedule that specifies what needs to be made when.

To make easier the demands of production

Businesses that see seasonal pattern in demand frequently accumulate inventory in the off-season in order to satisfy excessive demand during specific peak seasons. The term "seasonal inventories" is suitable for these stockpiles. Seasonal stocks are handled by businesses that process fresh fruits and vegetables. And the same goes for shops that sell Christmas trees, skis, snowmobiles, and greeting cards.

To separate the production-distribution system's components

In the past, industrial companies have relied on inventories as a means of preserving production continuity in the face of unforeseen circumstances like equipment malfunctions and accidents that result in temporary shutdowns of certain processes. While the issue is being fixed, other operations can be temporarily continued thanks to the buffers. Similar to this, businesses have employed completed goods inventory to protect sales operations from interruptions in manufacturing and raw material buffers to shield production from supplier delivery delays. Companies have recently looked more closely at buffer inventories, realizing the space and money they take up, and that identifying and removing sources of disturbance can significantly reduce the need to decouple activities.

To prevent stockouts

The possibility of shortages is increased by unanticipated rises in demand and delayed supply. Weather-related delays, supplier stockouts, incorrect material delivery, issues with quality, and other factors can all create delays. Keeping safety stocks, or supplies above typical demand to offset variations in lead time and demand, helps lower the chance of shortages.

To benefit from order cycles

A company frequently purchases in quantities more than what is needed right away in order to reduce purchasing and inventory expenditures. As a result, part or the entire purchase price must be set aside for future use. In a similar vein, producing in large rather than tiny numbers is typically more cost-effective. Further, extra output needs to be saved for later use. Thus, a company can buy and create in economic lot sizes thanks to inventory storage, eliminating the need to try to match short-term production or purchasing requirements with demand. Order cycles, or periodic orders, are the outcome of this. Cycle stock is the term for the resulting stock. Economic lot sizes are not the only basis for order cycles. Sometimes it makes sense to place orders in bulk or on a regular basis to be economical.

To benefit from bulk discounts or as a hedge against price hikes

Sometimes a company will buy more than usual when it thinks a significant price increase is coming up. This is done to protect itself from the hike. A company's ability to store extra inventory also enables it to benefit from discounts for larger orders.

To allow for operations

Because production processes are not immediate, they require a certain amount of time, which means that work-in-process (WIP) inventory is usually present. Furthermore, pipeline inventories in a production-distribution system are caused by intermediate stocking of goods, which includes raw materials, semifinished goods, finished goods, and goods kept in warehouses as well as at production sites.

6.3 PURPOSE OF INVENTORY

Both understocking and overstocking of products can be caused by insufficient inventory control. Understocking causes production bottlenecks, late deliveries, lost sales, and unhappy customers; overstocking wastes money that could be better spent elsewhere. Overstocking may seem like the better of two evils, but when inventory holding costs are high – the cost of excessive overstocking may be astounding, and things can quickly spiral out of control. Managers finding out that their company has a 10-year supply of a certain commodity are not unheard of. (The company certainly made a nice purchase on it!)

Concerns about inventory management are twofold. The first is the quality of customer service, which is having the appropriate products in the correct amounts at the right location at the right time. The other is the expense of placing orders and maintaining inventory.

Maintaining affordable inventory expenses while providing customers with acceptable service is the overarching goal of inventory management. The decision-maker attempts to attain stocking equilibrium in order to do this. The time and size of orders (i.e., when to order and how much to order) are the two main judgments that he or she must make. Models that can be used to help with those decisions take up the majority of this unit.

Managers can assess the efficacy of inventory management using a variety of performance metrics. Of course, the most evident is customer satisfaction, which can be measured by looking at the quantity and number of backorders as well as customer complaints. Inventory turnover, or the ratio of average inventory investment to annual cost of goods sold, is a commonly used metric. The number of times the inventory is sold annually is shown by the turnover ratio. In general, a larger ratio is preferable as it suggests a more effective utilization of inventory. This measure's ability to compare businesses of various sizes within the same industry is one of its advantages. Days of inventory on hand, a metric that represents the anticipated number of days of sales that can be met with current inventory, is another helpful indicator. In this case, balance is preferred; a high number of days may indicate excess inventory, whilst a low number may indicate a possibility of stock outs.

6.4 CONDITIONS FOR SUCCESSFUL INVENTORY MANAGEMENT

When it comes to inventory, management has two primary responsibilities. The first is to set up the inventory tracking system, and the second is to decide what to order and when to order it. The following are necessary for management to be effective:

1. A method for tracking the available and ordered inventories.
2. An accurate demand prediction that provides a possible forecast error indicator.
3. Understanding lead times and their variability.
4. Reasonable estimations of the expenses associated with ordering, shortages, and carrying inventory.
5. A system of categorization for inventory items.

Let's examine each of these prerequisites in more detail.

6.4.1 SYSTEMS FOR INVENTORY COUNTING

Systems for counting inventory might be continuous or periodic. In a *periodic system*, the determination of how much to order of each item is based on a physical count of the inventory items conducted at regular intervals (e.g., weekly, monthly). A lot of small retailers employ this strategy: A manager periodically counts the number of items on hand by inspecting the stockroom and shelves. The manager then determines the order quantity based on an estimate of the amount that will be required before the next delivery period. This kind of system has the benefit of allowing orders for many items to be placed simultaneously, which can save money on order processing and shipping. Periodic evaluations have a number of drawbacks as well. A deficiency of control occurs in between reviews. Another is the requirement to keep extra stock on hand to guard against shortages in between review periods.

In order to provide information on the current level of inventory for each item, a system of perpetual inventory, commonly referred to as *continuous review* system, tracks the removals from inventory continuously. A specific quantity, Q, is ordered when the amount in stock falls below a predefined minimum. The control that this system offers through ongoing inventory withdrawal monitoring is evident. The fixed-order quantity is another benefit; management may choose the ideal order quantity. The additional expense of record keeping is one drawback of this strategy. Moreover, mistakes, theft, spoiling, and other issues that can lower the effective amount of inventory necessitate the frequent physical count of stocks in order to confirm records. Customer deposits and withdrawals from banks are instances of ongoing inventory change reporting.

There are many different levels of complexity in continuous inventory review systems. A basic system known as a "*two-bin system*" keeps inventories in two containers. Before the first bin's contents are depleted, items are removed from it. It's then time to place a new order. There are occasions when an order card is tucked under the first bin. A buffer of excess stock in the second bin helps to lessen the likelihood of a stockout in the event that the order is delayed or that usage exceeds expectations. The buffer of stock will last until the order is filled. This method has the benefit of not requiring a record of each inventory withdrawal; nevertheless, it has the drawback that the reorder card might not be returned for a number of reasons (e.g., misplaced, the person responsible forgets to turn it in).

6.4.1.1 CONTINUOUS INVENTORY REVIEW SYSTEM

Every item's inventory level is continuously recorded in a continuous inventory review system. When the available inventory falls below a certain level – known as the *reorder point* (ROP) – a fresh order is issued to top off the stock. To reduce the overall cost of inventory, a fixed quantity order is issued. A more thorough discussion of this amount, also known as the *economic order quantity*, is provided later in this unit.

The benefit of the continuous review system is that management is always aware of the inventory situation because the inventory level is regularly reviewed. This is helpful for necessities like replacement components, pharmacy supplies, raw materials and supplies. On the other side, keeping an ongoing track on the quantity of inventory on hand can also be expensive.

A simple record that many pharmacy owners keep is an illustration of a continuous inventory system. Reorder cards are a common component of office inventory systems. They indicate when a new order has to be placed and are typically placed at the bottom of cases of paper clips or pens, or inside stacks of stationery.

These days, inventory systems frequently use digital information technology solutions to increase data entry speed and accuracy. One well-known example is the automated checkout system that many supermarkets and other establishments utilize, which is equipped with a laser scanner. When a product package's bar code, or Universal Product Code (UPC), is read by a laser scanner, the transaction is immediately logged and the inventory level is updated. This kind of technology is not only fast and precise, but it also gives managers up-to-date information on inventory levels. Bar code systems and handheld laser scanners are also used by distributors and suppliers to many manufacturing organizations to inventory materials, supplies, equipment, in-process parts, and finished goods.

ALONG THE INVENTORY REVIEW SYSTEM

RFID

Developed in the 1980s for tracking and access purposes, radio frequency identification (RFID) is a relatively recent automated identification and data capture (AIDC) technology. Because these wireless AIDC systems enable non-contact reading, they work well in harsh settings like manufacturing and other places where barcode labels would not hold up. Because RFID can follow moving items, it has made a name for itself in a variety of applications, such as automatic vehicle identification (AVI) systems and animal identification. Globally, the technology is now a major component of automated systems for data identification, gathering, and analysis.

The non-contact, non-line-of-sight feature of RFID technology is a major advantage for all types of systems. Barcodes and other optically read technologies would be worthless in visually demanding situations like snow, fog, ice, paint, crusted filth, and other materials. However, tags can read through a range of materials. RFID tags may also be read remarkably quickly in difficult conditions; most of the time, they react in less than 100 milliseconds. An active RFID system's read/write functionality is also a big benefit for interactive applications like maintenance tracking and work-in-process monitoring. RFID has become essential for a variety of automated data collecting and identification applications that would not be possible otherwise, even though it is a more expensive technology than barcode.

6.4.1.2 PERIODIC INVENTORY REVIEW SYSTEM

The inventory on hand is counted at predetermined intervals, such as once a week or at the end of each month, in a periodic inventory review system, also known as a *fixed-time-period system*. Following the determination of the amount of inventory in stock, an order is placed for the quantity necessary to restore the inventory to the target level. This technique has the benefit of requiring little or no record keeping because the inventory level is not tracked at all during the time between orders. Less direct control is the drawback. Because of this, periodic inventory systems usually have higher inventory levels than continuous review systems in order to prevent unplanned stockouts early in the specified period. Every time a periodic order is placed, a new order amount must likewise be calculated according to such a method.

A college or university bookstore serves as an illustration of a periodic inventory assessment procedure. Textbook orders are typically placed using the periodic approach, and during the first few weeks of a semester or quarter, a count of the number of textbooks in stock (for each course) is made. Next, based on the quantity still in stock and the anticipated course enrollments for the upcoming term (i.e., demand), an order is placed for new textbooks for the upcoming semester. Periodic systems are occasionally used by smaller retail establishments, pharmacies, grocery stores, and offices. Typically, a vendor checks the stock level every week or month to determine how much has to be ordered.

The most common kind of bar code scanner for customers is the one used on retail cash registers. In most cases, the bar code is a single line consisting of 11 digits, the first 6 of which identify the manufacturer and the final 5 of which are allotted to a particular product. This employee is scanning a bar code for inventory control using a portable, handheld bar code scanner. Not only can it identify the goods, but it can also provide information about its origin, intended destination, and handling instructions while in transit.

6.4.2 INFORMATION ABOUT LEAD TIMES AND FORECASTS FOR DEMAND

Having accurate forecasts of the quantity and timing of demand is crucial since inventories are utilized to meet demand requirements. In a similar vein, it's critical to ascertain the estimated time of order delivery. Furthermore, managers must understand the degree to which lead time (the interval of time between placing an order and receiving it) and demand may differ; the higher the possibility of variability, the higher the requirement for extra stock to lower the chance of a shortage in between deliveries. Consequently, forecasting and inventory management are closely related.

Real sales are electronically recorded by point-of-sale (POS) systems. Accurate sales information can significantly improve inventory control and forecasting: These systems provide real-time information on actual demand, allowing management to adjust replenishment decisions as needed. By granting suppliers access to this data, these systems are being highlighted more and more as crucial components of efficient operations.

6.4.3 INFORMATION OF COSTS

Inventories have three fundamental costs: holding, transaction (ordering), and shortage costs.

Carrying or holding costs are associated with having things in physical storage. Interest, insurance, taxes (in certain states), depreciation, deterioration, spoiling, pilfering, breakage, and warehousing expenses (heat, light, rent, and security) are among the expenses. They also include the potential expenses incurred by having money tied up in goods that could be spent elsewhere. Keep in mind that the relevant part of these costs is the variable portion.

The importance of the different holding cost components varies depending on the kind of item; nonetheless, taxes, insurance, and interest are often calculated using an inventory's dollar worth. Theft is more likely to occur with items that are extremely expensive (such as TVs and cars) or readily disguised (such as calculators, transistor radios, and pocket cameras). Fresh produce, seafood, meats, and poultry, as well as baked items, can quickly deteriorate and spoil. There are other goods with short shelf lives, like film, medications, salad dressings, dairy products, and batteries.

Holding or carrying costs can be expressed as a dollar total per unit or as a percentage of the unit price. Either way, the average yearly holding costs for an item are between 20 and

40 percent of its worth. Put another way, it might cost $20 to $40 to store a $100 item for a year. The costs associated with handling, insurance, storage facilities, theft, obsolescence, breakage, depreciation, taxes, and the opportunity cost of capital are all included in holding costs. It goes without saying that high holding costs encourage frequent replenishment and low inventory levels.

The price of purchasing and receiving inventory is known as the **ordering cost**. These are the expenses that change depending on when an order is really placed. These include figuring out how much is required, creating invoices, paying for shipment, checking the goods for amount and quality when they arrive, and putting them in temporary storage. Regardless of the quantity of the purchase, ordering expenses are often stated as a set dollar amount every order. Ordering costs can include the expenses related to keeping up the technology that is required to track orders.

Analogous to ordering costs, **machine setup costs** are expressed as a fixed charge each production run, regardless of run size. Examples of these expenses include adjusting the machine, changing cutting tools to prepare the equipment for the task, acquiring the requisite materials, and removing the prior material stock.

There would be numerous small lots created if there were no expenses or delays associated with switching from one batch to another. This would result in lower inventory levels and cost savings. Reducing these setup costs to allow for smaller lot sizes is one of the challenges facing modern manufacturing (a Just-in-Time (JIT) system aims to do this, as it will be covered later in this unit).

When demand outpaces the available supplies, **shortage costs** arise. These expenses may consist of late fees, lost customer goodwill, missed opportunities, and other such expenses. Furthermore, the cost of downtime of machine is regarded as a shortage cost if the shortfall affects an item transported for internal use (such as to supply an assembly line). These expenses may potentially reach several hundred dollars per minute or higher. Costs associated with shortages can occasionally be evaluated subjectively and are challenging to quantify.

An order for an item that runs out of stock must be canceled or postponed until the item's supply is restored. Stockout is the term used to describe the situation where orders are canceled due to unmet demand. When an order is placed and then held until the item's inventory is replenished, it's referred to as a backorder. Carrying inventory to meet demand requires a trade-off with the expenses associated with stockouts and backorders. Because it may not be able to estimate lost income, the impact of lost clients, or lateness penalties, this balance can occasionally be challenging to attain. The presumed scarcity cost is often merely an estimate, though typically a range of such prices might be specified.

Finding the lowest overall cost that results from the addition of the four separate costs – holding, ordering, setup, and shortage – is necessary to determine the appropriate amount to order from the supplier or the size of lots submitted to the manufacturing facilities. Of course, a crucial element that could affect inventory costs is the timing of these orders.

A manufactured F-150 Lightning. Ford's adoption of Just-In-Time inventory management (Source: https://www.nytimes.com/2022/06/10/business/henry-ford-supply-chain.html)

The use of "just in time" inventory by Ford, which involves maintaining lean warehouses to reduce expenses, is attributed to the financial markets and their emphasis on return on invested capital.

ALONG THE INVENTORY MANAGEMENT

HAIER'S ZERO INVENTORY MANAGEMENT MODEL

The Haier Group is the world's fifth-largest producer of "white electric appliances" and the biggest in China. This $8.6 billion corporation employs over 30,000 people, produces 13,000 distinct items, and sells its goods in 160 countries. Haier Group builds an internal supply chain system, ERP system, logistics and distribution system, capital flow management and settlement system, distribution management system, and customer service response system throughout the nation, connecting and integrating subsystems with order information flow as the core.

Haier Group combines the zero inventory concepts with the national conditions of China. The production line can produce a mixed flow of various product categories thanks to Haier's CIMS system. In addition, Haier has created six auxiliary systems, such as the ERP system, JIT three-fixed distribution system, and EOS (business system). The ERP and CRM systems work together to remove barriers to accurate information transmission and synchronous communication, allowing Haier Group to meet customer demands and deliver products on time, ultimately leading to zero inventory. Haier's CRM system achieves zero-distance sales.

Issues with Haier's Zero Inventory Control

1. *Inadequate forecasting and analysis of the market*: Because Haier's estimation of the market's sudden orders is too inaccurate, the excess demand in orders cannot be filled in a timely way.
2. *No limitations on reserved safety stocks*: Because Haier's ultimate goal is zero inventory, the company has no excess inventory to support it and will be extremely passive when faced with unexpected demand in the market. If the market experiences a sudden spike in demand or encounters unforeseen circumstances like natural disasters, for example, the company may experience complete production stagnation, disrupt the original regular production timing, create tension throughout the entire supply chain, and incur significant financial losses. While Haier has benefited greatly from the zero inventory model in terms of cost and capital structure optimization, there will be significant hazards if the company pursues extreme zero inventory without setting aside safety stock limits.
3. *Although there is a lot of reliance on suppliers, the evaluation criteria are overly rigid*: A steady and dependable supplier is a crucial requirement for businesses to achieve zero inventory goals, and the zero inventory management models strengthen the cooperative relationship between them and their suppliers. After receiving an order, suppliers to the business request quick delivery in order to guarantee that the business can meet its deadlines for production, distribution, delivery, and other processes. As a result, businesses rely heavily on their suppliers; if one of them fails to deliver on time, it will negatively impact the enterprise's subsequent links, including customer satisfaction and market profitability. Therefore, in order to screen and monitor suppliers, more thorough standards must be established.

Haier's options for action

Based on the prior knowledge, it is evident that Haier benefits from the zero inventory management strategy in terms of supply chain, logistics, and cash flow. Haier can begin optimizing the enterprise model by focusing on the following areas.

1. *Enterprise process optimization driven by the market*: Haier's zero inventory management strategy cannot be sustained by sticking with the old "demand and supply" approach; instead, it must bolster a

more thorough market demand prediction. The Haier Company can set up a dedicated department to work on market forecasting, fully utilize big data from online and offline platforms and affiliated businesses, anticipate and analyze potential windows of demand fluctuation, and select the right amount of inventory reserves based on various scenarios.

2. *Establish a minimum quantity for safety stock*: Use the prior market prediction to determine the minimal safety stock in order to be ready for demand changes brought on by market emergencies, avoid missing out on business opportunities, and retain clients.
3. *Zero inventories cannot fully replace safety stock*: Furthermore, this portion of the safety stock may be given to outside logistics firms to be stored. By doing so, Haier can avoid missing out on opportunities due to fluctuations in demand, avoid adding to its initial logistics workload, avoid having to spend more money on labor and materials, increase operational efficiency and financial gains, and lower operating costs associated with logistics.

6.5 A SYSTEM OF CLASSIFICATION

The fact that things kept in inventory are not equally important in terms of money invested, potential for profit, volume of sales or usage, or stockout penalties is a crucial component of inventory management. A manufacturer of automobiles, for example, may stock electrical systems, engine assemblies, and various nuts and bolts. Giving each of these things the same amount of attention would be unfeasible. A more sensible strategy would be to divide up control efforts based on the relative value of different inventory items. Giving each of these things the same amount of attention would be unfeasible. A more sensible strategy would be to divide up control efforts based on the relative value of different inventory items.

The A-B-C strategy divides control efforts across inventory items based on their relative importance, which is often determined by multiplying the dollar value per unit by the annual utilization rate. Items are often categorized into three classes: A (extremely significant), B (moderately important), and C (least important). Nevertheless, the precise count of categories could range throughout organizations, contingent upon the degree to which a company desires to distinguish its control initiatives. Goods typically make up 15–20 percent of the total number of items in inventory, while 60–70 percent of the dollar utilization is attributed to these three classes of items. On the other hand, C items could make up roughly 60% of the total number of products in an inventory, but just 10% of its total dollar usage. These percentages differ from company to company, but generally speaking, a small number of goods will bear a disproportionate amount of the value or expense of an inventory, and control efforts ought to be directed at these things more heavily. For example, to ensure that customer service standards are met, A items should be closely monitored through regular checks of the amounts on hand and, when possible, control over withdrawals.

Only loose control (two-bin system, bulk orders) should be applied to the C products, while controls for the B items should fall somewhere in the middle of the two extremes.

Within the automotive industry, engine and chessis would be classified as A items that require daily or weekly replenishment; tires, batteries, oil, and transmission fluid could be classified as B items that require ordering every two or four weeks; and C items would include things like valve stems, fan belts, radiator caps, hoses, and windshield wiper blades, among other things. Due to the minimal penalty for stockouts, C products may be ordered every two or three months, or they may even be permitted to stockout before being restocked.

Example: Value-based inventory utilization annually

Part Number	Dollar Usage Per Year ($)	Percentage of the entire value (%)
0022	96,000	40.79
0068	76,000	32.29
0027	26,000	11.04
0003	16,000	6.80
0082	12,000	5.09
0054	7,000	2.97
0036	1,000	0.42
0019	700	0.30
0023	400	0.17
0041	250	0.11
Total	235,350	100.00

A-B-C Inventory item grouping

Classification of Parts	Part Number	Dollar Usage Per Year ($)	Percentage of the entire value (%)
A	0022, 0068	172,000	73.08
B	0027, 0003, 0082	54,000	22.94
C	0054, 0036, 0019, 0023, 0041	9,350	3.97
Total		235,350	100.00

A-B-C Inventory classifiation (inventory value for each group versus the group's portion of the total list)

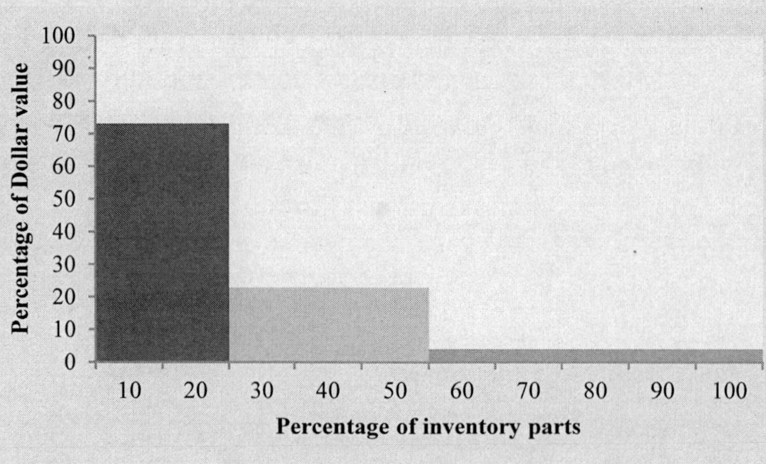

Keep in mind that C items are not always trivial; an assembly line shutdown caused by a stockout of C items, such as the nuts and bolts needed to assemble produced goods, can be very expensive. However, ordering some things in higher quantities or a little early would not result in substantially more expense because of the low annual dollar volume of C items.

6.6 ECONOMIC ORDER QUANTITY MODELS

In a continuous, or fixed-order-quantity, system, a fixed amount is ordered when inventory hits a certain level, often known as the reorder point. The economic order quantity (EOQ), or economic lot-size model, is the most popular and conventional method for figuring out how much to order in a continuous system. Ford Harris, a worker at Westinghouse, is credited with publishing the first documented derivation of the fundamental EOQ model formula in 1915.

The EOQ model's purpose is to identify the ideal order size that reduces overall inventory expenses. The EOQ model comes in a few different forms, based on different assumptions on the inventory system. The production quantity model and the fundamental EOQ model will be discussed.

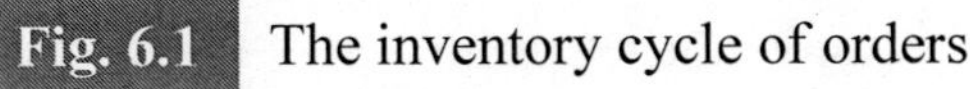
Fig. 6.1 The inventory cycle of orders

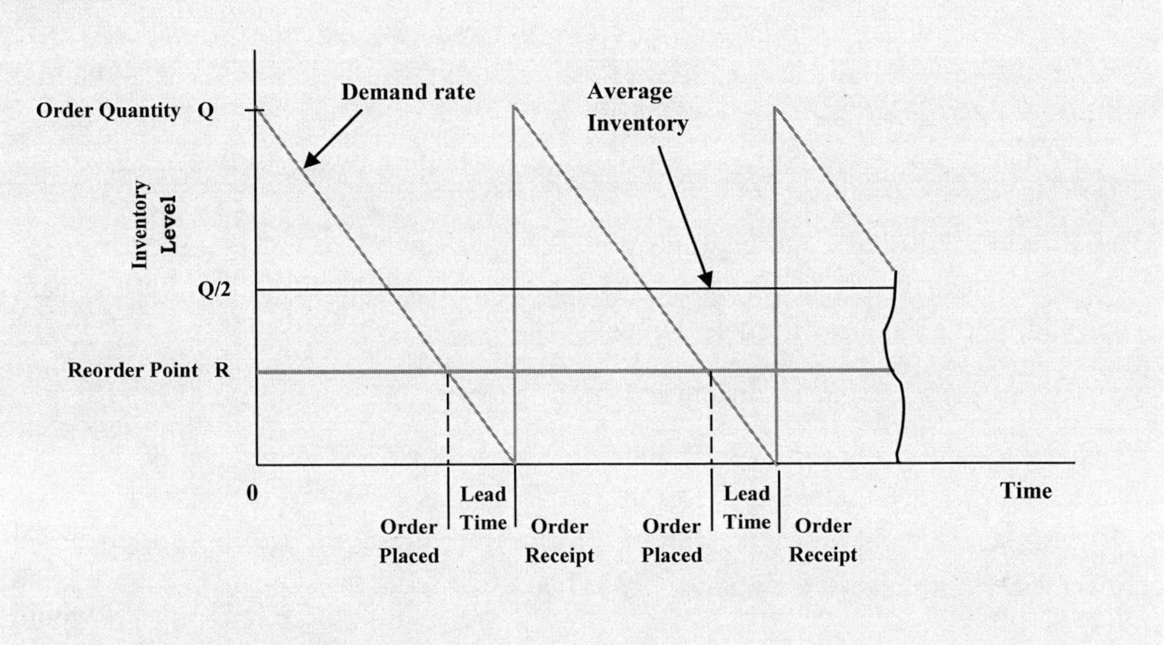

6.6.1 THE BASIC EOQ MODEL

A method for figuring out the optimal order size that minimizes the total of carrying and ordering costs is the foundation of the EOQ model. Under the following constrictive and simplifying assumptions, the model formula is derived:

- Demand is known for sure and remains constant over time.
- Shortages are not permitted.
- Orders are received with a consistent lead time.
- All order quantities are received simultaneously.

Fig. 6.1, which outlines the continuous-inventory order cycle system built into the EOQ model, reflects these fundamental model assumptions. Order quantity Q is received and depleted at a steady rate throughout time. A new order is placed when the inventory level drops to the reorder point, R; delivery takes a certain amount of time, known as the *lead time*. There won't be any shortages because the order is received all at once right before demand uses up the entire inventory, or until the inventory level drops to zero. As a result, the cycle is continually repeated with the same order quantity, lead time, and reorder point.

The order size that minimizes the total of carrying and ordering costs is known as the economic order quantity. The relationship between these two expenses is inverse. The ordering cost will decrease as the order size grows because fewer orders are needed, but the carrying cost will increase since there will be more average inventory on hand. Therefore, the optimal order quantity is essentially a compromise between these two costs that are inversely connected.

The cost per order, shown as C_o, is multiplied by the total number of orders placed over the year to get the overall yearly ordering cost. Given the assumption of known and constant annual demand, *D*, the number of orders will equal *D*/*Q*, where *Q* is the order size and

$$\text{Annual ordering cost} = \frac{C_o D}{Q}$$

In this equation, *Q* is the only variable; C_o and *D* are constant values. Consequently, the order quantity affects how much the ordering cost is relative to other costs.

The average inventory level is multiplied by the yearly per-unit carrying cost, denoted by C_c, to get the total annual carrying cost. Fig. 6.1 illustrates that the average inventory level is half of *Q* or *Q*/2.

$$\text{Annual carrying cost} = \frac{C_c Q}{2}$$

The ordering and carrying costs add up to the total annual inventory cost:

$$TC = \frac{C_o D}{Q} + \frac{C_c Q}{2}$$

The ordering cost and carrying cost inversely relate to one another, as seen by the convex total cost curve in Fig. 6.2.

Fig. 6.2 The Cost Model for EOQ

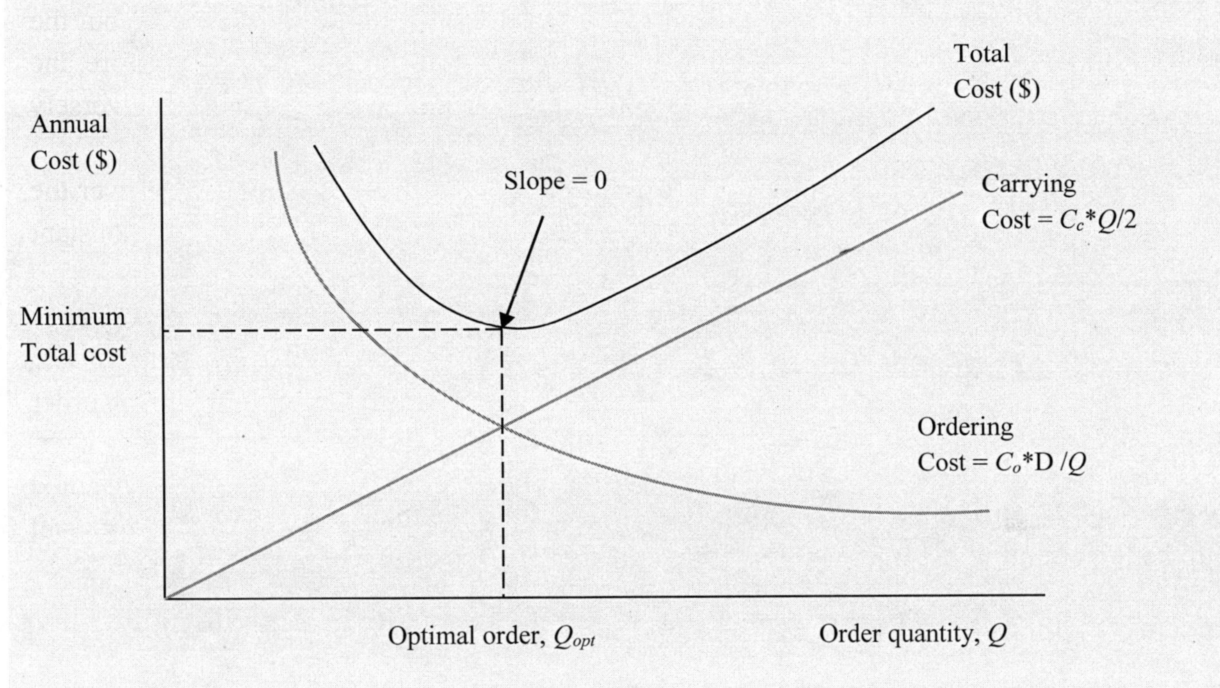

The point in Fig. 6.2 where the total cost curve is at its minimum – exactly where the ordering cost curve and the carrying cost curve intersect – is the location of the optimal order quantity. This allows us to solve for Q by equating the two cost functions and determining the optimum value of Q:

$$\frac{C_o D}{Q} = \frac{C_c Q}{2}$$

$$Q^2 = \frac{2C_o D}{C_c}$$

$$Q_{opt} = \sqrt{\frac{2C_o D}{C_c}}$$

As an alternative, the optimum value for Q can be found by differentiating the total cost curve with respect to Q, solving for Q, and setting the resultant function's slope to zero (the minimum point on the total cost curve):

$$TC = \frac{C_o D}{Q} + \frac{C_c Q}{2}$$

$$\frac{\partial TC}{\partial Q} = -\frac{C_o D}{Q^2} + \frac{C_c}{2}$$

$$0 = -\frac{C_o D}{Q^2} + \frac{C_c}{2}$$

$$Q_{opt} = \sqrt{\frac{2C_o D}{C_c}} \qquad \ldots (6.1)$$

By entering Q_{opt}, the value for the optimal order size, into the total cost calculation, one can find the total minimal cost:

$$TC_{min} = \frac{C_o D}{Q_{opt}} + \frac{C_c Q_{opt}}{2} \qquad \ldots (6.2)$$

Example 6.1: The Economic Order Quantity

The aCart automobile shop stocks spare parts in its store and sells it online on its website. The store stocks several brands of spare parts; however, its biggest seller is Perfect Components Company.

The company wants to determine the optimal order size and total inventory cost for spare parts given an estimated annual demand of 9,000 parts, an annual carrying cost of \$0.50 per part, and an ordering cost of \$125 per order. It would also like to know the number of orders that will be made annually and the time between orders (i.e., the order cycle).

Solution

$$C_c = \$0.50 \text{ per part}$$

$$C_o = \$125 \text{ per order}$$

$$D = 9{,}000 \text{ parts}$$

The optimal order size is

$$Q_{opt} = \sqrt{\frac{2C_oD}{C_c}}$$

$$= \sqrt{\frac{2(125)(9000)}{(0.50)}}$$

$$= 2{,}121 \text{ parts}$$

By substituting Q_{opt} to the total cost calculation, the total annual inventory cost may be found:

$$TC_{min} = \frac{C_oD}{Q_{opt}} + \frac{C_cQ_{opt}}{2}$$

$$= \frac{(125)(9000)}{2121} + \frac{(0.50)(2121)}{2}$$

$$= 530 + 530$$

$$= \$1060$$

The formula used to determine the annual number of orders is as follows:

$$\text{Number of orders per year} = \frac{D}{Q_{opt}}$$

$$= \frac{9000}{2121}$$

$$= 4 \text{ orders per year}$$

The order cycle, assuming that the business processes orders for 320 days a year, is:

$$\text{Order cycle time} = \frac{320}{D/Q_{opt}}$$

$$= \frac{320}{4} = 80 \text{ days}$$

Since it is based on estimations of carrying and ordering costs as well as deterministic demand, the optimal order quantity found in this example and generally is an approximation (although all of these factors are treated as known, certain values in the EOQ model). It is preferable to round the Q values to a practical value that is close by in practice. Generally speaking, a decimal place's precision is not required. In addition, mistakes in fluctuations in the cost parameters and demand tend to be dampened because the optimal number of orders is calculated from a square root. For instance, in Example 6.1, the optimal order size would have been $2000 (i.e., marginally reduced by 6%) if the order cost had actually been 20% higher, or $150, and the carrying cost by 50% higher (i.e., $0.75 instead of $0.50). Since the two inventory costs are inversely related, variations in one will typically negate the other. Because of this, the EOQ model is stable and comparatively resilient to inaccuracies in demand and cost predictions, which has served to increase its recognition.

6.6.2 THE MODEL OF PRODUCTION QUANTITY

The production quantity model, also known as the gradual usage and non-instantaneous receipt model, is a variant of the fundamental EOQ model. The requirement that all orders be received at once is relaxed in this EOQ model. Over time, the order quantity is progressively received, and the inventory level is being replenished while also being decreased. When the producer and inventory user are the same, like in a manufacturing process when a part is made to be used in a larger assembly, this kind of scenario is frequently encountered. This can also happen when orders are supplied on a regular basis or when a retailer additionally handles production.

The progressive replenishment model's assumptions are comparable to those of the EOQ model; however, units are received gradually during production as opposed to orders being received in a single delivery. These are the assumptions:

- There's only one item at work.
- Demand annually is known.
- The rate of utilization never changes.
- Although production happens on a sporadic basis, usage happens continuously.
- The rate of production never changes.
- There is no variation in lead time.
- Discounts for larger quantities are not available.

Fig. 6.3 shows how creating a batch of a specific item on a regular basis affects inventory. Inventory builds at a rate equal to the difference between production and utilization rates during the cycle's production phase. For instance, inventory will accumulate at the rate of 30 – 10 = 20 units per day if the daily production rate is 30 and the daily usage rate is 10. The inventory level will rise as long as manufacturing is underway and start to fall as soon as production is stopped. As a result, the inventory level will peak at the point of production discontinuation. Production is restarted and the cycle continues until the available inventory is depleted.

Fig. 6.3 EOQ complemented by progressive replenishment of inventories

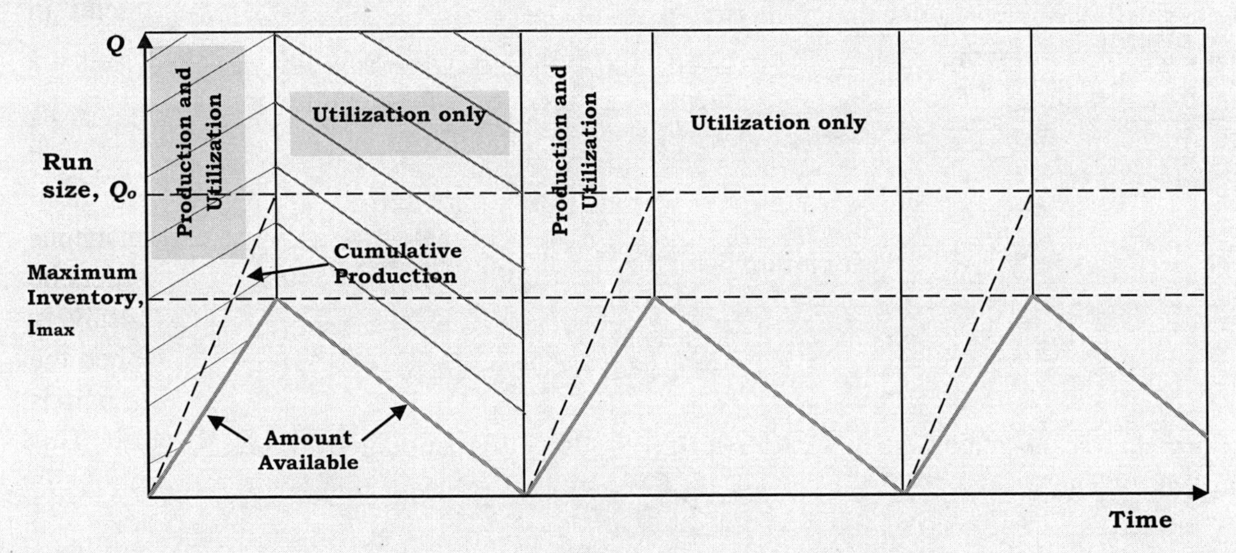

Since the company produces the product on its own, there are no actual ordering costs. However, setup costs are associated with each manufacturing run, or batch; they are the expenses incurred to get the equipment ready for use, including cleaning, adjusting, and replacing fixtures and tools. Because setup costs are unaffected by the size of the lot (run), they are similar to ordering expenses. They receive the exact same treatment in the formula.

The maximum inventory level in this model isn't Q; instead, it's a value that's been adjusted to account for the order quantity being used up during the order receipt time. We define the following model-specific parameters in order to calculate the average inventory level:

p = daily rate at which the order is received over time, also known as the production rate.

d = daily rate at which inventory is demanded.

Since we are still assuming that there won't be any shortages, the demand rate cannot exceed the production rate. Additionally, if $d = p$, there won't be an order size because products will be consumed at the same rate as they are produced. This model requires that the production rate be higher than the demand rate ($p \geq d$).

Looking at Fig. 6.3, we can see that the order quantity divided by the production rate, or *Q*/*p*, determines how long it takes to complete receiving an order. For instance, an order of 120 units will be received over the course of 4 days if the manufacturing rate, *p*, is 30 units per day. The demand rate, *d*, is multiplied to get the amount of inventory that will be consumed or depleted over the given time period (i.e., (*Q*/*p*)*d*). For instance, 40 units would be consumed if the order takes 4 days to arrive and during that period the inventory runs out or 10 units are used every day. Consequently, the order-size less the amount used up during the receiving period, calculated as follows, represents the maximum amount of inventory on hand.

$$\text{Maximum inventory level} = Q - \frac{Q}{p}d$$

$$= Q\left(1 - \frac{d}{p}\right)$$

Since this is the maximum inventory level, dividing this amount by 2 yields the average inventory level.

$$\text{Average inventory level} = \frac{1}{2}\left[Q\left(1 - \frac{d}{p}\right)\right]$$

$$= \frac{Q}{2}\left(1 - \frac{d}{p}\right)$$

When average inventory is used, the total carrying cost using this method is

$$\text{Total carrying cost} = \frac{C_c Q}{2}\left(1 - \frac{d}{p}\right)$$

In this instance, the production setup cost, C_o, is frequently the ordering cost.

Thus, the following formula is used to compute the total annual inventory cost:

$$TC = \frac{C_o D}{Q} + \frac{C_c Q}{2}\left(1 - \frac{d}{p}\right) \qquad \text{... (6.3)}$$

When we differentiate (*TC*) in relation to *Q* and set its value to zero, we obtain

$$\frac{\partial(TC)}{\partial Q} = -\frac{D}{Q^2}C_o + \frac{1}{2}\left(1 - \frac{d}{p}\right)C_c = 0$$

The optimal value of Q is

$$Q^* = \sqrt{\frac{2DC_o}{C_c\left(1-\frac{d}{p}\right)}} \quad \ldots (6.4)$$

Other Characteristics of the Model

1. Optimal number of production run per year

$$N^* = \frac{D}{Q^*} = \sqrt{\frac{\left(1-\frac{d}{p}\right)C_cD}{2C_o}} \quad \ldots (6.5)$$

2. Length of each lot size production run

$$T_{p^*} = \frac{Q^*}{p} = \sqrt{\frac{2DC_o}{C_c p(p-d)}} \quad \ldots (6.6)$$

3. Total minimum inventory cost

$$TC^* = \frac{D}{Q^*}C_o + \frac{Q^*}{2}\left(1-\frac{d}{p}\right)C_c$$

$$= DC_o + \sqrt{\frac{2DC_o}{C_c}\left(\frac{p}{p-d}\right)} + \frac{1}{2}\left(1-\frac{d}{p}\right)C_c\sqrt{\frac{2DC_o}{C_c}\left(\frac{p}{p-d}\right)}$$

$$TC^* = \sqrt{2DC_oC_c\left(1-\frac{d}{p}\right)} \quad \ldots (6.7)$$

Example 6.2: The gradual usage and non-instantaneous receipt model

Assume that aCar dealership in automobiles owns a manufacturing plant where it makes pistons. The cost of setting up the production process to create a piston is known as the ordering cost, or C_o. C_o is equal to $125. Remember that D = 9,000 units annually and C_c = $0.50 per unit. The manufacturing plant makes 150 pistons every day and is open on the same days as the store, or 320 days in total. Find the optimal order size, the overall cost of inventory, the time it takes to receive an order, the annual number of orders, and the maximum amount of inventory.

Solution

$$C_o = \$125$$

$$C_c = \$0.50$$

$$D = 9{,}000 \text{ units}$$

$$d = \frac{9{,}000}{320} = 28$$

$$p = 150 \text{ units per day}$$

The following formula is used to get the optimal order size:

$$Q^* = \sqrt{\frac{2DC_o}{C_c\left(1 - \frac{d}{p}\right)}}$$

$$= \sqrt{\frac{2(125)(9000)}{0.50\left(1 - \frac{28}{150}\right)}} = 2{,}352 \text{ units}$$

The following formula is used to obtain the total minimum annual inventory cost by substituting this amount.

$$TC^* = \sqrt{2DC_oC_c\left(1 - \frac{d}{p}\right)}$$

$$= \sqrt{2 * 9000 * 125 * 0.50 * \left(1 - \frac{28}{150}\right)} = \$957$$

The term "production run" refers to the duration of time it takes to receive an order for this kind of manufacturing process.

$$\text{Production run} = \frac{Q}{p}$$

$$= \frac{2352}{150} = 15.68 \text{ days per order}$$

The number of production runs that will be made is actually equal to the number of orders placed annually:

$$\text{Number of production runs (from orders)} = \frac{D}{Q}$$

$$= \frac{9000}{2352} = 3.83 \text{ runs per year}$$

Finally, the maximum possible inventory level is:

$$\text{Maximum inventory level} = Q\left(1 - \frac{d}{p}\right)$$

$$= 2352\left(1 - \frac{28}{150}\right) = 1913 \text{ units}$$

As a result, aCart Company will need to reserve enough storage space to hold these 1,913 piston units.

6.7 QUANTITY DISCOUNTS

A quantity discount is an item's price reduction if a set number of units are ordered. An advertisement for a company may appear in the back of a magazine, promising to make specific clothing with an organization or company emblem. The price per shirt will be \$25 for orders of 100, \$20 for orders of 200, or \$15 for orders of 500 or more. When manufacturing companies place huge orders for supplies and materials, they often receive price discounts; similarly, when retail stores place large orders for merchandise, they sometimes receive discounted prices.

The basic EOQ model can be used to determine the optimal order size with quantity discounts; however, the application of the model is slightly altered. The total inventory cost function must now include the purchase price of the item being ordered:

$$TC = \frac{C_o D}{Q} + \frac{C_c Q}{2} + PD \qquad \dots (6.8)$$

where

P = Price of the item per unit

D = Yearly demand

Because purchase price had no bearing on the optimal order size, it was not taken into account in our previous basic EOQ formulation. The following formula uses *PD* as a constant value that would not change the overall cost curve's basic shape; that is, the curve's minimum point would remain at the same location and correspond to the same value of *Q*. Thus, regardless of the purchase price, the optimal order size is always the same. When a discount price is offered, however, it is linked to a certain order quantity, which could differ from the optimal order quantity. As a result, the client must weigh the trade-off between the EOQ cost and potentially higher carrying costs with the discount quantity. Therefore, when a discount is offered, the purchase price does influence the choice of order size.

6.7.1 QUANTITY DISCOUNTS WITH CONSTANT CARRYING COST

For a price schedule with two discounts, d_1 and d_2, the EOQ cost model with constant carrying costs is shown in Figure 4 for the following discounts:

Size of Order	Price
1 - 99	$10
100 - 199	$8
200+	$6

Each unit price has its own U-shaped total-cost curve when bulk discounts are available. Again, adding unit prices only elevates each curve by a certain amount. Nevertheless, each curve is raised by a different amount due to the variations in the unit prices: A total-cost curve will rise more slowly for smaller unit prices than for greater unit prices. Keep in mind that each curve only covers a fraction of the range of quantities; none of the curves applies to the whole range (see Fig. 6.4). Therefore, at the price breaks – the lowest quantities required to receive the discounts – the relevant or feasible total cost falls, curve by curve, from its original position on the curve with the highest unit price. As a result, the price breaks at 100 and 200 units in the above discount table. A total-cost curve with steps at the price breaks is the final result.

Every curve has a minimum, but those points are not always feasible. For instance, Fig. 6.4's $6 curve looks to have a minimum point of roughly 195 units. On the other hand, the discount table's pricing list suggests that 195 boxes will cost $8 per unit for an order size of that magnitude. The solid lines represent the actual total-cost curve; only those price-quantity combinations are practical. Finding the order quantity that will represent the lowest total cost for the full set of curves is the aim of the quantity discount model.

The model consists of two general cases. In one, carrying costs are expressed as a percentage of purchase price (e.g., 20% of unit price); in the other, carrying costs are expressed as a constant (e.g., $2 per unit). There will only be one minimal point when carrying costs are constant, and that minimum point will be at the same quantity for all curves. As a result, as seen in Fig. 6.4A, the total-cost curves line up vertically and only differ in that the lower unit costs are reflected by lower total-cost curves. (The horizontal purchasing cost lines have been removed for illustration purposes.)

If carrying costs are expressed as a percentage of unit price, the minimum point of each curve will vary. Lower pricing will result in lower carrying costs and larger minimum points since carrying costs are a function of price. The minimum point of each curve will therefore be to the right of the minimum point of the subsequent higher curve as the price drops. Refer to Fig. 6.4B.

Fig. 6.4 A portion of each price's total-cost curve makes up the total cost curve with quantity discounts.

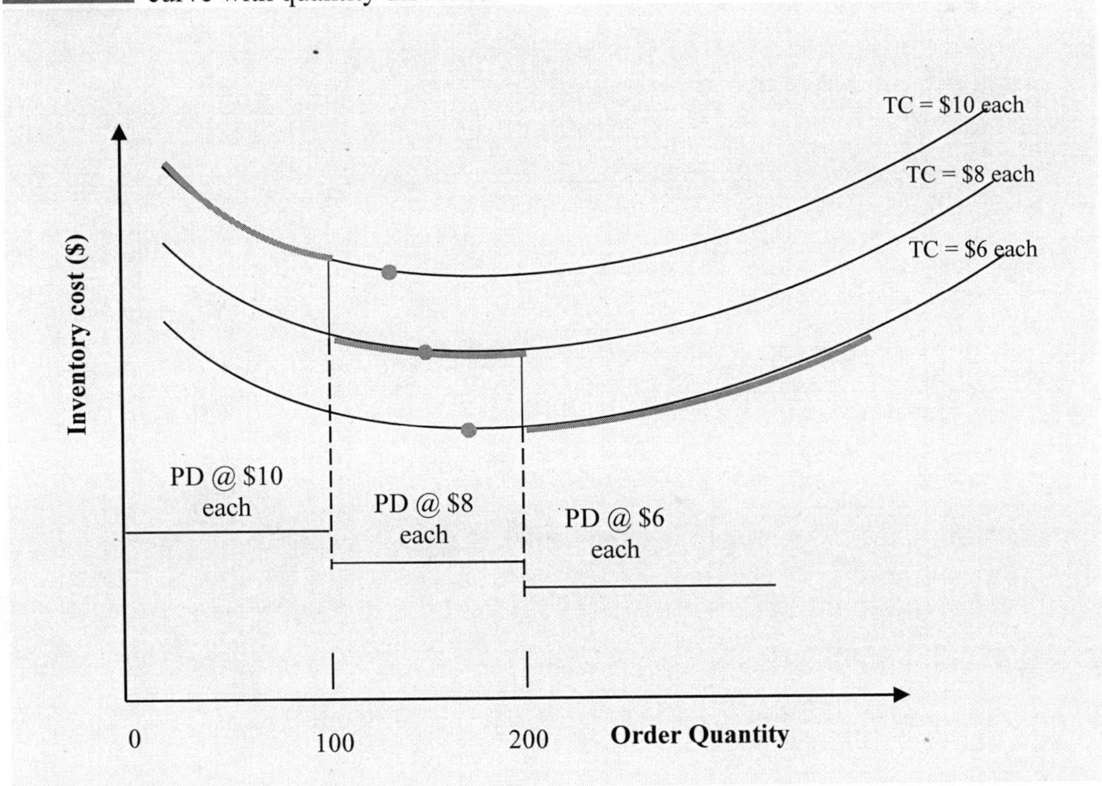

Depending on which of these two scenarios is important, there are subtle differences in the process for calculating the overall EOQ. The process for carrying costs that are constant is as follows:

1. Determine the common minimum point.
2. Since the ranges do not overlap, only one of the unit prices will have the lowest point in its viable range. Determine that range.
   a. The optimal order quantity is found in the lowest price range, where the feasible minimum point is located.
   b. Compute the total cost for the minimum point and the price breaks of any lower unit prices if the feasible minimum point falls into any other range. Examine the overall expenses; the optimal order quantity is the quantity (minimum point or price break) that results in the lowest overall cost.

Fig. 6.4A Comparison of the constant carrying costs (TC) curves; the minimum of each curve is at the same quantity

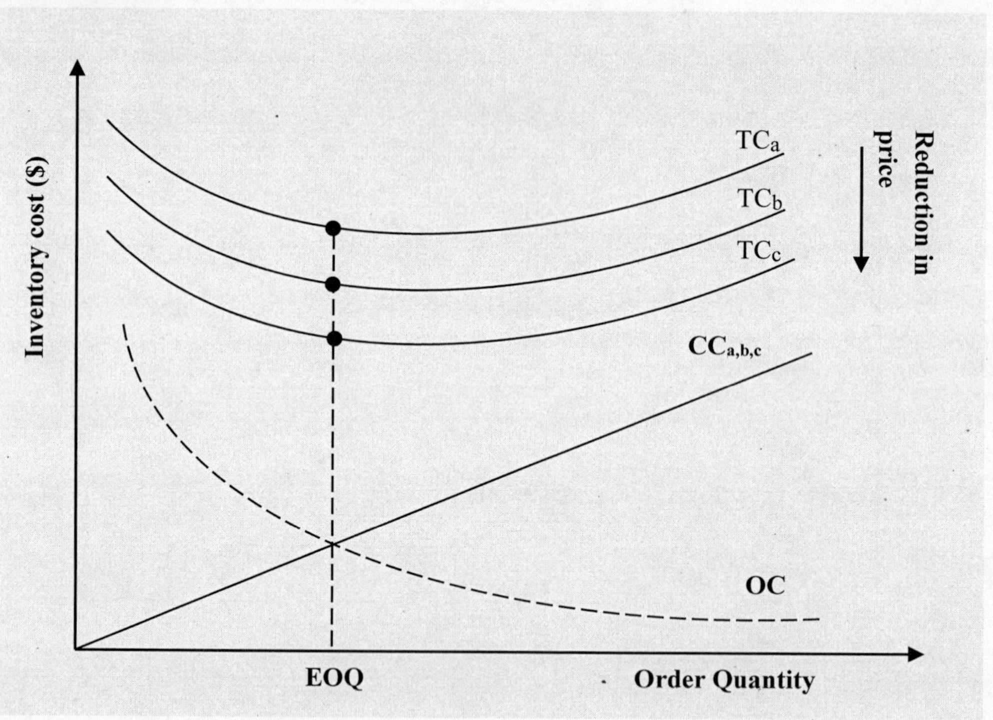

Fig. 6.4B Comparison of the varying carrying costs (TC) curves; the minimum of each curve is at different quantity

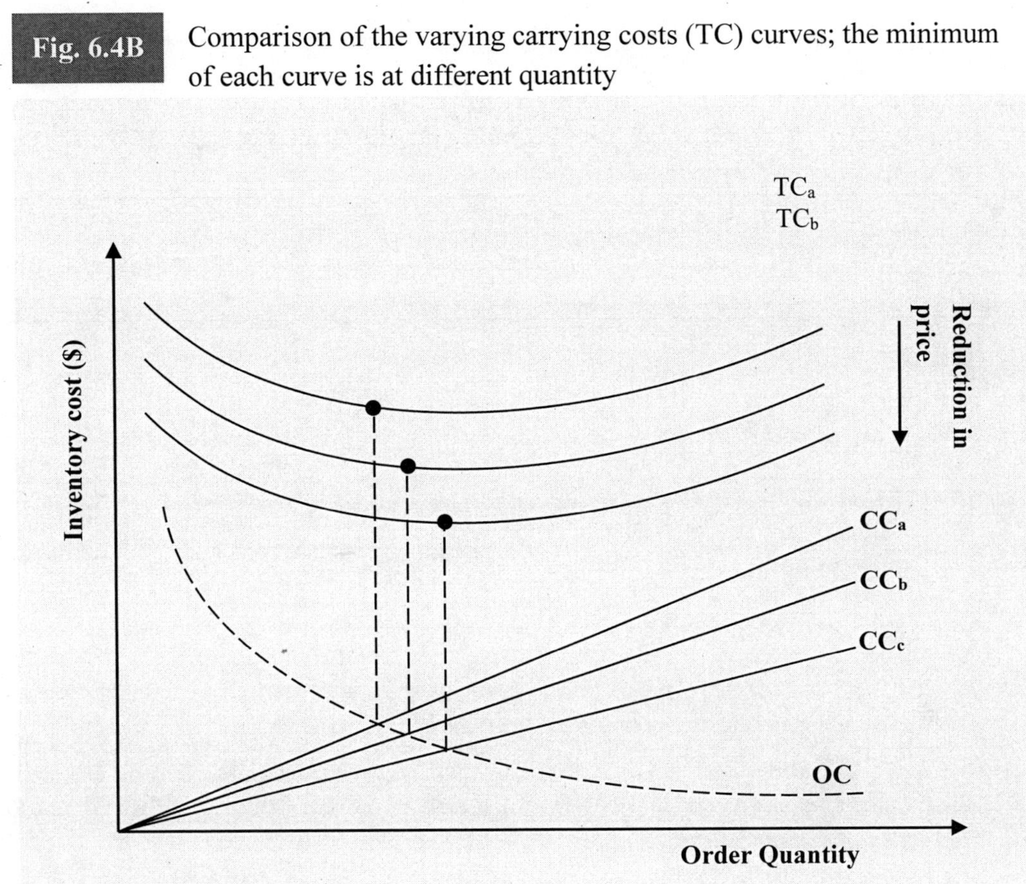

Example 6.3: A constant carrying cost quantity discount

Precision Measurement Company wishes to minimize its substantial microscope inventory. It has provided a quantity discount pricing plan, as follows, to a nearby chain of distributors:

Quantity	Price
1 – 79	\$1500
80 – 144	\$1200
145+	\$1000

The anticipated yearly demand for this specific kind of microscope is 180 units, while the annual carrying cost for the stores is \$150 and the ordering cost is \$3000. The distributors are trying to figure out if they should order the standard EOQ order size or take advantage of this discount.

Solution

Using the basic EOQ approach, first ascertain the optimal order size and total cost.

$$C_o = \$3000$$
$$C_c = \$150 \text{ per Microscope}$$
$$D = 180 \text{ Microscopes per year}$$

$$Q_{opt} = \sqrt{\frac{2C_oD}{C_c}}$$

$$Q_{opt} = \sqrt{\frac{2(3000)(180)}{150}} = 85 \text{ Microscopes}$$

Since the Q_{opt} = 85 units is elligible for the initial \$1200 discount, the total cost is calculated using this price.

$$TC_{min} = \frac{C_oD}{Q_{opt}} + \frac{C_cQ_{opt}}{2} + PD$$

$$= \frac{(3000)(180)}{85} + \frac{(150)(85)}{2} + (1200)(180)$$

$$TC_{min} = \$228{,}727$$

This total cost of \$228.727 needs to be compared to the total cost with an order size of 145 units and a discounted price of \$1000 because there is a discount for greater order sizes than 80 units (i.e., the range of quantity from 145 units and higher).

$$TC = \frac{C_oD}{Q} + \frac{C_cQ}{2} + PD$$

$$= \frac{(3000)(180)}{145} + \frac{(150)(145)}{2} + (1000)(180)$$

$$= 14599 + 180000 = \$194{,}599$$

Given that the overall cost is lower (\$194,599 < \$228,727), 145 units should be ordered at the maximum discount price. Given that the minimum point on this total cost curve has already been established at 85 units, we know that no order size greater than 145 units would result in a lower cost.

6.8 DECISIONS ABOUT ORDER TIMING FOR FIXED-ORDER QUANTITY MODEL

The timing of replenishment orders is discussed in this section using the order point rules from Fig. 6.1. To do this, the *reorder point* (*ROP*) must be determined. A replenishment order for a defined amount Q is issued when the stock level reaches the ROP, and it is assumed that the inventory level is *continuously* monitored (reviewed). Four elements affect the determination of the reorder point:

- The rate of demand,
- The amount of lead time needed to replenish inventory,
- The degree of uncertainty in both the rate of demand and the lead time for replenishment, and
- The management policy governing the acceptable degree of customer service.

Safety stock is not necessary and the reorder point can be easily determined when there is no uncertainty regarding the item's demand rate or lead time. A reorder point of 5 units, for instance, offers enough inventory to fulfill demand until the replenishment order is received, assuming, for example, that the laptop demand rate is exactly 5 units per day and the replenishment lead time is exactly one day, i.e.,

$$ROP = d * LT$$

where

d = demand rate per period (e.g., units per day or week)

LT = lead time in days or weeks

Note: Same time units must be used for demand and lead time.

Example 6.4: The Basic EOQ Model's Reorder Point

The Precision Product Company is accessible for business 320 days a year. Identify the reorder point for piston replenishment if the yearly demand of pistons is 9,000 and the lead time for receiving an order is 10 days.

Solution

$$ROP = d * LT$$

$$= \left(\frac{9000}{320}\right)(10)$$

$$= 281 \text{ units of pistons}$$

A fresh order is placed when there are just 281 pistons left in the inventory. Observe that neither the optimal order quantity nor any of the inventory costs have any influence on the reorder point.

6.8.1 SAFETY STOCKS

When the inventory level in Example 6.4 reaches the reorder point, an order is placed. The stock that is still on hand will be depleted at a steady pace of demand during the lead period, meaning that the new order quantity will arrive precisely when the stock reaches zero. Practically speaking, lead time and demand are both unpredictable. During the lead time period, the inventory level may be depleted faster. Fig. 6.5 illustrates this for a constant lead time and uncertain demand. When demand exceeds available inventory, a *stockout* may happen. During lead time, a *safety stock* of inventory is often added to the anticipated demand as a precaution against stockouts in cases of uncertain demand.

The introduction of safety stock into the reorder point setting is seen in Fig. 6.5. The quantity of inventory (R – S) needed to meet average demand $(\bar{d})$ during the average replenishment lead time (LT) and safety stock level S contribute to the reorder point R in this figure. These two add up to the reorder point, which is $R = (\bar{d}) + S$.

When a replenishment order is issued (at point a), demand variations during the replenishment lead time mean the inventory level can drop to a point between b and e. When demand equals the average demand rate or less, the inventory level reaches a point between b and c, and the safety stock is not needed. However, when the demand rate exceeds the average demand rate, and the inventory level drops to a point between c and e, a stockout will occur unless safety stock is available.

Fig. 6.5 Safety stock as a buffer against variations in demand

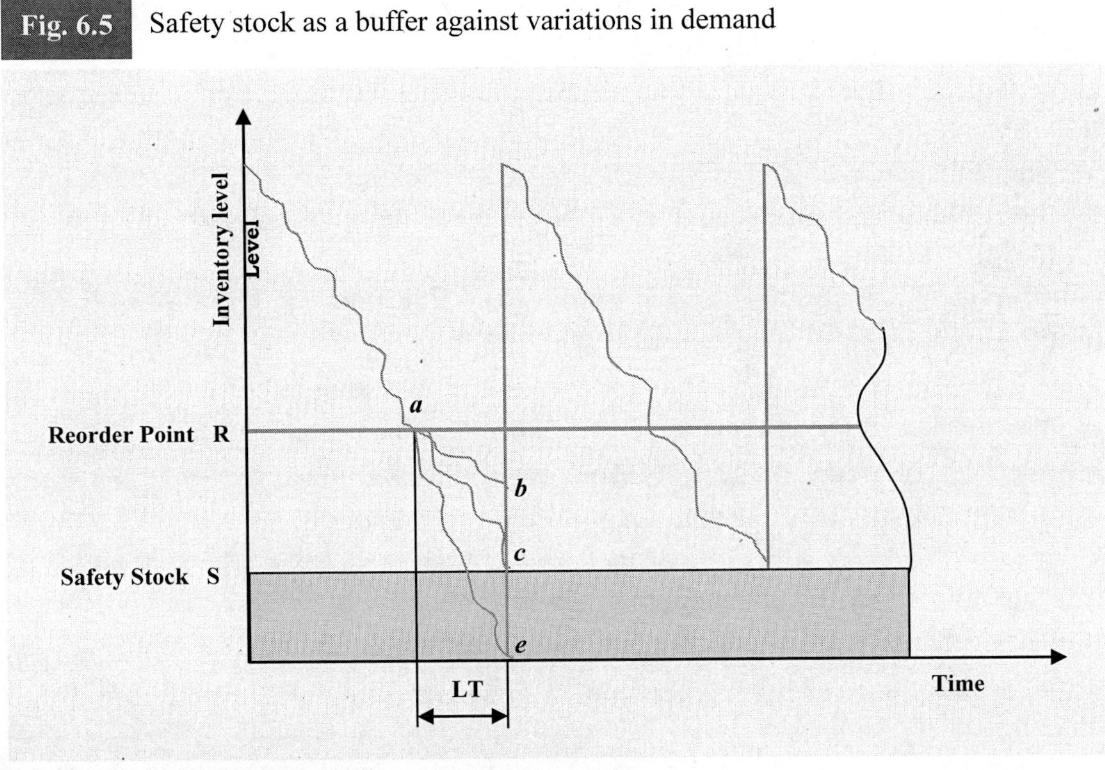

6.8.1.1 ESTABLISHING THE SAFETY STOCK

We need to set a criterion for evaluating how much protection against inventory shortages is appropriate before setting the safety stock level. Usually, one of two criteria is applied: either the fill rates, which indicate the desired degree of customer service in meeting product demand directly out of inventory, or the probability of stocking out in any particular replenishment order cycle. We provide illustrations of both criteria below.

6.8.1.2 PROBABILITY APPROACH TO DETERMINE SAFETY STOCK

It is very easy to determine safety stock using the probability criterion. We assume that the demand over a certain period of time is normally distributed with a mean and a standard deviation when using the models covered in this chapter. Furthermore, keep in mind that this method solely takes into account the likelihood of running out of stock – not the actual number of units we need. We can easily create a normal distribution for the predicted demand and observe where the amount we have on hand lies on the curve to find the probability of stocking out over the given time period.

Let's demonstrate this with a few straightforward instances. Let's say we know the standard deviation is 10 units and we anticipate demand to be 100 units over the course of the next month. We know that we have a 50% chance of stocking out if we start the month with just 100 units. We would anticipate demand to be greater than 100 units in half of the months and lower than 100 units in the other half. Extending this, we would anticipate running out of inventory in six months of the year if we ordered 100 units of inventory at a time and received it at the beginning of the month.

In order to lower the risk of stocking out, we would want to carry excess inventory if running out this frequently was unacceptable. Carrying an additional 10 units of inventory for the item could be one idea. In this scenario, we would still place one order for a month's supply at a time, but we would plan for delivery to happen when we had 10 units left in stock. This would provide us with that small safety stock cushion to lessen the probability of stocking out. We would be carrying one standard deviation's worth of safety stock if the standard deviation related to our demand was 10 units. A probability of 0.8413 can be obtained by moving 1 standard deviation to the right of the mean and looking at the cumulative standard normal distribution (Appendix 6.1). Consequently, we would anticipate not to stock out 84% of the time and do so 16% of the time. Now, if we placed an order every month, we might anticipate running out of supply for about two months out of the year ($0.16 \times 12 = 1.92$).

Companies that employ this strategy frequently set the probability of not stocking out at 95% confidence. This indicates that, in our example, we would carry 16 units ($1.64 \times 10 = 16.4$), or roughly 1.64 standard deviation of safety stock. Remember once more that this does not imply that we would order an additional 16 units every month. Instead, it means that each time, we would continue to order a month's supply, but we would plan the receipt so that we could anticipate having 16 units in stock at the time of the order. In this scenario, we would anticipate stockouts happening once every 19 months or roughly 0.63 months out of the year.

6.8.2 SERVICE LEVEL

Creating a safety stock that will satisfy a given service level is the second strategy. The possibility that there will be enough inventories on hand during the lead time to meet anticipated demand, or the probability that a stockout won't happen, is known as the service level. The term "service level" refers to the likelihood that a customer's demand will be satisfied, or that the client will be serviced, based on the probability that inventory will be on hand. With a 95% service level, there is a 0.95 probability that demand will be satisfied within the lead time, and a 5% probability that there will be a stockout. Usually, policymakers base their choice of service level on a variety of considerations, such as carrying costs for excess safety stock and potential sales losses in the event that customer demand is not satisfied.

You will see later on how the annual service level and the order cycle service level are related. The following variables determine the necessary quantity of safety stock in a particular scenario:

1. Average lead time and average rate of demand.
2. Variability in lead times and demand
3. The level of service that is wanted.

The more variations there is in lead time or demand rate for a given order cycle service level, the more safety stock will be required to meet that service level. Similarly, increasing the quantity of safety stock will be necessary to achieve an increase in service level for a given degree of change in lead time or demand rate. The choice of a service level may be based on policy considerations (e.g., the manager wishes to attain a specific service level for a particular item) or it may represent stockout costs (e.g., lost sales, customer dissatisfaction).

Fig. 6.6 Service Level Reorder Point

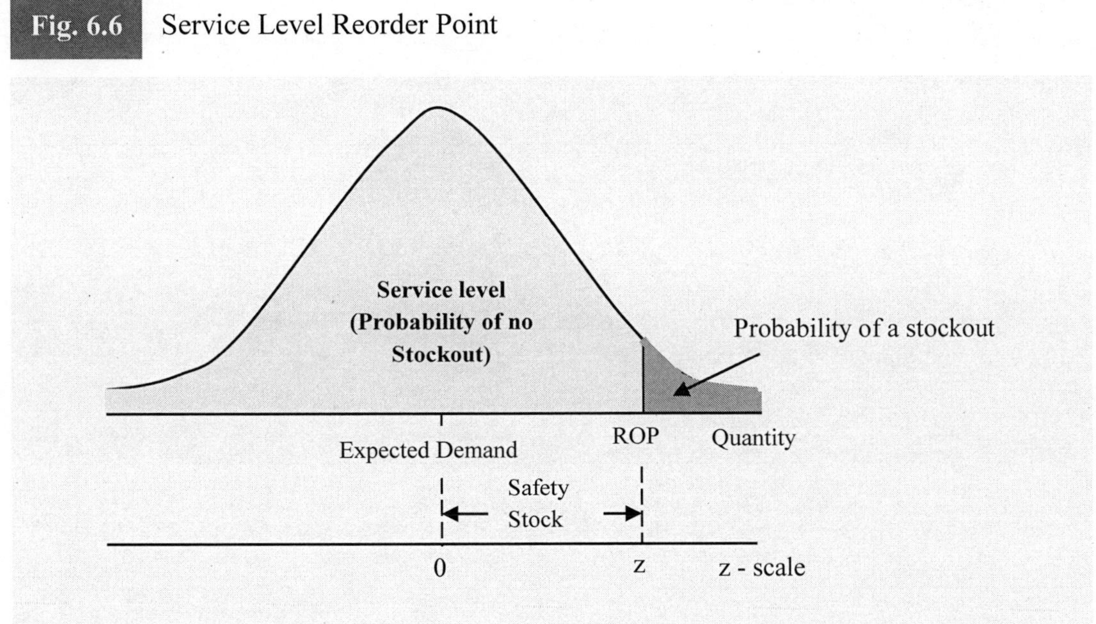

Let's examine a few models that can be applied when there is variability. If an estimate of the expected demand during the lead time and its standard deviation are provided, the first model can be applied. The equation is

$$ROP = \text{Expected demand during lead time} + z\sigma_{dLT} \quad \ldots (6.9)$$

where

z = No. of standard deviations

σ_{dLT} = The lead time demand standard deviation

Generally speaking, the model assumes that a normal distribution can properly reflect any fluctuation in lead time or demand rate. This need is not strictly enforced, though, as the models nonetheless yield approximations of reordering points in cases where the actual distribution deviates from the normal distribution. The manager's willingness to take on stockout risk determines the value of z (see Fig. 6.6) in a given situation. In general, the value of z increases with the amount of risk the manager is willing to take. To find the value of z given a desired service level for lead time, use the table in the Appendix 6.1.

Example 6.5: Reorder point for variable demand

Let's say the manager of a car repair shop calculated the typical annual demand for grease during lead time using previous data. Furthermore, let's say the management concluded that a normal distribution with a mean of 100 Kilograms and a standard deviation of 5 Kilograms might adequately characterize the demand during the lead period. Respond to these inquiries, presuming that the manager is ready to take a maximum 3 percent stockout risk.

(a) What is a suitable value for z?

(b) What is the appropriate amount of safety stock to hold?

(c) What reordering point is appropriate to use?

Solution

Expected lead time demand = 100 Kgs.

σ_{dLT} = 5 Kgs.

Risk = 3%

(a) Using a service level of 1 – 0.03 = 0.9700, you can calculate z = + 1.88 from Appendix 6.1.

(b) Safety stock = $z\sigma_{dLT}$ = 1.88(5) = 9.4 Kgs.

(c) ROP = Expected demand during lead time + Safety stock = 100 + 9.4 = 109.4 Kgs.

Equation (6.9) cannot be applied when lead time demand data are not easily accessible, i.e., when lead time demand is uncertain, independent, and well-described by a normal distribution on each lead time day. The average daily demand for the days of the lead time, which is also the result of multiplying the average daily demands by the lead time, adds up to the average demand for the lead time. In a similar vein, the total daily variances for the number of days in the lead time equal the variance of the distribution. These parameters allow us to calculate the ordering point as follows in order to satisfy a given service level:

$$ROP = \bar{d}LT + z\sigma_d\sqrt{LT} \qquad \text{... (6.10)}$$

where

$\bar{d}$ = average daily demand

LT = Lead time

σ_d = the standard deviation of daily demand

z = number of standard deviations corresponding to the service level probability

$z\sigma_d\sqrt{LT}$ = Safety stock

In this calculation for average daily demand $\bar{d}$ would be calculated as:

$$\bar{d} = \frac{\sum_{i=1}^{n} d_i}{n}$$

where n is the number of days.

Further, for the reorder point, the term $\sigma_d\sqrt{LT}$ represents the square root of the total daily deviations throughout the lead time:

$$\text{Variance} = (\text{daily variance}) \times (\text{number of days of lead time})$$

$$= \sigma_d^2 LT$$

$$\text{Standard deviation} = \sqrt{\sigma_d^2 LT}$$

$$= \sigma_d\sqrt{LT}$$

ALONG THE INVENTORY MANAGEMENT FOR STOCKOUTS

For most consumer goods companies worldwide, poor fill rates, stockouts, and inventory buildups are serious problems. Research indicates that inventory problems are causing organizations to lose as much as 12% of their yearly sales. Agile supply chains that can swiftly adapt to changes in supply or demand can help minimize stockouts and waste. The secret to developing agile supply chains is having precise demand forecasts that are updated regularly, taking into account the effects of external and business factors like changes in pricing, and continuously coordinating these forecasts with supply side constraints to provide the best suggestions for raw material inventory levels that should be maintained from a manufacturing perspective in order to meet the constantly shifting demands of the market.

Challenge for the company

An *ABC Food & Beverages* medium-sized company based in India is a producer of more than 70 specialty beverages that are available in a variety of packaging formats, including pouches, tetra packs, and single servings. They sell via more than 200 channels, which are divided into direct websites, modern and general trade, and e-commerce marketplaces. The company, like many of their peers, is always dealing with the problem of stockout, which results in millions of dollars' worth of lost income. Demand planning, obtaining raw materials, and restocking completed goods are all done manually and primarily based on intuition. Their approach to demand planning is based on static min-max days norms and average daily orders. They are consequently unable to smoothly match the manufacturing side of things to the anticipated demand.

Additionally, because they work with a wide range of raw materials and several suppliers for each one, they have limited insight into the performance of their raw material providers. For ease of use, the company frequently chooses their default suppliers above those with the best lead times, fill rates, or pricing. Additionally, their replenishment strategies rely heavily on stockout-influenced backward-looking daily averages. Naturally, taking into account previous stockouts results in lower average sales, which in turn results in less-than-ideal replenishment quantities, which may cause additional stockouts. Because of this, companies are unable to promptly adjust to the constantly shifting preferences of their customers, match their needs with the appropriate suppliers, and restock their stores with the appropriate amount of merchandise at the appropriate moment.

Remedies performed by the company

1. Demand projections at the retailer level were translated into the raw materials needed utilizing the Bill of Materials from a manufacturing perspective. In order to dynamically calculate safety stock based on historical errors and estimate the appropriate quantities to order given the projected demand and current inventory runway, this is then coupled with existing inventory and purchase order data.

2. For each stock keeping unit (SKU) in each geography/channel, the deployed solutions were designed to scale while taking into account the effects of seasonality, holidays, and neighborhood effects. Replenishment quantities and safety stocks were calculated using forward-looking daily demand predictions rather than the more conventional min-max based systems. Furthermore, proactive measures to reduce sales loss were aided by early alerts on stockout.

Other variants of calculating ROP

Fig. 6.7 Demand in the lead time

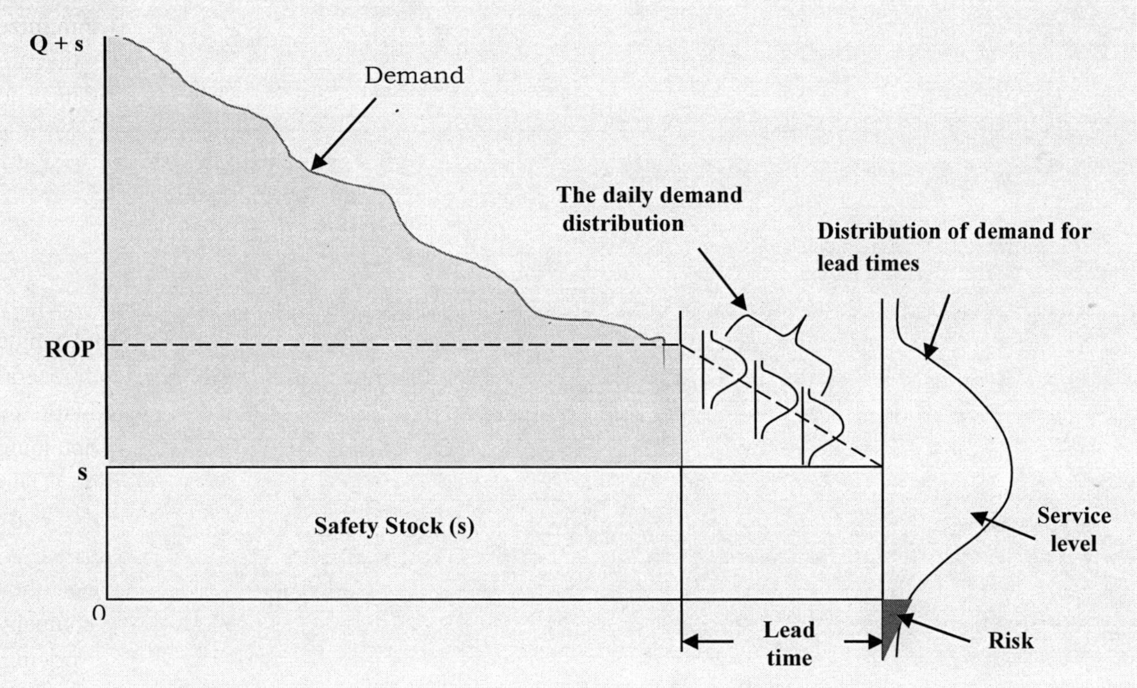

1. If only *lead time is variable,* then

$\sigma_{dLT} = d * \sigma_{LT}$, and reorder point is

$$ROP = d \times \overline{LT} + zd\sigma_{LT} \quad \ldots (6.11)$$

where

d = daily demand

$\overline{LT}$ = Average lead time

σ_{LT} = Standard deviation of lead time in days or weeks

2. If *both demand and lead time are variable*, then

$\sigma_{dLT} = \sqrt{\overline{LT}\sigma_d^2 + d^2\sigma_{LT}^2}$, and the reorder point is

$$ROP = \bar{d} \times \overline{LT} + z\sqrt{\overline{LT}\sigma_{\bar{d}}^2 + d^2\sigma_{LT}^2} \quad \dots (6.12)$$

REMARK

We make some observations when examining the reasoning behind the three ROP formulas (Equations 6.10 through 6.12) that were previously covered. Each formula starts with expected demand, which is the result of multiplying the number of days (or weeks) of lead time by the daily (or weekly) demand. The formula's second element is equal to *z* times the lead time demand standard deviation. The daily (or weekly) demand is expected to be normally distributed and to have the same mean and standard deviation as illustrated in Fig. 6.7for the formula where demand is the only variable. Summing the daily (or weekly) demand variances yields the standard deviation of demand for the full lead period, and since standard deviations are not additive like variances, you can get the square root of that value after that.

As a result, if the lead time is four days, the lead time demand variance will equal the total of the four variances, or $4\sigma_d^2$, assuming the daily standard deviation isσ_d. The square root of this, or $2\sigma_d$, is the standard deviation of lead time demand. This usually becomes$\sqrt{LT}\sigma_d$ and, so the final component of the formula (6.10).

The explanation is significantly easier when lead time is the only variable. The constant daily demand multiplied by the lead time standard deviation yields the standard deviation of lead time demand.

The formula looks really good when both lead time and demand are variable. Still, it's just the product of squaring the variances of the two earlier calculations to get their standard deviations, adding them up, and then calculating the square root.

Example 6.6: Calculating ROPs for three cases of uncertainty of demand and lead time

(a) Every day, a laundry receives about 500 orders from neighboring hotels to wash bed linens. The real figure often fluctuates depending on how many visitors are in the city on any given day. A normal distribution with a mean of 500 and a standard deviation of 10 bedsheets per day can be used to approximate usage. Two days are needed to get a large quantity of soiled bedsheets from every hotel. What is the minimal quantity of cleaned bedsheets that need to be on hand at the time of reorder, and what portion of that quantity can be classified as safety stock, if the owner of the loundary maintains a 2 percent stockout risk?

Solution

$\bar{d} = 500$

LT = 2 days

$\sigma_d = 10$ Risk = 2%, so service level = 98%

From Appendix 6.1 the value of z = 2.055

Since in this case demand is variable and lead time is constant, the ROP would be computed as:

$$ROP = \bar{d}LT + z\sigma_d\sqrt{LT}$$

$$= (500)(2) + 2.055(10)\sqrt{2}$$

$$= 1000 + 29.06 = 1{,}029 \text{ bedsheets approximately}$$

Safety stock is approximately 29 bedsheets. This can be demonstrated through a normal distribution curve as shown below.

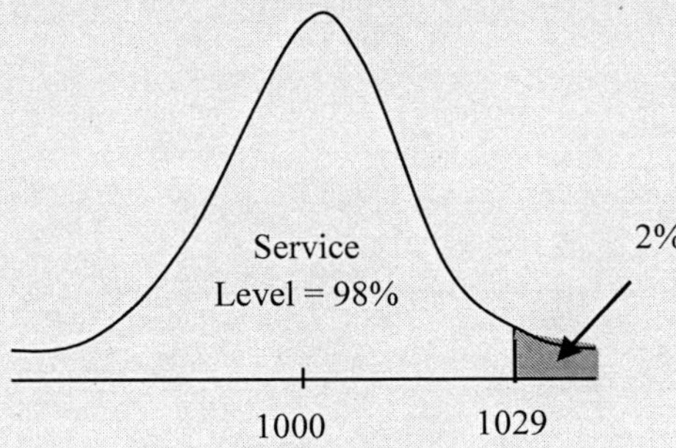

(b) The laundry company in the aforementioned example utilizes roughly 150 packs of detergent per day, with little variation in that amount. The lead time for the detergent pack delivery has a mean of 5 days and a standard deviation of 1.5 days. It is normally distributed. It is desired to have a 90% service level. Find the ROP.

Solution $\bar{d} = 150$ packs Service level = 90%, so $z = +1.28$ (see Appendix 6.1)

$\overline{LT} = 5$ days $\sigma_{LT} = 1.5$ days

$$ROP = d \times \overline{LT} + zd\sigma_{LT}$$

$$ROP = (150)(5) + (1.28)(150)(1.5) = 750 + 288 = 1{,}038 \text{ packs of detergents}$$

Safety stock is approximately 288 packs of detergents. This can be demonstrated through a normal distribution curve as shown below.

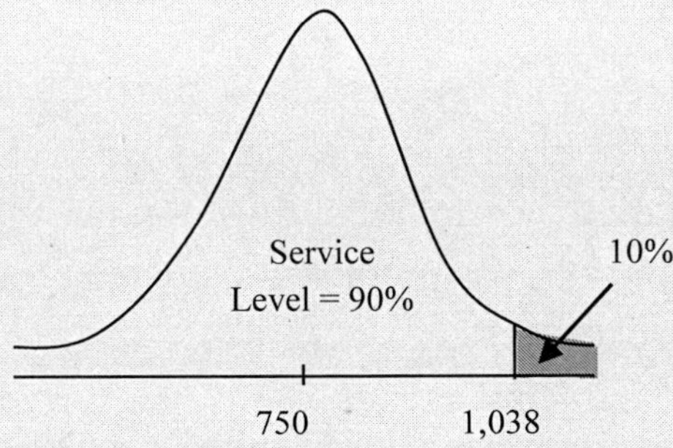

(c) 20 cloth-clips a day are replaced by the loundary owner to dry the bedsheets in case they break. This quantity has historically tended to normally distributed, with a standard deviation of 3 cloth-clips every day. With a standard deviation of 0.5 days and an average of 2 days, the lead time is normally distributed. In order to reach the 95 percent service level, find ROP.

Solution

$\bar{d} = 20$ cloth – clips per day $\qquad \overline{LT} = 2$ days

$\sigma_d = 3$ cloth – clips per day $\qquad \sigma_{LT} = 0.5$ days

Service level = 95%, so the value of z = +1.65 (see Appendix 6.1)

$$ROP = \bar{d} \times \overline{LT} + z\sqrt{\overline{LT}\sigma_d^2 + d^2\sigma_{LT}^2}$$

$$= (20)(2) + (1.65)\sqrt{(2)(3)^2 + (20)^2(0.5)^2} = 58 \text{ cloth-clips approximately}$$

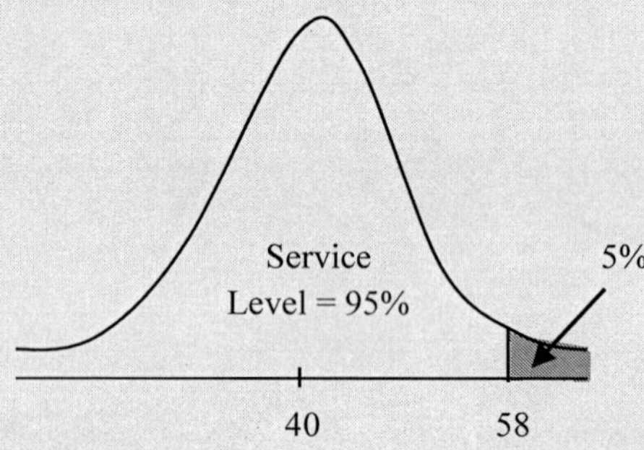

6.9 DECISIONS ABOUT ORDER TIMING FOR FIXED-TIME PERIOD MODEL

A continuous or fixed-order-quantity model was described in the preceding section as one in which the order quantity was ordered and the interval between orders fluctuated. Our conversation has thus far centered on this kind of inventory system. A system with a fixed order size and a constant order interval between orders is known as a periodic or fixed-time-period inventory system. Only specific intervals, like once a week or once a month, are used to count the inventory. Businesses that occasionally utilize a fixed-period inventory approach include grocery retailers. Spices, breads, cakes, biscuits, soaps, toothpaste, and many more household goods are available at grocery stores.

The suppliers of these goods to the store typically visit on a regular basis, perhaps once a week or once a month, to count the inventory that is available for various products. A further order for the quantity needed to replenish the inventory will be placed if it runs out or reaches a predefined reorder point. Between vendor visits, the grocery store owner typically relies on the vendor to take inventory rather than keeping an eye on the amount of inventory.

By combining numerous little, inexpensive things into a single order and delivery under this arrangement, the vendor would save money. Larger safety stockpiles won't be too expensive because the items are typically inexpensive. Furthermore, it won't matter much if there is a stockout if the things are noncritical.

But since inventory in fixed-time period models is only counted at the designated review time, there's a chance that a high demand will cause the stock to run out immediately after the purchase order is placed. This condition might not be detected until the subsequent review cycle. Even after that, it will take some time for the fresh order to arrive. As a result, there's a chance that stock will run out during the evaluation period (*T*) and order lead time (*LT*). Therefore, safety stock needs to guard against stockouts both throughout the review period and the lead time between placing an order and receiving it.

6.9.1 SAFETY STOCK FOR FIXED-TIME PERIOD MODEL (PERIODIC REVIEW MODEL)

For a fixed-time period system with a review cycle of *T* and a constant lead time of *LT*, the on-hand inventory level is shown in Fig. 6.8. Given the random distribution of demand around a mean *d*, the quantity to order, or *Q*, is as follows:

$$Q = \bar{d}(T + LT) + z\sigma_d\sqrt{T + LT} - I \qquad (6.13)$$

where

$\bar{d}$ = average demand rate

T = the fixed time between orders

LT = lead time

σ_d = standard deviation of demand

$z\sigma_d\sqrt{T + LT}$ = safety stock

I = inventory in stock

This formula's first part, $\bar{d}(T + LT)$, is the average demand for the order cycle time plus the 'protection interval,' which is the lead time and order interval added together. The protection interval shows how much inventory will be required to cover both the lead time until the order is received and the duration between this order and the next.

Fig. 6.8 Timing for fixed-period model

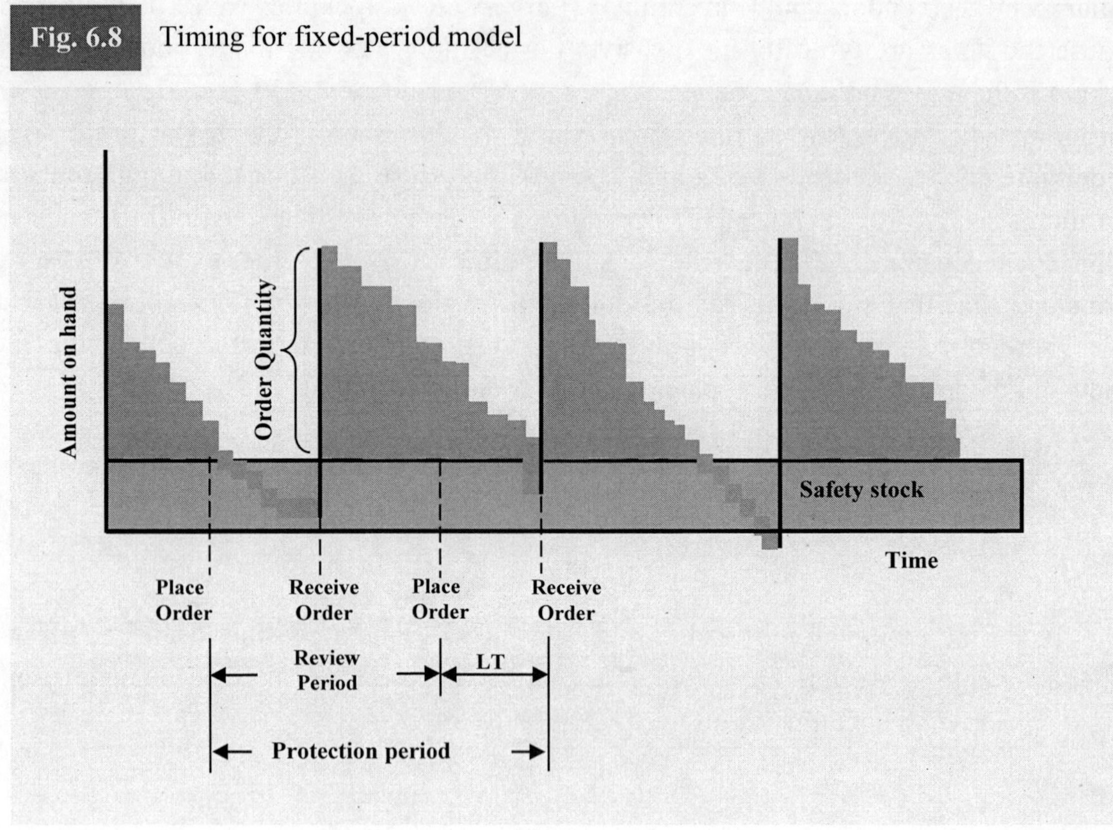

The safety stock for a certain service level is represented by the second component, $\sigma_d\sqrt{T + LT}$, which is calculated in a manner similar to that previously explained in the continuous review inventory system for reorder point. The total of these two components represents the desired level of inventory to be kept or the reorder point. When an order is placed and the inventory level is verified, the amount of inventory on hand, *I*, is the last component.

The other variant of the formula for reorder point in fixed-interval model could be a case when both demand and lead time are variable.

$$ROP = \bar{d}(T + LT) + z\sqrt{\sigma_d^2(T + LT) + \bar{d}^2\sigma_{LT}^2} \quad \ldots (6.14)$$

If the order interval or review period (T) is very small (hourly or daily), Equation (6.14) is similar to Equation (6.12) of fixed-quantity or continuous review systems in which T can be considered very small.

Depending on how much of the product is consumed, a person can order at any appropriate interval (weekly or monthly) under the fixed-interval approach. The order would be delivered to them soon (lead time) thereafter. But compared to the fixed-quantity (continuous review) model, the fixed-interval strategy requires more safety stock. Take note, for instance, of the fixed-interval model's higher dip into safety stock in Fig. 6.8 during the second order cycle.

Although in somewhat different ways, both the periodic review and continuous review models are responsive to lead time and demand. Higher-than-normal demand or longer lead times result in more frequent orders in the fixed-quantity (continuous review) model because of an increase in the ROP value; in the fixed-interval (or periodic review) model, on the other hand, a bigger order-size is the outcome. Another distinction is that the fixed-quantity approach necessitates careful inventory monitoring; that is, a constant evaluation to determine when the quantity on hand has reached the reorder point. To order an amount that protects the next review period and lead time, the fixed-interval model just requires a periodic check of inventory levels.

Example 6.7: Order size in a fixed-period model with varying lead time and demand

One well-known brand of spices is carried by the Vmart supermarket. Six packets of spices are ordered on average each day, with a standard deviation of 2 spice packs. Every 30 days, a vendor representing the spice company inspects Vmart's inventory. Vmart had 5 bundles available when he visited. This well-known spice brand's supplier is located distant from Vmart, thus there is supply variability with a mean lead time of 5 days and a standard deviation of 1.5 days. Find the order size that will allow Vmart to keep a 95% service level during this order period.

Solution

$\bar{d} = 6$ packs of spices $\quad \sigma_d = 2 \quad T = 30$ days $\quad LT = 5$ days $\quad \sigma_{LT} = 1.5$ days

$I = 5$ packs

Using Equation (6), the order size will be:

$$ROP = \bar{d}(T + LT) + z\sqrt{\sigma_d^2(T + LT) + \bar{d}^2\sigma_{LT}^2}$$

$$= 6(30 + 5) + (1.65)\sqrt{2^2(30 + 5) + 6^2(1.5)^2} = 234.53$$

$$\text{Order size} = 234.53 - I = 234.53 - 5 = 230 \text{ (approximately)}$$

6.10 THE SINGLE-PERIOD INVENTORY MODEL

When ordering perishables (fresh fruits, vegetables, seafood, cut flowers) and things with a short shelf life (newspapers, magazines, spare parts for specialist equipment), the single-period model – also known as the "newsboy problem" – is employed. Assuming that the parts cannot be utilized for other equipment, the spare part period is equal to the equipment's lifespan. The fact that unsold or unused items are normally not carried over, at least not without penalty, from one period to the next is what makes them unique. For example, day-old baked goods are frequently sold at reduced prices; leftover seafood may be thrown away; and outdated publications may be donated to used-book stores at a discount. Similar to this, it is quite challenging to sell T-shirts with a team's emblem to spectators at Indian Premier League (IPL) cricket matches, as it is unclear which team will be the crowd favorite and how many people would really purchase the shirts. The T-shirts that are sold after the game will need to be drastically reduced, while those that are sold before the game can likely be sold at a premium price.

Even the expense of disposing of leftover items can apply. The two costs of shortage and excess are typically the subject of analysis of single-period scenarios. The opportunity cost of lost sales as well as a charge for a reduction in consumer goodwill may be included in the shortage cost (C_s). Shortage cost is typically just unrealized profit per unit. That is,

$$C_s = \text{Revenue per unit} - \text{Cost per unit}$$

Shortage cost is the true cost of production lost when a shortage or stockout affects a machine spare part or an item required in manufacturing.

Items that remain at the end of the period are considered excess cost. Excess cost (C_e) is essentially the difference between salvage value and buying cost. That is,

$$C_e = \text{Purchase cost per unit} - \text{Salvage cost per unit}$$

The salvage will be negative and raise the excess cost per unit if there are expenses related to disposing of extra items.

Finding the order quantity, or stocking level, that will minimize long-run excess and shortage costs is the aim of the single-period model.

In this scenario, the newsperson selling papers at the sales stand had gathered data over a few months and discovered that, on average, 120 papers were sold on Saturdays, with a standard deviation of 15 papers. It is assumed that the newspapers were intentionally overstocked during this period to prevent shortages, allowing the newsperson to determine the true demand. The newsperson might easily express a service rate that is deemed acceptable with the use of these facts. For instance, the newsperson may wish to ensure, at least 90 percent of the time, that they won't run out of papers on Saturdays.

If we stocked exactly 120 papers every Saturday morning, the risk of stocking out would be 50 percent based on our knowledge of probability and the assumption that the probability distribution associated with the paper's sales is normal. This is because 50 percent of the time, we expect demand to be less than 120 papers, and 50 percent of the time, we expect demand to be greater than 120. We need to carry a few additional papers to ensure that we don't stock out by ninety percent. From the cumulative standard normal distribution chart given in Appendix 6.1, we see that we need around 1.28 standard deviation of extra sheets to be 90 percent sure of not stocking out. Using Microsoft Excel's NORMSINV(probability) function, one can quickly determine the precise number of standard deviations required for a certain probability of stocking out (=NORMSINV(0.9) = 1.28). Using the Excel result, which is more precise than the table results, the number of additional papers would be 1.28 × 15 = 19.2, or 19 papers.

It would be beneficial to genuinely take into account the possible profit and loss connected with stocking either too few or too many papers on the stand in order to make this more helpful. Assume that the newspaper person purchases each paper for $0.10 and sells it for $0.60 per unit. The lost profit of $0.50 is the marginal shortage cost in this instance of underestimating demand or supply. In a similar vein, $0.10 would be the marginal excess cost if the demand was overestimated, that is, if there was excess stock on hand. Using the marginal analysis, the best stocking level is reached when carrying the next unit is predicted to result in more benefits than expenses. Remember that the particular advantages and expenses vary depending on the problem at hand.

In mathematical terms, the expected marginal cost equation is transformed into the following through incorporating probabilities:

$$P(C_e) \leq (1 - P)C_s$$

where

C_e = Excess cost margin resulting from overestimating demand
C_s = Cost of the marginal shortage when demand is underestimated

P = The unit's cumulative probability of not being sold
(1-P) = The unit's cumulative probability of being sold
Next, by calculating P, we arrive at

$$P \leq \frac{C_s}{C_e + C_s}$$

According to this equation, we should keep increasing the order size as long as the likelihood of selling the items we order is either the same or less than the ratio of $C_s/C_e + C_s$.

Going back to our newspaper problem, we have a cost of underestimating demand (C_s) of \$0.50 and a cost of overestimating demand (C_e) of \$0.10 per unit of newspaper. Consequently, the chance is 0.50/(0.10 + 0.50) = 0.83. The point on our demand distribution that corresponds to the cumulative probability of 0.83 must now be located. The number of standard deviations (also known as the *z*-score) of additional newspapers to carry can be calculated using the NORMSINV function. The result is 0.954, which indicates that we need to stock 0.954(15) = 14.31, or 14 extra papers. The total number of newspapers for sale on each Saturday should be 134 newspapers.

Applications in manufacturing and services cover a broad range of uses for single period inventory models. For instance, reservations made for a certain flight with an airline is an interesting example. Overbooking or making reservations for more seats than are available can be thought of as inventory for perishable goods since they cannot be sold after the flight has taken place. In this case, the demand is represented by the number of no-shows. According to this view, the expense of overbooking (too much overbooking) would be the cost of paying customers who were bumped, and the cost of underordering (too little overbooking) would be the lost profit from vacant seats.

Example 6.8: A small one-speed girl bicycle

The distributor has been notified by the manufacturer that a certain model of girl's bicycle, which has one speed, is being discontinued. Based on historical data, the average number of bicycles on this model each day is 10, with a standard deviation of 2 bicycles per day around Christmas. The cost of a bicycle is \$1500 on average. The seller was offering the bicycle for a discounted price of \$1200 because the model is going out of production. How many bicycles should the distributor keep on hand?

Solution

The shortage cost due to underestimating the demand (C_s) = \$1500 – \$1200 = \$300

The excess cost due to overestimating the demand (C_e) = \$1500

$$P \leq \frac{300}{1500 + 300} = 0.1666$$

The z-score obtained by using Microsoft Excel's NORMSINV(0.1666) is -0.9677. We should stock by a value less than the average of 10 bicycles, according to the negative value. Actually, there should be 2 bicycles less than 10, or -0.9677(2) = 1.93. By Christmas, the distributor ought to have 8 bicycles in stock.

Discrete probability distribution for stocking levels

Using real data and marginal analysis, a discrete probability distribution is a popular technique for analyzing this kind of issue. The service level calculated using the ratio C_s/C_e+C_s typically does not match with a practical stocking level when stocking levels are discrete (e.g., the best amount may be between 2 and 3 units). The solution is to stock at the next higher level (e.g., 3 units). Stated differently, determine the stocking level in a way that will either match or above the intended service level.

In order to estimate the consumption of spares for the aforementioned problem, historical records on bicycle spare parts have to be used. Stockouts result in lost time costs associated with bicycle assembly and expedited ordering. These are $6000 short per unit on average. Unused parts have no salvage value, and spares cost $500 per unit. Establish the ideal level of stocking.

Number of spares used	Relative frequency	Cumulative frequency
0	.10	.10
1	.50	.60
2	.30	.90
3	.10	1.00
4 or more	.00	

Solution

$C_s = \$6000$ $C_e = \$500$ $P \leq 6000/500+6000 = 0.9231$

The cumulative frequency column reflects the proportion of time when demand did not exceed (was equal to or less than) certain quantity. For instance, the demand is met 60% of the time with one spare and 90% of the time with two spares. Thus, in order to obtain a service level of atleast 92.31 percent, it will required to stock 3 spares (i.e to proceed to the next higher stocking level).

UNIT SUMMARY

- ***Types and Purpose of Inventory*** – Covers raw materials, work-in-progress (WIP), finished goods, and MRO (Maintenance, Repair, and Operations) inventory.
- ***Inventory Review Systems*** – Explains continuous review systems (real-time tracking) and periodic review systems (fixed-interval tracking).

- ***Inventory Costs*** – Discusses carrying costs, ordering costs, and shortage costs, balancing them for efficiency.
- ***Economic Order Quantity*** (EOQ) Model – Introduces EOQ as an optimal order quantity model to minimize total inventory costs.
- ***Production Quantity Model & Quantity Discounts*** – Explains inventory replenishment strategies and price discount considerations.
- ***Order Timing Decisions*** – Covers reorder points, safety stock calculations, and service levels for both fixed-order quantity and fixed-time period models.
- ***ABC Classification*** – Prioritizes inventory items into A (high value), B (moderate value), and C (low value) for better control.
- ***Real-World Applications*** – Includes case studies like Ford's Just-in-Time (JIT) system and Haier's Zero Inventory Model, demonstrating strategic inventory control.

EXERCISES

MULTIPLE CHOICE QUESTIONS

6.1 What is the primary goal of inventory management?

(a) To maximize the number of items in stock	(b) To minimize inventory holding costs
(c) To ensure there is always excess inventory	(d) To track employee performance

6.2 Which of the following is NOT a typical inventory type in inventory management?

(a) Raw materials	(b) Work-in-progress
(c) Finished goods	(d) Customer feedback

6.3 Which type of demand is associated with inventory items that are used in the production of other items?

(a) Independent Demand	(b) Dependent Demand
(c) Seasonal Demand	(d) Speculative Demand

6.4 What is the key characteristic of independent demand inventory?

(a) It is determined by the demand for other products	(b) It is directly related to production requirements
(c) It is determined by customer purchases and market conditions	(d) It is used to support inventory replenishment cycles

6.5 For which type of demand would companies use methods like Material Requirements Planning (MRP) to manage inventory levels?

(a) Independent Demand	(b) Dependent Demand
(c) Seasonal Demand	(d) Strategic Demand

6.6 What is the primary purpose of maintaining buffer inventory?

(a) To increase sales revenue	(b) To prevent stockouts and ensure continuous operations
(c) To minimize storage space	(d) To reduce production costs

6.7 What is a stockout in inventory management?

(a) An excess of inventory that exceeds storage capacity	(b) The situation where inventory levels are higher than the demand
(c) The condition where inventory is depleted and cannot meet demand	(d) An error in the inventory accounting system

6.8 How can inventory be used as a hedge against price hikes?

(a) By purchasing additional stock when prices are low to avoid future cost increases	(b) By reducing inventory turnover rates
(c) By increasing the frequency of inventory audits	(d) By limiting the range of products offered

6.9 What role does inventory play in balancing supply and demand?

(a) It allows for the purchase of raw materials at lower prices	(b) It maintains a sufficient stock level to meet customer demand while minimizing shortages
(c) It increases the company's production speed	(d) It reduces the need for a marketing strategy

6.10 What is the purpose of holding safety stock in inventory management?

(a) To accommodate for unexpected variations in demand or supply chain disruptions	(b) To reduce the cost of goods sold
(c) To increase the speed of production	(d) To eliminate the need for inventory audits

6.11 In a continuous review system, when is an order placed for replenishment?

(a) At fixed intervals	(b) When inventory reaches reorder level
(c) When demand exceeds supply	(d) When a new product is introduced

6.12 In a digitized continuous review system, which technology is commonly used to automatically track inventory levels and trigger reorders?

(a) Barcode scanning	(b) Manual ledger entries
(c) Paper-based inventory logs	(d) Periodic physical audits

6.13 Which of the following is a potential disadvantage of a periodic review inventory system?

(a) It allows for real-time adjustments based on immediate demand changes	(b) It may lead to higher stockholding costs due to larger, less frequent orders
(c) It requires fewer inventory checks compared to continuous review systems	(d) It typically results in fewer stockouts compared to continuous review systems

6.14 A grocery store chain typically uses a periodic review inventory system. What is one reason this system is suitable for grocery stores?

(a) High variability in product demand	(b) Large number of product types with stable demand patterns
(c) High-value inventory items	(d) Complex supply chain logistics

6.15 Which of the following examples represents a situation where periodic review inventory might be less effective compared to a continuous review system?

(a) A chain of convenience stores where products are replenished weekly	(b) A company managing spare parts for manufacturing machinery with unpredictable breakdowns
(c) A warehouse that stocks non-perishable goods with consistent, predictable demand	(d) A supermarket managing bulk orders for everyday household items

6.16 When optimizing inventory levels, which of the following would be considered a trade-off between carrying costs and ordering costs?

(a) Increasing the order quantity to reduce the frequency of orders	(b) Decreasing the reorder point to minimize carrying costs
(c) Increasing the safety stock to avoid stockouts	(d) Reducing the lead time to lower the ordering cost

6.17 In which situation would a company most likely experience high shortage costs?

(a) When holding large amounts of inventory in a warehouse	(b) When inventory turnover is very high, leading to frequent reordering
(c) When there are frequent stockouts and backorders due to insufficient inventory	(d) When the carrying costs of inventory are minimal

6.18 What does the A-B-C classification system primarily categorize inventory items based on?

(a) The size and weight of inventory items	(b) The frequency of use and financial impact
(c) The type of product and its manufacturing process	(d) The supplier and lead time for delivery

6.19 What is the primary objective of the Economic Order Quantity (EOQ) model?

(a) To determine the optimal reorder point for inventory	(b) To minimize the total cost of inventory, including ordering and carrying costs
(c) To maximize the inventory turnover rate	(d) To forecast future inventory needs based on historical data

6.20 What happens if the actual order quantity deviates from the EOQ in the EOQ model?

(a) Increased holding costs	(b) Increased stockouts
(c) Increased ordering costs	(d) Decreased lead time

6.21 In the Production Quantity Model, which factor is unique compared to the Economic Order Quantity (EOQ) model?

(a) The fixed ordering cost	(b) The carrying cost per unit
(c) The production rate and demand rate	(d) The annual demand

6.22 When using the Economic Order Quantity (EOQ) model with quantity discounts, what is the primary consideration?

(a) To determine the maximum discount possible for each order quantity	(b) To find the order quantity that minimizes the total cost including ordering, carrying, and discount costs

(c) To ensure that the quantity discount does not affect the overall carrying cost	(d) To adjust the reorder point to account for the discount levels

6.23 How do total cost curves help in determining the optimal order quantity in quantity discounts?

(a) By identifying the point where ordering costs equal holding costs	(b) By analyzing the impact of lead time on total costs
(c) By considering the effect of demand variability on total costs	(d) By comparing total costs at different order quantities

6.24 In the Fixed-Order Quantity model, how is the reorder point (ROP) typically calculated?

(a) By multiplying the average demand by the lead time	(b) By summing the carrying cost and ordering cost
(c) By adding the safety stock to the average demand during lead time	(d) By dividing the annual demand by the order quantity

6.25 If the lead time in the Fixed-Order Quantity model increases, what happens to the reorder point (ROP)?

(a) The reorder point decreases	(b) The reorder point increases
(c) The reorder point remains unchanged	(d) The reorder point becomes unpredictable

6.26 In the Fixed-Order Quantity model, how does variability in demand impact the order timing and reorder point?

(a) Variability in demand increases the reorder point to account for higher uncertainty	(b) Variability in demand decreases the reorder point to reduce excess inventory
(c) Variability in demand has no effect on the reorder point	(d) Variability in demand reduces the need for safety stock

6.27 When using the Fixed-Order Quantity model, how does an increase in lead time impact the required level of safety stock?

(a) Safety stock requirements decrease as longer lead times mean fewer orders are needed	(b) Safety stock requirements increase to account for the longer period of uncertainty during the lead time
(c) Safety stock remains unchanged regardless of lead time	(d) Safety stock becomes irrelevant as lead time does not affect inventory levels

6.28 What is the primary goal of using the probability approach to determine safety stock in the Fixed-Order Quantity model?

(a) To reduce the number of inventory items	(b) To minimize the total order quantity
(c) To ensure a specified service level by calculating safety stock based on demand variability	(d) To eliminate the need for safety stock calculations

6.29 If a company aims for a 95% service level in a fixed order quantity model, what does this imply about stockouts?

(a) Stockouts will occur 5% of the time.	(b) The company will never experience stockouts.
(c) Stockouts will occur 95% of the time.	(d) The probability of stockouts is zero.

6.30 Which of the following factors most directly impacts the safety stock required to maintain a specific service level in a fixed order quantity inventory system?

(a) The lead time for replenishment.	(b) The average cost per unit.
(c) The fixed order quantity.	(d) The frequency of order placement.

6.31 In the context of the fixed order quantity inventory model, what effect does increasing the desired service level have on the safety stock?

(a) The safety stock decreases.	(b) The safety stock remains unchanged.
(c) The safety stock increases.	(d) The safety stock becomes zero.

6.32 What is a key advantage of the Fixed-Time Period Model compared to the Fixed-Order Quantity Model?

(a) It allows for more precise control of inventory levels.	(b) It simplifies inventory management by ordering at regular intervals rather than varying order quantities.
(c) It eliminates the need for safety stock.	(d) It reduces the frequency of orders.

6.33 If the cost of understock (lost sales) is higher than the cost of overstock (excess inventory), what effect does this have on the order quantity in the Single-Period Inventory Model?

(a) It increases the order quantity to reduce the risk of stockouts.	(b) It decreases the order quantity to avoid excess inventory.
(c) It has no effect on the order quantity.	(d) It makes the order quantity constant regardless of costs.

Answers of Multiple Choice Questions

6.1 (b), 6.2 (d), 6.3 (b), 6.4 (c), 6.5 (b), 6.6 (b), 6.7 (c), 6.8 (a), 6.9 (b), 6.10 (a), 6.11 (b), 6.12 (a), 6.13 (b), 6.14 (b), 6.15 (b), 6.16 (a), 6.17 (c), 6.18 (b), 6.19 (b), 6.20 (c), 6.21 (c), 6.22 (b), 6.23 (d), 6.24 (c), 6.25 (b), 6.26 (a), 6.27 (b), 6.28 (c), 6.29 (a), 6.30 (a), 6.31 (c), 6.32 (b), 6.33 (a)

SHORT AND LONG ANSWER TYPE QUESTIONS

Category I

6.1 What are the main types of inventories used in business, and how do they differ from each other?

6.2 Explain the distinctions between independent and dependent demand, providing an example from a pizza restaurant like Dominos or Pizza Hut.

6.3 Explain the differences between a fixed-time period system and a fixed-order quantity system, and provide an example of each.

6.4 Explain why the responses to the two fundamental questions that inventory management addresses vary for periodic and continuous inventory systems.

6.5 Describe the main cost categories and how they relate to one another in an inventory analysis.

6.6 Describe how the basic EOQ model is used to determine the order quantity.

6.7 What are the fundamental EOQ model's assumptions, and how much do they restrict the model's applicability?

6.8 In inventory analysis, how do lead time and reorder point relate to each other?

6.9 What are the differences between the basic EOQ model and the noninstantaneous receipt model?

6.10 If the cost of the shortfall is very large, how will this affect the EOQ model with shortages?

6.11 In what way does the basic EOQ model application need to change to account for quantity discounts?

6.12 What would happen in the noninstantaneous receipt EOQ model if the production rate increased and the demand rate decreased, eventually leading to a negligible ratio d/p?

Category II

6.13 Discuss the various types of inventory that businesses typically manage. In your discussion, explore how each type contributes to the overall inventory management strategy, and analyze the potential challenges and benefits associated with managing each type. Additionally, provide examples of industries or businesses where each type of inventory is particularly critical and explain why.

6.14 In inventory management and production planning, understanding the nature of demand is crucial for effective decision-making. Explore the concepts of independent and dependent demand, highlighting their key differences. Discuss how each type of demand influences inventory management strategies and production scheduling. Additionally, provide examples of products or components that typically exhibit independent versus dependent demand and analyze how these distinctions impact inventory control and supply chain management in different industries.

6.15 In the realm of inventory management, two common systems used for managing stock levels are the fixed-time period system and the fixed-order quantity system. Examine the fundamental differences between these two inventory management systems. In your discussion, consider how each system impacts inventory control, ordering processes, and overall supply chain efficiency. Provide examples of scenarios or industries where each system might be more advantageous, and analyze the potential trade-offs associated with adopting one system over the other. How do these differences influence decisions related to inventory planning and operational performance?

6.16 Inventory management often employs various models to determine the optimal order quantity and control costs. Compare and contrast the basic Economic Order Quantity (EOQ) model with the noninstantaneous receipt model. In your analysis, discuss how each model addresses inventory replenishment and demand over time. Evaluate how the assumptions and limitations of each model impact their practical applications in different business scenarios. Additionally, provide examples of industries or situations where one model might be more suitable than the other, and explain how these models influence decisions related to inventory management and operational efficiency.

NUMERICAL PROBLEMS

6.1 A specific brand of car shockers is stocked and sold by Perfect Products Company. Every time the company ordered shockers from the manufacturer, it had to pay $450. One shocker costs $170 to keep in stock for a full year. The store manager projects that there would be a consistent demand rate for the shockers for the entire year, amounting to 1200 units. Minutes after an order is placed, it is picked up from a nearby warehouse that the manufacturer keeps in order. Stockouts of shockers are never permitted in the store. Every day of the year, barring Christmas Day, the store is open for business. Ascertain the following:

a. The optimum order quantity per order
b. The lowest possible total annual inventory costs
c. The optimum number of orders per year
d. The optimum order-to-order (in working days) interval

6.2 The Precision Products Company makes motorcycle connecting rods. The company is able to create 64 connecting rods every day, five days a week, and 52 weeks a year. After the manufacturing line for connecting rods is set up, the company continues to produce until a predefined quantity (Q) is produced. The manufacturing line is utilized to make other products when it is not making connecting rods. $500 is the setup cost for a connecting rod production run. Five dollars a connecting rod is the annual cost of keeping them in stock. There is a steady yearly demand of 5,000 units for connecting rod. Find out the following:

(a) The optimum quantity of a production run (Q)
(b) The total yearly cost of inventory
(c) The optimum number of manufacturing runs in a year
(d) The ideal cycle time (interval between runs)
(e) Run length in terms of working days.

6.3 Vegetable oil is available in bottles at the V-Mart Supermarket. Every year (365 days), there is a demand of 4,000 boxes for vegetable oil bottles. Vegetable oil costs the store $60 per order, and keeping the oil in stock costs $0.80 per box annually. The order from a food wholesaler takes four days to arrive once it is placed for vegetable oil. Ascertain the following:

(a) Ideal order size
(b) Minimum annual total cost of inventory
(c) Reorder point

6.4 A food processing unit ships different items in excellent box packaging to its dealer. On an average, every year, 4000 new packaging boxes are purchased to replace the broken and damaged ones. The carrying cost of the boxes in inventory is 50% and cost of placing an order is $40. The supplier of the boxes quotes the following discount prices:

Size of Order	Price per box ($)
Below 500	0.75
501 to 1000	0.72
1001 to 2000	0.70
Over 2000	0.69

While the purchase department is attracted by gradual discount on bulk-purchase, what should be the optimal order quantity?

6.5 The amount of denim that the Levis Jeans Company uses every day to produce jeans is normally distributed with a standard deviation of 600 yards and an average of 3000 yards. An order for denim from the textile mill always requires a lead time of six days. If the Levis Jeans Company wants to keep the probability of a stockout and work stoppage to 5%, determine:

(a) The safety stock and reorder point.

(b) How much service level would be offered in the event that 2,000 yards of safety stock were provided?

6.6 Every day, FreshOn fast food shop purchases fresh noodles for $1.40 per pound and sells them for $1.90. Any noodles that remain at the end of each business day are sold for 80 cents per pound to a dog food manufacturer. A normal distribution with a mean of 80 pounds and a standard deviation of 10 pounds can be used to approximate daily demand. What is the optimum level of stocking?

6.7 Given the items in the list below,

(a) Categorize them as A, B, and C.

(b) Calculate each item's economic order quantity, rounding to the closest whole unit.

Item	Estimated Annual Demand	Ordering Cost	Holding Cost (%)	Unit Price
I4-010	20,000	50	20	2.50
I5-201	60,200	60	20	4.00
Q6-400	9,800	80	30	28.50
Q6-401	16,300	50	30	12.00

Q7-100	6,250	50	30	9.00
Q9-103	4,500	50	40	22.00
US-300	21,000	40	25	45.00
US-400	45,000	40	25	40.00
US-041	800	40	25	20.00
VS-001	26,100	25	35	4.00

REFERENCES AND SUGGESTED READINGS

1. Arnold, U., and Hesse, R. Cost Analysis of Inventory Systems: A Review of Classical and Modern Approaches. *International Journal of Production Economics*, Vol. 128(1), 1-12, 2010.

2. Ballou, R. H. *Business Logistics/Supply Chain Management*, 5th Edition, Pearson Prentice-Hall, 2004.

3. Cachon, G. P., and Terwiesch, C. Inventory Classification and Management for Multi-Echelon Systems. *Operations Research*, Vol. 57(6), 1424-1435, 2009.

4. Dev, N. K., Shankar, R., and Debnath, R. M. Supply chain efficiency: a simulation cum DEA approach. *International Journal of Advanced Manufacturing Technology*, Vol. 72, 1537-1549, 2014.

5. Harris, F. W. The Theory of Factory Management. *Harvard Business Review*, 11(1), 13-22, 1913.

6. Harris, R. L., and Hill, T. Comparing Continuous and Periodic Inventory Systems: An Analytical Study. *International Journal of Production Research*, Vol. 37(9), 2251-2264, 1999.

7. Harrison, J. P., and Van Houtum, G. J. Optimizing Order Timing in Fixed-Time Period Models with Safety Stock. *European Journal of Operational Research*, Vol. 224(2), 343-355, 2012.

8. Heizer, J., Render, B., and Munson, C. *Operations Management: Sustainability and Supply Chain Management*, 12th Edition, Pearson, 2017.

9. Jacobs, F. R., and Berry, W. L. *Manufacturing Planning and Control for Supply Chain Management*, 6th Edition, McGraw-Hill Education, 2014.

10. Nahmias, S. Safety Stock and Service Level Analysis in Fixed-Order Quantity Systems. *Journal of Operations Management*, Vol. 29(6), 516-527, 2013.

11. Silver, E. A., and Peterson, R. *Inventory Management and Production Planning and Scheduling*, 3rd Edition, Wiley, 1985.

12. Slack, N., Chambers, S., and Johnston, R. *Operations Management*, 6th Edition, Pearson Education, 2010.

13. Tersine, R. J., and Hasegawa, H. *Principles of Inventory and Materials Management*, 6th Edition, Prentice-Hall, 2004.

14. Vollmann, T. E., Berry, W. L., and Whybark, D. C. *Manufacturing Planning and Control for Supply Chain Management*, 5th Edition, McGraw-Hill Education, 2004.

15. Waters, D. The Role and Purpose of Inventory in Manufacturing. *Journal of Operations Management*, Vol. 20(4), 423-440, 2002.

16. Wright, P. L. *Operations Management*: *Theory and Practice*, 4th Edition, McGraw-Hill Education, 2010.

APPENDIX 6.1

Table of the standard normal distribution values ($z \leq 0$)

$-z$	0.00	0.01	0.02	0.03	0.04	0.05	0.06	0.07	0.08	0.09
0.0	0.50000	0.49601	0.49202	0.48803	0.48405	0.48006	0.47608	0.47210	0.46812	0.46414
0.1	0.46017	0.45621	0.45224	0.44828	0.44433	0.44038	0.43644	0.43251	0.42858	0.42466
0.2	0.42074	0.41683	0.41294	0.40905	0.40517	0.40129	0.39743	0.39358	0.38974	0.38591
0.3	0.38209	0.37828	0.37448	0.37070	0.36693	0.36317	0.35942	0.35569	0.35197	0.34827
0.4	0.34458	0.34090	0.33724	0.33360	0.32997	0.32636	0.32276	0.31918	0.31561	0.31207
0.5	0.30854	0.30503	0.30153	0.29806	0.29460	0.29116	0.28774	0.28434	0.28096	0.27760
0.6	0.27425	0.27093	0.26763	0.26435	0.26109	0.25785	0.25463	0.25143	0.24825	0.24510
0.7	0.24196	0.23885	0.23576	0.23270	0.22965	0.22663	0.22363	0.22065	0.21770	0.21476
0.8	0.21186	0.20897	0.20611	0.20327	0.20045	0.19766	0.19489	0.19215	0.18943	0.18673
0.9	0.18406	0.18141	0.17879	0.17619	0.17361	0.17106	0.16853	0.16602	0.16354	0.16109
1.0	0.15866	0.15625	0.15386	0.15151	0.14917	0.14686	0.14457	0.14231	0.14007	0.13786
1.1	0.13567	0.13350	0.13136	0.12924	0.12714	0.12507	0.12302	0.12100	0.11900	0.11702
1.2	0.11507	0.11314	0.11123	0.10935	0.10749	0.10565	0.10384	0.10204	0.10027	0.09853
1.3	0.09680	0.09510	0.09342	0.09176	0.09012	0.08851	0.08692	0.08534	0.08379	0.08226
1.4	0.08076	0.07927	0.07780	0.07636	0.07493	0.07353	0.07215	0.07078	0.06944	0.06811
1.5	0.06681	0.06552	0.06426	0.06301	0.06178	0.06057	0.05938	0.05821	0.05705	0.05592
1.6	0.05480	0.05370	0.05262	0.05155	0.05050	0.04947	0.04846	0.04746	0.04648	0.04551
1.7	0.04457	0.04363	0.04272	0.04182	0.04093	0.04006	0.03920	0.03836	0.03754	0.03673
1.8	0.03593	0.03515	0.03438	0.03363	0.03288	0.03216	0.03144	0.03074	0.03005	0.02938
1.9	0.02872	0.02807	0.02743	0.02680	0.02619	0.02559	0.02500	0.02442	0.02385	0.02330
2.0	0.02275	0.02222	0.02169	0.02118	0.02068	0.02018	0.01970	0.01923	0.01876	0.01831
2.1	0.01786	0.01743	0.01700	0.01659	0.01618	0.01578	0.01539	0.01500	0.01463	0.01426
2.2	0.01390	0.01355	0.01321	0.01287	0.01255	0.01222	0.01191	0.01160	0.01130	0.01101
2.3	0.01072	0.01044	0.01017	0.00990	0.00964	0.00939	0.00914	0.00889	0.00866	0.00842
2.4	0.00820	0.00798	0.00776	0.00755	0.00734	0.00714	0.00695	0.00676	0.00657	0.00639
2.5	0.00621	0.00604	0.00587	0.00570	0.00554	0.00539	0.00523	0.00509	0.00494	0.00480
2.6	0.00466	0.00453	0.00440	0.00427	0.00415	0.00403	0.00391	0.00379	0.00368	0.00357
2.7	0.00347	0.00336	0.00326	0.00317	0.00307	0.00298	0.00289	0.00280	0.00272	0.00264
2.8	0.00256	0.00248	0.00240	0.00233	0.00226	0.00219	0.00212	0.00205	0.00199	0.00193
2.9	0.00187	0.00181	0.00175	0.00170	0.00164	0.00159	0.00154	0.00149	0.00144	0.00140
3.0	0.00135	0.00131	0.00126	0.00122	0.00118	0.00114	0.00111	0.00107	0.00104	0.00100
3.1	0.00097	0.00094	0.00090	0.00087	0.00085	0.00082	0.00079	0.00076	0.00074	0.00071
3.2	0.00069	0.00066	0.00064	0.00062	0.00060	0.00058	0.00056	0.00054	0.00052	0.00050
3.3	0.00048	0.00047	0.00045	0.00043	0.00042	0.00040	0.00039	0.00038	0.00036	0.00035
3.4	0.00034	0.00033	0.00031	0.00030	0.00029	0.00028	0.00027	0.00026	0.00025	0.00024
3.5	0.00023	0.00022	0.00022	0.00021	0.00020	0.00019	0.00019	0.00018	0.00017	0.00017

Table of the standard normal distribution values ($z \geq 0$)

z	0.00	0.01	0.02	0.03	0.04	0.05	0.06	0.07	0.08	0.09
0.0	0.50000	0.50399	0.50798	0.51197	0.51595	0.51994	0.52392	0.52790	0.53188	0.53586
0.1	0.53983	0.54380	0.54776	0.55172	0.55567	0.55962	0.56356	0.56749	0.57142	0.57535
0.2	0.57926	0.58317	0.58706	0.59095	0.59483	0.59871	0.60257	0.60642	0.61026	0.61409
0.3	0.61791	0.62172	0.62552	0.62930	0.63307	0.63683	0.64058	0.64431	0.64803	0.65173
0.4	0.65542	0.65910	0.66276	0.66640	0.67003	0.67364	0.67724	0.68082	0.68439	0.68793
0.5	0.69146	0.69497	0.69847	0.70194	0.70540	0.70884	0.71226	0.71566	0.71904	0.72240
0.6	0.72575	0.72907	0.73237	0.73565	0.73891	0.74215	0.74537	0.74857	0.75175	0.75490
0.7	0.75804	0.76115	0.76424	0.76730	0.77035	0.77337	0.77637	0.77935	0.78230	0.78524
0.8	0.78814	0.79103	0.79389	0.79673	0.79955	0.80234	0.80511	0.80785	0.81057	0.81327
0.9	0.81594	0.81859	0.82121	0.82381	0.82639	0.82894	0.83147	0.83398	0.83646	0.83891
1.0	0.84134	0.84375	0.84614	0.84849	0.85083	0.85314	0.85543	0.85769	0.85993	0.86214
1.1	0.86433	0.86650	0.86864	0.87076	0.87286	0.87493	0.87698	0.87900	0.88100	0.88298
1.2	0.88493	0.88686	0.88877	0.89065	0.89251	0.89435	0.89617	0.89796	0.89973	0.90147
1.3	0.90320	0.90490	0.90658	0.90824	0.90988	0.91149	0.91308	0.91466	0.91621	0.91774
1.4	0.91924	0.92073	0.92220	0.92364	0.92507	0.92647	0.92785	0.92922	0.93056	0.93189
1.5	0.93319	0.93448	0.93574	0.93699	0.93822	0.93943	0.94062	0.94179	0.94295	0.94408
1.6	0.94520	0.94630	0.94738	0.94845	0.94950	0.95053	0.95154	0.95254	0.95352	0.95449
1.7	0.95543	0.95637	0.95728	0.95818	0.95907	0.95994	0.96080	0.96164	0.96246	0.96327
1.8	0.96407	0.96485	0.96562	0.96638	0.96712	0.96784	0.96856	0.96926	0.96995	0.97062
1.9	0.97128	0.97193	0.97257	0.97320	0.97381	0.97441	0.97500	0.97558	0.97615	0.97670
2.0	0.97725	0.97778	0.97831	0.97882	0.97932	0.97982	0.98030	0.98077	0.98124	0.98169
2.1	0.98214	0.98257	0.98300	0.98341	0.98382	0.98422	0.98461	0.98500	0.98537	0.98574
2.2	0.98610	0.98645	0.98679	0.98713	0.98745	0.98778	0.98809	0.98840	0.98870	0.98899
2.3	0.98928	0.98956	0.98983	0.99010	0.99036	0.99061	0.99086	0.99111	0.99134	0.99158
2.4	0.99180	0.99202	0.99224	0.99245	0.99266	0.99286	0.99305	0.99324	0.99343	0.99361
2.5	0.99379	0.99396	0.99413	0.99430	0.99446	0.99461	0.99477	0.99492	0.99506	0.99520
2.6	0.99534	0.99547	0.99560	0.99573	0.99585	0.99598	0.99609	0.99621	0.99632	0.99643
2.7	0.99653	0.99664	0.99674	0.99683	0.99693	0.99702	0.99711	0.99720	0.99728	0.99736
2.8	0.99744	0.99752	0.99760	0.99767	0.99774	0.99781	0.99788	0.99795	0.99801	0.99807
2.9	0.99813	0.99819	0.99825	0.99831	0.99836	0.99841	0.99846	0.99851	0.99856	0.99861
3.0	0.99865	0.99869	0.99874	0.99878	0.99882	0.99886	0.99889	0.99893	0.99896	0.99900
3.1	0.99903	0.99906	0.99910	0.99913	0.99916	0.99918	0.99921	0.99924	0.99926	0.99929
3.2	0.99931	0.99934	0.99936	0.99938	0.99940	0.99942	0.99944	0.99946	0.99948	0.99950
3.3	0.99952	0.99953	0.99955	0.99957	0.99958	0.99960	0.99961	0.99962	0.99964	0.99965
3.4	0.99966	0.99968	0.99969	0.99970	0.99971	0.99972	0.99973	0.99974	0.99975	0.99976
3.5	0.99977	0.99978	0.99978	0.99979	0.99980	0.99981	0.99981	0.99982	0.99983	0.99983

UNIT 7

JUST-IN-TIME SYSTEMS

UNIT SPECIFICS

This unit elaborately discusses the following topics:

- Goals of JIT
- Modules of JIT system (Product design and process design)
- Manufacturing planning and control (Pull system)
- Kanban system
- Close vendor relationship

The cutting-edge ideas of the subjects are examined in order to promote greater creativity and curiosity. In addition to a number of multiple-choice questions, the questions are divided into short and long answer categories according to Bloom's taxonomy's lower and higher orders. In keeping with the content, the unit also provides an additional section ("Along the...") after the unit's related topic. It has been thoughtfully written to benefit the book's reader. This content primarily emphasizes the amazing facts about the issue being addressed in the contemporary, fascinating industrial setting in order to spark interest in the subject.

It is significant to note that parts have included QR codes that can be scanned to obtain pertinent supporting material on a variety of interesting topics.

RATIONALE

This unit explores Just-In-Time (JIT) manufacturing, focusing on its goals of reducing waste and improving efficiency. It discusses key modules of the JIT system, including product and process design, which are essential for streamlined operations. The chapter emphasizes the pull system in manufacturing planning and control, highlighting its role in responding to actual demand. Additionally, the Kanban system is examined as a tool for managing inventory flow, while the importance of close vendor relationships is addressed to ensure timely material supply and enhance collaboration.

UNIT OUTCOMES

List of outcomes of this unit is as follows:

U7-UO1: Define JIT Goals

U7-UO2: Identify JIT Modules

U7-UO3: Explain the Pull System

U7-UO4: Utilize the Kanban System

U7-UO5: Assess Vendor Relationships

U7-UO6: Analyze JIT Implementation Challenges

UNIT-7 Outcomes	EXPECTED MAPPING WITH COURSE OUTCOMES (1-Weak Correlation; 2-Medium Correlation; 3-Strong Correlation)					
	CO-1	CO-2	CO-3	CO-4	CO-5	CO-6
U7-UO1	2	2	3	3	2	2
U7-UO2	2	2	3	3	2	2
U7-UO3	2	2	3	3	3	2
U7-UO4	1	2	3	3	2	2
U7-UO5	2	2	3	3	3	1
U7-UO6	1	2	3	3	3	2

Several businesses, particularly in the manufacturing sector, are implementing a just-in-time strategy in an effort to optimize processes and save inventory costs. Rather than storing inventory, businesses aim to run in a just-in-time (JIT) environment with as little inventory as possible. This necessitates building a system that functions in this way and collaborating closely with suppliers to ensure that supplies and pieces are delivered exactly when needed, or just in time. Producing only what is required, when required, and maintaining a continuous workflow with the least amount of resources is the aim of a just-in-time (JIT) system. Exceeding the required amount is considered waste. A significant decrease in work-in-process and finished goods inventories, as well as a corresponding decrease in the amount of working capital allocated to inventories, are two clear advantages of a JIT system. Reduced waste, balanced manufacturing, and excellent quality are further advantages.

Businesses are always looking for more efficient ways to run their operations. For some, this entails switching to what are now known as lean operations from the conventional methods of operating. Because of their highly synchronized activities and just-in-time delivery of commodities, lean systems are sometimes known as just-in-time systems. There is very little "fat" in lean manufacturing processes (e.g., excess inventory, superfluous labor, wasted space). JIT is concerned with when components and materials enter the system and when services are rendered. Businesses that use the just-in-time (JIT) or lean production approach generally have a competitive edge over those that follow a more traditional strategy. This is because they may launch new or better products faster, with lower processing costs, fewer faults, and more flexibility.

JIT is one of the two fundamental techniques to manufacturing planning and control, the other being material requirements planning. One component of JIT is production planning and control. While MRP is thought of as a system for batch production, JIT is occasionally seen as a solution for repetitive manufacturing processes. Though the two systems operate significantly differently, they are occasionally applied to situations that are comparable. Due to their complexity, MRP systems necessitate comprehensive and intricate shop floor controls. JIT systems require very few shop floor controls, making them significantly simpler. Furthermore, JIT depends on auditory or visual signals to initiate production and delivery, while MRP depends on a computer-based component scheduling system.

7.1 INTRODUCTION

Since World War II, full employment through industrialization has been the national aspiration of the Japanese. Targeting particular product categories has been the method for achieving market domination. The Japanese Ministry of International Trade and Industry only considered industries with a competitive edge when deciding which ones to target for improvement. They brought in technology to make their nation more competitive. Their focus was mostly on the production floor in order to attain high productivity and reduced unit costs. They also made an effort to raise the quality and reliability of their product above those offered by rivals. The removal of waste was a key focus of their activities. The Japanese developed a strong sense of waste and inefficiency, which is not surprising. They considered extra inventory to be a burden since it locks up resources and takes up space, and scrap and rework to be waste. Urban Lehner's book "The Nuts and Bolts of Japan's Factories" offers valuable insights into the just-in-time manufacturing methodology and explains some of the factors that have contributed to the success of Japanese manufacturers.

Toyota gained a significant deal of knowledge by observing Ford's operations and used that knowledge to inform their JIT strategy. But Toyota managed to achieve what Ford was unable to: a system that could accommodate variation.

A common misconception about Just-In-time manufacturing scheduling is that it's just another inventory and work-in-process scheduling system. But in its purest form, just-in-time manufacturing is a philosophy that touches on every stage of the process, from product design to post-sale support. The idea is to develop a system that runs efficiently with the least amount of inventory, waste, space, and transactions. The system needs to be resilient to disturbances and adaptable in terms of the range of products and volumes it can manage. The ultimate objective is to create a balanced system that enables materials to move through it quickly and easily.

Quality is intrinsic to the process as well as the product in JIT systems. Businesses that employ JIT have attained a quality standard that allows them to operate with tiny batch sizes and constrained timetables. The JIT system is very reliable; significant causes of disruption and inefficiency have been removed, and employees have received training on both how to operate the system and how to continuously enhance it.

ALONG THE JIT SYSTEMS

Apple

The IT giant Apple has successfully implemented JIT principles in its production process. Apple takes a different tack when it comes to JIT since they use their suppliers to help them meet their objectives. With just one main warehouse located in the US and roughly 150 important suppliers across the globe, Apple has established smart and robust partnerships with their suppliers. Apple became leaner as a result of this production outsourcing, which also cut expenses and decreased overstock. Most of their merchandise is kept at their retail locations because they only have one central warehouse in the US. Apple started to use dropshipping, which added even more to the JIT mix. This lowers the cost of storage, waste, and transportation.

Key elements influencing Apple's success

- Suppliers' readiness to maintain stock on hand, relieving Apple of this obligation
- keeping stock at their retail locations
- Set up dropshipping for internet purchases

The other companies benefited from JIT policy

Apparel industry

Nike's disjointed production facilities throughout Southeast Asia were improved with the implementation of a just-in-time delivery system. Using just-in-time production and lean inventory approaches was the aim. Since then, research indicates that the company has shortened lead times by 40%, raised productivity by 20%, and sped up the introduction of new models by 30%.

Retail industry

The retailer Zara benefits from just-in-time delivery since it keeps production and sales regionally synchronized and guarantee that each location receives only the inventory they require. In this fast-fashion era, Zara can react to shifting fashion markets more swiftly.

Watch industry

JIT delivery gives luxury watchmaker Grayton a competitive advantage in their sector. Grayton increased their cash flow by 70% and became the first company in the watch business to embrace lean production practices.

Computer industry

Dell was able to flourish early on due of its lean operations. When Dell first began selling directly to customers in the 1980s, they only ordered parts when customers made purchases. Instead of keeping an entire warehouse full of pre-assembled computers, Dell shortened lead times, lowered prices, and finally rose to prominence in their sector.

Fast food industry

Every day in their kitchens, Burger King locations apply the just-in-time delivery philosophy. Food is only prepared upon request, even though they maintain an inventory of the necessary ingredients. Here, ordering food is done using the JIT delivery method, which keeps food fresh and minimizes waste.

Remarks

Mostly JIT is used by manufacturers to make commodities like automobiles, which allow them to meet client demand and prevent significant accumulations of finished goods inventory. It is not as likely to be employed in the manufacturing of consumer products.

These firms often work in a make-to-stock manner, manufacturing goods that are kept in inventory until they are needed, as opposed to the make-to-order mode. They can do this because they produce standard items on the basis of a marketing forecast. However, the forecast is subject to error due to demand variability. Finished goods inventories buffer these manufacturers from disruptions caused by differences between the forecast and actual demand.

7.2 GOALS OF JIT

A balanced system, or one that accomplishes a seamless, quick flow of materials through the system, is the ultimate goal of just-in-time (JIT). The goal is to use resources as efficiently as possible in order to minimize the process duration. The success of some supporting goals determines the extent to which the main goal is accomplished. These objectives are:

1. Remove disruptions
2. Provide for system flexibility
3. Shorten lead and setup times
4. Reduce the amount of inventory
5. Remove waste

The performance of the system is negatively impacted by disruptions in the efficient flow of products through it. It is necessary to stop these disruptions. Numerous variables, including low-quality equipment malfunctions, schedule modifications, and delayed delivery, are responsible for these disruptions. As far as feasible, these should all be removed. As a result, there will be less ambiguity for the system to handle.

A flexible system is one that is strong enough to manage a variety of goods, frequently on a daily basis, and can adapt to variations in output level without compromising balance or throughput speed. The system is able to handle some uncertainty as a result of this.

Lead times for setup and delivery elongate a procedure without improving the quality of the final output. Additionally, lengthy lead and setup periods have a detrimental effect on the system's adaptability. Therefore, cutting down on setup and lead times is crucial and one of the goals of continuous improvement.

Inventory is a wasteful resource that increases system costs and takes up space. It needs to be reduced to the barest minimum.

Waste is an indicator of non-value-adding activity[2]; removing waste can improve production efficiency and free up resources. Among the wastes in the JIT system are: (i) excessive use of manufacturing resources resulting overproduction, (ii) requiring extra space for waiting time in work-in-process, (iii) increase of handling due to unnecesssary transporting, (iv) unused resources, unreported quality problems, and production inefficiencies brought on by inventories, (v) waste as a result of needless production processes and scrap generation, (vi) inappropriate layout, ineffective work techniques, and patterns of material movement all contribute to an increase in work-in-process inventory, (vii) rework charges and potential revenue losses as a result of dissatisfied customers brought on by defects in the product. The fact that these wastes exist suggests that things may be improved. These may also point up possible areas for continuing attempts at improvement.

7.3 FUNDAMENTAL MODULES OF JIT SYSTEM

JIT goals can be achieved by the design and operation of a system, which provides the fundamental basis for success. Four modules make up the fundamentals: product design, process design, manufacturing planning and control, and organizational and personnel aspects.

7.3.1 PRODUCT DESIGN

Standard parts, modular design, and quality are the three fundamental elements of product design that JIT systems depend on.

Repeatability is increased by part commonality, or the *standardization of components*. A firm that produces ten products with a thousand different components, for instance, could update its products to have only one hundred components with significant daily requirements. Repeatability grows when component requirements rise, meaning that every worker must carry out a standardized activity or work process more frequently every day. Employees that are trained to do tasks more effectively tend to be more productive. JIT

[2] Non-value-adding refers to activities within a company that do not directly contribute to satisfying end consumers' requirements

systems aim for high productivity and low inventory, and this can be achieved in part by standardizing components and labor processes.

In order to more effectively organize complicated designs and processes, *modular design* essentially breaks large systems down into smaller, more manageable modules. The idea was first presented by (Starr 1965), who suggested using modular products in production as a novel way to increase variety. The idea of modular design has been used to numerous design and production domains. Modular design offers three key benefits: cost savings, augmentation, and design flexibility. The designer can more simply alter each module rather than the entire design since the components are grouped into distinct modules. Furthermore, the system may be enhanced by adding new features by only plugging in a new module, allowing the system to be expanded within a predetermined range.

An expansion of standardization is modular design. Modules are groups of components that are handled as a single entity. Because there are a lot less pieces to manage, assembling, buying, handling, training, and other tasks become much easier. A further advantage of standardization is that it reduces the number of distinct parts that are included in the bill-of-materials for different products, making the bill of materials simpler.

Inability to alter a standard design and reduced product variety are drawbacks of standardization. These drawbacks are somewhat mitigated in cases where various products share some components and modules. A management can postpone choosing which end-items to generate while the standard portions are being produced by employing a strategy known as *delayed differentiation* or some times referred to as *postponement*.

Understanding modularity in the automotive business requires setting it apart from a "*system*." A module is a self-contained assembly that adheres to standards and performs a specific function inside a larger system; on the other hand, a system is a collection of interdependent pieces that work together as a whole. A car seat is a self-contained unit that can be produced by a separate manufacturer and added as a module when the automobile is being assembled. However, the brake system is one that cannot be made by a single manufacturer and installed as a module when the automobile is being assembled. It is equipped with interconnected systems that use fluid under pressure to travel from the brake pedal to the wheels and are connected to the engine. The car's entire electrical system is connected. System is always constructed from several components. Nonetheless, it is impossible to design a module and ignore how it interacts with the system.

Assuring that goods and services fulfill requirements for performance, safety, and high standards is known as *quality control*. Quality control is crucial to JIT production in order to prevent errors, holdups, and dissatisfied consumers. Inspection and testing of the arriving supplies, the production procedures, and the finished products are all part of JIT quality control. Additionally, it entails locating and removing the primary drivers of waste, variance, and errors. As opposed to a reactive and remedial strategy, quality control in JIT necessitates a proactive and preventive one.

JIT manufacturing processes and consumers can gain a great deal from quality control, including lower inventory and storage costs, increased customer satisfaction and loyalty, and increased productivity and efficiency. Quality control saves space, money, and resources by reducing the requirement for buffer stocks, rework, and excess inventory. Additionally, it makes the manufacturer more competitive and reputable, which attracts more devoted and satisfied customers. In addition, it reduces cycle and lead times, optimizes resource utilization, and streamlines manufacturing processes, all of which boost output and efficiency.

Since just-in-time (JIT) manufacturing depends on suppliers delivering materials on a regular basis, any disruption or delay in the supply may have an impact on the output's quantity and quality. This calls for tight coordination and communication with the providers in addition to having a backup plan in place for unforeseen circumstances. Furthermore, as there is little room for error or modification in JIT production, any flaw or variance in the final product may lead to consumer complaints or returns.

Three parts make up the JIT system's quality approach. Creating a high-quality product and production method is one aspect of it. High quality levels can be achieved with Just-In-Time (JIT) systems, which generate standardized goods that result in uniform manufacturing techniques, job familiarization for workers, and the usage of standardized production equipment. Furthermore, it is possible to spread the cost of product design quality – that is, adding quality into the design phase – over a large number of units, resulting in a low cost per unit. Selecting the right quality levels for the final client and manufacturing capacity is also crucial. As a result, process design and product design need to go simultaneously.

7.3.2 PROCESS DESIGN

Small Lot Sizes – Users of JIT systems preserve inventory with the smallest lot sizes feasible rather than accruing a buffer of inventory. There are three advantages to small lots. First off, cycle inventory – the extra inventory held between orders – is decreased by small lot sizes (see Unit 6).

Fig. 7.1 Effects for cycle inventories with respect to small and large lot sizes

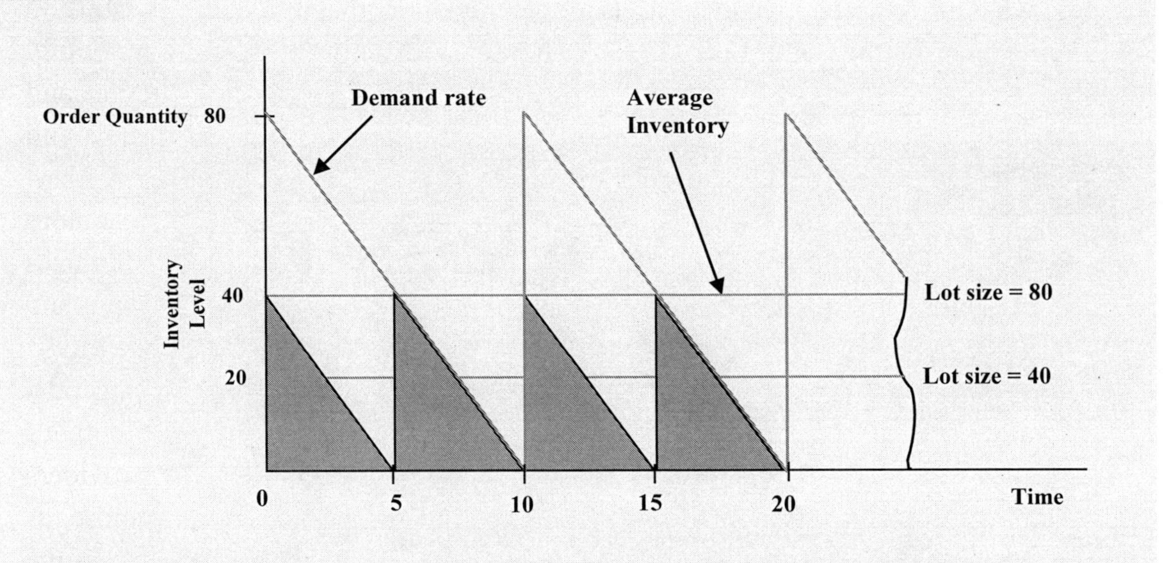

On average, cycle inventory is half the size of the lot; cycle inventory decreases as the lot size decreases. The amount of time and space needed for production and inventory holding is decreased by reducing cycle inventory. The impact of decreasing the lot size from 80 to 40 on cycle inventory for a consistent demand of 8 units per hour is depicted in Fig. 7.1. Half of the cycle inventory has been eliminated.

Secondly, lead times are shortened by modest lot sizes. Because large lots require more overall processing time at each workstation than small lots do, a decrease in lead time also reduces pipeline (work-in-process) inventory. Additionally, after one workstation completes processing a large lot, the next one frequently has to wait longer to process a large lot. Large lots also result in greater delays if any defective items are found because the lots as a whole needs to be inspected in order to identify every item that requires rework.

Last but not least, small quantities contribute to a consistent operating system workload. Large lots make scheduling more difficult because they take up a lot of workstation processing time. Planners can use capacities more effectively by judging small lots more effectively. Furthermore, small batches shorten manufacturing wait times, enabling workstations to handle mixed-model production (more than one variant of item).

Assume, for example, that a company offers three product variants: X, Y, and Z. In a conventional system, the pattern would repeat after a lengthy run of variant X (for example, spanning two or three days or longer), a long run of variant Y, and a long run of variant Z. A JIT system, on the other hand, would usually switch from producing X to manufacturing Y and Z when using small lots. Because of their adaptability, just-in-time (JIT) systems can create exactly what is required, when it is required, allowing them to react to shifting customer requirements for output faster. Fig. 7.2 shows the difference between small and large lot sizes.

Fig. 7.2 Comparison of JIT with large-lot run sizes

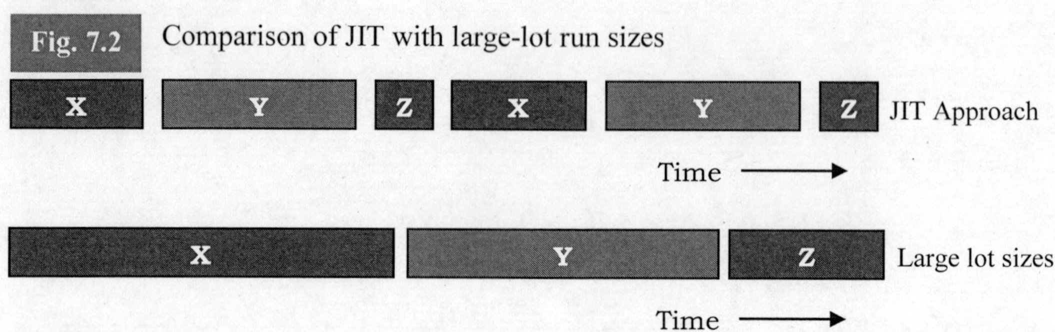

Short Setup Durations – Regular setups are necessary due to small quantities and fluctuating product combinations. The time and expense involved in doing these tasks may be prohibitive unless they are simple and inexpensive. A system frequently educates employees to perform their own installations. In addition, the system makes use of programs to cut down on setup time and expenses in order to accomplish the intended goals; workers are typically an important component of the process and conscious effort is needed.

SCAN ME
For Virtual Cellular Manufacturing

Standardized and easy-to-use setup processes are required for both setup equipment and tools. Equipment or attachments with many uses might speed up setup. One way to significantly cut down on job changeover time is to have a machine with numerous spindles that can be readily rotated into place to suit different project requirements. By using commonalities in recurrent tasks, group technology can also minimize setup costs and times. For example, pieces with comparable shapes, materials, and so forth, might need extremely similar configurations. Sequential processing on the same apparatus can minimize the necessity for a setup modification; only small adjustments might be required.

Group technology typically takes advantage of the design similarities between products and processes. By shortening the setup time, family-based dispatching (FBD) rules tackle the problem of better lead time performance. One could think of FBD rules as a component of the virtual cellular manufacturing (VCM) idea. This is accomplished by classifying products into families for cooperative dispatching that have comparable system setup needs. The manufacturing of discrete parts in small batches benefits from the implementation of these criteria. Decisions about dispatching are done under the assumption of a two-phase process, wherein selecting a family comes before selecting a particular job from the range of jobs that are accessible for the family. Alternative guidelines for family-based dispatching usually only differ in how families select priorities and which jobs each family chooses to perform. Productivity is increased by using the proper dispatching rule under exchange of information at the individual workstation and cellular shop levels. The evaluation of the impact of implementing a specific dispatching rule under information capabilities can improve the overall performance of the supply chain and provide the system extraordinary flexibility.

You may save setup time by making better selections by keeping an eye on your equipment

Cellular manufacturing – Multiple production cells are a feature of many Just-in-Time (JIT) systems. The cells hold the equipment and machinery required to process families of parts with comparable processing needs. The cells are essentially extremely efficient, highly specialized production hubs in the manufacturing process. Reduced changeover times, high equipment utilization, and simplicity of cross-training operators are a few of the manufacturing cells' major advantages. Very little work-in-process inventory is produced by the combination of small lot sizes and high cell efficiency.

Although cellular setting in service sector is rare, but an interesting example do come out of health sector – instead of routing patients all over different sections of a hospital for carrying out various tests, exams, X-rays, and injections – are reorganizing their services into work groups based on the type of problem. Teams that treat only traumas are common are common, but other work groups have been formed to treat less immediate conditions like hernias.

Adding cellular manufacturing to the JIT manufacturing workflow has the following benefits:

- Improved conditions for production and quality assurance
- Increased ability to quickly generate a wide range of high-volume items
- Significant decrease in waste and delay time in production
- Reduced inventory of work-in-progress (WIP)
- Create a highly adaptable and efficient staff

Expansion of Quality – The strong connection between Just-In-Time (JIT) and Total Quality Management (TQM) is widely acknowledged. The TQM (discussed in detail in Unit 14) movement's main goal is to reduce quality issues in the production and design system by emphasizing process analysis and improvement. TQM also places a strong emphasis on minimizing waste, particularly that which is related to quality. Not only do these methods align with JIT principles, but they also form the core of a JIT implementation.

Sometimes, JIT systems use autonomy (automated defect detection during production) in a production setting to minimize defects. It is applicable to machinery and, more recently, *image processing*, for defect detection which finds extensive application in several industries. Stopping the production causes the issue to be addressed right away, which is followed by an investigation and the implementation of remedial measures to fix the issue.

SCAN ME
for
Image processing
for defect detection

Production Flexibility – The ability to process a variety of products in a seamless flow is the ultimate goal of a just-in-time (JIT) system. Bottlenecks that arise from overloaded areas of the system are one possible hindrance to this goal. A flexible production system is necessary to get beyond this challenge. In the literature, many flexible production systems are thoroughly investigated. The variety of responses to the manufacturing system management is impacted by these flexibilities. A few of the various kinds of manufacturing flexibilities that are discussed below are briefly explained here.

Volume flexibility is the first category of manufacturing flexibility. It is described as the capacity to adjust production levels to changes in consumer demand. In the event of fluctuating demand, volume flexibility necessitates tight collaboration between the manufacturer and its supplier. This cooperation could involve the exchange of data about lead times or the inventory of a raw material supplier. Product modularity is crucial for volume flexibility since it standardizes components and boosts customisation. Volume flexibility successfully handles out-of-stock situations.

"Machine flexibility" is the second category of manufacturing flexibility. Highly flexible workstations have a variety of features, such as the ability to quickly change the program according to the task at hand, a user-friendly programming language, an advanced part-loading and tool-changing system, an ample supply of pallets and fixtures, automatic chip removal, control to optimize metal removal, integration with Computer Aided Design (CAD)/Computer Aided Manufacturing (CAM). Workstations with Computerized Numerical Control (CNC) machining centers are incredibly versatile.

"Process flexibility" is the third category of manufacturing flexibility. It is the system's ability to manufacture various parts without requiring extensive setups. This adaptability makes possible the JIT system, which lowers inventory levels and requires smaller batch sizes. Machine flexibility and volume flexibility are inherited by process flexibility. Group technology can be viewed as the foundation for process flexibility, where different family-based dispatching rules allow for a reduction in setup time. In this instance, volume flexibility can be defined as the various part families that a given cell is capable of handling.

SCAN ME
for
Family-based dispatching rules

The flexibility related to "Routing" is the fourth category in production – the capability to transport the component for production through different paths within the system. Different machines, different processes, or a different order of operations can all be thought of as alternative pathways. This can also be viewed from the perspective of group technology in that the part may route or balk to another machine with a different path in circumstances such as machine unavailability. On the other hand, using a different machine requires a flexible procedure. Flexible routing facilitates the creation of effective part scheduling. Thus, in the context of a short product life cycle, it helps to improve customer due-date performance.

The ability to route flexible requires prospective information and communication (ICT) skills at both the intra – and interorganizational levels. This is because routing to different machines necessitates the determination of priority based on certain factors, such as processing times for various part types or minimal setup times. Real-time information at the point of sale is necessary for due-date choice.

Preparedness to improve consistently – JIT methods promote consistent improvement in efficiency and quality by highlighting areas that require attention. The idea behind JIT systems' constant improvement is illustrated in Fig. 7.3. The water surface in manufacturing is a representation of the inventory levels of products and components. The water surface in services refers to the staffing levels and other capacity of the service system. The rocks stand in for issues that arise during production or service delivery. Because the large inventory level hides issues, the ship passes over the rocks when the water level is high enough. Rocks become more visible as inventory decreases. Ultimately, if the water surface indicating inventory levels declines enough, the ship will run into trouble on a variety of unfavorable, difficult circumstances. With JIT systems, employees, managers, engineers, and analysts use techniques for continuous improvement, such as statistical quality control (SQC), total quality management (TQM), and others, to break down the visible rocks of troublesome issues. In JIT systems, material flows must be coordinated in order for the pull system – discussed in the section ahead – to identify issues and take corrective action in a timely manner.

Reduced inventories are the outcome of a long-term, effective process of issue solutions. Moreover, it is imperative to have the ability to promptly address issues when they arise, as it is improbable that every issue will be identified and fixed. Therefore, in order to keep new issues from interfering with the efficient flow of work through the system, it is constantly necessary to recognize problems and find quick solutions for them.

Direct delivery of supplies from suppliers to the manufacturing floor reduces inventory storage in a Just-In-Time (JIT) system by doing away with the need to hold incoming components and materials. Finished goods are kept in less storage at the other end of the process since units are transported out as soon as they are ready. These characteristics, when combined with minimal work-in-process inventory, lead to systems that run with very little stock. Fewer inventories, however, comes with certain hazards as well: First and foremost, there is no safety stock in case issues develop. Missed opportunities arise when the system fails to react promptly to them.

SCAN ME
for
Vendor Managed
Inventory

However, to overcome the problem of less safety stock, one option is the vendor-managed inventory (VMI) system, in which the supplier of raw materials (the vendor) receives real-time information about the manufacturer's production plans or the retailer's demand in real-time and arranges their own supplies and production accordingly. As a result, the uncertainties that cause inventory levels to rise are removed.

Fig. 7.3 Inventory conceals failures and wastes

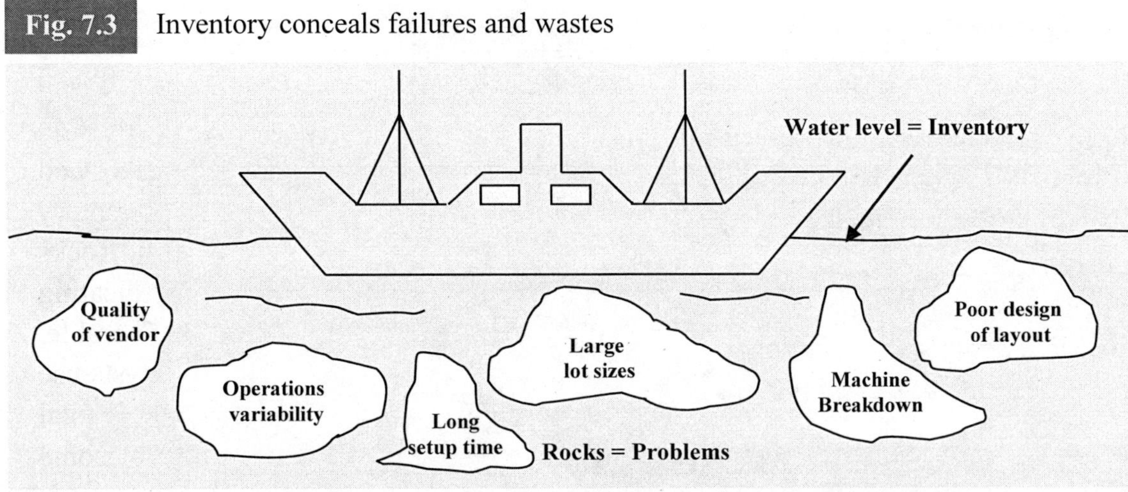

ALONG THE EFFORTS OF CONSISTENT IMPROVEMENT

Howard Bank, a Community Bank Maximizes Performance With Business Process Improvement

During the account establishing procedure, Howard Bank desired additional time to establish a connection with its clients. To help reach this objective through increasing process efficiency, the bank selected Fiserv's Business Process Improvement for Financial Institutions. The bank was able to engage in meaningful interactions with consumers and gain a better understanding of their actual financial needs by implementing more efficient operations.

Leaders at Howard Bank looked at account opening procedures to find methods to shorten the process so they could spend more time with customers. This was done out of a desire to provide outstanding customer service. They chose to pursue business process improvement as a means of achieving long-term value after identifying several areas for improvement.

Wade Barnes, chief marketing officer and director of product and delivery innovation, stated, "We didn't have the time to do that with our existing account opening process. Our strategy is to deliver outstanding service by having meaningful conversations with our customers."

Opening an account with Howard Bank took about an hour and a half prior to the implementation of business process improvement. Fiserv assisted the bank in streamlining the account opening process from the front desk to the back office and combining vital business data. By automating the account opening procedure, the bank was able to eliminate paper records and reduce processing times by more than 75%. Howard Bank accounts can now be opened in just 20 minutes. Bank employees may spend more time with customers and have in-depth talks to learn how they can best service their financial needs because they have a lot less paperwork to handle.

7.3.3 MANUFACTURING PLANNING AND CONTROL

There are five elements of manufacturing planning and control which are particularly important from JIT systems point of view.

1. Uniform production levels
2. Pull systems
3. Kanban or visual systems
4. Close interactions with vendors
5. Less processing of transactions

7.3.3.1 UNIFORM PRODUCTION LEVELS

Leveling or smoothing demand throughout the planning horizon is one method of reaching consistent output; this technique is called heijunka. Demand is broken down into tiny time intervals and dispersed as uniformly as feasible to ensure that the same quantity of each item is produced every day. Production of individual items is also distributed throughout the day in minute amounts. The models placed in sequence on the final assembly line determine the mix.

Diet Coke, Coke Zero, Vanilla Coke, and other soft drink varieties are produced by the Coca-Cola Company. Starting with each product or variant's daily production requirements, the mixed-product sequencing process is initiated. Let us choose three different variations of Coke: Diet Coke (X), Coke Zero (Y), and Vanilla Coke (Z), each having a daily requirement of 1000, 1500, and 500, respectively. Each variant is produced in batches of 100. There are three problems that require attention. Three questions need to be answered: first, what sequence (Z-Y-X, X-Y-Z, etc.) to employ; second, how many cycles (i.e., repetitions) of the sequence should be performed each day; and third, how many units of each variant to manufacture in each cycle.

The daily production amounts determine the number of cycles in a day. The number of cycles will be indicated by finding the smallest integer that can be evenly divided into each variety's daily quantity if producing every variant in every cycle is the aim, which is frequently the case. Five cycles (5, that can be equally divided into each quantity) should be used for variants X, Y, and Z. A manager may choose to use fewer cycles due to high setup costs, which would trade off setup cost reductions and level production. A manager may choose to use the smallest production amount to choose a number of cycles if dividing by the smallest daily quantity does not generate an integer value for each variant. In order to make up the difference, they can then produce more of some items in some cycles.

Occasionally, a manager will divide the daily production quantity of each variant by the total number of cycles to find the number of units of each variant in each cycle. 200 units of X, 300 units of Y, and 100 units of Z could be produced by using five cycles per day.

Because of limitations on packing lot sizes, certain amounts might not be feasible. Because variant Y, for instance, might be packaged 400 units to a carton, making 300 units per cycle would occasionally require waiting for finished units (inventory) to become available in sufficient quantities to fill an entire carton. Similar to this, multiple batch sizes may be used in some production processes in the order of operations. An example of this would be a bottle-washing fixture that can handle up to fifty bottles at once. The bottles could not be grouped if the various variants required different fixture sizes. An examination of the trade-off between setup costs for changing fixtures and the benefit of level production is required in this case.

7.3.3.2 THE PULL SYSTEMS

In the car manufacturing industry, the main challenge is to coordinate the needs of the final assembly line, subassembly production, and material and part delivery with each other. A single automobile requires the production of thousands of little and huge components by thousands of workers, which is why the process is complex rather than the technology. Large stocks have historically been kept on hand as a safety measure against coordination errors. Ohno spent five years attempting to devise a system that would enhance process coordination and reduce the requirement for substantial inventories. Ultimately, the super market – another American classic – gave him the idea for his pull method. Ohno discovered (after reading) that Americans do not maintain substantial food reserves at home. Rather, they shop at neighboring stores often and buy things as needed. In response, the stores keep a close eye on their stock, adding new things to their shelves only when old ones are taken out. The things that customers require are truly "pulled through" the system; stores never order more than they can sell.

Push systems function by reversing the standard process/information flow from the production point of view. A push system pushes finished work from one workstation to the next once a schedule for the group of workstations is prepared using forecasting techniques. With the ***pull system***, workers return to their prior positions, taking only the components or resources they require so they can start processing right away.

Hero of the Toyota Production System, Taiichi Ohno

Workers at the preceding station know when to start creating more when their output is generated; they replenish the exact amount, and the workers at the succeeding station just took away. Workers at the preceding station simply cease producing if their output is not taken; no extra is produced. Operations are compelled by this system to cooperate with one another. Only the necessary quantities are produced, preventing both overproduction and underproduction. "Necessary" is determined by the shop floor's operation, including unforeseen events and performance variances, not by the projected schedule that outlines what should be needed. When looking at the sequence of operations from a wider angle, each subsequent procedure is seen as a buyer or a customer, while the preceding operation is seen as a supplier that fulfills the demand from the subsequent operation.

Pull production system implementation can be challenging despite its seemingly straightforward notion because it deviates significantly from standard scheduling practice. With the advancement of information and communication technology, Ohno discovered that after testing with the pull method for several years, it was necessary to implement *Kanban* in order to have more control over the pull process on the shop floor.

7.3.3.3 THE KANBAN SYSTEM

The Toyota Kanban system is one of the JIT systems that have received the most attention. The Japanese word "Kanban," which means "card" or "visual record," describes the cards used in factories to regulate the flow of production. Each container containing manufactured items has a card attached to it in the simplest Kanban system. A percentage of an item's daily requirements are shown on this card. The card is taken out of the container and placed on a receiving post when the parts user empties a container. The storage facility is where the empty container is brought. The card indicates that more of the part has to be produced. After filling the container again, the card is placed on it and it is put back in a storage room. When the parts user picks up the container with the card inside, the cycle starts over.

Fig. 7.4 Kanban system with two cards

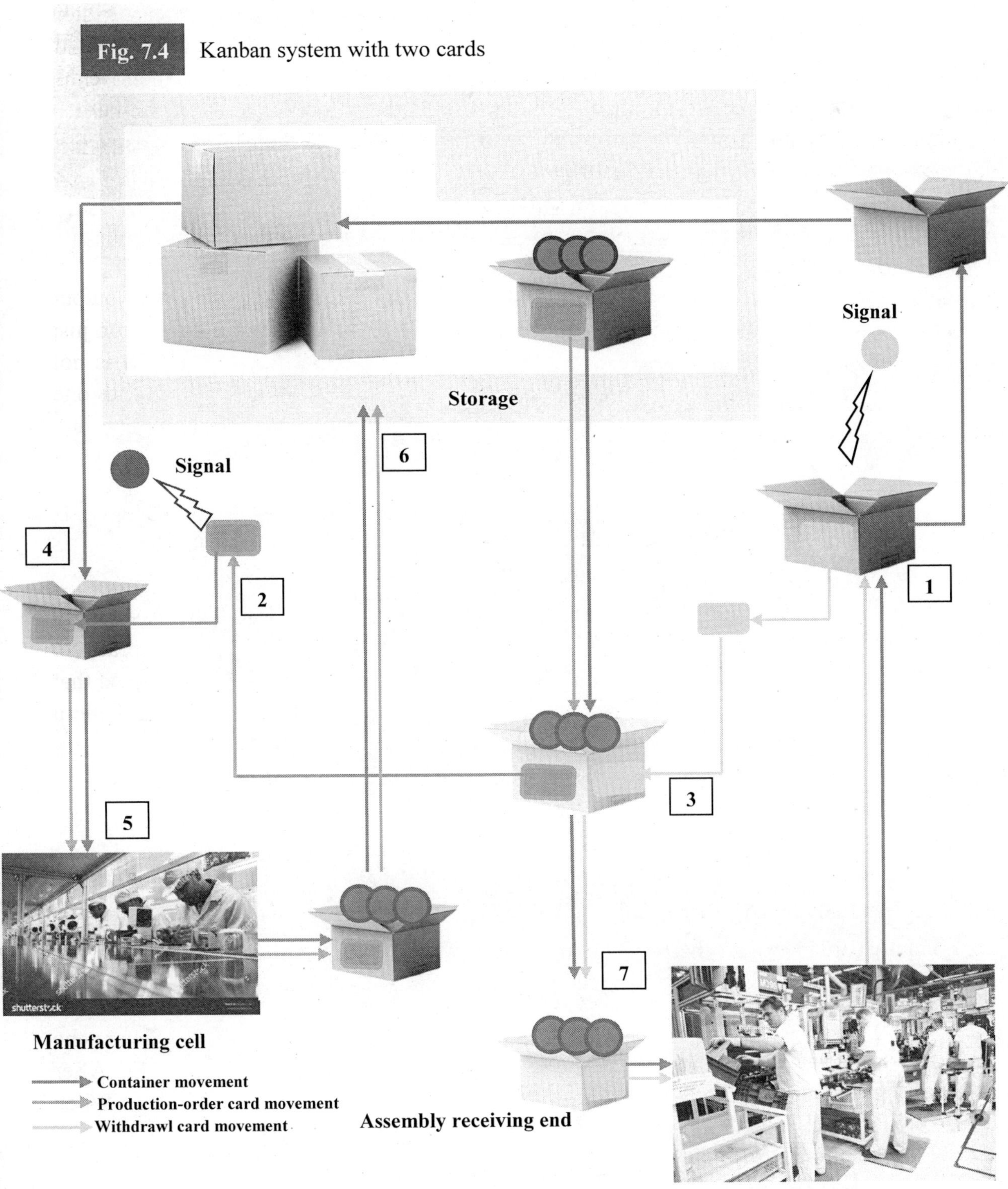

To further regulate withdrawal quantities, Toyota has implemented a two-card system that consists of a production-order card and a withdrawal card. The withdrawal card details the product, the amount that the user should take from the manufacturer, and the stocking locations for both the user and the manufacturer. The production-order card details the item to be created, the amount to be produced, the materials needed and their location, as well as the location of storage for the completed goods. Without a withdrawal card, materials cannot be removed, and without a production-order card, manufacturing cannot start. When production starts, the cards are fastened to containers. We can see the two-card setup in Fig. 7.4. Between the manufacturing cell and the assembly line moves the container (red arrow). The assembly line uses the withdrawal card (green arrow) to obtain additional materials. Along with the container, the production card (blue arrow) gives the manufacturing cell permission to make additional parts.

To keep things simple, we will discuss a manufacturing process that supplies an assembly line; however, the concept is applicable to any process that supplies another process.

Step 1. Removed from the assembly line and placed in the storage area are accumulated empty containers with withdrawal cards attached on. After removing the withdrawal cards from the containers, they are stored for later use (step 3).

Step 2. Full containers are swapped out for empty ones. Every full container has its production-order card removed and put on the receiving post; thereby send the signal of availability of card.

Step 3. Once the contents of the full containers match the requirements listed on the withdrawal card, each full container has a withdrawal card attached to it. The containers are moved to the assembly line's arriving stock point. The withdrawal card loop is finished with this step.

Step 4. The withdrawal of the production-order cards starts on receiving the signal of availability of card for the manufacturing cell's production process. Prior to being manufactured, they undergo screening and sorting.

Step 5. In accordance with the production-order cards, the pieces are manufactured in that order. The manufacturing cell receives the production-order cards that are attached to empty containers.

Step 6. The manufactured components along with the production-order card are sent to the storage.

Step 7. When the final phase's signal of a withdrawal card's availability in the shelf is received, the completed units are moved from storage to the assembly receiving end to meet the demands of the assembly line's output. This completes the loop of the production-order card.

Just-in-time material amounts are provided by coordinating all supplier and workstation tasks in a same manner. For processes based on pull systems, information sharing within a production system is crucial. In addition to the Kanban system, the CONWIP (CONstant Work in Process) system is another prominent pull system in the modern pull-based industries. A single set of cards is used by the CONWIP pull system, which is similar to a single-stage Kanban system, to regulate the overall work in progress (WIP). Only when there is a demand does material enter a CONWIP system, and the raw material is issued a card allowing entry. The material can proceed through the system and finish manufacture with authorization from the same card.

SCAN ME
for
CONWIP

7.3.3.4 CLOSE VENDOR RELATIONSHIP

Companies who have effective, long-term buyer-seller partnerships have a competitive advantage. Because of this, it's critical for businesses to comprehend the variables affecting their partnerships with other businesses. Determining the relative importance of these elements can help a business concentrate its efforts on the areas that matter most, increasing the long-term competitive advantage that results from that relationship. Relationships are influenced by a number of elements, including mutual goals, power and dependency, reputation, performance satisfaction, trust, social linkages, and the degree of comparison in trust.

In the past, buyers have been responsible for keeping an eye on the quality of the products they have purchased, examining shipments to ensure both quantity and quality, and returning subpar products to the vendor for repair. Because JIT systems have minimal margin for error, subpar products impede the efficient operation of the business. Furthermore, because it does not enhance the value of the product, the screening of arriving items is seen as inefficient. The vendor now bears the responsibility for guaranteeing quality for these reasons. Stock shipments need to happen often, with short lead times, and on time. A supplier may be required by a contract to deliver goods to a factory up to multiple times a day. Local vendors are often used by manufacturers who use JIT systems.

JIT consumers also discover that a cooperative attitude toward suppliers is crucial. The JIT premise is to search for methods to streamline operations and lower stock levels across the whole supply chain. A win-win situation can arise when businesses and their suppliers work closely together. As we covered for the VMI model in section 7.3.2, improved communication of component requirements, for instance, permits the supplier to plan inventory and schedule distribution more effectively. It is advisable to involve suppliers in the design process of new goods to prevent wasteful component design before production starts. Suppliers ought to be viewed as partners in a project where both sides are motivated to keep a lucrative, long-lasting partnership.

UNIT SUMMARY

- ***Goals of JIT*** – The primary objective is to eliminate waste, reduce inventory levels, shorten lead times, and improve system flexibility.
- ***Fundamental Modules of JIT*** – Discusses product design (standard parts, modularity, quality), process design (small lot sizes, cellular manufacturing), and continuous improvement (Kaizen).
- ***Manufacturing Planning & Control*** – Covers key elements like: (i) Pull System – Ensures production aligns with actual demand, (ii) Kanban System – A visual signaling tool to control workflow and inventory, (iii) Close Vendor Relationships – Emphasizes collaboration with suppliers for timely material delivery.
- ***Comparison with MRP*** (Material Requirements Planning) – Highlights the differences between JIT (lean, low inventory, simple control) and MRP (batch production, high inventory, complex control).
- ***Real-World Applications*** – Case studies of Apple, Nike, Zara, Dell, and Toyota demonstrate how JIT enhances efficiency, cost savings, and responsiveness.

EXERCISES

MULTIPLE CHOICE QUESTIONS

7.1 What is the primary objective of the Just-in-Time (JIT) production philosophy?

(a) To increase the inventory levels to meet unpredictable demand	(b) To minimize the waste of resources by producing goods only as needed
(c) To maximize the use of labor through overtime and shift work	(d) To expand production capacity rapidly to cover future demand

7.2 How does Just-in-Time (JIT) help to remove disruptions in the production process?

(a) By increasing the amount of inventory held to buffer against supply chain disruptions	(b) By implementing strict, long-term contracts with suppliers to ensure uninterrupted supply
(c) By synchronizing production schedules with actual demand and maintaining minimal inventory levels	(d) By automating production processes to reduce the need for human intervention

7.3 How does Just-in-Time (JIT) enhance system flexibility?

(a) By maintaining high levels of inventory to accommodate any production changes	(b) By using large production batches to standardize processes and reduce setup times
(c) By enabling quick adjustments to production schedules in response to actual demand	(d) By outsourcing all production activities to third-party providers for increased adaptability

7.4 How does Just-In-Time (JIT) manufacturing help reduce lead times and machine setup times in a production process?

(a) By increasing the frequency of production runs, reducing batch sizes and by standardizing production processes	(b) By using high levels of inventory to avoid delays and ensure materials are always available
(c) By standardizing equipment and processes to eliminate variability in production runs	(d) By outsourcing production to third-party manufacturers with advanced automation

7.5 How does Just-In-Time (JIT) manufacturing help reduce inventory levels?

(a) By increasing the amount of raw materials purchased in bulk to avoid stockouts	(b) By producing goods in large batches and storing them until needed
(c) By aligning production schedules closely with actual demand and receiving materials just in time for production	(d) By implementing automated systems to track and manage larger inventory volumes efficiently

7.6 How does Just-In-Time (JIT) manufacturing help reduce waste?

(a) By increasing inventory levels to ensure a buffer against any production issues	(b) By producing large quantities of goods to benefit from economies of scale

(c) By eliminating excess inventory and focusing on producing only what is needed, when it is needed

(d) By using automated systems to handle large volumes of materials and minimize human error

7.7 How does product design impact the effectiveness of a Just-In-Time (JIT) manufacturing system?

(a) Complex designs with multiple components are preferred to utilize the full capacity of the production line

(b) Simple and standardized designs are favored to reduce production time and facilitate smoother workflows

(c) Custom designs are encouraged to create a unique product offering and justify higher inventory levels

(d) Designs with extensive tolerances are preferred to minimize the need for precision in production

7.8 In a JIT system, why is modular product design beneficial?

(a) It allows for bulk production of individual modules and storage until needed

(b) It simplifies assembly and enables quick adjustments to production based on demand

(c) It increases the need for extensive inventory to accommodate various module combinations

(d) It discourages flexibility by requiring extensive retooling for each product variation

7.9 How does delayed differentiation help reduce inventory levels in a JIT system?

(a) By producing customized products in advance and storing them until needed

(b) By allowing companies to produce generic products in bulk and complete customization only when orders are received

(c) By increasing the variety of products held in inventory to meet diverse customer needs

(d) By focusing on long-term forecasts to maintain high levels of safety stock

7.10 In a JIT system, what is the preferred lot size for production?

(a) Large lot sizes to maximize economies of scale

(b) Medium lot sizes to balance between production efficiency and inventory holding

(c) Small lot sizes to reduce inventory levels and increase flexibility

(d) Variable lot sizes based on historical sales data

7.11 How does small lot size in JIT affect setup times?

(a) It generally increases setup times due to more frequent changes in production setups	(b) It reduces setup times by allowing more efficient and standardized changeovers between different products
(c) It has no impact on setup times as setup processes remain the same	(d) It leads to longer setup times because more complex setups are required for each lot

7.12 In the context of family-based dispatching rules, what is a key strategy for minimizing setup times?

(a) Producing a single product type continuously to avoid any setup changes	(b) Scheduling production in small batches with frequent changes between different product families
(c) Grouping products with similar setup requirements into families and scheduling them together	(d) Focusing on complex product designs to enhance production flexibility and setup efficiency

7.13 In a JIT system, how does cellular manufacturing affect setup times?

(a) It increases setup times by requiring frequent reconfigurations of equipment across different cells	(b) It reduces setup times by allowing each cell to specialize in a specific set of operations for similar products
(c) It has no impact on setup times, as each cell handles a wide range of products	(d) It increases setup times by requiring larger batches of products to be processed in each cell

7.14 How does continuous improvement (Kaizen) contribute to the effectiveness of a Just-In-Time (JIT) system?

(a) By maintaining static processes and avoiding frequent changes to ensure stability	(b) By systematically identifying and eliminating inefficiencies to enhance production processes and reduce waste
(c) By increasing production batch sizes to manage improvements more effectively	(d) By focusing solely on increasing inventory levels to handle potential disruptions

7.15 What advantage does a pull system offer in a JIT environment?

(a) It increases lead times by producing goods in advance of demand	(b) It reduces excess inventory and minimizes the risk of overproduction

(c) It requires extensive safety stock to cover potential fluctuations in demand	(d) It simplifies production scheduling by allowing large batch sizes

7.16 What is the primary purpose of the Kanban system in a JIT environment?

(a) To forecast future demand and plan production schedules accordingly	(b) To signal when to reorder materials and components, ensuring a smooth flow of production
(c) To increase inventory levels to handle potential disruptions in supply	(d) To standardize production processes and minimize equipment maintenance

7.17 How does close vendor relationship support flexibility and responsiveness in a JIT system?

(a) By maintaining rigid schedules and fixed delivery dates regardless of production changes	(b) By enabling vendors to quickly adapt to changes in order quantities and production schedules
(c) By encouraging vendors to produce large batches of materials to cover all potential future needs	(d) By standardizing all product designs to simplify procurement and reduce vendor variability

Answers of Multiple Choice Questions
7.1 (b), 7.2 (c), 7.3 (c), 7.4 (a), 7.5 (c), 7.6 (c), 7.7 (b), 7.8 (b), 7.9 (b), 7.10 (c), 7.11 (b), 7.12 (c), 7.13 (b), 7.14 (b), 7.15 (b), 7.16 (b), 7.17 (b)

SHORT AND LONG ANSWER TYPE QUESTIONS

Category I

7.1 How does JIT reduce production disruptions by minimizing inventory levels?

7.2 How does the implementation of JIT contribute to faster response times to changes in customer demand?

7.3 In what way does JIT's focus on small batch production help in managing unexpected production issues?

7.4 In what way does JIT facilitate quicker adaptation to changes in customer demand or market conditions?

7.5 How does JIT's emphasis on reducing batch sizes contribute to shorter setup times in production processes?

7.6 In what way does JIT's focus on minimizing safety stock impact the overall amount of inventory held?

7.7 How does JIT's focus on producing only what is needed, when it is needed, help in eliminating excess production and associated waste?

7.8 How does the use of standardized modules in a JIT system facilitate easier and faster adaptation to changes in product design or customer requirements?

7.9 What role do small lot sizes play in enhancing flexibility and responsiveness to changes in customer demand within a JIT system?

7.10 What is the impact of family-based dispatching on improving workflow and reducing idle time between different productions runs in a JIT environment?

7.11 How does vendor-managed inventory support the principles of Just-In-Time by aligning supplier deliveries more closely with actual consumption and production needs?

7.12 How does the pull system facilitate better flow of materials and products through the production process in a JIT system?

7.13 How does the Kanban system improve communication and coordination between different stages of production in a JIT system?

7.14 What impact does maintaining a strong vendor partnership have on the flexibility and responsiveness of the supply chain in a JIT system?

Category II

7.15 How does the Just-In-Time (JIT) inventory management system mitigate disruptions within the supply chain, and what are the underlying mechanisms that contribute to this reduction in operational and logistical disruptions? Analyze how JIT reduces the impact of variability in demand and supply, enhances the flexibility of production processes, and improves overall system synchronization.

7.16 In a Just-In-Time (JIT) inventory system, how does the implementation of small batch production contribute to managing and mitigating unexpected production issues? Discuss the role of small batch production in enhancing flexibility, reducing lead times, and improving response times to disruptions or changes in demand. Analyze how producing in smaller quantities influences quality control, inventory management, and overall production efficiency. Additionally, consider the potential challenges associated with small batch production, such as increased setup times and the need for more frequent changeovers. Provide examples of industries or companies that have successfully integrated small batch production within a JIT framework, and evaluate how these implementations have addressed or mitigated production issues.

7.17 In the context of a Just-In-Time (JIT) inventory system, how does the use of standardized modules contribute to optimizing production processes and inventory management? Discuss the mechanisms by which standardized modules enhance efficiency, reduce lead times, and improve flexibility in response to demand variability. Analyze the impact of modularization on production setup times, quality control, and supply chain coordination. Additionally, evaluate the potential challenges and trade-offs associated with implementing standardized modules, such as the risk of reduced product differentiation and the need for robust module management systems. Provide examples of industries or companies that have successfully integrated standardized modules within a JIT framework, and assess how these implementations have addressed or mitigated production and inventory challenges.

7.18 How does the implementation of a pull system within a Just-In-Time (JIT) inventory management framework enhance the flow of materials and products through the production process? Discuss the mechanisms by which a pull system improves material handling, reduces lead times, and minimizes waste, while maintaining alignment with actual customer demand. Analyze how the pull system contributes to the synchronization of production stages and inventory levels, and its impact on operational efficiency and responsiveness. Additionally, examine the potential challenges associated with implementing a pull system, such as the risk of over-reliance on real-time data and the need for effective communication across the supply chain. Provide examples of industries or companies that have successfully utilized pull systems to optimize their production processes within a JIT environment.

REFERENCES AND SUGGESTED READINGS

1. Aquilano, N. J., and Chase, R. B. The role of product and process design in Just-In-Time (JIT) systems. *International Journal of Production Research*, Vol. 37(6), 1361-1376, 1999.

2. Cachon, G. P., and Fisher, M. *Supply Chain Management: A Strategic Perspective*. McGraw-Hill, 2000.

3. Heizer, J., Render, B., and Munson, C. *Operations Management: Sustainability and Supply Chain Management*, 12th Edition, Pearson, 2017.
4. Hernandez, M., and Gregory, M. Building close vendor relationships in a JIT environment. *International Journal of Production Economics*, Vol. 71(3), 233-245, 2001.
5. Hopp, W. J., and Spearman, M. L. To pull or not to pull: What is the question? *Production and Operations Management*, Vol. 17(1), 1-8, 2008.
6. Jacobs, F. R., and Berry, W. L. *Manufacturing Planning and Control for Supply Chain Management*, 6th Edition, McGraw-Hill Education, 2014.
7. Koskela, L. An exploration of the principles of Just-In-Time (JIT). *International Journal of Production Research*, Vol. 38(2), 317-336, 2000.
8. Lee, H. L., and Billington, C. Material Management in Decentralized Supply Chains. *Operations Research*, Vol. 41(5), 835-847, 1993.
9. Liker, J. K. *The Toyota Way: 14 Management Principles from the World's Greatest Manufacturer*. McGraw-Hill, 2004.
10. Monden, Y. The application of Kanban systems in managing inventory. *Journal of Manufacturing Science and Engineering*, Vol. 128(4), 907-915, 2006.
11. Monden, Y. Toyota Production System: *An Integrated Approach to Just-In-Time*, 4th Edition, CRC Press, 2011.
12. Shah, R., and Ward, P. T. Lean manufacturing: Context, practice bundles, and performance. *Journal of Operations Management*, Vol. 21(2), 129-149, 2003.
13. Slack, N., Chambers, S., and Johnston, R. *Operations Management*, 6th Edition, Pearson Education, 2010.
14. Starr, M. K. Modular production: A new concept. *Harvard Business Review*, Vol. 43(6), 131-142, 1965.
15. Womack, J. P., Jones, D. T., and Roos, D. *The Machine That Changed the World: The Story of Lean Production*, Free Press, 2007.
16. Yin, Y., and Stecke, K. E. An integrated approach to JIT systems. *International Journal of Production Research*, Vol. 44(5), 999-1023, 2006.
17. Zhang, G., and Dong, J. Collaboration and close vendor relationships in JIT supply chains. *International Journal of Production Economics*, Vol. 77(1), 23-31, 2002.

UNIT 8

SUPPLY CHAIN MANAGEMENT

UNIT SPECIFICS

This unit elaborately discusses the following topics:

- Current supply chain management (SCM) requirements
- SCM evolution
- SCM approach and objectives
- SCM framework and complexity
- Value of information (Bullwhip effect)
- Strategies for SCM for uncertain demand (Managing supply chain risk)
- Outsourcing for procurement in supply chain
- Logistics and distribution in SCM (Warehouse management, outsourcing of distribution, Last mile delivery)
- Sustainable supply chain
- Information technology in logistics industry

To encourage greater innovation and curiosity, the topics' innovative concepts are explored. According to the lower and higher orders of Bloom's taxonomy, the questions are separated into short answer and long answer categories, in addition to some multiple-choice questions. After the unit's related topic, there is a further section ("Along the...") that is consistent with the content. It was prepared with consideration for the reader's benefit. For the purpose of generating interest in the topic, this content mainly highlights the incredible facts about the problem being addressed in the modern, intriguing industrial world. One noteworthy feature is the inclusion of QR codes, which may be scanned to access relevant supporting information on a range of intriguing topics.

RATIONALE

This unit delves into the essential components of contemporary supply chain management (SCM), examining the evolving landscape and current requirements that shape effective practices. It outlines the objectives and strategic approaches of SCM while addressing the inherent complexities within its framework. The unit highlights the critical value of information, particularly in mitigating the bullwhip effect, and discusses strategies for managing supply chain risks associated with uncertain demand. Additionally, it explores the role of outsourcing in procurement, logistics, and distribution, including warehouse management and last-mile delivery. Emphasizing the importance of sustainability, the unit also examines the transformative impact of information technology on the logistics industry, underscoring its significance in enhancing efficiency and responsiveness in supply chains.

UNIT OUTCOMES

List of outcomes of this unit is as follows:

U8-UO1: Understand Current SCM Requirements

U8-UO2: Trace SCM Evolution

U8-UO3: Articulate SCM Objectives

U8-UO4: Analyze SCM Framework and Complexity

U8-UO5: Mitigate the Bullwhip Effect

U8-UO6: Assess Sustainable Supply Chain Practices

UNIT-8 Outcomes	EXPECTED MAPPING WITH COURSE OUTCOMES *(1-Weak Correlation; 2-Medium Correlation; 3-Strong Correlation)*					
	CO-1	CO-2	CO-3	CO-4	CO-5	CO-6
U8-UO1	3	3	3	3	3	3
U8-UO2	2	3	3	3	3	2
U8-UO3	3	3	3	3	3	3
U8-UO4	2	3	3	3	3	3
U8-UO5	1	2	3	2	3	2
U8-UO6	2	2	3	3	3	2

8.1 INTRODUCTION

The business environment is changing quickly these days, and organizations are forced to learn new things or risk being forced out of the market. The current dynamics of business encourage mapping self-competency and creating a strong chain of these capable actors to provide goods and services to clients in a cheap, effective, and efficient manner. This understanding of competency alliance is the foundation of the Supply Chain Management (SCM) paradigm. In actuality, a strong partnership between the manufacturer, supplier, and client leads to efficient supply chain management.

8.1.1 THE CURRENT SCM REQUIREMENT

Due to growing customer expectations and the introduction of products with shorter life cycles, businesses are being compelled to invest in and pay closer attention to their supply chains in today's competitive market. In business, the focus now lies on tactics that build enduring relationships with customers. Consumers don't perceive many differences between two rivals' products' functionalities and technical aspects. What sets the rivals apart is their customer service, specifically their prompt order fulfillment. The supply chain, which permits the constant delivery of services in terms of reaching the right product, at the right time, at the right cost, in the right condition (quality), and to the appropriate consumer, is the means by which effective customer service is accomplished. Generally, goods are manufactured at one or more factories using raw materials, then they are sent to warehouses for temporary storage before being delivered to retailers or clients (see Fig. 8.1). Because the supply chain must consider the interactions among its echelons at different levels in order to cut costs and improve customer service levels, it is viewed as a component of an organization's overall strategy. Several firms have discovered that supply chain management is their primary strategy, which has put them in a highly competitive position.

The principles and insights that are crucial for managing both the supply chain's distribution and procurement ends are presented and explained in this unit. According to the conversation above, a supply chain is defined as follows:

"Supply chain management is a set of approaches utilized to efficiently integrate suppliers, manufacturers, warehouses, and stores, so that merchandise is produced and distributed at the right quantities, at the right locations, and at the right time, in order to minimize system wide costs while satisfying customer service level requirements."

Fig. 8.1 Supply chain structure and its approach

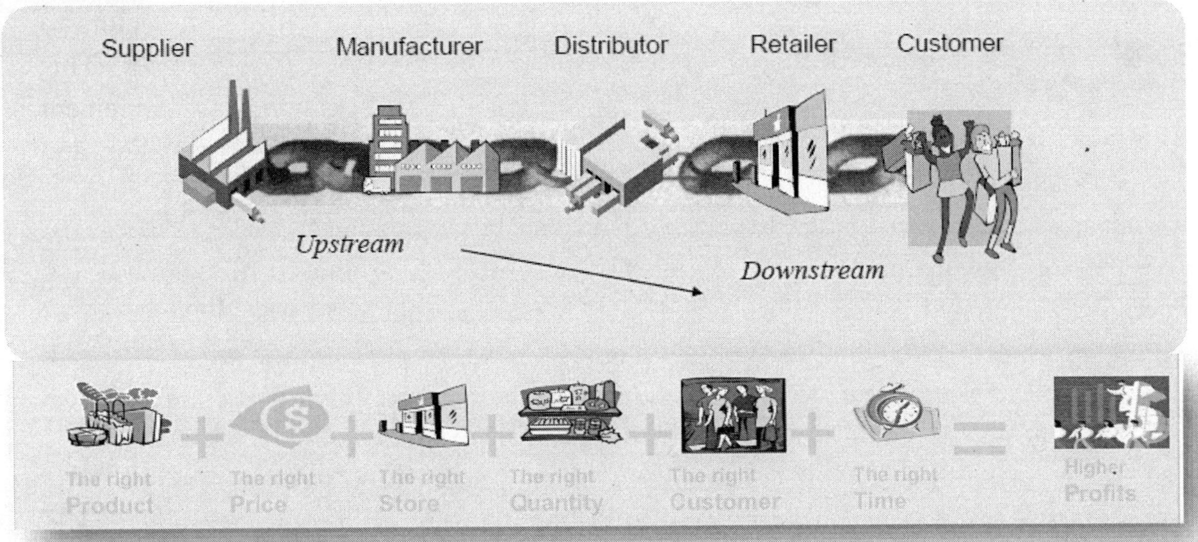

8.1.2 SUPPLY CHAIN MANAGEMENT EVOLUTION

Following the first industrial revolution, corporations used a fragmented supply chain strategy in their factory systems, whereby each department functioned independently of other trading organizations such as suppliers, wholesalers, dealers, and so on. Following the Second Industrial Revolution, their organizations began to change with the introduction of MRP systems, MRP-II systems, and eventually ERP (discussed in Unit 4) systems. ERP gave the companies access to the closely knit, or partnerships, that are formed between trading organizations. The outcome of this development is supply chain management. The development of manufacturing management and logistics management roles together gave rise to supply chain management (SCM). Sales and distribution management, along with materials management, jointly evolved into the idea of logistics management. That's what Figure 8.2 depicts.

Fig. 8.2 SCM function evolution

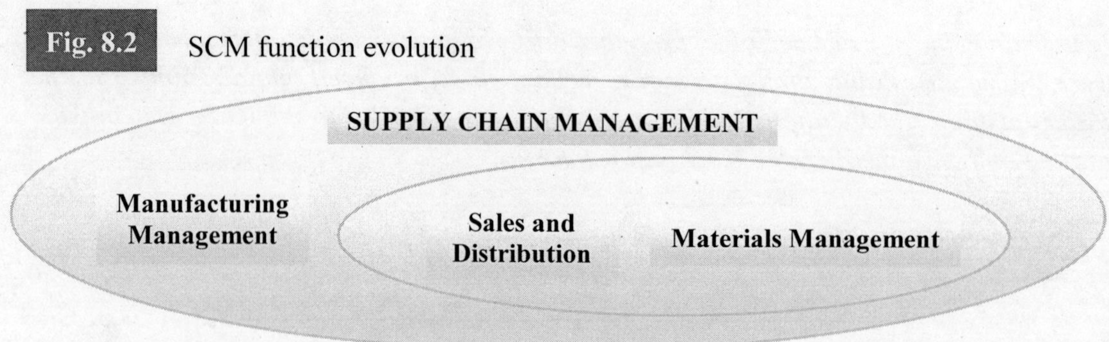

Usually, various functions were in charge of overseeing the organization's movements of goods and services from supplier to client. The distribution manager was in charge of ensuring that the downstream supply chain entities – dealers, wholesalers, retailers, and customers – functioned effectively, while the materials manager was in charge of maintaining consistent relationships with suppliers. A supply chain is thought of as a link between supply and demand. It delivers the supply to the demand point and communicates the demand to the supply point. The supply chain manager of today is in charge of the entire material flow, including demand planning, sourcing, acquisition, value addition, and distribution to the customer at the end. As a result, the majority of the roles are included in the organization's overarching SCM strategy.

8.2 THE SCM APPROACH

Initially, SCM operations were conducted in isolation, with each department working to locally optimize its own operations. The lack of a worldwide perspective on operations meant that there was no actual coordination between the various supply chain groups. Nonetheless, a few observations are made in light of the concept of supply chain in the current situation.

1. Supply chain management takes into account every facility that affects the functioning of the supply chain, from manufacturing and supplier facilities to warehouses and distribution centers to retail establishments.
2. The goal is to manage the supply chain throughout the system, from transportation and distribution to inventories of raw materials, work-in-process, and finished goods, employing a systems approach to supply chain management. This goes beyond just making the supply chain efficient and effective from local perspectives.

3. Supply chain management encompasses supply chain operations at the strategic, tactical, and operational levels since it centers on the effective integration of manufacturers, suppliers, warehouses, and retailers.
4. Every supply chain carries some level of risk and uncertainty since it is impossible to predict consumer demand precisely, lead times cannot be guaranteed, and equipment and logistics will eventually break down. Similar to this, current practices that aim to improve supply chain performance – such as outsourcing, offshoring, and lean manufacturing – also make supply chains more vulnerable and fragile. Supply chains must therefore be viewed from the perspectives of risk and uncertainty.

8.3 OBJECTIVE OF SCM

A supply chain's ultimate goal is to produce the most value overall. The gap between the customer's willingness to purchase the product and the supply chain's attempts to meet the customer's needs indicates the value of the supply chain. The majority of supply networks assess their worth using the concept of supply chain profitability, which measures the discrepancy between total costs incurred across the chain and revenue received. The entire supply chain should be considered when measuring supply chain profitability, not only the profits made at each particular stage. A list of requirements is given in Table 8.1 for enhancing the supply chain's value. Obtain answers to the following questions.

Table 8.1 List of requirements for enhancing the supply chain's value

- To what extent is the item required, does it have the potential to create value, or can it be removed?
- Which other sources are there for this item?
- Is it possible to provide the item internally?
- Are there any benefits to the current arrangement?
- Is it possible to use a different component, substance, or service?
- How may fewer, less-stringent requirements save money and time?
- Is it possible to separate parts into modules?
- How may reduced processing work result in cost savings?
- Can the providers/suppliers propose ways to improve?
- Are recommendations for improvements accepted from the staff?
- How can the packing be made better financially?

One well-known case study of the Narayan health model is available, showing how Narayana Health has saved money by employing effective staffing practices, telemedicine, and equipment utilization. Over the past ten years, the health system in India has established dependable and affordable supply chains, and it takes advantage of economies of scale to further reduce costs.

SCAN ME
for
Narayan Health
model study

8.4 SUPPLY CHAIN PROCESSES FRAMEWORK

A supply chain is made up of several interconnected and intraechelon activities and flows that work together to meet consumer demand for a particular product. The supply chain's operations are executed through a sequence of interface steps, often referred to as cycles between various echelons. A broad cycle of activities in all the echelons of a supply chain is shown in Fig. 8.3. We envision a three-tier supply chain that functions similarly to a business-to-business (B2B) transaction, with a supplier, a manufacturer, and a retailer.

Fig. 8.3 Broad activities in an echelon of a supply chain

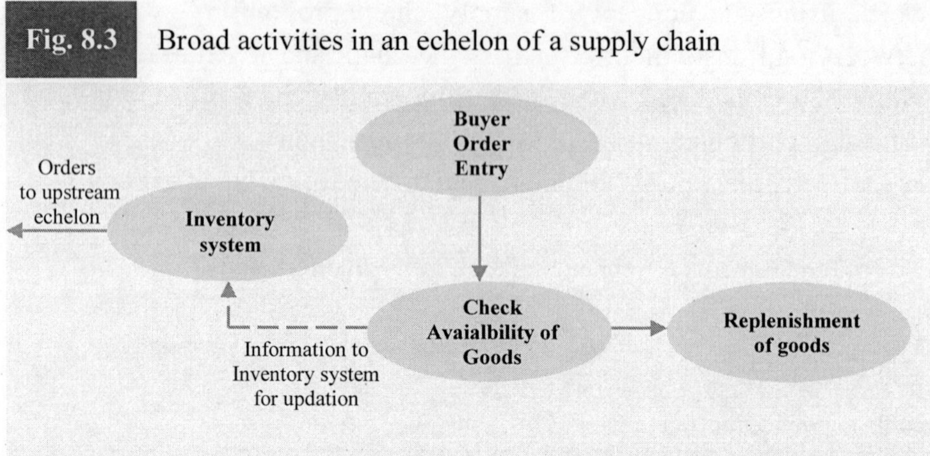

The cycle, which begins at the echelon interface, includes all of the tasks necessary to replenish an echelon's inventory. An echelon initiates the process of replenishing its stock when it places an order. Effectiveness and efficiency are the two primary objectives at each echelon, which is to optimize product availability while keeping inventory replenishment costs to a minimum. The replenishment cycle includes orders to the next upstream echelon, replenishments of items, and requests from buyers, and determining whether goods are available (Fig. 8.3). Modern supply chains communicate real-time information on commodities replenishment to the inventory system, which updates the information in real-time.

In case of manufacturer echelon, if the manufacturer knows the point-of-sale demand through modern real-time information systems, the retailer initiates the manufacturing cycle, otherwise the manufacturer forecasts the demand. The manufacturing system's "push" or "pull" approach, which determines whether production is started in response to actual demand (pull) or in anticipation of demand (push), determines the amount of the production order.

At the procurement end of supply chain if a supplier manages the inventory for the whole supply chain and is connected to the point-of-sale, their performance can be improved. Unit 7 covered this topic in relation to vendor managed inventory (VMI). There could be multiple supplier tiers and multiple suppliers at each tier in a real world supply chain.

8.5 THE COMPLEXITY OF THE SUPPLY CHAIN

A supply chain's focal point is a manufacturer. Before the manufacturing process is carried out, a manufacturer's echelon receives information from several phases of development processes as shown in Fig. 8.4. Development procedures in a supply chain include decisions on sourcing, production schedules, and activities related to the product design phase. In particular, decisions about product architecture, what to manufacture in-house and what to purchase from outside vendors – also known as inhouse versus outsourcing decisions – supplier selection and supply contracts are all part of the development process.

The supply chain is impacted by the features of the development phase since the activities conducted there are related to the supply chain's manufacturing echelon. Therefore, it makes sense that we would also anticipate the integration of development activities in the opposite scenario, when actions made in the supply chain have an impact on the features of the development process. The system-wide supply chain integrated solution is a challenging issue for a number of reasons. The supply chain is, first and foremost, a dynamic system that changes with time. There is tremendous demand on manufacturers and suppliers to provide a wide range of high-quality items, which eventually results in customized products, because of products having shorter life cycles and rising client expectations. Second, dualities can be used to illustrate supply chain uncertainty. The retailer's end of the supply chain is where demand is met, with an emphasis on customer differentiation strategy and mass customization. In the actual world, customer differentiation is prevalent. Many companies classify the customers they serve in an effort to increase revenue and deliver superior customer service. For instance, a lot of retailers offer memberships. Customers who have memberships are eligible for a variety of privileges, including free delivery and discounts. An additional factor contributing to the level of unpredictability in demand at the downstream end of the supply chain is the presence of competitors' pricing tactics, trends, advertising and promotions, and seasonal swings.

Supply unpredictability, whether at the upstream or supply end, has become a major source of interruption for supply chain streamlining activities. There are many different things that might create supply disruptions, including as terrorism, natural disasters, equipment failures, worker strikes, unstable political environments, and traffic jams. Disruptions in supply could have serious consequences. For example, the global industries had a severe downturn during the COVID-19 pandemic and the ensuing supply interruption. By scanning the provided QR code, one may learn how supply chains have adjusted to the disruptions and what efforts the firms are taking to address short-and long-term supply chain issues.

SCAN ME for Resilience to disruption due to pandemic

Fig. 8.4 Impact of internal and external complexity in a supply chain

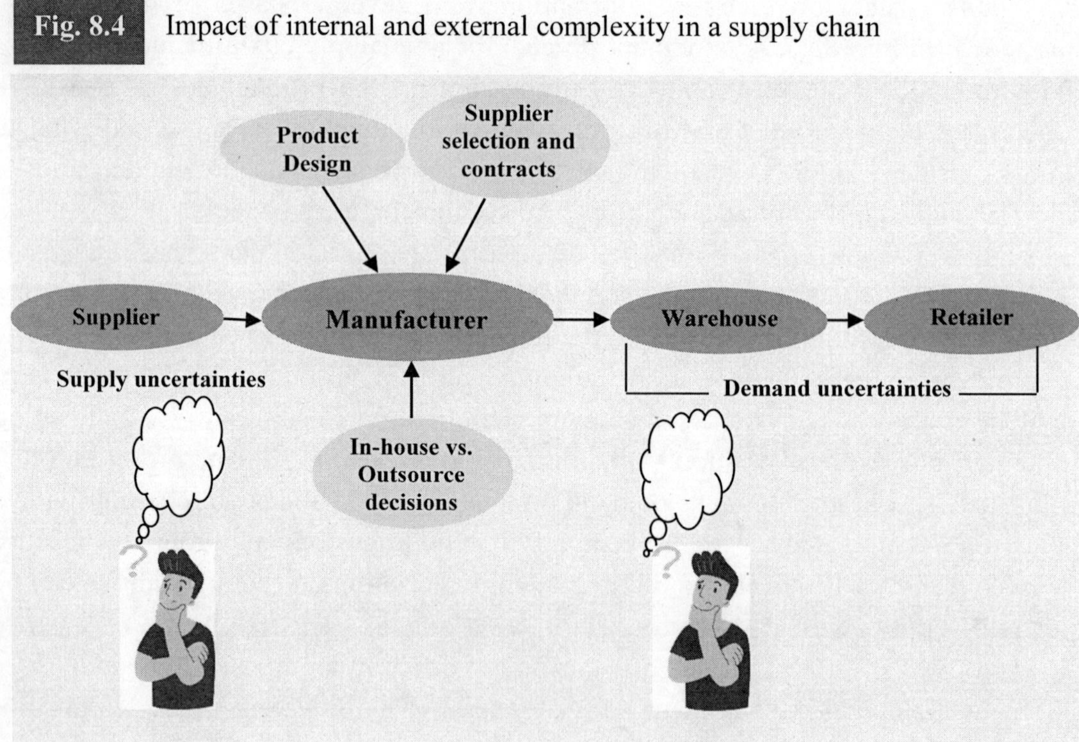

In addition to the external interruptions that affect the supply chain, there are competing goals within it. For example, most manufacturers would prefer to have long production runs in order to be able to adapt to the changing demands of their customers. However, suppliers usually require manufacturers to promise to buy in bulk at consistent volumes with flexible delivery schedules. Therefore, a major obstacle to streamlining the system-wide supply chain is the manufacturer's capacity to match demand and supply operations in the absence of demand information at the manufacturing end. From the foregoing, it is clear that the key to simplifying the integrated supply chain is managing the activities, which are mostly determined by the decisions made at the focal unit, the manufacturer. Fig. 8.4 shows how the development chain is integrated and how an external disruption affects the manufacturer. From now on, we will examine what operations are all about and how a single company's operations fit within a bigger supply chain. Here are a few of the main points that will be covered in-depth in this unit. We will address some of the supply chain challenges that include trade-off choices in handling various complexities.

8.6 VALUE OF INFORMATION

The implications of information availability in the modern business setting are immense. Experts in supply chains have even gone so far as to state that "*information has completely replaced inventory in modern supply chains*." To a certain extent, we agree, but ultimately, customers require products in addition to information. Nevertheless, a lack of cooperation across various supply chain echelons defeats the organization's goals. If there is no delay or dissonance in information between and among various echelons, supply chain coordination is smooth.

The goal from the perspective of the entire supply chain is disrupted as a result of each echelon trying to maximize its own performance due to a lack of coordination. The supply chain of today may comprise hundreds or even thousands of separately held businesses. A few of the major supply chains are Apple, McDonald's, Amazon.com, and so on. In the US alone, Apple has over 250 retail locations. Due to incomplete or delayed information sharing between echelons, information is skewed as it passes through the supply chain. This distortion is further exacerbated by the many product mixes that the company produces. For example, Amul and Gujarat Cooperative Milk Marketing Federation deal in a variety of product mixtures that include butter, milk powder, ghee, cheese, and milk, among other items.

SCAN ME
for
Top supply chains of the world

8.6.1 THE BULLWHIP EFFECT

The Bullwhip effect, which occurs when orders fluctuate more as one moves up the supply chain from retailers to wholesalers to distributors to manufacturers, affects a lot of businesses. For example, while analyzing the market for Pampers disposable diapers, Procter & Gamble officials saw a noteworthy occurrence. The product's retail sales were comparatively consistent; demand did not significantly fluctuate on any given day or month. It was discovered, meanwhile, that wholesale distributor orders to manufacturers vary significantly more than retail sales. Also, there is still greater fluctuation in the manufacturer's orders to suppliers. The ***Bullwhip Effect*** refers to this rise in unpredictability as we move up the supply chain.

Fig. 8.5 The Bullwhip effect

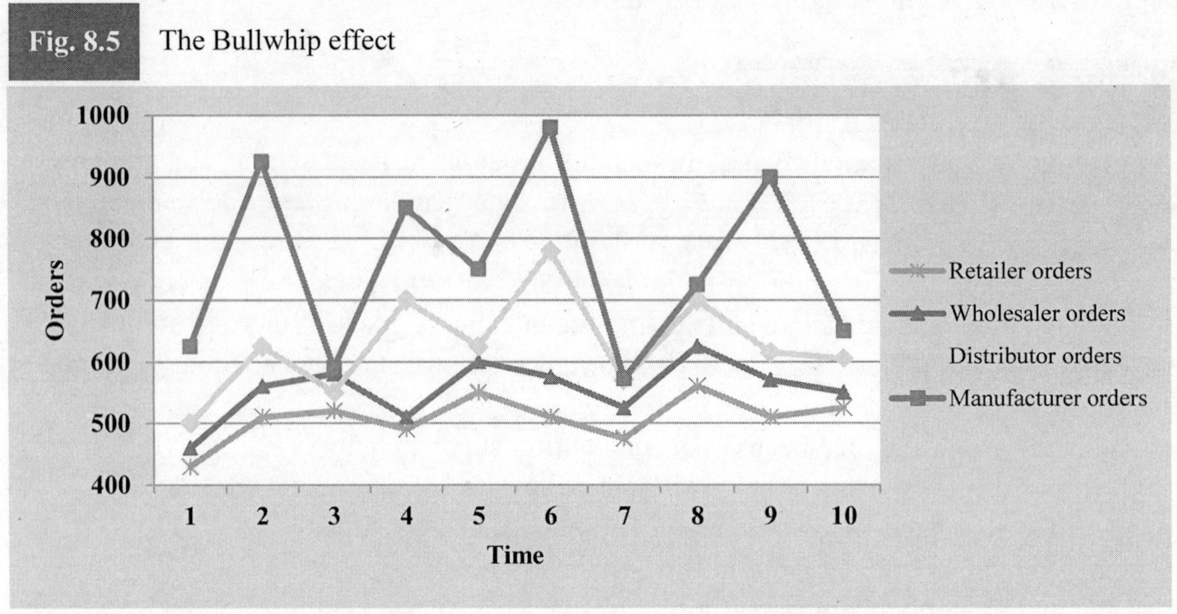

A retailer monitors consumer demand and arranges orders with a wholesaler in a four-stage supply chain that includes a distributor, manufacturer, wholesaler, and retailer. The distributor sends orders to the producer, who then delivers the goods to the wholesaler. A graphical illustration of demand placed by various echelons over a horizon of ten time units is shown in Fig. 8.5. The increase in variability throughout the supply chain is obviously depicted in the graphic. The fundamental aspect of this variability is that, in the lack of information on the demand of the immediate downstream echelon (i.e., the customer's demand in the instance of the retailer acting as the downstream echelon for the wholesaler), each upstream echelon must anticipate the demand of the immediate downstream echelon.

For instance, the wholesaler is compelled to carry higher safety inventories than the retailer because to the significant demand unpredictability of the retailer. This approach is followed all the way to the manufacturer in the supply chain, which raises inventory levels even further and thus raises expenses at the upstream levels. "Bullwhip" was first used by executives in the logistics industry. Procter & Gamble (P&G), Hewlett-Packard (computer business), Bristol-Myers Squibb (pharmaceuticals industry), and Wal-Mart (retail) are among the companies that have encountered this issue.

As a result, it became necessary to determine certain strategies for reducing or managing the bullwhip effect, or managing the rise in supply chain variability. The supply chain's increased variability is mostly caused by the following variables.

1. *Forecasting demand* – The bullwhip effect is caused by the standard inventory management practices used in the supply chain. When there is demand fluctuation, an inventory management strategy typically sets a base stock that is equal to the average demand for the lead time and review period (if periodic review monitoring is in place) plus a multiple of the demand standard deviation for the lead time and review period. Safety stock is the term used to describe the later amount. In the majority of real-world scenarios, managers estimate average demand and demand variability using basic forecasting smoothing approaches. A key component of all forecasting methods is the quantity of data that is observed. The more data collected, the more stable the demand estimates become. Because base-stock level and safety stock are usually dependent on estimations of demand mean and standard deviations, the user must adjust the order quantity, which increases unpredictability. Businesses are extensively using Computer Assisted Ordering (CAO) to streamline information exchange in an effort to alleviate the bullwhip effect.

   A lot of businesses have implemented continuous inventory review policies (CRPs), such as Campbell Soup, Scott Paper, M&M/Mars, Procter and Gamble (P&G), Nestle, Nabisco, and Quaker Oats; in contrast, Apple, Motorola, and Texas Instruments use vendor managed inventory (VMI) policies as part of their channel alignment strategies to lessen the bullwhip effect. Eliminating middlemen in the distribution process is one way to lessen the bullwhip impact. By selling directly to customers instead of through a distribution system, companies like Dell are able

SCAN ME
for
B2C

to minimize the bullwhip impact. This operates similar to B2C in which the businesses sell their products directly to the customer eliminating wholeseller or distributors.

2. *Lead time* – Regarding the inventory management process once again, lead time is one of the variables that affects base-stock and safety-stock levels. Actually, the two supply chain variations operate from two distinct supply chain ends. Lead time variability occurs from the upstream to the downstream end, whereas demand fluctuation occurs from the downstream to the upstream. The two forms of uncertainty are, in a way, mirror reflections of one another. In actuality, the combined effects of lead time variability and demand fluctuation further raise order variability when estimating safety stock and base-stock levels.

   An upstream echelon can give the downstream echelon information on lead times, inventory levels, resource capabilities and capacity, shipment schedules, and cost for supply chain planning purposes. As soon as the downstream partner receives information from the upstream, the supply conditions become evident. Significantly useful information can be obtained from second-or third-tier suppliers. Businesses are more vulnerable to supply chain disruptions as supply chains get more intricate as a result of the global reach of today's supply chain networks. Interactions between the supply chain and its surroundings, such as disruptions brought in by external hazards as we have seen during COVID 19 pandemic. Disruption to the supply chain is defined as:

   "*An exposure to serious disturbance, arising from risks within the supply chain, as well as risks external to the supply chain.*"

   Thus, to lower supply chain vulnerability overall, risk management both inside and outside of the chain should be handled with a coordinated strategy by chain participants. Supply chain risk management has never been more difficult than it is right now. It appears that external disruptions to the supply chain create delays. In addition to stopping supply chain activities, delays cause the impacted system to take longer to recover if proper planning and precautions are not taken. Risk resulting from supply delays is the possibility of an event that could have a major negative impact on downstream echelons. Managing inventory is a practical approach to handling these kinds of interruptions.

3. *Purchasing in bulk* – When batch ordering, the upstream echelon will see a bigger order, followed by a number of periods without any orders, another large order, and so on, if an echelon is employing a min-max policy or a (Q, R) inventory policy

(discussed in Unit 6). Consequently, a distorted and very varied pattern of commands is found by the upstream echelon. It is important to note that the companies employ batch ordering for various purposes.

A company must implement (*Q*, *R*) or (*s*, *S*) inventory policies because of fixed ordering costs. Batch ordering results from this. Additionally, a downstream echelon may order amounts that enable them to benefit from transportation discounts (e.g., full-truck load) as transportation costs become more substantial. Finally, a lot of organizations have annual or quarterly sales goals or incentives, which might lead to abnormally variable orders across specific time periods.

SCAN ME
for
(Q, R) and (s, S)
inventory policies

Dividing order batches is one way to counteract the bullwhip effect caused by big batch sizes. Businesses can place orders more frequently and at a lower cost by using electronic data interchange (EDI). Additionally, in order to offset the high cost of transportation, businesses can engage third-party logistics (3PL) organizations to manage shipment or send a variety of products in a truckload.

4. *Variations in price* – The bullwhip effect can also result from price fluctuations. When the price is cheap, retailers stock their inventories. In genuine business, forward buying – the practice of offering discounts at specific dates or for specific quantities – is standard procedure. In this instance, the retailer purchases large quantities during times when the manufacturer or distributor is implementing promotion methods, and purchases comparatively smaller quantities during other times. Businesses such as Procter & Gamble, Kraft, Walmart, and Pillsbury use the Everyday Low Price (EDLP) strategy to reduce price volatility and, in turn, the bullwhip effect.

5. *Anticipating a product shortfall* – Retailers and distributors place larger purchases initially and then reduce them to normal size orders when they foresee a product shortage in the near future. Demand estimations become distorted and vary as a result. Products are distributed by corporations such as General Motors, HP, and Texas Instruments according on historical sales data or orders. By entering into contracts, businesses also exchange data on sales, capacity, and inventory. By adopting harsher return and cancellation rules, many corporations encourage their sellers to overstate their needs and cancel purchases.

Along with the aforementioned elements, some experts believe that human conduct is a significant contributor to the bullwhip effect. These elements consist of: (i) decision-making delays while placing orders; and (ii) stock-out anxiety.

ALONG THE REVERSE BULLWHIP EFFECT

RIPPLE EFFECT AND SUPPLY CHAIN RISK

A *ripple effect* is not the same as the popular bullwhip effect. It appears when a disturbance to the supply chain cannot be isolated to a single area of the supply chain and instead cascades downstream, having a significant negative influence on the chain's performance. Bullwhip effect characterizes oscillations in operational parameters; ripple effect takes into account the dynamics of the structural network in the SC. A severe disruption is the catalyst for the ripple effect, which is the description of how this disturbance spreads downstream along the SC. For example, the ripple effect can be used to explain how a severe disruption causes demand fulfillment to downscale. In more extreme situations, such as when there is a lack of materials, the ripple effect may temporarily turn off specific nodes and arcs in the network. On the other hand, a slight operational variation causes the bullwhip effect, which is anticipated to increase upstream.

Although the causes of the bullwhip effect have been thoroughly investigated over the past 20 years, the ripple effect is a relatively recent phenomenon, and further study is needed to fully understand its effects. These effects could be disastrous and include decreased sales, delivery delays, reputational damage, loss of market share, and a decline in stock returns. Table 8.2 shows how the ripple and bullwhip effects differ from one another.

Table 8.2 Difference between Bullwhip and Ripple effect

Feature	Bullwhip effect	Ripple effect
What kind of uncertainty?	Arbitrary uncertainty	Danger and profound uncertainty
What kind of risks?	Operational, ongoing risks (such as variations in demand)	Unpredictability and unusual risks (like the COVID-19 pandemic)
What might be agitated?	operational criteria like inventory and lead time	Structures and crucial performance indicators (like revenue or supplier unavailability)
How are variations avoided?	Coordination of information	Proactive redundancy as well as adaptability
What takes place following the disruption?	Short-term coordination to maintain supply and demand equilibrium	Stabilization for the short term as well as recovery for the medium and long terms; strong coordination and investment
What is the influence on performance?	Existing performance may decline, as seen by daily or weekly stock outages or overages.	There may be a decline in output performance, as seen in annual revenues or profits.

Order instability and unpredictability result from supply chain participants not considering the optimal time to place an order when there are delays in making ordering choices. Order delays result in shipping delays, delivery delays, and ultimately a delay impact on the entire supply chain system. Bullwhip effect can be minimized by shortening this delay. Second, elite players frequently put large orders because they worry about running out of product and losing clients as a result. Bullwhip effect-causing extreme order fluctuation could result from this behavior.

8.7 STRATEGIES FOR THE SUPPLY CHAIN FOR UNCERTAIN DEMAND

Supply chain strategies are created using Fisher's paradigm in response to product demand uncertainty. Demand depends undoubtedly on the kind of products. Within this framework, products are categorized as either **innovative** or **functional**. Demand for innovative products, such high-tech things like integrated circuits and high-end computers, is quite erratic. The market for functional goods is steady and includes consumables for the home like food and groceries.

Efficient Supply Chains – The supply chains employ a variety of techniques to achieve high cost effectiveness. The techniques that contribute to cost efficiency are minimizing waste, utilizing economies of scale, and making the most use of available capacity. Functional products have a steady and predictable demand, therefore production and distribution schedules can be optimized by forecasting demand while staying below capacity limits.

Responsive Supply Chains – These supply chains employ strategies to be adaptable and sensitive to the ever-changing demands. Businesses employ mass customization techniques, such as engineer to order and make to order, to cater to the unique requirements of their customers. Information technology plays an important role in shaping such supply chain. The responsive supply chains exploit the concept of differentiation (discussed in Unit 7) or commonly referred to as the *customer order decoupling point* (CODP) or *push-pull boundary*.

Companies can learn from the behavior of demand and other environmental factors by delaying activities. This offers a chance for businesses to make decisions based on more real information (like customer demand, for example). In light of this, the differentiation or sometimes referred to as postponement might be seen as a strategy for bringing the supply chain into harmony. Time buffers are introduced at those times where the streamline flow could be destroyed by a lack of information. Stated differently, it gives procedures that call for additional information more time. Activities intended to postpone consumption are typically positioned nearer the time and location of consumption. As illustrated in Fig. 8.6, four different delay tactics can be developed depending on the state of inventories.

Fig. 8.6 Postponement strategies and the location to place the customer-order decoupling point

Source: Yang, B. and Burns, N.D. (2003). Implications of postponement for the supply chain.Int. J. Prod. Res. 41(9), 2075-2090.

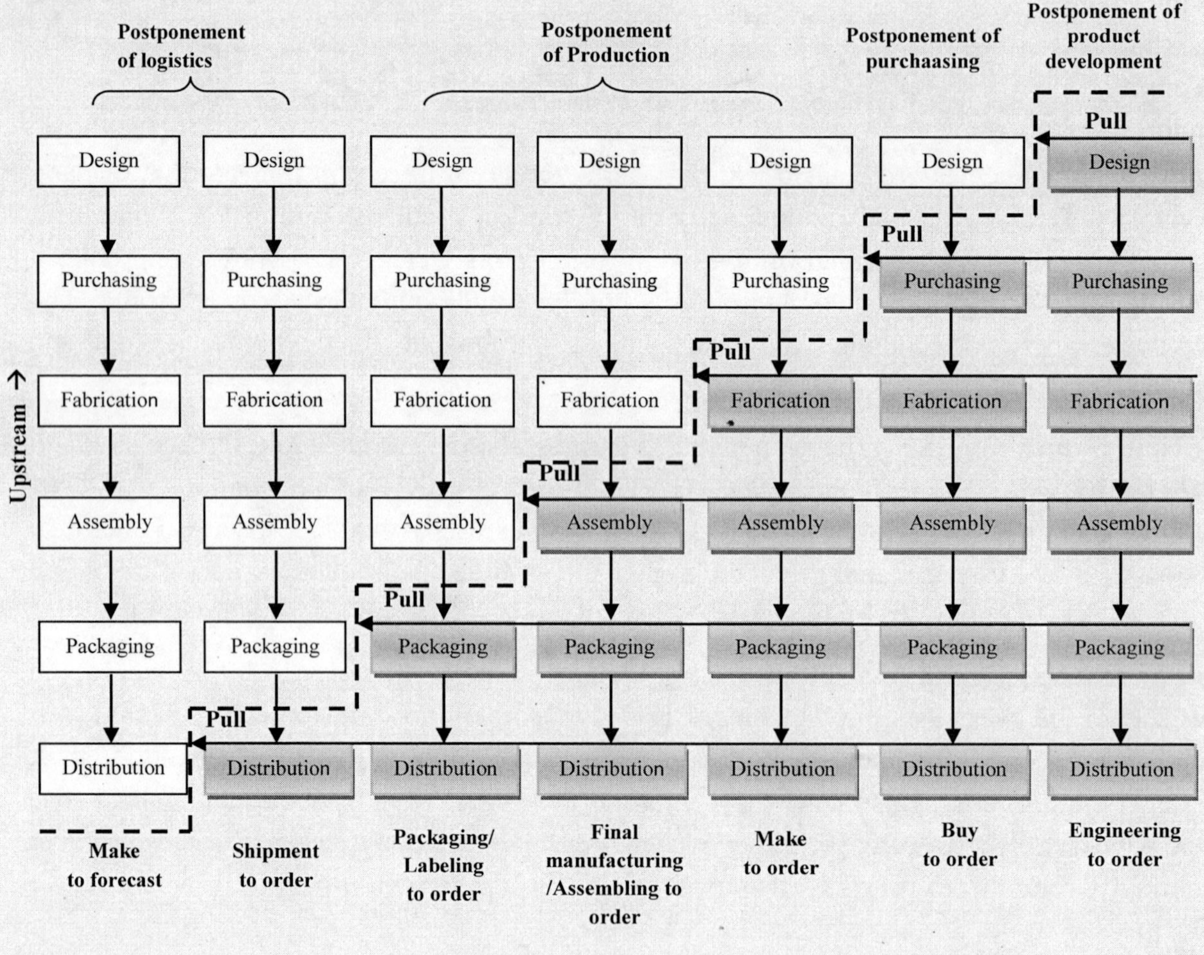

First, *logistics postponement* (finished goods) searches for postponement chances in the last product flow to the client. These products have reached their final form ahead of customer orders. The development of the internet (e-commerce) has made this easier. By delaying the location of merchandise to their distributor, a downstream supply chain echelon, until the client orders come, online retailers can manage their stocks to fulfill orders. Typically, Amazon.com chooses to collaborate closely with US postal services and its vendors in order to be able to employ this kind of postponement technique (drop-shipping). Second, holding onto semi-finished goods for as long as feasible during a *manufacturing postponement* will improve a business's adaptability to shifts in client demand. Third, enterprises can defer the acquisition of incoming raw materials or components until after demand is established by using *purchasing postponement* (components or raw material). By doing this, the chance of having outdated inventory on hand is decreased. In addition to postponing manufacturing, this strategy enables businesses to prevent stockpiling completed goods in anticipation of upcoming purchases. This kind of postponement strategy can be used in conjunction with vendor managed inventory (VMI), and involves the raw material supplier handling the retailer's customer demand. Fourth, there is a *postponement of product development* (no inventory case).

Postponing product creation is seen as an extreme type of customization, with all work, including product design, done after an order is placed. Additionally, in this instance, the clients are involved from the start of the design process. Given that a fully customized approach results in longer delivery times, this strategy is preferred when the downstream clients are willing to wait for longer delivery times.

Risk Hedging supply chains – These supply chains make use of strategies designed to combine and distribute resources among a chain's participants in order to distribute the risks associated with supply disruptions. A solitary entity within a supply chain may be susceptible to supply disruptions; nevertheless, the danger of disruption is mitigated in the event that several supply sources or alternate resources are accessible. To mitigate the risk of a disruption in supply, a company may decide to increase the safety stock of a vital component. The expense of keeping this safety stock might be borne by sharing it with other locations that require the same component. When multiple retail outlets or dealerships share inventory, this kind of strategy is prevalent in the retail industry. Because real-time data on demand and inventory enables the most cost-effective management and transshipment of goods between partners sharing the inventory, information technology is critical to the strategies' success.

The supply chains of numerous firms have become particularly vulnerable to coronavirus (COVID 19) pandemics due to their lean and globalized structures. Thus, the topic of the survivability of the market and society was brought up. In other supply chains, on the other hand, the decline in supply and demand has led to production halts (automotive industry, for example), the

SCAN ME
for
Intertwined supply chains

risk of bankruptcies, and the need for government assistance. The issues of supply chain survival surfaced in this situation. Examining the idea of viability, under which the concept of intertwined – which is made up of a collection of overlapping supply chains that are sharing their resources – evolved is an intriguing study area to take the conversation to the level of survival. Supply chain intertwined can also occur in industrial sharing, such as when many business and humanitarian supply chains share warehouse space or when commercial and humanitarian logistics are shared. By scanning the provided QR code, one can learn more about the intricate details of the intertwined supply chain.

Agile supply chains – A complex collection of procedures known as an agile supply chain helps companies better allocate resources, improve inventory control, and boost output. By using this procedure, businesses can more effectively manage the supply of materials and goods to meet customer demand and allocate resources more wisely to large orders. An agile supply chain is used by organizations to manage inventory, expedite, and regulate manufacturing and delivery. Through this procedure, businesses may monitor the state of their products, determine when they are required, and make necessary adjustments. By doing this, waste from possible overproduction or underproduction is ideally avoided. Agile supply chains are characterized by their resilience, or their capacity to bounce back from setbacks like a breakdown or failure affecting the entire chain. Determine the sources, associated risks, and possible outcomes in order to manage disruptions. Upon completion, you can proceed with developing mitigation protocols and backup plans to guarantee the supply chain maintains its strength. The advantages of "hedged" and "responsive" supply chains are combined in agile supply chains. Because they can minimize the risks of supply disruptions in the back-end while responding quickly to the ever-changing, diversified, and unpredictable demands of customers, they are considered agile. Understanding supply chain strategies can be facilitated by using the paradigm of demand and supply uncertainty. Innovative products have a significant difficulty due to their erratic demand and dynamic supply chains. A company's supply chain strategy must be dynamically adjusted and adopted due to the ever-shorter product life cycles.

8.7.1 MANAGING SUPPLY CHAIN RISK

Over the course of more than ten years, supply chain risk management emerged as one of the most significant subjects for both practice and study. A variety of supply chain risk classifications were established in recent research. Seven categories include these classifications (Quang and Hara, 2017):

- *External risks* are those that "address threats to SC from an external perspective that may arise from economic, sociopolitical, or geographic factors." Natural disasters, fire incidents, economic downturns, external legal issues, corruption, and cultural differences are a few examples. The topic on risk hedging has addressed how to deal with such risk, and intertwined supply chains are one suggestion made by the literature.
- *Time risks* are associated with delays in supply chain procedures. High capacity utilization, inflexibility, and low quality or yield from the supply source is some of the factors that cause delays. As indicated earlier, we talked about using a postponement approach to manage this kind of risk.
- *Systems risks* include misinformation, information breaches, information infrastructure issues, and breakdowns in team communication.
- *Financial risks*, such as currency volatility, inflation, interest rate levels, and stakeholder requests.
- *Supply risks* include those associated with suppliers, such as supplier insolvency, price swings, and inconsistent input quality and quantity. We talked about this problem in terms of close vendor relationships and VMI strategies in Unit 7, which might significantly reduce supply risks.
- *Operational risks* are those brought on by issues that arise inside a company's organizational boundaries, such as improvements in technology and design, bottlenecks, accidents, and labor disputes.
- *Forecast risks* because of erroneous projections brought on by small client bases, short life cycles, seasonality, long lead times, and product variety.
- *Demand risks* include fluctuations in demand, fierce competition in the market, client insolvency, and fragmentation of the customer base.

We limit our discussion to the effects of inventory issues and demand risk at this point. Supply chains that span large distances and numerous places worldwide increase risk and uncertainty. Little redundancy and slack (i.e., inventory) characterize lean supply chains, so when a disruption occurs – natural or man-made – the impacts can spread throughout the chain, slowing or halting regular activities and ultimately leading to the fulfillment of client orders. One strategy to reduce uncertainty is to carry excess inventory at different stages of the supply chain.

A business must offer a greater service level of demand fulfillment in order to draw in and keep customers. Because companies need to hold inventory to do this, a large portion of their capital is invested in three categories of inventories: raw materials, work-in-process, and finished goods. Inventory holding costs can result in a shortage of capital, opportunity costs, increased product costs, and a whole or partial loss of value in such stocks should market conditions or demand change.

Here, we especially address how the ***risk pooling*** approach enhances the effectiveness and efficiency of operations and/or services, particularly with regard to supply chain management and logistics. According to the statistical theory of risk pooling, demand variability can be decreased by combining demand across products, geographical areas, or even time. Actually, aggregation lowers variability and uncertainty according to a statistical concept. There is a higher likelihood that a client's strong demand will be offset by a client's low demand when demand from several places is combined. Because there is less unpredictability and correspondingly less demand for safety stock, the average inventory falls.

The accuracy of demand forecasts for specific markets or products is constantly questioned. Demand forecast aggregation, however, is more accurate than demand forecasting done in reverse. For this reason, the risk pooling approach might be applied. One needs to understand both ***centralized*** and ***decentralized*** inventory holding systems in order to comprehend risk pooling. It is a common belief that having a decentralized system (Fig. 8.7) will improve demand fulfillment efficiency and lower the likelihood of stock outs. Furthermore, a reduced lead time would come from situating the warehouse closer to the market. It is true that having more warehouses and being closer to the market results in shorter lead times and better demand fulfillment, but it also means that more safety stock is being kept, and any significant variability in demand will either cause a stock out or an overstock of products; the former will likely increase supplier demand and create a bullwhip effect, while the latter will increase holding costs.

Having one or more centralized stores to service many neighboring retailers through risk pooling is a more efficient approach because the demand fluctuation in one store or retailer can be counterbalanced by the demand variability in another. The same holds true for the product's demand variability. The strong demand for Product A, which generates profit, can counteract Product B's lackluster performance in a particular market. As a result, safety stock will be decreased while maintaining or increasing service levels (refer to the retailers

A, B, and C in Fig. 8.7). The expense of maintaining safety stock at each warehouse and the capital that is stranded in inventory will be rather significant if the warehouses for the three of them are managed independently. On the other hand, demand aggregation through risk pooling will lower the cost and requirement for safety stock. Additionally, unless all retailers exhibit positive demand fluctuation simultaneously, any variability in one retailer's demand would be countered by the variability in the other.

Risk pooling offers several benefits and can maximize service level while lowering costs, but like every tool or technique, it has its drawbacks. A few possible detrimental effects include the following:

- Transportation costs would rise as a result of the potential likelihood of rising costs owing to increased distance between different markets.
- Longer lead times may potentially result from the greater distance.
- Any kind of unforeseen circumstances may result in a lack of substitute possibilities.

Fig. 8.7 Decentralized and Centralized supply chain system

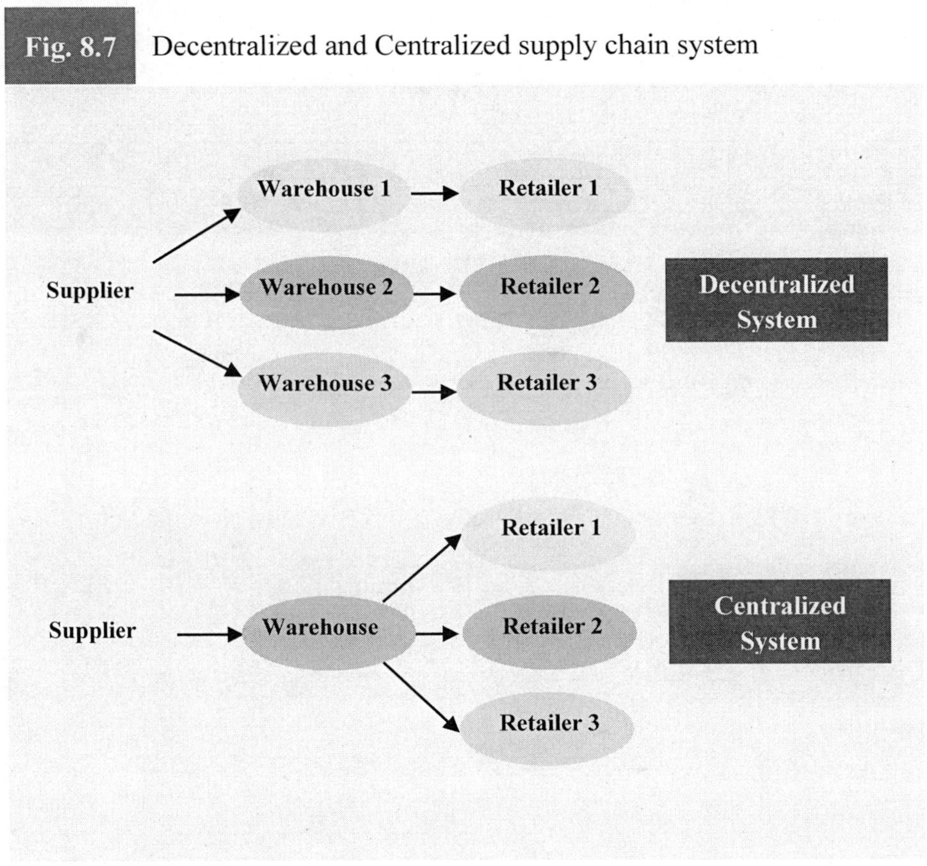

Example 8.1

Let's look at a business that has two distinct product distribution scenarios – a decentralized system and a centralized system – for products A and B. With a one-day lead time, two warehouses in the decentralized system deliver items to two different retailers.

Each unit will cost \$1.05 for transportation. The transportation cost for a centralized system is \$1.10. In all scenarios, the ordering cost is \$60, the carrying cost is \$0.27 per week, and the service level is 97%. The historical data of demand of each product is given below. We consider product B to be a slow-moving item.

Week	1	2	3	4	5	6	7	8
Product A to Retailer 1	33	45	37	38	55	30	18	58
Product A to Retailer 2	46	35	41	40	26	48	18	55
Product B to Retailer 1	0	2	3	0	0	1	3	0
Product B to Retailer 2	2	4	0	0	3	1	0	0

Solution

The average and standard deviation of demand for each product in both the centralized and decentralized systems are summarized in the following table.

Warehouse	Product	Average Demand	Standard Deviation	Coefficient of Variation	ROP (s)	Order-upto-level (S)	Average Inventory	Percent Decrease
Retailer 1	A	39.3	13.2	0.34	65	197	91	
Retailer 2	A	38.6	12.0	0.31	62	193	88	
Retailer 1	B	1.125	1.36	1.21	4	29	14	
Retailer 2	B	1.25	1.58	1.26	5	29	15	
Centralized	A	77.9	20.7	0.27	118	304	132	36%
Centralized	B	2.375	1.9	0.81	6	39	20	43%

1. The value of ROP for each product with respective retailers is calculated using Eq. 6.12 of Unit 6.

$$ROP = s = \bar{d} \times \overline{LT} + z\sqrt{\overline{LT}\sigma_d^2 + d^2\sigma_{LT}^2}$$

For instance, at Retailer 1, the ROP for product A is given by

$$= 39.3(1) + 1.89\sqrt{1(13.2)^2 + (39.3)^2(0)} \approx 65$$

$$Note\text{: } for\ 97\%\ service\ level, the\ value\ of\ z = 1.89$$

2. For calculating 'S', suppose we use the order quantity eqaul to EOQ, then

$$S = s + Q^* = s + \sqrt{\frac{2DC_o}{C_c}} \text{ (using Eq. 6.1 of Unit 6 for EOQ)}$$

For instance, at market 1, the S for product A is given by

$$S = 65 + \sqrt{\frac{2(39.3)(60)}{0.27}} = 197$$

3. For calculating 'Average Inventory', the relation is:

$$\text{Average inventory=safety stock+Average lot size}$$
$$= z\sqrt{LT\sigma_d^2 + d^2\sigma_{LT}^2} + \frac{Q}{2}$$
$$= 1.89(13.2) + \frac{132}{2} \approx 91$$

4. The difference in average inventory between the centralized and decentralized systems is indicated by the value of decreasing percent, which is given by:

$$\frac{\text{Decentralized average inventory-Centralized average inventory}}{\text{Centralized inventory}}$$

For instance, Product A's average inventory is lowered by

$$= \frac{(91 + 88) - 132}{132} \approx 36\%$$

when we move to a centralized system from a decentralized one.

Observations from the above case

(a) Keep in mind that the average demand that the two warehouses in the decentralized system combined to form the average demand that the centralized warehouse faced.

(b) The cumulative variability experienced by the two warehouses in the decentralized system is significantly more than the variability faced by the centralized warehouse, as indicated by the standard deviation or coefficient of variation.

8.8 OUTSOURCING FOR PROCUREMENT IN SUPPLY CHAIN

The process of buying products and services that were once created internally from an external supplier is known as outsourcing. As a temporary fix for issues like an unanticipated spike in demand, equipment and plant malfunctions, product testing, or a brief shortage of plant capacity, firms have been outsourcing for decades. Yet rather of being merely a tactical short-term choice, outsourcing has evolved into a long-term strategic choice. An increasing number of production, service, and inventory responsibilities are being delegated to suppliers by businesses, particularly large multinational companies.

In order to concentrate more on their core competencies – that is, what they do best – many businesses are outsourcing as a strategic decision. They delegate to a supplier the tasks that the company lacks the expertise or knowledge to perform, and that the supplier is best suited to perform. In the past, a lot of businesses – especially big ones – tried to own and run every source of supply and distribution throughout the supply chain. This gave them direct administrative control and lessened their reliance on suppliers who may turn out to be untrustworthy. They believed it to be more economical as well. However, this put a strain on these businesses' resources, and they found they lacked the knowledge to handle everything effectively. Additionally, it was frequently challenging to maintain a convoluted, complicated supply chain. Large stockpiles were maintained along the whole supply chain as a safeguard against uncertainty and subpar handling techniques. Companies now have more flexibility and resources to concentrate on their own core strengths thanks to the recent outsourcing trend, and their supplier partnerships have given them control. Furthermore, a growing number of businesses are outsourcing under supervision to nations like China and India, where labor and supplier costs are lower.

The discussion above leads us to the conclusion that outsourcing and flexibility go hand in hand, with businesses using outsourcing to take advantage of flexibility. However, modularity – the uniformity of parts – exploits flexibility, as we saw in Unit 7. This indicates that outsourcing has a close relationship with modularization. The easier it is to outsource manufacturing or its component parts, the more modularized the system is. Thus, the decisions on postponement (process design) and modularization-based outsourcing will work together to boost the possibility of improved supply chain performance. Therefore, outsourcing should not be viewed as a distinct activity from postponing activity in the context of modularization. While it might not be feasible to achieve the highest degree of postponement and modularization in every product, there might be technological limitations that limit postponement (such as in the steel industry) or organizational structure limitations that limit collaboration (such as in decentralized organizational structures that limit integration).

One can examine the supply chain structure from both an outbound and an inbound logistics standpoint. While the postponement can be evaluated from outbound logistics, the degree of modularization can be viewed from inbound logistics. Therefore, the amount of decisions made internally versus externally is captured by inbound logistics. A very vertically integrated supply chain is indicated by a low inbound modularization. Conversely, high inbound modularization usually indicates a decentralized supply chain where the majority of the components are outsourced.

8.9 LOGISTICS AND DISTRIBUTION IN SUPPLY CHAIN

Distribution includes all of the routes, procedures, and activities that a product goes through en route to the ultimate consumer (end user), such as transportation and warehousing. It is the actual transportation of materials and goods between locations. Managing the handling of goods and supplies at receiving ports, warehousing goods and materials, packing, and order shipment are all part of distribution management. *Order fulfillment* is the main goal of distribution and what it achieves. It is the procedure used to guarantee that customers' orders are delivered on schedule.

The process of moving manufactured goods from the production facility to the consumer is a crucial consideration in the design of an excellent supply chain. Moving goods from a manufacturing facility to a warehouse and finally to a retail location is a common process for consumer goods. Consider all the products that have the label "Made in China" on them. You probably don't think about this very often. A pair of trousers manufactured there has most likely traveled farther than you will ever. There is no way to know how quickly trouser completed the trip, therefore it must be done as efficiently as possible to keep the price low. It may have traveled by truck for a portion of the journey and by boat or airplane for the remaining distance. The transportation of commodities through the supply chain is the focus of logistics.

The scientific field of logistics studies the flow of information and goods to meet customer demand and keep total cost of ownership as low as feasible while organizing inventory.

"What's the difference between logistics and supply chain management?" is one question that is commonly asked. One definition of logistics would be that it is an SCM subset operating within a wider framework. The practice of allocating and scheduling goods to create value is known as logistics. Integrated logistics, which links and synchronizes the entire chain as a continuous operation, is essential to a smooth and effective supply chain.

Originally, the term "logistics" only applied to the transportation management role. It was actually considered a pretty low-profile position that primarily included coordinating – rather than arguing – with drivers or haulers. The situation has drastically altered recently. Organizations began to examine all aspects of transportation, purchasing and supply, physical distribution, and sales management as logistical tasks with an emphasis on integration, visibility, cycle time reduction, and seamless channels as supply chain management principles evolved. Operations like transportation, material handling, inventory control, warehousing, location analysis, and packing are all facilitated by the integration, which starts with the processing of customer orders and ends with after-sale services. The key to these operations' success is the corporate leadership's system-wide vision, which promotes transformation in a company's internal and external relationships. Furthermore, the primary competitive element in today's industry is logistics, which has a direct impact on the organization's service standards, expenses, and earnings. Thus, today's strategic perspective on logistics is possible.

Fig. 8.8 Logistics' development over several decades

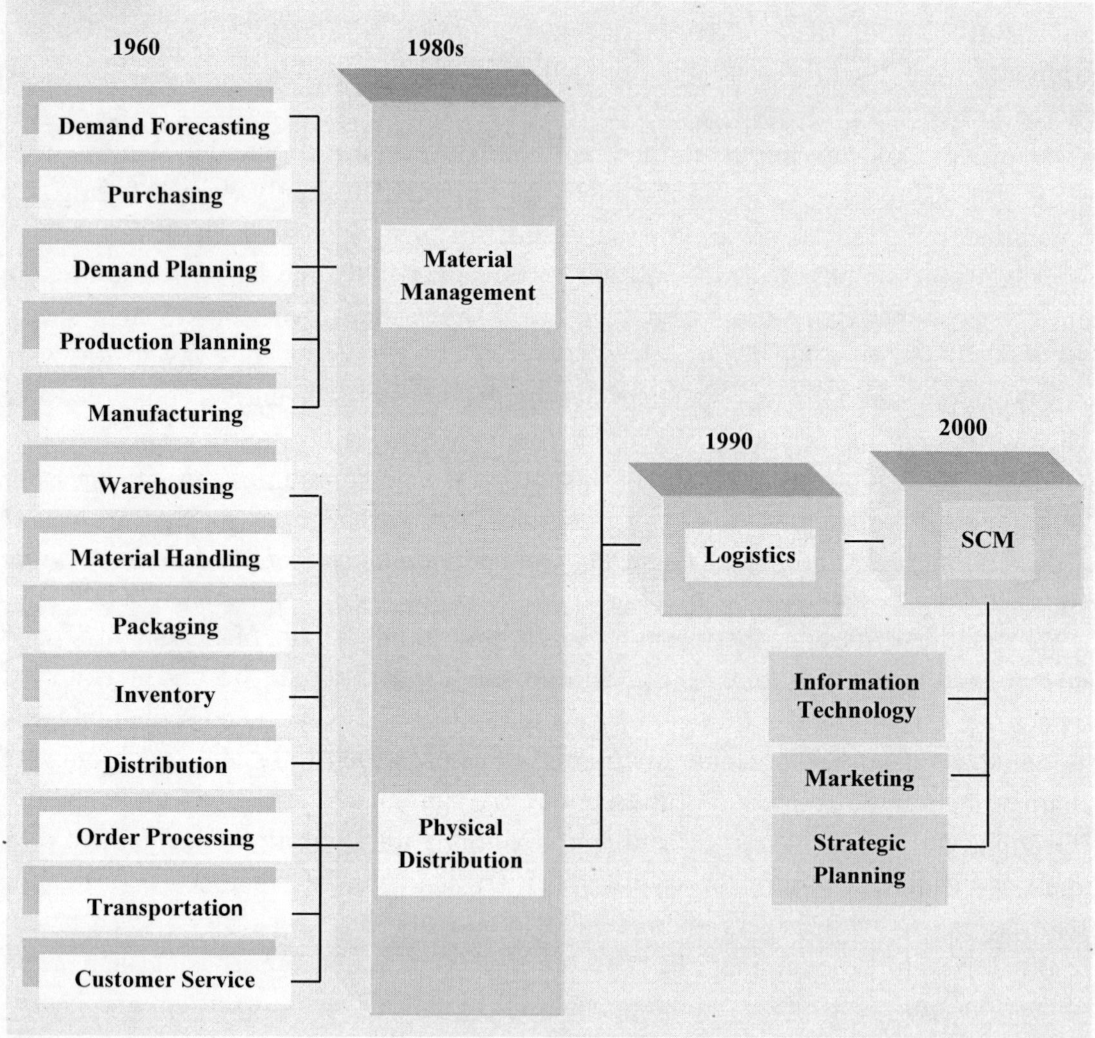

There are three phases to the evolution of logistics. The first phase of logistics began in the 1960s and 1970s, when it was thought to be limited to the actual transportation of commodities. To supply their stores, major retailers created their own distribution networks, which were based on the idea of local or regional distribution depots. The application of information technology concepts and the integration of distinct logistics tasks occurred in the late 1980s and early 1990s. At the time, logistics was defined as the physical distribution of goods along with material management (inbound and outbound logistics). Eventually, businesses began to recognize that logistics adds value in the year 2000 and beyond (Fig. 8.8).

ALONG AN EFFECTIVE DISTRIBUTION CASE

THE DABBAWALLAHS OF MUMBAI

The lunch box delivery workers in Mumbai, known as Dabbawallahs, pick up and deliver lunch boxes from homes or restaurants to the customer's workplace within a predetermined window of time. They subsequently return the empty box to the pickup location. It exemplifies how procedures can be crucial in facilitating logistics coordination. In order to offer British workers in Mumbai with lunch delivery and pickup, the Nutan Mumbai Tiffin Box Charity Trust was founded in 1891. Afterwards, it rose to prominence as the city's top lunch delivery cooperative. Every day, it picks up, delivers, and returns 200,000 lunchboxes in a typical container to the pickup location. The company employs 5000 workers for pickup and delivery, with an annual turnover of roughly $12 million; all of them lack formal education. Less than ten boxes are incorrectly delivered or left unpicked in a month – what an incredible accomplishment. The group's operations have garnered international recognition and numerous accolades. They are part of an expanding network of logistics-connected service providers that offer specialized services and add value for the client.

Teams that are arranged hierarchically are responsible for pick-up, consolidation, and delivery (as well as reverse logistics for empty boxes, which involves switching the roles of the teams). Every dabba or lunch box typically travels up to 6 km each way and goes through more than four pairs of hands. The window for pickup is 7.30 am to 9:00 am, the window for delivery is 12:00 pm to 1:00 pm, and the window for return is 2:00 pm to 5:00 pm. These stand for a group of twenty to twenty-five people who are employed under rigid schedules and are managed by a team leader who also covers for absentees. A single individual handles about thirty pick-ups. The boxes are bicycled to the closest train station in a special fixture, where they are consolidated according to their final destination. This is done by a consolidation team, which also loads the boxes onto the train, frequently carried to its target station on a third train along with boxes that originate from different areas. When the delivery is accomplished, the lunch boxes from different sources are once more separated at the destination station. Ultimately, a delivery team picks up their boxes, that is, the boxes they will deliver to particular owners in particular buildings, rides their bicycles to the owner's workplace, and drops the boxes off. The same individual picks up the empty box later in the afternoon, follows through with the reverse logistics, and eventually delivers the box to its original location, which is either a restaurant or a house.

Given this complexity, what could be the cause of the comparatively low mistake rates?

Since they are in charge of delivering food to clients, the group members actually regard their function as quite significant. This strengthens their social commitment to their work and creates a vital customer-service provider bond.

8.9.1 WAREHOUSE MANAGEMENT SYSTEMS

Companies used sophisticated, highly automated warehouse management systems (WMS) to manage daily operations of a distribution center and track stocks in order to meet the emerging trends and needs of distribution management. The WMS locates and retrieves items from storage (a pickup), packs items, and dispatches them via a carrier. It also stores items at a designated location (a putaway). The product is acknowledged by the WMS as being ready for shipping; if it isn't, the system will instantly find out from suppliers when it will be.

Orders are routed via an order management system (OMS) into a WMS. The distribution center (DC) can add, amend, or cancel orders in real time with the OMS. The online order information from customers is received by the OMS, which uses EDI (Electronic Data Interchange) to get a picture of product availability from suppliers and the WMS. When an item is out of stock, the OMS finds out when it will be available by checking the supplier's manufacturing schedule. After determining a delivery date and allocating inventory from the warehouse to fulfill an order, the OMS forwards these orders to the transportation management system for fulfillment.

Yard management sets dock appointments and controls activities at the facility to minimize bottlenecks; labor management plans, oversees, and documents warehouse staff performance levels. The transportation management system enables the distribution center to track incoming and outgoing shipments, to consolidate and build economical loads, and to choose the best carrier based on cost and service. By optimizing the "slotting" (placement) of products in the warehouse according to product groups, demand, and item physical attributes, warehouse optimization manages the inventory. Custom labelling and packaging are also made by a WMS. ***Cross-docking***, which Walmart invented, enables a DC to route incoming shipments directly to a shipping dock in order to fulfill outbound orders, obviating the need for expensive putaway and picking activities. This is made possible with the help of a WMS. A cross-docking system involves continuously delivering goods to a warehouse for storage, repackaging, and distribution to retailers without allowing them to languish in inventory. It typically takes 48 hours or less for goods to "cross" from one loading dock to another.

8.9.2 OUTSOURCING OF DISTRIBUTION

As was previously mentioned, outsourcing enables the business to concentrate on its core strengths. Additionally, it makes use of the knowledge that distribution businesses have built up. Distribution tasks can be outsourced to third-party logistics (3PL) organizations, which can help reduce inventory levels, save costs for the outsourcing firm, and free up resources for the company to concentrate on its core capabilities.

The necessity for transportation businesses to provide their customers with additional services led to the development of the 3PL concept. Generally speaking, 3PL refers to the practice of contracting out transportation and logistics tasks to third-party businesses that are neither consignees nor consignors. In actuality, a variety of tasks, including transportation, warehousing, and storage, are outsourced. 3PL emerged in the 1980s as the freight transport sector was deregulated, and it developed further in the 1990s as information technology advanced. A shift in the roles within transport/logistics operations could be used to characterize the party logistics pyramid from 1PL to 5PL (Fig. 8.9).

Fig. 8.9 Pyramid from 1PL through 5PL

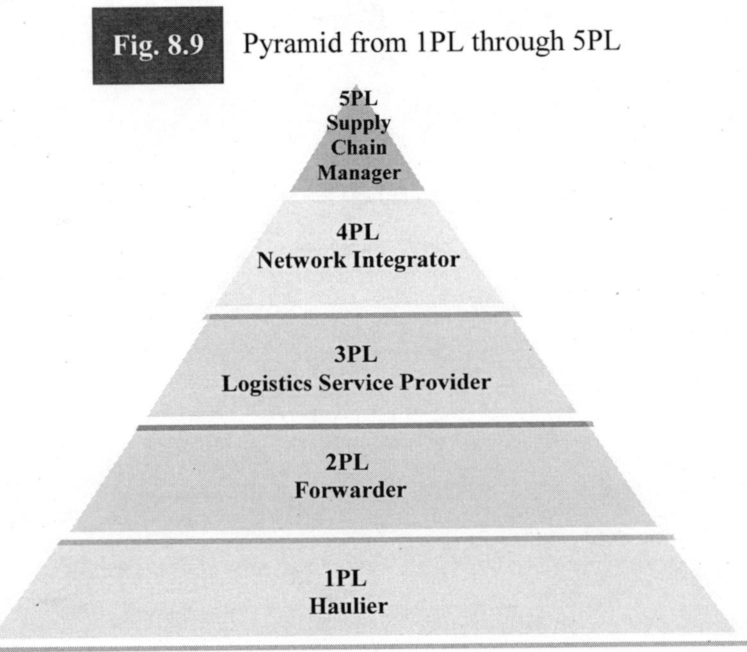

1PL is made up of small companies that do both purchasing and selling in one place. The manufacturer's logistics border grows as the business does. A 2PL provider is typically a supplier of commodity capacity, like a trucking company or a warehouse operator. A single or limited number of supply chain functions are serviced by a 2PL. Many 2PLs have expanded into 3PLs by merging their operations and adding additional logistics capabilities in response to the growing demand for one-stop solutions. It might or might not entail ownership of assets. A more general phrase commonly used to refer to contract logistics or freight forwarding operations is 3PL (Fig. 8.10). It handles a big percentage of a client's supply chain logistics, and its value addition is predicated on knowledge and information as opposed to providing non-differentiated transportation services at the lowest possible price. For the manufacturer's logistics outsourcing needs, the 4PL provider functions as a sort of logistics integrator or point of contact. They are in charge of managing end-to-end solutions and establishing connections between 2PL and 3PL suppliers. With its comprehensive understanding of the supply chain and its robust information technology and logistical capabilities, the 4PL provider can provide the manufacturer highly valuable added services.

Fig. 8.10 3PL System

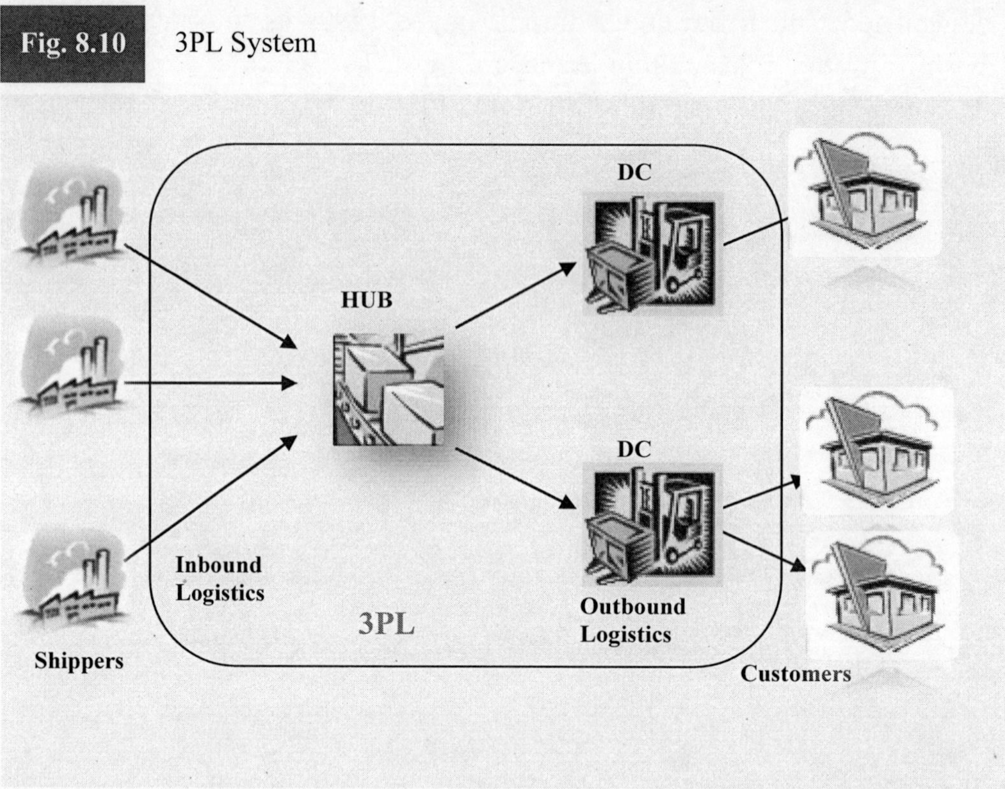

5PL is a recently developed new logistics model. The goal of the 5PL solutions is to offer comprehensive supply chain logistics solutions. The goal of supply chain management (SCM) is to gain a competitive edge by integrating the operations related to the movement and transformation of goods in the corresponding logistics networks through enhanced supply chain relationships founded on shared collaborative performance measurement and well-coordinated network relationships.

In logistics and supply chain management, selecting the right method of transportation can increase a company's ability to collaborate, cut costs, and scale up or down in response to demand. By scanning the provided QR code, you may learn more about different modes of transportation systems and how they work.

SCAN ME
for
Modes of Transports

8.9.3 DISTRIBUTOR STORAGE WITH LAST-MILE DELIVERY

When creating a distribution network, there are two important choices to make:
(i) How far away will the product delivery be made from the customer?
(ii) How would the distribution be made?

The renowned Chinese philosopher Lao-Tzu once stated, "A journey of a thousand miles begins with a single step." He was right. However, we believe that in this context, the 999th step marks the start of the true trip. The "final" step makes the voyage worthless, even if we travel 999 miles. Within the business system, an idea starts the journey and continues through various supply chain operations, marketing, distribution, and production. The "last-mile," or reaching the final customer, is the concluding phase in the supply chain, which guarantees the supply all the way to the end of the distribution channel.

Delivering a product to a customer's home by the distributor/retailer rather than through a package carrier is known as "last-mile delivery."

As seen in Figure 8.11, last mile delivery necessitates the distributor warehouse being somewhat closer to the client than package carrier service. The distributor warehouse in a last-mile delivery system must be located considerably closer to the customer. Compared to package delivery, more warehouses must be created due to the last-mile delivery's constrained service radius. With the exception of retail outlets, distributors offering last-mile delivery of fast-moving consumer goods (FMCG) with tailored requirements need to maintain larger inventory levels than other options due to the higher demand uncertainty and lower level of aggregation. However, last-mile deliveries come with a considerable expense of transportation, particularly when they are made to private homes. Package carriers used to achieve economies of scale by aggregating deliveries across numerous shops. If the delivery is being made in a densely populated city and the quantity is substantial, last-mile transportation makes sense. Large amounts, however, are uncommon for specific clients.

Fig. 8.11 Distribution in conjunction with last-mile delivery

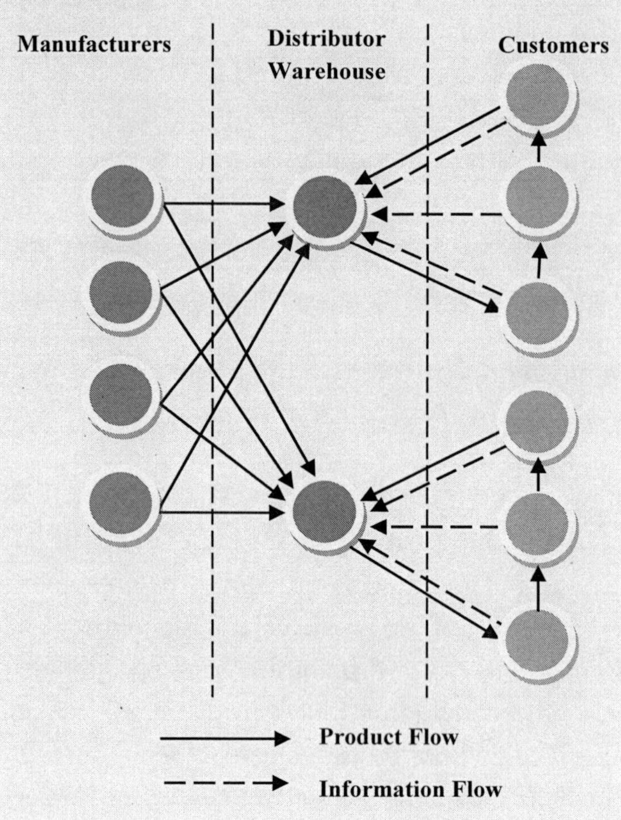

The ability to schedule deliveries is further required by information capabilities such as Enterprise Resource Planning (ERP), since last-mile delivery necessitates a very narrow window of time. Faster response times are required. With the exception of retail outlets, the expense of ensuring product availability is higher than for any other choice. Product variety availability will be less than that of distributor storage plus package carrier delivery. As there are several ways to assemble or produce the product employing a delay approach at upstream echelons, product variety availability is always higher when delivery is started from upstream in a supply chain. The provided QR code can be used to study the "milk run" delivery strategy, another well-known distribution scheme.

SCAN ME
for
Milk run
distribution system

8.10 SUSTAINABLE SUPPLY CHAIN

The World Commission on Environment and Development (WCED) first defined sustainability, or sustainable development, as follows in 1987:

"*Development that satisfies current needs without compromising the ability of future generations to satisfy their own needs*."

The notion of sustainability is thought to have originated with the practices of numerous ancient thinkers, even though it wasn't until the 1970s that it made its way into contemporary writing. However, the WCED definition of sustainability from 1987 elevated it from a collection of technical ideas into the mainstream of politics and industry. Based on the Triple Bottom Line (TBL) approach, which advocates for equal consideration of the economy, ecology, and society – the three pillars of sustainability – sustainable supply chain management (SSCM) literature typically incorporates sustainability into the theory of supply chain management. Sustainability, therefore, is characterized as follows from a TBL perspective:

In order to achieve the goals of sustainable development – economic, environmental, and social – companies along the supply chain must collaborate and manage the flows of capital, information, and materials while keeping in mind the needs of customers and stakeholders.

The five broad areas that make up the SSCM practices are: (i) supportive, (ii) permanence, (iii) collaborative, (iv) risk management, and (v) innovative.

1. Supportive – One of the main ingredients for an efficient SSCM program is upper management's supportiveness. It is far more likely that sustainability will be adopted and propagated throughout the organization with the backing of top management. Incorporating sustainable objectives into routine supply chain procedures is crucial. When pursuing competing sustainability goals, managers should be cognizant of potential trade-offs. However, win-win situations should be reached; for example, cutting waste reduces pollution burdens on society, improves the environment, and saves money for the business over time.

2. Permanence – The structure of a supply chain is made up of permanent elements that facilitate cooperation amongst its many participants. Having positive, mutually beneficial connections is one of the basics of SSCM. Such stability in the partnership is taken into account when evaluating the overall systemic supply chain performance, rather than just the individual supply chain members' performance when sharing

profits and risks. By investing in a "Long-term relationship" with at least the major supply chain partners, it is evident that the aims of permanence can be pursued.

3. Collaboration – Collaboration must be operationally and structurally focused. On the one hand, it facilitates and supports the use of IT infrastructure to support collaboration and on the other, it examines at the operational level how cooperation is actually accomplished in the SC. the process of cooperation designed to ensure that a supply chain's sustainability goals are truly met. "The potential for inter-organizational learning is the source of the value of collaboration in the supply chain," it is said. Generally speaking, collaboration is focused on the long term. In teamwork, trust is a crucial factor. Once more, "information sharing" is a technique that is necessary for a cooperative approach. Transmitting sustainability standards to suppliers is made possible through the exchange of information.
4. Risk management – It's a widely held view that businesses who use SSCM methods and are involved in sustainability are subject to different, and occasionally even greater, risks than those associated with traditional SCM. Among these risks are, for example, the possibilities of supply chain disruption brought on by a reduced pool of suppliers or the potential for reputational damage in the event that non-governmental organizations (NGOs) expose flaws. Reducing the supplier base and fostering greater collaboration, on the other side, are ways to lessen a SC's complexity and uncertainty, which eventually lowers risk.
5. Innovation – Businesses that use sustainable practices are seen as proactive since they frequently implement new techniques and technology to promote innovation in their supply chain. According to the SSCM, businesses who decide to implement sustainability strategies make investments in the creation of environmentally friendly goods and services. These goods are already designed with the option of recycling and reusing in mind for the post-use phase. To improve one aspect of sustainability, additional research on sustainability performance measures focuses on estimating and lowering the carbon footprint of goods along the supply chain.

Based on the above discussion on sustainability categories, it is evident that risk-management, innovation, and cooperation entail a range of procedures that are associated with Triple Bottom Line (TBL), including information exchange, standardization and certification, and innovation. Because operations have the largest environmental consequences of all a manufacturer's business functions, it is imperative to incorporate TBL into the activity of greening operations (i.e., the transformation processes that generate usable goods and services).

The three main tasks of the supply chain are distribution/material transit, manufacturing/material management, and purchasing/material sourcing. Green purchasing, manufacturing/materials management, distribution/marketing, and reverse logistics can all be considered components of ***green supply chain management*** (GSCM) when considering the various functions involved in a more environmentally conscious and sustainable "green" context. To access an in-depth study of the green supply chain, simply scan the provided QR code. The fully integrated, green supply chain has all the components of the conventional supply chain; however, it goes beyond to create a closed loop that involves the recycling, reuse, and/or remanufacturing of products and packaging, resulting in a reverse logistics approach. Scan the corresponding QR code to gain access to an in-depth study of the reverse logistics.

SCAN ME
for
Green Supply Chain

SCAN ME
for
Reverse logistics

8.11 INFORMATION TECHNOLOGY TRENDS IN LOGISTICS INDUSTRY

Warehouses in India usually run at sixtyfive percent of their capacity. The time lost in between tasks is the primary cause of this. Optimizing the process of receiving, sending out, and storing merchandise as well as managing resources is crucial. A thoughtfully planned warehouse management system aids in cutting expenses, raising customer happiness, lowering inventory levels, and enhancing quality control. The warehouse management system and logistics can both be greatly enhanced by the application of sophisticated information resources.

Global Positioning System (GPS) – GPS technology provides shipment origin and destination information. It assists in giving the precise location of the shipment during transit. One may follow movement and notify consumers about cargo status and estimated delivery time in a proactive manner with the help of advanced GPS maps and technology. Logistics businesses can trace the position of their goods with the use of GPS systems. Furthermore, these systems can be utilized for load temperature tracking in refrigerated vehicles, which enables the monitoring and recording of critical temperature changes – which are necessary for certain pharmaceutical and food chain items. According to estimates, the global market for GPS tracking devices has generated $3.1 billion in sales in 2023.

Enterprise Resource Planning (ERP) – A remarkable advancement in computer hardware and software systems over time was the ERP system. The majority of businesses created, developed, and deployed centralized computing systems in the 1960s, typically organizing their inventory control systems using inventory control packages. These were developed using the programming languages FORTRAN, ALGOL, and COBOL. Systems for material requirement planning (MRP) were created in the 1970s, primarily for the purpose of scheduling product or part requirements in accordance with the master production schedule (MPS). The 1980s saw the development of new software systems, the result of which was manufacturing resource planning (MRPII). By aligning the materials with the demands of production, this program focused on streamlining manufacturing processes. Aspects of MRPII encompassed project management, engineering, finance, human resources, and shop floor and distribution management. With the power of company-wide inter-functional coordination and integration, ERP systems initially emerged in the late 1980s and early 1990s.

Each entity in the supply chain is involved in three main processes: production, distribution, and supply. Material management, production planning, and distribution are the three main logistic modules of the ERP system that are integrated in these three processes. There are two stages in the development of information exchange or integration: process and data. An intermediate ERP system should be present in supply chain systems in order to link different levels. The information is taken from ERP databases that have been set up at various stages of the supply chain by the intermediate system, which then transfers it to ERP databases and formats it so that other ERP systems may receive it. This intermediate software's technology transfers data via EDI, HTML, and XML formats.

The data resources are linked across the supply chain in order to exchange information at the data level. Information is shared between ERP databases, which are updated between them. The functional routine of some organizational processes should also be integrated if information sharing is done at the process level, meaning that the two organizations' processes should be tied to one another. For instance, the supplier receives access to the vendor's warehouse data. After the data has been processed by the supplier's system, the supplier will be notified if the warehouse stock level is below the allowable threshold.

SCAN ME
for
Advantages and disadvantages of ERP system

Integration can be developed in the intermediary software at the process level, such as in the supply chain planning procedure. The processes that need to be put into place at various supply chain levels are: master production schedules (MPS) for each manufacturing echelon; dispersed requirement planning throughout the chain; and cumulative pre-demand across the chain. Additionally, the ERP master production schedule should be used as the operating basis for every production unit. Various stages of the chain will each see the implementation of the integrated process (Fig. 8.12).

Fig. 8.12 ERP's function in the supply chain procedure

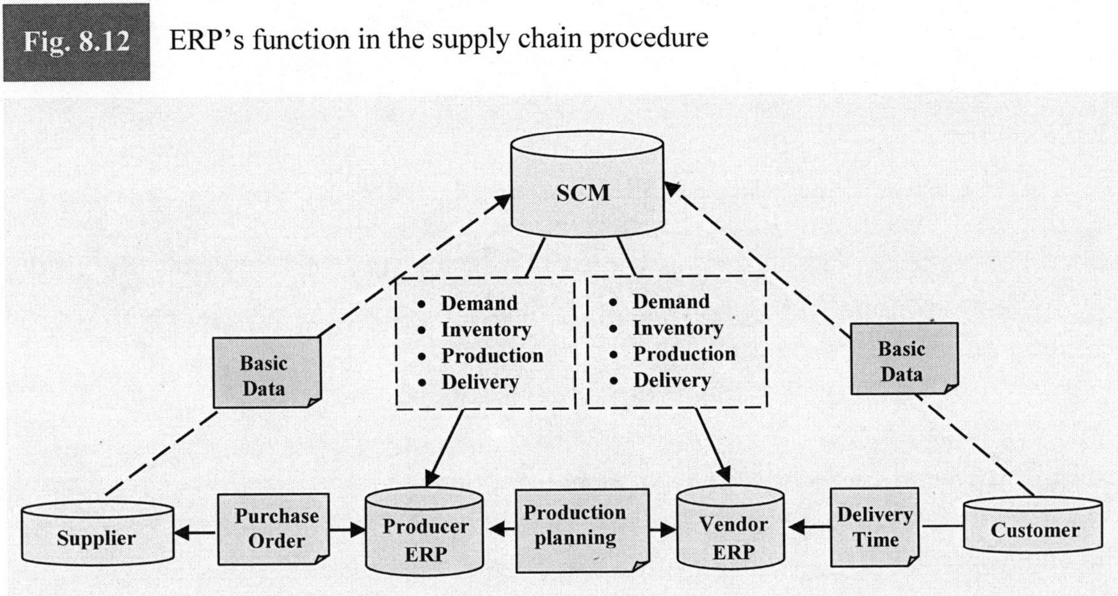

Bar Codes and Radio Frequency Identification (RFID) – A bar code is a tiny pattern of lines and spaces used to identify a certain product number, person, or place. It can be attached to goods, identity cards, and mail. Practically every facet of supply chain management has been impacted by bar codes. Bar code use has improved the supply chain's efficiency, simplification, and integration. Bar codes are a useful identifying tool that lowers error rates in product tracking. Accuracy, portability, and affordability characterize bar code technology. Bar codes are widely used and recognized worldwide in supply chain management as a result of these benefits.

Bar codes are used in inventory control procedures to provide quick and precise information that improves warehouse productivity and reduces the amount of inventory on hand. Organizations are able to base their judgments on reliable, real-time information that is available thanks to the bar codes. Businesses can use this information to improve their supply chain management strategies and gain a competitive edge. For example, the organization may be able to implement Just-In-Time (JIT) inventory policies and function with a lower inventory on hand or a larger storage capacity provided they receive accurate and fast information.

Nonetheless, the use of bar code technology in the supply chain is declining as attention shifts to the labor demands imposed by bar code scanning's physical character. This is a result of both the growing acceptance of radio frequency identification (RFID) technology, which is unrestricted by optical line-in-sight characteristics, and the technical line-in-sight characteristic of bar codes.

An automatic identifying system known as radio frequency identification (RFID) uses tags, or transponders, to store and partially retrieve data. It makes it possible for logistics service providers to more effectively and efficiently track, monitor, report on, and manage people, products, documents, and assets as they travel between locations at any time. An RFID tag is integrated into a product in order to identify it by radio frequency identification. Certain tags have a significant reading range. In order to process information, these RF tags – which might be active or passive – need an interface computer and a reading device.

SCAN ME
for
Bar codes and RFID

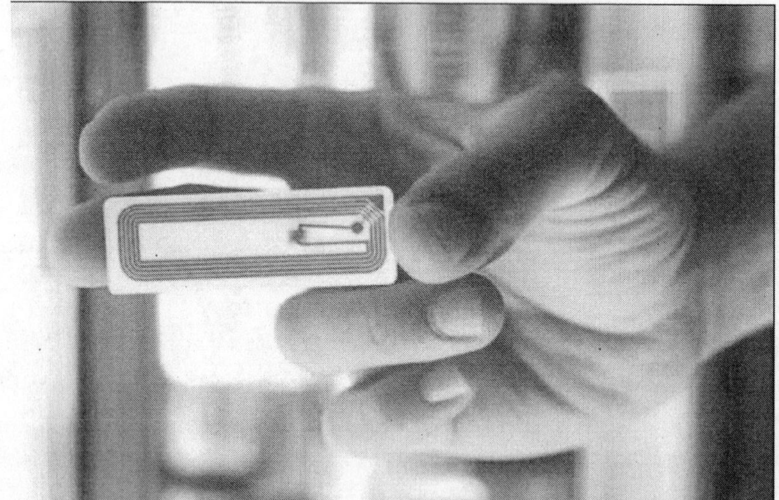

ALONG THE INFORMATION AND DISTRIBUTION CAPABILITIES IN SUPPLY CHAIN

Amazon.com – An Internet Company

One of the best companies that have moved past theory is Amazon, which is currently using its capabilities to investigate supply chain opportunities and unexpected synergies. For online retailers such as Amazon.com, where supply and distribution make up nearly all of the supply chain, distribution is a crucial component. These businesses only sell and distribute goods that they purchase from suppliers; they don't engage in any kind of production. They are propelled by distribution at the back end of the supply chain rather than the website, which is the front end. The ability to ship each order when the consumer needs or wants it is ultimately what determines their success. You can obtain a comprehensive analysis of the Amazon supply chain by scanning the provided QR code.

SCAN ME
For
Amazon.com

UNIT SUMMARY

- ***SCM Evolution*** – Traces the historical development from fragmented supply chain functions to integrated SCM, driven by ERP systems and global trade networks.
- ***SCM Objectives & Complexity*** – Focuses on cost minimization, efficiency, risk management, and customer satisfaction, while addressing challenges like demand unpredictability and supply disruptions.
- ***Bullwhip Effect*** – Explains demand distortion in supply chains and strategies to mitigate fluctuations using information sharing, inventory management, and technology.
- ***SCM Strategies for Uncertain Demand*** – Covers: Efficient Supply Chains (cost minimization for predictable demand), Responsive Supply Chains (adaptability for fluctuating demand), Risk Hedging & Agile Supply Chains (balancing risk and flexibility).
- ***Outsourcing & Procurement*** – Highlights the growing trend of third-party logistics (3PL) and supplier partnerships to improve cost-effectiveness and flexibility.
- ***Logistics & Distribution*** – Discusses: Warehouse management & last-mile delivery, Information technology in logistics (RFID, GPS, ERP systems), Sustainable SCM & Green Supply Chains.

EXERCISES

MULTIPLE CHOICE QUESTIONS

8.1 What is the primary goal of Supply Chain Management?

(a) To increase the number of suppliers	(b) To manage the flow of goods and services from production to consumption
(c) To reduce the workforce in manufacturing	(d) To maximize the number of transactions in the supply chain

8.2 In the context of SCM, what does the term 'logistics' refer to?

(a) The strategic planning of a company's long-term goals	(b) The process of moving and storing goods within the supply chain
(c) The development of new products	(d) The negotiation of supplier contracts

8.3 Which of the following best describes the term 'supply chain integration'?

(a) The process of improving customer service levels	(b) The coordination of all supply chain activities and entities to optimize performance
(c) The elimination of all intermediaries in the supply chain	(d) The increase of inventory levels to prevent stockouts

8.4 The rise of which technology in the 1990s significantly advanced supply chain visibility and data management?

(a) Artificial Intelligence	(b) Internet of Things (IoT)
(c) Enterprise Resource Planning (ERP) systems	(d) Blockchain

8.5 What is a major characteristic of the modern supply chain compared to its earlier forms?

(a) Emphasis solely on cost reduction	(b) Focus on linear and siloed processes
(c) Integration of end-to-end visibility and real-time data	(d) Exclusively domestic operations

8.6 Which approach helps enhance supply chain value by aligning supply chain operations with customer needs and preferences?

(a) Product Lifecycle Management (PLM)	(b) Demand-Driven Supply Chain Management
(c) Cost Leadership Strategy	(d) Centralized Warehousing

8.7 What is a major factor contributing to the increased complexity of modern supply chains?

(a) Simplified distribution channels	(b) Increased globalization and international sourcing
(c) Reduced number of suppliers	(d) Decreased consumer demand for variety

8.8 Which of the following is a challenge associated with multi-echelon supply chains?

(a) Limited inventory visibility across different stages	(b) Reduced need for information sharing between partners
(c) Simplified logistics and transportation	(d) Uniformity in supplier capabilities

8.9 What is the primary benefit of information sharing in a supply chain?

(a) Improved coordination and decision-making	(b) Increased costs and inefficiencies
(c) Reduced transparency among partners	(d) No impact on supply chain operations

8.10 How does real-time data contribute to supply chain performance?

(a) Enables quick response to changes in demand and supply	(b) Leads to increased lead times and delays
(c) Has no effect on supply chain efficiency	(d) Only benefits the customers

8.11 What role does accurate forecasting play in the value of information in a supply chain?

(a) Optimizes inventory levels and reduces stockouts	(b) Leads to overstocking and excess inventory
(c) No impact on supply chain performance	(d) Only benefits the manufacturers

8.12 How does information sharing impact supply chain resilience?

(a) Enhances the ability to respond to disruptions	(b) Decreases flexibility and adaptability
(c) Increases operational inefficiencies	(d) Only benefits the suppliers

8.13 What is the bullwhip effect in a supply chain?

(a) The amplification of demand variability as it moves upstream in the supply chain	(b) A decrease in demand variability as it moves upstream in the supply chain

(c) A phenomenon that only affects downstream partners in the supply chain	(d) A situation where demand remains constant throughout the supply chain

8.14 How does the bullwhip effect impact inventory levels within the supply chain?

(a) It leads to consistently low inventory levels across the supply chain.	(b) It causes inventory levels to fluctuate significantly, leading to both stockouts and overstock situations.
(c) It results in perfectly balanced inventory levels.	(d) It has no impact on inventory levels.

8.15 How can technology help in reducing the bullwhip effect in a supply chain?

(a) By enabling real-time data sharing and visibility across the supply chain	(b) By increasing order batching and lead time variability
(c) By limiting communication among supply chain partners	(d) By ignoring demand fluctuations and inventory levels

8.16 What is the customer order decoupling point (CODP) in a supply chain?

(a) The point at which inventory is replenished based on forecasts	(b) The point at which customer orders trigger production and replenishment activities
(c) The point where raw materials are sourced from suppliers	(d) The location where finished goods are stored before distribution

8.17 In a make-to-stock (MTS) production strategy, where is the CODP typically located?

(a) At the final assembly stage	(b) At the raw material sourcing stage
(c) At the finished goods inventory stage	(d) At the order fulfillment stage

8.18 Which of the following is a common risk hedging strategy used to manage supply chain disruptions?

(a) Single sourcing	(b) Multi-sourcing
(c) Just-in-time (JIT) inventory	(d) Reducing safety stock levels

8.19 How does the practice of "postponement" contribute to agility in a supply chain?

(a) By centralizing all manufacturing activities in one location	(b) By delaying the final production or assembly of products until customer orders are received
(c) By increasing the amount of finished goods inventory held at each distribution center	(d) By standardizing all product offerings and eliminating customization

8.20 Which of the following is an example of a risk pooling strategy?

(a) Maintaining separate inventories for each individual store in a retail chain	(b) Centralizing inventory at a central warehouse and fulfilling orders from this location for multiple regions
(c) Increasing the number of suppliers to spread risk	(d) Implementing a just-in-time (JIT) inventory system for each production facility

8.21 How does a decentralized inventory system impact lead times?

(a) It generally increases lead times due to the need for inventory replenishment from multiple locations.	(b) It reduces lead times by keeping inventory closer to end customers.
(c) It has no effect on lead times.	(d) It decreases lead times by centralizing inventory control.

8.22 Which inventory system is more likely to achieve economies of scale in purchasing and reduce overall inventory carrying costs?

(a) Centralized inventory system	(b) Decentralized inventory system
(c) Hybrid inventory system	(d) Just-In-Time (JIT) inventory system

8.23 How does cross-docking enhance efficiency in a distribution system?

(a) By increasing the need for extensive warehousing and storage	(b) By minimizing handling and storage time by moving products directly from inbound to outbound transportation
(c) By centralizing inventory in a single location for all distribution activities	(d) By relying on multiple distribution centers to handle all inbound and outbound shipments

8.24 What distinguishes 4PL (Fourth-Party Logistics) providers from 3PL providers?

(a) 4PL providers focus on a single aspect of logistics, such as transportation or warehousing	(b) 4PL providers manage and oversee the entire supply chain, integrating multiple 3PL providers and offering strategic solutions
(c) 4PL providers handle only internal logistics operations without external partnerships	(d) 4PL providers are involved in the actual physical handling of goods and inventory

8.25 Which logistics provider level is most likely to offer technology-driven solutions and advanced analytics to optimize supply chain performance?

(a) 1PL	(b) 2PL
(c) 3PL	(d) 5PL

8.26 What is the primary focus of last-mile delivery in the supply chain?

(a) Managing the transportation of goods from the supplier to the distribution center	(b) Optimizing the delivery of products from the distribution center to the final customer
(c) Coordinating the movement of raw materials from suppliers to manufacturers	(d) Handling bulk shipments from manufacturers to retail stores

8.27 What distinguishes a green supply chain from a traditional supply chain?

(a) Focus on maximizing profits without considering environmental impact	(b) Implementation of practices that reduce environmental impact and improve sustainability throughout the supply chain
(c) Emphasis on increasing resource consumption and waste generation	(d) Solely focusing on enhancing logistical efficiency without environmental considerations

8.28 Which of the following is a key component of a sustainable supply chain?

(a) Reducing the use of renewable energy sources	(b) Increasing the carbon footprint of transportation activities
(c) Implementing practices that minimize waste, optimize resource use, and promote recycling and reuse	(d) Ignoring regulatory requirements related to environmental impact

8.29 What is the primary benefit of using RFID technology in the supply chain?

(a) Reduced cost of raw materials	(b) Enhanced visibility and tracking of inventory throughout the supply chain
(c) Simplified manual inventory counts	(d) Increased reliance on paper-based documentation

Answers of Multiple Choice Questions

8.1 (b), 8.2 (b), 8.3 (b), 8.4 (c), 8.5 (c), 8.6 (b), 8.7 (b), 8.8 (a), 8.9 (a), 8.10 (a), 8.11 (a), 8.12 (a), 8.13 (a), 8.14 (b), 8.15 (a), 8.16 (b), 8.17 (c), 8.18 (b), 8.19 (b), 8.20 (b), 8.21 (b), 8.22 (a), 8.23 (b), 8.24 (b), 8.25 (d), 8.26 (b), 8.27 (b), 8.28 (c), 8.29 (b)

SHORT AND LONG ANSWER TYPE QUESTIONS

Category I

8.1 How does supply chain management aim to reduce operational costs?

8.2 What role does supply chain management play in improving customer satisfaction?

8.3 Why is supply chain integration important for businesses?

8.4 In what way does ERP support better forecasting and planning in supply chain management?

8.5 What distinguishes the modern supply chain from earlier supply chains in terms of technology use?

8.6 How has the approach to inventory management evolved in modern supply chains compared to earlier practices?

8.7 How does complexity in coordination affect multi-echelon supply chains?

8.8 How does information sharing improve supply chain visibility?

8.9 How can companies improve their supply chain resilience to handle disruptions?

8.10 What causes the bullwhip effect in supply chains?

8.11 How does the location of the CODP impact the responsiveness of a supply chain?

8.12 How does postponement contribute to supply chain agility?

8.13 How does risk pooling help in managing demand variability?

8.14 What is a key advantage of implementing flexibility through outsourcing and modularization?

8.15 What is a major advantage of using cross-docking in distribution?

8.16 What is a primary function of 5PL (Fifth-Party Logistics) providers in the supply chain?

8.17 How does a milk-run delivery system impact transportation efficiency?

8.18 How can companies measure the effectiveness of their green supply chain initiatives?

8.19 How does the Internet of Things (IoT) benefit supply chain management?

Category II

8.20 In what ways does supply chain integration enhance visibility, transparency, and responsiveness across the entire supply chain network, ultimately leading to better decision-making and risk management?

8.21 How does supply chain resilience play a crucial role in mitigating disruptions and ensuring continuity in operations during unforeseen events or crises, such as natural disasters, geopolitical issues, or global pandemics?

8.22 What is the bullwhip effect in the context of supply chain management, and how does it impact inventory levels, production planning, and overall supply chain performance?

8.23 How does the customer order decoupling point (CODP) help in providing flexibility in the supply chain, and what are the implications of managing the CODP effectively?

8.24 What are the key differences between centralized and decentralized inventory systems, and how does each of these approaches impact supply chain management and overall business operations?

8.25 What are the key principles of a sustainable and green supply chain, and how do these principles impact business operations, environmental performance, and stakeholder relationships?

8.26 What is the role of digitalization in supply chain management, and how does it transform traditional supply chain practices to enhance efficiency, visibility, and agility?

REFERENCES AND SUGGESTED READINGS

1. Ballou, R. H. *Business Logistics/Supply Chain Management*, 5th Edition, Pearson Prentice-Hall, 2004.
2. Bowersox, D. J., and Closs, D. J. *Supply Chain Logistics Management*. McGraw-Hill, 2001.
3. Carter, J. R., and Kaufmann, L. *The Purchasing and Supply Chain Management Handbook*. McGraw-Hill Professional, 2007.
4. Chopra, S., and Meindl, P. *Supply Chain Management: Strategy, Planning, and Operation*, 6th Edition, Pearson, 2016.
5. Christopher, M. *Logistics and Supply Chain Management*, 5th Edition, Pearson, 2016.
6. Cox, A., and Chicksand, D. The role of procurement in managing the supply chain. *International Journal of Operations & Production Management*, Vol. 25(5), 1221-1243, 2005.

7. Cox, A., and Lamming, R. Managing supply chains: The evolution of the discipline. *International Journal of Purchasing and Materials Management*, Vol. 33(3), 10-16, 1997.
8. Dev, N.K., Shankar, R., Gunasekaran, A., and Thakur, L.S. A hybrid adaptive decision system for supply chain reconfiguration. *International Journal of Production Research*, Vol. 54(23), 7100-7114, 2016.
9. Harland, C. M., Lamming, R. C., and Cousins, P. D. *Supply Chain Management: A Strategic Perspective*, Prentice Hall, 2001.
10. Harrison, A., and van Hoek, R. *Logistics Management and Strategy: Competing through the Supply Chain*, 5th Edition, Pearson, 2014.
11. Kannan, D., and Tan, K. C. Supply chain management: An integrated approach. *International Journal of Production Economics*, Vol. 93-94, 153-165, 2005.
12. Klaus, P., and Dillon, W. R. Outsourcing logistics: A strategic approach. *Journal of Business Logistics*, Vol. 34(1), 19-34, 2013.
13. Kleindorfer, P. R., and Saad, G. H. Managing risk in supply chains. *Production and Operations Management*, Vol. 14(1), 14-27, 2005.
14. Lee, H. L., Padmanabhan, V., and Whang, S. The bullwhip effect in supply chains. *Sloan Management Review*, Vol. 38(3), 93-102, 1997.
15. Quang, H. T., and Hara, Y. (2017). Risks and performance in supply chain: the push effect, *International Journal of Production Research*, Vol. 56(2), 1-20, 2017.
16. Rushton, A., Croucher, P., and Baker, P. *The Handbook of Logistics and Distribution Management*, 5th Edition, Kogan Page, 2014.
17. Seuring, S., and Müller, M. From a literature review to a conceptual framework for sustainable supply chain management. *Journal of Cleaner Production*, Vol. 16(15), 1699-1710, 2008.
18. Simchi-Levi, D., Kaminsky, P., and Simchi-Levi, E. Managing *the Supply Chain: The Definitive Guide for the Business Professional*, 2nd Edition, McGraw-Hill, 2008.
19. Tang, C. S. Robust strategies for mitigating supply chain disruptions. *International Journal of Logistics Research and Applications*, Vol. 9(1), 33-51, 2006.
20. Van der Vorst, J. G. A. J., and Beulens, A. J. M. Supply chain management and information technology. *Journal of Operations Management*, Vol. 20(4), 529-546, 2002.
21. Wilding, R. D. The supply chain risk management: A systematic review. *International Journal of Production Economics*, Vol. 79(3), 249-260, 2002.

UNIT **9**

FORECASTING

UNIT SPECIFICS

This unit elaborately discusses the following topics:

- Domains of forecasting (SCM, Quality management, etc.)
- Attributes of forecasts
- Components of effective forecasts
- Steps involved in forecasting
- Qualitative techniques of forecasting (Delphi, marketing research, panel consensus, visionary model, views of sales force)
- Quantitative techniques of forecasting (Moving average, weighted moving average, exponential smoothing, Trends, trend adjustment in exponetial smoothing, seasonality)
- Forecasting accuracy and control

The topics' real-world applications are examined in order to enhance problem-solving skills and promote greater creativity and curiosity. The unit includes a list of references, suggested readings, and assignments through a number of numerical problems in addition to a number of multiple-choice questions and questions with short and long answer types divided into two groups according to lower and higher order of Bloom's taxonomy. You can fill these out to practice. In line with the content, an additional part ("Along the...") has been introduced after the unit's related topic. It has been thoughtfully written to benefit the book's reader. The use of QR codes, which may be scanned to obtain pertinent supporting material on a variety of interesting topics, is one notable aspect.

RATIONALE

In this unit, we explore the multifaceted domains of forecasting, including supply chain management and quality management, which underscore the critical role of accurate predictions in organizational success. We examine the essential attributes of forecasts that contribute to their effectiveness. The unit outlines the systematic steps involved in forecasting, highlighting both qualitative techniques – like the Delphi method, and marketing research – and quantitative methods, such as moving averages and exponential smoothing. These techniques are vital for capturing trends and seasonality in data. Additionally, we discuss the importance of forecasting accuracy and control, emphasizing how these elements are crucial for informed decision-making and strategic planning across various sectors.

UNIT OUTCOMES

List of outcomes of this unit is as follows:

U9-UO1: Understanding Domains of forecasting

U9-UO2: Evaluating Forecast Attributes

U9-UO3: Components of Effective Forecasts

U9-UO4: Forecasting Steps

U9-UO5: Qualitative and Quantitative Techniques

U9-UO6: Accuracy and Control in Forecasting

UNIT-9 Outcomes	EXPECTED MAPPING WITH COURSE OUTCOMES (1-Weak Correlation; 2-Medium Correlation; 3-Strong Correlation)					
	CO-1	CO-2	CO-3	CO-4	CO-5	CO-6
U9-UO1	2	2	3	2	2	2
U9-UO2	1	2	3	3	2	3
U9-UO3	2	3	3	2	2	2
U9-UO4	1	2	3	3	3	2
U9-UO5	2	3	3	3	2	2
U9-UO6	2	3	3	3	3	2

9.1 INTRODUCTION

A forecast is an anticipation of future events. The majority of significant planning decisions are based on a projection of product demand. Customer demand influences planning decisions on work force, distribution, purchasing, scheduling, inventory, manufacturing, and other areas. Top management bases its long-term strategic plans on predictions about the kinds of goods that consumers will want in the future as well as the size and geography of product marketplaces.

It is crucial to keep the forecasting goal in mind while deciding the forecasting methodology to employ. A few projections pertain to extremely advanced demand analysis. Let's say we forecast the demand for a certain set of products for the upcoming year. A few projections are utilized to help determine the overall plan for meeting demand. We'll refer to these as ***strategic forecasts***. For example, decisions about overall strategy, capacity, manufacturing and service process design, location and distribution design, sourcing, and sales and operations planning are best made using strategic forecasts. These are all long-and medium-term decisions about how demand will be strategically satisfied.

Forecasts are also required to ascertain the daily operations of a company's processes. For instance, how much manufacturing should be planned for an item next week, or when should the inventory for an item be refilled? In these ***tactical forecasts***, estimating demand for the next several weeks or months is the main objective. These estimates are crucial to ensuring that, in the near future, we can fulfill lead time commitments made by customers and other requirements pertaining to the accessibility of our goods and services.

9.1.1 FORECASTING IN SUPPLY CHAIN MANAGEMENT

For every product line, sales and operational planning forecasting span several months to a year into the future. Therefore, the projections must likewise span the same (or a larger) number of periods and be aggregated to the product family level. Data on customer plans and existing demand is a critical component of the forecast used in sales and operations planning. Through initiatives like customer relationship management and vendor-managed inventory (VMI), current data on inventory balances, demand levels, and product mix preferences can be added to insights into customers' future plans. These are valuable sources of information for creating the operations and sales plans. Add the estimates for each individual product in each product line to get an aggregated forecast for sales and operational planning. Knowledge of consumers' plans, prevailing patterns, and any marketing initiatives that could affect demand can all be taken into account when adjusting these totals. Even so, when utilizing the forecasts to create strategies, managerial judgment and insight are crucial. Creating the plan is not the same as creating the forecast.

Demand management provides precise estimates almost continuously, which helps the master production scheduling module make decisions. A declaration of how many completed goods or components to produce and when to do so is the outcome of the MPS decisions. As the market and industrial environment shift, these decisions are made on a regular basis. As a result, the MPS receives regular and comprehensive forecast data.

Control decisions that alter the order of importance for production, inventory distribution, and shipment destinations also occur continuously. All aspects of the process experience changes that necessitate adjustments as products progress from the purchase of raw materials to the delivery of finished goods. In order to maintain the product moving toward the customer in spite of these changes, control choices need to be made fast and effectively. The plans for their parents (the items they are used on), can be used to determine the timing and amounts of a dependent demand; an independent demand will need to be forecasted. Frequent, thorough, and timely forecasting is necessary to manage these daily control decisions.

The idea of decoupling points covered in Unit 8 on supply chain management. In order to enable independent operation of processes or entities within the supply chain, inventory is positioned at these decoupling points. For instance, when a product is stocked in a store, the manufacturer is never notified when a customer places an order because the buyer takes the item off the shelf. To keep the consumer and the manufacturing process apart, inventory serves as a buffer. A strategic choice that affects inventory investment and customer lead times is where to locate the decoupling point. The customer can be supplied more quickly the closer this point is to them. Because completed goods inventory is more expensive than raw material inventory, there is typically a trade-off involved when responding to consumer demand more quickly comes at the expense of increased inventory investment. Furthermore, for "last mile" and "milk run" distribution system operations – which are covered in Unit 8 on supply chain management – accurate demand forecasting enables inventory levels at various hubs to precisely meet all customers' predicted need in terms of timing and quantity.

The "bullwhip effect" and its detrimental effects on the supply chain were discussed in Unit 8 on supply chain management. The information about product demand, including forecasts, is distorted when they are sent back to suppliers across the supply chain; a phenomenon known as the bullwhip effect. Demand fluctuates more significantly and demand forecasts become less accurate the further away demand is from the final end-user.

This greater variance may lead to more expensive and excessive safety stock inventories at every point in the supply chain, as well as worse customer service.

When information flows back upstream in the supply chain, slight demand variability gets amplified, this results in the bullwhip effect. It arises when supply chain participants place orders based only on their own interests and without accurate demand projections from other supply chain participants. Each supply chain participant will accumulate excess inventory to make up for its lack of confidence in its ability to accurately predict the demand for the next member it supplies. In other words, the participant builds a security blanket of inventory. Creating demand projections that will lower uncertainty and encouraging supply chain participants to share them are two strategies to counteract the bullwhip effect. The creation of future projections for each supply chain member backup along the supply chain should ideally be based on a single demand estimate for the supply chain's end customer.

9.1.2 FORECASTING IN QUALITY MANAGEMENT

In a quality management setting, forecasting is equally essential. Customers increasingly believe that receiving a high-quality product when they need it equates to receiving good service. For businesses engaged in manufacturing and services, this is valid. When customers enter McDonald's to place an order, they don't anticipate having to wait a lengthy time for their purchases to be processed. They anticipate placing their orders quickly and that McDonald's will have the item they desire. In order to deliver high-quality service, McDonald's needs to estimate customer traffic flow and product demand well enough to schedule enough servers, stock adequate food, and schedule food production. Poor quality results from service breakdowns brought on by inaccurate forecasts. Customers expect parts from manufacturing processes, particularly suppliers, to be available as needed. Predicting client demand with accuracy is essential to delivering excellent service.

9.2 ATTRIBUTES SHARED BY ALL FORECASTS

There are several different forecasting methods in use. As you will soon see, they differ greatly from one another in a number of ways. However, there are some characteristics that all share, and it's critical to identify them.

1. Forecasting methods often operate under the assumption that the underlying causal system will remain unchanged from the past into the future. Unplanned events can

seriously affect forecasts, thus a management cannot just assign forecasting to models or computers and walk away. Events connected to the weather, changes in taxes, and adjustments to the features or costs of rival goods and services, for example, can all significantly affect demand. As a result, a management needs to be aware of these things and prepared to deviate from forecasts that rely on a steady causal system.

2. Actual results typically deviate from forecast values; forecasts are rarely precise. A flawless forecast is impossible due to unpredictability and the inability to anticipate with precision how a wide range of linked factors will affect the variable under consideration. It's important to account for errors.

3. Since forecasting errors among items in a group typically have a neutralizing effect, forecasts for groups of items typically have higher accuracy than forecasts for individual items. If components or raw materials are used in several products, or if a good or service is required by several separate sources, then opportunities for grouping could present themselves.

4. The longer the time horizon or the timeframe covered by the forecast, the less accurate the forecast becomes. In general, short-term projections are more accurate because they have fewer uncertainties to contend with than longer-term forecasts. The requirement for a shorter forecasting horizon in industries that operate on "pull" systems – those that must react swiftly to changes in demand – means that these sectors will benefit from more accurate short-term projections than their push system competitors.

9.3 COMPONENTS OF EFFECTIVE FORECASTS

A forecast that has been adequately developed should meet the following criteria:

1. Creating the foundation – Before we begin the forecasting process, we must conduct a comprehensive investigation, study, and analysis of the company, its goods, its market share, its organizational structure, and the industry. The prediction should be precise. A forecast's data response usually requires a certain amount of time. For example, increasing capacity overnight or rapidly changing inventory levels are not feasible. For this reason, the forecasting horizon needs to account for the lead time needed to carry out such revisions. The idea is to lay the groundwork for estimating needs in the future.

2. Comparing the predicted and actual outcomes – Monitoring and investigating the causes of significant discrepancies between the actual and expected business outcomes on a regular basis. In order to measure and compare actual growth and results, forecast estimations for the upcoming years give as benchmarks. Prediction accuracy is required, and it must be stated to what degree. Customers can therefore take into consideration any mistakes and have a baseline against which to compare various estimates. Customers using a method that yields estimates that are sometimes accurate and other times inaccurate would be hesitant to invest in it every time a new estimate is made available.
3. Improving the forecasting procedure – Developing proficiency in projecting the company's future through experience makes it simple to refine the methodology and streamline the process. As forecasting is a talent that can only be mastered through practice and experience, these ongoing adjustments, modifications, and enhancements would hence increase forecasting experience and skills. It must be simple to apply and understand the forecasting process. Users sometimes have little faith in forecasts produced by sophisticated procedures because they are not aware of the limitations or circumstances under which the methods are appropriate. Technique misuse is an obvious consequence. Not surprisingly, since customers are more comfortable with them, rather basic forecasting techniques are frequently employed.
4. Documenting the forecasts – Documentation of the forecast is required. This will at least increase the chance, even if there's no guarantee that everyone is using the same data. Moreover, a recorded forecast will provide an unbiased foundation for evaluating the forecast after actual outcomes are known.

9.4 THE STEPS INVOLVED IN FORECASTING

The following are the main steps in the forecasting process, presented in an understandable and basic manner:

1. Clearly define your objectives – Selecting what to anticipate and why should be your first step. Ascertain the forecast's objective and decide on the time horizon that interests you – short –, medium –, or long-term.

2. Collect data – Get historical information that is relevant to your projection, such as sales figures, trends in the market, or indicators of the weather. To acquire the most accurate forecast, make sure the data is accurate, reliable, and current.
3. Select a technique – Selecting the best forecasting method depends on your objectives and the facts at hand. There are several techniques, including quantitative and qualitative techniques (will discuss in forthcoming sections).
4. Analyze the data – Examine the data using the selected methodology to search for trends, patterns, or connections. You'll be able to forecast future occurrences and results with greater knowledge thanks to this analysis.
5. Develop a forecast – Make educated assumptions about potential future events based on your study. When you make your predictions, bear in mind the limitations of predicting and the unpredictability of the future.
6. Examine and modify – When new information becomes available or circumstances alter, periodically examine, and modify your forecast. Remember to remain adaptable and ready to change your ideas and projections as necessary.

9.5 TECHNIQUES OF FORECASTING

Forecasting is generally approached in two ways: qualitatively and quantitatively (Fig. 9.1). The primary inputs used in qualitative approaches are subjective and frequently difficult to accurately quantify numerically. When using quantitative methods, historical data is expanded upon or associative models are created in an effort to foresee by using causal (explanatory) variables. Generally speaking, qualitative forecasting methods rely heavily on expert knowledge and judgment. These methods usually entail procedures that are clear to everyone taking part in the forecasting activity. For instance, predicting the demand for a specific meal at a restaurant depends primarily on feedback from regular patrons who share their preferences. The key point is that this entails a methodical and well-considered approach to decision-making; it is not a series of wildly optimistic estimates of the predicted demand.

Fig. 9.1 Forecasting techniques

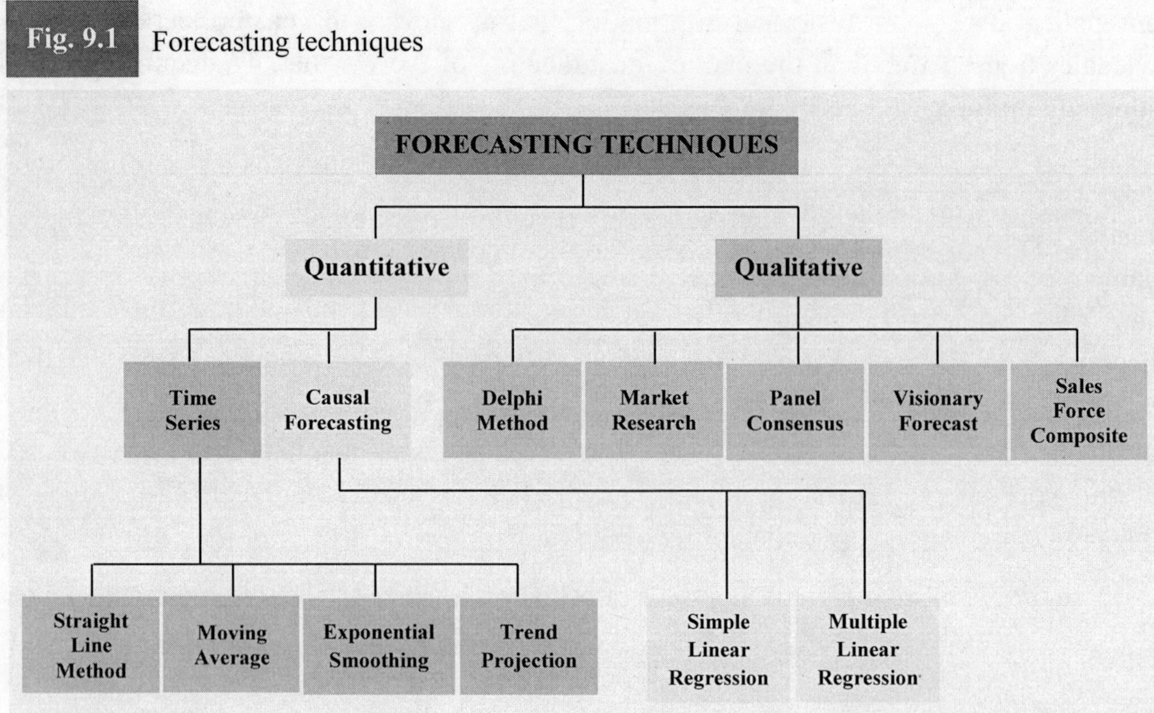

These strategies work best when the product is brand-new or there is limited prior sales experience in the target market. In certain circumstances, forecasters may need to make decisions rapidly since they may not have enough time to collect and evaluate the data. Other times, particularly when political and economic circumstances are changing, the information that is currently available may be outdated, and more recent information may not yet be accessible. Here, it may be crucial to have knowledge of related items, local consumer behavior, and the way the product will be marketed and introduced in order to accurately forecast demand. When estimating predicted demand, it can even be helpful in some situations to take industry data and rival companies' experiences into account.

Following are the approaches of qualitative techniques.

9.5.1 DELPHI METHOD

One with a higher level of authority will probably be given more weight when making statements or voicing opinions. In the worst situation, lower-level individuals refrain from contributing their true beliefs because they feel intimidated. The identity of the study participants is concealed through the *Delphi method* in order to avoid this issue. To arrive at a consensus forecast, the Delphi method is an iterative process. Those who have the knowledge and capacity to make significant contributions were asked to distribute a series of questionnaires as part of this strategy.

Since responses are kept anonymous, it is less likely that one person's viewpoint will win over and more likely that candid responses will be given. Every time a new questionnaire is created, data from the prior one is incorporated to expand the amount of information available for participants to use when making decisions. The Delphi technique has been used in many different contexts, not all of which include predicting. This topic is restricted to its application as a tool for predicting.

The Delphi approach is a valuable tool for technological forecasting, which evaluates technical advancements and their effects on an organization. Predicting when a particular event will happen is frequently the aim. A Delphi forecast might be used, for example, to estimate when video phones will be placed in at least 50% of residential houses or when a disease vaccine will be created and available for widespread distribution. The majority of the time, these are long-term, one-time forecasts, and as such, the problem does not lend itself to analytical methodologies because there is typically very little hard data to work with or expensive data to get. Instead, the opinions of specialists or other people with the information to make forecasts are used.

The Delphi method's step-by-step process is as follows:

- Select which experts will participate. There must to be a diversity of experts in various fields.
- Ask each participant for their projections, along with any presumptions or qualifications, via a questionnaire (or email).
- Provide a summary of the findings and provide the participants with them along with fresh, pertinent questions.
- Review, improving the conditions and forecast, and pose fresh queries.
- If required, repeat step 4 again. Share the finished results with each and every participant.

In three rounds, the Delphi approach typically yields good findings. The amount of time needed depends on how many people are participating, how much work they have to do to create their projections, and how quickly they respond.

9.5.2 MARKETING RESEARCH

Using the market research method, existing or future customers are consulted. Businesses carry out market research to gather data that will help them forecast the size, scope, demography, and purchasing patterns of a specific niche or market for goods and services. A variety of methods, including consumer surveys, interviews, and panels, are used in market research to gather qualitative, subjective data. Market research is the main instrument used by many consumer product companies for predicting.

The main goal of qualitative market research is to comprehend people's opinions, beliefs, and feelings about the circumstances, as well as the elements that ultimately drive their behavior. Market research is mostly used for product research, which includes finding new product ideas, identifying consumer preferences for competitive items within a given class, and so forth. Recall the wildly popular television program Desperate Housewives? And how many times have you seen women invite friends around for a couple of drinks or a cup of tea to talk about the gaudy new things they just bought? In a different situation, you get calls inquiring about your income, habits, preferred products, and other things. These calls ultimately have data collection as their main objective.

9.5.3 PANEL CONSENSUS

A qualitative forecasting method known as panel consensus, or expert opinion, involves experts or staff members from various organizational levels (from low-level to executive) discussing a good or service. As if they were a focus group, the members share their ideas and suggestions to create a forecast. Everyone is free to speak throughout the conversation, although occasionally, because of their inexperience in the industry, lower-level employees may be afraid to voice their opinions. This is among this model's shortcomings. For example, a salesperson in a particular product line may have a good estimate of future product demand but may not speak up to refute a much different estimates given by high level executive of marketing. The Delphi technique aforementioned takes care of this impairment to free exchange. However, if a large number of people participate in the forecasting process, the results are more accurate and balanced than those of a single person. After everyone has come to an agreement, the meeting will adjourn.

The phrase "executive judgement" is typically used when forecasting decisions are made at a higher, more general level (such as when launching a new product line or addressing strategic product decisions like new marketing areas). The name should go without saying – it refers to a higher degree of management.

9.5.4 VISIONARY MODEL OF FORECAST

A relevant and experienced individual's personal ideas, assessments, and insights form the foundation of the visionary forecasting model. To forecast future events, the projections are supported by facts, figures, and statistics. Historical analogies can also be used to make predictions about the future when they are accessible. Stated differently, the "visionary" makes predictions about the future based on an analysis of past occurrences and advancements. Consequently, this model is purely dependent on one person's conjecture and imagination, making it subjective and non-scientific in character. The sole potential drawback to visionary forecasting is the possibility of confirmation bias, as visionaries might only consider data that confirms their own theories and ignore any opposing data.

This model can also be applied in the event that historical data is not available. This model could be useful since it can be used for steps in the business planning process that don't require the usage of historical data, such analyzing the present financial condition, researching the company's competitors, creating future scenarios, or utilizing industry trends.

9.5.5 VIEWS OF SALES FORCE

The sales and customer support teams are frequently excellent sources of information due to their frequent interaction with customers. They frequently know about any future plans their clients may be thinking of. This strategy does have a few disadvantages, though. One is that they might not be able to discern between what clients genuinely want to do and what they would prefer to accomplish. Another is that these individuals are occasionally unduly impacted by recent encounters. Therefore, their estimates may tend to grow pessimistic after multiple periods of poor sales. Following multiple instances of strong sales, people could become overly hopeful. Furthermore, there will be a conflict of interest if predictions are used to set sales quotas as it is in the salesperson's best interest to produce low sales estimates. When you need to project sales for certain regions and territories in the near future with more accuracy, the sales force views can be helpful.

Technological forecasting has grown more and more important in the current business climate in order to compete.

Businesses always have access to cutting edge machinery and equipment, improved computer technology, and innovative production techniques. They can now launch more new products into the market more quickly than ever thanks to the advancements. By scanning the provided QR code, you may read a more in-depth analysis on the technology forecasting that is common in today's world.

SCAN ME
for
Technological forecasting

The development of information technology has led to the recent addition of "Data mining" as one of the technological forecasting strategies to the toolkit of approaches and techniques that businesses can use for forecasting. It is a procedure and toolkit for examining vast amounts of data to find patterns, trends, and connections within and between consumer, market, and product groupings. The enormous volumes of data that businesses already have access to from numerous electronic transactions throughout their business entities enable data mining. You can scan the provided QR code to learn more about data mining.

SCAN ME
for
Data mining in forecasting

9.6 QUANTITATIVE TECHNIQUES OF FORECASTING

The available historical demand data is plotted as the first phase in the quantitative forecasting process. The components of historical data, which are explained in the section that follows, may include trends, seasonal, or cyclical factors, among others. Using the linear regression technique, we address causal forecasting, which makes the assumption that demand is influenced by one or more underlying environmental factors.

Time Horizon – Forecasts might be long-range or short- to mid-range. Based on the company and the industry, short-range (to mid-range) projections are usually for sales demand on a daily, weekly, or monthly basis for a maximum of two years in the future. They are mostly used to set inventory levels and decide on production and delivery schedules. Hewlett-Packard prepares monthly printer forecasts twelve to eighteen months ahead of time, but Levi Strauss prepares weekly denim forecasts five years ahead of time.

A long-range forecast typically covers a horizon of more than two years. Strategic planning typically uses a long-range forecast to set long-term objectives, plan new goods for shifting markets, enter new markets, build new facilities, develop technologies, create supply chain designs, and carry out strategic initiatives. These distinctions are broad generalizations. There isn't always an apparent difference between short- and long-range forecasts. A long-term outlook for some businesses may be expressed in terms of months, whereas a short-term estimate may be expressed in terms of many years. How quickly the product market changes and how vulnerable the industry is to technical advancements are two factors that greatly influence how long a prediction should last.

Behaviour of Demand – Demand can exhibit erratic, random behavior at times. Other times, its behavior is consistent. Generally speaking, there are six components that make up the demand for goods and services: the average demand for the time being, a trend, seasonal and cyclical features, random variation, and auto correlation.

A demand curve spanning four years is depicted in Fig. 9.2, together with the average, trend, seasonal, cyclical, and random components around it. Chance events give rise to ***random*** variances. According to statistics, the percentage of demand that cannot be explained leaves behind after deducting the entire amount of demand from all known reasons (i.e., average, trend, seasonal, cyclical, and autocorrelative). We consider this remaining to be entirely random chance if we are unable to determine its cause.

When creating a forecast, ***trend*** lines are typically the first step. Following that, these trend lines are modified to account for cyclical factors, seasonal influences, and any other anticipated events that might have an impact on the final projection. Four of the most prevalent trend types are displayed in Fig. 9.3. It goes without saying that a linear trend (Fig. 9.3(a)) is a continuous, straight line. Products with rapid growth often follow an exponential curve (Fig. 9.3(b)). Given the exponential trend, it may not be prudent to assume that sales will increase at an ever-increasing rate. A product's growth and maturity cycle is typified by an S-curve (Fig. 9.3(c)). Where the trend shifts from slow to fast growth or from fast to slow growth is the most significant point on the S-curve. When a trend is asymptotic (Fig. 9.3(d)), demand growth is greatest in the beginning and eventually levels off. A curve similar to this one might be observed when a company enters an already-existing industry with the intention of saturating it and taking a substantial market share.

Data is plotted using a popular forecasting technique, which then looks for the best-fitting curved pattern (such as an exponential, S-curve, asymptotic, or linear one). This method's advantage is that it makes finding values for future time periods simple because the equations governing the curve are understood.

An oscillating movement in demand that repeats itself and happens on a regular basis (in the short run) is called a ***seasonal*** pattern. Often, seasonality is tied to whether. Every winter, there is an increase in demand for skis and snow blowers, and the Christmas season generally results in higher retail sales. On the other hand, a daily or weekly seasonal rhythm may manifest. Weekend demand for theaters and retail mall stores is typically higher than that of restaurants, for instance, which are busier at lunch than at dinner. The month of the year, the day of the week, the day of the month, and other holidays are examples of seasonalities at FedEx. The seasonal pattern seen in Fig. 9.3(c) repeats the same demand behavior at the same time every year.

Demand behavior commonly exhibits multiple of these traits at once. Over time, there has been an increasing trend in the construction of new homes, despite the fact that housing starts exhibit cyclical behavior. Ski demand is cyclical, although in recent years, demand for gear related to winter sports has increased. The combination of two demand patterns, a trend with a seasonal pattern, is seen in Fig. 9.2.

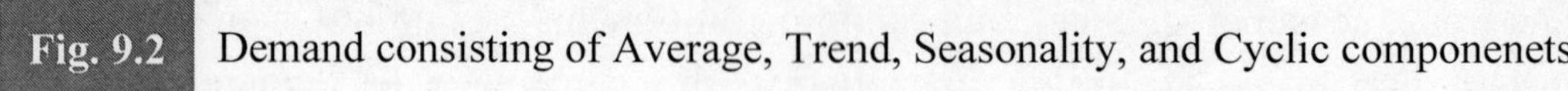
Fig. 9.2 Demand consisting of Average, Trend, Seasonality, and Cyclic componenets

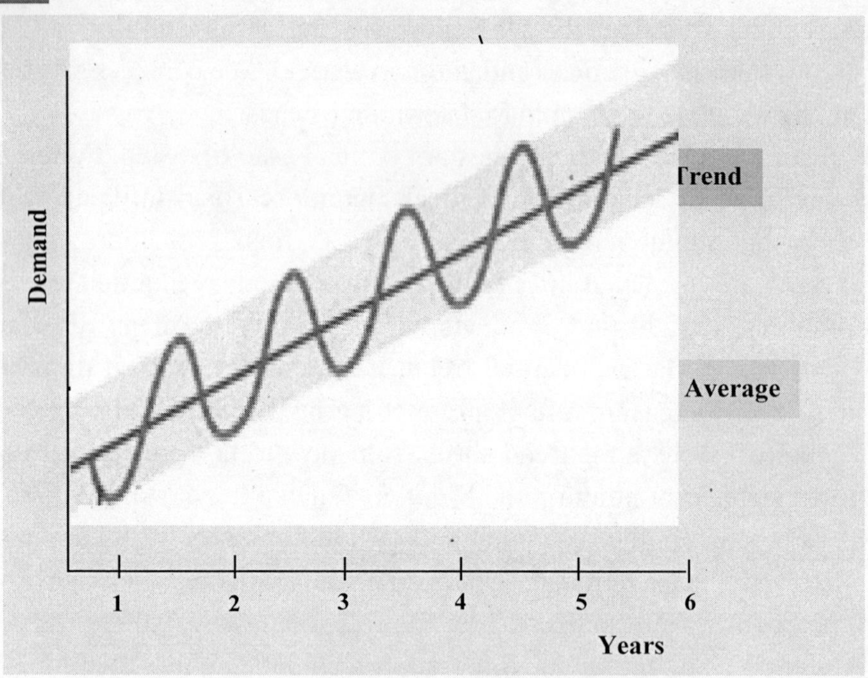

A *cycle* (i.e., greater than a year) is a demand pattern that varies up and down over an extended period of time. Cyclical factors, on the other hand, are more challenging to identify since the cause of cycle may not be taken into account or the time duration may be unclear. The construction of new buildings and the products that go along with it usually follow economic cycles. Events such as war, social pressure, or political elections can also have a cyclical effect on demand. Another example of cyclical demand is the demand for winter sports equipment, which peaks every four years before and after the winter Olympics. Fig. 9.2 depicts a demand cycle's dynamics.

Occasionally, it appears that none of the standard curves fits our data. This could be the result of multiple factors simultaneously impacting the data in different ways. Plotting data for these situations can yield a straightforward but frequently accurate forecast.

Fig. 9.3 Types of Trends of Demand: (a) Linear, (b) Exponential, (c) S-curve, (d) Asymptotic

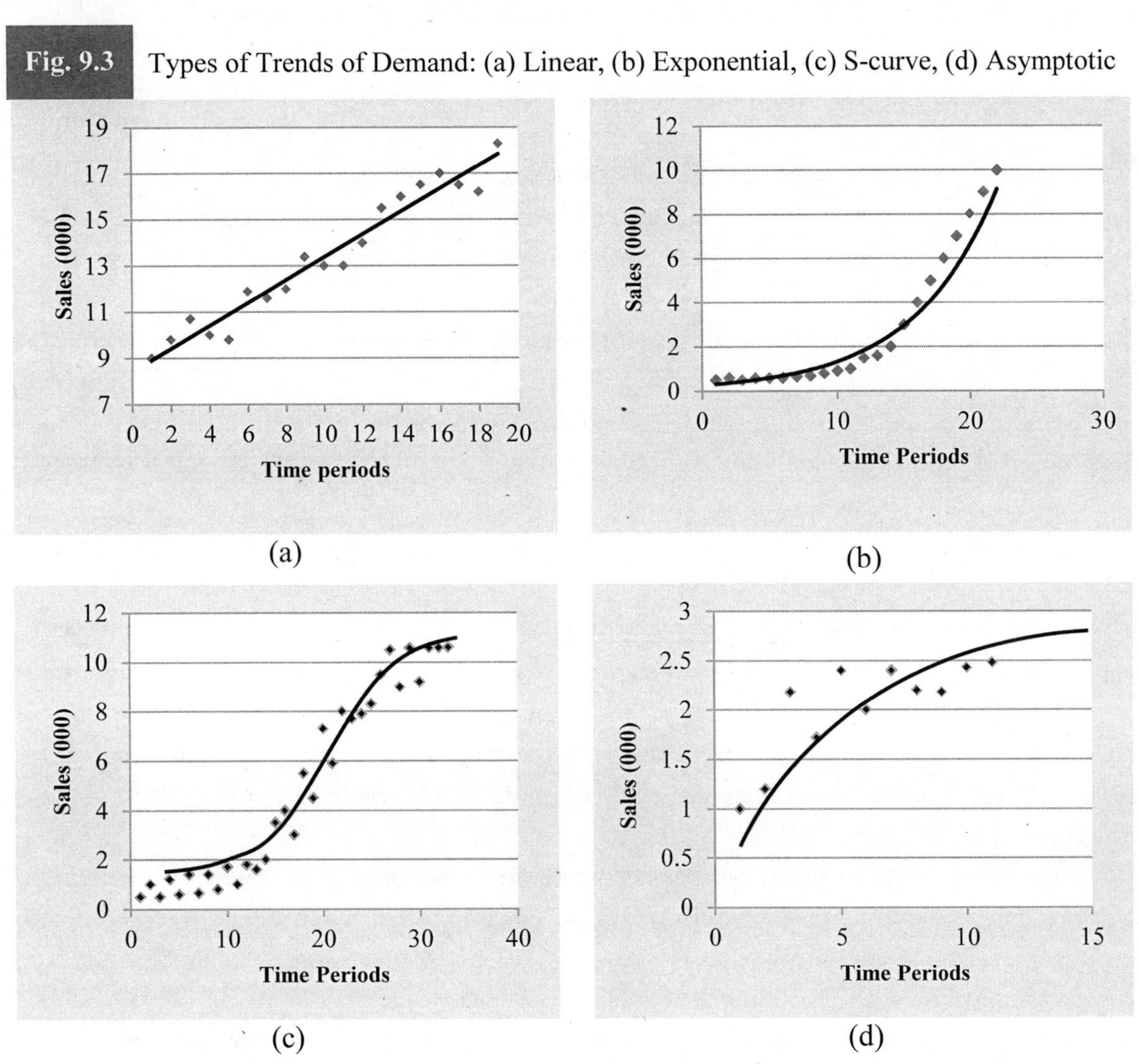

9.6.1 THE TIME SERIES APPROACH

Time series approaches are statistical methods based on historical data that has been collected over a period of time. The time series approach makes the assumption that historical events will recur in the future. These methods tie the forecast to just one factor, time, as the name "time series" suggests. A time series is an ordered succession of time-series observations (hourly, daily, weekly, monthly, quarterly, and annual) that are collected at regular intervals over a given period of time. Measurements of the consumer price index, output, precipitation, productivity, shipping, earnings, profits, and accidents are some examples of the data. These approaches are frequently utilized, often producing pretty excellent results, although little attempt is made to identify variables that influence the series.

The moving average, exponential smoothing, and linear trend line are a few of the time series techniques that are most often used by industrial and service organizations for short-term forecasting. Utilizing demand from the current period to predict demand from the next can be a straightforward method of creating a time series forecast. This forecast is sometimes referred to be *naive* or *intuitive*. For instance, if demand is 100 units this week, then 100 units are predicted for the following week; if demand is 90 units instead, then 90 units are predicted for the following week, and so on. This kind of forecasting technique just considers demand in the present and ignores demand behavior in the past. It responds immediately to the regular, random fluctuations in demand.

9.6.1.1 MOVING AVERAGE

To create a forecast, the simple ***moving average*** (MA) approach takes into account a number of previous demand numbers. These tend to attenuate, or smooth out, a single-period forecast's random increase and decline. When projecting demand that is steady and does not exhibit any prominent demand behavior, such as a trend or seasonal pattern, the simple moving average can be quite helpful.

Depending on how much the forecaster wants to "smooth" the demand data, moving averages are calculated for predetermined periods of time, such as three or five months. Moving averages tend to be more sensitive (responsive) when there are fewer data points in the average. A moving average comprising very few data points ought to be employed if responsiveness is deemed significant. This will allow for rapid adaptation to changes in the data, such as a step shift, but it will also make the forecast somewhat responsive to random fluctuations. On the other hand, moving averages with a larger sample size will smooth out more but react less to "real" fluctuations. As a result, the decision-maker has to balance the expense of reacting to data changes more slowly compared to the expense of reacting to variations that could just be chance. Making this judgment can be aided by reviewing the forecast errors.

A moving average prediction has the benefit of being simple to calculate and comprehend. The fact that every value in the average is weighted equally could be a drawback. For example, every value in a 20-period moving average has a weight of 1/20. As a result, the weight of the oldest value is equal to that of the most recent. A moving average forecast may take a while to respond to a change in the series, particularly if the average contains a big number of data. The weight of more recent values is increased when the average has fewer values, but this comes at the cost of perhaps losing information from less recent values.

The formula for computing the simple moving average is:

$$MA_n = \frac{\sum_{i=1}^{n} D_i}{n} \quad \ldots (9.1)$$

where

n = number of periods in the moving avaerage

D_i = demand in period i

This approach can generally produce accurate short-term forecasts, but it shouldn't be used for too long.

Example 9.1

Products are sold to the market by Perfect Precision. The company's manager is concerned about having enough goods on hand to meet demand as soon as possible. For this reason, the management needs to be able to predict the quantity of orders that will be placed over the course of the upcoming month (i.e., to estimate the need for delivers). The management has gathered the following data for the last ten months from the accessible data from prior months, and it wishes to compute three- and five-month moving averages from the data below.

Weeks	Orders	Weeks	Orders
1	700	16	1,600
2	1,500	17	1,500
3	1,200	18	1,800
4	1,400	19	2,200
5	1,800	20	2,600
6	1,700	21	1,900

7	1,300	**22**	2,600
8	1,500	**23**	2,200
9	1,400	**24**	2,200
10	1,700	**25**	2,500
11	1,700	**26**	2,400
12	2,300	**27**	2,100
13	2,300	**28**	2,500
14	2,000	**29**	2,200
15	1,000	**30**	2,300

Solution

Let's say the end of week 29 has arrived. The next week in the series, in this case 30 is usually covered by the projection produced by either the three- or nine-week moving average. Equation (9.1) is used to calculate the moving average based on the demand for orders for the previous three weeks in the sequence.

$$MA_3 = \frac{\sum_{i=1}^{3} D_i}{3}$$

$$= \frac{2200 + 2500 + 2100}{3} = 2267 \text{ orders for week 30}$$

Using demand data from the previous 9 weeks, the 9-week moving average is calculated as follows.

$$MA_9 = \frac{2200 + 2500 + 2100 \ \ldots + 2200 + 2600 + 1900}{9} = 2289 \text{ orders for week 30}$$

A plot of the data in Fig. 9.4 shows the effects of using diferent numbers of periods in the moving avaerage. We see the growth trend to show almost a consistent demand thereafter. The 3-week moving average is more responsive to this change than the 9-week average, although overall, the 9-week average is smoother.

Fig. 9.4 Comparison of MA_3 and MA_9 with actual demand

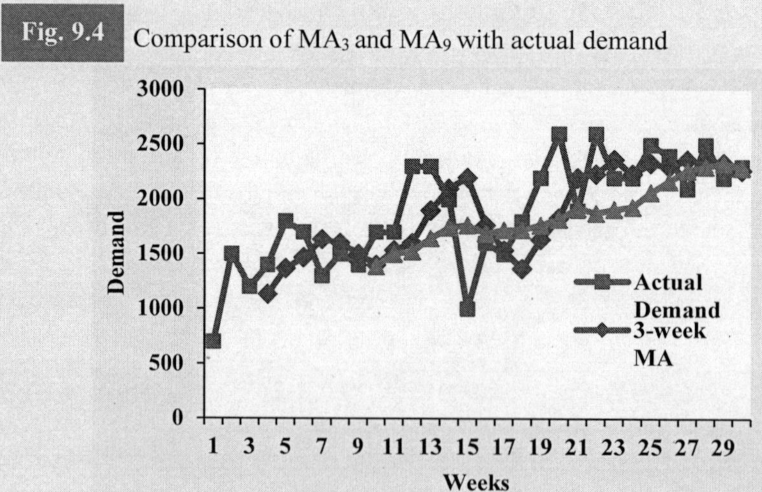

9.6.1.2 WEIGHTED MOVING AVERAGE

A ***weighted moving average*** (WMA) permits the assignment of any weights to any element of the moving average data, as long as the total of all weights is equal to one. This is in contrast to the basic moving average, which gives equal weight to each component of the moving average data according to following formula:

$$WMA_n = \sum_{i=1}^{n} W_i D_i \qquad \dots (9.2)$$

where

W_i = the weight for period i, between 0 and 100 percent

$\sum w_i = 1.00$

It normally takes some trial-and-error testing to figure out the exact weights to use for each data period and how many periods to include in the moving average. The prediction may overreact to an erratic change in demand if the most recent periods are given an excessive amount of weight. Should they be overly simplified, the projection may fail to account for real shifts in demand patterns. For example, it would be more accurate to predict the revenue or plant capacity for the upcoming month based on the previous month's data rather than the data from several months prior. But weights should be set appropriately, for instance, if the data are seasonal. In the Indian context, woolen sales in January of the previous year ought to be given greater weight than those in June.

Example 9.2

The medical shop's analyst has given the demand from the most recent week weights of 0.70, the demand from one week ago weights of 0.20, and the demand from two weeks ago weights of 0.10. Utilizing the information from Example 9.1 for the previous three weeks, compute the weighted moving average prediction for week 31.

Solution

The average demand in week 31 will be:

$$WMA_{31} = 0.70(2{,}300) + 0.20(2{,}200) + 0.10(2{,}500) = 1610 + 440 + 250 = 2{,}300$$

Suppose actual demand for week 31 turned out to be 2,350. Then, the forecast for the week 32 would be

$$WMA_{32} = 0.70(2{,}350) + 0.20(2{,}300) + 0.10(2{,}200) = 1610 + 440 + 250 = 2{,}325$$

9.6.1.3 EXPONENTIAL SMOOTHING

An additional averaging technique that gives the most recent data a higher weight is ***exponential smoothing***. As a result, the prediction will respond more strongly to recent variations in demand. This is helpful if there have been notable and unexpected changes in the data recently rather than merely sporadic swings (for which a basic moving average forecast would suffice).

For a number of reasons, exponential smoothing is one of the more often used and well-liked forecasting methods. Exponential smoothing needs very little information. All that is required are the current period's forecast, current period's actual demand, and a weighting factor known as a ***smoothing constant***. The amount of smoothing and the rate at which variations between anticipated and actual events occur are determined by this smoothing constant. The manager's perception of what makes for a good response rate, as well as the nature of the product, both influence the constant's value. The reaction rate to variations in actual and predicted demand, for instance, would typically be modest, maybe within 5 or 10 percentage points, if the company produced a common item with a reasonably consistent demand. To give greater weight to recent growth experience, a higher reaction rate – perhaps 15 to 30 percent points – would be ideal if the company were expanding. Higher reaction rates are appropriate for faster growing populations. Simple moving average users occasionally choose to employ exponential smoothing instead, but they still prefer to maintain a forecast that closely resembles the simple moving average. The constant in this instance, commonly represented as α, can be roughly expressed as $2/(n+1)$, where n represents the total number of time periods in the related simple moving average.

The technique's mathematics is simple enough for management to comprehend. Exponential smoothing modules are included in almost all computer software packages for forecasting and since historical data is used sparingly, computer storage requirements are minimal. Above all, exponential smoothing has demonstrated efficacy in the past. Many businesses have used it over the years because they believe it to be a reliable forecasting technique.

The following formula is used to calculate the exponential smoothing forecast:

$$F_{t+1} = \alpha D_t + (1 - \alpha) F_t \qquad \dots (9.3)$$

where

F_{t+1} = the forecast for the upcoming period

D_t = current demand as it actually exists

F_t = the forecast that had previously been determined for the current period

α = a weighting factor known as the smoothing constant

Rearranging Eq. 9.3 results in

$$F_{t+1} = \alpha D_t + F_t - \alpha F_t = F_t + \alpha(D_t - F_t) \quad \text{... (9.4)}$$

where

$(D_t - F_t)$ represent the forecast error and α is a percentage of error.

The range of the smoothing constant, α, is 0.0 to 1.0. The weight assigned to the latest demand data is reflected in it. As an instance, if α = 0.20,

$$F_{t+1} = 0.20D_t + (0.80)F_t$$

It indicates that, as forecast F_t is generated from past demands and forecast, our projection for the upcoming period is based on 20% of recent demand (D_t) and 80% of historical demand.

If we work on extremeties, i.e., let α = 0.0, then

$$F_{t+1} = F_t$$

that is, this period's forecast and the one for the following period are identical. Or, to put it another way, the prediction completely ignores the most current demand. Conversely, in case α = 1.0, then,

$$F_{t+1} = D_t$$

that is, only demand in the current period is taken into account. Thus, a larger α value indicates less smoothing and a more sensitive projection to recent changes in demand. Greater damping, or smoothing, effect occurs when α approaches zero. In response to variations in the actual and predicted demand, the forecast will react and change more slowly as α gets closer to zero. Within the range of 0.01 to 0.5, α are most frequently utilized values. But α is normally determined through subjective trial-and-error testing, which makes it judgmental. The predictive power of this method may be restricted by an imprecise approximation of α. The prediction matches the naive outcome as α gets closer to 1.0.

Example 9.3

AccuProd Company performs local service calls in addition to computer repairs at its center. They purchase used computers and give them a refurbished. For this reason, they require an accurate estimate of the demand for repairs in order to decide how many specialists to hire as well as what kind of computer components to buy and stock.

After gathering demand data for repair over the last 12 months, as indicated in the accompanying table, the company wishes to evaluate exponential smoothing projections with smoothing constants (α) set at 0.30 and 0.70.

Weeks	Demand	Weeks	Demand
1	37	**7**	43
2	40	**8**	47
3	41	**9**	56
4	37	**10**	52
5	45	**11**	55
6	50	**12**	54

Solution

We will begin with week 1 and use α = 0.3 to generate the forecast for week 2 in order to create the series of forecasts for the data in this table. We don't have the value of the previous period's forecast to estimate the value of the forecast for week 2, which is another need of the exponential smoothing formula. As a result, we shall utilize the forecast value for week 1 which is equal to the demand value (i.e., 37). As an alternative, we can make a subjective estimate or take the average of the first three or four periods to get the starting forecast. Consequently, week two's forecasting is

$$F_2 = 0.30D_1 + (0.70)F_1$$

$$F_2 = 0.30(37) + (0.70)(37) = 37 \text{ repair estimates}$$

The forecast for week 3 is computed similarly:

$$F_3 = 0.30D_2 + (0.70)F_2$$

$$= 0.30(40) + (0.70)(37) \approx 38 \text{ repairs}$$

The remainder of the weekly forecasts are calculated in similar way for α = 0.3 and α = 0.7. The exponential smoothing curves for α = 0.3 and 0.7 can be seen in comparison to actual demand in Fig. 9.5.

Fig. 9.5 Comparison of forecasted demand with α = 0.3 and 0.7 with actual demand.

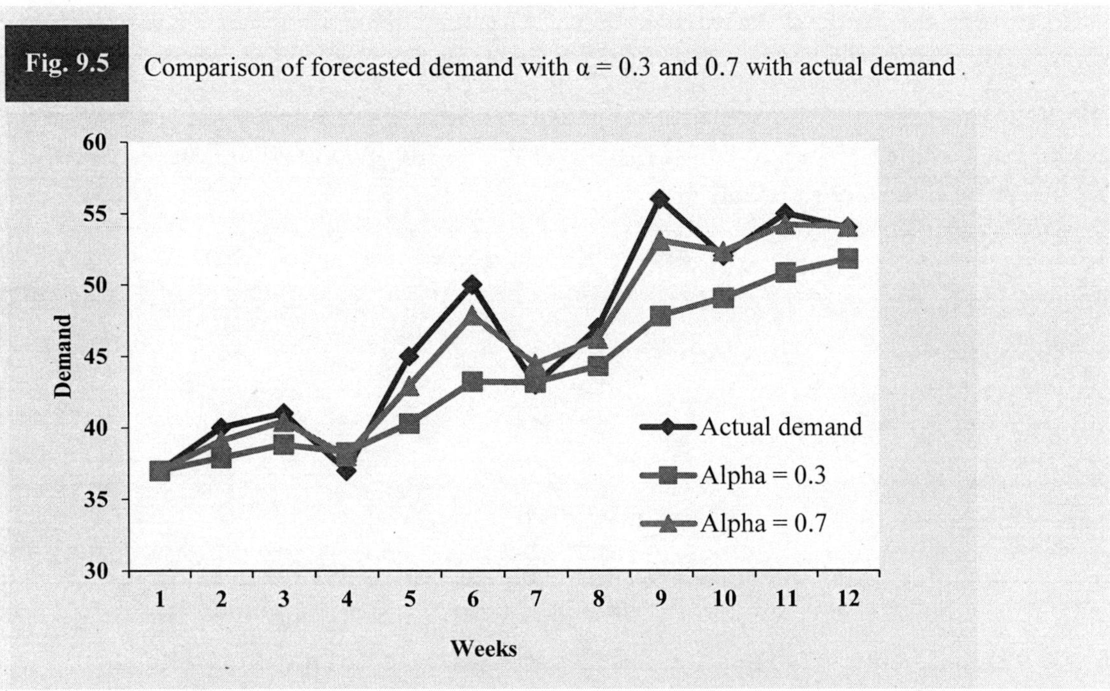

In Example 9.3, the prediction with α = 0.7, the larger smoothing constant, appears to respond more strongly to changes in demand than the forecast with α = 0.3, even though both forecasts smooth out the forecast's random variations. Take note of how both projections are behind the real demand. Just by looking at the two forecasts, it appears that α = 0.7 is the more accurate one because it closely resembles the real data. A modest number for α is more appropriate to smooth out the forecast when the actual demand is basically consistent throughout without any trend.

Certain methods of exponential smoothing monitor the forecast's accuracy by calculating the difference between the actual and forecast values. In an effort to adjust the forecast to the actual data, α is adjusted (higher or lower) if these differences get bigger. Nonetheless, trend effects can also be taken into account when adjusting the exponential smoothing forecast.

9.6.1.4 METHODS FOR ANALYZING TRENDS

The process of trend analysis entails creating an equation that, if trend is present in the data, adequately describes the ***trend***. It is possible for the trend component to be nonlinear. The

presence and type of a trend can frequently be determined by straightforward data visualization. Since linear trends are somewhat common, these are the only ones discussed here. In situations where a pattern is evident, forecasts can be created using two key methods. A trend equation is used in one, and exponential smoothing is extended in the other.
The form of a linear trend equation is

$$F_t = a + bt \qquad \text{... (9.5)}$$

where
F_t = Forecast for period t
a = value of F_t at t = 0, which is the y intercept
b = Slope of the line
t = Specified number of time periods from t = 0

Take the trend equation F_t = 50 + 4t, for instance. Since the slope of the line is 4 and the value of F_t is 50 at t = 0; on average, this indicates that the value of F_t will increase by four units for each time period. The forecast, F_t, is 50 + 4(8) = 82 units if t = 8.
The coefficients of the line, a snd b, are based on the following two equations:

$$b = \frac{n\sum ty - \sum t \sum y}{n\sum t^2 - (\sum t)^2} \qquad \text{... (9.6)}$$

$$a = \frac{\sum y - b\sum t}{n} \; or \; \bar{y} - b\bar{t} \qquad \text{... (9.7)}$$

where
n = number of periods
y = value of the time series
The only difference between these two equations and those used to calculate a linear regression line is that t is substituted for x in the first equation.

9.6.1.5 ADJUSTING FOR TREND IN EXPONENTIAL SMOOTHING

In situations where a time series shows a linear trend, a variant of simple exponential smoothing may be applied. To distinguish it from plain exponential smoothing, which is only appropriate when data are very close to average or exhibit step or gradual changes, it is also known as trend-adjusted exponential smoothing, or occasionally double smoothing. When basic smoothing is applied to a trending series, the resulting forecasts will lag behind the trend: Every projection will be too high if the data are falling, and too low if they are increasing.

Two components make up the trend adjusted forecast (TAF): a trend factor and a smoothed error.

$$TAF_{t+1} = S_t + T_t \quad \text{... (9.8)}$$

where

S_t = Previous forecast plus smoothed error

T_t = Current trend estimate

and

$$S_t = TAF_t + \alpha(D_t - TAF_t) \quad \text{... (9.9)}$$

$$T_t = T_{t-1} + \beta(TAF_t - TAF_{t-1} - T_{t-1}) \quad \text{... (9.10)}$$

where

α = Smoothing constant for average

β = Smoothing constant for trend

To employ this technique, one must first create an initial forecast and an estimate of the trend, as well as choose values for α and β (sometimes by trial and error).

Example 9.4

Precision Products Company wishes to create an adjusted exponentially smoothed projection, using the demand for 10 week period displayed in the table below. The forecast will be exponentially smoothed with $\alpha = 0.50$ and a trend smoothing constant of $\beta = 0.30$.

Solution

Weeks (t)	Actual demand (D_t)		
1	725	Trend estimate $= \frac{760 - 725}{3} = 11.66$	
2	730		
3	720	Starting forecast = 760 + 11.66 = 771.66	
4	760		
		Using Eq. (9.9)	Using Eq. (9.10) for T_t
5	775	771.66 + 0.5(775 – 771.66) = 773.33	11.66 + 0.3(0) = 11.66

6	760	784.99 + 0.5(760 – 784.99) = 772.49	11.66 + 0.3(784.99 – 771.66 – 11.66) = 12.16
7	780	784.65 + 0.5(780 – 784.65) = 782.33	12.16 + 0.3(784.65 – 784.99 – 12.16) = 8.41
8	750	790.74 + 0.5(750 – 790.74) = 770.37	8.41 + 0.3(790.74 – 784.65 – 8.41) = 7.49
9	805	777.86 + 0.5(805 – 777.86) = 791.43	7.49 + 0.3(777.86 – 790.74 – 7.49) = 1.38
10	825	792.81 + 0.5(825 – 792.81) = 809.00	1.38 + 0.3(792.81 – 777.86 – 1.38) = 5.45
11		809 + 5.45 = 814.45	

Fig. 9.6 Comparison of trend adjusted exponential smoothing with actual demand

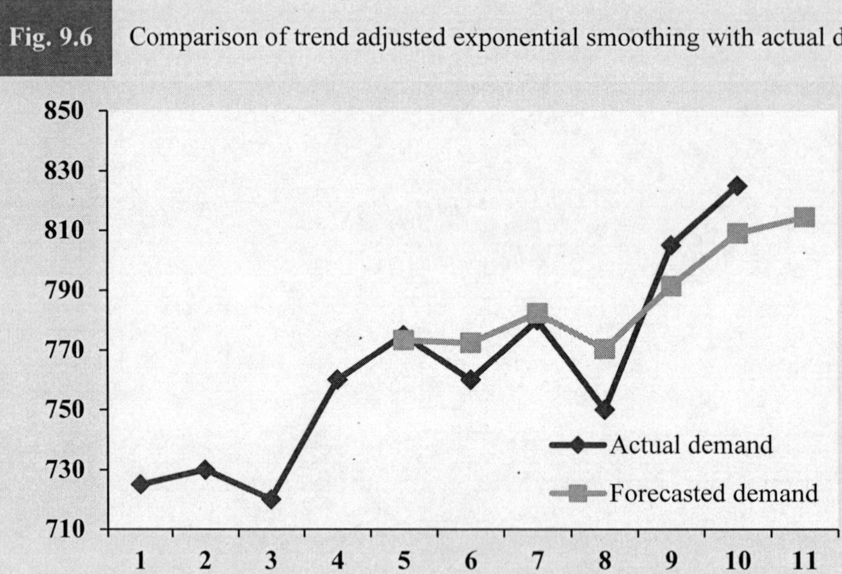

9.6.1.6 SEASONALITY TECHNIQUES

Recurring upward or downward movements in series values that are connected to periodic occurrences are known as ***seasonal*** fluctuations in time series data. Regular yearly fluctuations are one example of seasonality. Greeting card sales, airline travel, vacations, and visits to tourist and resort areas are also common instances of seasonality, as are weather fluctuations (e.g., purchases of winter and summer clothes). Seasonal variation also refers to trends in data that occur on a daily, weekly, monthly, and other regular basis. For instance, there are two instances of rush hour traffic each day: one in the morning and one in the late afternoon. Weekly demand patterns are common for restaurants and theaters, with demand peaking later in the week.

The degree of deviation between actual values and the series average is how seasonality in a time series is expressed. In case the series exhibits a tendency to fluctuate around a mean value, seasonality is represented using that mean (or a moving average); if a trend is discernible, seasonality is articulated using the trend value.

There are two different models used to illustrate seasonality: multiplicative and additive models. Seasonality is taken into account by means of the additive model, which expresses it as a number (such as 30 units) that is either added to or subtracted from the series average. The amplitude of the upward and downward movement in series for each periodic occurrence along the trend line stays constant in the additive model. In other words, additive seasonal variation only makes the assumption that the seasonal quantity is constant, independent of the trend or means value.

Forecast including trend and seasonal = Trend + Seasonal

Seasonality is taken into account in the multiplicative technique by expressing it as a percentage of the average (or trend) amount and multiplying it by the series value. The trend line's upward and downward movements have greater amplitudes in a multiplicative model. In other words, in a multiplicative seasonal variation, the seasonal components multiply the trend.

Forecast including trend and seasonal = Trend × Seasonal factor

We will only be focusing on the multiplicative model because businesses actually utilize it significantly more frequently than the additive one. In the multiplicative model, the seasonal percentages are called seasonal relatives or seasonal indexes. Assume that a store's June bicycle sales volume has a seasonal relative of 1.30. This shows that the month's bicycle sales were 30 percent higher than the average for the month. Sales in July are 80 percent of the monthly average, according to a seasonal relative of 0.80 for the month. Understanding the degree of seasonality in a time series can help one eliminate seasonality from the data (seasonally adjust data) so that other patterns or the absence of patterns in the series can be identified. This is also called ***decomposition*** of a time series in which the components of demand: trend, seasonal, cyclical, autocorrelation, and random are separated out.

Example 9.5

The Perfect Products Company made 1,000 product sales in the previous year. The average quarterly sales of the products are 200 units during the first quarter, 350 units during the second, 300 units during the third, and 150 units during the fourth. *The quantity sold during each quarter divided by the average for all quarters is the seasonal factor, often known as an index.*

Calculate the quarterly demand using multiplicative season factors if the company anticipates 1,200 units of demand throughout the next year.

Solution

The average sales of product across the year is 1000/4 = 250. The seasonal factor or indexes are:

	Past Sales	Average Sales for each Quarter	Seasonal factor
Quarter I	200	250	200/250 = 0.8
Quarter II	350	250	350/250 = 1.4
Quarter III	300	250	300/250 = 1.2
Quarter IV	150	250	150/250 = 0.6
Total	1,000		

With these variables, we may predict demand to happen as follows if we assume 1,200 units of demand the following year:

	Next year expected demand	Average Sales for each Quarter	Next year seasonal forecast
Quarter I		300	300 × 0.8 = 240
Quarter II		300	300 × 1.4 = 420
Quarter III		300	300 × 1.2 = 360
Quarter IV		300	300 × 0.6 = 180
Total	1,200		

Periodically, as new data becomes available, the seasonal factors might be modified.

The determination and application of seasonal indexes to forecast (i) a straightforward computation based on historical seasonal data and (ii) the trend and seasonal index from regression line are demonstrated in the following examples. The data decomposition and least squares regression forecasting process will then be carried out utilizing a more structured approach.

Example 9.6 Computing Trend and Seasonal factor from a linear regression line

Forecast the demand for each quarter of the next year using trend and seasonal factors. Demand for the past two years is in the following table:

Quarter	Amount	Quarter	Amount
I	300	V	520
II	200	VI	420
III	220	VII	400
IV	530	VIII	700

Solution

First, we find the values of a and b by using regression Equations (8.6) and (8.7), we get

$$b = \frac{n\sum ty - \sum t \sum y}{n\sum t^2 - (\sum t)^2}$$

$$= \frac{8(17{,}000) - 36(3{,}290)}{8(204) - 1296} = 52.3$$

$$a = \frac{\sum y - b\sum t}{n}$$

$$= \frac{3290 - 52.3(36)}{8} = 176.1$$

Therefore, the trend adjusted forecast equation is $TAF_t = 176.1 + 52.3t$

Quarter	Actual demand	$TAF_t = 176.1 + 52.3t$	Ratio of Actual / Trend	Seasonal factor (Average of same quarters of both years)
2022				
I	300	228.4	1.31	
II	200	280.7	0.71	
III	220	333.0	0.66	1.25
IV	530	385.3	1.38	0.78
2023				0.70
V	520	437.6	1.19	1.28
VI	420	489.9	0.86	
VII	400	542.2	0.74	
VIII	700	594.5	1.18	

Then, by comparing the real data with the trend line, we may calculate a seasonal indicator. By averaging the same quarter every year, the seasonal component was created. Including trend and seasonal factor (TAFs), we can calculate the forecast for the upcoming year as follows:

$$TAF_t = TAF \times \text{Seasonal factor}$$

$$TAF_9 = [176.1 + 52.3(9)] * 1.25 = 809.1$$

$$TAF_{10} = [176.1 + 52.3(10)] * 0.78 = 548.7$$

$$TAF_{11} = [176.1 + 52.3(11)] * 0.70 = 525.4$$

$$TAF_{12} = [176.1 + 52.3(12)] * 1.28 = 1025.9$$

Please take note that as these calculations were performed in Excel, there may be some variation as a result of rounding off the numbers.

9.6.2 FORECASTING ACCURACY AND CONTROL

One of the most important parts of forecasting is accuracy and control. It's crucial to keep an eye on forecast errors while creating regular projections in order to assess if they fall within acceptable ranges. Corrective action will be required if they aren't. The discrepancy between the value that really occurs and the value that was anticipated for a specific time period is known as the forecast error. Therefore, error is equal to actual demand minus forecasted demand.

$$e_t = D_t - F_t \qquad \text{... (9.11)}$$

Positive error results when the forecast is too low, negative errors when the forecast is too high. For example, if actual demand for a week is 150 units and forecast demand was 140 units, the forecast was too low; the error is 150 – 140 = +10.

Accuracy of forecast – When choosing between forecasting options, forecast accuracy is a crucial consideration. The past error performance of a forecast serves as the foundation for accuracy. The **mean squared error (MSE)** and the **mean absolute deviation (MAD)** are two metrics that are frequently used to quantify historical errors. The average of squared errors is called MSE, and the average absolute error is known as MAD. The formula to compute MAD and MSE are:

$$MAD = \frac{\sum_{t=1}^{n} |D_t - F_t|}{n} \qquad \text{... (9.12)}$$

where

t = period number
D_t = Actual demand for the period t
F_t = Forecast demand for the period t
n = Total number of periods
$|D_t - F_t|$ = Absolute value of error (i.e., disregarding positive and negative signs)

The MAD is correlated with the standard deviation of the error terms when the forecast errors are normally distributed, which is the typical situation.

$$1 \text{ standard deviation} \approx \sqrt{\frac{\pi}{2}} \times \text{MAD, or } 1.25 \text{ MAD}$$

1MAD, on the other hand, is roughly 0.8 times standard deviation. With ±3 standard deviations (or ±3.75 MADs) as the control limits within the normal distribution, 99.7% of the data points would fall into these ranges.

The **mean absolute percent error (MAPE)** is an additional error measure that is frequently helpful. This metric calculates the inaccuracy as a percentage of the demand. For instance, the value of MAPE would be 10% (=5/50) if the error was 5 units and the actual demand was 50 units. MAPE is computed as follows.

$$MAPE = \frac{100}{n}\sum_{t=1}^{n}\left[\frac{|D_t - F_t|}{D_t}\right] \qquad \ldots (9.13)$$

When estimates for various product demands show disparities in average demand values, the true usefulness of MAPE becomes apparent. Even with a better estimate, if you use the MAD, the product with the higher demand would have the higher MAD.

A **tracking signal** (TS) is a measurement that shows if any real changes in demand, either upward or downward, are being kept up with by the predicted availability. A forecast is considered skewed when it is regularly high or low. A normal distribution with a mean of 0 and a MAD of 1 is depicted in Fig. 9.7. Therefore, we may conclude that the prediction model is producing forecasts that are far above the mean of the actual occurrences if we compute the tracking signal and find it to be equal to minus 3.

The arithmetic total of forecasted deviations divided by the mean absolute deviation can be used to get the tracking signal (TS):

$$\text{TS} = \frac{\text{RSFE}}{\text{MAD}} \qquad \ldots (9.14)$$

where

RSFE = The forecast error running total, taking into account the type of error (negative errors cancel out positive errors and vice versa).

MAD = The mean of all forecast errors, regardless of the direction of the deviations. It is the average of the absolute deviations.

Fig. 9.7 Mean = 0 and MAD = 1 in a normal distribution

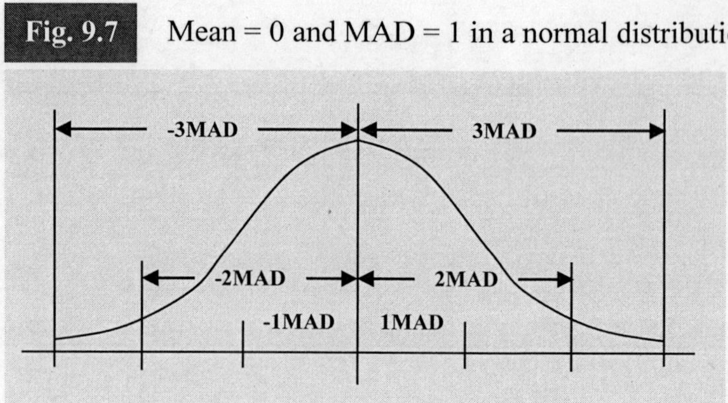

After an intitial value of MAD has been computed, MAD can be updated using exponential smoothing:

$$MAD_t = MAD_{t-1} + \alpha(|Actual - Forecast|_t - MAD_{t-1}) \quad \text{... (9.15)}$$

Instead of using cumulative errors, as is the case with a tracking signal, the control chart approach sets upper and lower bounds for individual forecast errors. The limits are MSE square root multiples.

$$s = \sqrt{MSE} \quad \text{... (9.16)}$$

In practical application, the standard deviation of the error distribution is estimated using the square root of the mean square error (MSE). This approach makes the assumptions that there is a normal distribution of errors and forecast errors are randomly distributed around a mean of zero. Remember the standard deviation limits, where 99.7% of data should lie within $\pm 3s$ of zero. Consequently, the following formula is used to get the upper control limit (UCL) and lower control limit (LCL):

$$UCL = 0 + z\sqrt{MSE}$$

$$LCL = 0 - z\sqrt{MSE}$$

where

z = Number of standard deviations from the mean.

Example 9.7

The following table displays the monthly demand for products during the last 24 months, along with projections and mistakes for those months. Check whether the forecast is accurate by use these methods:

1. A tracking signal that updates the MAD using exponential smoothing starting in month 10. Make use of ±3 and $\alpha = 0.3$ limitations.
2. A 3*s* limit control chart. Create the control chart using the data from the first eight months, and use the control chart to assess the remaining data.

Month	Demand (*D*)	Forecast (*F*)	Error '*e*' (*D-F*)	|*e*|	Cumulative |*e*|
1	48	43	5	5	5
2	52	44	8	8	13
3	53	50	3	3	16
4	55	48	7	7	23
5	49	54	-5	5	28
6	48	51	-3	3	31
7	38	35	3	3	34
8	33	44	-11	11	45
9	24	46	-22	22	67
10	25	32	-7	7	74
11	30	25	5	5	
12	35	26	9	9	
13	44	51	-7	7	
14	57	50	7	7	
15	60	34	26	26	
16	55	51	4	4	
17	51	55	-4	4	
18	48	54	-6	6	
19	42	38	4	4	
20	31	43	-12	12	
21	25	50	-25	25	
22	28	27	1	1	
23	38	27	11	11	
24	35	32	3	3	

Solution

1. The cumulative absolute error as of the tenth month is 74. As a result, 74/10 = 7.4 is the first MAD. Equation (9.15) is utilized to update the ensuing MADs. The following table displays the findings.

The tracking signal for any month is:

$$\frac{\text{Cumulative error at that month}}{\text{Updated MAD at that month}}$$

t (Month)	|*e*|	Updated MAD using Eq. (9.15)	Cumulative Error	TS = Cumulative error / MAD_t
10			– 22	– 22/7.4 = – 2.97
11	5	= 7.4 + 0.3(5 – 7.4) = 6.68	– 17	– 17/6.68 = – 2.54

12	9	= 6.68 + 0.3(9 – 6.68) = 7.38	– 8	–8/7.38 = – 1.08
13	7	= 7.38 + 0.3(7 – 7.38) = 7.26	– 15	– 15/7.26 = – 2.07
14	7	= 7.26 + 0.3(7 – 7.26) = 7.18	– 8	– 8/7.18 = – 1.11
15	26	= 7.18 + 0.3(26 – 7.18) = 12.82	18	18/12.82 = 1.40
16	4	= 12.82 + 0.3(4 – 12.82) = 10.17	22	22/10.17 = 2.16
17	4	= 10.17 + 0.3(4 – 10.17) = 8.32	18	18/8.32 = 2.16
18	6	= 8.32 + 0.3(6 – 8.32) = 7.62	12	12/7.62 = 1.57
19	4	= 7.62 + 0.3(4 – 7.62) = 6.53	16	16/6.53 = 2.45
20	12	= 6.53 + 0.3(12 – 6.53) = 8.17	4	4/8.17 = 0.49
21	25	= 8.17 + 0.3(25 – 8.17) = 13.22	– 21	– 21/13.22 = – 1.59
22	1	= 13.22 + 0.3(1 – 13.22) = 9.55	– 20	– 20/9.55 = – 2.09
23	11	= 9.55 + 0.3(11 – 9.55) = 9.98	– 9	– 9/9.98 = – 0.90
24	3	= 9.98 + 0.3(3 – 9.98) = 7.88	– 6	– 6/7.88 = – 0.76

There is no indicator of an issue because the tracking signal is within ±3 every month.

2. (a) A large average would indicate a biased forecast, therefore make sure the average error is close to zero.

$$\text{Average error} = \frac{\sum \text{errors}}{n} = \frac{-6}{24} = -0.25$$

(b) Calculate the standard deviation for the first nine values as per the question.

$$s = \sqrt{MSE} = \sqrt{\frac{\sum e^2}{n-1}}$$

$$= \sqrt{\frac{5^2 + 8^2 + 3^2 + 7^2 + -5^2 + -3^2 + 3^2 + -11^2}{8-1}} = 6.67$$

(c) Determine 3*s* control limits:

$$0 \pm 3s = 0 \pm 3(6.67) = \pm 20.01$$

(d) Verify whether or not every error is within the allowed range. We see in Fig. 9.8 that certain errors (encircled points in graph) are exceeding both positive and negative control limits, necessitating corrective measures in the forecasting process. Even if the entire forecast errors are within acceptable limits, this will lead to reduced fluctuation in the errors. We discover that this non-randomness was not disclosed by the tracking signal.

Comment: In general, the tracking signal strategy is inferior to the control chart approach. The tracking signal approach's usage of cumulative errors is one of its main weaknesses: individual errors can be hidden so that significant positive and negative values cancel each other out. On the other hand, every error is evaluated separately when using control charts. Therefore, depending solely on a tracking signal method to keep an eye on errors may be deceptive. The tracking signal approach actually has historical roots that go back before computers were used for business purposes.

The idea of a tracking signal was created since, at the time, calculating standard deviations was far more complex than calculating average deviations. Standard deviations can now be easily obtained using computers. However, tracking signal use has continued, most likely due to consumers' ignorance about the superiority of the control chart approach.

Fig. 9.8 Plot of errors in ± 3s

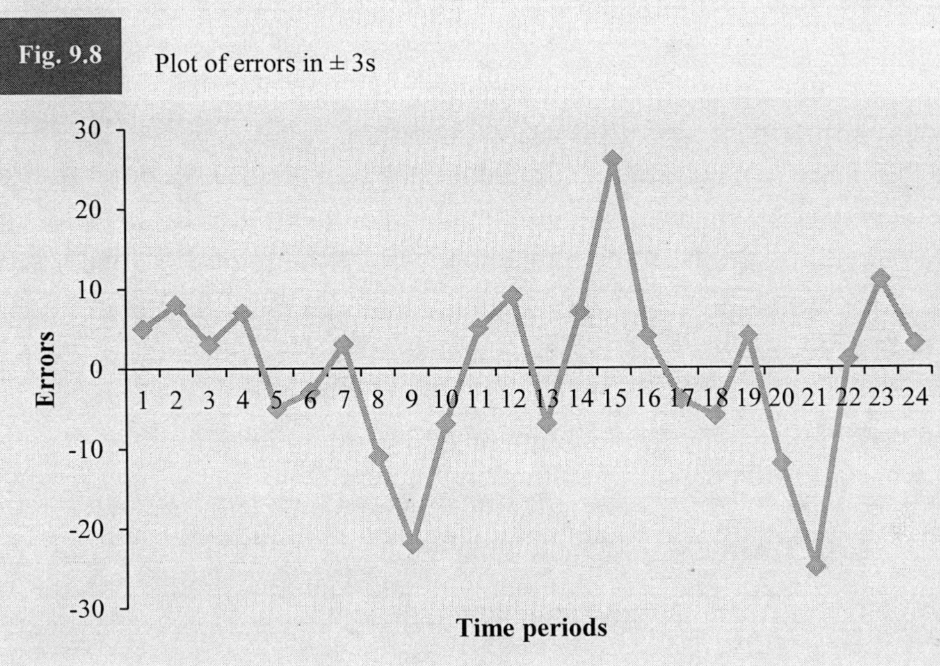

ALONG THE FORECASTING APPROACHES

Web-Based Forecasting

A web-based technology called **Collaborative Planning, Forecasting, and Replenishment** (CPFR) is used by supply chain trading partners for collaborating on demand forecasts, production and purchase planning, and inventory replenishment. The model was developed by Benchmarking Partners, a software and strategy consultancy, Wal-Mart, and Cambridge University. It was then submitted to the Voluntary Inter Industry Commerce Standards Committee (VICS) to become the global standard. You can view a more thorough analysis of CPFR by scanning the provided QR code.

SCAN ME for CPFR

A remarkable overview of Amazon's journey from a forecasting perspective, this QR code can be scanned to read about the company's successful application of cutting-edge forecasting techniques throughout the years.

SCAN ME for Amazon's Forecasting history

UNIT SUMMARY

- ***Domains of Forecasting*** – Discusses its role in SCM, quality management, and decision-making.
- ***Attributes & Components of Effective Forecasts*** – Covers essential elements such as historical data analysis, trend identification, and seasonal patterns.
- ***Forecasting Methods***: (i) Qualitative Techniques – Delphi method, market research, expert panel consensus, visionary models, and sales force inputs, (ii) Quantitative Techniques – Moving averages, exponential smoothing, trend projection, and seasonality adjustments.
- ***Forecast Accuracy & Control*** – Introduces Mean Absolute Deviation (MAD), Mean Squared Error (MSE), and Tracking Signals to evaluate forecasting reliability.
- ***Practical Applications*** – Explores case studies on demand planning, business strategy, and inventory management, including Amazon's use of advanced forecasting methods.

EXERCISES

MULTIPLE CHOICE QUESTIONS

9.1 What is the primary goal of forecasting in supply chain management?

(a) To accurately predict future demand	(b) To minimize costs in the supply chain
(c) To maximize profits for the company	(d) To optimize inventory levels

9.2 How does forecasting play a role in quality management within the supply chain?

(a) By ensuring timely delivery of products	(b) By reducing defects and improving product quality
(c) By increasing production speed	(d) By minimizing transportation costs

9.3 What is a common feature of all forecasting methods when used to make predictions?

(a) Use of a single variable	(b) Dependence on past data or trends
(c) Ignoring external influences	(d) Exclusion of statistical analysis

9.4 Which of the following is a critical criterion for a forecast to be considered useful?

(a) It should be highly complex and difficult to understand	(b) It should be consistent with historical data and trends
(c) It should require minimal data inputs	(d) It should rely solely on subjective opinions

9.5 Which of the following is typically the first step in the forecasting process?

(a) Analyzing historical data	(b) Selecting the forecasting method
(c) Defining the forecasting objectives and scope	(d) Implementing the forecast

9.6 What is the primary purpose of the Delphi Method in forecasting?

(a) To utilize historical data for predictions	(b) To gather expert opinions and reach a consensus on future events
(c) To create statistical models based on past data	(d) To implement real-time forecasting techniques

9.7 In marketing research, which method involves observing customer behavior and collecting data without direct interaction?

(a) Focus groups	(b) Surveys
(c) Ethnographic studies	(d) Experiments

9.8 In IT-managed forecasting, which type of system helps automate the process of generating forecasts based on historical data and predictive models?

(a) Enterprise Resource Planning (ERP)	(b) Customer Relationship Management (CRM)
(c) Predictive Analytics System	(d) Document Management System

9.9 Which technology is often used to visualize forecast data and trends, helping stakeholders understand predictions and make informed decisions?

(a) Geographic Information System (GIS)	(b) Data Visualization Tools
(c) Content Management System (CMS)	(d) Virtual Private Network (VPN)

9.10 Which type of forecasting is most likely to use a time horizon of less than one year?

(a) Strategic forecasting	(b) Tactical forecasting
(c) Operational forecasting	(d) Scenario planning

9.11 What does the "trend" component in demand forecasting typically represent?

(a) Periodic fluctuations due to seasonality	(b) Long-term movement or direction in the data over time
(c) Unpredictable variations in demand	(d) Economic cycles affecting demand

9.12 In demand forecasting, which component is characterized by regular and predictable fluctuations within a fixed period, such as daily, weekly, or monthly?

(a) Random	(b) Trend
(c) Seasonal	(d) Cyclical

9.13 Which component of demand forecasting is most likely to be influenced by factors such as economic recessions, technological advancements, or major market shifts?

(a) Seasonal	(b) Random
(c) Trend	(d) Cyclical

9.14 Which technique is generally preferred when the time series data shows a clear trend and needs to account for recent observations more heavily?

(a) Moving Average	(b) Exponential Smoothing
(c) Linear Trend Line	(d) Seasonal Decomposition

9.15 In Exponential Smoothing, what is the primary advantage of using the smoothing constant (α)?

(a) It allows the forecast to rely solely on historical averages	(b) It provides a weighted average where more recent observations have more influence
(c) It eliminates all randomness from the data	(d) It integrates seasonal effects into the forecast

9.16 Which forecasting technique is primarily used to identify and estimate long-term movements in a time series?

(a) Random Forecasting	(b) Trend Analysis
(c) Seasonal Adjustment	(d) Cyclic Forecasting

9.17 What is the primary purpose of decomposing a time series into its component parts?

(a) To eliminate the need for any further forecasting	(b) To understand and analyze the underlying patterns and structures in the data
(c) To generate new data for testing models	(d) To reduce the complexity of the data by averaging out variations

9.18 Which of the following statements is true about the Mean Squared Error (MSE) compared to the Mean Absolute Deviation (MAD)?

(a) MSE is less sensitive to large errors compared to MAD	(b) MSE penalizes larger errors more heavily than MAD
(c) MAD is more computationally intensive than MSE	(d) MSE provides a better measure of central tendency compared to MAD

9.19 If a tracking signal shows a consistently positive value over time, what might this indicate about the forecasting model?

(a) The model is consistently underestimating the actual values.	(b) The model is consistently overestimating the actual values.
(c) The model is correctly predicting the actual values with minimal error.	(d) The model is accurately capturing seasonal variations.

Answers of Multiple Choice Questions

9.1 (a), 9.2 (b), 9.3 (b), 9.4 (b), 9.5 (c), 9.6 (b), 9.7 (c), 9.8 (c), 9.9 (b), 9.10 (c), 9.11 (b), 9.12 (c), 9.13 (d), 9.14 (b), 9.15 (b), 9.16 (b), 9.17 (b), 9.18 (b), 9.19 (b)

SHORT AND LONG ANSWER TYPE QUESTIONS

Category I

9.1 How can forecasting help improve customer satisfaction in both supply chain management and quality management?

9.2 How does historical data influence the choice of forecasting methods?

9.3 How do you select a forecasting model, and what factors should be considered?

9.4 What is a key advantage of using qualitative forecasting methods?

9.5 What is IT-managed forecasting, and how does it integrate with overall business processes?

9.6 What is the primary focus of strategic forecasting, and how does it differ from tactical forecasting?

9.7 How does the trend component in time series forecasting help in predicting future values?

9.8 What is the role of the seasonal component in time series forecasting, and how is it typically accounted for?

9.9 How can time series forecasting models incorporate both trend and seasonal components?

9.10 How does Mean Absolute Error (MAE) differ from Mean Squared Error (MSE)?

9.11 Why is it important to monitor the tracking signal regularly?

Category II

9.12 Explain how different types of historical data – such as sales data, inventory levels, and production metrics – affect the selection of forecasting models. Provide examples of how historical data can guide the decision-making process in selecting an appropriate forecasting model and its impact on managing supply chain and quality issues.

9.13 Compare and contrast the different types of qualitative forecasting models, including the Delphi Method, Market Research, Sales Force Composite, and Expert Judgment. For each model, describe its methodology, advantages, and limitations. How does each model address uncertainty and what factors should be considered when choosing the appropriate qualitative forecasting model for a given scenario?

9.14 Explain how IT-managed forecasting systems support strategic, tactical, and operational forecasting within organizations. Discuss the role of technology in enhancing forecasting accuracy and efficiency at each level. Include examples of IT tools and techniques used in these forecasting processes and describe how they contribute to improved decision-making and organizational performance.

9.15 Explain the different components of time series data: random, trend, seasonal, and cyclical. For each component, describe its characteristics, the role it plays in time series forecasting, and the methods used to identify and model each component. Additionally, discuss how these components interact within a time series and can improve forecasting accuracy. Provide examples of practical applications where identifying and modeling these components are crucial for accurate predictions.

9.16 Discuss the following time series forecasting techniques in detail: Moving Average, Trend Analysis, Exponential Smoothing, and Seasonal Decomposition. For each technique, explain its underlying principles, methods of implementation, typical use cases, advantages, and limitations. Additionally, describe how each technique handles different aspects of time series data and how selecting the appropriate technique can impact forecasting accuracy. Provide examples to illustrate the application of each technique.

NUMERICAL PROBLEMS

9.1 The information below displays the value of manufactured wool clothing imports into the United States over a seven-year period, together with the exports of raw wool:

	Thousands of $						
Exports	42	44	58	55	89	98	60
Imports	56	49	53	58	67	76	58

Find the import-export regression equation and calculate the import when the export in a given year reaches a value of $70 thousands.

9.2 The following lists the amount of raw material that Precision Products Ltd. bought during the year 2023 at the prices mentioned:

Month	Price per Kg ($)	Quantity (Kg)	Month	Price per Kg ($)	Quantity (Kg)
January	96	250	July	112	220
February	110	200	August	112	220
March	100	250	September	108	200
April	90	280	October	116	210
May	86	300	November	86	300
June	92	300	December	92	250

(a) Find the regression equations based on the above data.

(b) Could you calculate the approximate amount that will probably be bought if the price increases to $124 per kilogram?

(c) Consequently, find the correlation coefficient between the amount demanded and the current price.

9.3 To calculate sales for 2025, apply the least squares approach. The following information is provided:

Year	2019	2020	2021	2022	2023
Sales of refrigeratos	100	110	130	125	160

9.4 Calculate the 3-year simple moving average for year 2025, using the time series data in the following table.

Year	Sales	Year	Sales
2006	2000	2016	2350
2007	1350	2017	2005
2008	1945	2018	1355
2009	1975	2019	1940
2010	3100	2020	1970
2011	1751	2021	3110
2012	1550	2022	1750
2013	1300	2023	1555
2014	2200	2024	1310
2015	2775		

9.5 For the data given in problem 9.4, calculate a 6-year weighted moving average for year 2025, using the weights: 0.1, 0.1, 0.1, 0.2, 0.2, and 0.3 from the oldest to the most recent years.

9.6 Using an α of 0.2, calculate the year 2025 forecast using the simple exponential smoothing model. Use the data of problem 9.4 and assume a 2024 forecast as 1800.

9.7 Using the method of least squares, find the regression equation for the time series data shown in problem 9.4. Use the regression equation to forecast sales for the year 2025.

9.8 After charting demand across four periods, AccuProducts Company determined that a trend-adjusted exponential smoothing model would be a suitable tool for demand forecasting. There are calculations displayed for the ensuing five periods. Based on the net change of 30 for the three periods spanning from 1 to 4, the initial estimate of trend is based on an average of +10 units. Employ $\alpha = 0.5$ and $\beta = 0.4$. Find the forecast value of 10th period.

Hint: Do similar to Example 9.4

	Period t	Actual A_t
Model development	1	210
	2	224
	3	229
	4	240
Model Test	5	255
	6	265
	7	272
	8	285
	9	294

9.9 A steel company faced the following demand for its products during past few months. Presently, the company is using last year's corresponding monthly sales as this year forecast.

Month	Forecasted Demand	Actual Demand
July	21100	20000
August	23600	22000
September	22400	21000
October	27500	26500

Calculate MAD, Bias, MSE, and Tracking signal and interpret them.

REFERENCES AND SUGGESTED READINGS

1. Armstrong, J. S., and Collopy, F. Error Measures for Generalizing About Forecasting Methods: Empirical Comparisons. *International Journal of Forecasting*, Vol. 8(1), 69-80, 1992.

2. Bovas, A. *Forecasting Methods for Business and Economics*. McGraw-Hill, 2010.

3. Bovas, A., and Goodwin, P. *Business Forecasting: A Practical Approach*. Wiley, 2004.

4. Bunn, D. W., and Salo, A. Forecasting in Supply Chain Management: The Role of Forecasting and Coordination in the Context of Business Strategy. *European Journal of Operational Research*, Vol. 143(1), 50-60, 2002.

5. Cai, F., and Dufresne, E. Improving Forecast Accuracy in Sales and Operations Planning. *International Journal of Production Economics*, Vol. 87(3), 347-356, 2004.

6. Fildes, R., and Bunn, D. W. The impact of forecast information in supply chain planning. *International Journal of Forecasting*, Vol. 10(4), 517-527, 1994.

7. Fildes, R., and Goodwin, P. *Principles of Business Forecasting. Thomson South-Western*, 2007.

8. Gärtner, R., and P. K. Ghosh A Review of Qualitative Forecasting Techniques. *Journal of Forecasting*, Vol. 32(3), 176-188, 2013.

9. Heizer, J., and Render, B. *Operations Management*, 12th Edition, Pearson, 2017.

10. Hyndman, R. J., and Athanasopoulos, G. Forecasting: principles and practice. *International Journal of Forecasting*, Vol. 34(2), 263-272, 2018.

11. Makridakis, S., Wheelwright, S. C., and Hyndman, R. J. *Forecasting: Methods and Applications*, 3rd Edition, Wiley, 1998.

12. Montgomery, D. C., and Johnson, L. A. *Forecasting and Time Series: An Applied Approach*, 2nd Edition, Wiley, 2009.

13. Sharma, S., and Raj, V. *Forecasting Methods and Applications: A Comprehensive Approach*, Springer, 2016.

14. Snyder, D. L., and Koehler, A. B. (2012). Forecasting: Principles and Practice. Online textbook (available for free at forecastingbook.com).

15. Stewart, T. R. *The Handbook of Forecasting: A Manager's Guide*. Wiley-Interscience, 2003.

UNIT **10**

FACILITY LAYOUT

UNIT SPECIFICS

This unit elaborately discusses the following topics:

- Facility layout objectives
- Fundamental facility layouts (Process layout, Product layout, Fixed position layout, Combination layout)
- Designing process layout (Minimization transportation cost or distance, Relationship rating)
- Designing product layout (Line balancing)
- Cellular layouts
- Flexible manufacturing systems

In order to foster increased creativity and curiosity as well as improve problem-solving abilities, the topics' practical applications are investigated. Along with several multiple-choice questions and questions with short and lengthy answer types categorized into two groups based on lower and higher order of Bloom's taxonomy, the unit also includes a list of references, recommended readings, and assignments through a number of numerical problems. You can practice by completing these. According to the content, the unit's linked topic has been followed by an extra section ("Along the..."). It was carefully crafted with the reader of the book in mind. One noteworthy feature is the use of QR codes, which can be scanned to provide relevant supporting information on a range of interesting topics.

RATIONALE

In this unit, we explore the critical objectives of facility layout, which aim to optimize workflow, enhance efficiency, and reduce costs. We examine the four fundamental types of layouts: process, product, fixed-position, and combination layouts, each serving distinct operational needs. The design of process layouts focuses on minimizing transportation costs and leveraging relationship ratings to enhance workflow. In contrast, product layouts emphasize line balancing to streamline production processes. Additionally, we delve into cellular layouts, which promote flexibility and responsiveness, as well as flexible manufacturing systems that adapt to varying production demands. Together, these elements underscore the importance of strategic facility layout in achieving operational excellence.

UNIT OUTCOMES

List of outcomes of this unit is as follows:

U10-UO1: Understand Facility Layout Objectives

U10-UO2: Identify Fundamental Layout Types

U10-UO3: Apply Process Layout Design Principles

U10-UO4: Implement Line Balancing in Product Layouts

U10-UO5: Evaluate Cellular Layouts

U10-UO6: Explore Flexible Manufacturing Systems

UNIT-10 Outcomes	EXPECTED MAPPING WITH COURSE OUTCOMES (1-Weak Correlation; 2-Medium Correlation; 3-Strong Correlation)					
	CO-1	CO-2	CO-3	CO-4	CO-5	CO-6
U10-UO1	3	2	2	3	2	2
U10-UO2	2	2	2	3	2	1
U10-UO3	3	2	2	3	2	2
U10-UO4	2	2	2	3	3	3
U10-UO5	2	2	2	3	2	2
U10-UO6	3	2	2	3	3	3

10.1 INTRODUCTION

Facilities have an impact. Through their ability to enable and utilize the newest process principles, they can offer a competitive edge. Quality and productivity are impacted by the design of a facility. Facilities have an impact on the productivity of employees, the volume and speed at which items may be produced, the difficulty of automating a system, and the system's ability to adapt to changes in the demand volume, product mix, or design of goods or services. Facilities need to be organized, located, and designed.

ALONG THE FACILITY LAYOUT

The first airport built entirely new following airline deregulation was Pittsburgh International Airport. It is made to work with the "hub-and-spokes" system, which has travelers from different cities arrive at a hub and change to other planes to get to their final destinations.

Hub airports need to be able to move quickly and efficiently while managing high passenger and flight volumes. Passengers at Pittsburgh are taken to remote gates in eleven minutes or fewer via moving sidewalks and shuttle trains. In order to accommodate the bigger people, the gates are also larger.

From flight to flight, baggage is bar-coded and directed by sophisticated laser scanners along six miles of conveyor belts. Because of its X-design, the terminal itself can accommodate planes arriving from any angle.

To cut down on takeoff line wait times, the terminal is surrounded by dual taxiways that run in opposite directions. According to USAir, the runway layout alone helps the airline save over $12 million in fuel expenses annually.

Source: Edwin McDowell, "For Pittsburgh, a Model Airport at an Immodest Price," New York Times, November 8, 1992.

Pittsburgh International Airport with X-design "hub-and-spokes" system

The configuration of equipment, workstations, storage spaces, passageways, and common areas within a current or planned facility is referred to as the **facility layout**. A firm's quality, productivity, and competitiveness are significantly impacted by its layout. The decisions made about system layout have a big impact on how well employees can perform their tasks, how quickly products can be produced, how hard it is to automate a system, and how adaptable the system is to changes in the product mix, demand volume, and design of products or services.

More than ever, facility layouts can be customized. Manufacturers who used to locate their shipping and receiving divisions at one end of the structure are now designing their facilities to allow deliveries to be made straight to production sites (as in the case of JIT systems). A plan that works well can serve a variety of objectives.

10.1.1 FACILITY LAYOUT OBJECTIVES

Ensuring that labor, supplies, personnel, and information move through the system smoothly is the main objective of the layout choice. Additionally, effective layouts:

- Reduce the expense of material handling;
- Make effective use of both space and labor;
- Get rid of bottlenecks;
- Effectively facilitate communication within the organizational hierarchy;
- Enhance the metrics for manufacturing performance;
- Encourage the right flow of people, goods, and materials while removing unnecessary movement or back tracking[3] at the same time;
- Encourage high-quality goods and services;
- Promote appropriate maintenance practices while implementing safety and security measures at the same time;
- Utilizing state-of-the-art systems provide operations or activities real-time control so they can be flexible enough to adjust to changing situations.

---

[3] Backtracking occurs when materials are moved upstream in a manufacturing line along a linear track, which is the opposite of the typical downstream flow. By placing machines at the right places along the line to reduce backtracking, management aims to streamline the job flow.

10.2 FUNDAMENTAL FACILITY LAYOUTS

There are numerous distinct types of facility layouts. Prior to discussing more advanced layouts like cellular layouts, flexible manufacturing systems, and mixed-model assembly lines in later sections, we first cover three fundamental layout types in the next section.

10.2.1 PROCESS LAYOUTS

Similar tasks are grouped together in departments or work centers according to the process or function they carry out in **process layouts**, sometimes referred to as **functional layouts**. In a machine shop, for instance, there would be one work center with all the drills, another with the lathes, and still another with the milling machines. Within a department store, there are distinct sections dedicated to women's, men's, children's, cosmetics, and shoe departments. Intermittent operations, job shops, service shops, and batch production – all of which cater to various customers with varying needs – all have process layouts in common. The quantity of orders placed by each customer is minimal, and the order in which they must be completed can differ significantly. Workers in a process layout have the necessary skills to operate the general-purpose machines in their specific area. This layout has the following advantages.

1. Flexibility of workcenters – It is possible to make changes in operations and their order without affecting the current arrangement. Any point in the process sequence allows for the addition of a new operation.

2. Reduced expenditure due to a relatively smaller number of machines – Generally speaking, general purpose machines are inexpensive. There is no machine duplication. Moreover, general purpose machines do not age out as quickly as machines designed for specific purposes.

3. Greater utilization of the production facilities – Any machine failure does not cause the process to stop entirely. The machine experiencing a breakdown can assign its work to other machines.

4. Greater potential for expansion – This kind of arrangement allows for the expansion of various capacity lines. It is possible to add more workers and machines without disrupting the current workflow.

5. Supervisor develop specialization – Supervisors gain extensive understanding by managing a range of tasks.

The following are some disadvantages of process layout:

1. There may be backtracking, which lowers the efficiency of material handling.
2. Material handling cannot be mechanized due to the possibility of backtracking, which increases costs.
3. Batch processing lengthens process times by decreasing inventory turnover and raising investment in inventories, meaning that work-in-process inventory is high.
4. Different batches processing methods make it challenging to plan and control production.
5. It is necessary to offer additional storage space near machines to hold material that is waiting processing due to the relatively high work-in-progress inventory.
6. Decreased productivity as a result of several setups from various product-mix batches.

Fig. 10.1 A process layout in manufacturing industry

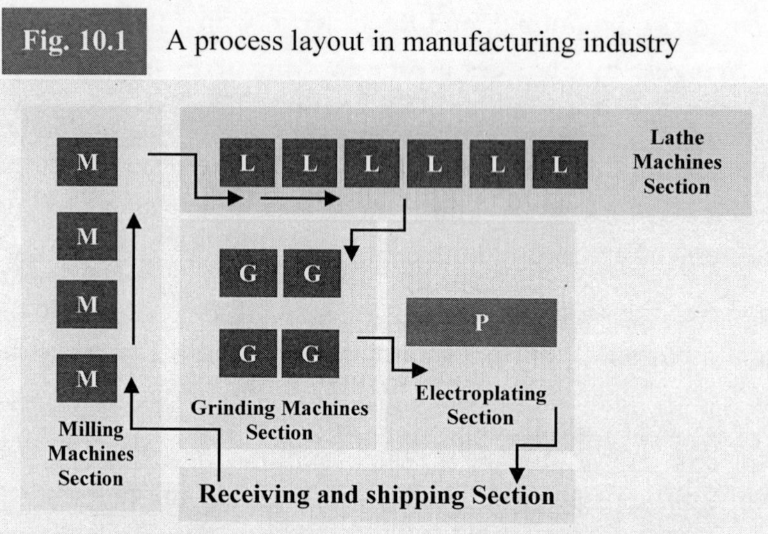

Schematic design of process layout in manufacturing is displayed in Fig. 10.1. In the service industry, process layout is comparable to that of manufacturing. For example, in a mall, numerous sections are devoted to different commodities, such as housewares, sports goods, clothing for women, children, and men, and so forth. Workers' workloads frequently vary, ranging from queues of jobs or customers waiting to be processed to idle time in between jobs or customers, even though they may run many machines or carry out multiple activities in a single department. As such, staffing in process layout is another challenging job.

Flexible material handling tools, such as forklifts, carts, or automated guided vehicles (AGVs), are essential to manufacturing process layouts because they can move in programmed guided courses, follow various paths, and transport heavy loads of work while in process. The different priority rules covered in Unit 4 are used to determine how movements should be scheduled.

Service companies' process layouts need to have wide aisles for consumers to walk along and lots of display area to meet a range of client preferences. The primary layout consideration for a process layout is the optimal placement of the departments or machine centers with respect to one another. Certain paths will be more prevalent than others, even if every project or customer may have a unique route through the facility. It is possible to create patterns of flow through the store by using historical data on client orders and forecasts of future orders. In addition, it ought to be balanced between the expense and the efficiency of the material flow.

10.2.2 PRODUCT LAYOUTS

Product layouts, sometimes known as line layouts, arrange tasks in a line based on the order in which they must be completed. This is comparable to the sequence of tasks carried out on a product assembly line. Every product has a "line" that is specifically designed to meet its requirements. Moving from one workstation to the next along the assembly line until a final product comes off the end of the line; the job is done in an efficient and well-organized manner. Special machinery can be purchased to fulfill a product's specific processing requirements, since the line is built up for a single type of product or service. Product layouts work well for repetitive tasks or mass production where volume and demand are both steady. The product or service is a basic offering intended for a general market rather than a specific customer. Product layouts are more automated than process layouts due to the high degree of demand, and worker roles have changed. In process layout, personnel who execute strictly defined assembly tasks are paid less than those who conduct more varied duties.

Product layouts tend to counterbalance their high equipment costs by achieving high labor and machine utilization. Items flow swiftly from one operation to the next, therefore there is rarely much work-in-process. As a result, operations are interdependent to such an extent that a mechanical malfunction or a high rate of absenteeism could lead the system as a whole to fail. One crucial process that should be used in product layouts to lower the likelihood of malfunctions during operation is preventive maintenance. The following are product layouts' primary benefits:

1. Low cost per unit from high production rate offsets the expensive cost of special purpose machinery employed in product layout.
2. In comparison to process layout, routine work in product layout provides for lower labor costs and fewer supervisory skills.
3. Minimal material handling cost per unit; material handling is made simpler by the uniform sequence of operations across units.
4. Because routing and scheduling are built into the system from the beginning, they don't need as much maintenance after its operational, which leads to a high labor and machine utilization rate.
5. Inventory control, purchasing, and accounting are all somewhat standard procedures.

The primary disadvantages of product layouts include:

1. When it comes to adapting to changes in output volume, different product variants, or process design, the system is somewhat rigid.
2. The system is quite vulnerable to significant absenteeism or machine breakdowns.
3. The extra costs are associated with the need for preventive maintenance, the ability to fix problems quickly, and the inventory of spare parts for unexpected replacement of worn-out components.
4. Due to the possibility of employee dissatisfaction when incentives are intended, a highly balanced line from a cycle time perspective at each workstation along the line is required.
5. Jobs that require a lot of repetition have limited room for growth, can be demoralizing, and can cause repetitive stress injuries.

The main goal of a product layout is to balance the assembly such that no workstation obstructs the flow of work through the line and causes a bottleneck. Material must be moved along the assembly line in a single direction and consistently in the same pattern for a product layout. The most popular material handling tool for product design is the conveyor. Conveyors can be unpaced, meaning that workers can start and stop them at their own speed. Assembly work can be done off the moving line or on the moving conveyor (offloading a car from the assembly line is how a vehicle is put through a strenuous test).

Significant changes in product design may require that a new assembly line be built and new machines be purchased. The material is moved only in one direction and not very far, and the conveyor is a necessary component of the assembly process, with workstations typically located on either side, thus the aisles are limited. The only thing to consider when scheduling conveyors is the pace they should run when they are installed. Due to in-process inventory used in the product's assembly as it passes down the assembly line, storage space along an assembly line is relatively modest. When sent to dealers or stores to be sold, finished items, however, might need to be stored in a different warehouse.

U-shaped arrangements – While a straight production line can seem more natural, a U-shaped line (see Fig. 10.2) has several benefits that make it a viable option. A lengthy, straight line has the drawback of obstructing worker and vehicle cross-traffic. A U-shaped production line is more compact and often requires half the length of a straight line. Additionally, because workers are grouped together, a U-shaped line encourages teamwork and increases communication amongst line members. Workers can manage stations on both sides of the route in addition to nearby stations, increasing flexibility in work assignments.

Furthermore, a U-shaped line simplifies material handling if materials enter the facility at the same location as finished goods exit it. Of course, not all scenarios are suitable for U-shaped layouts; for example, collaboration and communication are less necessary in highly automated lines. Additionally, the building's entry and exit locations could be on different sides. Additionally, concerns like as noise or contamination may need the separation of operations.

During the COVID-19 pandemic, there was an acute demand for critical care beds. As a result, the Indian government, through the national health mission, initiated the COVID-19 emergency response and health system preparedness package. The goal of this program was to hasten the health system's readiness for COVID-19 pandemic prevention, early detection, and management. It was determined that the room's design should enable the actual visualization of every patient from a central hub. The beds were arranged in a U-shaped layout around the central station to accomplish this. The reader can scan the provided QR code to view a comprehensive case study.

SCAN ME
for
U-shaped layout
case study

Fig. 10.2 U-shaped product layout

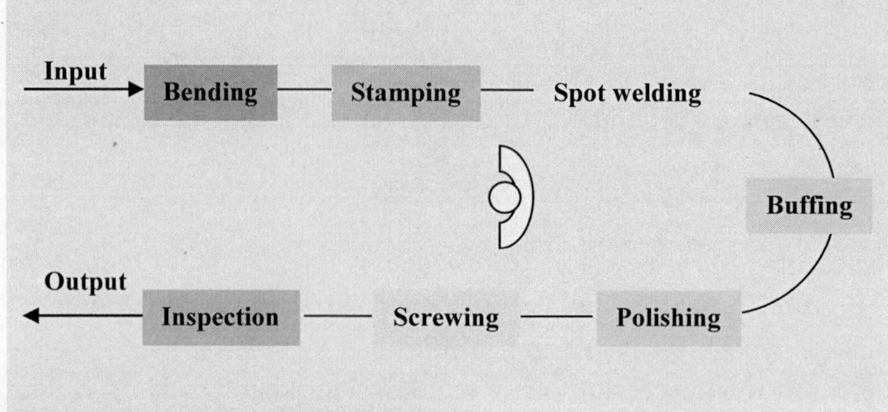

10.2.3 FIXED-POSITION LAYOUTS

Fixed-position layouts are commonly used in projects where the final product is too heavy, unwieldy, or fragile to be moved. Examples include buildings, ships, airplanes, large vehicles (see in the picture, workers performing work on-site). The product in this arrangement stays in one place during the whole manufacturing process. Resources such as labor, materials, equipment, and other are brought to the production location. The reason for low equipment usage is that moving equipment back and forth is frequently more expensive than leaving it idle where it will be needed again in a few days.

Fixed-position layouts are commonly used in projects where the final product is too heavy, unwieldy, or fragile to be moved. Examples include buildings, ships, airplanes, large vehicles (see in the picture, workers performing work on-site). The product in this arrangement stays in one place during the whole manufacturing process. Resources such as labor, materials, equipment, and other are brought to the production location. The reason for low equipment usage is that moving equipment back and forth is frequently more expensive than leaving it idle where it will be needed again in a few days.

Since the equipment is only utilized seldom, it is frequently rented or subcontracted. The laborers dispatched to the job site possess exceptional proficiency in carrying out the specific task assigned to them. For example, at one point in the production process, pipe fitters might be required, and at another, electricians or plumbers. These laborers make far more money than the minimum wage. Therefore, the fixed cost would be relatively low (because the equipment might not belong to the company) and the variable cost would be high (because of high labor costs and the expense of leasing and moving equipment) if we were to examine the cost breakdown for the fixed position layouts. The following are some of the main benefits of plants with fixed-position layouts:

1. Reduceded expenses – Goods move infrequently or never.
2. Customization – Customizing a project is easier when it involves building a house to a client's specifications or fabricating a huge caravan vehicle, for instance.
3. Fragility – Shipping and transportation-related product damage is less common.

This setup has a few drawbacks as well, such as:

1. Moving equipment around the facility is expensive when it is used frequently.
2. Demand for skilled personnel is higher than usual.
3. Space restrictions
4. Increased likelihood of longer project completion timelines and delays

When starting a project with a fixed-position design, location is the most important factor to take into account. The project setup is essentially permanent once it is finalized, hence placement is important. Among the factors are:

- Zoning restrictions or environmental requirements.
- The standard of living for locals living near the plant or warehouse.
- The ability to grow as the project or company progresses.
- The site's accessibility to skilled labor, suppliers, consumers, and resources.

Additionally, keep in mind that workers frequently have to assemble product parts offsite due to restricted space at the project site. After that, you'll need to move those parts to the permanent place. You might also require room to assemble the parts. For operations to run well, the workflow must be designed. Large machinery like cranes are frequently used in fixed-position layout projects to handle materials, so the facility needs to have enough room to store and run this heavy machinery.

10.2.4 COMBINATION LAYOUTS

Process layouts, product layouts, and fixed-position layouts are all combined to create combination layouts. Because they incorporate elements from the different primary layout styles, these are sometimes known as "hybrid layouts". Combination design, with a variety of components, may enable some businesses to optimize productivity in light of the various tasks they must complete, the kinds of items they handle, and the range of products they deal with on a daily basis. For example, a company might utilize a product plan with assembly lines to create components but a fixed-position arrangement for the product's final assembly.

The majority of the manufacturing sections are set up in a process configuration, with manufacturing lines appearing sporadically wherever the circumstances allow. Combination layouts are conceivable when several types and sizes of the same item are produced.

Fig. 10.3 Product and process layouts combined to form Combination layout

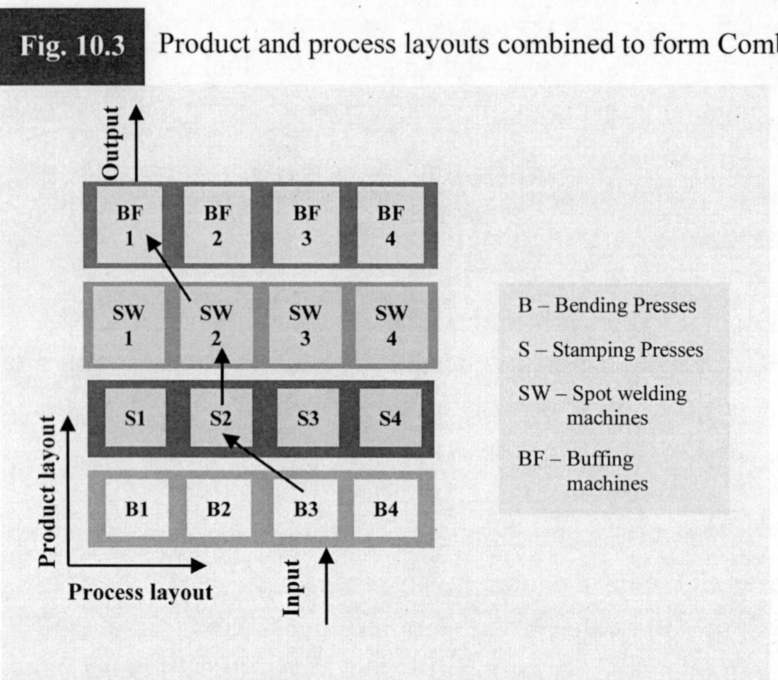

In these situations, the machinery is set up in a process layout, but the process grouping – a collection of several similar machines – is then set up in a certain sequence to produce a range of goods in terms of sizes and types. It's important to remember that the process stays the same or is somewhat comparable regardless of the product's type and size. A combination type of architecture for producing sheet metal components of various sizes is shown in Fig. 10.3.

Similar combination layouts are created in supermarkets by integrating line and process layouts. In a process layout, specific items are arranged in discrete sections, while fixed-path line layouts are represented by material handling equipment like belt and roller conveyors at the cash registers and in the stockroom. While hospitals employ a fundamental process layout with distinct treatment areas, an operation theater functions more like a fixed-position layout where patients are attended to by nurses, doctors, and specialized equipment. By scanning the provided QR code, which shows how tyres of various sizes are processed to depict combination arrangement, one can observe how combination layout functions.

SCAN ME for Functioning of Combination Layout

10.3 DESIGNING PROCESS LAYOUT

The relative placement of the departments involved is the primary focus when designing process layouts. Locations must be allocated to departments. Creating a comparatively decent arrangement is the challenge; certain arrangements will be more appealing than others. Certain departments might benefit from being located next to each other, while others ought to be kept apart. A department with heavily vibrating machinery would not put delicate lab equipment near it. On the other hand, proximity to two departments that utilize some of the same equipment would be advantageous. External elements that affect layouts include windows, loading docks, elevators, entrances, and places with reinforced flooring. Safety, noise levels, and the layout and dimensions of restrooms are all crucial factors.

10.3.1 MINIMIZATION TRANSPORTATION COST OR DISTANCES

Reducing transportation expenses and distances traveled are the most often sought-after objectives when creating process architectures. Under such circumstances, *from-to charts* such as the ones shown in Tables 10.1 and 10.2 can be a very useful tool for summarizing the relevant facts. Table 10.1 shows the distance between each location, and Table 10.2 shows the work flow between each pair, either as it is now or as it is expected to be. For example, the distance chart shows that it will take 20 meters to get from site A to location B (distances are typically measured between departments). Assume, for the sake of simplicity, that there is always a fixed distance, independent of direction, between any two sites. The assumption that interdepartmental work flows are equal, however, is not realistic; there is no reason to believe that department 1 will send department 2 as much work as department 2 sends to 1. For instance, items may be sent to packaging from multiple departments, but packaging may only send to the shipping department. From-to charts is another useful tool for summarizing transportation costs; however, for simplicity, consider that costs are a direct, linear function of distance.

Example 10.1

Handtools are manufactured by Precision Inc. Divided into three locations, X, Y, and Z, and spaced apart by the distances indicated in Table 10.1, is the small-job business that produces hand tools. Precision Inc. would like to know if a similar architecture should be used or if a better layout can be built, as they anticipate the need for a new facility for other hand tool activities shortly. In order to decrease transportation costs, you are to assess the current arrangement.

Solution

Our aim would be to assign departments with the greatest interdepartmental work flow first to those locations that are closest to each other.

Table 10.1 Distance between locations (meters)

		Location		
From	**To**	**X**	**Y**	**Z**
X		–	30	60
Y		30	–	50
Z		60	50	–

Table 10.2 Interdepartmental work flow (loads per day)

		Department		
From	**To**	**1**	**2**	**3**
1		–	20	70
2		40	–	20
3		70	90	–

In order to evaluate we need to calculate the composite, or back-and-forth, movements between departments as shown in Table 10.3.

Table 10.3 Composite values of work flow and distances

Composite department movement	Work flow	Composite Location	Distance
1↔3	140	X↔Y	60
2↔3	110	Y↔Z	100
1↔2	60	X↔Z	120

These lists show that locations X and Y are the closest, while departments 1 and 3 have the highest interdepartmental work flow. As a result, it makes sense to think about allocating 1 and 3 to locations X and Y, even though it's not yet clear which department belongs in which location. 2 and 3 should likely be positioned closer together than 1 and 2, since further examination of the work flow list indicates that they have a higher work flow than 1 and 2. Therefore, it makes sense to arrange 3 between 1 and 2, or at the very least, to centralize that department in relation to the other two. The assignments that arise could look like the ones shown below.

1	3	2
X	Y	Z

The number of loads for each department multiplied by the journey distance will give you the total daily transportation cost for this assignment if the cost per meter to transfer any load is $1.

Composite department movement	Work flow (Load)	Location	Distance	Load × distance
1↔3	140	X-Y	30	4,200
2↔3	110	Y-Z	50	5,500
1↔2	60	X-Z	60	3,600
			Total	13,300

This plan costs $13,300 per day at $1 per load meter. Although this configuration seems to result in the lowest shipping cost, you cannot be certain of that without calculating the total cost of all the other options and contrasting them with this one. This might be done in this case, because there are just 3! = 6 possible arrangements, but in problems involving more departments, there are probably too many options to even consider looking at each one. To find a workable, if not ideal, solution, instead depend on selecting appropriate heuristic principles like the ones mentioned above.

10.3.2 RELATIONSHIP RATING

When quantitative data are available, the solution procedure that came before it is suitable for creating process architectures. Subjective feedback from analysts or managers can, however, take the role of the load summary chart in circumstances when quantitative data are hard to come by or do not sufficiently address the layout issue. Muther's grid is a format created by Richard Muther to show manager preferences for departmental locations.

The five vowels – A, E, I, O, and U – as well as the letter X – are linked to six categories that correspond to the preference data. For the purpose of placing two departments near to one another, as illustrated in Figure 10.4, the vowels correspond to the first letter of the closeness ranking. Similar to distance charts on a road map, the diamond-shaped grid is read. According to Figure 10.4, for instance, it is "okay" if the offices are next to manufacturing; it is "absolutely necessary" that the stockroom be next to manufacturing; it is "important" that shipping be next to manufacturing; it is "especially important" that the finishing operation be next to manufacturing; and it is "absolutely necessary" that the toolroom be nearest to manufacturing.

Fig. 10.4 Muther's Grid

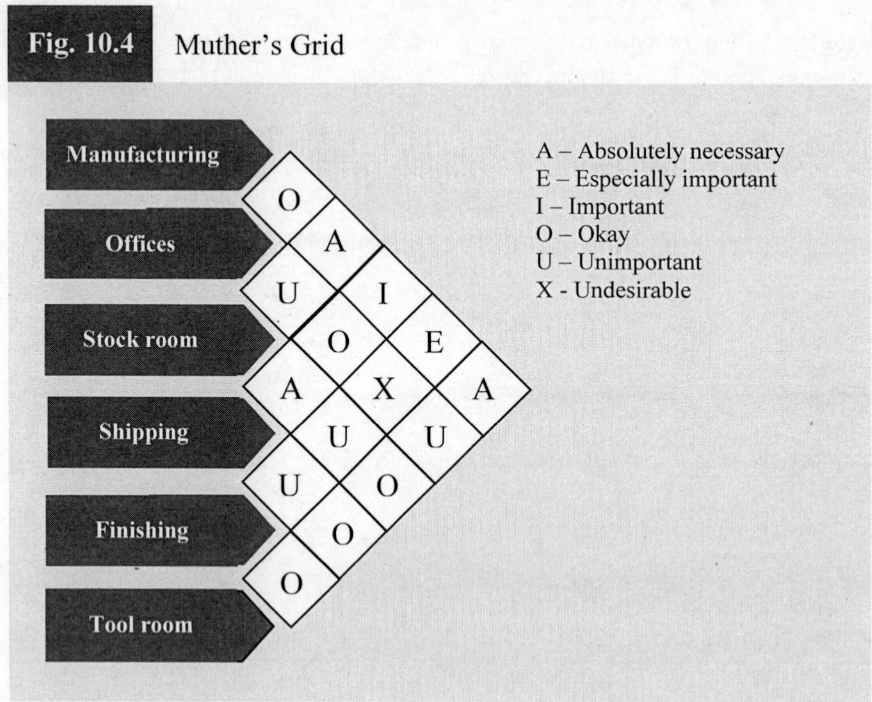

Muther's grid data can be utilized to create a relationship diagram that assesses suggested or current patterns. Take a look at the relationship diagram in Fig. 10.5(a). A 2×3 grid has a schematic illustration of the six departments from Fig. 10.5. Department to department, lines are drawn with varying widths. The departments for which it is important, especially important, or absolutely necessary that they be situated adjacent to one another are indicated by the thickest lines, which indicate the closeness ratings with the highest priority. As lines get thicker, the priority increases. A zigzagged line indicates judgments of undesirable closeness. Short, thick lines without any zigzag lines would be the ideal visual representation (unwanted places are only indicated if they are close together). Because thin lines signify unimportant or okay, can be any length, they are occasionally excluded from examination.

It is clear from Fig. 10.5(a) that the offices and finishing process are too close to one another, and that manufacturing and shipping are situated too far from the stockroom. A relationship diagram is used to assess the updated layout, which is depicted in Fig. 10.5(b). The updated design seems to meet the preferences listed in Muther's grid. The short, thick lines are inside the grid's bounds. There are no zigzagged lines and the long lines are narrow.

Fig. 10.5 Relationship diagram

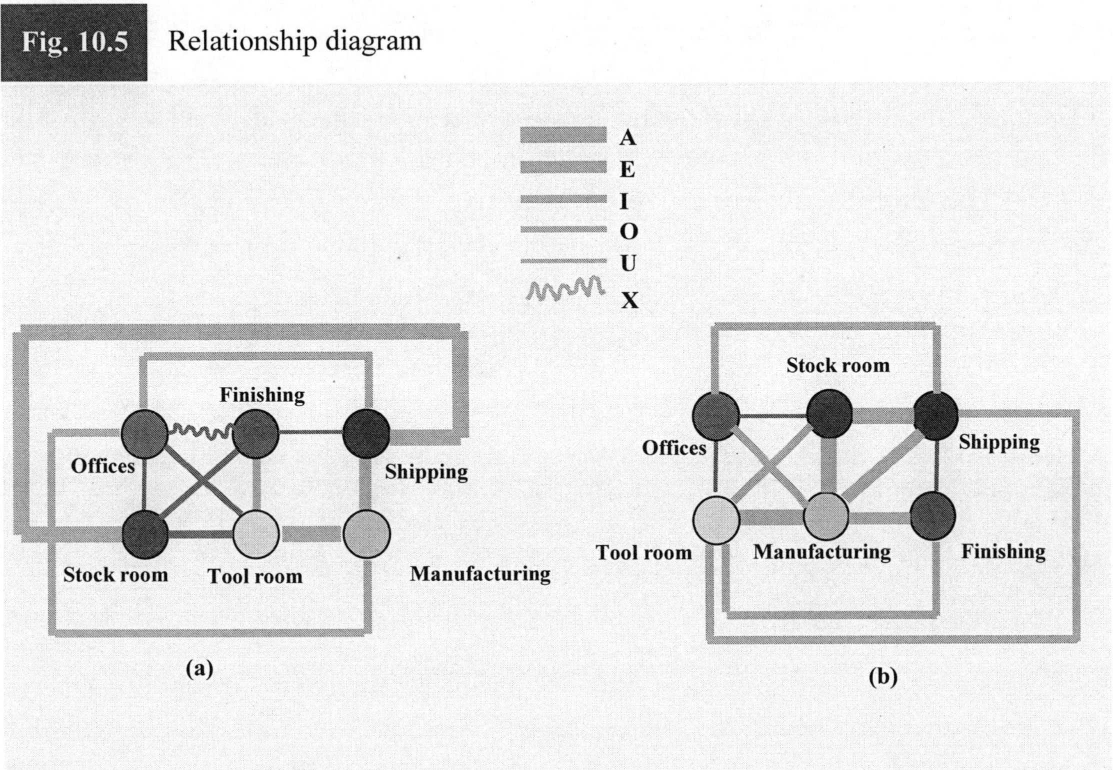

10.4 DESIGNING PRODUCT LAYOUT

A product arrangement sets up equipment or workers in a line based on the tasks required to assemble a certain product. This description suggests that the layout might be found by simply following the assembly sequence listed in the product's bill of materials. This is true to some degree. An essential factor in the decision-making process regarding product layout is precedence requirements, which outline which tasks must come before others, which can be completed simultaneously, and which must wait until later. However, there are more elements that add to the complexity of the choice.

For high-volume production, product layouts or assembly lines are employed. Jobs are divided into their smallest indivisible parts, referred to as work elements, in order to achieve the desired output rate as effectively as feasible. The small size of the task parts prevents them from being completed by several employees or at multiple workstations. However, when the product moves through his or her workstation, it is typical for one employee to complete many tasks. Ensuring smooth product flow along the assembly line involves deciding how to group these work pieces into workstations as part of the designing process. Any place on the assembly line that needs a minimum of one machine or person is called a workstation. Products will go sequentially from workstation to workstation on the assembly line if each workstation takes the same amount of time to complete the allocated task elements. This means that neither a product nor an employee will need to wait. **Line balancing** is the process of adjusting the workload at each workstation to be equal.

When there is little variation in the times needed to complete the individual subassemblies, assembly-line systems function effectively. Operators farther down the line might not be able to keep up with the flow of parts from the previous workstation or might have too much idle time if the duties are reasonably difficult, which would lead to a higher assembly-time variance. An assembly line without conveyors can be replaced with a series of workstations connected by gravity conveyors that serve as breaks in between jobs.

10.4.1 LINE BALANCING

The aim of line balancing is to achieve work groupings that roughly correspond to equal time needs. This leads to a high worker and equipment utilization rate and reduces idle time along the line. Task timings that differ between workstations – some are able to produce at higher rates than others – lead to idle time. In order to prevent work accumulation between stations, these "fast" stations will occasionally have to wait for the output from slower stations or else be pushed into idleness.

Unbalanced lines are undesirable because they utilize labor and equipment inefficiently and may affect employee morale at slower stations where workers are required to work continually. Work will flow more smoothly along precisely balanced lines since all activities are coordinated to maximize the use of both manpower and equipment. The primary hindrance to achieving a perfectly balanced line is the challenge of creating job bundles with identical durations. One reason for this could be that some tasks are incompatible or too different to include in a single bundle (e.g., risk of grease contamination from electroplating), or it might not be possible to include them all in one bundle. It can also be difficult since cycle time would match the operation with the maximum task time, so merging jobs does not always compensate for differences in elemental task lengths. Third, an unfulfilled line might be explained by a necessary technological sequence of operations or precedence requirements that prevents otherwise desired task combinations.

The physical sequence in which tasks are completed on an assembly line is limited by precedence constraints. When a worker has the opportunity to package a product before it is passed to the next person in line, we would not, for instance, ask them to do so until all the components were joined. Precedence needs are sometimes expressed in the form of a **precedence diagram** to aid in line balancing. Precedence relationships are shown by directed line segments connecting the nodes in the precedence diagram, which is a network with work elements represented by circles or nodes. The second constraint on line balancing, **cycle time**, is the maximum duration that the product can be left at each workstation in order to attain the desired production rate. The number of units scheduled to be produced divided by the time available for production yields the desired cycle time:

$$C_d = \frac{\text{Production time available}}{\text{desired units of output}} \qquad \ldots (10.1)$$

Assume a business had a daily goal of producing 96 units in an 8-hour shift. The required cycle time to complete the batch of manufacturing is

$$C_d = \frac{8 \text{ hours} \times 60 \text{ minutes/hour}}{96 \text{ units}} = 5 \text{ minutes}$$

The interval of time between finished goods leaving the assembly line can alternatively be thought of as cycle time. Take a look at this three-station production line.

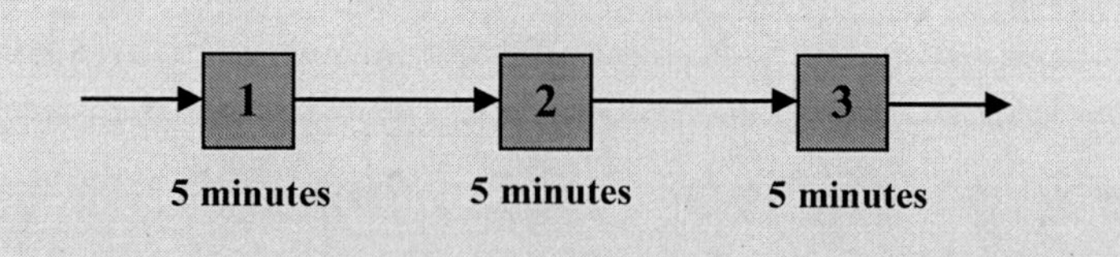

For every item on the assembly line, it takes 15 minutes (5+5+5) to go through all three stations. An item's flow time, also known as lead time, is the amount of time needed to finish it. The assembly line, however, does not work on a single item at a time. When the line is completely functional, three objects in varying stages of assembly – one at each workstation – will be processed at once. Every five minutes, a new item starts to move through the line at workstation 1, another item moves from workstation 1 to workstation 2, and a finished item exits the assembly line. As a result, per five minutes, a finished product comes off the assembly line. The line's real cycle time is this 5-minute interval.

The maximum workstation time on the line is known as the actual cycle time, or C_a. When the production lot (batch-size) is not met by the system's maximum output, the cycle time deviates from the intended one. Sometimes the amount of time needed for one task element is so great that the production lot cannot be met. The situation can be rectified by setting up parallel stations for the bottleneck part or by revising the batch-size downward.

In essence, line balancing is a process of trial and error. Taking into account time and priority restrictions, we organize the components into work stations. We are able to evaluate every possible combination of parts in basic issues. We must know when to give up on trying various workstation configurations for more complex issues. One kind of guideline can be obtained from the line's efficiency, while another can be obtained from the theoretically minimal number of workstations. The efficiency (E) and minimum number of workstations (N) formulas are:

$$E = \frac{\sum_{i=1}^{j} t_i}{nC_a} \quad \text{... (10.2)}$$

$$N = \frac{\sum_{i=1}^{j} t_i}{C_d} \quad \text{... (10.3)}$$

where

t_i = completion time for element i

j = number of work elements

n = actual number of work elements

C_a = actual cycle time

C_d = desired cycle time

Balance delay, or the line's total idle time, is computed as (1 – efficiency). Typically, efficiency and balance delay are given as percentages. Achieving the theoretical number of workstations or 100% efficiency in practice could be challenging.

Example 10.2

Line Balancing

A component is made by a sheet metal product firm. The table below lists the order and duration of each step in the process of creating the sheet metal assembly. Every 40-hour workweek, the firm produces 4800 sheet metal assemblies to meet demand. Create an assembly line with the fewest possible workstations to meet production lot requirements without going against precedence rules.

	Work Element	Precedence	Time (Minutes)
A	Cutting out Strips	–	0.1
B	Blanking	A	0.2
C	Piercing	A	0.4
D	Inspection and packaging	B,C	0.3

Solution

The precedence diagram is first drawn as follows.

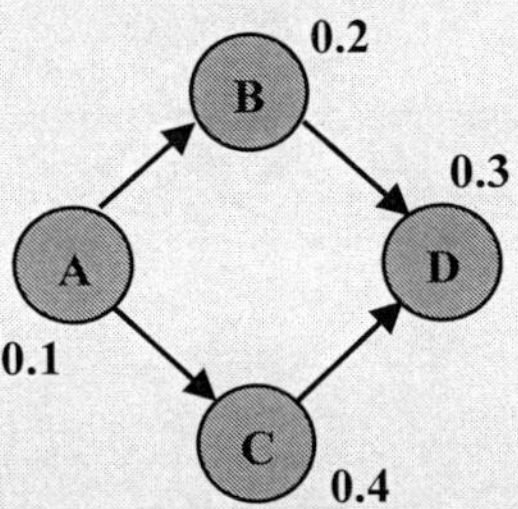

The desired cycle time (Eq. 10.1) and the theoretically minimal number of workstations (Eq. 10.3) are then determined:

$$C_d = \frac{40 \text{ hours} \times 60 \text{ minutes/hour}}{4800 \text{ units}} = 0.5 \text{ minutes}$$

$$N = \frac{0.1 + 0.2 + 0.3 + 0.4}{0.5} = 2$$

We must arrange the components into workstations so that the total element duration at each workstation is less than or equal to the planned cycle time of 0.5 minutes. Let's begin by looking at element A because it is the only one in the precedence diagram without precedence. Workstation 1 assignment is assigned to A. At this point, B and C can be assigned. We combine A and C to workstation 1 because doing so on the same workstation equals a cycle time of 0.5. Workstation 1 cannot have any more components added to it due to cycle time limitations. After then, D and B are assigned to the second workstation, resulting in a cycle time of 0.5. The components organized into workstations on the precedence diagram are

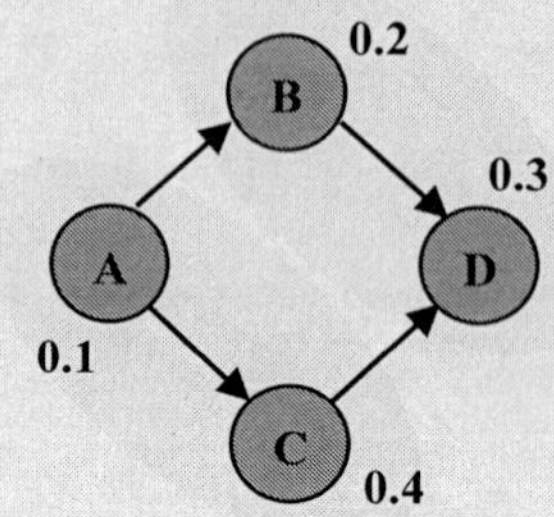

Workstation diagram will be:

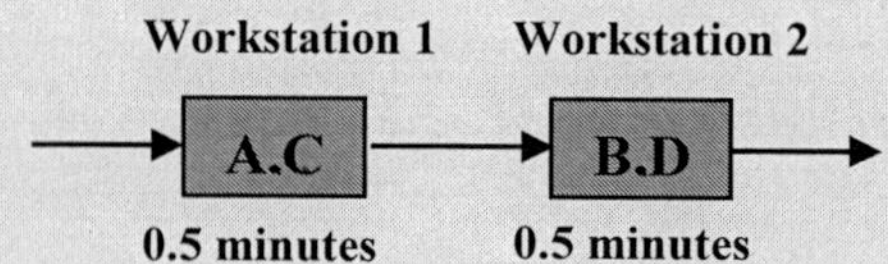

We can conclude that we have effectively balanced the line because the theoretical minimal number of workstations was two.

The efficiency of the assembly line is

$$E = \frac{0.1 + 0.2 + 0.3 + 0.4}{2(0.5)} = 1.0$$

While we have attained 100% efficiency in this task, huge networks of processes may not always allow for such an achievement. You can scan the QR code to view the line balancing of a more complicated problem in a more complicated network.

SCAN ME
for
Line Balancing
Numerical Analysis

The procedures outlined in the section above are often completed by hand. This does not mean that it cannot be used on a digital computer. In actuality, a number of the heuristic approaches have served as the foundation for computer programs. Nevertheless, compared to a manual solution method, the computer allows for a more thorough listing of all potential solutions to a line balance problem. To learn more about other computerized line balancing techniques, scan the provided QR code.

SCAN ME
for
Computerized line balancing

10.5 CELLULAR LAYOUTS

Cellular layouts aim to bring together the productivity of a product layout and the adaptability of a process plan. To process parts with similar shapes or processing requirements (commonly called part families shown in picture below), dissimilar machines are organized into work centers, or cells, based on the idea of group technology[4] (GT). The arrangement of the cells is designed to reduce the movement of material among them. Huge, immobile machines are positioned close to the cells that utilize them, or at their point of usage.

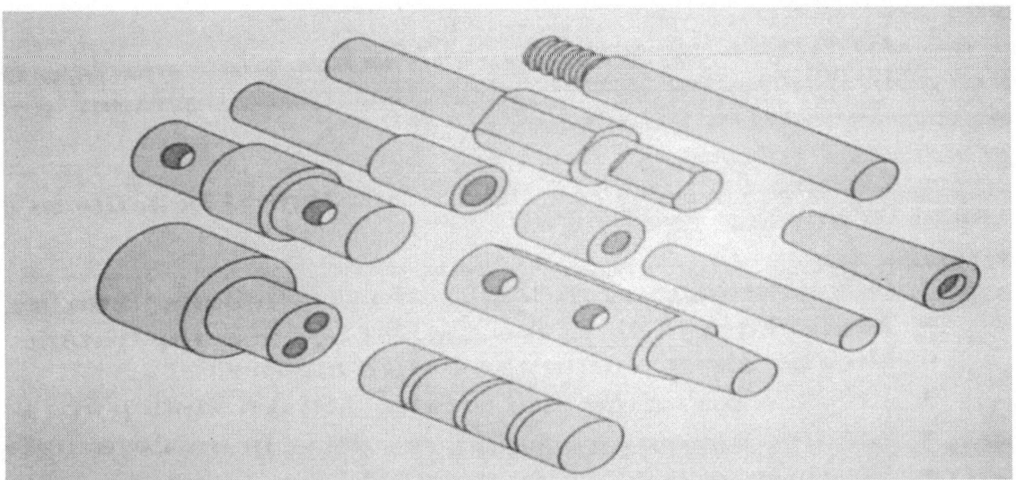

Source: https://industri.fatek.unpatti.ac.id/wp-content/uploads/2019/03/245-Automation-Production-Systems-and-Computer-Integrated-Manufacturing-Mikell-P.-Groover-Edisi-4-2015.pdf

Each cell's machine arrangement is similar to a little manufacturing line. Thus, the machines within the cell can be arranged using line-balancing processes with some modification. A

[4] Group technology is an approach in which similar parts, called part family, are identified and grouped together in order to take advantage of the similarities in design and production.

process layout is one that is created between cells. Thus, cells and any remaining equipment in the facility can be found using computer applications like CRAFT.

Production flow analysis (PFA) – This method was developed by J. Burbidge and is used for machine cell construction and part family identification. In this procedure, the machines are divided into different departments based on their functions. Consider the process layout shown in Fig. 10.6. On the assembly line, component parts made in the factory's process layout department are eventually put together to create a finished good. Different paths for the parts flow through the shop. Parts A, B, and C have three representative routings displayed in the figure. Take note of the distance that every component needs to cover to be completed as well as the uneven part routing. A significant quantity of paperwork is required to ensure that every step is taken correctly and to guide the flow of each individual portion. Workers are usually able to operate multiple machines at once and are proficient in operating the sorts of machinery found in a specific department.

Fig. 10.6 Initial process layout

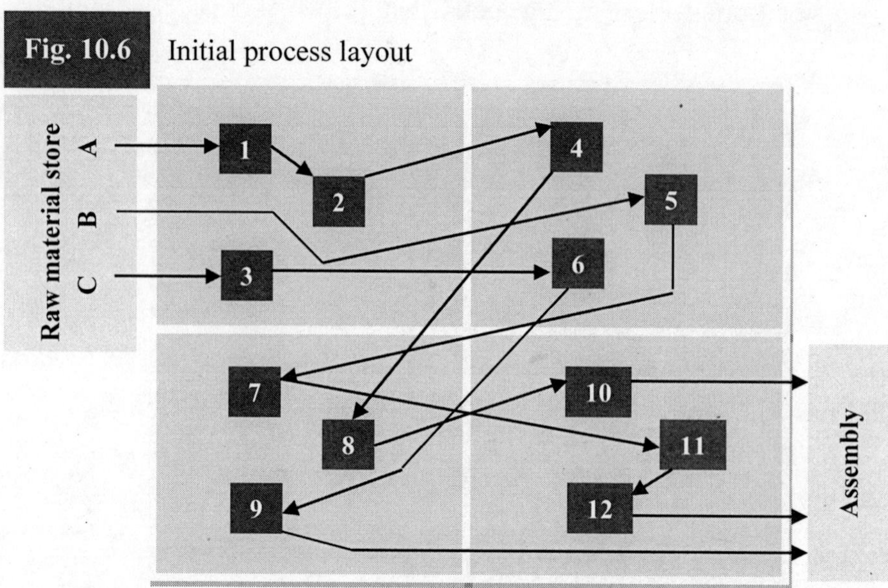

The part routing matrix for all eight parts that were processed by the facility is provided in Fig. 10.7. The routings don't seem to follow any pattern as they are right now. Part routing matrices are rearranged using production flow analysis (PFA) to find part families with related processing needs. Reordering parts can be as easy as noting which parts share four machines, then which parts share three, two, and so on, or it can be as complex as artificial intelligence's pattern-recognition algorithms.

The outcome of rearranging Fig. 10.7 is displayed in Fig. 10.8. The cell structures and part families are now evident. Cell 1 will process parts A, D, and F, Cell 2 will process products C and G, and Cell 3 will process parts B, H, and E. Cell 1 is made up of machines 1, 2, 4, 8, and 10. Cell 2 is made up of machines 3, 6, and 9. Cell 3 is made up of machines 5, 7, 11, and 12. Fig. 10.9 provides a complete cellular structure with the three cells feeding a final assembly line.

Fig. 10.7 Part routing matrix

	Machines											
Parts	1	2	3	4	5	6	7	8	9	10	11	12
A	*	*		*				*		*		
B					*		*				*	*
C			*			*			*			
D	*	*		*				*		*		
E					*	*						*
F	*			*				*				
G			*			*			*			*
H							*				*	*

Fig. 10.8 Rearranged part routing matrix to underline specific cells

	Machines											
Parts	1	2	4	8	10	3	6	9	5	7	11	12
A	*	*	*	*	*							
D	*	*	*	*	*		Cell 1					
F	*		*	*								
C						*	*	*				
G			Cell 2			*	*	*				*
B									*	*	*	*
H						Cell 3				*	*	*
E							*		*			*

Compared to the part flows in the process layout, the representative part flows for parts A, B, and C are substantially more direct. The parts travel a shorter distance to be processed, and there is no backtracking or traversing of paths. It is evident that portions G and E cannot be processed in their allotted cells, 2 and 3, in their entirety. Nonetheless, the two compartments are positioned so that there is minimal additional movement required for the transfer of parts between them.

Fig. 10.9 Redesigned layout with three cells

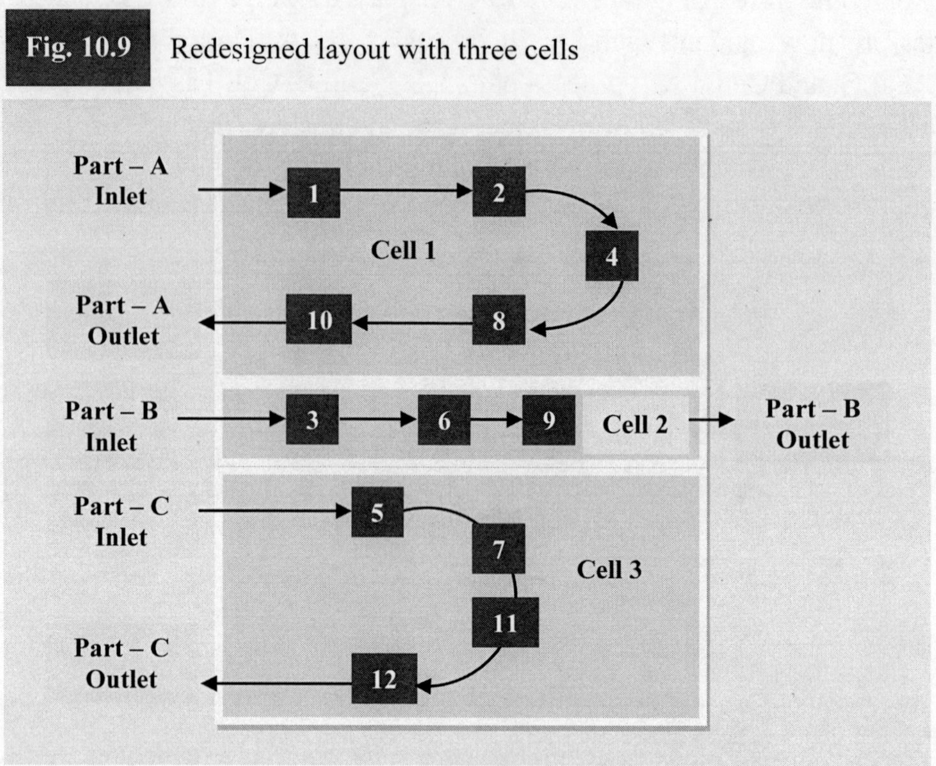

A common configuration for production cells is the U-shaped arrangement of cells 1 and 3, which makes it easier for workers to switch between many machines. As with the process layout, workers in a cellular layout usually run many machines. But workers assigned to each cell now need to be multifunctional, meaning they should be able to operate multiple types of machines instead of just one, as in the process arrangement. Furthermore, employees are given a route to follow when operating the equipment, which might or might not match the path the product takes through the cell.

Certain packs frequently do not fit into any kind of logical classification. These components could be dissected to see whether a new process sequence that falls into one of the categories can be created. If not, a traditional process layout will need to be used to create these parts. To study a methodical approach known as ***rank-order clustering***, which may be utilized to carry out the cluster analysis, the reader can scan the QR code.

SCAN ME
for
Rank order clustering method for cell formation

10.6 FLEXIBLE MANUFACTURING SYSTEMS

A flexible manufacturing system (FMS) is a highly automated GT machine cell made up of one or more processing stations (often CNC machine tools) coupled by an automated material handling and storage system and managed by a distributed computer system. The Flexibility of the FMS lies in its ability to process several part types at separate workstations simultaneously. It also allows for the adjustment of production volumes and part styles in response to shifting demand patterns.

The foundation of group technology is an FMS. There is no manufacturing method that is totally adaptable. The variety of parts or goods that can be produced in an FMS has its limitations. As a result, a flexible manufacturing system is made to create goods or parts that fall within a specific range of sizes, styles, and methods. Put otherwise, an FMS can generate a single part family or a small number of different part families.

FMS would be better described as a flexible automated manufacturing system. This kind of production technology would be distinguished from other flexible but non-automated manufacturing systems, like a manned GT machine cell, by the usage of the term "automated." It would be distinguished from other highly automated but non-flexible production systems, such a traditional transfer line, by the term "flexible."

Flexibility – The three characteristics that make a manufacturing system flexible are: (1) the capacity to recognize the various incoming parts or product styles that the system processes; (2) the ability to quickly switch between operating instructions; and (3) the ability to quickly switch between physical setups. This quality of flexibility is applicable to both automated and manual systems. The human operators in manual systems are frequently the ones who make the system flexible.

To explore the idea of flexibility in an automated manufacturing system, have a look at the machine cell seen in Fig. 10.10. This machine cell consists of two CNC machine tools that are loaded and unloaded from a parts storage system by an industrial robot. The cell runs for long stretches of time without supervision. A worker must periodically remove finished parts from the storage system and swap them out for fresh work pieces. This is an automated manufacturing cell by definition, but is it also a flexible manufacturing cell? Its flexibility may be argued to stem from the fact that the cell is made up of CNC machine tools, and CNC machines are adaptable due to their ability to be programmed to produce various part configurations. However, this does not qualify as flexible manufacturing if the cell only works in batch mode, when both machines make the same part style in lots of several hundred units.

For an automated manufacturing system to be considered flexible, it must meet the requirements of the four flexibility tests listed below.

- Test for part variety: Is the system able to handle various product or part styles in a mixedmodel (non-batch) mode?
- Test for schedule changes: Is the system able to easily accommodate modifications to the production schedule, such as adjustments to the part mix or production quantities?
- Test for error recovery: Is there a way for the system to gracefully bounce back from equipment failures and malfunctions without totally interrupting production?

Fig. 10.10 An automated manufacturing cell

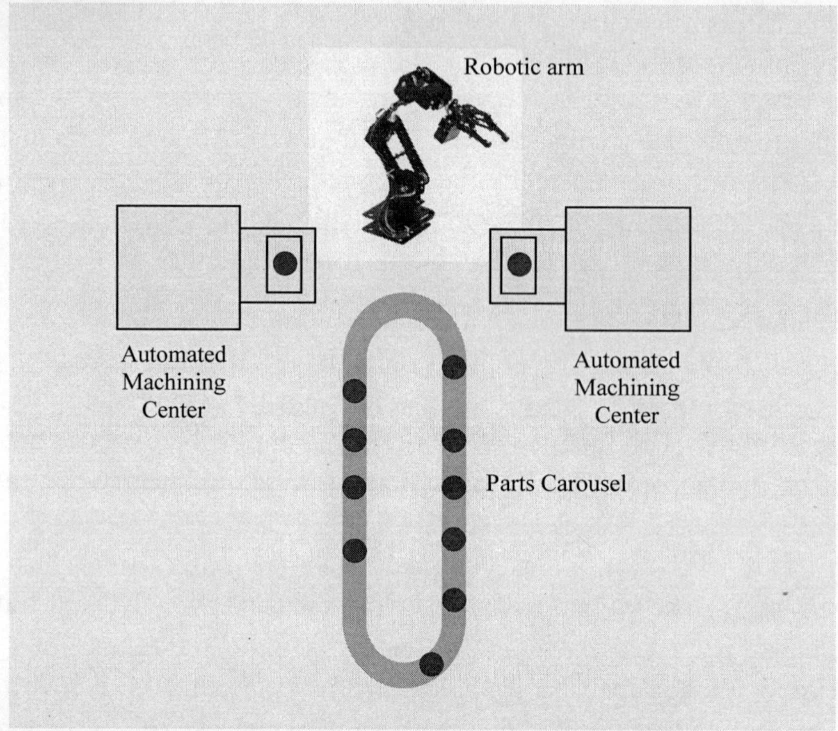

10.6.1 CONFIGURATIONS FOR THE FMS LAYOUT

The FMS arrangement is determined by the material handling system. Four types of layout configurations are commonly seen in modern flexible production systems: in-line layout, loop layout, open field layout, and robot-centered cell.

Fig. 10.11 FMS loop layout

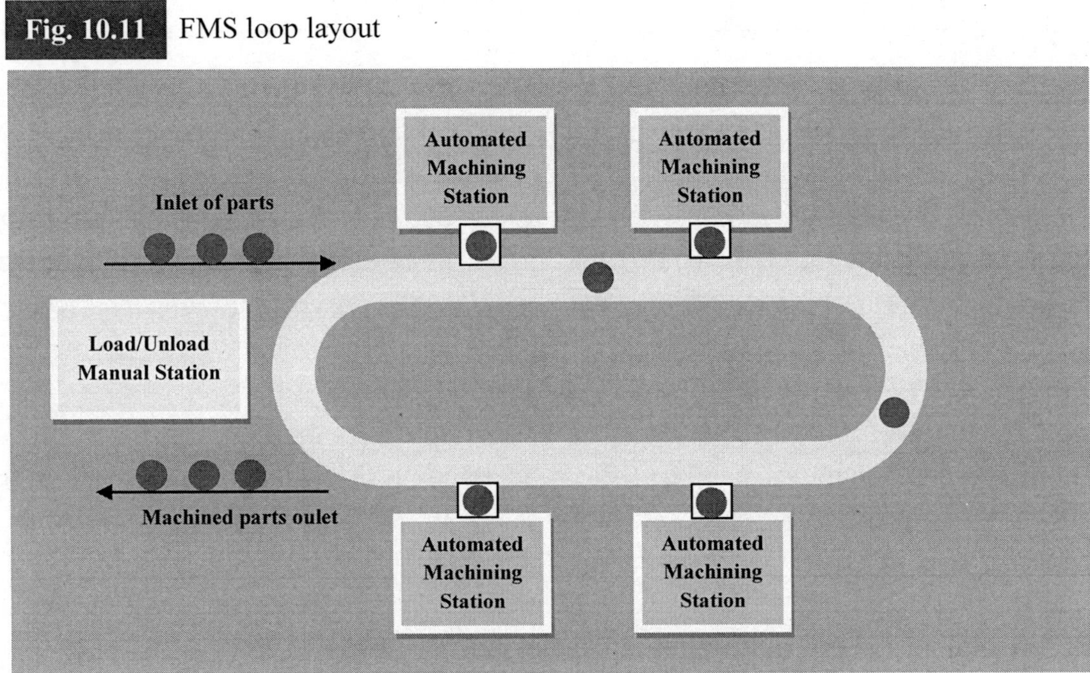

As in the preceding section, we describe the cellular layout system that is analogous to the loop layout system. Workstations are arranged in a loop in the loop configuration (Fig. 10.11), which is served by a parts-handling system of the same form. While having the potential to pause and be moved to any station, parts often flow around the loop in a single direction. To facilitate the free flow of components around the loop, a secondary handling system is displayed at each workstation. On one end of the loop is usually where the load/unload station(s) are positioned.

Setup and queue lengths/queue times are reduced to increase an FMS's efficiency. Before the part enters the machine, setup is completed. A machine is only given components and equipment that are ready to be used right away. Pallets are kept in a queue area at each machine so they are ready to go as soon as the equipment completes processing a piece. Pallets can also be used as work platforms, saving time when moving workpieces from pallet to machine or arranging and fixing parts. Five-axis CNC machining centers, for example, are examples of advanced FMSs where a single machine can execute up to five operations on a workpiece at once, which would typically need multiple machines to complete.

UNIT SUMMARY

- ***Facility Layout Objectives*** – Focuses on minimizing material handling costs, maximizing space utilization, reducing bottlenecks, and improving workflow efficiency.
- ***Fundamental Facility Layouts***: (i) Process Layout – Organizes similar functions together, suitable for job shops, (ii) Product Layout – Follows a sequential flow, ideal for mass production, (iii) Fixed-Position Layout – Used for large, immobile projects like shipbuilding, (iv) Combination Layout – A hybrid approach integrating elements of different layouts.
- ***Layout Design Techniques***: (i) Process Layout Optimization – Uses transportation cost minimization and relationship ratings, (ii) Product Layout Optimization – Focuses on line balancing to ensure smooth production flow.
- ***Advanced Layouts***: (i) Cellular Layouts – Groups machines for similar tasks to reduce movement and setup times, (ii) Flexible Manufacturing Systems (FMS) – Automates material handling and processing for high adaptability.
- ***Practical Applications*** – Case studies like Pittsburgh International Airport's hub-and-spokes model, demonstrating efficient layout design.

EXERCISES

MULTIPLE CHOICE QUESTIONS

10.1 What is the primary purpose of studying facility layout in operations management?

(a) To design marketing strategies	(b) To optimize the arrangement of physical resources for efficient production
(c) To enhance customer service protocols	(d) To determine employee compensation

10.2 Which key factor is commonly considered when designing a facility layout?

(a) Employee vacation schedules	(b) Location of competitors
(c) Efficient flow of materials and information	(d) Advertising budget

10.3 How does an effective facility layout contribute to cost savings?

(a) By increasing the number of workstations	(b) By reducing the need for additional training programs
(c) By optimizing space utilization and reducing operational costs	(d) By expanding the building's physical size

10.4 In what way could an effectively designed facility layout contribute to a company's long-term competitive advantage?

(a) By increasing the frequency of product updates	(b) By improving the efficiency of internal processes and reducing production lead times
(c) By elevating employee salaries	(d) By expanding the range of marketing strategies

10.5 How could optimizing the layout of a manufacturing facility indirectly benefit customer satisfaction metrics?

(a) By increasing the frequency of customer feedback sessions	(b) By streamlining production processes, leading to faster delivery times and more reliable service
(c) By enhancing product customization options	(d) By reducing the need for customer support

10.6 Which of the following best describes a potential effect on operational efficiency from adopting a functional layout in a manufacturing facility?

(a) Decreased productivity due to increased worker specialization	(b) Improved flexibility in handling varied production processes and job functions
(c) Reduced capacity for handling diverse product lines	(d) Increased need for advanced technology integration

10.7 Which of the following challenges is often associated with a functional layout?

(a) Increased material handling and movement between different functional areas	(b) Difficulty in adjusting the layout for different types of products
(c) Enhanced worker specialization and reduced training needs	(d) Reduced need for maintenance due to simpler equipment arrangements

10.8 What type of production process is most appropriate for a product layout?

(a) Job-shop production with custom orders	(b) High-volume production with standardized products
(c) Batch production with varied product types	(d) Project-based production with large, unique products

10.9 Which of the following is a common disadvantage of a product layout?

(a) Increased material handling costs due to dispersed workstations	(b) Reduced efficiency in handling large product variations
(c) Enhanced flexibility in production scheduling	(d) Simplified equipment maintenance due to similar machinery

10.10 How does a product layout typically affect the flexibility of production scheduling?

(a) It enhances flexibility by allowing easy adjustments to production schedules	(b) It has no impact on flexibility
(c) It limits flexibility due to the fixed sequence of operations for specific products	(d) It improves flexibility by enabling quick changes in production volume

10.11 What is a primary advantage of a U-shaped facility layout?

(a) Enhanced communication and coordination between workstations due to proximity	(b) Increased space utilization by maximizing floor area
(c) Reduced flexibility in handling various product types	(d) Simplified equipment maintenance due to centralized location

10.12 Which of the following best describes the type of products typically produced in a fixed-position facility layout?

(a) Small batch items	(b) Standardized mass-produced items
(c) Perishable goods	(d) Custom or large-scale products

10.13 In a combination layout, what is a typical reason for integrating both process and product layout elements?

(a) To increase the amount of available floor space.	(b) To simplify training for employees.
(c) To minimize the need for equipment maintenance.	(d) To cater to both high-volume production and customized product requirements.

10.14 What is a critical consideration when integrating multiple layout types in a combination facility layout?

(a) The ease of training employees to handle multiple layout types	(b) The ability to standardize equipment across all layout types
(c) The potential for increased operational complexity and the need for effective coordination	(d) The necessity to use only one type of layout for all processes to minimize confusion

10.15 Which of the following best describes the main feature of Muther's Grid?

(a) It plots departments on a grid to assess the importance of their proximity to each other.	(b) It provides a detailed analysis of cost per square foot of facility space
(c) It uses a flow diagram to visualize product routes through the facility	(d) It calculates the total area needed for different departments

10.16 In line balancing, what is the primary goal of achieving a balanced line?

(a) To minimize the number of workers required	(b) To ensure that each workstation has the same cycle time
(c) To maximize the throughput of the production line	(d) To reduce the total production cost

10.17 In a line balancing problem, what does the term "bottleneck" refer to?

(a) The process of eliminating redundant tasks in the production line	(b) The point in the production process where the flow of products is most constrained and limits the overall production rate
(c) The software used to simulate production line efficiency	(d) The method used to calculate the total labor cost in the production line.

10.18 How does the concept of "smoothness index" help in evaluating line balancing performance?

(a) It calculates the percentage reduction in production lead time	(b) It measures the cost-effectiveness of different workstation setups
(c) It assesses the total time required to train employees on the new production line	(d) It evaluates the degree to which work is evenly distributed across workstations, aiming to minimize idle time and imbalance

10.19 What is the primary goal of implementing a cellular layout in a manufacturing facility?

(a) To separate different types of production processes into distinct areas to avoid cross-contamination	(b) To standardize workstations and processes across the entire facility for uniformity
(c) To reduce the transportation time and handling costs by grouping machines and workstations that process similar parts or products	(d) To maximize the use of available space by creating a compact, centralized area for all operations

10.20 Which of the following best describes a situation where a cellular layout would be most beneficial?

(a) Custom manufacturing of diverse products	(b) Batch production of standardized items
(c) Continuous flow production	(d) High-volume production of a single product

10.21 In a flexible manufacturing system, which of the following components is essential for achieving flexibility?

(a) Dedicated machinery for each product	(b) Fixed workstation layouts
(c) Automated material handling systems	(d) Manual assembly processes

10.22 Which of the following industries is most likely to benefit from implementing a flexible manufacturing system?

(a) High-volume food processing	(b) Mass production of consumer electronics
(c) Standardized furniture manufacturing	(d) Custom automobile manufacturing

Answers of Multiple Choice Questions

10.1 (b), 10.2 (c), 10.3 (c), 10.4 (b), 10.5 (b), 10.6 (b), 10.7 (a), 10.8 (b), 10.9 (b), 10.10 (c), 10.11 (a), 10.12 (d), 10.13 (d), 10.14 (c), 10.15 (a), 10.16 (c), 10.17 (b), 10.18 (d), 10.19 (c), 10.20 (a), 10.21 (c), 10.22 (d)

SHORT AND LONG ANSWER TYPE QUESTIONS

Category I

10.1 What is the main goal of optimizing facility layout in operations management?

10.2 How can facility layout influence customer service in a manufacturing or service setting?

10.3 What role does workflow play in the design of a facility layout?

10.4 What is the significance of considering future expansion when designing a facility layout?

10.5 How does an optimized facility layout impact inventory costs?

10.6 How does a well-designed facility layout support flexibility and adaptability in meeting market demands?

10.7 What is the primary characteristic of a functional layout in facility design?

10.8 What is a potential drawback of using a functional layout in terms of workflow efficiency?

10.9 What is the main feature of a product layout in facility design?

10.10 How does a product layout impact inventory management?

10.11 What is a potential challenge associated with implementing a U-shaped facility layout?

10.12 What is a potential drawback of using a fixed-position layout in terms of production efficiency?

10.13 How does a combination layout address the needs of facilities with varying product types and production processes?

10.14 How does Muther's Grid help in determining the most efficient layout for a facility?

10.15 How does line balancing impact production cycle time?

10.16 What is a common method used to achieve line balancing in assembly lines?

10.17 How does cellular manufacturing support flexibility in production?

10.18 How does flexible manufacturing enhance production efficiency?

Category II

10.19 In a real-life manufacturing or service setting, how does optimizing facility layout contribute to enhancing customer service, and what are the specific ways in which improvements in layout can positively impact customer satisfaction and service quality? Discuss the various elements of facility layout optimization and also provide examples of how different industries might implement these changes to achieve better customer service outcomes.

10.20 What are the specific strategies and design elements that enable a facility to quickly adjust to changes in product types, production volumes, and customer preferences? Discuss the various ways in which different industries implement these strategies to enhance their ability to respond to dynamic market conditions. Provide examples of how a flexible facility layout can help companies remain competitive and efficiently meet evolving market demands.

10.21 In a real-life manufacturing or service setting, how do different types of facility layout designs affect operational efficiency, production flexibility, and overall effectiveness? Discuss the specific advantages and disadvantages of each layout type, and provide examples of how different industries implement these layouts to optimize their operations. Explain how choosing the right layout can impact a company's ability to meet customer expectations and remain competitive in the market.

10.22 In the context of flexible manufacturing systems (FMS), how does the facility layout contribute to operational flexibility and efficiency, and what are the key design considerations for implementing an effective FMS layout? Provide real-life examples of industries or companies that have successfully implemented FMS layouts to enhance their production capabilities and responsiveness to market demands. Highlight the specific benefits and challenges associated with these implementations, and explain how the facility layout supports the overall goals of flexibility and efficiency in a dynamic manufacturing environment.

NUMERICAL PROBLEMS

10.1 Pensioners' advisory department (A), pensioners' responsibility scheduling department (B), pensioners' employment calculation department (C), and pensioners' complaints department (D) are the four departments that make up a government treasury office. Each department is assigned a certain responsibility. The office is twenty feet broad and eighty feet long. Each 20-by-20-foot chamber is constructed. Departments A, B, C, and D are currently located in a straight line. The number of interactions that each advisor in one department has with advisors in another department is displayed in the load summary. Assume that this value is the same for each advisor:

Load summary: AB = 10, AC = 20, AD = 30, BC = 15, BD = 10, CD = 20.

(a) Apply the material handling cost approach to this layout's evaluation.

(b) Reorganize the arrangement by switching roles within departments. Use the same approach as in (a) to demonstrate how much you have improved.

10.2 The following jobs need to be completed according to sequence and within the allotted time on an assembly line.

Task	Task time (seconds)	Task that must precede
A	50	–
B	40	–
C	20	A
D	45	C
E	20	C
F	25	D
G	10	E
H	35	B, F, G

(a) Draw the schematic diagram.

(b) In order to meet the estimated demand of 400 units each 8-hour day, what is the theoretical minimum number of stations required?

(c) In order to generate 400 units each day, balance the line in the bare minimum of stations using the longest task time criteria.

10.3 Create a 2 × 3 grid arrangement that meets the following requirements.

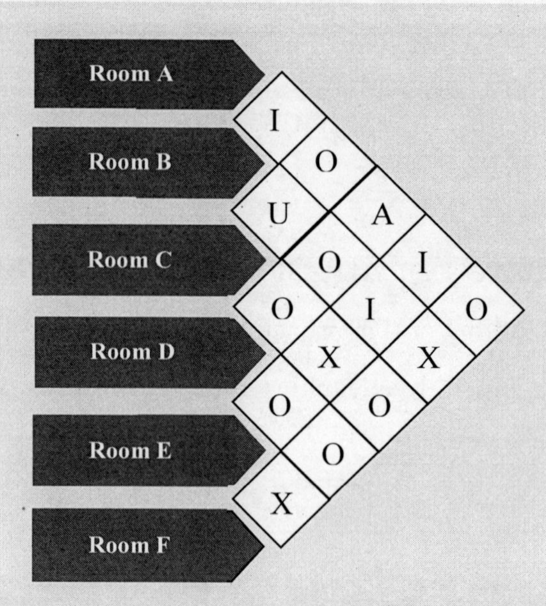

10.4 The manufacturing company AccuComp was engaged in a new project aimed at producing commercial drones. To assist them in choosing the most efficient manufacturing method to satisfy the anticipated demand for this new product, they engaged the services of a production consultant. It was suggested by the consultant that they employ an assembly line. In order to fulfill the anticipated demand, he informed the manufacturing engineers that the line needed to be able to produce 600 drones every day. Eight hours a day are worked by the plant's employees. Below is the task information for the new commercial drone.

TASK	TASK TIME (SECONDS)	TASKS THAT MUST PRECEDE
A	28	–
B	13	–
C	35	B
D	11	A
E	20	C
F	6	D, E
G	23	F
H	25	F
I	37	G
J	11	G, H
K	27	I, J
Total	236	

(a) Draw the schematic layout.

(b) Based on an eight-hour workday, what is the necessary cycle time to meet the estimated demand of 600 commercial drones per day?

(c) Given the response in item (b), what is the theoretically minimal number of workstations?

(d) To break ties and create 600 drones a day, use the longest task time in alphabetical order and balance the line in the bare minimum of stations.

(e) To generate 600 trucks every day, balance the line in the fewest number of stations and use the shortest task time and the greatest number of subsequent tasks as the tiebreaker.

10.5 PrecisionSemiCon Company began as a semi conductor production company and has expanded into a full-service factory with the ability to handle a variety of tasks, including printed circuit board manufacturing, scanning, soldering, testing, and basic semiconductor assembly. The company wants to set up its sixteen processes in a way that is both flexible and efficient since it is moving to a new facility. The process manual chart below lists the most common jobs along with the corresponding processes. Divide the processes into cells to guarantee a flexible and effective operation.

	Processes															
Jobs	1	2	3	4	5	6	7	8	9	10	11	12	13	14	15	16
A	X	X										X				
B						X		X								
C	X						X							X		
D	X	X					X							X		
E				X		X										
F						X		X			X					
G	X	X										X				
H					X					X					X	
I	X	X	X											X		
J						X					X					
K										X					X	X
L				X		X					X			X		
M		X							X			X				
N										X					X	X
O					X					X					X	X
P				X		X					X					
Q								X								

REFERENCES AND SUGGESTED READINGS

1. Askin, R. G., and Huo, J. Facility layout design: A review. *International Journal of Production Research*, Vol. 39(1), 1-22, 2001.
2. Browning, T. R., and Heath, R. A. Reevaluating the performance of layout types in manufacturing facilities. *International Journal of Production Research*, Vol. 47(8), 2277-2293, 2009.
3. Burbidge, J. L., Production Flow Analysis, *Production Engineer*, Vol. 41, 742, 1963.
4. Chung, W. W., and Lee, H. H. A study of flexible manufacturing systems and their integration with facility layout. *International Journal of Advanced Manufacturing Technology*, Vol. 20(3), 164-170, 2002.
5. Francis, R. L., and White, J. A. The influence of process and product layouts on overall plant performance. *International Journal of Operations & Production Management*, Vol. 27(8), 1091-1109, 2007.
6. Gupta, A., and Jain, A. Facility layout design for small-scale manufacturing: A case study. *International Journal of Advanced Manufacturing Technology*, Vol. 74(5-8), 811-822, 2014.
7. Heizer, J., and Render, B. *Operations Management*, 12th Edition, Pearson, 2017.
8. Krajewski, L. J., and Ritzman, L. P. *Operations Management: Processes and Supply Chains*, 10th Edition, Pearson, 2012.
9. Meller, R. D., and Gau, K. Y. A review of the state of the art in facility layout. *European Journal of Operational Research*, Vol. 98(1), 3-18, 1996.
10. Muther, R. *Systematic Layout Planning*, 2nd Edition, PWS Publishing Company, 1984.
11. Reid, R. D., and Sanders, N. R. *Operations Management: An Integrated Approach*, 7th Edition, Wiley, 2019.
12. Sarin, S. C., and Huo, J. Designing cellular manufacturing systems: A review of methodology and future research. *Journal of Manufacturing Systems*, Vol. 33(4), 648-660, 2014.
13. Slack, N., Chambers, S., and Johnston, R. *Operations Management*, 6th Edition, Pearson Education, 2010.
14. Tay, W. M., and Goh, M. Designing process layouts: Approaches and techniques for minimizing transportation costs. *International Journal of Production Economics*, Vol. 93(1), 85-99, 2005.
15. Tompkins, J. A., White, J. M., Bozer, Y. A., and Tanchoco, J. M. A. *Facilities Planning*, 4th Edition, Wiley, 2020.
16. Vakharia, A. J., and Shapiro, M. A. Survey of the line balancing techniques in product layout design. *International Journal of Production Research*, Vol. 38(1), 43-64, 2000.

UNIT **11**

MATERIAL HANDLING

UNIT SPECIFICS

This unit elaborately discusses the following topics:

- Objectives of material handling
- Principles of material handling
- Selection of material handling equipment
- Types of material handling equipment (Pallets, Conveyors, Cranes and hoists)
- Relationship between plant layout and material handling
- Automated guided vehicles and its types

The topics' contemporary, real-world applications encourage greater creativity and curiosity. In addition to a number of multiple-choice questions and questions with both short and long answer types, the unit also includes a list of references, suggested readings, and assignments that are divided into two groups according to the lower and higher order of Bloom's taxonomy. These can be completed as practice. An additional part ("Along the...") has been added after the unit's related topic, per the content. The book's reader was the primary focus of its meticulous creation. One notable aspect is the utilization of QR codes, which can be scanned to yield pertinent supplementary data on a variety of interesting topics.

RATIONALE

This unit addresses the vital objectives of material handling, emphasizing its role in optimizing efficiency, reducing costs, and ensuring safety in operations. We will explore key principles of material handling, which guide the selection and utilization of appropriate equipment to streamline processes. A detailed examination of various types of material handling equipment – such as pallets, conveyors, cranes, and hoists – will highlight their specific functions and applications. Additionally, the unit will discuss the critical relationship between plant layout and material handling, demonstrating how strategic layout decisions can enhance material flow. Finally, we will delve into automated guided vehicles (AGVs) and their types, showcasing their significance in modern material handling systems and their potential to improve operational efficiency.

UNIT OUTCOMES

List of outcomes of this unit is as follows:

U11-UO1: Comprehend Material Handling Objectives

U11-UO2: Understand Principles of Material Handling

U11-UO3: Select Appropriate Material Handling Equipment

U11-UO4: Differentiate Types of Material Handling Equipment

U11-UO5: Analyze Plant Layout and Material Handling Relationships

U11-UO6: Explore Automated Guided Vehicles (AGVs)

UNIT-11 Outcomes	EXPECTED MAPPING WITH COURSE OUTCOMES (*1-Weak Correlation; 2-Medium Correlation; 3-Strong Correlation*)					
	CO-1	**CO-2**	**CO-3**	**CO-4**	**CO-5**	**CO-6**
U11-UO1	2	2	3	2	3	2
U11-UO2	2	2	3	3	3	2
U11-UO3	2	2	3	3	3	2
U11-UO4	2	1	2	2	2	2
U11-UO5	3	2	3	3	2	2
U11-UO6	2	2	2	3	3	2

11.1 INTRODUCTION

Material, labor, or machinery – the three fundamental components of production – must all move in order to transform raw materials into completed goods. Material handling is an important area of concern for the majority of industrial processes. The causes of this are as follows:

1. Over 90% of the time that material is on the shop floor, it is either being transported or left in waiting. This activity doesn't add any value. Material handling takes up close to 20 – 30% of this non-value-added time on average. Thus, some of this non-value-added time will be saved through effective processing.
2. In order to reduce congestion, ensure on-time delivery, and minimize machine idle time caused by material shortages, efficient material handling is essential.
3. Economical material handling is a crucial concern. Material movement typically makes up 10 to 90% of the entire production cost, which is, on average, estimated to be around 25%. As such, a thorough examination of substitute means of material transportation is crucial.
4. Improved material handling aids in maintaining proper housekeeping. This lessens scraps, loss, breakage, and waste.

Material handling is required throughout the manufacturing system's supply chain. Sub-assemblies or raw materials are sent from the supplier to the plant's in-coming store. Subcontractors occasionally provide semi-finished goods. Road, rail, or ship transportation is required for this. Transporting raw materials or semi-finished goods to the different machinery happens at the plant level. Not only can material move down the floor, but it can also move vertically, that is, against or along a garvity.

"*Moving, packing, and sorting materials in any form using gravity, human labor, or machinery with power is the art and science of this process.*"

– American Materials Handling Society

11.2 OBJECTIVES OF MATERIAL HANDLING

1. Cut down on material handling expenses.

2. Reduce the amount of delays and disruptions by having the supplies available at the point of use in the appropriate quantity and at the appropriate time.
3. Improve productivity and make efficient use of available capacity to raise the production facilities' productive capability.
4. Material handling safety through enhanced operational conditions.
5. Making the most of material handling machinery.
6. Preventing material damage.
7. Less money spent on inventory used in processes.

11.3 PRINCIPLES OF MATERIAL HANDLING

Material management is governed by a few guiding principles. These are:

1. Minimize wasteful movement – This requires choosing the quickest route to get to the goal.
2. Minimize congestion and bottlenecks – This call for removing obstacles and bottlenecks in the material handling process.
3. Layout of a scientific factory – In doing so, fewer trips will be made, overall material movement will be minimized, and transportation expenses will be lowered.
4. Utilizing conventional material handling machinery – This makes it easier to maintain material handling equipment because replacement parts are easily obtained.
5. Schedule a minimal amount of loading and unloading – This lessens the possibility of breaking. It also saves money and time when loading and unloading.
6. To move material as far as possible, use gravity.
7. Make use of automated material handling machinery – Dependency on human labor is decreased as a result.
8. Employ basic, secure equipment when handling materials – Operator security ought to come first. Material handling equipment may include a bell or sound and a blinking light attached to alert surrounding workers.
9. Material handling equipment should never be loaded above its designed capacity.
10. The unit size load concept ought to be utilized. Aggregating material into a longer unit, container, or pallet of a standard size accomplishes this.

11. Instead of using zigzag flow and/or backtracking, which takes longer and creates more congestion, apply the concept of straight line flow.
12. It is best to carry the load in both directions. This implies that some stuff might be picked up and delivered to both the origin and an intermediate location while returning.
13. In order to ensure that the material position during unloading meets the requirements of the destination point, the part orientation principle should be used. Parts should be orientated to accommodate the most material with the least amount of damage during transit as well.
14. The material handling system should be integrated with other facilities, including receiving, assembly, packing, inspection, and storage, by using system principles.
15. When more efficient handling techniques or equipment can enhance performance, replace antiquated procedures and/or equipment.
16. Assign all handling equipment to routine maintenance or repair.
17. Using cost per unit handled as the key criterion; ascertain the handling performance's efficiency.

11.4 SELECTION OF MATERIAL HANDLING EQUIPMENT

The selection of material handling is crucial since it affects the handling system's efficiency and cost. Considerations for choosing material handling equipment include the following:

1. **Characteristic of the operations**
   - If handling is temporary or ongoing.
   - If there are random or continuous flows.
   - The direction of material flow: horizontal or vertical.
   - Layout type, such as combination, process, or product layouts.
2. **Materials to be managed**
   - The material's dimensions and form.
   - Material weight and quantity.
   - Material properties.
   - Material susceptibility to damage during handling.

3. **The material's intended movement distance**
    - Work station.
    - Long distance.
    - Fixed distance.
4. **Costs associated with installation and operation**
    - The initial outlay
    - Costs associated with operation and upkeep.
5. **Facilities for plants**
    - Building types
    - Floor load capacity.
6. **Engineering elements**
    - Dimensions of doors and ceilings.
    - Traffic safety.
    - Floor conditions and structural strength.
7. **Reliability of the equipment**
    - Using parts that are standard.
    - Service providers.
    - The reliability of the supplier.
8. **Safety considerations**
    - Policies pertaining to material handling and health and safety must be addressed.
    - It is important to address some hazards, such as mismaintained lifting apparatuses, broken racking and storage units, collisions with moving machinery, etc.

11.5 TYPES OF MATERIAL HANDLING EQUIPMENT

The following factors are used to categorize material handling equipment:

i. Service types needed – lifting, moving, stacking, and positioning.
ii. The equipment's relative mobility – its ability to move across large distances and between stationary locations. There are fixed path equipments such as: elevator, conveyors, chutes, automated guided vehicles (AGVs), etc.
iii. Equipment movement – Underground, above ground, on the floor, etc.

11.5.1 PALLETS

Pallets are used as bases for assembling loads of material. Forklifts can be used to raise pallets, which are specifically made platforms. Because of several factors, pallets are now considered essential in the material handling industry. The following are some benefits of using pallets.

1. Pallets offer a standardized and practical way to organize and move items, which can simplify operations and improve overall productivity.
2. Pallets are adaptable platforms that maximize storage space by permitting product stacking, which also makes it possible for forklifts and other material handling equipment to move many things at once. This efficiency guarantees seamless handling along the whole supply chain and reduces damage.
3. Pallet sizes that are standard allow material handling operations to become more organized, which decreases the amount of time spent on manual handling, lowers the possibility of product damage, and boosts output.
4. The usage of pallets transformed the way warehouses function. Prior to its creation, products were usually kept in boxes, crates, or barrels, which made handling and organizing them challenging.
5. Pallets made inventory turnover more quickly, improved accessibility, and enhanced organization possible. Pallets offer a uniform unit for counting and tracking things, which further streamlines inventory management.
6. Palletized warehouses make it simple to load, unload, and rearrange merchandise, guaranteeing that it is always ready for shipping and cutting down on critical downtime.
7. For cost-effectiveness in the storage and warehousing industry, space optimization is essential. Pallets make effective use of vertical space by stacking, allowing warehouse capacity to be maximized by erecting racks in accordance with available horizontal and vertical space.
8. Pallets have become the main component of contemporary supply networks because of their consistent size and shape. Palletization makes it possible to stack and load cargo into trucks, airplanes, and containers quickly and efficiently while maintaining cargo security and expediting transportation.
9. Palletized loads save time during shipping and distribution since they are simpler to handle and stack. Faster turnaround times, lower shipping costs, and a lower chance

of product damage are the outcomes of this optimized procedure. Fig. 11.1 shows the palletized pallet patterns.

10. Additionally, pallets have improved sustainability initiatives. A lot of pallets are made to last, providing a sturdy option that is reusable several times. Pallet recycling and reuse also contributes to a circular economy by reducing waste.

Fig. 11.1 Palletized pallet patterns

Source: https://verbruggen-palletizing.com/about-us/news-blogs/what-is-a-palletizing-pallet-pattern-chart/

11.5.2 CONVEYORS

For the automatic movement of goods and materials inside a space, a conveyor system is a quick and effective mechanical handling device. In addition to other advantages, this technique lessens labor expenses, workplace hazards, and human error. Moving big or heavy objects from one place to another is made easier with their assistance. Time is saved while moving goods from one place to another with conveyor systems. They facilitate the easier process of moving objects up and down floors, which can be inclined to span numerous levels. Manually performing this task by hand can be physically taxing for humans.

When choosing the best conveyor system for your distribution or storage operation, there are a number of things to take into account. You should think about the needs for the process and the product at the same time. A perfect conveyor system should be:

- Safe to operate
- Energy-efficient
- Dependable (with long-lasting parts and components)
- Flexible enough to accommodate evolving requirements
- Economical

The operational effectiveness of a warehouse will be swiftly compromised by installing the incorrect conveyor system, which will increase costs and decrease customer satisfaction before finally depriving the company of its competitive edge.

Product requirements for selecting a conveyor system

The design, size, and kind of conveyor system to be built are often determined by the kind of item(s) to be moved. The answers to the following questions can help you determine design and configuration requirements and assist in calculating things like horsepower and belt draw for specific conveyors when you're looking for the ideal conveyor system for your facility:

1. What kind of goods is being transported?
2. How much weight does a product typically weigh per foot?
3. What is the items' maximum weight?
4. What are the product's length, width, and height, that is, its lowest, maximum, and average dimensions?
5. What are each product's dimensions data?
6. In what direction and how are the products being conveyed?

Process requirements for selecting a conveyor system

Process requirements address the particulars of the operational environment as well as the parameters controlling the conveyor's movement. Among these factors are:

1. The length of time that goods must travel between functional regions.
2. Is there a path it follows that has bends, diversions, elevation changes, or stops?
3. Product orientation – Do things need to be arranged a specific way (to facilitate barcode reading, transfer, etc.)?

4. Transfer speed – Is it better to go quickly or slowly?
5. The surrounding atmosphere.
6. Available area

Flow rate requirements for selecting a conveyor system

The average transfer rate at your facility as well as times when demand is at its highest because of seasonal variations should be supported by the conveyor system. Conveyor length and speed depend on how many products you need to move in an hour or minute. Additionally, some conveyor types work best with particular products. For moving plastic-footed pallets, a huge plastic chain conveyor works well; for moving wooden pallets, a chain-driven roller conveyor works best.

11.5.2.1 TYPES OF CONVEYORS

Modular belt conveyor

A modular belt conveyor is a flexible system with one or more belts that is driven by sprockets. These belts follow a straight path and can be made to any length or width to meet the needs of a variety of industries.

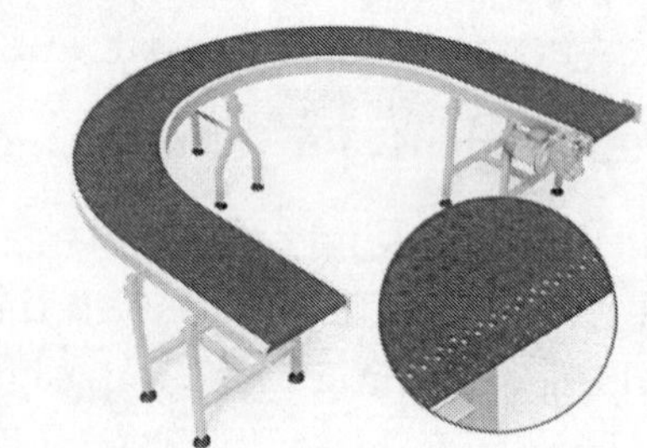

1. **Telescopic belt conveyor**

With their extendable lengths, telescopic belt conveyors enable safe and effective loading and unloading. They work in the post, home appliance, food, tobacco, and light manufacturing industries, as well as logistics, ports, stations, airports, and warehouses.

Straight belt conveyor The straight belt conveyor is a crucial transition piece in the conveying process and is composed of a flat PVC/PVK belt. It can handle many different types of bulk goods as well as single-piece items like cartons and packaging bags,

particularly the lighter ones.

2. Curve belt conveyor

The curve belt conveyor, which is made of flat PVC/PU/PVK material, is essential for enabling turns in the conveying line. With the ability to perform turns at 45°, 90°, 180°, or to your own degree, it is widely used in the printing, express, food, tobacco, and logistics industries.

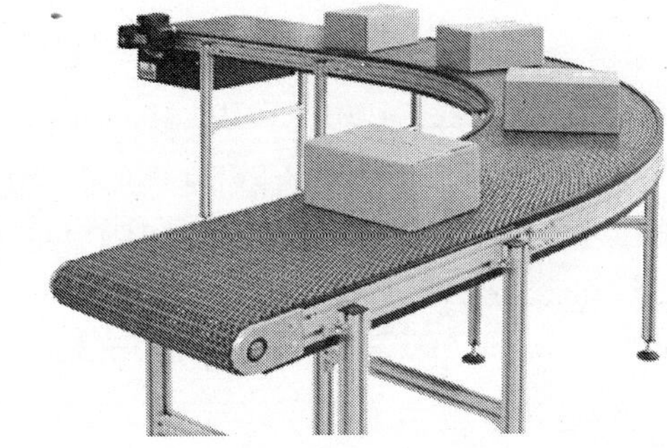

3. Flexible roller conveyor

The production, distribution, and warehousing industries are revolutionized by flexible roller conveyors. Operational efficiency is improved by its flexibility in accommodating curved routes and changes in the structure of production lines. Because of its large load capacity, this conveyor increases productivity by reducing the need for manual handling.

4. Straight roller conveyor

The straight roller conveyor smoothly moves goods over curved routes by using cone rollers as carriers. Offering both single- and double-chain drive options, it is a crucial transitional element in the entire conveying process. Its uses are widespread in the printing, tobacco, tire, and

logistics sectors.

5. Curve roller conveyor

Similar to its straight version, the curve roller conveyor uses cone rollers to move products around curves. With fully adjustable turning angles of 45°, 90°, 180°, or other bespoke degrees, it provides a smooth transition between turning portions of the conveying line. For effective material handling, this conveyor is essential to the printing, express, tobacco, and logistics industries.

6. Flexible chain conveyor

Flexible chain conveyors provide a range of product moving options due to their variable widths. They serve a wide range of applications, including (i) material flow along production lines, particularly in industries with changing production needs; (ii) suitable for tasks like moving ingredients, processing products, and packaging operations in food and beverage processing plants; and (iii) conveying pharmaceutical products, medical devices, and equipment in production and distribution facilities. They are capable of conveying products horizontally, around corners, on inclines, declines, and even vertically.

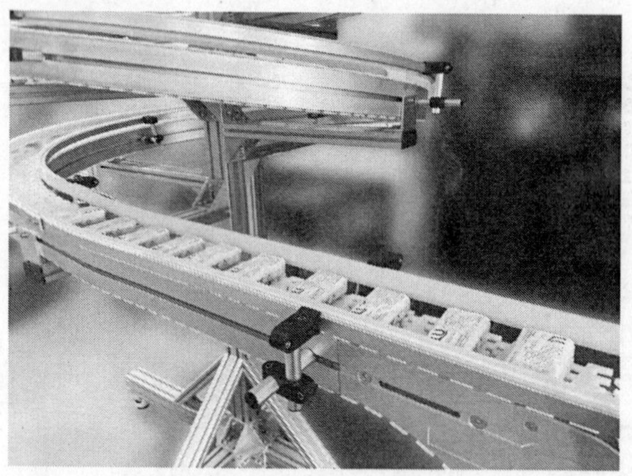

11.5.3 CRANES AND HOISTS

Cranes and hoists are examples of material handling equipment that is commonly utilized. Compared to loads carried by conveyors, loads handled by cranes typically have greater shape and weight variability. Cranes are usually equipped with hoists that are used to raise, lower, and move loads or goods. The following are general characteristics of hoists and cranes:

1. Material management loads are moved both vertically and horizontally within the covered area of the material handling equipment using cranes and hoists.
2. Compared to conveyors, material handling cranes and hoists provide more mobility.
3. Conveyors are unable to carry loads of different forms and weights; material handling cranes and hoists can.
4. There are several ways to operate a crane and hoist using a remote control, the driver's cabin, a suspension panel, or a combination of these.
5. Cost of floor space – The quantity of floor space needed varies depending on the type of crane and hoist.
6. Lifting height – High, adaptable to certain requirements.
7. Load capacity – Adaptable to specific load needs.
8. Intermittently moving different loads within the cranes' and hoists' rated capacities to any location within their coverage areas.

Overhead Cranes

Four fundamental configurations of material handling overhead cranes are available to accommodate almost any kind of lifting requirement in your establishment:

1. A bridge girder and two end trucks combine to form a **single girder**. Since they are less expensive, simpler and faster to build, and function in a safe and convenient manner, single girder cranes are perfect for light duty and moderate service.

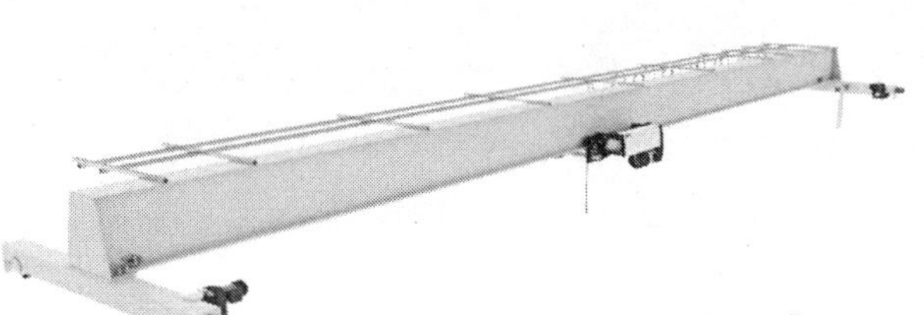

2. Two bridge girders and two end trucks make up a **double girder bridge**. The best crane for heavy-duty applications is a two-girder crane. It is more durable and efficient than a single-girder overhead crane.

3. **Top running crane** is the most widely used crane system. A top running crane has the capacity to lift several hundred tons due to its greater span and higher lifting height.

4. An **underhung crane** is one that is suspended from the ceiling or roof of a building. The overhead material handling crane maximizes the width and height of the structure and offers a great side approach.

Gantry Cranes

One of the most widely used overhead traveling cranes is the gantry crane. Freestanding Goliath gantry structures come in full or semi-gantry designs, with single or double girder crane configurations for indoor and outdoor material handling. Gantry crane specifications range from 500 kg to 320 tons, with models including 2 ton, 3 ton, 5 ton, and 6 ton gantry cranes. Following pictures show some of the common gantry cranes.

Single girder gantry crane

Portable gantry crane

Double girder gantry crane

Semi gantry crane

Jib Cranes

When it comes to short-distance transfers, Jib cranes are the best lifting apparatus. Jib cranes come in different varieties for material handling, such as wall mounted, pillar, and wall travelling cranes. movement of materials A large overhead crane system can be supplemented, materials can be transferred from one work cell to another, a line load can be safely lifted up to its rated capacity, and jib cranes can lift and transport materials in semicircles or full circles around their support structures. Following pictures show some of the commonly used Jib cranes.

Free standing pillar Jib crane

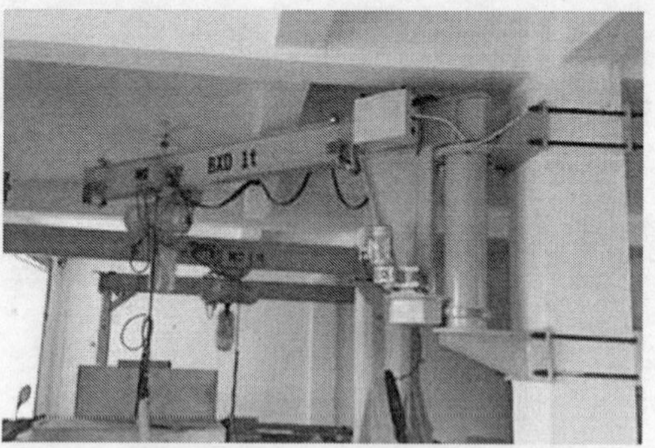

Wall mounted Jib crane

Wall travelling Jib crane

Portable Jib crane

11.6 RELATIONSHIP BETWEEN PLANT LAYOUT AND MATERIAL HANDLING

Material management and plant layout are closely related to one another. Minimal material handling and no rehandling are guaranteed by a well-designed layout.

1. Although it cannot be completely avoided, material handling should be kept to a minimum because it adds no value to the product. The methodical plant layout is the only thing that makes this feasible. An effective layout hence reduces handling.
2. If workers need to travel a great distance to obtain materials, tools, etc., their productive time will be lost. In order to maximize production time and reduce searching and travel time, a well-designed layout guarantees that workers make the fewest possible trips.
3. Space is a crucial factor. A well-designed layout that incorporates a material handling system allows for the integration of all human and material movements throughout the plant.

4. An effective plant layout makes material handling shorter, faster, and more cost-effective. A well-designed layout ensures manufacturing effectiveness by minimizing material backtracking and needless worker movement.

Material handling in Product type layout

Gravity chutes can be used effectively in this type of layout where the nature of the product permits it. Material handling techniques and machines, like the layout itself, tend to be special purpose in nature. This type of layout requires some direct means of transportation between various operations.

Commercial conveyors are available in a wide range of sizes, shapes, and weights to suit various uses. These conveyors might be a good fit for the product kind of layout. While the material is moving, a number of operations, including cleaning, painting, drying, and weighing in the case of some liquid materials, may occur. It is frequently worthwhile to develop specialized handling equipment that is so fully integrated with processing that the entire line functions as a single integrated machine due to the particular purpose nature of product layout design.

Material handling in Functional layout

Flexibility is a fundamental prerequisite for material handling techniques utilized in functional layouts, including flexibility in terms of load size, weight, and shape as well as flexibility in course. Material handling equipment that meets this criteria includes, but is not limited to, mobile trucks, tractors, trains, forklifts, lifts, trucks, and cranes. The time it takes to pick up or set down a load is a crucial feature of an effective material handling device. As a result, pallets and skids have become solution to rapid pickup systems. When the worker completes his operation on the part, he can immediately load the material onto a pallet or skid.

A skid truck, fork lift truck, or pallet truck can swiftly pick up the full items and transport it to its destination without the need for additional handling. Therefore, making sure that all processes are easily accessible by effective material handling equipment is a crucial factor to take into account while establishing the layout's details. At the work stations, additional cranes are frequently required to move big tasks to and from the equipment. Large, heavy jobs are moved and positioned within of a fixed space using overhead cranes.

11.7 AUTOMATED GUIDED VEHICLES (AGVs)

Automatic guided vehicles, or AGVs, are computerized vehicles that employ software to guide them in terms of location, movement, and positioning. With the use of an electric motor or battery, they may carry out various tasks like loading, warehousing, and manufacturing without the need for human intervention. Self-powered AGVs can carry out tasks that were formerly undertaken by people, including as load transfers, pallet movement and stacking, assembly completion, and towing heavy loads. They have increased production productivity, kept people out of potentially hazardous situations, and prevented human error.

Even though the name "automated guided vehicle," or "AGV," might sound self-explanatory, there are really a number of ways that AGVs get their programming and instructions. These methods include technology such as radio waves, lasers, cameras, wires embedded in the floor, and other forms of technology. AGVs were first used to tow trailers in order to increase production speed. They were seen as pleasant extras that saved time at the time. AGV technology offers a wide range of capabilities, purposes, and functions as a result of designers' exploration of additional methods to employ the technology to enhance manufacturing conditions in the later half of the 20th century.

11.7.1 FEATURES OF AGV

AGV systems have following important features:

1. The automated storage and retrieval system (AS/RS), CNC machines, robots, and other flexible manufacturing system (FMS) modules can all be readily interfaced with an AGV system. It is a crucial component of the FMS system, without which efficient material handling could not be possible.
2. The AGV system provides a great deal of flexibility since it can adjust to changes in both production and product.
3. An AGV system provides a manufacturing system with a great deal of expansion flexibility. Depending on the situation, the number of vehicles or the area that the AGV will cover can be readily changed.
4. Computer integrated manufacturing systems (CIMS) are well adapted to the AGV material handling system. The AGV's on-board controller is to blame for this. The on-board controller can communicate with other CIMS modules via a host computer.

It is simple to establish information links between material handling systems and other production processes.

5. Productivity gains and production system efficiency optimization are made possible by the integrated material handling system.
6. Thc AGV system offers less transit damage and the elimination or reduction of labor.
7. The AGV system can adapt to changes in product routing or fluctuation in the manufacturing rate.
8. In contrast to traditional material handling systems, it can easily adjust to modifications in product design and machine layout without requiring significant capital expenditure.
9. It can move materials with low to medium volume unit loads across a sizable amount of the factory without any issues.
10. The AGV system gives more flexibility in terms of plant layout planning than a dedicated conveying system. This is because the AGV moves easily along the guidance path in both directions (forward and backward).
11. The AGV system requires little maintenance. When one AGV breaks down, another can be added to the same route and the broken AGV can be moved into the parking lot for maintenance or repair.
12. The AGV system has minimal noise and disruption levels.
13. The absence of labor is a major factor in operational safety.
14. The factory information system's successful adoption could be aided by an AGV system. Relevant data about inventory control, production, administration, procurement, and shipment is generated by the AGV system. Such data must be integrated into the industrial information system.
15. The study that is contributing to the creation of green production systems has received more attention lately. In this system, the AGV might serve as a supporting component. For each procedure, an AGV may transport the jobs to a closed space, which could be uncomfortable for the environment.

11.7.2 TYPES OF AGV SYSTEM

AGV systems provide movement options throughout warehouses and buildings using industrial batteries or power. The majority of industries, including greenhouses, general manufacturing, plastics and metal, newspapers and mail, automotive, aerospace, food and beverage processing, and packaging, can employ these solutions for material handling, transportation, assembly, delivery, and storage.

These systems can be used with free range systems or fixed guidance systems. In order to direct vehicle that react to antennae, signal emissions, and frequencies on straightforward pathways, fixed guiding uses magnetic tape, colored paint, or implanted wiring. While fixed guiding systems are dependable and efficient, they are not always appropriate for all situations and applications. Additionally, their rigidity restricts the capabilities of AGVs. Thankfully, most automated guided vehicles are not constrained by stationary guidance systems. Rather, free range is used by the majority of modern AGV systems. Supervisory control systems and onboard microprocessors enable computer control of free range systems. Without restriction AGV systems, which are managed by computer software and have global navigation capabilities, can modify a vehicle's route in response to traffic patterns and potential obstacles, making the factory floor a safer place to work. These characteristics of AGVs are summarized in brief as follows.

The kind of computerized navigation that an AGV system uses is one of the most important factors to take into account. The type of navigation system used depends on the specific requirements of each industry and user when implementing AGVs. Generally speaking, the guidance system chooses the AGV's path and operations. The quality of the system and how it is installed have a significant impact on the AGV's performance. The guidance systems used by manufacturers for AGV vehicles are very diverse. These include magnetic navigation, LiDAR navigation, magnetic spot navigation, wired navigation, optical navigation, vision navigation, and laser guided navigation (LGV). They differ based on whether they are free ranging or fixed path. Every variety has advantages and is made for a certain use.

1. **LGV – Laser Navigation**

A laser positioning device installed on the roof of the car is used by the LGV system. It is guided by targets in its workspace. Targets receive laser signals from the navigation system, and the targets return signals to the AGV navigation device. The AGV has to detect three targets in order to determine its position. There are adjustments every 30 to 40 seconds. In comparison to industry norms, LGVs are very precise and simple to install.

SCAN ME
for
Laser Guided Vehicle

2. **Magnetic Tape**

Magnetic tape AGVs have magnetic sensors installed, and they adhere to a well-defined route delineated by magnetic tape. Line modifications can be accommodated for in the tape induction system. In order to ensure that the AGV is always centered on the tape, the sensor gauges the distance from the tape's center and transmits the data to the controller, which modifies the steering and course.

for
Magnetic tape guided vehicle

3. LiDAR Navigation

LiDAR (Light Detection and Ranging) navigation is sometimes called natural navigation. Various sensors, including lidar, cameras, and lasers, are employed in this system to map the surroundings for security reasons. To help the AGV define and calculate its position, all of the data is integrated with an internal inertial measurement unit (IMU). SLAM, or simultaneous localization and mapping, is a sophisticated algorithm that performs a variety of calculations.

for
LiDAR Navigation

4. Wire guided AGVs

In order to guide the tug, Mr. Barrett strung a wire from the ceiling when he created the first AGV. He moved the wire from the ceiling to the floor and reinserted it as he worked on his gadget. Some manufacturers continue to employ his original wire design despite the advancements in technology. A wire guide has only to be buried approximately an inch into the ground. It sends signals to the AGV so that it can use its location to control steering. As depicted in Fig. 11.2, the working aisle is divided by a small groove of 1/8″ width and 3/8″ depth. An LDU (line driver unit), is a device that generates signals by passing a frequency across wires. Due to its tuning to this frequency, the vehicle guidance system is able to recognize the guiding path and drive the car automatically. Nothing needs to be changed about the rack or floor. An inductive guide-path is followed by these AGVs. Floor embedded wires are grouped into closed loops and are designed to convey alternating current. The AGV's guidance path is established by these loops. Every closed loop transports low voltage, low amperage current at various frequencies. Every loop uses AC current up to a frequency range of 15 kHz.

Fig. 11.2 Working of wire guided vehicle

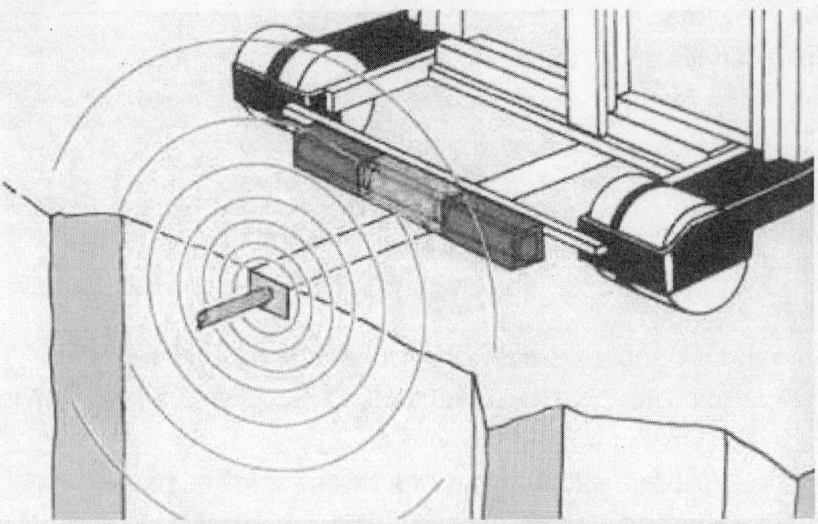

Source: http://www.pmh-co.com/EKweb/PMH%20Guideance/B_guidance9.html

5. AGVs having optical navigation

On their guide-path, these AGVs make use of an optical magnetic material strip. The car's proximity sensor is able to identify it. For instance, when ultra-voilet rays from the AGV strike the chemical guide-way, the path becomes energized. They then re-emit waves that are visible. As a result, the beams' contrast ratio is enhanced. The contrast ratio is interpreted to determine the guide path's location and the direction of the vehicle.

6. Dead Reckoning AGVs

These AGVs store distance tables for stations, speed, steering information, and acceleration/deceleration data in memory within their on-board microcomputer. Odometry serves as its foundation. At first, the AGV's current location in relation to the fixed positions in the surrounding reference plane is known. The vehicle's next position is determined by precisely tracking the rotation and velocity of each driving wheel. Dead reckoning offered the greatest benefit in that it removed the requirement for cut radius turns at intersections. The cars could break free from the wire, revolve in a predetermined circle, and then re-attach themselves to the wire to resume their journey. Installation was much simplified, but the path still needed several wires in the floor. The primary benefit of dead reckoning was that it removed the requirement for cut radius turns at intersections.

7. Free ranging AGVs

The free ranging AGV does not adhere to a physical guide path like the wire-guided AGV does. The following methods can be employed with the help of the free-ranging AGV:

Position reference beacons: The AGV controller is aware of the factory positions of certain beacons in this system. The precise distance and direction of the AGV in relation to beacons are measured by on-board equipment. The position of the AGV (Fig. 11.3) is determined using this data.

Fig. 11.3 AGV with collimated beam

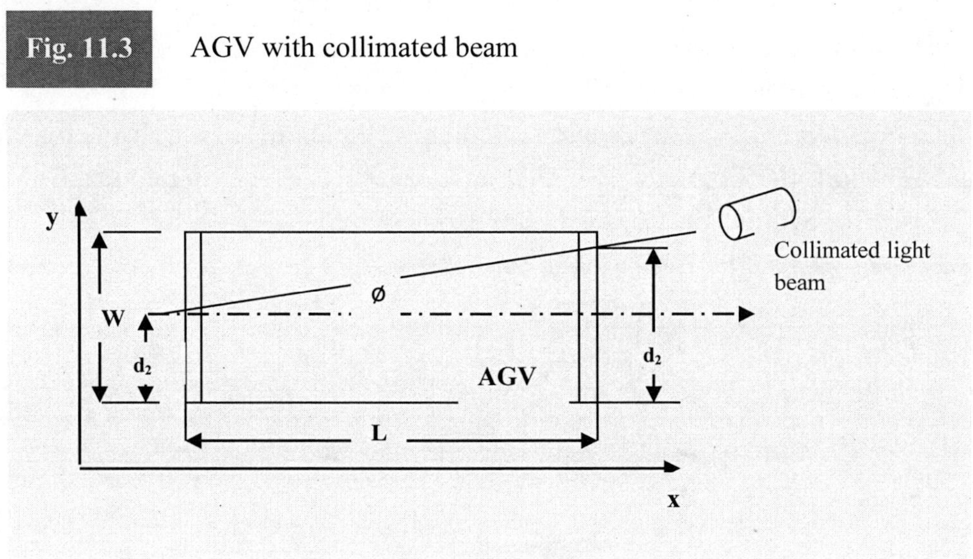

By scanning the provided QR code, the reader can learn more about smart automated vehicles for manufacturing in the context of Industry 4.0.

SCAN ME
for
Smart Automated Vehicle in Industry 4.0

UNIT SUMMARY

- ***Objectives of Material Handling*** – Includes cost reduction, minimizing delays, improving productivity, enhancing safety, and preventing material damage.
- ***Principles of Material Handling*** – Covers minimizing wasteful movement, congestion, and handling steps, using gravity and automation for efficiency.
- ***Selection of Material Handling Equipment*** – Considers operation type, material characteristics, cost, safety, and reliability.
- ***Types of Material Handling Equipment***: (i) Pallets – Standardized platforms for efficient storage and transport, (ii) Conveyors – Automated systems for moving goods, (iii) Cranes & Hoists – Used for lifting heavy loads in industrial settings.
- ***Relationship Between Plant Layout & Material Handling*** – Explores how an efficient layout minimizes handling costs and time.
- ***Automated Guided Vehicles*** (AGVs) – Self-guided transport systems using lasers, LiDAR, wire guidance, and optical navigation.

EXERCISES

MULTIPLE CHOICE QUESTIONS

11.1 What is the primary objective of material handling in industrial settings?

(a) To reduce energy consumption	(b) To ensure products are manufactured quickly
(c) To move materials efficiently and safely within a facility	(d) To increase the cost of production

11.2 Which material handling principle focuses on reducing the movement of materials?

(a) The Principle of Minimal Handling	(b) The Principle of Continuous Flow
(c) The Principle of Maximum Load	(d) The Principle of Balanced Workload

11.3 In material handling, what does the term "unit load" refer to?

(a) A single item that can be handled individually	(b) A collection of items packaged together as a single unit for handling
(c) A type of machinery used for lifting heavy loads	(d) The weight limit of a material handling system

11.4 To maintain a high level of efficiency in handling materials, a business should focus on:

(a) Increasing the number of handling stages	(b) Using the same handling procedures for different materials
(c) Reducing the number of times materials are handled	(d) Prioritizing complex processes over simplicity

11.5 To ensure that materials are moved efficiently and with minimal disruption, which approach would likely be most beneficial in a busy warehouse setting?

(a) Using multiple routes with frequent changes	(b) Designing a consistent and clear material flow path
(c) Randomly positioning handling equipment	(d) Employing various handling methods for the same material

11.6 To maximize efficiency and reduce unnecessary costs in handling materials, what strategy should be employed?

(a) Handling materials multiple times before reaching the final destination	(b) Consolidating materials into larger, manageable loads
(c) Using different equipment for each step in the handling process	(d) Increasing the frequency of material transfers

11.7 When setting up a new storage system in a facility, which approach ensures optimal use of the available space?

(a) Placing storage units arbitrarily without regard for layout	(b) Using vertical storage solutions and organizing inventory logically
(c) Minimizing the use of space-saving techniques	(d) Storing items based on convenience rather than efficiency

11.8 When selecting equipment for handling materials, which aspect ensures the equipment will fit well into existing processes and workflows?

(a) Aligning equipment capabilities with operational requirements	(b) Choosing equipment based on the latest trends

(c) Opting for the most expensive available option	(d) Selecting equipment with minimal user reviews

11.9 In terms of material handling efficiency, which of the following is a key benefit of using standardized pallets?

(a) They make it harder to fit goods into storage racks	(b) They require frequent adjustments to handling equipment.
(c) They reduce the uniformity of the material handling process	(d) They increase the versatility and efficiency of loading and unloading operations

11.10 When designing a conveyor system for a high-speed production line, which combined factors should be evaluated to ensure optimal performance?

(a) Conveyor speed and load capacity	(b) Conveyor length and type of materials handled
(c) Conveyor speed, load capacity, and system integration with existing workflows	(d) Conveyor design complexity and operational efficiency

11.11 In a facility where space is constrained, which factors should be combined to maximize conveyor system efficiency?

(a) Conveyor's modular design and layout flexibility	(b) Conveyor speed and type of materials handled
(c) Conveyor length and operational noise	(d) Conveyor's brand reputation and visual design

11.12 To accommodate future changes in material handling requirements, which factors should be considered in the conveyor system design?

(a) Conveyor's visual appeal and initial cost	(b) Conveyor's brand and market trends
(c) Conveyor's speed and load capacity alone	(d) Modularity, scalability, and compatibility with potential upgrades

11.13 Which type of conveyor is best suited for transporting items across long distances with minimal friction?

(a) Roller conveyor	(b) Belt conveyor
(c) Chain conveyor	(d) Screw conveyor

11.14 What is a primary advantage of using an overhead conveyor system in a manufacturing plant?

(a) It requires more floor space	(b) It is suitable for large, heavy items
(c) It helps to free up floor space for other operations	(d) It is less efficient than ground-level conveyors

11.15 What is the primary application of a jib crane in material handling?

(a) Moving materials across large outdoor areas	(b) Transporting materials vertically between floors
(c) Handling bulk materials in a conveyor system	(d) Lifting and rotating loads within a limited range around a fixed point

11.16 Which type of crane is commonly used for loading and unloading materials from trucks and railcars in industrial settings?

(a) Jib crane	(b) Gantry crane
(c) Tower crane	(d) Crawler crane

11.17 What type of material handling equipment is commonly used in product type layouts to transport materials horizontally between workstations?

(a) Conveyor belt	(b) Crane
(c) Jib crane	(d) Hoist

11.18 In a functional type layout, which of the following material handling equipment is most commonly used to move materials between departments?

(a) Jib cranes	(b) Gantry
(c) Conveyors	(d) Pallets and forklifts

11.19 Which technology is commonly used by AGVs for navigation?

(a) GPS only	(b) Infrared sensors
(c) Magnetic tape or markers	(d) Manual control

11.20 AGVs can be programmed to perform which of the following tasks?

(a) Only transporting materials	(b) Only loading and unloading
(c) A variety of tasks including transporting, loading, and unloading	(d) None of the above

11.21 AGVs are often equipped with which of the following technologies to improve their functionality?

(a) Basic mechanical systems	(b) Advanced sensors and cameras
(c) Only manual controls	(d) None of the above

11.22 In a laser navigation system, how do AGVs detect obstacles in their path?

(a) By using cameras only	(b) By employing ultrasonic sensors
(c) By emitting laser beams and measuring the time it takes for the reflection to return	(d) By relying on human operators

11.23 What is one of the primary advantages of using LiDAR navigation in AGVs?

(a) Limited range of operation	(b) High sensitivity to environmental changes
(c) Ability to create detailed 3D maps of the surroundings	(d) Dependence on physical markers for navigation

11.24 Which of the following is a limitation of wire-guided AGVs?

(a) Inability to navigate around obstacles	(b) Limited payload capacity
(c) High initial setup costs	(d) Dependence on battery power

11.25 In which scenario would a free-ranging AGV using collimated beam technology be particularly beneficial?

(a) In a highly dynamic environment with frequent layout changes	(b) In a controlled environment with fixed paths
(c) In outdoor applications with GPS navigation	(d) In environments with minimal obstacles

Answers of Multiple Choice Questions

11.1 (c), 11.2 (a), 11.3 (b), 11.4 (c), 11.5 (b), 11.6 (b), 11.7 (b), 11.8 (a), 11.9 (d), 11.10 (c), 11.11 (a), 11.12 (d), 11.13 (b), 11.14 (c), 11.15 (d), 11.16 (b), 11.17 (a), 11.18 (d), 11.19 (c), 11.20 (c), 11.21 (b), 11.22 (c), 11.23 (c), 11.24 (a), 11.25 (a)

SHORT AND LONG ANSWER TYPE QUESTIONS

Category I

11.1 What is the impact of effective material handling on workflow continuity and efficiency?

11.2 How can modular shelving units contribute to maximizing space in a storage system?

11.3 Why is it crucial to consider the load capacity of material handling equipment relative to current operational needs?

11.4 What is the impact of standardized pallets on inventory management?

11.5 What role does conveyor system capacity play in supporting a high-speed production line?

11.6 What factors should be considered when designing a long-distance conveyor system to ensure its efficiency and reliability?

11.7 How does a gantry crane differ from a jib crane in terms of structure and application?

11.8 What is the primary function of a conveyor belt system in a product-type layout?

11.9 How do roller conveyors contribute to the efficiency of horizontal material transport in a product-type layout?

11.10 In what situations are belt-driven roller conveyors preferred over traditional belt conveyors?

11.11 What role do automated guided vehicles (AGVs) play in horizontal material transport within a product-type layout?

11.12 Why are trolleys or carts used in functional type layouts for material handling?

11.13 How do magnetic-guided AGVs navigate within a facility?

11.14 What is the main advantage of LiDAR navigation for AGVs compared to other navigation methods?

11.15 In what type of application would you prefer using wire-guided AGVs, and why?

Category II

11.16 Discuss the impact of effective material handling on workflow continuity and efficiency within a production or supply chain environment. How does efficient material handling contribute to the overall performance of a facility? Illustrate your answer with a real-life example from a specific industry or company, detailing the practices they implemented, the challenges they faced, and the outcomes achieved.

11.17 Explain the crucial role of load capacity in material handling equipment and its impact on meeting current operational needs in a production setting. How does ensuring that equipment load capacities align with operational requirements affect overall efficiency, safety, and cost management? Illustrate your discussion with a real-life example from a specific industry or company, detailing how mismatched load capacities led to challenges and how aligning them with operational needs resulted in improved outcomes.

11.18 Analyze the role of conveyor system capacity in supporting a high-speed production line. How does conveyor system capacity impact the overall performance of such production lines, and what strategies are employed to ensure that long-distance conveyor systems maintain efficiency and reliability? Provide a detailed explanation supported by a real-life example from a specific industry or company, illustrating how conveyor system capacity was managed to enhance production speed and reliability.

11.19 Examine the role of material transport in product-type and functional-type layouts within manufacturing and production environments. How does the layout type influence the efficiency and effectiveness of material handling processes? Discuss the advantages and challenges associated with material transport in each layout type, and illustrate your analysis with a real-life example from a specific industry or company, detailing how material transport was managed and optimized within each layout type.

11.20 Discuss the different types of Automated Guided Vehicle (AGV) navigation systems and their respective applications within a facility. How do these navigation systems impact the efficiency and flexibility of material handling operations? Provide a detailed explanation of the various navigation methods, and illustrate your discussion with a real-life example from a specific industry or company, describing how the chosen navigation system addressed specific operational needs and contributed to overall facility performance.

REFERENCES AND SUGGESTED READINGS

1. Ahuja, S., and Hegde, S. *Material Handling and Automation: Concepts and Techniques*. Wiley, 2017.
2. Baker, J. R., and Bell, R. L. Palletization and Conveyor Systems: Optimal Design for Efficient Material Handling. *International Journal of Production Research*, Vol. 46(9), 2331-2344, 2008.
3. Chauhan, S. S., and Sharma, R. R. Relationship between Plant Layout and Material Handling Systems. *Journal of Operations Management*, Vol. 37(4), 251-265, 2018.

4. Cheng, C. Y., and Wang, J. H. *Selection of Material Handling Equipment*, Springer, 2006.
5. Chien, C. F., and Cheng, T. C. E. A Study on the Integration of Automated Guided Vehicles with Conveyors in Material Handling Systems. *International Journal of Production Economics*, Vol. 118(2), 426-435, 2009.
6. Groover, M. P. *Automation, Production Systems, and Computer-Integrated Manufacturing*, 4th Edition, Pearson, 2016.
7. Gupta, A., and Jain, A. Designing Efficient Material Handling Systems for Manufacturing. *International Journal of Operations & Production Management*, Vol. 30(8), 809-832, 2010.
8. Jäkel, D., and Jäkel, A. *Fundamentals of Material Handling*, 2nd Edition, CRC Press, 2010.
9. Kumar, S., and Saini, M. *Handbook of Material Handling*, Springer, 2011.
10. Lurato, P., and Mroczkowski, M. *Material Handling Equipment Handbook*, McGraw-Hill, 2009.
11. Narayan, A., and Goh, M. Material Handling Systems: A Review of Equipment Selection. *International Journal of Production Research*, Vol. 48(3), 663-678, 2010.
12. O'Neill, M. M., and Hernandez, G. Material Handling and Its Integration with Lean Manufacturing. *Journal of Industrial Engineering*, Vol. 13(2), 113-127, 2011.
13. Pahl, G., and Beitz, W. Selection of Material Handling Equipment for Automated Guided Vehicle Systems. *International Journal of Advanced Manufacturing Technology*, 38(9-10), 1014-1025, 2007.
14. Pietrosanti, M., and Pasquali, R. *Material Handling: Principles, Equipment, and Applications*, Wiley, 2013.
15. Sharma, A., and Gupta, A. *Material Handling: Principles and Applications*. PHI Learning, 2012.
16. Sung, J. H., and Kuo, Y. H. An Efficient Method for Selecting Material Handling Equipment. *Journal of Manufacturing Science and Engineering*, Vol. 138(2), 021009, 2016.
17. Tompkins, J. A., White, J. M., Bozer, Y. A., and Tanchoco, J. M. A. *Facilities Planning*, 4th Edition, Wiley, 2010.
18. Zhou, Q., and Wu, J. Automated Guided Vehicles: Types, Control, and Applications in Material Handling. *Journal of Manufacturing Systems*, Vol. 33(2), 268-277, 2014.

UNIT **12**

LEAN AND GREEN MANUFACTURING

UNIT SPECIFICS

This unit elaborately discusses the following topics:

- Lean manufacturing milestones
- Principles of lean manufacturing (Value stream mapping, Pull-based production, PDCA)
- Building blocks of lean manufacturing (Pull system, Kanban systems, manufacturing cells, TQM, SMED, 5S, Concurrent engineering)
- Principles of Green manufacturing (Design for environment)
- Integration of Lean and Green manufacturing

More creativity and curiosity are stimulated by the topics' current, practical applications. The unit has a list of references, recommended readings, and assignments that are categorized into two groups based on the lower and higher order of Bloom's taxonomy, in addition to several multiple-choice questions and questions with both short and lengthy answer types. One can practice by completing these. According to the content, a section ("Along the...") has been included following the unit's associated topic. The unit was meticulously created with the reader in mind. The use of QR codes, which may be scanned to provide relevant additional information on a range of interesting topics, is one noteworthy feature.

RATIONALE

This unit explores the critical milestones in lean manufacturing, emphasizing its foundational principles such as value stream mapping, pull-based production, and the PDCA cycle. It delves into the essential building blocks that support lean practices, including pull systems, Kanban systems, manufacturing cells, Total Quality Management (TQM), Single-Minute

Exchange of Die (SMED), 5S methodology, and concurrent engineering. Furthermore, it highlights the principles of green manufacturing, particularly design for environment, underscoring the importance of sustainability in production processes. By integrating lean and green manufacturing approaches, the unit demonstrates how organizations can enhance efficiency while minimizing environmental impact, ultimately fostering a holistic framework for sustainable industrial practices.

UNIT OUTCOMES

List of outcomes of this unit is as follows:

U12-UO1: Understand Lean Milestones

U12-UO2: Apply Lean Principles

U12-UO3: Analyze Lean Building Blocks

U12-UO4: Explore Green Manufacturing Principles

U12-UO5: Integrate Lean and Green Practices

U12-UO6: Evaluate Performance Metrics

UNIT-12 Outcomes	EXPECTED MAPPING WITH COURSE OUTCOMES (*1-Weak Correlation; 2-Medium Correlation; 3-Strong Correlation*)					
	CO-1	CO-2	CO-3	CO-4	CO-5	CO-6
U12-UO1	2	2	3	3	2	2
U12-UO2	2	2	3	3	2	2
U12-UO3	3	2	3	3	2	1
U12-UO4	1	2	2	3	2	1
U12-UO5	2	3	3	3	2	1
U12-UO6	1	2	2	3	2	2

12.1 INTRODUCTION

Relaxations of regulations trading off worldwide manufacturing companies now have more market opportunities thanks to "Liberization, Privatization, and Globalization" (LPG). Because of this, there is more rivalry for high-quality items globally, which leads to various strategies for improving competency. Competition is being impacted by worldwide phenomena such as global climate change, political unrest, technological advancements, financial instability, and strict regulations. Because supply and demand are never in balance, the cost of energy and resources is constantly rising, which has a direct impact on production economics and operating expenses. Reducing resource waste from inefficient operations and production techniques is a crucial competitive strategy for industries.

The lean approach has been adopted by several large industries to increase competition globally. The concept of lean is incredibly well-known and widely used at many companies, such as Toyota, Boeing, and Ford. There have been a lot of definitions of lean that have made it difficult to understand its impact. The term "lean" itself is difficult to define. Some have said that lean is more about concept than it is about tools. Conversely, a workable and systemic strategy illustrates lean as a collection of waste reduction techniques. A structure that aims to eliminate waste is also known as lean. Regardless, the common lean plan emphasizes reducing waste. The manufacturing framework can benefit from the methodology, tools, practices, and methodologies provided by lean strategies, which will reduce waste and resource consumption. Manufacturing facilities have been implementing lean manufacturing since the Toyota Production System's efficient use.

Lean Manufacturing is defined as a production methodology that eliminates all non-value-added operations. Lean focuses on the operational aspect, whereas "**green**" considers the environment. In addition to addressing ecological balance, green also targets specific concerns such waste, air, water, and land pollution, as well as recycling management to increase productivity. The European Commission articulated green principles and practices in cooperation with other buffer zones, resulting in the creation of a green economy that raises product value while using fewer environmentally friendly resources everywhere possible. The green economy is a vital means of driving economic growth in the direction of decreasing carbon emissions from processes and goods. Green growth is development that is resilient to typical risks, effective in using normal resources, and limits contamination and natural consequences. Green is also known as the modern Lean, where companies are starting to offer assistance. It has been demonstrated that the main focus of the "green" component is reducing contamination by boosting value and wisely using resources.

Green manufacturing is a trading strategy that emphasizes productivity through proactive, environmentally conscious processes that are responsive and active. It is also thought to represent a revival of the manufacturing industry. It refers to any manufacturing facility that uses innovation and renewable energy sources, while "green" describes actions taken to reduce waste and contamination through resource reduction. The research indicates that sectors that have adopted creative approaches to environmental management have advanced and met buyer demands to improve their standing with regulators and the general public. By reducing waste and producing value products, the lean and green collaboration will promote and enhance performance. Numerous analysts have blended and found this mixture intriguing. The lack of a Lean green domain expert poses a significant obstacle to its use, delaying its implementation and lowering industry competitiveness. This Unit examines lean green manufacturing standards and implementation techniques. Also addresses their future prospects, difficulties, and measures related to Lean Green manufacturing.

12.2 LEAN MANUFACTURING

After the industrial revolutions, lean manufacturing became a crucial part of contemporary manufacturing facilities. It eliminates events and activities that don't improve the value of the product. The milestones of Lean Manufacturing are shown in Fig. 12.1. When Eli Whitney launched the first industrial revolution in the UK in the early 1800s, machines were employed for the first time in manufacturing. His concept of interchangeability allowed for the employment of a large number of unskilled laborers in the musket industry, which at the time was seen to be a skilled vocation performed only by craftsmen. The economic scale of the production units was significantly increased as a result. Up until the late 1890s, when F.W. Taylor introduced time study to shorten processing times, the manufacturing units heavily relied on specialized technologies. This method establishes "Standard time" to perform a specific activity by using a stopwatch to measure and analyze the amount of time required for an operator to complete the given job. Frank and Lilian Gilbreth's Process Control Chart came next, and a Motion Study was conducted in the early 1900s. In order to optimize the manufacturing process, corrective and remedial measures are implemented using the process control chart, which is designed to provide an accurate image of the process. The motion study approach was used to cut down on pointless movements needed to complete the assignment. These days, motion study and time study are combined, enhanced, and referred to as method engineering. It evaluates how much time people spend using electronics and provides guidance to help them do tasks efficiently. Regarding motion and inactivity, which are regarded as types of waste in Lean Manufacturing, these innovators are the ones that first introduced waste removal.

Fig. 12.1 The post-industrial revolution roadmap for lean manufacturing

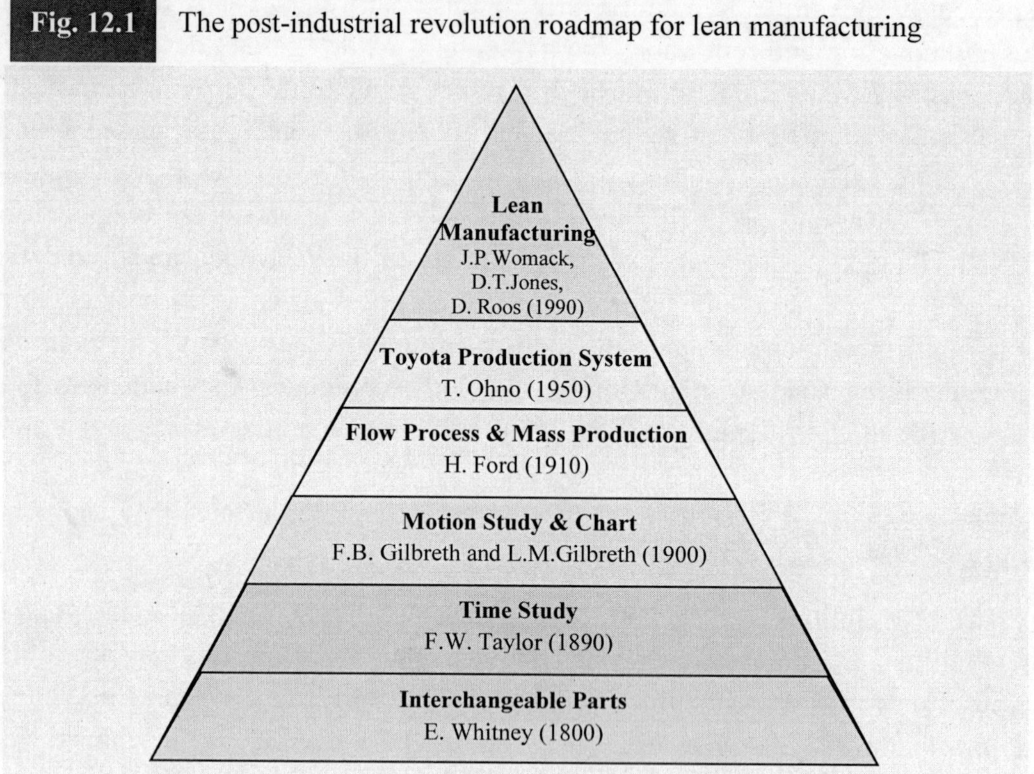

12.2.1 PRINCIPLES OF LEAN MANUFACTURING

Fundamentally, lean manufacturing is about increasing productivity while decreasing waste – two things that must happen for a business to succeed greatly. Lean manufacturing is therefore defined by five fundamental ideas:

1. **Define Value** – If all three of the following criteria are satisfied, an action in a process is considered value contributed.

(i) For the activity to take place, the client must be willing to pay.

(ii) In order to bring the product closer to the final product that the consumer needs and is willing to pay for, the activity must modify it.

(iii) The task needs to be completed correctly the first time, minimizing wasted time.

Eliminating time waste, however, does not mean what the pictures suggest. Therefore, any action that does not create value is a waste of time, money, or effort. Since they might be avoided by implementing a production strategy that produces goods without flaws, testing and inspection procedures are also regarded as waste.

Activities that don't provide value from the perspective of the consumer but occasionally are required from the perspective of production are referred to as non-value added activities. For instance, the outsourced material must be inspected upon arrival at the facility, as are other processes over which the parent company has no influence. But with time, because of long-term relationships, the reliability-checking procedure might be dropped. Lean places a strong emphasis on customer value because cutting costs in one production stage may result in higher costs in another.

The most expensive step in the production process is the design phase. As a result, the designers make every effort to standardize the parts; if not, they typically specify more costly materials that they are acquainted with. This shortens the design process but raises the product's total cost. The customer-oriented method is far simpler; company profit will rise by lowering the cost of production and eventually selling more products if total manufacturing costs are decreased while maintaining quality.

2. **Identify Value Stream** – Value stream mapping (VSM), which is often referred to as lean process mapping, is a method for examining and removing waste from processes. There are made system maps showing both the present and the future states. Unlike standard flowcharts, VSM features a number of unusual icons, some of which are displayed in Fig. 12.2. These include several kanban types, material and information flows for both push and pull systems, and lean production approaches. All of the value-added and non-added values needed to create the product are included in value stream mapping.

Steps to make use of VSM:

(i) *Observe the current conditions* – Choosing the product or product family, determining the improvement objective, and preparing the team for value stream mapping are the initial steps. Assemble a cross-functional team with representation from all process stakeholders. Next, follow the material or information flow's physical course. All of the primary and secondary flows must be mapped. For every stage of the process, measurements should be provided. The type of project you are working on will determine the steps you take. You must have the answer to the following questions.

- What is affordable for you to measure? Because, measuring some processes is more difficult or costly than others.
- What is the most likely time, or average time?
- What is the average time?
- Is there a transition period or preparation time needed?
- How long is the uptime?
- Which resources are needed for each step?
- How many workers and how many shifts are there?
- What are the capabilities of the machine?
- What is the delivery performance and step throughput?
- How much is piled up in inventory?

(ii) *Value Stream Mapping* – Firstly, examine the current performance of the process with all stakeholders by analyzing the value stream map in its current state. Next, determine the bottlenecks, shortcomings, and limiting aspects of the current process. Quantification of each limiting factor's cost and performance is necessary. Take a look at the waste generated and the value provided. Make a note of any wastes, such as downtime, rework, wait time, and retooling, among others. Make a note of any unnecessary steps in the procedure. Determine the cycle time, or how long it takes for a product (a finished good or a physical good) to go through all of the steps necessary to produce one piece at a time. The entire amount of time invested in a process physically. Because waste is not included in, this differs from the total amount of time needed to finish a task or process step in a stream. A cycle time in sales, for instance, can begin when a potential customer contacts your business and conclude when they finish their transaction.

(iii) *Enhance* – For the improvement in the process, we must look into the following.

- How may the wastes we identified be eliminated, reduced, or avoided?
- Which steps in our procedure are the bottlenecks?

- Which process stream stage has the slowest cycle time or throughput?
- Is there a method to increase the effectiveness of that?

Before putting the future state value stream map into action, consult with all parties involved and seek their agreement. After that, the adjustments must be put into practice, which will require modifying the training materials, bills of materials, and procedures that are impacted. Employees should get training based on the new policies and guidelines. Lastly, a declining priority system should be used to facilitate the changes' implementation. The goal is to finish a service or create a product for a customer faster, using less resources while yet keeping outstanding quality, not to get a high score for each individual process step.

(iv) *Reinforce* – Effective key performance indicators should be used to define and measure performance and cost-related metrics in order to verify and validate the implemented modifications. The new standard operating procedures need to be regularly observed and reinforced.

Fig. 12.2 VSM symbols

VSM Symbol	Description	VSM Symbol	Description	VSM Symbol	Description
	Inventory		Time line		Customer or supplier
	Finished goods movement		Kanban stockpoint		Material Pull
	MRP/ERP		Safety Stock		Process
	Electronic information flow		Kaizen Burst		
	Manual information flow		Truck Shipment		
	Operator	P	Kanban Production		
	Kanban batches	W	Kanban withdrawl		

Example 12.1

AccuBatt is a company that produces batteries. Depending on their need, the distribution agency (client) receives these batteries. The lead plate process, assembly, battery charging, and, in the end, daily battery shipping to the distribution agency are all part of AccuBatt's battery production process. The supplier delivers lead coils and other parts twice a week. The future state of VSM of battery manufacturing process is displayed in Figure below. VSMs are crucial to a business's sustainability initiatives, which help cut down on material and energy consumption.

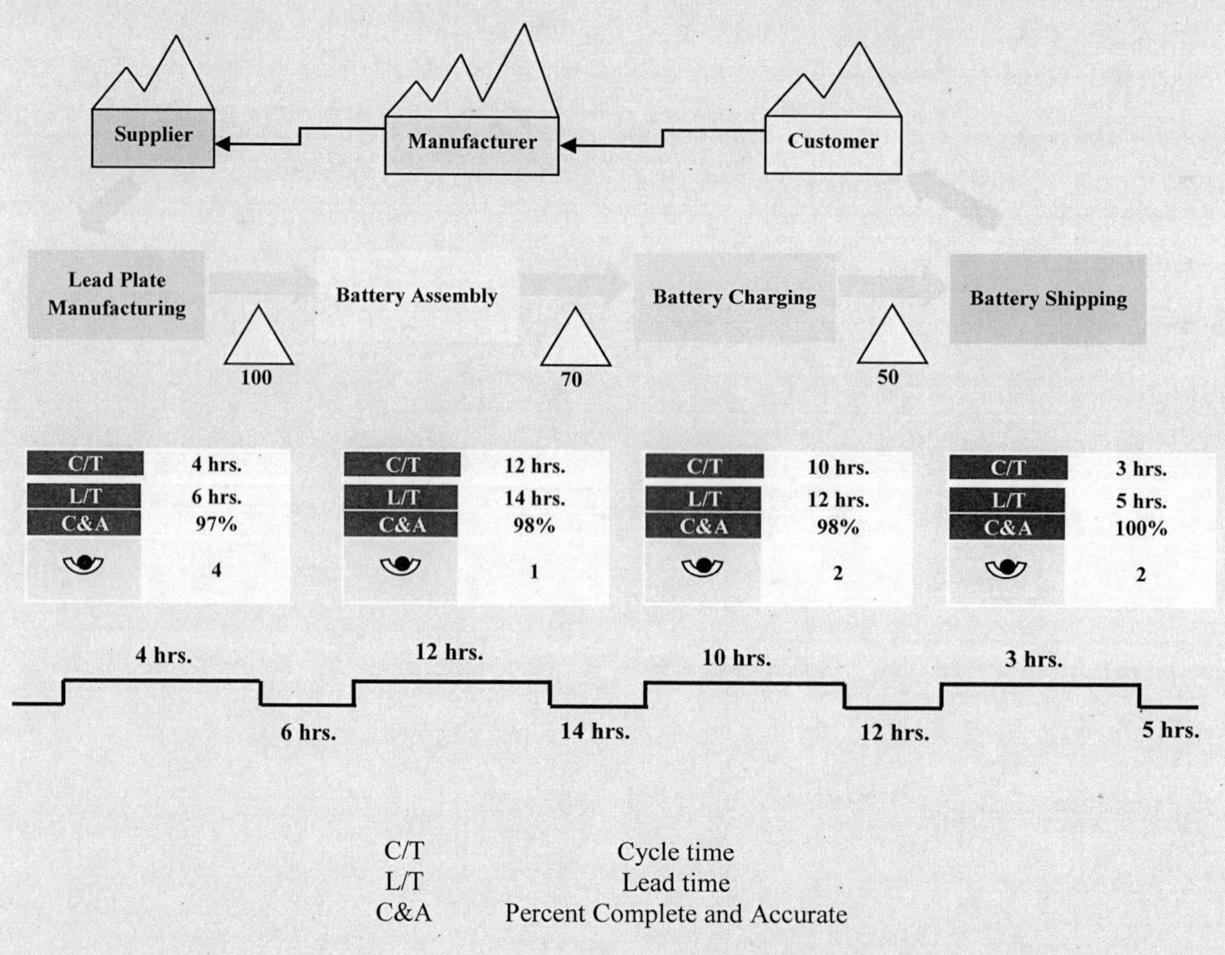

C/T	Cycle time
L/T	Lead time
C&A	Percent Complete and Accurate

3. **Establishing a flow** – In the context of Lean, flow is a fundamental idea. In order to create a flow of value, you want to make sure that everything runs smoothly from the moment you receive an order until you deliver it to the consumer. This is because any form of waiting is a waste. You can't have a smooth flow if your process is full with bottlenecks. You should monitor how work moves through your workflow as a manager. Pay close attention to any places where work tends to become stalled. In this manner, you can delve farther and determine the reason behind it initially. Waiting for outside stakeholders, capacity constraints at a certain point, etc., can all result in bottlenecks.

   The just-in-time (JIT) system used by Toyota, where businesses plan their strategy by precisely forecasting supply and demand so that manufacturing may be put on autocontrol, is honored by the modern flow concept. Manufacturing disruption brought on by erroneous supply and demand planning, in which companies find themselves with either too much or too little inventory at any given time, is a major source of waste. As a result, production operations must stop abruptly and then swiftly resume.

4. **Implement Pull-based Production** – Create a pull system (discussed in Unit 7 on JIT) that only starts manufacture of products when there is a demand for them, eliminating waste. Pull systems reduce waste at every level of the process, but only if the right planning is started as part of an all-encompassing approach. If an organization produces things only in response to demand, it must make sure that it can accurately predict demand in order to maintain manufacturing throughout fluctuations in demand rather than having it cease altogether. However, there must be a healthy balance because excessive supply or insufficient demand might result in high storage costs, which means there will be more waste and less value for customers.

   Again, a just-in-time system can be used to establish pull. Utilizing inventory Kanban signals as a basis, the Just-In-Time system produces goods only as required. This approach guarantees that the right amount of product is created at the right time and helps lessen the need for surplus stock.

5. **Pursue excellence** – In order to readily identify areas for improvement in the pursuit of improving the customer experience, it is important to continuously analyze metrics. In an ideal world, the amount of time, information, and resources needed to get products to end users would all continue to decrease along with the number of steps in the product life cycle. Organizations can improve the value they provide to consumers and cut costs and waste by eliminating weak points in their processes and streamlining them through the collection and analysis of data from multiple sources. Though it may not be literally possible to achieve perfection, there is always space for more development. Businesses

can continuously find and remove waste from their systems by using the continuous improvement process technique. In order to pinpoint problem areas and implement adjustments that will have an effect on the bottom line, this strategy also makes use of data and statistics.

Plan, Do, Check, Act (PDCA) is a continuous improvement process that was introduced by Dr. W. Edwards Deming, one of the pioneers of quality management. The Plan-Do-Check-Act (PDCA) methodology highlights the need to continuously seek out new methods to improve after improvements have been recognized and put into practice. To read a thorough analysis of the PDCA technique for continuous improvement, scan the provided QR code.

SCAN ME
for
PDCA approach

12.3 BUILDING BLOCKS OF LEAN MANUFACTURING

Lean employs a variety of tried-and-true, practical techniques or building blocks to reduce or eliminate waste. Key components of lean include the following:

- Pull systems
- Kanban systems
- Manufacturing cells
- Total quality management
- Total productive maintenance
- Point-of-use-storage
- Quick changeover/SMED (Single Minute Exchange of Die)
- Reduction of batch size
- 5S
- Visual control
- Concurrent engineering

These apply equally to service organizations as they do to industrial ones. In the Table 12.1, these are summarized, some of which have already been discussed in Unit 7 on JIT. Lean principles have been successfully implemented by numerous organizations globally, including manufacturing and service organizations, which have experienced both operational and administrative gains.

Table 12.1 Building blocks of lean manufacturing

S.No.	Building Block	Description
1.	Pull System	Manufacturing according to consumer request, Make-to-order (MTO), with regard to precise specifications and time. This goes against Make-to-stock (MTS), capacity-driven systems, and push systems.
2.	Kanban	Producing using timely and correct information provided on a card, with the material being transported between stages in accordance with the timely information. Either a single card or two cards Kanban system can be used. The volume of demand and production economics is used to determine the number and size of Kanbans.
3.	Manufacturing Cells	Improved labor, material, and other resource flow is the main objective of lean methodology. The resources are arranged according to the needs of the completed task.
4.	Total Quality Management (TQM)	The foundation of lean is TQM, which emphasizes the importance of every department within the company. It acknowledges the power of cooperation and human resources.
5.	Total Productive Maintenance	Using the expertise and collaboration of individuals, suppliers, and other resources, it is predicated on a proactive or preventative maintenance strategy. For higher throughput, it looks for and fixes malfunctions while strengthening system reliability.
6.	Point-of-use-Storage	The goal of this lean strategy is to keep the necessary resources close to the point of usage. For instance, the tools and equipment required at the work center are stored there - an indicator to the commitment of resources.
7.	Quick Changeover/SMED	Its main goal is to cut down on lengthy adjustments, which are expensive both in terms of money and time. It permits smaller lots and more frequent modifications.
8.	Reduction of Batch Size	Manufacturing companies used to produce in order to lower setup costs. Small batch sizes are better suitable for the pull method, which will lead to low work-in-process, excellent quality, cheap cost, etc.
9.	5S	When applied, the five-step 5S approach results in a more orderly and effective workspace. The five Ss are: Seiri (sort), Shitsuke (sustain), Seisou (shine), Seiton (straighten), and Seiketsu (standardize). The implementation of more sophisticated lean manufacturing tools and procedures is based on 5S.
10.	Visual Controls	Visual controls are used in practically every part of business by businesses like Toyota, Honda, Canon, Sony, Samsung, and others because they increase efficiency and visibility and are simple to understand when implemented.
11	Concurrent Engineering	This method makes use of cross-functional teams and significantly cuts lead times. In particular, this feature speeds up the time it takes for new goods and services to reach the market.

12.4 GREEN MANUFACTURING

Increased environmental awareness is a result of popular concern over global warming. A disregard for environmental performance has been revealed by the manufacturing sector's lean improvement of operational performances. Environmentally friendly operational practices, both proactive and reactive, are the emphasis of green manufacturing's profitable sustainable manufacturing business strategy. With the emergence of ecő-innovation in the early 1990s, Green manufacturing was primarily introduced. Eco-innovation is a production approach that reduces environmental risk and other negative effects of resource use. It is new to the organization. Green manufacturing is thought of as an economical and environmentally friendly way to reduce waste streams through product and material use, as well as process design. The green manufacturing strategy considerably improves economy without sacrificing the environment. Any activity that reduces waste is considered to be green productive. The total industrial performance may be impacted by the potential of green productivity. The first Environmental Management System (EMS) standard, known as ISO14001, was issued globally by the International Standard Organization (ISO). The EMS system serves as a tool for continuous development by offering an organized approach to handling environmental-related issues inside a company.

12.4.1 PRINCIPLES OF GREEN MANUFACTURING

Green manufacturing requires the right method to be established in order to attain a healthy environmental performance in the manufacturing process. Table 12.2 outlines the concepts of green manufacturing as the standards for process design. It has been stressed that assessments of energy and material input and output, as well as product lifetime assessments, must be fundamentally non-hazardous. Additionally, emphasis has been placed on the need to take energy and environmental emission issues into account. Regarding green manufacturing, innovative technologies that can enhance environmental performance, the use of green energy, and the design of sustainable production should all be taken into account. It has been found that during the design of a product or process, 80% of the impact on the economy, society, and environment, which is referred to as "tripple bottom line" (TBL), is decided. In order to incorporate a green element into process design, Design for Environment (DfE) is established. When designing a product, DfE typically considers how the product would affect the environment across its whole life cycle.

Table 12.2 Principles of green manufacturing

S. No.	Principle	Description
1.	Fundamentally non-hazardous material	As much as feasible, make sure that every input and output of materials and energy is intrinsically non-hazardous.
2.	Rather than treating, prevent	Waste should be avoided rather than treated or cleaned up after it has already occurred. Waste is a byproduct of an inefficient procedure or usage of energy in an operation.
3.	Create a separation-focused design	Energy and materials are used extensively in the production process during the product separation and purification stages. The design of separation and purification processes should take minimum energy consumption and material use into account.
4.	Optimize the efficiency of mass, energy, space, and time	When the use of mass, energy, space, and time is less than its maximal efficiency, a process is said to be inefficient. Not only may mass and energy be used to remove waste, but also space and time. Maximizing the efficiencies of mass, energy, space, and time is crucial in the design of products, processes, and systems.
5.	Pull system	Production is dependent on customer demand, meaning that resources like energy or materials are only used when necessary.
6.	Keep complexity simple	High complexity and reuse ought to go hand in hand. The complexity benefit of the material should be achieved without requiring changes to the current manufacturing process. When deciding which design decisions to make toward recycling, reuse, or good disposition, embedded entropy and complexity must be considered investments.
7.	Durability as opposed to immortality.	An environmental issue will typically arise from a product that lasts far longer than its commercial life. A product's anticipated lifespan should be taken into account during design. It is better to aim for durability in design rather than immortality.
8.	Satisfy needs while reducing excess.	An overdesigned system may have significant material and energy cost operating costs. It is a design mistake to include extra capacity or capabilities in a design.
9.	Reduce the variety of materials.	Reduced material diversity will encourage disassembly and value retention in multicomponent goods.
10.	Include the flow of materials and energy locally.	This concentrates on material recovery and heat using current processes. Designing systems, processes, and products with accessible energy and material flows integrated and interconnected is essential.
11.	Develop for the "afterlife" market.	Product design ought to take recycling into consideration. This makes it possible to use the present product in the next generation of products. Systems, procedures, and products ought to be created with performance in a commercial "afterlife" in mind.

12.	Regenerative as opposed to exhaustible.	A recyclable or renewable source is one that uses waste products from one process as a fuel for another. It is possible to recycle the renewable resources. Renewable resources should be used instead of finite ones for materials and energy.

ALONG THE GREEN MANUFACTURING

General Motors

Apart from its comprehensive Corporate Responsibility Report, which offers an overview of the company's environmental endeavors, General Motors company has a series of indicators that quantify the energy consumption and greenhouse gas emissions of its several sites. Additionally, the business has begun installing solar panels on the rooftops of its buildings. Its attempts to encourage sustainable building methods include this approach. Additionally, General Motors has started training staff members on the application of the Design for the Environment concept. The goal of this initiative is to assist them in lowering their emissions and increasing the vehicles' fuel efficiency.

General Motors has established targets for lowering the quantity of hazardous and non-hazardous waste produced at its sites in terms of waste management. Multiple techniques and procedures are implemented in order to carry out this program. One of these is the decrease in systems that burn coal. The corporation has also started using cleaner-burning natural gas to prevent pollution of the air and water. The company is also creating reverse logistics systems – which will enable it to gather and repurpose end-of-life vehicles – through partnerships. Additionally, it ought to raise the percentage of recycled or reused materials to 95%.

Volkswagen Group

There are five sections to the report on Volkswagen's environmental activities. It includes a range of topics related to the business's operations, including management and strategy, operations, and data and statistics. The company's attempts to establish green building principles are not mentioned at all. Volkswagen Group seeks to investigate the long-term potential of non-carbon fuels in addition to environmental concerns. According to the company's analysis, rising economic growth in emerging nations would result in a greater demand for transportation, therefore increasing the efficiency of its cars won't be sufficient to cut emissions. For this reason, the business is always searching for methods to increase fuel efficiency. Volkswagen has been able to cut back on its waste management efforts by using cutting edge recycling systems. The majority of the recycling done by the company happens in Europe.

A product's life cycle assessment (LCA) is comparatively significant during the early stages of design. LCA examines the possible effects on the environment at each stage of a product's life cycle, including raw material, manufacture, usage, and disposal. Reducing environmental waste or emissions is intimately tied to the relationship between LCA and DfE. A management concept known as the "triple bottom line" aims to balance social, environmental, and economic performance, as shown in Figure 12.3 below. This promotes sustainable development. By historical standards, the TBL-concept emphasizes how crucial it is for organizations to strike a balance between the three TBL blocks and not just concentrate on the economic side. TBL is more than just a management toolkit; rather, it is a multifaceted approach that highlights how sustainability is shared by all parties involved.

Fig. 12.3 Trippple Bottom Line

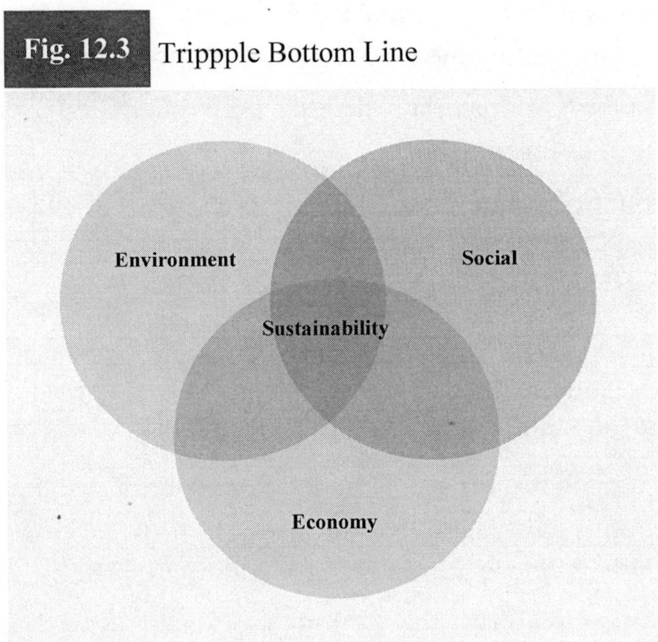

12.4.2 DESIGN FOR ENVIRONMENT (DfE)

The goal of design for environment (DfE) is to lessen the influence that product design has on a product's or service's surroundings. It considers all aspects of the life cycle, not only the appropriate use of recycled materials, packaging, or disposal. The Design for Environment strategy has five components that track a product's life cycle and help businesses operate in a more ecologically responsible manner. The materials and extraction process; (2) production; (3) transport, distribution, and packaging; (4) use; and (5) end of life, design for disassembly and design for recycling are these five aspects.

1. **Material Extraction**
    - To reduce harmful emissions during manufacturing as well as poisonous and/or hazardous emissions in later life stages, avoid or employ materials that are hazardous, toxic, or environmentally unfriendly in any other way.
    - Reducing the amount of non-renewable resources that need to be mined from the earth can be achieved by using materials that are recyclable, renewable, and/or recycled, and by minimizing the use of thermosets or mixed polymers.
    - Reduce the quantity of materials that need to be mined from the ground by designing products in this manner.
    - Reduce the amount of materials used as much as possible and use recyclables that are simple to sort.
2. **Manufacturing**
    - During production, try to avoid or utilize as little as possible dangerous, poisonous, or ecologically unfriendly materials. As a result, fewer dangerous gaseous, liquid, and solid emissions will be produced.
    - Recycle waste and leftovers from production processes, either inside or outside the manufacturing facility. As a result, fewer raw materials will be needed, and less waste will be produced during the production process.
    - Reduce production facility losses through efficient design, upkeep, and quick repairs. Additionally, maximize the insulation of the pipes, walls, and ceilings to guard against leaks, large boilers, and inadequate insulation-related losses.
3. **Transport, Distribution, and Packaging**
    - Transportation by rail or container ship is better than transportation by truck or airplane because the latter two methods use a lot of emissions and energy, respectively.
    - Reduce long-distance transportation as much as possible by utilizing local suppliers and markets. By doing this, long-distance transportation's energy consumption as well as its emissions would be reduced.
    - Increase the efficiency of transportation by using bulk packing, including Europallets, standardized transport packaging, and the simultaneous shipment of bigger quantities of commodities.

- Reduce the quantity of packing material used and the quantity of (virgin) materials used in the packaging. By doing this, less material would be required for packaging and less waste would be generated, which would facilitate material recycling.
- When possible, make the most of reused or refillable containers to reduce the quantity of packing material required.
- Avoid using unsuitable materials for packaging, such as PVC and aluminum, in order to reduce the amount of toxic, dangerous, or valuable items that end up in waste.

4. **Utilization**

- Maximize the lifespan of the product by enhancing reliability and durability. This would result in less demand for new items and less need for raw materials and energy during manufacture.
- Modular product structure design would allow for later product upgrades, extending their lifespan.
- Reduce the amount of working products disposed of because of outmoded aesthetic design. To do this, stay away from designs whose technological usefulness outlives their aesthetic value.
- Increase a product's potential lifespan by developing it to accommodate potential user needs in the future.
- Reduce the amount of gaseous emissions, such as CO_2 and tetraethyl lead, as well as any other undesired emissions, during the life cycle of the product.

5. **Design for Recycling, Disassembly, and End of Life**

The three practices known as the "3Rs" – Reduce, Reuse, and Recycle – define a product's sustainable life cycle. These endeavors evoke the general concept of the "circular economy." Reduce refers to the amount of substance used in the process of manufacture and consumption. Reuse involves increasing the time intensity of a product or service; and Recycle concentrates on the regeneration of renewable resources following usage. The traditional one-way linear economic model of "resource-product-waste" is replaced by the feedback circular economy mode of

SCAN ME
for
Circular Economy

"resource-product-waste-renewable resource," which is in line with the idea of sustainable development and more efficiently uses resources and safeguards the environment to produce the greatest possible economic and social benefits at the lowest possible cost to the environment and resource consumption. To a certain extent, the circular economy encourages the application of the green operations approach by heightening awareness of resource conservation and environmental protection. By scanning the provided QR code, the reader can learn more about the circular economy in detail.

The 3Rs include the waste management hierarchy, which leads to the Green paradigm. Managers can use the waste hierarchy to help them look into the most environmentally friendly ways to change a resource's or product's life cycle. The waste hierarchy can be represented by the six-layer inverted pyramid shown in Fig. 12.4. In order to achieve a more environmentally friendly post-production condition, managers can assess material efficiency (ME) processes with the use of the 3R concept. The general principles of ME are to use less organizational resources per completed product, or to produce less waste. Towards sustainability, ideas related to material efficiency include flow cost accounting, greener production, eco-efficiency, and reverse logistics.

Fig. 12.4 The hierarchy pyramid of waste management

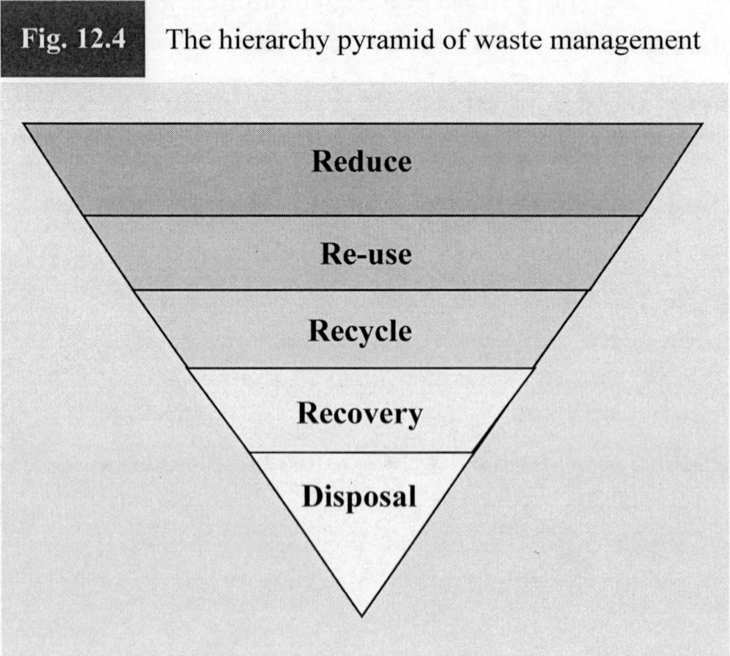

In view of our above discussion, the following recommendations regarding the product's life cycle are developed:

- Increase a product's potential lifespan and hence reduce the demand for new ones by encouraging repurposing it through sound design that keeps it from becoming technologically outdated too soon.
- Reduce the requirement for new products by extending the potential lifespan of parts and components. Encouraging potential remanufacturing/refurbishing through:
  a) A modular design,
  b) Making use of removable points,
  c) Usage of standardized joints,
  d) Positioning joints to reduce the amount of product movement required during disassembly, and
  e) Marking opening instructions for non-destructive disassembly.
- Reduce the requirement for virgin resources by encouraging the potential recycling of parts and materials by using recyclables in an already-existing market (i.e., adopting the concept of cradle-to-cradle concept in which designing a product with a long life cycle and eventually recyclability).

ALONG THE REVERSE LOGISTICS AND CLOSED LOOP SYSTEM

WHIRLPOOL CORPORATION

The American multinational company Whirlpool Corporation is the world's biggest producer and marketer of household appliances. For a century, the company has been in business. With over 67,000 people and over 70 industrial centers worldwide, the corporation generates over US$ 20 billion in revenue annually. Operating under thirteen distinct brand identities, the corporation has activities in over twelve countries.

Principal Concern

In Canada, Whirlpool Corporation dominated the market for home appliances, which included clothes washers, dryers, and kitchen ranges. Introduced in 2002, the Waste Diversion Act (WDA) was the primary legislation in Ontario designed to manage trash by reducing, recycling, or reusing it in accordance with a waste diversion program. In order to run the trash diversion program efficiently, this program was developed in cooperation with government agencies and local officials.

Whirlpool's Issues

Whirlpool had to deal with three main problems. How to abide by the law was the first significant concern. To make sure that the old appliances' diversion aims were met, it was necessary to hunt them down during their entire lifespan. The most essential component of the recently authorized ERP system was the tracking and data management of electronic gadgets.

It was crucial to identify the second significant concern, which was that the manufacturers would have to compete with unregulated recyclers based on their financial interests. The ongoing development near the waste material was the third main worry. Various manufacturers implemented rigorous procedures to ensure that the balance of compounds that deplete the ozone layer was maintained during the manufacturing process. Provincial regulations and government agencies that mandated recyclers to manage ozone depleting compounds of major concern at "end of life" in an effective manner were obtained in order for this to be implemented.

By using the closed loop approach, Whirlpool Corporation was able to obtain total control over its consumer goods and overall expenses to both the company and its customers. Whirlpool was able to maintain total control over the design, reuse, and waste management of its products thanks to the closed loop technology. Additionally, it balanced the degree of competition and safeguarded the product design. The closed loop system's drawback was that it would severely tax Whirlpool Corporation's logistics network, which is primarily focused on the sale and distribution of electronic products. The inability of the trucks used to bring goods to retailers and the vehicles used by retailers to deliver goods to customers to pick up outdated appliances posed the second problem with the closed loop system's deployment.

Finally, the company's regional distribution facilities were not built to handle a huge volume of returns and trash products at this time. Fighting the ERP laws was the last resort when dealing with Whirlpool Corporation. This option existed because there was a substantial body of pertinent data available that showed the ways in which industry was improving waste management without the need for this legislation. Nearly 95 to 99 percent of discarded household appliances are collected from landfills, according to industry statistics.

Recommendation

The closed loop system, which is seen to be a sustainable method of managing the product's life cycle and the materials that are not consumed safely, was the final recommendations to Whirlpool Corporation.

12.5 INTEGRATION OF LEAN AND GREEN MANUFACTURING

Value creation and waste reduction are two further ways that the "lean and green" approach can work in an integrated way to improve operational performance. Several companies are now interested in the lean and green technique in a combined framework. In-depth knowledge of how these strategies complement one another and how they both contribute to resource optimization in certain industrial sectors is required. More often than not, lean methods produce environmentally friendly outcomes. The fact that they collaborate well is nevertheless something to observe. Implementing lean methods can result in improved procedures within the green manufacturing sector. This is so that the complementary environmental and operational practices can be used to their full potential. By adopting environmental principles, a company can become both green and lean. It can decrease waste and become more efficient with the use of these techniques, which are also connected to the seven lean wastes.

Fig. 12.5 Integration of Lean, Green, and Sustainability

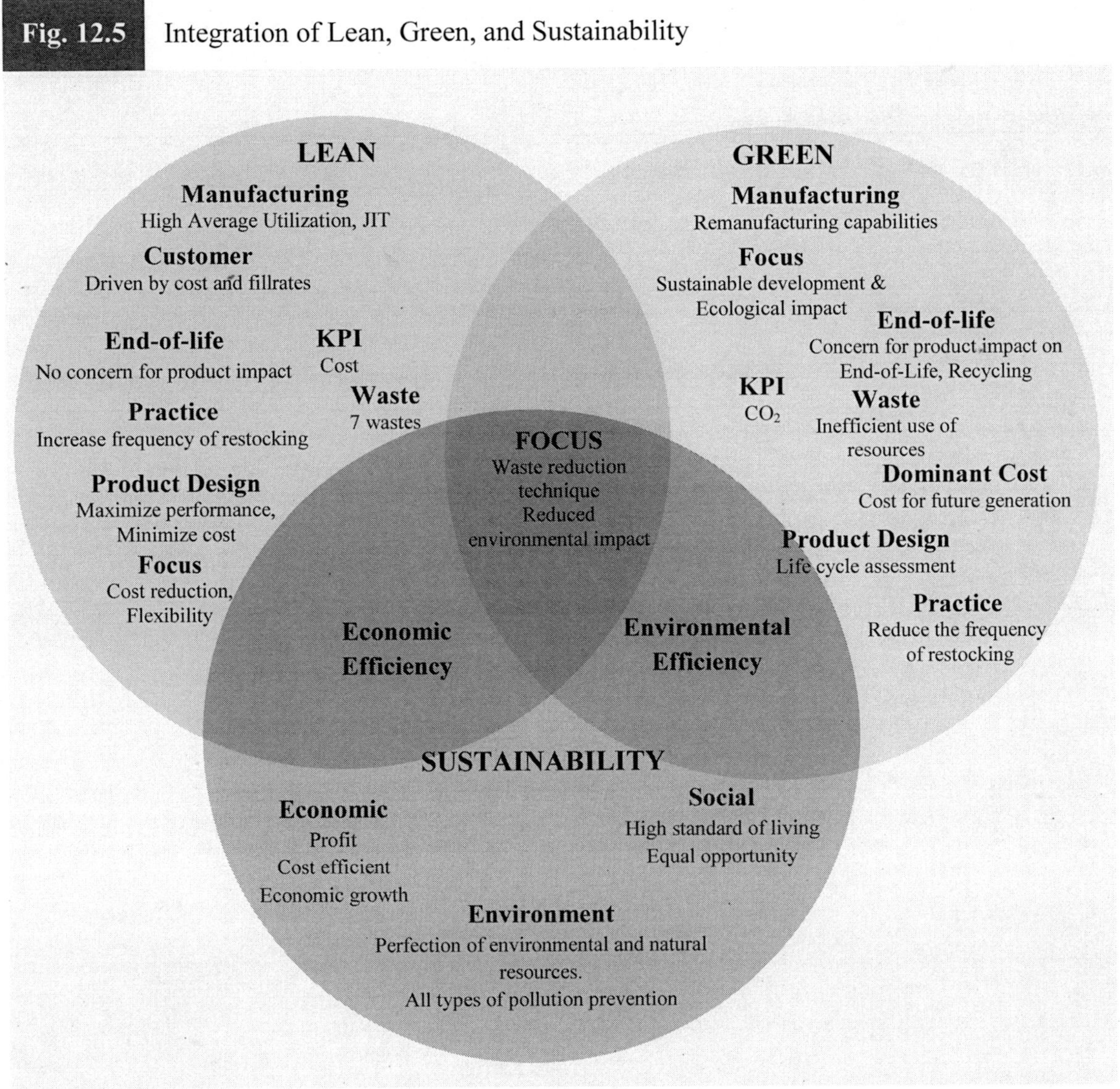

Lean must be able to advance green practices while simultaneously improving its own methods that lead to economic sustainability. To maximize value, lean must also be inclusive of the environment and society. Businesses that use green practices have a higher chance of outperforming those that don't. Therefore, it has been suggested that a combination of lean and green techniques be used to meet the required sustainability goals. By doing this, businesses will be able to lessen their shortcomings and strengthen their reputations and strengths. It should be mentioned that the integration of the two paradigms can result in a sustainable conclusion in any industry by creating a unified framework that incorporates the triple-bottom-line approach. Fig. 12.5 illustrates how overlapping principles of lean and green might be merged. Table 12.3 summarizes some of the distinctive characteristics of the Lean and Green paradigms as they are depicted in Fig. 12.5.

Table 12.3 Comparing the Lean and Green paradigms

Attribute	Lean Paradigm	Green Paradigm
Purpose	Increase profits by cutting expenses.	Improving the ecological efficiency of organizations and their partners while lowering environmental risks and impacts.
Focus	Prioritize cutting costs and enhancing flexibility by constantly getting rid of non-value-adding or wasteful processes in all areas of business.	Put an emphasis on sustainable development and the eradication of pollution and resource waste to lessen the ecological impact of industrial activity.
Customer satisfaction	Lowering expenses and lead times while ensuring client satisfaction.	Ensuring customer satisfaction by promoting green living.
System-wide lead time	Reduce lead time provided it doesn't raise expenses.	Shorten the lead time for transportation as long as it doesn't result in more CO_2 emissions.
Product Design	Optimize efficiency while reducing expenses.	Utilizing eco-design and life-cycle assessment to assess ecological risks and consequences.
Manufacturing	Keep a high average utilization rate and draw commodities through the system based on demand while implementing Just-In-Time (JIT) techniques.	Prioritize reducing waste and using resources efficiently to protect the environment, as well as building remanufacturing capabilities to incorporate recycled and reusable parts.
Sources of raw materials	High quality and low cost are characteristics of suppliers.	Green buying.
Inventory	Maximizes turnover and minimizes inventory across the system to cut expenses and free up resources.	Reduce unnecessary materials to free up space and minimize inventory; adding refurbished or reusable parts to the material inventory.

Transactions practice	Reduce the amount of material that is handled during manufacturing and promote regular, small delivery of supplies and finished goods.	Lower the frequency of replenishing to cut down on fuel use and greenhouse gas emissions.
End-of-life	After a product is sold, consideration ends; usage effects or end-of-life care are not taken into account.	Takes into account the effects of product use in addition to end-of-life recovery through recycling or reusing
KPI	Cost, Service Level	CO_2, Service Level
Techniques for Reducing Waste	Vision and Strategy, Innovation, Collaborations, Activities, and Support Roles; 7 Wastes: Removing waste from all operational processes, both internal and external, including those caused by overproduction, waiting, transit, improper processing, defects, needless inventory, and motion.	Product redesign, process redesign, internal consumption of byproducts, substitution, prolonged use, disassembly, remanufacturing, and reduction Packaging that can be returned, waste segregation, recycling, spreading risks, establishing markets, and alliances
Tools/practices	Inventory minimization, value stream mapping, greater rate of resource utilization, As information circulates over the network, Just in time, Reduced lead times	Reduced use of unnecessary and excess materials; efficient use of resources; and sustainable value stream mapping, Reducing waste (energy, water, raw materials, and non-product output), decrease in the lead time for transit, lowering the frequency of refill, Combining the information flow and reverse material in the closed loop system, sharing of environmental risk.

Due to ongoing dedication to lean production, most businesses are likely to implement green practices. This can be accomplished by creating new processes and a shared framework that promotes energy efficiency and optimal resource usage, which reduces waste. There are still points of contention between the Lean and Green practices paradigms, despite the significance of their relationship. Their divergent stances on the environment are the only distinction between Lean and Green. Although lean and green methods acknowledge the value of the environment, they can need to make special considerations to produce goods and services that are more environmentally friendly. For example, even though both strategies aim to raise the caliber of their goods and services, they might have to make concessions to create a more sustainable environment. Lean methods frequently recommend using a pull system and a JIT delivery method to enhance the frequency of replenishments. Conversely, green techniques seek to shorten transportation times and boost operational efficiency. Lean and green implementations as stand-alone systems typically aren't sufficient to ensure the balance between the three pillars of sustainability – economic, environmental, and social – as required by the contemporary global market, despite the practices' significant contributions to sustainability. Green and lean methodologies are proposed into a unified manufacturing strategy in this line. The following are some success elements for applying the lean-green method to achieve sustainability performance:

- Implementing the lean-green strategy gradually will enable businesses to establish priorities and important objectives.
- Sustainability concerns need to be included in the scope of operational duties and responsibilities.
- The development of sustainability metrics is necessary.
- To promote sustainability, effective information management is essential.
- Attaining sustainability standards requires the commitment of management.
- Green initiatives are more likely to be implemented in conjunction with lean techniques towards sustainability in a lean working environment that is made up of skilled, engaged, and dedicated people as well as a continuous improvements culture.
- A customer-centric approach and integration are essential for achieving long-term outcomes.
- To achieve sustainable results, teamwork and end-to-end supply chain integration are essential.
- Effective coordination and communication between different functional areas are essential to the successful use of the lean-green methodology.
- Sustainable results can be improved by evaluating and reviewing performance and target progress.

ALONG THE LEAN AND GREEN (SUSTAINABLE) ORGANIZATIONS

The following examples show how businesses across a range of sectors have effectively incorporated sustainable manufacturing methods into their operations, minimizing their negative effects on the environment and frequently realizing cost savings all while preserving or increasing their competitiveness.

Clothing brand **Patagonia**, based in California, is well known for incorporating sustainable practices into its business culture and product design. The company has also won numerous accolades, including the UN Champion of the Earth, the Fabric of Life Award, and the Corporate Excellence Awards for Climate Innovation. Using fair labor standards, renewable energy, and the introduction of programs like "Worn Wear" to encourage customers to purchase old items are some of the ways they have minimized their carbon impact.

Toyota is a global car manufacturer based in Japan that implemented lean manufacturing and waste reduction techniques. This led to notable decreases in energy usage and emissions, along with increased efficiency. They have a clear commitment to advancing recycling and end-of-life technology, enhancing water efficiency, and creating communities that coexist peacefully with the environment.

H&M, which was established in 1947 in Sweden, is sometimes criticized for deceptively portraying its items as more environmentally friendly than they actually are. But it has been able to hold onto a strong market position and rebuild its reputation by releasing an annual sustainability report, utilizing eco-friendly materials, recycling used clothing, and enhancing the energy efficiency of its retail locations and distribution hubs.

The American modular carpet manufacturer **Interface** launched a campaign known as "Mission Zero" to end all environmental harm. As a result, Interface is the only flooring company in the world to provide all of its products as carbon neutral throughout their whole life cycle. Their creative supply chain and manufacturing techniques have resulted in 97% fewer market-based greenhouse gas emissions, 67% less waste production, and an average of 52% recycled or biobased material content in their products. Additionally, 79% of the energy they utilize comes from renewable sources.

By 2033, **Ignitec®**, a UK-based design and technology firm, hopes to be net-zero. They can achieve supply chain agility, significant waste reduction, significantly lower emissions, and the capacity to draw in and keep more customers thanks to their in-house manufacturing skills and energy-efficient technologies, like their 3D printer. It has improved their bottom line, decreased operating costs, and increased team spirit to clearly state their approach and goals in their sustainability policy (e.g. recycle, switch to renewable energy, eliminate waste, and offset carbon).

NOTE ON THE SUSTAINABILITY IN HEALTHCARE SERVICES

Although healthcare facilities protect and enhance public health, their environmental effects may have a detrimental effect on the welfare of people and other living things. Thus, encouraging human well-being and health also depends on the sustainability of hospitals and other healthcare facilities. To benefit businesses as well as consumers, sustainability measures in healthcare structures must, however, guarantee that the standard of care offered by these institutions, as well as access to and cost of healthcare, are not compromised. Air pollution and waste disposal management are significant issues that need to be addressed in the context of sustainability in the healthcare industry.

One of the main sources of pollution in the world today, medical waste has a significant impact on the quality of the air, water, and land inside and surrounding healthcare facilities as well as the transmission of illness. As a result, it is essential for healthcare companies to have a multidisciplinary staff that handles many facets of healthcare sustainability. Several strategies have been put forth to help healthcare set sustainable development objectives and lessen their environmental impact. Some key suggestions concerning sustainable healthcare sector can be studied by scanning the QR code.

SCAN ME
for
Sustainability in Healthcare sector

UNIT SUMMARY

- ***Lean Manufacturing*** – Aims to eliminate waste and enhance productivity. Key principles include: (i) Value Stream Mapping (VSM) – Identifying waste and optimizing workflows, (ii) Pull-based Production & Just-in-Time (JIT) – Producing only as needed to reduce excess inventory, (iii) Continuous Improvement (PDCA Cycle, Kaizen) – A cycle of planning, implementing, and refining processes, and (iv) Lean Tools – Kanban, 5S, SMED, and Total Quality Management (TQM).
- ***Green Manufacturing*** – Focuses on sustainable practices by: (i) Design for Environment (DfE) – Reducing waste, improving recyclability, and using eco-friendly materials, (ii) Circular Economy & Cradle-to-Cradle Design – Reusing and recycling materials to minimize waste, and (iii) Life Cycle Assessment (LCA) – Evaluating a product's environmental impact from production to disposal.
- ***Integration of Lean & Green*** – Combining lean efficiency with sustainable practices to: (i) Reduce energy and resource consumption, (ii) Lower carbon footprint and improve environmental compliance, and (iii) Implement green supply chains and sustainable product designs.

EXERCISES

MULTIPLE CHOICE QUESTIONS

12.1 What is the primary goal of lean manufacturing?

(a) To increase production speed	(b) To reduce waste and improve efficiency
(c) To increase the number of products produced	(d) To minimize labor costs

12.2 What is the primary focus of green manufacturing?

(a) Increasing production speed	(b) Enhancing employee training
(c) Reducing environmental impact	(d) Expanding market share

12.3 How does integrating lean and green manufacturing benefit an organization?

(a) By focusing exclusively on cost reduction	(b) By prioritizing marketing over production

(c) By minimizing the use of advanced technologies	(d) By improving both operational efficiency and environmental sustainability

12.4 In lean manufacturing, what does the term "value stream" refer to?

(a) The series of steps and activities that create value for the customer from raw materials to finished products	(b) The financial flow associated with the production of goods
(c) The marketing and sales processes of a company	(d) The cost of materials used in production

12.5 What is the primary goal of "Just-In-Time" (JIT) manufacturing in the context of lean practices?

(a) To produce large quantities of products to meet future demand	(b) To produce and deliver products only as needed, reducing inventory and waste
(c) To increase the number of machines in production facilities	(d) To extend production lead times to accommodate more complex manufacturing processes

12.6 Which principle of lean manufacturing focuses on continuous improvement and incremental changes?

(a) Just-In-Time (JIT)	(b) Kaizen
(c) Total Quality Management	(d) Six Sigma

12.7 What does the 5S methodology aim to achieve in lean manufacturing?

(a) Enhancing product features	(b) Increasing marketing efforts
(c) Improving workplace organization and standardization	(d) Reducing labor costs

12.8 In lean manufacturing, what is the purpose of implementing "Kanban" systems?

(a) To increase production speed by adding more workers	(b) To extend production cycles to handle more orders
(c) To reduce the quality of products for cost savings	(d) To signal when new materials or components are needed in the production process

12.9 Which technique focuses on reducing setup times and streamlining changeovers between different production runs?

(a) Continuous Flow Manufacturing	(b) Total Productive Maintenance (TPM)
(c) Quick Changeover (SMED)	(d) Cellular Manufacturing

12.10 What is the main objective of "Cellular Manufacturing" in lean practices?

(a) To group similar equipment and processes into cells to reduce cycle time and improve efficiency	(b) To increase the number of production cells within a facility
(c) To create a centralized system for all production activities	(d) To isolate each production step in separate facilities

12.11 When designing a product, which principle considers how the product would affect the environment across its whole life?

(a) Design for Disassembly	(b) Efficient Resource Utilization
(c) Pollution Prevention	(d) Energy Efficiency

12.12 What is the concept of "cradle-to-cradle" in green manufacturing?

(a) Designing products that are made from biodegradable materials	(b) Utilizing renewable energy sources exclusively in production
(c) Reducing the physical size of products to save materials	(d) Designing products with a long lifecycle and eventual recyclability

12.13 What is the primary goal of implementing circular economy system?

(a) To increase product production speed	(b) To reduce the need for raw materials by recycling or reusing end-of-life products
(c) To enhance product marketability	(d) To maximize energy consumption

12.14 Which green manufacturing principle involves assessing and reducing the environmental impact of products throughout their entire lifecycle?

(a) Eco-Design	(b) Energy Efficiency
(c) Life Cycle Assessment	(d) Resource Efficiency

12.15 What is the primary goal of integrating the "Environment" aspect into the Triple Bottom Line framework in green manufacturing?

(a) To reduce the environmental footprint of manufacturing processes and products	(b) To focus solely on financial gains
(c) To increase production volume	(d) To outsource production to reduce environmental regulations

12.16 In the context of Design for Environment, what does the "Production" phase focus on?

(a) Reducing waste and energy consumption during the manufacturing process	(b) Minimizing the volume of goods transported
(c) Ensuring the product is easily recyclable	(d) Selecting biodegradable packaging materials

12.17 The "End of Life" component of Design for Environment focuses on:

(a) Improving the energy efficiency of the manufacturing process	(b) Designing products to be easily disassembled for recycling or disposal
(c) Reducing the cost of product transportation	(d) Enhancing product performance during use

12.18 How do lean and green paradigms generally intersect in practice?

(a) Both paradigms focus exclusively on cost reduction	(b) Green practices often hinder the implementation of lean principles
(c) Lean principles require exclusive use of renewable resources	(d) Lean practices can support green initiatives by reducing resource consumption

Answers of Multiple Choice Questions
12.1 (b), 12.2 (c), 12.3 (d), 12.4 (a), 12.5 (b), 12.6 (b), 12.7 (c), 12.8 (d), 12.9 (c), 12.10 (a), 12.11 (a), 12.12 (d), 12.13 (b), 12.14 (c), 12.15 (a), 12.16 (a), 12.17 (b), 12.18 (d)

SHORT AND LONG ANSWER TYPE QUESTIONS

Category I

12.1 In what way does lean manufacturing contribute to cost reduction?

12.2 What is a key objective of green manufacturing in terms of resource use?

12.3 How do lean and green manufacturing paradigms intersect to benefit an organization?

12.4 How can value stream mapping support continuous improvement in lean manufacturing?

12.5 How does the concept of "PDCA" relate to continuous improvement in lean manufacturing?

12.6 How does the Kanban system support continuous improvement in lean manufacturing?

12.7 What is SMED, and how does it contribute to reducing setup time?

12.8 How does Design for Disassembly impact the cost of product lifecycle management?

12.9 What role does product durability play in the Cradle-to-Cradle approach?

12.10 How does the concept of a circular economy relate to reducing the need for raw materials through recycling and reusing end-of-life products?

12.11 Which stages of a product's life are typically considered in a Life Cycle Assessment?

12.12 What is meant by "End-of-Life" in the context of Design for Environment (DfE)?

12.13 What is an example of a lean tool that supports green manufacturing objectives?

Category II

12.14 Describe how the integration of lean and green manufacturing can help the company achieve its objectives of reducing costs and optimizing resource use. In your response, discuss the specific goals and benefits of each approach, provide examples of practical strategies or tools that could be employed, and explain how these strategies might work together to enhance overall operational efficiency.

12.15 Explain how the PDCA cycle can be effectively applied to the company's lean manufacturing processes to achieve continuous improvement. In your response, outline each phase of the PDCA cycle, provide specific examples of how each phase can be applied in a manufacturing setting, and discuss the benefits and challenges associated with using PDCA for continuous improvement in lean manufacturing.

12.16 Discuss how implementing Design for Disassembly (DfD) can impact the cost of product lifecycle management. In your answer, elaborate on how DfD affects various stages of the product lifecycle, including design, production, maintenance, and end-of-life. Provide specific examples of how DfD can lead to cost savings or additional expenses, and explain how these impacts might influence overall lifecycle costs.

12.17 Discuss how the concept of a circular economy can help the furniture manufacturer reduce the need for raw materials through recycling and reusing end-of-life products. In your response, elaborate on how adopting circular economy principles can be applied in the furniture industry, provide specific examples of practices or strategies that could be implemented, and explain the potential benefits and challenges associated with this transition.

12.18 Explain how the company can apply Design for Environment (DfE) principles to effectively manage the end-of-life phase of its products. In your response, discuss how DfE strategies can be implemented to improve recycling, reuse, and disposal of products at their end-of-life. Provide specific examples of practices or design features that could be incorporated to achieve these goals, and analyze the potential benefits and challenges associated with implementing these end-of-life strategies.

REFERENCES AND SUGGESTED READINGS

1. Bicheno, J., and Holweg, M. *The Lean Toolbox: The Essential Guide to Lean Transformation*. PICSIE Books, 2009.
2. Dennis, P. *Lean Production for the Small Shop*. Industrial Press, 2007.
3. Dev, N. K., Shankar, R. Choudhary, A. Strategic Design for Inventory and Production Planning in Closed-Loop Hybrid Systems. *International Journal of Production Economics*, Vol. 183, 345-353, 2017.
4. Dev, N. K., Shankar, R. Using Interpretive Structure Modeling to Analyze the Interactions between Environmental Sustainability Boundary Enablers. *Benchmarking: An International Journal*, Vol. 23(3), 601-617, 2016.
5. Dev, N. K., Shankar, R., and Qaiser, F. H. Industry 4.0 and Circular Economy: Operational Excellence for Sustainable Reverse Supply Chain Performance. *Resources, Conservation, and Recycling*, Vol 153, 104583, 2020.
6. Emiliani, M. L. Lean Behavior: A New Paradigm for Sustainable Organizational Change. *Journal of Organizational Excellence*, Vol. 25(3), 57-66, 2006.
7. Fiksel, J. *Design for Environment: A Guide to Sustainable Product Development*. McGraw-Hill, 1996.
8. Hines, P., and Rich, N. The Seven Value Stream Mapping Tools. *International Journal of Operations & Production Management*, Vol. 17(1), 46-68, 1997.
9. Jabbour, C.J.C., and Jabbour, A.B.L.S. Lean Manufacturing, Green Innovation, and the Green Supply Chain: A Systematic Review and Future Directions. *Journal of Cleaner Production*, Vol. 112, 342-352, 2016.

10. King, A. Lean and Green: Integrated Perspectives on Green Manufacturing and Lean Practices. *Environmental Science & Technology*, Vol. 44(12), 4585-4592, 2010.

11. Krafcik, J. F. Triumph of the Lean Production System. *MIT Sloan Management Review*, Vol. 30(1), 41-52, 1988.

12. Lee, Y., and Lee, S. Integrating Lean and Green Manufacturing to Enhance Environmental and Operational Performance. *International Journal of Production Research*, Vol. 53(14), 4264-4283, 2015.

13. Liker, J. K. *The Toyota Way: 14 Management Principles from the World's Greatest Manufacturer*. McGraw-Hill, 2004.

14. Liker, J.K., and Meier, D. *The Toyota Way Fieldbook: A Practical Guide for Implementing Toyota's 4Ps*. McGraw-Hill, 2006.

15. Ohno, T. Toyota *Production System: Beyond Large-Scale Production*. Productivity Press, 1988.

16. Rother, M., and Shook, J. *Learning to See: Value Stream Mapping to Add Value and Eliminate MUDA*. Lean Enterprise Institute, 2003.

17. Rother, M., and Shook, J. Learning to See: Value Stream Mapping to Add Value and Eliminate MUDA. *International Journal of Production Research*, Vol. 37(13), 3173-3193, 1999.

18. Shingo, S. *A Study of the Toyota Production System from an Industrial Engineering Viewpoint*. Productivity Press, 1989.

19. Simons, D., and Langenberg, M. *Green and Lean: Integrating Lean Manufacturing with Environmental Management*. Springer, 2009.

20. Womack, J. P., Jones, D. T., and Roos, D. *The Machine that Changed the World: The Story of Lean Production*. Free Press, 1990.

UNIT 13

PROCESS ANALYSIS AND QUALITY DESIGN

UNIT SPECIFICS

This unit elaborately discusses the following topics:

- Overview of process analysis
- Measuring process performance (Little's law)
- Process with reduced throughput time
- System reliability
- Design for quality (Failure mode and effect analysis)
- Quality of design (Process capability and its measures)

The topics' practical applications are examined in order to promote greater creativity and curiosity as well as enhance problem-solving skills. The unit contains a list of references, suggested readings, and assignments through a variety of numerical problems in addition to a number of multiple-choice questions and questions with short and long answer types divided into two groups according to lower and higher order of Bloom's taxonomy. By completing these, you can get practice. The content indicates that an additional section ("Along the...") has been added after the unit's related topic. It was thoughtfully written with the book's reader in mind. The usage of QR codes, which may be scanned to yield pertinent supporting material on a variety of interesting topics, is one notable characteristic.

RATIONALE

This unit provides a comprehensive overview of process analysis, emphasizing its critical role in optimizing operational efficiency. We begin with an exploration of measuring process performance through Little's Law, illustrating how throughput time can be effectively quantified and managed. The discussion then shifts to strategies for reducing throughput time, which enhance overall system reliability. Additionally, we delve into Design for Quality, utilizing Failure Mode and Effect Analysis (FMEA) to proactively identify potential failures. Finally, we assess the quality of design through process capability and its measures, highlighting how these elements collectively contribute to superior operational performance and customer satisfaction.

UNIT OUTCOMES

List of outcomes of this unit is as follows:

U13-UO1: Understand Process Analysis

U13-UO2: Apply Little's Law

U13-UO3: Reduce Throughput Time

U13-UO4: Assess System Reliability

U13-UO5: Implement Design for Quality

U13-UO6: Measure Process Capability

UNIT-13 Outcomes	EXPECTED MAPPING WITH COURSE OUTCOMES (*1-Weak Correlation; 2-Medium Correlation; 3-Strong Correlation*)					
	CO-1	CO-2	CO-3	CO-4	CO-5	CO-6
U13-UO1	3	3	2	3	3	2
U13-UO2	1	1	3	2	2	2
U13-UO3	3	2	3	3	2	2
U13-UO4	2	2	2	3	3	3
U13-UO5	3	2	2	3	3	1
U13-UO6	2	2	2	3	2	2

13.1 INTRODUCTION

For a business to remain competitive, it is imperative that its processes are understood. Every minute the business is in business, it will be penalized by a procedure that is not tailored to its needs. For illustration, consider two fast-food chains. Whatever the second restaurant does, it can never make as much money as the first restaurant if it can provide a medium-sized pizza to a customer for \$10 in direct costs and the second business can only supply it for \$20. The procedure of assembling those pizzas requires careful consideration of numerous aspects. These elements include the price of the raw ingredients, the price of preparing the pizza, and the price of accepting an order and delivering the product to the client. Here, we have to be careful to take into account the processing cost of quality.

How do you define a process? Any component of an organization that transforms inputs into outputs that are hopefully more valuable to the organization than the original inputs is called a process. Think about a few instances of processes. The Manesar, India plant of Maruti Suzuki India Limited is where the car Ciaz is put together. Parts and components that have been manufactured specifically for the plant are received by the assembly plant. These parts and components are made into cars using energy, labor, and machinery on an assembly line. Similarly, Domino's uses ingredients including flour, baking powder, cheese, mozzarella, tomatoes, and yeast in all of its eateries. In order to make pizza, these inputs are combined with trained labor in the form of cooks and order takers, as well as capital equipment.

The processes in these two cases result in some products as an output. Nonetheless, many processes result in services as their outcome. For instance, in a hospital, highly skilled physicians, nurses, and technicians work alongside specialized equipment and another input – the patient. With the right care and attention, the patient recovers and becomes well. An additional illustration of a service organization is an airline. The airline transports passengers between destinations across the globe using aircraft, ground services, flight crews, reservation staff, and fuel.

A process's analysis enables the following crucial questions to be addressed: How many clients can the procedure handle per unit of time? What's the estimated time to service a customer? What modifications to the procedure are required to increase capacity? What is the cost of the process? Establishing the goal of the analysis is a challenging but crucial initial step in process analysis. Is the goal to resolve a conflict? Is it in an effort to comprehend the effects of a potential shift in the way business is conducted going forward? The goal of the study must be understood clearly in order to determine the level of detail in the process model. It is necessary to keep the analysis as basic as feasible.

The fact that a process is paced or unpaced is one way to classify it. The set time at which items are moved through a process is referred to as the **pacing**. The flow of items through each activity (or stage) in a serial process is frequently timed mechanically to keep the line in synchronization. The necessary cycle time for a process is found by dividing the amount of time needed to create a given good by the demand for it from customers. For instance, the cycle time is 50.4 seconds if a computer manufacturer wants to assemble 500 computers in a shift lasting 420 minutes on the assembly line (420 minutes/500 computers × 60 seconds/minute = 50.4 seconds/computer).

In engineering systems, reliability assessment is critical at every level of processing and control. In addition to assessing the **systems' reliability**, a crucial component is the examination of component importance. When it comes to determining the best course of action for an upgrade effort (reliability enhancement) in system design or offering advice on how to run and maintain system status, the component importance (reliability important index) is helpful. System reliability analysis's primary goals are to pinpoint a system's vulnerabilities and essential parts and to calculate the effect of a component failing.

The output of processes that deliver goods and services typically varies to some extent. These variations are the result of significant small elements working together, all of which are so unimportant that even if they could all be found and removed, the process variability would not change much. It's frequently called **random variation**. These variances could be the result of aging machinery, worn-out components, or the need for a machine redesign. Another is known as **assignable variation**, and it is the second type of variability in process output. As opposed to natural variations, assignable variations typically have a clear source that can be found and removed. Typical sources of assignable differences include tool wear, equipment that needs to be adjusted, defective materials, human factors (fatigue, distractions from noise, carelessness, following incorrect procedures, etc.), and issues with measuring devices.

It is commonly acknowledged that quality increases with fewer differences. It is intuitive to realize that sometimes. Schedules can be more precisely planned if raw material deliveries are consistently made on time. If a restaurant consistently serves hygienic food, ordering online can save time. However, the importance of reduced variability is hardly considered when considering such items. The knowledge is more precisely defined in the case of engineers. In order to avoid poor quality and unhappy customers, connecting rods should function smoothly, electronic parts should be compatible, and cereal boxes should have the appropriate number of raisins.

Engineers are aware that there can never be zero variability, though. Because of this, specifications were created by designers to specify acceptable bounds for an item's exact value in addition to its exact or nominal value. For instance, the design specifications might be $50^{\pm 0.2}$ millimeters if a dimension has a nominal value of 50 millimeters. The tolerance of the nominal size is the value denoted by the superscript (±0.2). This indicates that the limits of dimension 50, which range from 49.8 to 50.2 millimeters, have been set by the designer. The terms "upper" (50.2 millimeters) and "lower" (49.8 millimeters) allowable deviations from the nominal size of 50 millimeters are used to describe these intended limits. The difference between the upper and lower deviation values is called the tolerance. In this case the tolerance is 0.4 (= 50.2 – 49.8) millimeters.

13.2 MEASURING PROCESS PERFORMANCE

Decisions regarding the performance measures are made based on the industry or the company. A more consistent calculation of the metrics would make things easier. However, one common follow-up question is: "How to calculate that?" if a manager reports that his utilization is 90 percent or her efficiency is 115 percent. In the context of a certain process, metrics are frequently computed. The metrics that are defined to one industry may not exactly match the metrics used in the other industry. It's critical to comprehend the meaning of a term in the context of the case.

Benchmarking, or comparing a company's measurements to another, is a crucial practice. Metrics allow a company to determine whether improvements are being made. Process performance metrics provide an operations management with an indicator of how productive a process is currently running and how productivity is changing over time, much as the significance of financial measures to accounts. Operations managers frequently have to project the effects of suggested changes or enhance a process's effectiveness. To address these issues, the measurements discussed in this section are crucial. Fig. 13.1 illustrates the relationship between these metrics and its components. Utilization is arguably the most often used process metric. Utilization is the ratio of the amount of time a resource is really put to use to the total amount of time it is available. Every time a resource's utilization is measured, its intended capacity is taken into consideration. For instance, the ratio of the machine's actual production to its intended capacity is the machine's utilization. It's critical to understand the difference between utilization and productivity. The output to input ratio is known as **productivity**. The dollar amount of *total factor productivity* is often calculated by taking the total value of the output (i.e., goods and services sold) and dividing it by the total cost of all inputs (i.e., labor, material, and capital investment). On the other hand, *partial factor productivity* is calculated using a single input, most frequently labor. The question of how much output we can achieve from a given level of input – for instance, how many components are made by a worker in a production shop – is answered by partial factor productivity. Utilization evaluates how well a resource is really being used. That is, what proportion of the time does costly resource is actually been used? However, a situation could be that because of the cycle time, a machine in a production cell may only run once every minute. In that case, machine utilization is low despite the machine is efficient in its operation.

Fig. 13.1 Metrics for process performance

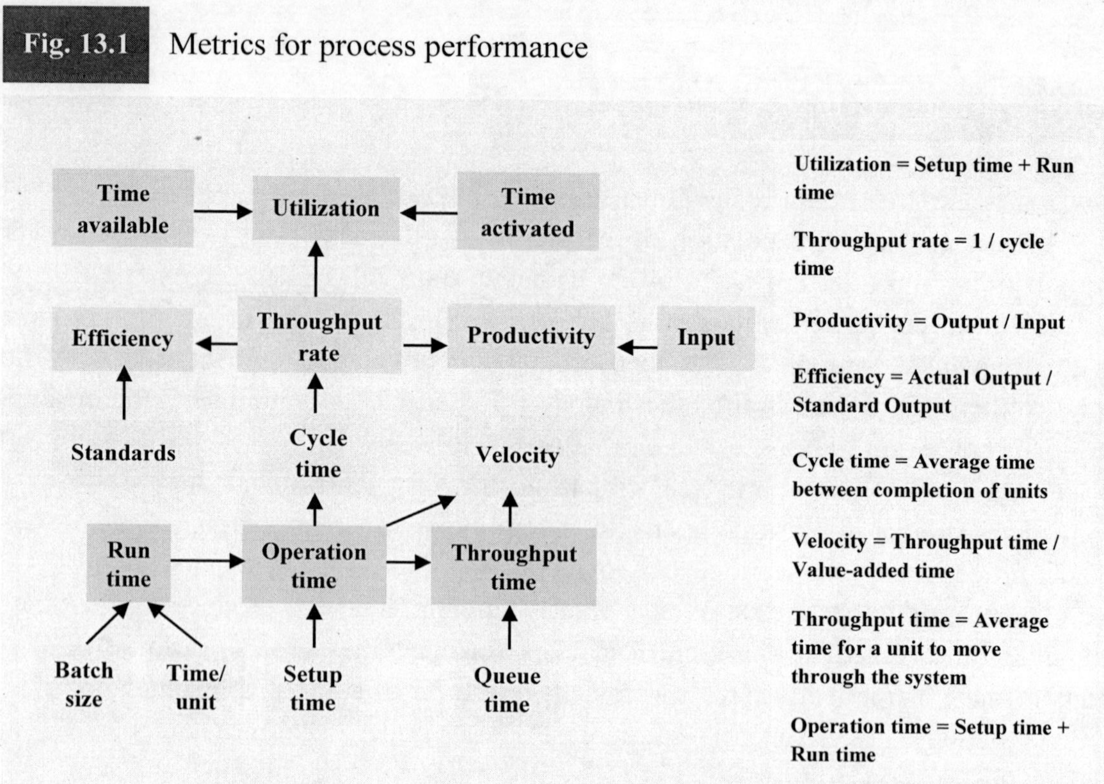

The actual output of a process relative to a standard is called its **efficiency**. Think of a machine that can produce components at a standard speed of 60 units per minute, for instance. The machine's efficiency is 120% if the operator actually produces at a rate of 72 units per minute (i.e., 72/60) ×100) during a shift. Measuring the gain or loss in a process is another method to apply the term efficiency. For instance, the operator in the aforementioned case creates 60 units but takes two minutes. In other words, the output rate is 30 boxes every minute. Consequently, there has been a 50% decrease in efficiency.

Run time is the amount of time needed to complete a batch of components. This is computed by multiplying the batch size by the amount of time needed to create each unit. The amount of time needed to set up a machine to produce a specific item is known as the **setup time**. Usually, parts are executed in batches on machines with large setup times. The total amount of time required for setting up and running a batch of parts on a machine is known as the **operation time**. Suppose you have a packing machine that can pack 20 products per minute. Three seconds (60/20) is the run time for every pack. A 20 minute setup is needed each time the machine is switched from one product type to another. A 1,000-product batch would take 4,200 seconds to complete (20 minutes × 60 seconds/minute + 3 seconds/pack × 1,000 packs), or 70 minutes.

The process's utilization frequently excludes setup time. Time spent on setup is essentially viewed as non-value-added work or downtime brought on by maintenance or other process interruptions. In order to compare how a machine or other resource is used, it is crucial to know precisely how the company classifies setup time, as this assumption can differ from business to business.

The amount of time that passes between beginning and finishing a task is called the cycle time. **Throughput time** is another word that is related. Throughput time is the sum of the unit's actual working time and its waiting time in a queue. Take, for instance, a timed assembly line with six stations and a 20-second cycle time. The throughput time is 2 minutes (20 seconds × 6 stations/60 seconds per minute) if the stations are arranged one after the other and parts travel from one station to the next every 20 seconds. The output rate that the process is anticipated to produce over time is known as the throughput rate. The assembly line's throughput rate is 180 units per hour (60 minutes × 60 seconds / minute ÷ 20 seconds/unit). Stated differently, the cycle time can be represented as the mathematical inverse of the throughput rate.

Units are frequently not worked on 100 percent of the time when they are being processed. Buffers are included in the process to enable individual operations to function independently, at least partially, because cycle times in processes are frequently somewhat variable. Think about the effects of adding ten more buffer positions to the six-station assembly line as shown in picture below. Assume that two units of these buffer locations are situated between the first and second workstations, the second and third workstations, and so on. With 16 locations altogether along the assembly line and average cycle duration of 20 seconds, the throughput time, if these places are constantly occupied, would be 5.33 minutes.

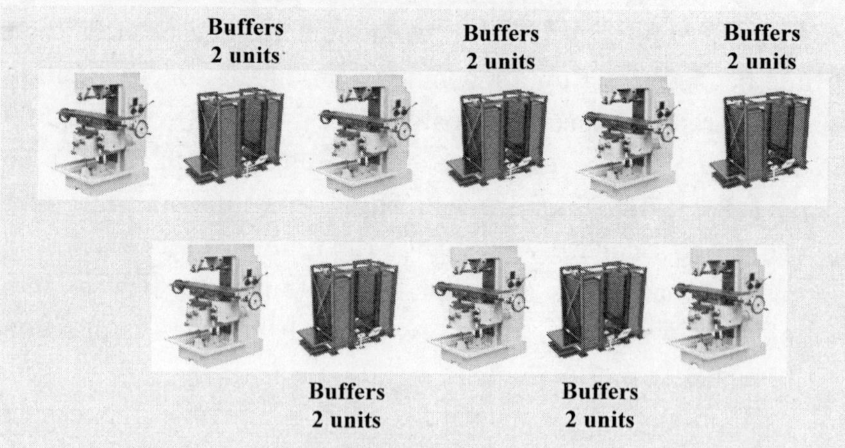

The ratio of the entire throughput time to the value-added time is called **process velocity**, or **throughput ratio**. The time when meaningful work is truly being done on the unit is known as **value-added time**. Value added time is the total of the activity operation times throughout the process, assuming that every activity is a value-added activity. Assuming the 10 extra buffer positions are used 100 percent of the time, the process velocity (or throughput ratio) for our assembly line with those positions is 2.66 (5.33 minutes / 2 minutes).

A mathematical link between throughput rate, throughput time, and the quantity of work-in-process inventory is stated by **Little's law**. Little's law, which may be used to determine the overall throughput time for a process, calculates the amount of time each item will spend in work-in-process inventory. Little's law is defined mathematically as:

$$\text{Throughput time} = \frac{\text{Work-in-process}}{\text{Throughput rate}}$$

Take note of how this law applies to the assembly line case where buffer inventory is absent. With 6 stations on the assembly line, each holding one unit of work-in-process, and a throughput rate of 3 units per minute (60 seconds / 20 seconds per unit), the throughput time would be 2 minutes (6 stations / 3 units per minute). When two of the three quantities are known, this equation is generally helpful. For instance, it is possible to determine the work-in-process if the throughput rate and throughput duration are given. Any process running at a steady rate can use this formula.

When we talk of steady rate, we imply that during the period under analysis, work is coming into and going out of the system at the same rate. 180 units enter our assembly line per hour, and 180 units leave it after processing. The system would not be running at a steady pace if, for instance, 210 units were entering the system every hour but only 180 units were leaving since 30 more units would be adding to the system every hour. The work-in-process that these thirty units add to would result in an hourly increase in the throughput time. Actually, there would be a 15-minute increase in throughput time per hour (30 units / 180 units per hour = 0.16 hour).

Example 13.1

An understanding of the steps involved in the manufacturing process of a gear is vital for a production shop manager. The gear-making process is depicted in a simplified form in Figure 13.2(a). To produce the component, there are two steps involved. Starting with the blank's turning process. And gear hobbing comes in second. Produced in 100-unit batches, the gears are made. Each hour, or one cycle of the operation, is completed by gear production in batches of 100 units. This 100 gear batch requires 0.75 hours for unloading and dispatch.

Fig. 13.2

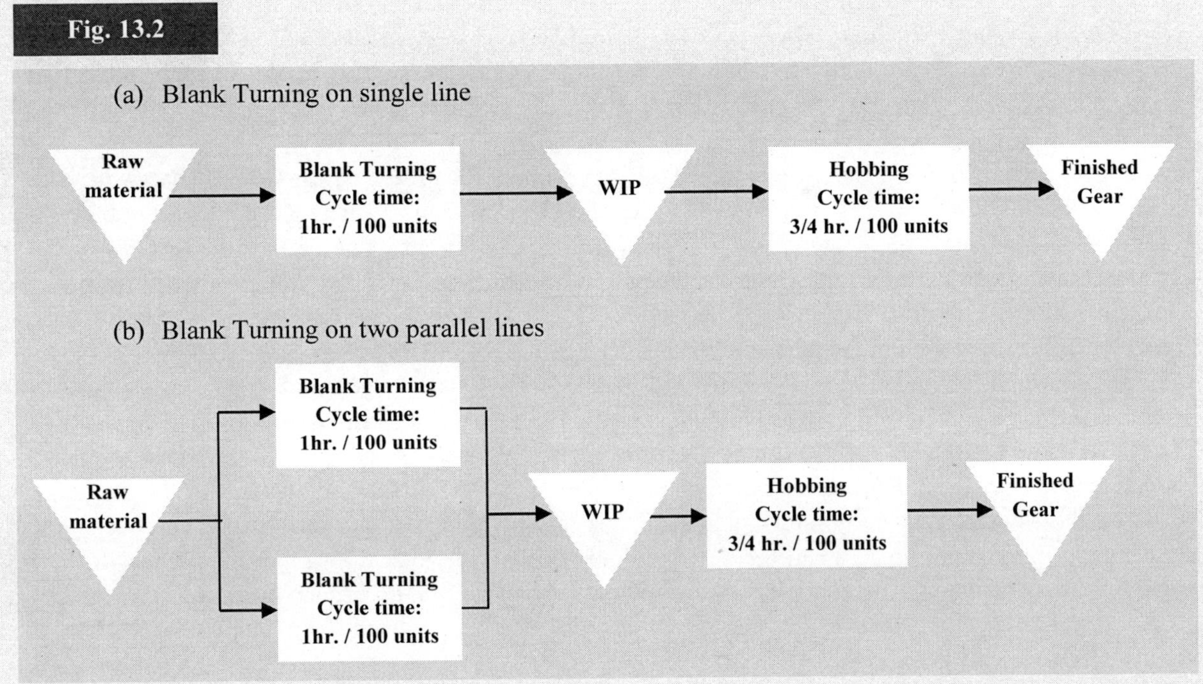

This indicates that blank turning is the process's bottleneck. The process step that restricts the process's total capacity is known as a bottleneck. Based on the assumption that the hobbing and blank turning processes run for the same length of time every day, the production facility can produce 100 gears every hour. Throughout the day, you will see that the hobbing process will pause for quarter-hour intervals during which the new batch of blank turning is being produced, but the hobbing has already been finished and the previous batch has been bagged. Under these circumstances, it would be expected that the hobbing procedure will be used 75% of the time.

Assume that, as seen in Figure 13.2 (b), we now have two concurrent processes for blank turning rather than just one. Every single blank turning process still has a cycle time of 100 units per hour. When both blank turning process lines are running simultaneously, the cycle time is thirty minutes. The hobbing operation is currently the bottleneck since it takes 0.75 hours to produce 100 units of gears. We do not have the capacity for the hobbing process, thus we would have to restrict the amount of gears that could be created if the blank turning and hobbing procedures were run for the same number of hours every day. On the other hand, if we ran the blank turning for two shifts and the hobbing process for three eight-hour shifts per day, then each process's daily capacity would be the same at 3,200 gears (this is assuming that the hobbing process begins an hour after the blank turning process). In order to accomplish this, work-in-process inventory must be built up daily to equal a shift's worth. Hobbing was going to bag this on the third shift. What is our gear manufacture shop's throughput time then?

Solution

Inventory would not accumulate between the blank turning and hobbing processes in the original operation with just single line of gear production, making this calculation simple. In this scenario, 1.75 hours would be the throughput time. The average wait in work-in-process inventory needs to be taken into account in the scenario when we run the hobbing operation for three shifts. The first 100 gears go straight into the hobbing process at the conclusion of the first hour if both blank turning operations begin at the same time, and the second batch of 100 gears waits. Until the hobbing operation is completed at the end of the second shift, the waiting period increases for every batch of 100 gears.

In this instance, Little's Law can be used to calculate how long the work-in-process gears will wait. We must calculate the average work-in-process between the blank turning and hobbing processes in order to apply Little's Law. Inventory increases from 0 to 1,200 ($0.75 \times 100 \times 16$) gears throughout the first two shifts. During this 16-hour period, the average work-in-process can be estimated to be 600 gears, which is half of the maximum. Inventory decreases from a maximum value of 1,200 gears to 0 over the last eight-hour shift. 600 gears are the average work-in-process once more. This means that the 24-hour average is just 600 gears total. This means that the 24-hour average is just 600 gears total. Assuming that the gears are packed in a batch, the hobbing method restricts the cycle time to 0.75 hours every 100 gears. This translates to a throughput rate of 133.3 gears per hour ($100/0.75 = 133.3$). According to Little's Law, gears are typically in the work-in-process state for 4.5 hours (600 gears / 133.3 gears/hour).

Together with the time spent on hobbing and blank turning processes, the gears' work-in-process time equals the entire throughput time. When this is taken into account, the total throughput time comes to 6.25 hours (1 hour for blank turning, 4.5 hours for work-in-process inventory, and 0.75 hours for hobbing process).

13.2.1 PROCESS WITH REDUCED THROUGHPUT TIME

The widely recognized principle that time equals money applies to critical activities. For instance, a consumer is more likely to move to a new vendor the longer they wait. The cost of investment increases with the length of time material is held in inventory. Bottlenecks are unavoidably caused by the fact that crucial operations frequently rely on certain, scarce resources. There are instances where throughput time can be decreased without investing in new hardware. Some recommendations that don't involve buying new equipment are listed below for shortening a process's throughput time.

1. **Carry out tasks concurrently** – In an operations process, the majority of the stages are carried out sequentially. When using a serial technique, the total throughput time of the process is equal to the total of all the individual stages plus the transit and step-to-step waiting times. A parallel technique yields higher quality results and can save throughput time by up to 80 percent.

A prime example is the current trend toward concurrent engineering in product development. Integrated teams complete all tasks in parallel rather than developing a concept, sketching, generating a bill of materials, and prioritizing tasks. There is a significant reduction in development time, and all parties' needs are met during the process.

2. **Change the order in which the processes are performed** – Parts are frequently backtracked between various machine components in functional arrangement. Cellular manufacturing uses group technology (discussed in Unit 7) to solve this issue by grouping part families with comparable sequences of operations together to prevent backtracking and enhance throughput performance.

3. **Minimize interruptions** – There are comparatively lengthy interruptions between the activities in many processes. Preventive maintenance, for instance, might only be carried out every other day. Timeliness is important for those who prepare preventive maintenance schedule that lead to maintenance operation since it can save many days of throughput time if these operations are timed better.

One of the fundamental skills required to comprehend how an organization runs is process analysis. Making a straightforward flowchart that illustrates how information or materials move through an organization can yield a great deal of knowledge. Every component of the operation should be shown in the diagram, along with how they work together. Don't forget to specify the location of the material storage or order queue. Frequently, waiting takes up 90% or more of the time needed to serve a customer. Therefore, just removing the waiting period can significantly enhance the process's performance.

13.3 SYSTEM RELIABILITY

The term "reliability" refers to the system's capacity to function effectively throughout time. It is the study of unplanned failures or unfavorable occurrences that happen at random when a physical system – a machine, a process, or any other kind of product – is in operation. The probability that a system will carry out its intended function for a predetermined period of time under typical operating conditions is known as **reliability**. Product warranties may have provided you with dependability information. A car warranty could be for 60,000 miles or three years. Regularly planned oil changes and other minor maintenance tasks would be considered normal conditions of usage. Not having an oil change or traveling more than 60,000 miles in three years would not be regarded as "normal" and would void the warranty.

A system's reliability depends on how reliable its operations are. It then depends on the components and their arrangement, as well as the reliability of the machinery, services, and parts. The system reliability is the product of the component part reliabilities if every portion of the equipment needs to work for the process or system to function. If R_s is the reliability of a system, then

$$R_s = (R_1)(R_2) \dots (R_n), \text{ where } R_n \text{ is the reliability of the } n\text{th component.}$$

In the event that a system requires two processes, each of which has a reliability of 0.80, the system's overall reliability would be 0.80 × 0.80 = 0.64, or 64%. The system can be seen as the following series of processes:

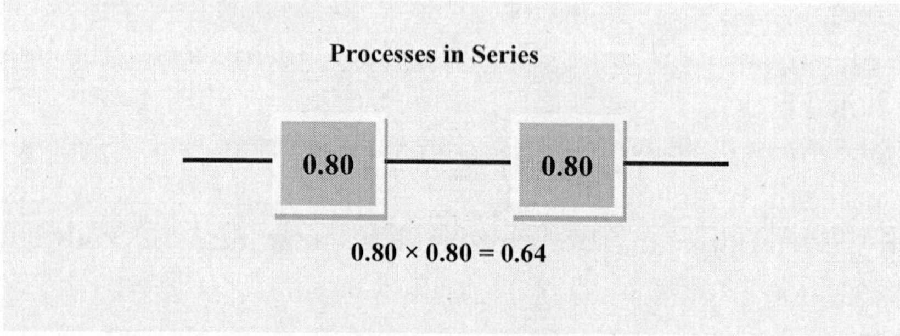

It should be noted that the 0.64 system reliability is significantly lower than the 0.80 individual process reliabilities. System reliability will keep decreasing as the number of serial processes rises. This presents a compelling case for a straightforward design with fewer steps.

The brake system of an automobile, for example, is one system whose failure can have more serious consequences than another. Redundant operations can be incorporated to support a failure in order to improve the reliability of each individual operation and, consequently, the system as a whole. Automobile emergency brakes are one example. Examine the subsequent parallel process design, where R_1 denotes the original process's reliability and R_2 the backup process's reliability.

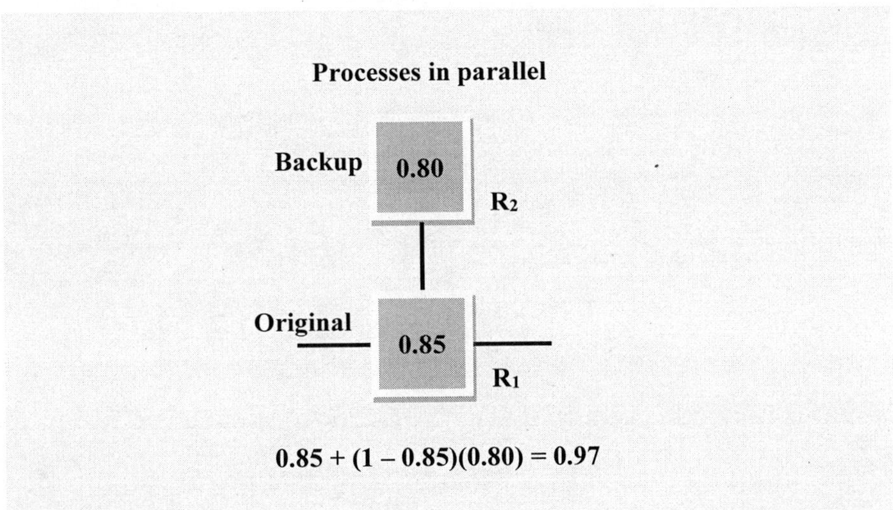

These processes are referred to as operating in parallel because, although it only happens 80% of the time, the backup process will automatically take over when the primary process fails (a 15% probability). Consequently, the system's reliability is:

$$R_s = R_1 + (1 - R_1)(R_2) = 0.85 + (1 - 0.85)(0.80) = 0.97$$

The mean time between failures (MTBF), which is another way to describe reliability, is the amount of time a process runs before failing. In this instance, the failure rate – the distribution of failures over time – is of interest. MTBF is equal to 1/failure rate, which is the reciprocal of the failure rate. For instance, the failure rate of your mobile phone battery would be 4/20 = 0.20 and its MTBF would be 1/0.20 = 5 hours if it fails four times in 20 hours of use.

Example 13.2

Determine the reliability of the system of components shown below.

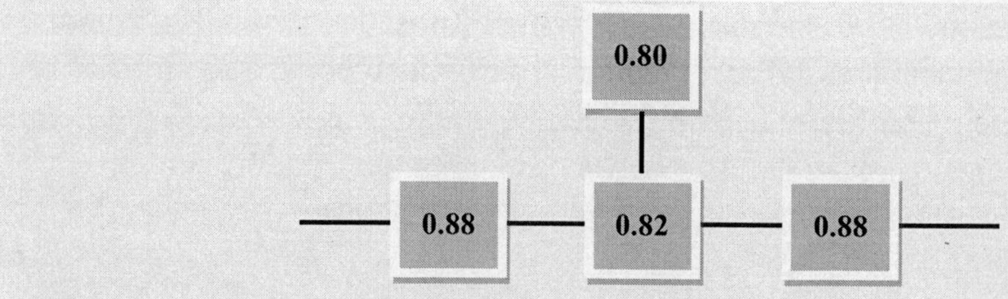

Solution

First, reduce the system to a series of three operations

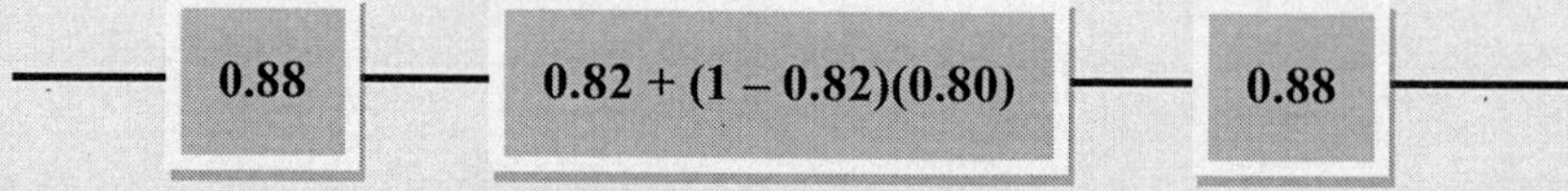

Then calculate the reliability of the system in series

$$= 0.88 \times 0.964 \times 0.88 = 0.746$$

Process design simplification, process improvement on an individual basis, or the addition of redundant processes can all increase reliability. Balanced and well-maintained assembly lines are more reliable.

13.3.1 MAINTAINABILITY

The term "maintainability" (also known as "serviceability") describes how simple and/or expensive it is to maintain or repair a good or service. Similar to cellular manufacturing, these processes are grouped based on comparable steps in the production process of a part, and a cell made up of various machines is established. If a machine breaks down, the parts can be diverted to another cell for a comparable machining operation until the broken machine is fixed. As a result, this kind of route scheme makes crucial replacement processes available.

Mean time to repair (MTTR) is one numerical indicator of maintainability. The average availability, or "uptime," of a system can be computed as follows when combined with the MTBF reliability measure:

$$\text{System Availability, SA} = \frac{\text{MTBF}}{\text{MTBF} + \text{MTTR}}$$

Example 13.3

AmaDay Company has to decide which service provider to use for her online store. If all else is equal, she will choose her choice based on the availability of the server. Which provider should she select based on the following server performance data?

Provider	MTBF (hr.)	MTTR (hr.)
X	50	3.0
Y	26	2.5
Z	30	1.5

Solution

$$SA = \frac{MTBF}{MTBF + MTTR}$$

$$SA_X = \frac{50}{50 + 3} = 0.9433 \text{ or } 94.33\%$$

$$SA_Y = \frac{26}{26 + 2.5} = 0.9122 \text{ or } 91.22\%$$

$$SA_Z = \frac{30}{30 + 1.5} = 0.9523 \text{ or } 95.23\%$$

AmaDay company should choose Provide Z.

13.4 DESIGN FOR QUALITY

Formal procedures for thoroughly evaluating the value of each part and component of an operation and analyzing potential failures should be followed before a design is finalized. Failure mode and effects analysis, fault tree analysis, and value analysis are three such methods.

13.4.1 FAILURE MODE AND EFFECT ANALYSIS (FMEA)

Failure Mode and Effects Analysis (FMEA) is a systematic method for identifying any failure in a product, service, or process design that might not have been noticed at the time of creation. With the use of this methodology, businesses should be able to foresee potential points of failure in the design phase and avoid any potential negative consequences down the road, such as delayed completion or overspending on capital projects.

Failure modes are the various ways that an equipment or end-product could fail. However, failures that result in waste, harmful results for the end user, or faults are known as effects. FMEA is therefore intended to detect failure modes, classify, rank, and ultimately prevent certain failure modes from ever happening.

During the design phase, you may recognize and handle failure modes with the help of the design FMEA. It entails dissecting the design into a number of constituent parts and examining the possible modes of failure. The analysis and upkeep of process control objectives is accomplished by the application of process FMEA. It is applied to processes rather than goods, as the name implies. You'll divide the procedure into different parts here, just like in design FMEA. Three fundamental criteria are used by a general FMEA technique to evaluate an issue. These are:

Severity – the degree to which the final consumer will be impacted. This criterion takes into account all standards that are significant to the particular industry. These can include environmental concerns, lost revenue, production continuity, safety regulations, and reputational harm.

Frequency – The problem's frequency. This criterion rates the likelihood of every failure mode over the anticipated lifetime of the process or product.

Detection – The problem's detection level or the degree of ease of detection. There are many challenges that arise, and they can be ranked according to how simple it is to identify issues and take proactive measures to avoid failure.

In order to complete an FMEA on a process or product, participants must decide on a ranking scale between 1 and 10. In the context of the aforementioned Severity, Frequency, and Detection criteria, 1 denotes very low and 10 high. For every failure mode that has been discovered, this needs to be done. Despite being a qualitative process, FMEA plays a crucial role in leveraging data to support and validate the conclusions the team takes about the ratings they provide. After assigning ratings to each of those modes of failure, we may get the Risk Priority Number (RPN). The formula for RPN is:

$$RPN = (Severity) \times (Occurrence) \times (Detection)$$

ALONG THE FAILURE MODE EFFECT ANALYSIS

The RPN finding under FMEA for some common manufacturing process follows.

Process Step	Potential Failure Mode	Potential Effects of Failure	Severety	Occurence	Detection	RPN	Action Taken
Material inspection	Incorrect material received	Products that are assembled might not fulfill requirements	8	3	5	120	Increased inspection checks and enhanced supplier communication
Cutting process	Machine tool wear	Varying dimensions of the parts	6	4	6	144	Frequent maintenance plans and a procedure for resharpening tools
Welding operation	Weld strength is insufficient	Failure of components' structure	9	2	4	72	More stringent quality controls and routine equipment maintenance
Assembly	Inaccurate order of assembly	Product failures and safety hazards	7	3	7	147	Visual aids and improved training for assembly line personnel
Quality inspection	Insufficient inspection	Shipped to customers defective goods	7	3	7	147	Process auditing, quality inspector certification, and training
Packaging	Mislabeled	Erroneous product identity	5	4	8	160	Automated technologies for tagging, more visual

In the analysis and remedial activity, the failure mode with the greatest RPN number should be prioritized. In the above case Packaging should be given the top priority for the FMEA.

For the purpose of studying “Fault Tree Analysis” and “Value Analysis,” the reader can scan the corresponding QR codes.

SCAN ME
for
Fault tree analysis

SCAN ME
for
Value analysis

13.5 QUALITY OF DESIGN

A product may not function properly due to poor factory manufacturing (quality of conformance) or poor design (quality of design). Quality of conformance is the main focus of quality control methods like statistical process control (SPC). Plotting periodic process samples on a chart to see whether the process is within statistical control limits is the method used to accomplish process control. One thing or a collection of items might serve as a sample. If a sample point is outside the range, the process can be out of control. In this case, the cause should be investigated in order to fix the issue.

No manufacturing method produces precisely the same products one after the other. Because of the inherent unpredictability in all processes, some variance across units is unavoidable. A process may differ for the two reasons stated in Section 13.1 above. The first is the process's intrinsic random variability, which is dependent on the machinery and equipment, the operator, the engineering, and the monitoring system. Naturally occurring events are the cause of this kind of fluctuation. The alternative explanation for variability is the presence of distinct or unusual causes that are observable and modifiable. If neglected, these nonrandom causes will eventually lead to low quality. These could include misaligned equipment, faulty materials, substitute parts or materials, worn-out machinery parts, operator tiredness, subpar work practices, or mistakes brought on by a lack of training.

Control charts are used to identify process errors at important points when the process has historically demonstrated a tendency to go out of control and at moments where going out of control can be costly and damaging. Control charts are graphs that indicate graphically if a sample falls inside the limits of statistical control. Establishing a process's control limits and then keeping an eye on it to spot instances of out-of-control behavior are their two main goals. There are control charts for variables and attributes, and there are various kinds of control charts within each category. Four typical charts are covered here: *p*-

SCAN ME
for
SPC charts

charts and c-charts for attributes, and mean X-bar and range R control charts for variables. By scanning the provided QR code, the reader can learn more about these charts.

Based on a number of standard deviations, z, from the process average (e.g., center line), a normal distribution is used to calculate the upper and lower bounds for control charts. The value of z is usually equal to 3.00, however it can also be equal to 2.00 on occasion. A normal chance of 95% is associated with a z value of 2.00, while 99.73% is associated with a z value of 3.00. Fig. 13.3, which displays a normal distribution, indicates the likelihoods associated with z values that are equivalent to 2.00 and 3.00 standard deviations (σ). The chart is more responsive to changes in the production process and the control limits are narrower the smaller the value of z. When referring to two standard deviations, control charts with $z = 2.00$ are said to have 2-sigma (2σ) limits, while those with $z = 3.00$ have 3-sigma (3σ) limits.

Since management want a high probability that the sample value will fall within the control limits if the process is under control, it typically chooses $z = 3.00$. Stated differently, if boundaries are broader, there is a decreased possibility that managers may mistakenly believe the process is uncontrollable, even if deviations from the limits are the result of typical, random fluctuations. On the other hand, changes in the process that are not random and have an assignable cause are more difficult to identify when the limitations are larger. A process that is identifiable with the tighter boundaries but not with the wider ones may alter due to a nonrandom, assignable cause. But businesses have always used the broader control boundaries.

Fig. 13.3 The Normal Distribution

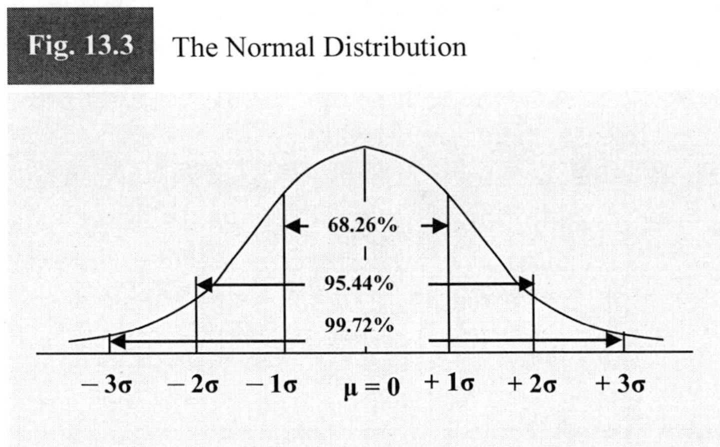

13.5.1 PROCESS CAPABILITY

An important factor affecting quality is process variability. Regarding the variability of process output, there are three phrases that are often employed. It is vital to distinguish between these concepts since each one pertains to a somewhat different component of that variability.

- The engineering design or the needs of the customer determine the *specifications* or *tolerances*. The range of values that each unit of output must fall within to be considered acceptable is indicated by them.
- Control limits are statistical limits that express the degree to which random variation alone can cause *sample statistics*, such as means and ranges, to differ.
- Process variability is a reflection of a process's inherent or natural variability, often known as random variability. The process standard deviation is used to measure it.

Process variability and control limits are closely linked since sampling variability is a function of process variability and control limits are dependent on it. However, neither control limits nor process variability is directly related to specifications. Instead of referring to the method used to create the good or service, they are described in terms of the product or service itself. Therefore, even if a process may be statistically in control, its output may not meet specifications in a particular situation. For this reason, considering a process's capabilities is equally essential. The inherent variability of process output in relation to the variance permitted by the design parameters is referred to as process capability.

CAPABILITY ANALYSIS

The purpose of capability analysis is to ascertain whether the process output's inherent variability is within the permissible variability range specified in the design requirements. When the process meets the requirements, it is deemed "capable." If not, the management has to make the decision about how to make things right.

Figure 13.4(a) illustrates the scenario whereby the design specification limits (the voice of the customer) and natural control limits (the voice of the process) coincide. The few items that go outside the process boundaries owing to random reasons will be among the few defective ones that arise from this. It is a reasonable quality target for a lot of firms. 99.72 percent of the probability exists between the limits if the process distribution is normally distributed and the natural control limits are three standard deviations from the process mean, or 3-sigma limits. The probability of good items is this. This indicates that there is a 0.28 percent area, or probability, outside the limits. This corresponds to 2.7 defects per thousand, or 2700 defects out of one million items. Strict quality philosophy, however, holds that this is inappropriate as a quality aim in situations involving human life.

Fig. 13.4 Process capability

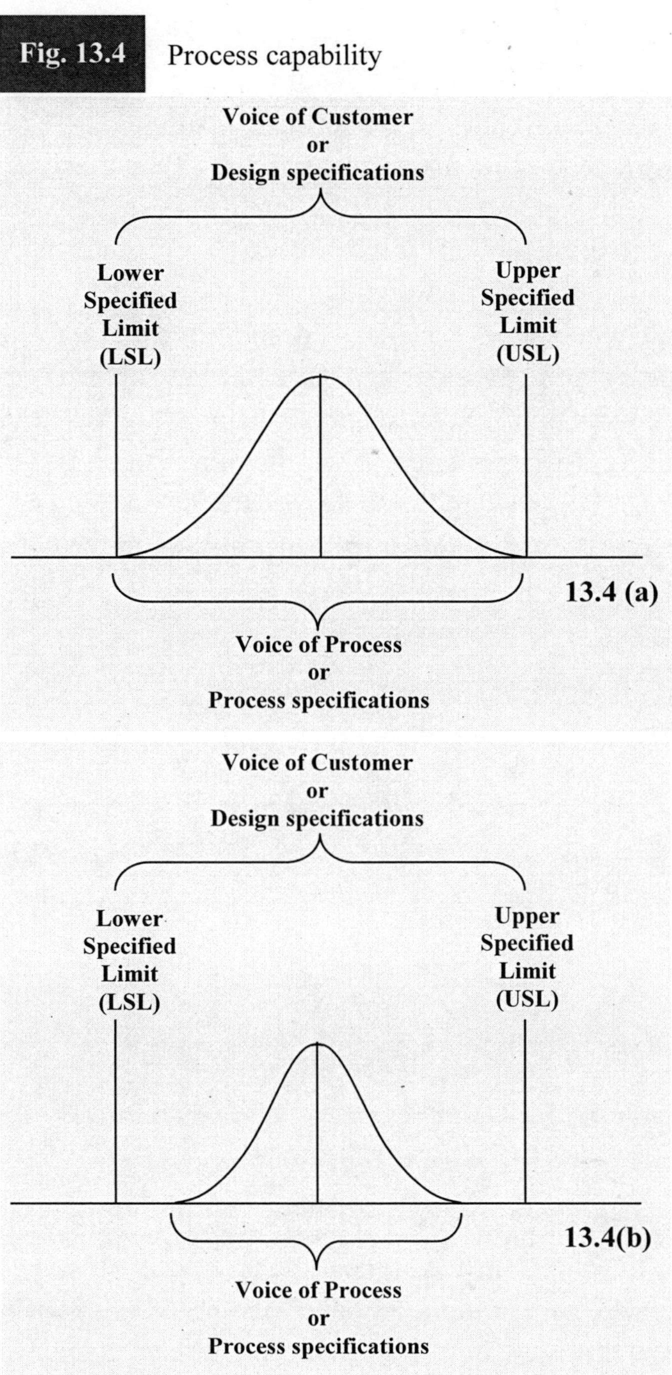

Consequently, many businesses have embraced "Six Sigma" quality. This means that twice as many specifications for product design are included as there are natural fluctuations, as indicated by 3-sigma control limits. Fig. 13.4 (b) provides a graphic representation of this kind of scenario, in which the design specifications beyond the natural control limits.

As long as the process mean is focused on the design target, the company anticipates that nearly all products will comply with the design specification. The statistical analysis indicates that a Six Sigma system would only generate 0.0000002 percent defects, or 0.002 defective parts per million (PPM), or 2 defects per billion. This was translated to 3.4 faults per million when Motorola stated in 1989 that it would reach Six Sigma quality in five years. From 2 flaws per billion to 3.4 defects per million, how did they do it? Motorola recognized that the process mean would not always match the design target exactly; in fact, it may deviate from the nominal design target by up to 1.5 sigma (the case shown in Fig. 13.4(c)), or 3.4 faults per million in Six Sigma terms. Since then, this value has evolved into the industry and company benchmark for Six Sigma quality. When the more common 3-sigma standard, which is utilized by most firms, is applied to the same scenario of a 1.5-sigma deviation from the process mean, the defect rate becomes 66,810 faults per million instead of 2700.

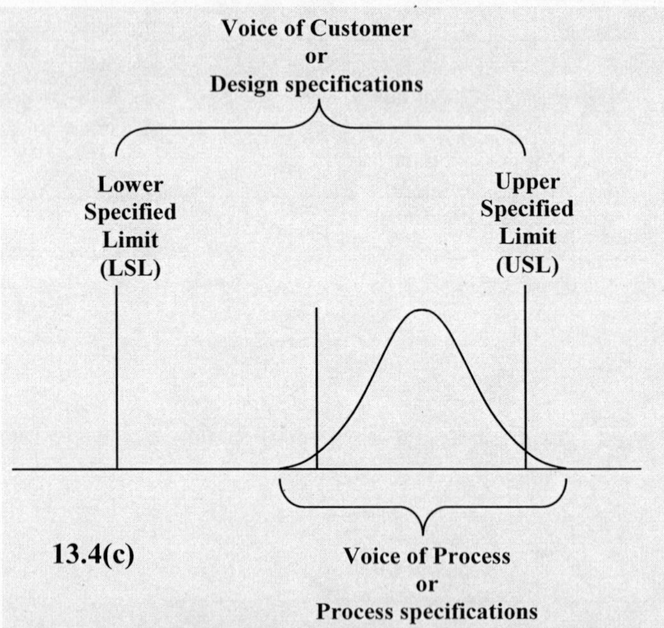

As can be seen, Fig. 13.4(c) illustrates the case where the process is off center but the design criteria exceed the process range of variation. Although the process is capable of achieving requirements, it cannot do so because it lacks control. In this instance, a portion of the output that is defective will go outside the higher design specification limit. Nearly majority of the output will match design requirements if the process is regulated such that the process center is centered and coincides with the design specifications.

In a similar vein, the natural variation of a process that exceeds the limits of the design specification is shown in Fig. 13.4(d). The procedure is unable to complete the tasks within the specified limits. Due to this circumstance, a significant percentage of the parts or products will be defective. A process cannot create a product in accordance with specifications if the limits of a control chart monitoring natural variation are greater than the product's planned standards or specification limits. There is more variance than intended because it will happen spontaneously and at random.

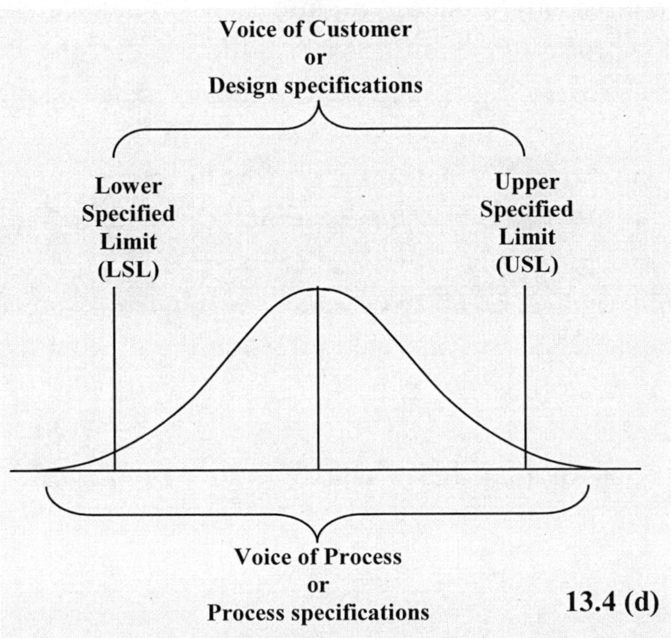

13.4 (d)

A company can better comprehend process variation by determining process capability. After determining the degree of quality that a process really achieves and how well it satisfies design standards, actions can be made to raise that level. The capability ratio (C_p) and the capability index (C_{pk}) are two metrics used to compare a process's ability to produce in accordance with design specifications.

13.5.2 PROCESS CAPABILITY MEASURES

The process capability ratio is one way to gauge a process's capacity to meet design specifications (C_p). It is defined as the ratio of the range of the designed specifications (the tolerance range) to the range of the process variation, which for most enterprises is usually $\pm 3\sigma$ or 6σ.

$$C_p = \frac{\text{tolerance range}}{\text{process range}}$$

$$= \frac{\text{upper specification limit (USL)-lower specification limit(LSL)}}{6\sigma}$$

The process is unable to consistently produce within design requirements if C_p is less than 1.0, which indicates that the process range is larger than the range of the design limitations. This is the scenario that is shown in Fig. 13.4(d). The tolerance range and the process range are nearly identical when $C_p = 1.0$, as illustrated in Fig. 13.4(a). The scenario shown in Fig. 13.4(b) occurs when C_p is more than 1.0, indicating that the tolerance range is larger than the process range. Companies would therefore naturally want a C_p of 1.0 or above, as this would suggest that the process is able to comply with specifications.

The process capability index (C_{pk}) is the second way to quantify process capability. In contrast to the C_p, the C_{pk} shows if and in which direction the process mean has deviated from the design target, or if it is off center. This is the scenario that Fig. 13.4(c) shows. The ability of the process in relation to the upper (USL) and lower (LSL) specifications is particularly measured by the process capability index.

$$C_{pk} = \text{minimum}\left[\frac{\bar{\bar{x}} - LSL}{3\sigma}, \frac{USL - \bar{\bar{x}}}{3\sigma}\right]$$

The process can satisfy the design parameters if the C_{pk} index is higher than 1.00. The process mean has shifted closer to either USL or LSL if C_{pk} is less than 1.00, and this will result in faults. The process mean is said to be centered on the design (nominal) target when $C_{pk} = C_p$.

A practical analysis like the one below could help us understand the process capability index better.

Fig. 13.5 Analogy of values of C_{pk}

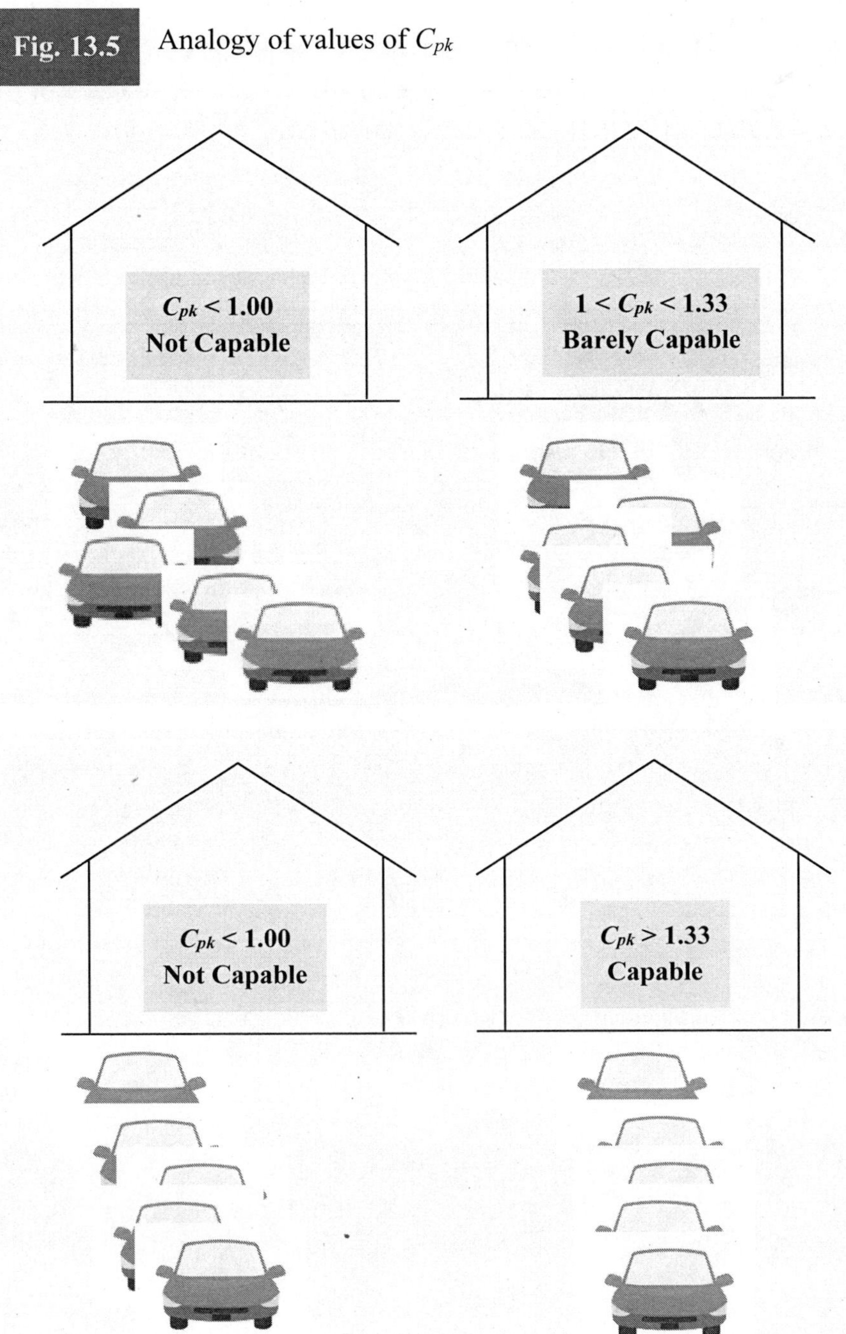

Let us assume that the width of the car is appropriate. It fits in the garage consistently because it's sufficiently narrow. Now, it is the driver's responsibility to park so that they don't damage the garage walls. A skilled driver would always keep the car well-centered and allow ample space on both sides to minimize the risk of scrapes or dents. On both sides, there's a plenty of space. On the other hand, an erratic driver could not always center the vehicle accurately. He's probably going to dent or scrape the car. Various car parking scenarios that correspond to the C_{pk} values are displayed in Fig. 13.5.

ALONG THE CAPABILITY ANALYSIS

Cleaning process for producing antibiotic drugs

It is generally known that in the purification processes of antibody drug substances the purified antibody proteins are likely to adhere onto the process equipment due to the process characteristics. A company needs to establish the quality of a cleaning process in producing antibody drug substances involving combination of many unit processes. The culturing process uses multiple reactors of varying sizes, while the purification process uses numerous tanks and chromatography equipment. Large areas need to be cleaned by numerous pieces of equipment in these operations.

An assessment of cleaning performance was carried out following the review and organization of previously collected cleaning data from the actual equipment used in the biopharmaceutical manufacturing process. This was done to make sure that cross-contamination was prevented and to guarantee that the cleaning process was carried out consistently.

The organization used the C_{pk} to statistically analyze the cleaning methods' capabilities in this investigation. Based on their production cleaning procedures, the manufacturing equipment for antibody drug substances was divided into equipment groups. The investigation showed that the cell separation and the bioreactor group's cleaning processes had excellent process capabilities. It also showed that, in comparison to other groups, the chromatography system group and the purification tank group had comparatively low C_{pk} values. The chromatography system's numerous horizontal and U-shaped piping parts, each with a diameter of less than 25.4 mm, making the system challenging to clean; this is thought to be the reason the chromatography system group's C_{pk} value was lower than that of the other groups. On changing the design aspects of the chromatography system, the company was able to bring the C_{pk} values within the control limits.

Example 13.4

Cereals at the grocery store are packaged in bags. With a tolerance of ±0.5 oz, the net weight of the cereals in each bag is intended to be 9.0 oz. Bags with a standard deviation of 0.12 oz and an average net weight of 8.80 oz are the product of the packaging procedure. The business want to ascertain whether

(a) The procedure can satisfy the design specifications.

(b) Whether or not the process mean is in the center.

Solution

(a) We know process capability

$$C_p = \frac{\text{USL} - \text{LSL}}{6\sigma}$$

$$= \frac{9.5 - 8.5}{6(0.12)} = 1.39$$

The process is therefore capable of operating within the design specification, as indicated by the process capability ratio of 1.39.

(b) Further, to know if the process mean is on center or not

$$C_{pk} = \text{minimum}\left[\frac{\bar{\bar{x}} - LSL}{3\sigma}, \frac{USL - \bar{\bar{x}}}{3\sigma}\right]$$

$$= \text{minimum}\left[\frac{8.80 - 8.50}{3(0.12)}, \frac{9.5 - 8.80}{3(0.12)}\right]$$

$$= \text{minimum}\ [0.83, 1.94] = 0.83$$

Despite the process being capable and being within the specified specification, as evidenced by the computed C_p of 1.39, the process mean is off center, as indicated by the C_{pk} value of 0.83. There will be underweight cereal packages made as a result of the shift toward the lower specification limit. As a result, the business must act to rectify the procedure and move the process mean closer to the designed goal.

UNIT SUMMARY

- ***Process Analysis & Measuring Performance***: (i) Defines processes as systems transforming inputs into valuable outputs, (ii) Introduces Little's Law to relate throughput time, work-in-process, and production rate, and (iii) Discusses bottlenecks and strategies to reduce throughput time.
- ***System Reliability***: (i) Explains reliability assessment methods in engineering systems, (ii) Covers series vs. parallel system reliability and methods to improve reliability, and (iii) Introduces Mean Time Between Failures (MTBF) and Mean Time To Repair (MTTR).
- ***Design for Quality*** (Failure Mode & Effect Analysis - FMEA): (i) Identifies failure modes, effects, and their severity, occurrence, and detection, and (ii) Uses Risk Priority Number (RPN) to rank and mitigate failure risks.

- ***Quality of Design & Process Capability***: (i) Discusses process control using Statistical Process Control (SPC) charts, (ii) Introduces process capability measures (Cp, Cpk) for assessing production quality, and (iii) Explains Six Sigma principles for process improvement.
- ***Practical Applications***: (i) Real-world case studies in manufacturing, service industries, and supply chain management, and (ii) Numerical problems and exercises for practical understanding.

EXERCISES

MULTIPLE CHOICE QUESTIONS

13.1 Which of the following best describes the term "processing time" in the context of process analysis?

(a) The total time taken to complete a batch of jobs	(b) The average time required to handle a single job or customer request
(c) The time taken to train employees on a new process	(d) The time required to develop a new process or system

13.2 When analyzing capacity issues in a process, what does the term "bottleneck" refer to?

(a) The process step that has the lowest cost	(b) The stage in the process that is the most expensive to operate
(c) The part of the process that limits the overall throughput or efficiency	(d) The stage that handles the most number of jobs

13.3 If a process has a job handling capacity of 50 jobs per hour and the average processing time for each job is 2 minutes, what is the maximum number of jobs that can be processed in a 10-hour shift?

(a) 200	(b) 300
(c) 500	(d) 600

13.4 What does the Reliability Importance Index measure in the context of a system's reliability?

(a) The contribution of a component to the overall system reliability	(b) The frequency of component failure
(c) The cost of replacing a component	(d) The ease of maintaining a component

13.5 Which of the following is a common cause of random variation in a manufacturing process?

(a) Ageing machinery	(b) Operator errors
(c) Variability in raw material properties	(d) Tool wear

13.6 Which of the following metrics is used as the ratio of the amount of time a resource is really put to use to the total amount of time it is available?

(a) Throughput	(b) Utilization Rate
(c) Defect Rate	(d) Downtime

13.7 In process performance metrics, what does "Throughput" measure?

(a) The total downtime experienced by the process	(b) The percentage of output that meets quality standards
(c) The average time to complete a single task	(d) The rate at which products are produced and delivered over a given time period

13.8 According to Little's Law, if the average arrival rate (λ) of customers to a service desk is 10 customers per hour and the average time (W) a customer spends at the desk is 15 minutes, what is the average number of customers in the system (L)?

(a) 2.5	(b) 10
(c) 15	(d) 25

13.9 Which assumption is essential for the application of Little's Law?

(a) The system must have a deterministic arrival and service time	(b) The system must be in a steady-state condition
(c) The arrival rate must be greater than the service rate	(d) The system must have no variability in arrival times

13.10 Which strategy is most effective for reducing the throughput time of a process?

(a) Increasing the number of inspections per unit	(b) Lengthening setup times to ensure higher quality
(c) Implementing streamlined workflows and reducing handoffs	(d) Increasing buffer sizes between process stages

13.11 What is the effect on the overall reliability if a system with components in series is redesigned to have components in parallel?

(a) The overall reliability decreases	(b) The overall reliability remains the same
(c) The effect on overall reliability cannot be determined	(d) The overall reliability increases.

13.12 Which metric is commonly used to assess the maintainability of a process?

(a) Mean Time Between Failures (MTBF)	(b) Return on Investment (ROI)
(c) Customer Satisfaction Score (CSAT)	(d) Market Share Growth

13.13 In FMEA, the "severity" rating is most closely related to which of the following?

(a) The cost of the components involved in the failure mode	(b) The potential consequences of the failure on the system or user
(c) The likelihood of the failure mode occurring	(d) The ease with which the failure can be detected

13.14 When calculating the Risk Priority Number (RPN) in FMEA, which factor is considered least relevant for assessing potential failure modes?

(a) The impact of the failure on user safety	(b) The likelihood of the failure occurring
(c) The ease of detecting the failure before it causes damage	(d) The number of users affected by the failure

13.15 Which type of control chart is typically used to monitor the mean and variability of a continuous process?

(a) P-chart	(b) C-chart
(c) X-bar chart	(d) NP-chart

13.16 When using a P-chart to monitor defect rates, which of the following factors is NOT typically adjusted to improve the chart's effectiveness?

(a) Sample size	(b) Control limits
(c) Number of defective items in each sample	(d) Sample frequency

13.17 When evaluating process capability, what does a Cp value greater than 1 indicate?

(a) The process is producing outputs that are consistently outside the specification limits	(b) The process variability is less than the specification range, but it does not account for process centering

(c) The process is perfectly centered between the specification limits with no variability	(d) The process mean is significantly different from the target value

13.18 If a process has a Cpk value of 0.75, what does this typically imply about the process?

(a) The process is operating within specification limits but is not capable of meeting the requirements	(b) The process is highly capable and consistently produces within the specification limits
(c) The process is not centered between the specification limits and may require significant improvement	(d) The process is perfectly centered but has high variability

Answers of Multiple Choice Questions

13.1 (b), 13.2 (c), 13.3 (c), 13.4 (a), 13.5 (a), 13.6 (b), 13.7 (d), 13.8 (a), 13.9 (b), 13.10 (c), 13.11 (d), 13.12 (a), 13.13 (b), 13.14 (d), 13.15 (c), 13.16 (d), 13.17 (b), 13.18 (c)

SHORT AND LONG ANSWER TYPE QUESTIONS

Category I

13.1 What strategies can be employed to alleviate a bottleneck?

13.2 How can the Reliability Importance Index influence decision-making in system design or maintenance?

13.3 Why might a component with a low failure rate still have a high Reliability Importance Index?

13.4 What role does operator skill play in assignable variation?

13.5 Why is utilization an important metric in manufacturing?

13.6 How can improving throughput benefit a manufacturing operation?

13.7 How is Little's Law applied in manufacturing processes?

13.8 How does adding more components in parallel affect the reliability of the system?

13.9 Why is MTBF an important metric in reliability engineering?

13.10 What do the three factors (Severity, Occurrence, and Detection) represent in the RPN calculation?

13.11 What is the primary difference between a variable control chart and an attribute control chart?

13.12 Which is the key difference between Cp and Cpk in process capability analysis?

Category II

13.13 In the context of designing a new industrial automation system for a manufacturing facility, you are tasked with evaluating and enhancing the system's reliability. The system includes various components such as sensors, actuators, controllers, and communication modules. Describe how the Reliability Importance Index (RII) can be utilized to improve the design of this system. Discuss the steps involved in calculating the RII for each component, how the results can guide design decisions, and the potential benefits of using the RII in this context.

13.14 Describe how you would differentiate between random variation and assignable variation in this manufacturing process. Explain the methods you would use to identify and analyze each type of variation, and discuss how addressing these variations can improve the overall quality and efficiency of the manufacturing process.

13.15 As part of an initiative to improve overall efficiency and productivity, you need to analyze and optimize the performance metrics of utilization and throughput across different stages of the production process. Describe how you would approach evaluating and improving these metrics. Explain the methods you would use to measure and analyze utilization and throughput, discuss how these metrics interrelate, and outline strategies to enhance both.

13.16 You are the operations manager at a busy warehouse that processes and ships customer orders. The warehouse is experiencing delays in order fulfillment and high levels of customer dissatisfaction. To address these issues, you decide to apply Little's Law to analyze the warehouse operations. Describe how you would use Little's Law to understand and improve the warehouse's efficiency. Include the following in your discussion:

- How you would collect and use relevant data for applying Little's Law.
- The specific steps involved in calculating and interpreting the key metrics using Little's Law.

- How you would use the results to identify operational bottlenecks and areas for improvement.
- Specific strategies you might implement to enhance warehouse performance based on your analysis.
- Potential challenges you might face in applying Little's Law in this context and how you would address them.

13.17 You are the reliability engineer for a company that designs and manufactures critical electronic systems for aerospace applications. The company is currently evaluating the reliability of two different system configurations: one with components connected in series and another with components connected in parallel. Describe how you would approach the reliability analysis for both series and parallel configurations on the following basis:

- The impact of component reliability on the overall system reliability in both configurations.
- Specific examples of real-life scenarios where each configuration might be preferable.

NUMERICAL PROBLEMS

13.1 A bike maker receives electrical circuit modules from a vendor and assembles bikes in a plant. Every electrical circuit module costs, on average, $45. When the electrical circuit module arrives at the plant, the bike manufacturer becomes the owner of the electrical circuit module. The plant produces 200 bikes in an eight-hour shift, taking precisely twelve hours to complete (the plant currently performs one shift each day). A single electrical circuit module is used in every bike. As a safety precaution, the manufacturer keeps 8000 electrical circuit modules in stock at the factory on average. Calculate the average total number of electrical circuit modules in the factory, including those in raw material inventory and work-in-process. What is the cost of these electrical circuit modules? What is the average number of days that electrical circuit modules inventory is retained in stock?

13.2 Bike silencers can be electroplated by a shop that specializes in electroplating. It is examining how things are done in its shop. The process's general flow is depicted as follows. At every stage of the process, a different person is engaged.

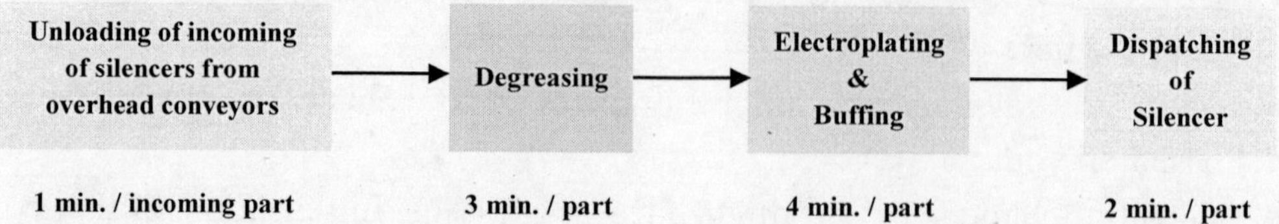

The manager is trying to determine the following for a typical eight-hour workday:

(a) What is the process's current maximum output?

(b) Where would we put the new employee and what would be the advantage?

(c) Would it help to move one minute from degreasing process to the unloading of arriving silencers? Assume we decide not to alter it in part (b).

(d) Would it help to switch one minute of labor from buffing to dispatching silencers? Assume that the modifications in parts (b) and (c) are not made.

13.3 SuperPrec, Inc.'s production manager is dedicated to the business's new quality initiatives. Making product components in-house is encouraged as part of the program to guarantee better quality standards and foster employee pride. All appears to be well with the system. One assembly is typically bought from a nearby supplier and requires a reliability of 0.95. It is now being put together in-house using three parts, each of which has a 0.96 reliability rating.

(a) In the three months since SuperPrec began handling its own assembly, the number of customer complaints has increased. Could you elaborate on why?

(b) What degree of component reliability is required to get the product back to its previous standard of quality?

(c) The manager can give each component a backup with a dependability of 0.90, but he cannot raise the reliability of any one component alone. How many backups will it take to get the assembly's reliability down to 0.95 if the backups have reliability of 0.90?

13.4 The production manager is attempting to determine which machine requires greater maintenance. The manager gathered information on the three machines in the manufacturing line's mean time to repair (MTTR) and mean time between failures (MTBF). Which of the three machines requires more maintenance care, considering that the cost and difficulty of the repairs are equal?

Machines	MTBF	MTTR
M1	20	1
M2	40	4
M3	80	6

13.5 The processing times for component machining in a manufacturing shop are displayed in the table below. There have been five samples, each consisting of four observations. Create upper and lower control limits for a mean chart and a range chart using the sample data and Table from this chapter's Appendix 13.1. Do the findings imply that the process is in control?

Sample 1	Sample 2	Sample 3	Sample 4	Sample 5
10.2	10.3	9.7	9.9	9.8
9.9	9.8	9.9	10.3	10.2
9.8	9.9	9.9	10.1	10.3
10.1	10.4	10.1	10.5	9.7

13.6 For each scenario, ascertain the two-sigma control limits using the relevant control chart:

(a) When inspecting each car being prepared for delivery to dealers, an inspector discovered an average of 3.9 scratches in the outside paint.

(b) An inspector tries to start each lawnmower before delivering it to a dealer, noting any that doesn't start on the first try. Four movers on average (4 percent) did not start out of the 100 movers in the lot.

13.7 Choose the most capable of these three processes.

Process	Mean	Standard Deviation	Lower Specification	Upper Specification
1	7.5	0.10	7.0	8.0
2	4.6	0.12	4.3	4.9
3	6.0	0.14	5.5	6.7

REFERENCES AND SUGGESTED READINGS

1. Clausing, D., and Dombrowski, D. *Design for Six Sigma: A Practical Approach to Building Quality into Products and Processes*. McGraw-Hill, 2013.
2. Cunningham, J. A., and Cunningham, M. P. *Applied Operations Research: A Practical Approach*. Springer, 2010.
3. George, M. L. *Lean Six Sigma: Combining Six Sigma Quality with Lean Production Speed*. McGraw-Hill, 2002.

4. Goh, T. N. The Quality of Process Capability: Process Capability Indices and Their Implications. *International Journal of Quality & Reliability Management*, Vol. 22(5), 486-500, 2005.
5. Goldratt, E. M. The Theory of Constraints: What Is This Thing Called Throughput? *International Journal of Production Research*, Vol. 28(5), 871-879, 1990.
6. Hass, S. System Reliability Engineering: Theory and Practice. *Journal of Reliability Engineering*, Vol. 16(4), 23-29, 2006.
7. Heizer, J., and Render, B. *Operations Management: Sustainability and Supply Chain Management*. Pearson, 2020.
8. Hopp, W. J., and Spearman, M. L. *Factory Physics: Foundations of Manufacturing Management*. McGraw-Hill, 2004.
9. Huang, L., and Zhang, Z. Reliability Optimization in Manufacturing Systems: A Review. *International Journal of Advanced Manufacturing Technology*, Vol. 88(5-8), 1185-1196, 2017.
10. Juran, J. M., and Godfrey, A. B. *Juran's Quality Handbook: The Complete Guide to Performance Excellence*. McGraw-Hill, 1999.
11. Kume, H. *Introduction to Statistical Quality Control*. Springer, 1999.
12. Kwak, Y. H., and Anbari, F. T. A New Approach to Throughput Time Reduction in Complex Manufacturing Systems. *International Journal of Project Management*, Vol. 24(7), 563-572, 2006.
13. Little, J. D. C. A Proof for the Queuing Formula: $L = \lambda W$. *Operations Research*, Vol. 9(3), 383-387, 1961.
14. Milenkovic, M., and Stojanovic, J. *Reliability Engineering: Theory and Practice*. CRC Press, 2010.
15. Montgomery, D. C. *Introduction to Statistical Quality Control*. Wiley, 2009.
16. Montgomery, D. C., and Runger, G. C. Process Capability Analysis and Control Charts. *Journal of Quality Technology*, Vol. 41(2), 1-17, 2009.
17. Porteus, E. L. *Foundations of Stochastic Inventory Theory*. Stanford University Press, 1990.
18. Pyzdek, T., and Keller, P. *The Six Sigma Handbook*. McGraw-Hill, 2014.
19. Shirose, M., and Takagi, A. *System Reliability and Optimization: A Practical Approach*. Wiley-Interscience, 2004.
20. Slack, N., Brandon-Jones, A., and Johnston, R. *Operations Management*, Pearson. 2019.
21. Stamatis, D. H. *Failure Mode and Effect Analysis: FMEA from Theory to Execution*. CRC Press, 2003.

22. Sunder, M. *Six Sigma and Beyond: Process Optimization*. CRC Press, 2009.
23. Suri, R. The Fundamentals of Process Improvement: Throughput Time Reduction and Capacity Expansion. *International Journal of Production Economics*, Vol. 89(1), 61-71, 2004.
24. Tavakkol, M., and Alizadeh, M. Application of Little's Law in Queuing Systems. *International Journal of Operations & Production Management*, Vol. 27(8), 862-870, 2007.
25. Womack, J. P., and Jones, D. T. *Lean Thinking: Banish Waste and Create Wealth in Your Corporation*. Free Press, 1996.
26. Woods, D. *Operations Management: A Supply Chain Approach*. Wiley, 2012.

APPENDIX 13.1

Factors for 3-sigma control limits for $\overline{X}$ and R charts

		FACTORS FOR R CHART	
No. of observations in Sample (n)	**Factor for Chart (A_2)**	**Lower Control Limit (D_3)**	**Upper Control Limit (D_4)**
2	1.88	0	3.27
3	1.02	0	2.57
4	0.73	0	2.28
5	0.58	0	2.11
6	0.48	0	2.00
7	0.42	0.08	1.92
8	0.37	0.14	1.86
9	0.34	0.18	1.82
10	0.31	0.22	1.78
11	0.29	0.26	1.74
12	0.27	0.28	1.72
13	0.25	0.31	1.69
14	0.24	0.33	1.67
15	0.22	0.35	1.65
16	0.21	0.36	1.64
17	0.20	0.38	1.62
18	0.19	0.39	1.61
19	0.19	0.40	1.60
20	0.18	0.41	1.59

UNIT **14**

TOTAL QUALITY MANAGEMENT

UNIT SPECIFICS

This unit elaborately discusses the following topics:

- Overview of Total Quality Management (TQM)
- Quality Gurus and their approaches to TQM
- Plan-Do-Study-Act (PDSA) cycle
- Objectives of TQM
- Quality improvement
- Cost of quality
- Elements of TQM
- Seven quality control tools
- ISO 9000 versus TQM

The topics covered in the unit encourage greater creativity and curiosity. Along with a number of multiple-choice questions and questions with both short and long answer types, the unit includes a list of references, suggested readings, and projects that are divided into two groups according to the lower and higher order of Bloom's taxonomy. By completing these, one can get practice. The reader was carefully considered when creating the unit. One notable aspect is the usage of QR codes, which can be scanned to yield pertinent extra information on a variety of interesting topics.

RATIONALE

This unit provides a comprehensive overview of Total Quality Management (TQM), highlighting its significance in enhancing organizational performance and customer satisfaction. It introduces key quality gurus – such as Deming, Juran, and Crosby – whose diverse approaches have shaped TQM principles. The Plan-Do-Study-Act (PDSA) cycle is examined as a fundamental method for continuous improvement. The objectives of TQM, including quality enhancement and cost reduction, are discussed alongside the concept of the cost of quality, emphasizing the financial benefits of investing in quality initiatives. Essential elements of TQM are outlined, along with the Seven Quality Control Tools that facilitate effective quality management. Finally, the unit contrasts ISO 9000 standards with TQM, illustrating their complementary roles in fostering a culture of quality within organizations.

UNIT OUTCOMES

List of outcomes of this unit is as follows:

U14-UO1: Understand the Fundamentals of TQM

U14-UO2: Identify contributions of Key Quality Gurus

U14-UO3: Apply the PDSA Cycle

U14-UO4: Set TQM Objectives

U14-UO5: Evaluate the Cost of Quality

U14-UO6: Differentiate ISO 9000 and TQM

UNIT-14 Outcomes	EXPECTED MAPPING WITH COURSE OUTCOMES (*1-Weak Correlation; 2-Medium Correlation; 3-Strong Correlation*)					
	CO-1	CO-2	CO-3	CO-4	CO-5	CO-6
U14-UO1	3	2	3	3	2	1
U14-UO2	2	1	2	3	1	-
U14-UO3	3	2	3	3	2	1
U14-UO4	2	2	2	3	2	1
U14-UO5	2	2	2	3	2	1
U14-UO6	2	1	2	3	2	1

14. 1 INTRODUCTION

The term "Total Quality Management," or "TQM," is widely used and is associated with the cultures of many industrial and service industries. Since many organizations are attempting to integrate TQM as a way of life, it is necessary to have a thorough awareness of the fundamental principles, major concerns, practical considerations, and potential pitfalls. There are a lot of misconceptions regarding TQM that are not at all true. A business that obtains ISO 9000 certification will reach its TQM objective. Is it true? This is untrue; merely obtaining an ISO 9000 certification does not guarantee complete quality: What then is the purpose of obtaining ISO certification? We have to have a thorough understanding of it. First things first, let's clarify: in TQM, what exactly are "total" and "quality"?

14. 2 WHAT IS TOTAL IN TQM?

Total in TQM refers to an organization's involvement in every facet in ensuring customer satisfaction. It seeks to achieve an objective that can only be realized if the value is acknowledged through the establishment of a partnership environment at every level of the business process, both inside and outside the organization. "Within the business process" refers to tasks that fall under organizational purview. When we talk about the outside, we imply a good customer-supplier relationship. This entails:

- A relationship of mutual trust and respect between the supplier and the customer. A win-win plan needs to be in place for both.
- Internal organization requirements as reported by clients.
- The supplier is aware of the needs of the client.
- Suppliers work together to create a situation where there is no rejection.
- The customer's routine observation of the supplier's operations and output.

14.3 WHAT IS QUALITY?

Customer's desire is quality. It is the opinion of the customer on how well the good or service fulfills his or her needs. As a result, the needs and expectations of the customer define quality. Similar to beauty, quality is subjective to the observer. When quality needs to be accurately defined, it becomes infinitely complex, even though it is simple to describe.

"Quality is equal to people plus the proper attitude to achieve excellence; meeting customer requirements and expectations; and producing error-free products and services on time." Delivering new goods and services that effectively meet the expectations of customers, both internal and external to the organization, is what is meant by quality.

In general, quality denotes the "excellence" of a good or service. A car, house, book, or other thing that a consumer utilizes is an example of a product. Services are similar to banks, post offices, hospitals, etc. We just spoke about the customer. There are two categories of customers in the context of TQM:

(i) Internal customer

(ii) External customer

One employee uses another's output inside the company system. On an assembly line, parts are passed between people as they work. The preceding person's internal customer is the subsequent person in this situation. Generally speaking, a department may also have internal customers. As an illustration, the production department's internal customer is the packaging department, and the packaging department's internal customer is the marketing department. The end-user of the product or service who is not affiliated with the organization is referred to as an external customer.

14.4 TOTAL QUALITY MANAGEMENT (TQM)

TQM is a systemic approach to managing quality. It means giving quality the utmost attention in every aspect of the company. Fig. 14.1 depicts a quality system plan. Total in Total Quality Management refers to an all-encompassing integrated approach to all domains of the system, including organization, people, resources, time, hardware/software, and even management commitments. TQM is an approach to organization management that is quality-focused, involves all members, and aims to achieve long-term success through customer satisfaction and benefits to the company's members as well as society (ISO 8402/IS 13999). According to MacDonald, Total Quality Management (TQM) is a procedure that is utilized to control environmental changes in order to guarantee that a corporation achieves its objective of total continuous improvement (TCI). Four pillars support Total Quality Management (TQM): SPC (statistical process control) tools, teamwork, top management commitment, and systems. Culture, communication, dedication, and client focus are the links between these pillars. TQM is a quality-focused organizational culture. Achieving excellence in every facet of the organization's operations is a journey. Every employee in the company, regardless of level of operation, is involved.

Fig. 14.1 A quality system plan

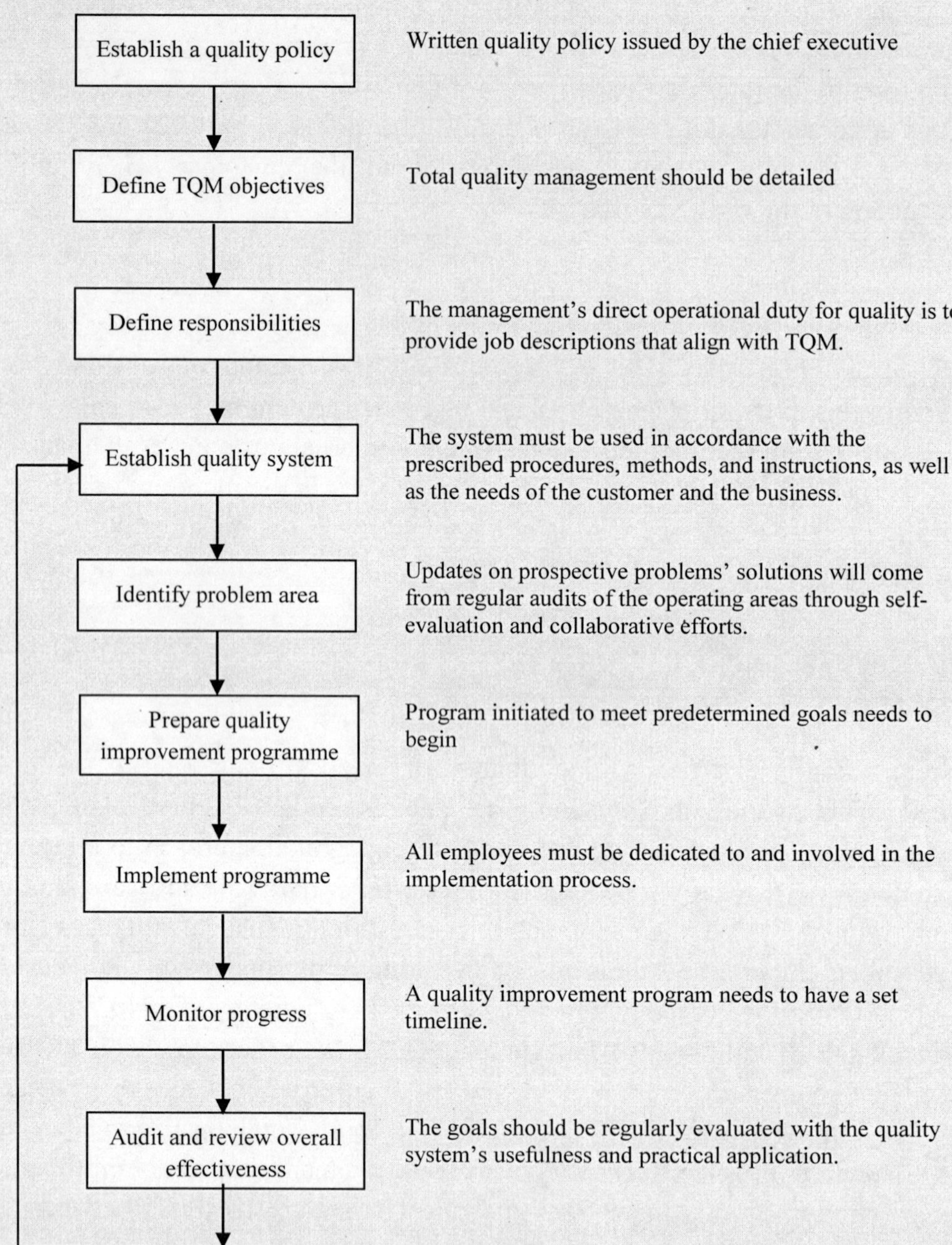

14.5 QUALITY GURUS

Few quality experts, or "Gurus," have made significant contributions in recent years to the popularization of the quality culture within organizations. Their primary focus has been on quality management strategies. We investigate the methods presented by a few of them, including Philip B. Crosby, W. Edwards, and Joseph M. Juran.

Philip B. Crosby approach to TQM

1. Definition – Quality is conformance to requirements; and not goodness.
2. System – Prevention, not appraisal.
3. Performance standard – Zero defect; and not "that's close enough."
4. Measurement – Not quality indicators, but the cost of non-conformance to requirements.

Crosby suggested fourteen steps for management to get more effective:

1. Emphasize the management's dedication to quality.
2. Assemble teams for quality enhancement that include members from every department.
3. Identify the areas that may have present or future quality issues.
4. Assess the cost of quality and describe how it can be used as a tool for management.
5. Increase each employee's awareness of quality and level of personal concern.
6. Implement solutions to issues found in the earlier phases.
7. Form a group to oversee the program to eliminate all faults.
8. Teach supervisors how to actively participate in the program for quality improvement.
9. Organize a "zero defect day" to inform all staff members of the change.
10. Motivate people to set personal and collective improvement objectives.
11. Encourage staff members to share with management the challenges they encounter in achieving their development objectives.
12. Give thanks and recognition to all who take part.
13. Create high-quality councils to facilitate regular communication.
14. Repeat the entire process to underline that the program for quality improvement never ends.

Deming's approach to TQM

Deming was one of the TQM concept's first proponents. His ideas for raising quality include the following fourteen points:

1. Strive to have a consistent purpose to enhance product and services.
2. Try to embrace the new mindset that aims to make the levels of errors, delays, and faults that are accepted undesirable.
3. Try to reduce your dependency on mass inspection since it doesn't ensure or enhance quality. Recall that the path to improvement lies in collaboration between the company and its suppliers.
4. Make an effort to cease granting contracts based solely on cost.
5. Seek to identify issues. The management needs to keep refining the system.
6. Make an effort to benefit from contemporary training techniques. When creating a training program, keep the following things in mind:
   - Strive to determine the company's goals.
   - Strive to identify your training objectives.
   - Aim for everyone to comprehend the objectives.
   - Aim for new hire orientation.
   - Emphasize providing supervisors with statistical thinking training.
   - Make a plan for team-building.
   - Try to analyze the necessity for instruction.
7. Try to implement contemporary methods of supervision.
8. Strive to eliminate fear so that each person can contribute to the best of their abilities.
9. Strive to eliminate departmental boundaries so that individuals can collaborate as a team.
10. Make an effort to get rid of things like objectives, signs, and catchphrases that demand higher prodictivity levels without also improving the techniques.
11. Strive to eliminate work standards that impose numerical quotas on your group.
12. Try to get rid of things that make workers less proud of their work.
13. Make an effort to create a training and education program that works.
14. Determine how to create a method that will continuously enhance the aforementioned 13 points daily.

Joseph M. Juran contributions to TQM

Juran suggested ten actions to raise the standard of quality:

1. Begin by raising awareness of the opportunity and need for improvement.
2. Establish attainable improvement targets.
3. Assemble to accomplish the objectives (using techniques to set up quality control, recognize issues, choose a project, form teams, and assign facilitators).
4. A focus on training.
5. Use projects to solve challenges.
6. Reports on progress are required.
7. Give praise to everybody who succeeds.
8. Share the findings with all parties involved.
9. Maintain your score by using numbers.
10. Keep up a consistent pace by integrating annual improvement into the company's systems and procedures.

14.6 PDSA CYCLE

Shewhart created the fundamental Plan-Do-Study-Act (PDSA) cycle, which Deming subsequently modified. It's a useful improvement strategy. As illustrated in Fig. 14.2, the seven phases of the PDSA cycle serve as the framework for the implementation of the continuous improvement process.

Phase 1: Identify the opportunity

This phase's aim is to recognize and rank opportunities for development. It is divided into three sections: defining the scope, forming the team (if none already exists), and identifying the problem.

Finding the problems provides a response to the query, "What are the problems?" The solution identifies the problems that need to be fixed the fastest and have the greatest potential for improvement. Problems can be identified using a variety of inputs, such as the following:

- Pareto examination of recurring external issues, including returns, complaints, field malfunctions, and other issues.
- Pareto analysis of repetitive internal issues, such as, sorting, rework, and scrap.

- Recommendations from important insiders, including union stewards, managers, and supervisors.
- Suggestions derived from suggestion schemes.
- Examination of user demands in the field.
- Information on rivals' performance (from lab testing and from users).
- Remarks from influential individuals outside the company (clients, vendors, reporters, and detractors).
- Locating the statements from independent labs and government regulators.
- Customer surveys.
- Employee questionnaires.
- Brainstorming within teams.

Fig. 14.2 Continuous improvement PDSA cycle

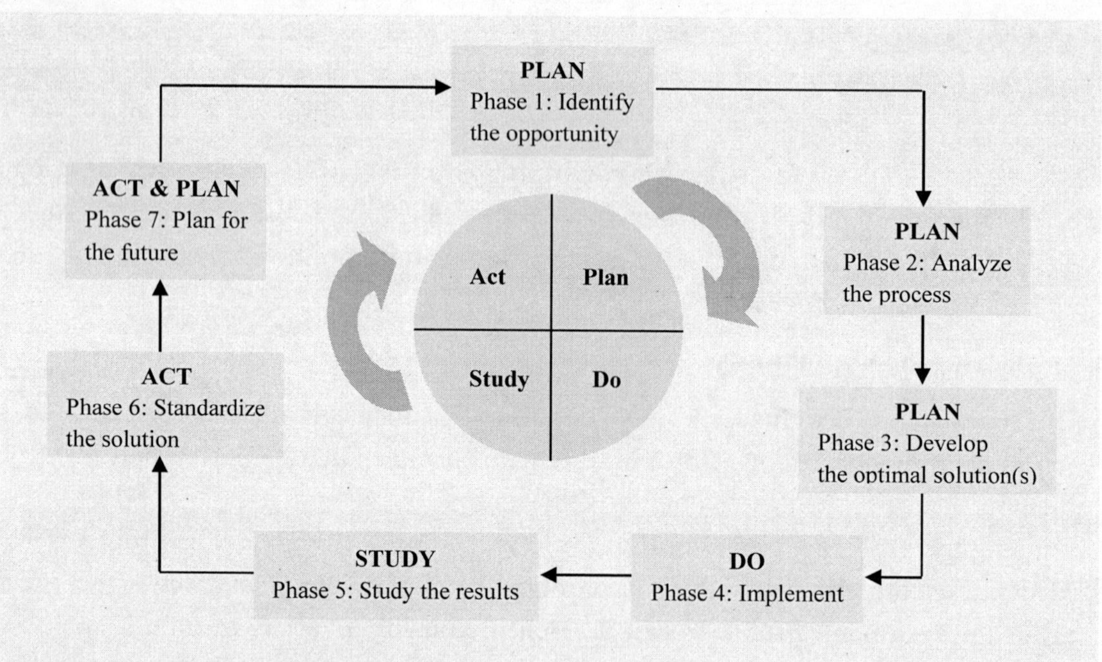

Phase 2: Examine the existing procedure

This phase's goal is to comprehend the procedure and the way it is currently carried out. The definition of process boundaries, outputs and customers, inputs and suppliers, and process flow are crucial tasks. Other activities include figuring out the necessary metrics and customer satisfaction levels, gathering data, and identifying root causes.

The team's initial task is to create a process flow diagram. A flow diagram simplifies complicated work into a visual representation that is simple to comprehend. The team finds this exercise to be "eye opening" because it is not often that everyone on the team is aware of every step of the procedure.

The target performance metrics are then specified. A key component of significant process improvements is measurement. Something cannot be made better if it cannot be measured. If new measurements are required, the team will:

- Establish performance measures in accordance with client needs.
- The team will assess if the measurements currently in use are sufficient to comprehend and enhance the process.
- Identify the information required to run the process.
- Get input from suppliers and customers on a regular basis.
- Set benchmarks for the timeliness, cost, and quality of inputs and outputs.

Phase 3: Workout for the optimal solution(s)

Establishing viable and workable solutions and advising the best course of action to enhance the process are the goals of this phase. As soon as all the data is in hand, the project team starts looking at potential fixes. To fix a situation, multiple solutions are usually needed. Sometimes a quick glance at the data analysis shows the answers to be very clear. During this stage, brainstorming is the main tool and creativity is the driving force. It needs innovation and creativity in addition to problem understanding to brainstorm potential solutions.

The next step is to evaluate or test the potential solutions after they have been identified. As previously indicated, there may be more than one way to handle the problem. Tests and/or evaluations are used to identify which potential solutions are most likely to succeed as well as their benefits and drawbacks.

Phase 4: Put adjustments into practice

The best option can then be put into practice when it has been chosen. The goals of this phase are to prepare the implementation strategy, secure approval, and put the process changes into action.

While the project team typically possesses some ability to initiate corrective measures, the permission of the quality council or other relevant authority is normally necessary. A report is provided, either verbally or in writing, if such approval is required. The implementation plan report's contents must provide a detailed description of:

- Why is it going to be done?
- How is it going to be carried out?
- When will it be completed?
- Who is going to do it?
- Where will it take place?

The answers to these queries will specify the necessary steps, allocate accountability, and set up an implementation milestone.

Phase 5: Examine the results

Through data collection and progress reviews, this phase aims to monitor and assess the change by recording and analyzing the efficacy of the improvement initiatives. To achieve continuous improvement, it is essential to establish continual monitoring and evaluation activities and institutionalize real change.

Throughout this phase, the team should get together on a regular basis to review the outcomes and determine whether further adjustments are needed or if the problem has been handled. The team will also want to determine whether the improvements have caused any unanticipated issues to arise. Some of the steps will need to be repeated if the team is not satisfied.

Phase 6: Make the solution standardized

After the team is agreed with the modification, it needs to be formally implemented through operator, process, and process certification as well as positive control. Important variables are guaranteed to remain under control thanks to positive control. It is an update of the monitoring activity that details the what, who, how, where, and when of the process.

Lastly, in order to understand what has to be done and how to execute it for a certain procedure, operators must be qualified. To guarantee job rotation and knowledge of the next client, cross-training in different roles within the process is also required. Complete product understanding is also preferred. Operator certification is a continuous process that needs to be done on a regular basis.

Phase 7: Consider future-oriented strategies

The goal of this stage is to raise the performance levels of the process. The process of improvement never ends, no matter how effective the initial attempts are. It's critical to keep in mind that Total Quality Management (TQM) covers both management quality and management. Everyone in the company is working together to create customer-focused, adaptable, and responsive procedures as part of a methodical, long-term effort to continuously enhance quality.

Continuous improvement is the state of constantly trying to better a process or work rather than just being satisfied with how it is done. Process measurement and team issue resolution are integrated into all work activities to achieve this. The goals of Total Quality Management (TQM) include cost, delivery, and quality improvement. Organizations need to reduce complexity, variation, and uncontrollable processes in order to consistently strive for excellence.

14.7 MAIN OBJECTIVES OF TQM

The following primary goals must be at the very least of a whole quality-oriented organization. The organization needs to set more detailed goals.

1. Customer pleasure and delight as the primary goal.
2. The organization's culture should be one of constant progress; it should be a way of life.
3. Cost reduction that is laser-focused, unwavering, and ongoing.
4. A laser-like commitment to constant, unwavering quality improvement.
5. To establish an environment in which all employees strive to make their company the greatest in its industry and to profit from the sense of accomplishment that comes with working for a top-tier company. An integrated TQM model needs to have a ten-dimensional framework with the following characteristics in order to accomplish these goals.
    - The communication of the quality policy.
    - Collaboration and involvement in a team.
    - Tools and methods for solving problems.
    - Standardization.
    - Quality system.
    - Measurement and costs of quality.
    - Process management.
    - Integration of suppliers and customers.
    - Training and education.
    - Audit and review of quality.

14.8 QUALITY IMPROVEMENT

TQM is an ongoing process of improvement. A mission statement outlining quality goals comes first. Subsequently, a customer requirements survey is conducted. The creation of the overarching corporate strategy and a study of the organization's capabilities come next. The overall improvement strategy should develop through the integration of functional strategies with the self, customer, and vendor evaluations. Sometimes benchmarking should be used on a case-by-case basis as a crucial technique to reach improvements. Fig. 14.3 illustrates the quality improvement strategy. The goal of the process is continuous improvement and it begins with senior management commitment. The quality manual's accurate and thorough documentation helps to sustain the quality system. To assure quality level, a variety of quality control (QC) technologies are utilized, including control charts and Pareto analysis. 5S and 3Mu contribute to enhancing system performance. The terms *Seiri* (straighten up), *Seiton* (organize things), *Seiso* (clean up), *Seiketsu*· (personal hygiene), and *Seitsuke* (discipline) represent the 5Ss. *Muda* (waste), *Muri* (strain), and *Mura* (discrepancy) are the 3 Mu. Removing 3Mu and implementing 5S both contribute to a better workplace by cutting down on waste and losses.

14.9 COST OF QUALITY

It involves both the expense of guaranteeing and assuring quality and the loss incurred when it is not met. Four categories can be used to group different aspects of the cost of quality assurance: appraisal, internal failure, external failure, and preventative costs (Table 14.1). Enhancing a TQM system's performance can be achieved through quality-cost management (Fig. 14.4). This is accomplished by making a deliberate effort to cut these expenses. The variance of failure, appraisal, and prevention costs at various levels of targeted quality is depicted in Figures 14.5 through 14.7.

Fig. 14.3 Methodology for enhancing the process

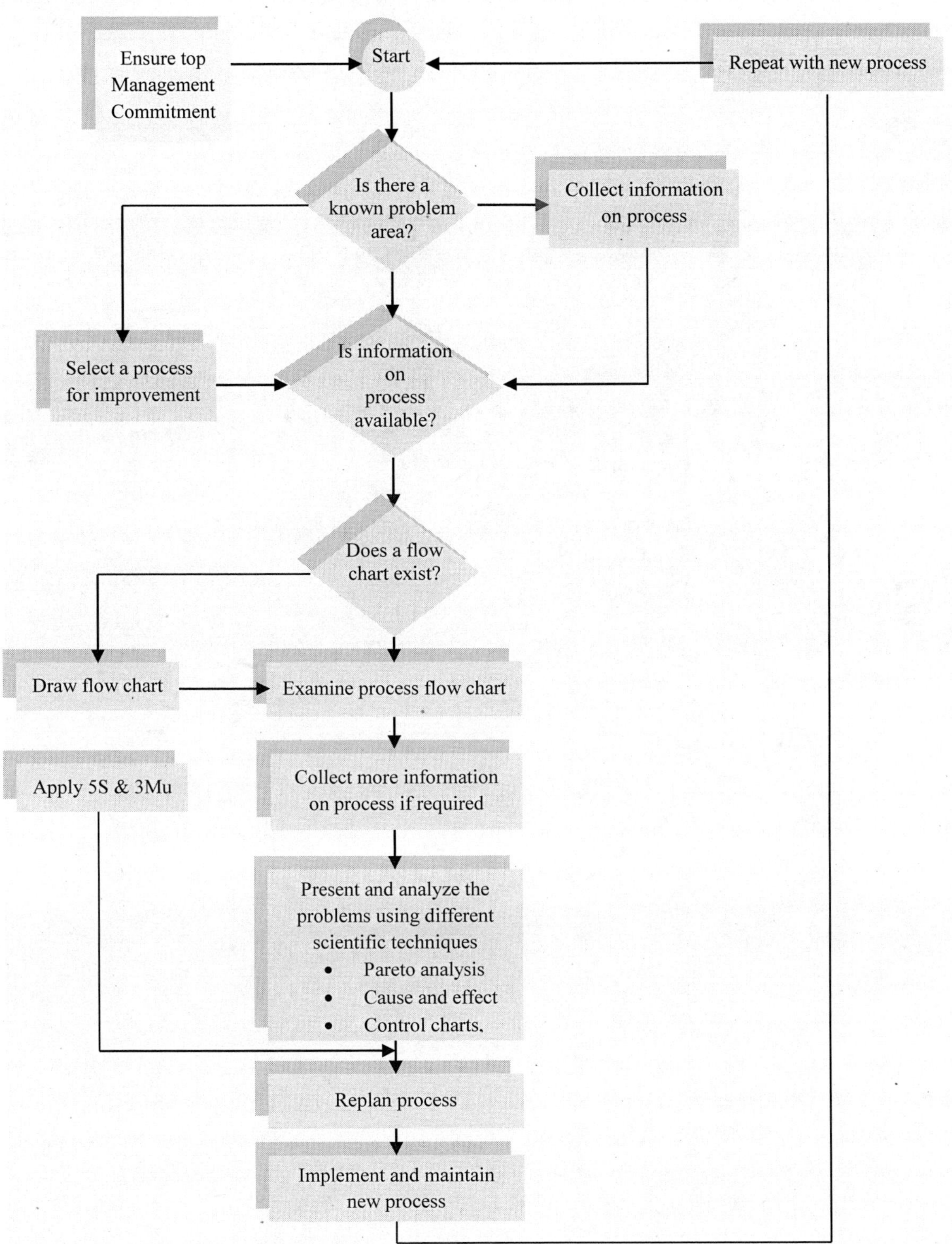

The pattern of the overall cost of quality at various quality levels is U-shaped when these expenses are pooled in a system (Fig. 14.8). It is significant to remember that a specific quality level results in the lowest possible overall cost for quality.

Table 14.1 Costs of quality assurance

Prevention cost	Appraisal cost	Internal failure cost	External failure cost
• Quality planning • QC administration and systems planning • Quality related training • Inspection of incoming process and final product • Process planning • Design review • Quality data analysis • Procurement planning • Market research • Vendor surveys • Reliability studies • System development • Quality measurement and control • Product qualification • Qualification of material	• Incoming inspection • Testing • Inspection in process • Quality audits • Incoming test and laboratory tests • Checking labour • Laboratory or other measurement service • Setup for test and inspection • Maintenance and caliberation work • Product engineering review and shipping release • Field testing	• Rejections • Scrap at full shop cost • Rework at full shopo cost • Failure analysis • Rework • Material procurement • Machine breakdown • QC investigation of failures • Material review activity • Repair and trouble shooting • Excess inventory	• Complaint handling • Goodwill loss • Warranty costs • Bad publicity • Field maintenance and product service • Returned material processing and repair • Fall in market share • Replacement inventories • Low employe morale • Strained distributor relations

The whole quality curve is flatter around the optimal quality level. Consequently, determining the precise quality level at the lowest possible overall cost is not required. The shop floor may identify this level and work within it through experience and iterations. It is nearly impossible to get an accurate quantitative evaluation of the various quality costs. This is a result of the several arbitrary cost components given in Table 14.1. As a result, industry can only acquire the necessary degree of quality through experience. A cost and value curve in relation to various quality levels is displayed in Figure 14.9. The cost of production goes up as the quality target is raised. The product's value to the consumer likewise rises. There are two places where these two curves cross.

Fig. 14.4 Enhancing performance by reducing quality costs

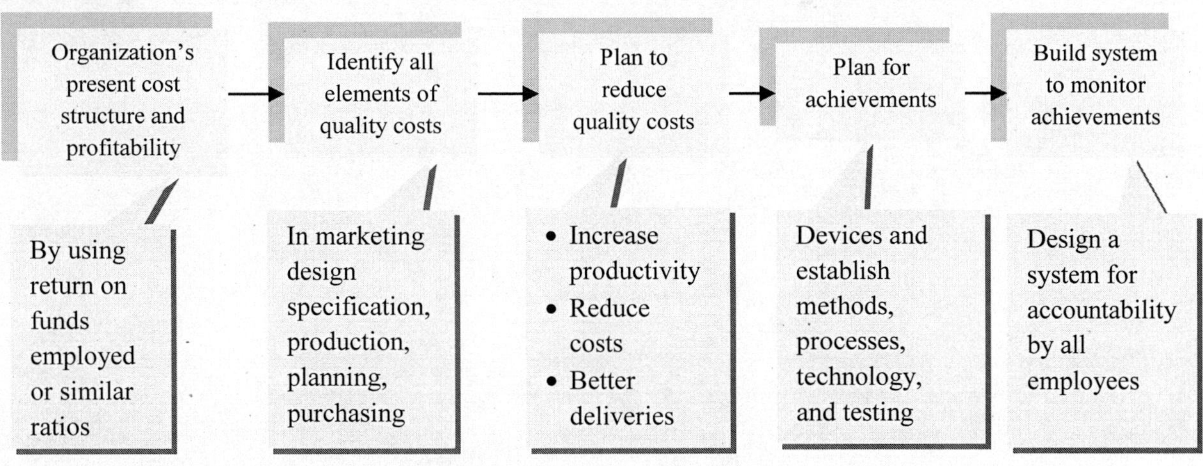

Fig. 14.5 Prevention costs

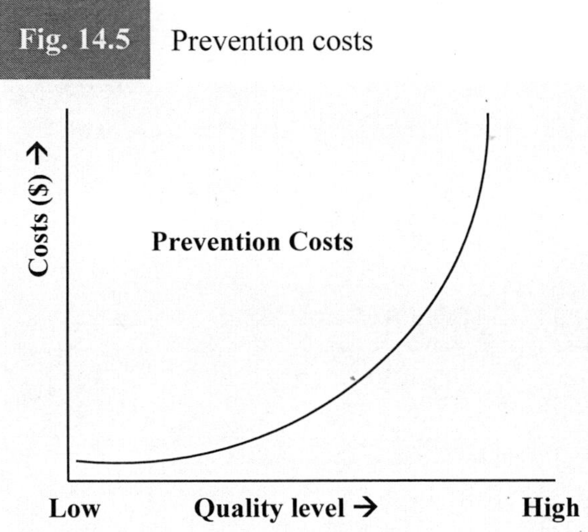

The desired level of quality target is the degree of quality at which the margin between value and cost is largest. Similar to Fig. 14.8, the margin is rather stable around this goal. Therefore, it is not crucial to estimate quality level precisely. In many situations in real life, intuition or guesswork based on experience proves to be effective. Industries can get the desired quality level by making small adjustments over practice.

Fig. 14.6 Appraisal costs

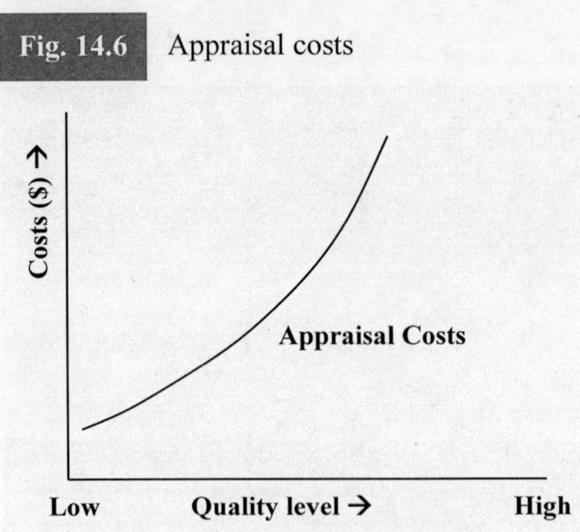

Fig. 14.7 Failure costs

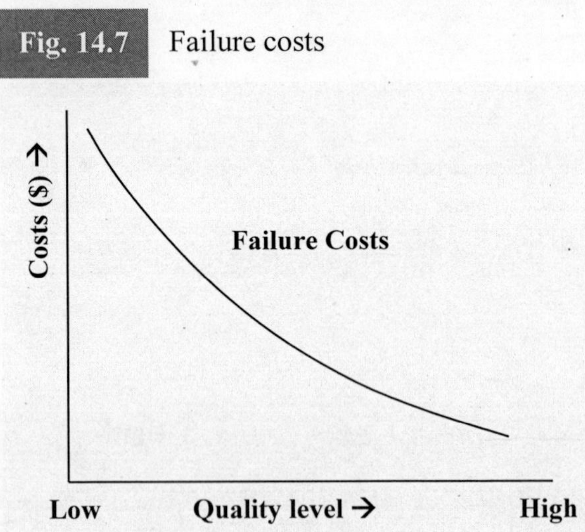

Fig. 14.8 Total quality costs

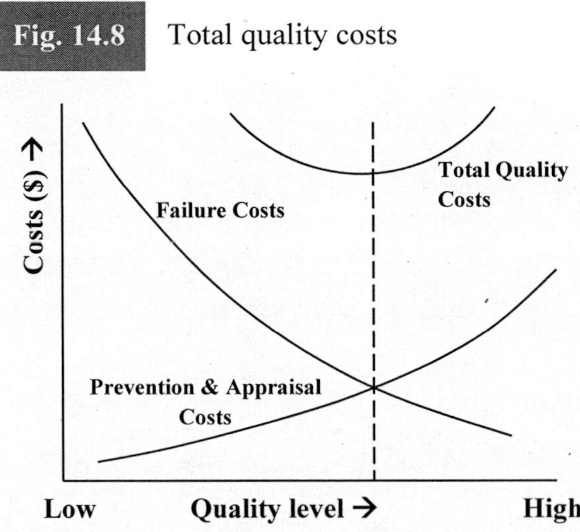

Fig. 14.9 Cost and values of qualities

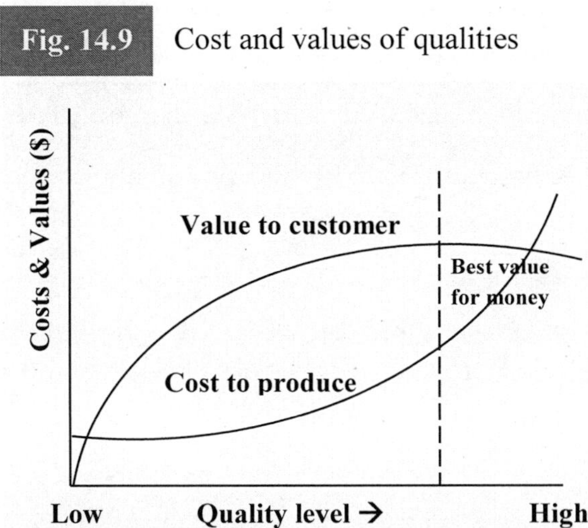

14.10 ELEMENTS OF TQM

1. **Customer satisfaction**: It serves as the foundation of TQM initiatives since it is the ultimate goal of the methodology. TQM uses the term "customer" to refer to the entire chain of customers, from the supplier to the external customer. Every step in the quality chain,

including processes, needs to make sure that the end result is satisfied customers. There are various aspects to customer happiness, such as:

- Suitability for use.
- The quality of life is determined by reliability.
- Worth of money that a consumer has spent.
- Customer support and after-sale services.
- Good packing.
- Customer right to accurate instruction and information.
- Reliability of the goods or services.
- A range of goods and services.
- Quick reaction time or speed of service.
- Civility in all aspects of life.
- Positive consumer perception of the business and trust in the organization stemming from previous experiences.

2. **Right first time**: TQM follows the zero defects or no error policy. This calls for a culture of "right first time" – rework and rejections are not an option.

3. **Corporate culture**: It needs to be more focused on people than on technology.

4. **Education**: Education is the formal application of rules that promote cooperation, the desire for progress, and a dedication to excellence.

5. **Continuous improvement (Kaizen)**: TQM aims to continuously improve quality. It never accepts to remain as it is. Long-term continuous improvement is built on a foundation of customer needs and comparisons with world-class enterprises. By creating a bridge between the "AS-IS" and "TO-BE" situations, this is accomplished.

6. **Benchmarking**: It is the process of comparing current performance to a set of benchmarks in order to determine which area has the best performance and to detect any gaps in the current state of affairs.

7. **Top mangement commitment and involvement**: The senior management's commitment to and continued involvement in product quality is essential. It is a tool for gaining market share and raising the quality of products.

8. **Customer involvemnt**: The TQM method is driven by customer expectations. The design and functionality of the product must incorporate the level of quality that the customer demands.

9. **Design product for quality**: Basic product qualities are determined by customer expectations. The customer expects quality. Service features, dependability, and strong performance can all contribute to this.

10. **Design process for quality**: A production system is made up of all its employees and processes. These ought to be made with customer-desired quality in mind.

11. **Control processes for quality**: Controlling the production processes is necessary to guarantee the quality of the products that are made.

12. **Building teams of empowered employees**: Employees need to be given the freedom to produce and serve in a flawless manner. They are the force behind TQM.

13. **Goals and performance measurement**: TQM promotes achievement celebration and measurement. It demands that arbitrary aims be eliminated without any kind of process. Encouragement is needed to help staff members assess their performance, compare it to the benchmark, and make improvements.

14. **Develop experts**: TQM emphasizes ongoing education and training. A culture of producing subject-matter specialists results from this. Experts are the catalysts that continuously spark improvements through involvement, encouragement, training, and education.

15. **Systematic approach**: Only with a methodical approach to TQM movement management will TQM be successful. TQM necessitates a thoroughly thought-out, integrated strategy that is based on the mission. The TQM goal of continuous improvement and customer delight can be more consistently achieved by implementing regular planning, effective leadership and motivation, teamwork, Kaizen, quality circles, and other practices.

16. **Customer-supplier relationship**: TQM requires that individuals receive training in understanding the interactions between suppliers and customers. At the top of the company, there should be a commitment to the demands of the customers. It is important to recognize and apply the idea of internal customers and suppliers. The company should operate in a way that promotes customer satisfaction.

17. **Total cost consideration**: Instead than emphasizing the cost of goods or services, TQM must concentrate on total cost. Performance, services, and product quality will all increase with continuous improvement. Reduced overall operating costs are achieved through continuous improvements.

18. **Supervision and training**: Adoption of contemporary techniques for training and monitoring is encouraged by TQM. It is not the purpose to point out errors. Honor

accomplishments and efforts. Recognize everyone's accomplishments. We ought to create the ideal setting for success.

19. **Better communication and quality circle**: TQM promotes strengthening departmental communications as a means of breaking down barriers. This would improve the process's integration. It will support teamwork, which is essential to the success of TQM. To solicit recommendations for undergoing improvement, there needs to be more transparency and communication. The quality circle, in which employees engage to solve work-related issues, is a useful tool for problem identification and resolution.

14.11 SEVEN QUALITY CONTROL TOOLS FOR IMPROVEMENT

The method of improving quality makes use of seven tools. These techniques are helpful in determining the issues and formulating improvement measures. These tools are:

- Scatter diagram
- Check sheets
- Graph and charts
- Histograms
- Pareto-diagram
- Cause-effect diagram
- Control charts

SCAN ME
for
QC tools for quality improvement

You can read more about these tools by scanning the provided QR code.

14.12 ISO 9000 VERSUS TQM

The International Organization for Standardization, or ISO, has its main office in Geneva, Switzerland. A documented set of standards known as ISO 9000 establishes a quality system. ISO documentation defines the fundamental components of the system. ISO guarantees an internationally recognized system that is consistent. A customer-focused quality system can be upheld with the help of ISO's methodical process documentation. Quality control in design/development, manufacturing, installation, and servicing is the focus of ISO 9001. A recognized, qualified registrar can grant an ISO 9000 registration to businesses that satisfy the requirements. ISO 9000, however, disregards the human aspect. Conversely, TQM emphasizes developing human components (Table 14.2).

Table 14.2 ISO 9000 vs. TQM

ISO 9000	TQM
Focus on: • Certification • Product conforms to specification • Audits and checks • Key processes • Quality system • External trust • Visibility of capability prior to delivery • Maintenance of what is documented • An assurance to external customer that a quality system is being pursued	**Focus on:** • Customer delight and satisfaction. • Total organization including 'invisible' and 'visible' resources. • Total quality management • Internal and external trust • Leadership • Internal customer • Human factor • Flexibility and change management • Top mangement commitment • Continuous improvement

It is not required for a business with an ISO certification to adhere to TQM principles. ISO just attests to the documentation of what is adhered to. The certifying organization is not accountable for ensuring that all procedures are correctly executed and in perfect order. To imply that an ISO company is a TQM company is actually inaccurate. TQM is an ongoing process that aims for quality perfection. It's crucial to remember that TQM and the ISO 9000 standard are not mutually exclusive. One is helping the other out. The ISO 9000 standard lays out the foundation for a management system that will boost an organization's productivity. It offers the fundamental building blocks needed to transition to TQM.

UNIT SUMMARY

- ***Fundamentals of TQM*** – TQM is a systematic approach that integrates quality into all aspects of an organization to achieve continuous improvement.
- ***Quality Gurus & Their Contributions*** – Examines key thinkers like: (i) Philip B. Crosby – "Quality is conformance to requirements," promoting zero defects, (ii) W. Edwards Deming – Focus on process improvement and statistical control, and (iii) Joseph M. Juran – Quality as "fitness for use" with a strong management focus.
- ***Plan-Do-Study-Act*** (PDSA) Cycle – A structured continuous improvement model.
- ***TQM Objectives*** – Customer satisfaction, cost reduction, and defect elimination.

- ***Cost of Quality*** – Breakdown of prevention, appraisal, internal failure, and external failure costs.
- ***Seven Quality Control Tools*** – Includes Pareto charts, cause-effect diagrams, control charts, and histograms.
- ***ISO 9000 vs. TQM*** – ISO 9000 focuses on standardization, while TQM is about continuous improvement.

EXERCISES

MULTIPLE CHOICE QUESTIONS

14.1 Can an organization that has achieved ISO certification be considered to have fully implemented Total Quality Management (TQM)?

(a) Yes, because ISO certification ensures all aspects of TQM are covered	(b) No, because ISO certification is just a formal recognition and does not ensure the ongoing TQM principles are being actively practiced
(c) Yes, as ISO certification includes a detailed TQM framework	(d) No, because TQM requires only periodic audits, while ISO certification is more frequent

14.2 Which aspect is NOT typically covered by ISO certification alone but is a crucial component of Total Quality Management (TQM)?

(a) Compliance with international standards	(b) Customer feedback and proactive quality measures
(c) Employee involvement and empowerment	(d) Continuous and systematic improvement of processes

14.3 What does "total" imply about the scope of quality management activities in TQM?

(a) Quality management activities are confined to specific projects	(b) Quality management activities are limited to product quality only
(c) Quality management activities encompass every aspect of the organization's operations, from processes	(d) Quality management activities are restricted to compliance and certification processes

to people	

14.4 Which component is essential for the successful implementation of a TQM system plan?

(a) An extensive market research report	(b) A clear quality policy and objectives
(c) High capital investment in new technology	(d) A detailed product launch schedule

14.5 In the context of a TQM system plan, what is the purpose of establishing performance metrics?

(a) To measure the effectiveness of quality management practices and identify areas for improvement	(b) To monitor compliance with industry regulations
(c) To increase production speed	(d) To evaluate the financial impact of quality initiatives

14.6 How does the TQM system plan typically address customer feedback?

(a) By incorporating feedback only in the final stages of the product development cycle	(b) By using customer feedback to continuously refine and improve processes and products
(c) By delegating feedback analysis to external consultants only	(d) By focusing feedback on marketing strategies rather than quality improvements

14.7 In Crosby's approach, what is the significance of the "quality is free" concept?

(a) It suggests that achieving high quality requires no investment in quality management systems	(b) It indicates that all quality-related costs are absorbed by the customer
(c) It implies that quality management is only relevant for high-end products	(d) It emphasizes that the cost of preventing defects is less than the cost of failing to prevent them

14.8 Which of the following is a key concept in Deming's philosophy that involves continually improving processes and products?

(a) The Pareto Principle	(b) The Law of Diminishing Returns
(c) The Kaizen approach	(d) The Hierarchy of Needs

14.9 When implementing the "Do" phase, which of the following practices is crucial to ensure the reliability of the test?

(a) Implement the changes across all departments to observe comprehensive results	(b) Conduct a pilot test with a controlled group and document deviations from the plan
(c) Ignore feedback from the team to prevent bias in the results	(d) Skip training sessions for staff to expedite the implementation process

14.10 In applying the PDSA cycle to a complex organizational process, which of the following strategies best ensures that the "Do" phase contributes to accurate and reliable results?

(a) Implement the changes incrementally while continuously gathering feedback to adjust the process dynamically	(b) Execute the full-scale changes immediately without interim evaluations to expedite results
(c) Delay implementation until all potential issues are fully resolved through exhaustive planning	(d) Restrict changes to a single department to avoid potential disruptions across the organization

14.11 In a quality management system, which of the following scenarios would most accurately reflect an investment in prevention costs?

(a) Conducting internal audits to detect defects before they reach the customer	(b) Performing detailed inspections and testing of finished products before shipment
(c) Implementing a comprehensive training program for employees to reduce defects and improve process knowledge	(d) Offering discounts and handling returns for products found to be defective after customer complaints

14.12 Which of the following best describes an effective approach to manage appraisal costs while ensuring product quality?

(a) Increasing the frequency of product inspections to catch defects before they are shipped	(b) Investing in advanced quality control equipment to enhance the accuracy and efficiency of inspections
(c) Reducing the number of quality control checks to cut costs and relying on final customer feedback	(d) Outsourcing quality inspections to reduce internal costs, despite potential risks of quality discrepancies

14.13 When analyzing quality-related costs, which strategy effectively balances the trade-offs between prevention, appraisal, internal failure, and external failure costs?

(a) Focus exclusively on reducing appraisal costs to minimize total quality expenses	(b) Prioritize increasing prevention costs to reduce both internal and external failure costs over time
(c) Allocate resources solely to managing external failure costs to address customer dissatisfaction directly	(d) Implement a balanced approach that integrates cost reductions in appraisal and internal failure areas while investing strategically in prevention measures

14.14 In TQM, how does the principle of "employee involvement" contribute to the success of quality management efforts?

(a) Employees are given limited roles in decision-making to maintain control over quality processes	(b) Involvement of employees at all levels in decision-making and problem-solving enhances ownership and accountability for quality outcomes
(c) Employee involvement is restricted to implementing pre-determined processes without input on improvements	(d) Employees focus only on their specific tasks without collaboration or input into broader quality initiatives

14.15 Which quality management tool is best used to visualize the relationship between two variables and identify potential correlations or patterns?

(a) Scatter Diagram	(b) Histogram
(c) Control Chart	(d) Pareto Diagram

14.16 In quality management, which tool is most effective for recording and summarizing data in a structured format to facilitate the identification of trends or issues?

(a) Cause-Effect Diagram	(b) Graph and Charts
(c) Histogram	(d) Check Sheet

14.17 When analyzing a process to determine potential causes of quality issues, which tool is best suited for identifying and mapping out possible causes and their effects?

(a) Histogram	(b) Scatter Diagram
(c) Cause-Effect Diagram (Ishikawa or Fishbone Diagram)	(d) Check Sheet

Answers of Multiple Choice Questions

14.1 (b), 14.2 (d), 14.3 (c), 14.4 (b), 14.5 (a), 14.6 (b), 14.7 (d), 14.8 (c), 14.9 (b), 14.10 (a), 14.11 (c), 14.12 (b), 14.13 (d), 14.14 (b), 14.15 (a), 14.16 (d), 14.17 (c)

SHORT AND LONG ANSWER TYPE QUESTIONS

Category I

14.1 Can obtaining ISO certification be considered sufficient for a company to claim it has fully implemented Total Quality Management (TQM)? Why or why not?

14.2 In what way does ISO certification contribute to the implementation of Total Quality Management (TQM) in an organization?

14.3 What are the essential components required for the successful implementation of a Total Quality Management (TQM) system plan?

14.4 What might be some challenges an organization could face when integrating performance metrics into a Total Quality Management (TQM) system plan?

14.5 What are the key principles of W. Edwards Deming's approach to Total Quality Management (TQM)?

14.6 What considerations might an organization need to address when transitioning between the different phases of the PDSA cycle to ensure effective implementation and evaluation of process changes?

14.7 What is an example of a prevention cost, and why is it important for overall quality management?

14.8 How do appraisal costs differ from internal failure costs, and can you provide an example of each?

14.9 What is an example of an external failure cost, and how does it impact customer satisfaction?

14.10 Why is it important for organizations to track all four types of quality costs (prevention, appraisal, internal failure, external failure), and how can this tracking benefit overall quality management?

14.11 How can a cause-effect diagram (Ishikawa or fishbone diagram) be utilized to analyze and address quality problems?

Category II

14.12 How does ISO certification contribute to the implementation of Total Quality Management (TQM) in an Indian industry? Provide a detailed real-life example from an Indian company to illustrate your points.

14.13 In the context of developing and implementing a Total Quality Management (TQM) system within a mid-sized manufacturing company, how can performance metrics be effectively integrated into the TQM plan to ensure continuous improvement and alignment with the company's strategic goals?

14.14 In the process of implementing a Total Quality Management (TQM) system in a global automotive manufacturing company, how can the approaches suggested by Philip Crosby, W. Edwards Deming, and Joseph Juran be effectively utilized to develop a comprehensive TQM strategy?

14.15 In the context of implementing a Total Quality Management (TQM) system in a mid-sized healthcare organization, how can the phases of the Plan-Do-Study-Act (PDSA) cycle be effectively utilized to drive continuous improvement in patient care and operational efficiency?

14.16 For a mid-sized electronics manufacturing company aiming to enhance its Total Quality Management (TQM) system, how can the organization effectively manage and balance the costs associated with quality, specifically prevention costs, appraisal costs, internal failure costs, and external failure costs? Illustrate your response with examples and strategies for each type of cost, and explain how the company can achieve a balanced approach to optimize overall quality and performance.

14.17 How can different tools used in Total Quality Management (TQM) be applied to improve quality in a manufacturing company? Provide a detailed explanation of at least five TQM tools, illustrating their use with real-life examples and explaining how each contributes to quality improvement.

REFERENCES AND SUGGESTED READINGS

1. Besterfield, D. H., Besterfield-Michna, C., and Besterfield-Sacre, M. The Impact of TQM on Financial Performance. *Journal of Total Quality Management*, Vol. 14(2), 267-276, 2003.

2. Besterfield, D. H., Besterfield-Michna, C., Besterfield-Sacre, M., and Besterfield, G. H. *Total Quality Management*, 4th Edition, Pearson, 2011.
3. Deming, W. E. *Out of the Crisis*. MIT Center for Advanced Educational Services, 1986.
4. Deming, W. E. Out of the Crisis: Quality, Productivity, and Competitive Position. *Harvard Business Review*, Vol. 60(1), 72-89, 1982.
5. Evans, J. R., and Lindsay, W. M. *Managing for Quality and Performance Excellence*, 10th Edition, Cengage Learning, 2019.
6. Goetsch, D. L., and Davis, S. B. *Quality Management for Organizational Excellence: Introduction to Total Quality*, 8th Edition, Pearson, 2016.
7. Ishikawa, K. The Role of the Quality Control Circle in Management. *International Journal of Production Research*, Vol. 23(5), 1221-1229, 1985.
8. Ishikawa, K. *What is Total Quality Control? The Japanese Way*. Prentice Hall, 1985.
9. Juran, J. M. The Quality Trilogy: A Universal Approach to Managing for Quality. *Quality Progress*, Vol. 19(8), 19-24, 1986.
10. Juran, J. M., and Godfrey, A. B. *Juran's Quality Handbook*, 5th Edition, McGraw-Hill, 1999.
11. Juran, J. M., and Gryna, F. M. Juran's Quality Handbook: The Complete Guide to Performance Excellence. *International Journal of Quality & Reliability Management*, Vol. 17(1), 9-22, 2000.
12. Linderman, K., and Schroeder, R. G. Six Sigma: The Role of Statistical Methods in Improving Organizational Performance. *International Journal of Quality & Reliability Management*, Vol. 20(6), 559-567, 2003.
13. Mitchell, A. *Quality Management: Creating and Sustaining Organizational Effectiveness*. Pearson, 2013.
14. Oakland, J. S. *Total Quality Management and Operational Excellence: Text with Cases*, 4th Edition, Routledge, 2014.
15. Oakland, J. S. TQM: Text with Cases. *International Journal of Operations & Production Management*, Vol. 23(3), 360-377, 2003.

UNIT **15**

DIGITALIZATION AND ADVANCED FACTORY SYSTEM

UNIT SPECIFICS

This unit elaborately discusses the following topics:

- Introduction to digitalization
- Industry 4.0 (Internet of Things and associated technologies)
- Smart manufacturing systems for Industry 4.0 (Smart wearable devices, CPS-based smart machine tools, Energy consumption monitoring, Cloud-based numerical control, Machine scheduling)
- Additive manufacturing
- Blockchain technology
- Artificial intelligence in operations management
- Machine learning

The topics' contemporary, real-world applications inspire greater creativity and curiosity. Along with a number of multiple-choice questions and questions with both short and long answer types, the unit includes a list of references, suggested readings, and assignments that are divided into two groups according to the lower and higher order of Bloom's taxonomy. By completing these, one can get practice. Following the unit's related topic, a section titled "Along the..." has been included in accordance with the content. The reader was carefully considered when creating the unit. One notable aspect is the usage of QR codes, which can be scanned to yield pertinent extra information on a variety of interesting topics.

RATIONALE

This unit introduces the transformative impact of digitalization in the context of Industry 4.0, exploring how technologies such as the Internet of Things (IoT) are reshaping manufacturing landscapes. It delves into smart manufacturing systems, highlighting innovations like smart wearable devices, cyber-physical systems (CPS)-based machine tools, and cloud-based numerical control, which enhance operational efficiency and energy management. The discussion extends to additive manufacturing and its role in customizing production processes. Furthermore, the unit examines the integration of blockchain technology to improve supply chain transparency and security, alongside the application of artificial intelligence (AI) and machine learning in operations management, which drive predictive analytics and automation. Collectively, these elements illustrate how digitalization is revolutionizing industry practices, fostering greater agility, and enabling data-driven decision-making.

UNIT OUTCOMES

List of outcomes of this unit is as follows:

U15-UO1: Comprehend Digitalization

U15-UO2: Explain Industry 4.0 Technologies

U15-UO3: Analyze Smart Manufacturing Systems

U15-UO4: Understand Additive Manufacturing

U15-UO5: Evaluate Blockchain Applications

U15-UO6: Understand application of AI and Machine Learning in Operations

UNIT-15 Outcomes	EXPECTED MAPPING WITH COURSE OUTCOMES (1-Weak Correlation; 2-Medium Correlation; 3-Strong Correlation)					
	CO-1	CO-2	CO-3	CO-4	CO-5	CO-6
U15-UO1	3	2	3	3	3	2
U15-UO2	3	2	3	3	3	2
U15-UO3	3	2	3	3	3	2
U15-UO4	2	2	2	3	3	1
U15-UO5	1	2	2	2	3	1
U15-UO6	2	2	3	3	3	2

15.1 INTRODUCTION

A phenomenon known as "digital disruption" has resulted from the information and communication technology's (ICT) extraordinary development. Within this framework, conventional business models that mostly rely on tangible operations are experiencing disruption and are transitioning towards digitalization. The progress of digitalization has implications for every industry. As a result, digital disruption has a substantial impact on many facets of society, including new connections and interactions with both individuals and organizations, in addition to businesses.

Through the application of cutting-edge technologies, manufacturers and providers of goods and services have enhanced the caliber of their enterprises in recent decades. This can be attributed to the industry's ongoing growth toward total digitization and intelligent production procedures that guarantee great efficiency. The new disruptive technologies like artificial intelligence (AI), cloud computing, big data analytics, and the Internet of Things (IoT) are constantly being developed. By elevating manufacturing processes to a smart level, these new technologies are gradually permeating the manufacturing sector and helping to handle contemporary difficulties including quicker time-to-market, improved quality, and increasingly customized requirements. Manufacturing equipment, for instance, has the ability to detect, act, and communicate with itself when sensors (such as machine tools) are used. Furthermore, these technologies make it feasible to record and distribute production data in real time, which may be utilized to make decisions quickly and accurately. Specifically, Cyber-Physical Production Systems (CPPS), a revolutionary production pattern that is a materialization of the general concept of Cyber-Physical Systems (CPS) in the manufacturing environment, are brought about by the connection of physical manufacturing equipment and devices over the Internet along with big data analytics in the digital world (e.g., the cloud). The advent of Industry 4.0, the fourth stage of industrial production, is signaled by the widespread use of CPS (or CPPS).

ALONG THE DIGITALIZATION

As a top producer of electrical and technological goods as well as aircraft engines, General Electric (GE) is essential to the development of several sectors, including the energy, healthcare, and aviation industries. The business experienced a number of financial difficulties, and in late 2000, as the economy was down, its profits began to fall. They realized that their current business strategy was not flexible enough to keep up with the rapid advancements in technology.

GE started its journey toward digital transformation in 2011 after seeing the potential of digital technology in the contemporary corporate environment. The company made investments in 3D printing and computer-aided design (CAD), which allowed them to reinvent product design.

In order to increase productivity and expedite the manufacturing process, the corporation also made investments in edge computing, advanced robotics, and the Industrial Internet of Things (IIoT). Additionally, GE made investments in data analytics and artificial intelligence, which gave them accurate information to maximize operational performance. Afterwards, GE proceeded with its digital transformation and ventured into the realm of online shopping. The massive electronics company increased revenue and improved customer satisfaction by launching an online store for kitchen and household goods. In an effort to advance the company's digital transformation, GE established GE Digital as a subsidiary in 2011. The company offers power generation, oil and gas, and other sectors software and IIoT services.

Predix is a cloud-based platform as a service (PaaS) for industrial-scale analytics created by GE Digital. It gathers and analyzes machine data to help businesses run more efficiently, produce more work, and cut expenses. GE's digital transformation has not been easy, but the corporation is still investing in digital technologies to spur its expansion. But the electronics giant was able to navigate difficult times thanks to the incorporation of digital technologies, making it one of the most fascinating cases of digital transformation.

15.2 INDUSTRY 4.0

Industry 4.0 was first presented in 2011 at the Hannover Fair. It was also formally unveiled as a German strategic initiative to lead industries that are now revolutionizing the manufacturing sector. The Fourth Industrial Revolution is signified by the term Industry 4.0. The incorporation of intelligent digital technologies into industrial and manufacturing processes is known as Industry 4.0. It includes a range of technologies such as robotics, automation, artificial intelligence (AI), big data, industrial Internet of Things (IoT) networks, cyber-physical systems (CPS), and cloud computing. Intelligent factories and smart production are made possible by Industry 4.0. It seeks to improve manufacturing and supply chain operations' productivity, efficiency, and flexibility while facilitating more thoughtful decision-making and customization. A new generation of industrial systems, known as "smart factories", is emerging to deal with the complexity of production in a cyber-physical environment. Industry 4.0 uses technologies like embedded systems, semantic machine-to-machine communication, IoT, and CPS to integrate the virtual and physical worlds.

There have been three industrial revolutions since the 1800s. The reason they were referred to as "revolutions" was that the invention behind them radically changed how work and things were produced, rather than only marginally increasing productivity and efficiency. The Fourth Industrial Revolution, or Industry 4.0, is now underway. Fig. 15.1 provides a visual representation of the history of industry from Industry 1.0 to Industry 4.0, along with an ICT roadmap for industrial information integration and industrial integration for the upcoming IoT and CPS age.

Fig. 15.1 Industry 1.0 to Industry 4.0 evolution

4th Industrial Revolution: Cyber Physical System Age
The Industry 4.0 idea was formally introduced in 2013.

CPS Age

3rd Industrial Revolution: Information Age
Automation-related electronic and ICT systems were introduced. The idea of integrating industrial information with newly developed ICT was introduced in 2005.

Information Age

2nd Industrial Revolution: Electricity Age
Introduction of electric power-based mass production

Electricity Age

1st Industrial Revolution: Steam Age
Mechanical manufacturing systems using steam and water power were introduced.

Steam Age

The foundation of industry 4.0 includes nine technology pillars. These developments create a link between the digital and physical realms and enable intelligent, self-governing systems. Even while some of these cutting-edge technologies are currently in use by businesses and supply chains, Industry 4.0 really stands out when these technologies are combined.

15.2.1 INTERNET OF THINGS AND ASSOCIATED TECHNOLOGIES

When the term "Internet of Things" (IoT) initially appeared, it was used to describe radio-frequency identification (RFID) technology-enabled, uniquely identifiable, interoperable connected things. When an RFID reader is connected to the Internet, it can automatically and uniquely identify and track things that have tags attached to them in real time. The Internet of

Things is this. Subsequently, the Internet of Things was integrated with additional technologies, including sensors, actuators, mobile devices that are controlled by Wi-Fi, Bluetooth, cellular networks, or near field communication (NFC), and the Global Positioning System (GPS). The worldwide network infrastructure that underpins the Internet of Things is made up of a large number of interconnected devices that rely on networking, sensing, communication, and information processing technologies. Wireless sensor networks (WSN) and RFID are thought to be the two key components that make the Internet of Things possible. RFID technology makes it possible for microchips to wirelessly communicate identification data to a reader. Users may instantly identify, track, and keep an eye on any object marked with RFID tags by using RFID readers.

Numerous industries, including transportation, package delivery, healthcare, materials management, retail, and defense, have used RFID. Conversely, WSN uses a network of intelligent sensors that are connected to one another for sensing and monitoring. There have been several documented uses of WSN, including transportation, industrial, environmental, healthcare, and other monitoring applications. The growth of IoT is greatly aided by advancements in WSN and RFID. Along with other pertinent technologies like barcodes, smart phones, cloud computing, location-based services, near field communication, and social networks, the core technologies are RFID and WSN.

Manufacturing companies have new opportunity to analyze and apply design, production, sourcing, and inventory data to help them realize their modernization goal thanks to Industry 4.0, also known as smart manufacturing and cognitive manufacturing. Industry 4.0 analyzes real-time data from numerous machines, processes, and systems using data science and analytical models; it then automates manufacturing in accordance with the results. Industry 4.0 also leverages Industrial IoT (IIoT) applications and cognitive computing approaches. IoT and IIoT have so far been used by a number of manufacturing industries to improve manufacturing process production, distribution, transportation, service, and maintenance. Here are a few current IoT uses in the manufacturing sector.

(a) **Application of IoT to Product Lifecycle Management** – Product Lifecycle Management (PLM) gathers and organizes data on product concept, process, and decision across the whole product development stage in IoT applications in the manufacturing business. Because PLM goods are disposed of in a dispersed, mobile, and collaborative environment, they are not only disposed of intra-organizationally but also inter-organizationally. For this reason, unique identities for products or parts are crucial for PLM systems throughout the predetermined lifecycle. The abundance of diverse data combined with a rapidly changing environment can make the associated data and information difficult to exchange and share. To integrate heterogeneous and scattered product information for manufacturing within and between organizations, it entails setting up a flexible information model and an open, configurable software platform for IoT-based applications that span the whole product lifecycle.

The developments in RFID, WSN, and IoT are shown in Fig. 15.2. Currently, a strong technological basis is formed by RFID, WSN, and IoT to support both CPS and the newly emerging ICT. Consequently, Industry 4.0 can create a new breed of production systems that synchronize and integrate real-time data between physical objects and the cyber computational domain.

Fig. 15.2 Evolution of IoT

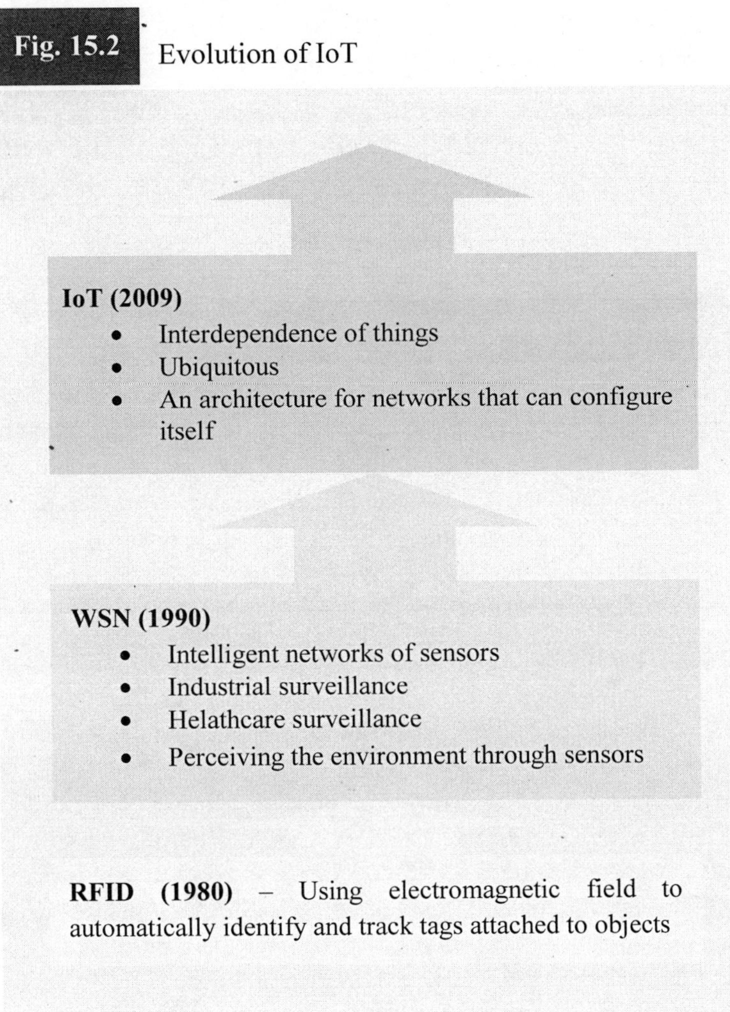

(b) **Integrating IoT with systems used in industrial manufacturing** – The IoT environment is composed of three layers:

- IoT platform layer,
- IoT application layer, and
- IoT industrial solutions layer.

After connecting several devices to receive and transmit data, the IoT platform layer streams data from the devices to the application layer. In order to assess the dynamic, complex aspects that affect production, the application layer assesses the condition of the equipment and combines the Internet of Things with cognitive techniques like automation, data analytics, and machine learning. The solution layer obtains the domain information from the industry application layer. Knowledge management expertise, analytical techniques, and industry-specific standards are all adapted to the production process. The goal of the multi-layer IoT system can be to strike the ideal balance between flexibility and efficiency, which will save costs and increase customization.

ALONG THE APPLICATIONS OF INTERNET OF THINGS

ZillionSource Technologies is an internationally renowned IoT enterprise that specializes in supply chain management and asset tracking. ZillionSource gives businesses insights into their supply chain commodities or asset monitoring by fusing the power of modern technologies with hardware. Apart from travel notes and worldwide map tracing, the IoT platform also analyzes data and displays it in graphs and reports.

With millions of devices, the extensible and scalable platform continues to function flawlessly. Its powerful pattern-recognition rule engine and business cloud application for dynamic control handle customization and security devices by enabling users to develop and modify rules based on their preferences.

Daimler, a German automaker, is using IoT innovation to make cars safer and more efficient, and consequently, the roads they drive on. The company envisions a transportation sector in which there are no fatal crashes. By creating a system for its trucks that enables highly assisted or driverless operations, Daimler is building on previous innovations and enhancing road safety while reducing driver fatigue. Daimler has consistently been among the top adopters of IoT technologies in its vehicles. In order to improve road safety, Daimler is now developing a car that can be purchased commercially and fitted with a "Highway Pilot System," which will relieve the driver during potentially hazardous portions of the journey. In comparison to operating a traditional truck, Daimler discovered that the help of onboard technology decreased driver tiredness by 25% if the driver was able to partake in other activities while the automated system operated the vehicle.

Daimler is fully embracing the technological advancements that are drastically altering the way we travel and live. Daimler is demonstrating the transformative power of the Internet of Things revolution by embracing the potential provided by IoT technologies and concentrating on using those innovations to benefit its customers, the roads they drive on, and other drivers on those roads. This is an example that businesses in every industry could follow.

John Deere, the American agricultural business is utilizing the IoT to link every one of its vehicles to a mobile online platform called JDLink. This allows dealers and farmers to view fleet location, utilization, and diagnostic data remotely for any equipment. Its John Deere Operations Center provides farmers with a wide range of IoT options, such as real-time weather and crop reporting, mobile monitoring, and wireless data streaming of production data.

By ensuring that equipment is running dependably, networked sensors and historical and current data on weather, soil, and crop status help farmers increase the value of their operations. They maximize every task by making sure crops are planted and harvested at the optimal times and in the most productive ways. They also accomplish what John Deere refers to as "agronomic optimization" by enlisting the help of the farmer's reliable partners to conduct data analysis and make recommendations for upcoming crop years.

To enable quicker, smarter IoT solutions, **Intel** is combining edge computing, 5G connectivity, and artificial intelligence. The company consistently interacts with ecosystem partners to deliver ready-to-deploy solutions that expedite insights, optimize investments, and safeguard data, and works with industry leaders to prioritize industry standards. Intel provides several Internet of Things (IoT) solutions for telehealth, medical imaging, and diagnostics to improve patient outcomes. These technologies can be applied in a variety of industries, including retail and healthcare.

Siemens provides a wide range of IoT solutions, such as industrial IoT and smart buildings, to satisfy the demands of all types of organizations. The industrial Internet of things (IIoT) powers smart manufacturing through Siemens' Insights Hub, formerly known as Mindsphere. It allows users to enhance business operations and obtain actionable insights from asset and operational data. In the meantime, its IoT solutions for smart buildings increase building operational efficiency, boosting employee productivity and occupant wellbeing while optimizing space and asset use.

The Internet of Things has a huge and expanding potential value and is used in a variety of industries, including manufacturing and transportation. According to McKinsey, the worldwide value might reach up to US$12.5 trillion by 2030. In view of above discussion we found that IoT has its application in large areas. Here we discuss some of the benefits of IoT in the area of manufacturing.

1. **Enhanced efficiency** – Automating processes can help manufacturers increase their operational efficiency, which is the main advantage of industrial IoT (IIoT). Manufacturing processes can be streamlined and productivity increased by using robotics and automated technology, which can operate more correctly and effectively. Furthermore, software can be linked to hardware by sensors that continuously track performance. As a result, producers are able to gain deeper understanding of how well both individual equipment units and entire fleets operate. Manufacturers are empowered by IIoT-enabled data systems to increase operational efficiencies by:

- Utilizing automated, digital processes in place of human ones.
- Making judgments about all aspects of manufacturing based on data.

- Tracking performance from any location, whether thousands of kilometers away or on the factory floor.

2. **Reduced Time to Market** – Increased manufacturing process speed and efficiency are also made possible by higher operational efficiencies. Employees can communicate directly with network components through the use of industrial IoT solutions, which:

- Allows for quicker decision-making in response to changes in the market.
- Increases supply chain operational insights and expedite interruption response.
- Allows for improved optimization across several lines by identifying inefficiencies in the product cycle time.

3. **Decreased Inaccuracies** – Industrial IoT gives manufacturers the ability to digitalize almost every aspect of their operations. Manufacturers can minimize human error, the largest risk related to manual work, by decreasing manual processes and entries. This extends beyond simple manufacturing and operational mistakes. IIoT solutions can also lessen the chance of human error-related cyber and data breaches. Human mistake is at blame for 95% of cybersecurity problems, according to the World Economic Forum's Global Risks Report. Programs and devices with AI and machine learning capabilities may handle a large portion of the necessary computation on their own, removing the possibility that someone could make a small error and jeopardize the manufacturer's data.

4. **Predictive Machine Downtime** – Machine downtime has the worst possible effects on a manufacturing operation. According to experts, an average producer encounters 800 hours of equipment downtime annually, resulting in $50 billion in unanticipated expenses for the industry as a whole. What could be the source of such severe problems that manufacturers are unable to function? The explanation is straightforward: improper and haphazard machine maintenance. Manufacturing companies are trapped attempting to determine what the problem is, how to fix it, and how much it will cost when maintenance is reactive rather than proactive. Industrial IoT solutions enable predictive maintenance, which resolves all those problems.

Manufacturers are able to establish a baseline when they regularly monitor the function and performance of their machinery. Businesses are equipped with the knowledge necessary to identify problems before they arise thanks to this baseline and the associated data. Then, they can plan maintenance ahead of downtime, which helps them because, they:

- Possess the parts needed for the task.
- Have a budget in place and be aware of the project's cost in advance.
- Shift production to a different area of the plant to maintain product quotas.
- Make sure all equipment is running as efficiently as possible.

5. **Enhanced safety** – Workplace safety is being strengthened by all of the sensors and data needed for an IIoT manufacturing operation to run smoothly. "Smart manufacturing" is evolving into "smart security" as a result of the IIoT sensors monitoring worker and workplace safety collectively. One more recent idea that several manufacturers are implementing is allowing their staff to wear wearable technology. Although wearables have been a component of IoT since its inception, industrial IoT operations are only now beginning to make use of them. Leadership may enhance work conditions and possibly boost performance by using wearables to monitor things like staff posture and noise levels in the area. Additionally, by warning staff members when they are not adhering to the relevant workplace safety protocols, they can make the necessary corrections and maintain their safety while working.

6. **Line optimization** – It is easier to improve operations across entire facilities when industrial IoT solutions provide the standardization of work output throughout a manufacturing line. Let's take an example where you have six facilities with various production lines and capacities. With the help of industrial IoT, you can examine the manufacturing process at each facility and assess several aspects such as equipment capabilities, capacity, and availability. These insights simplify the process of figuring out where to manufacture a particular product most efficiently across all sites and how to enable operation efficiencies across various processes in many locations.

7. **Digital Twins** – The term "digital twins" describes precise virtual replicas of real-world things made possible by cloud computing, machine learning, IoT, and artificial intelligence. Managers can simulate various processes, run experiments, identify problems, and attain necessary outcomes without compromising or causing damage to physical assets by utilizing virtual replicas of equipment and replacement parts.

Digital twins also make it possible to see the wider picture while a production line is running, which improves performance and efficiency evaluation. You can step back for a more comprehensive perspective of the entire process or delve deep into a representation of a particular machine through digital recreations. This lets you see potential performance bottleneck locations. For instance, if your feeder is sluggish, an examination of the digital depiction of the manufacturing line may indicate packing system inefficiency.

8. **Decreased Expenses** – Manufacturers are receiving the knowledge they need to cut expenses and increase revenue through IIoT solutions. Businesses can be guided toward profitability with the help of data-driven insights into operations, production, marketing, sales, and other areas.

A manufacturer will see an increase in profitability from all of the aforementioned advantages of IoT, including predictive maintenance, reduced errors, enhanced quality control, and optimal efficiencies. The most useful tool available to manufacturing firm leaders is probably industrial IoT's ability to provide insights at any time and from any location.

15.2.2 RADIO-FREQUENCY IDENTIFICATION (RFID)

Among the pillars of the Internet of Things is RFID, a notion developed from RFID-enabled tracking and identifying technology. RFID has been extensively employed in several industries, including manufacturing, since the 1980s as a means of tracking and identifying things. Sufficient real-time information about IoT objects can be obtained with an RFID system. One technology that uses wireless communication is RFID. RFID was first created for tracking and identification, but as interest in its many other potential uses has grown, a new generation of RFID-based wireless sensor devices has been created. More automated industries are made possible by the autonomous and continuous sensing capabilities of RFID, which often reduce the need for human labor in the data collecting process.

Logistics managers can track and manage goods and assets in the supply chain in a variety of ways thanks to RFID. With applications ranging from inventory management to automation, RFID tags and scanners have the ability to enhance product and material handling both inside and outside the warehouse environment. These are a few advantages that RFID can offer the supply chain.

1. **Enhances product tracking by integrating warehouse management system** – The receipt, storage, and distribution of commodities are monitored by warehouse management systems. Product locations, inventory levels, reordering information, and other data that users would need for supply chain management are all stored in a WMS. Users may be able to increase the speed, ease, and accuracy of product tracking by integrating RFID technology with a WMS. Employees can use an RFID scanner to scan the items on each pallet as soon as they arrive at the warehouse and update the new stock to the WMS. Employees can enable location tracking by scanning the product and the bin number when they are being stored in the warehouse. Additionally, pickers have the option to scan each RFID tag as they choose items and subsequently designate them as leaving the distribution center.

2. **Enhances the efficiency of product handling** – RFID tags can also be used for managing items both inside and between supply chain locations and for planning routes. Workers in

warehouses can outfit trucks, containers, forklifts, and other material handling equipment with RFID tags so that they can swiftly retrieve equipment to transport goods and always know where it is.

3. **Speeds up the counting of inventories** – Inventory counting and reconciliation can be accelerated with RFID tags and scanners because warehouse staff can quickly and precisely scan RFID tags with handheld RFID equipment. While some scanners can count each tag individually for each item, others can count every tag in a certain area almost simultaneously. Accurate inventory management can also be achieved through faster and more regular inventory counting.

4. **Helps rectify inaccurate inventory counts** – RFID technology facilitates the process of locating the root cause of problems related to product distribution, storage, or receipt. RFID allows warehouse staff to track the movement of a specific product and look into the cause of any discrepancies. An RFID scanner might detect the tag somewhere else and notify the user, for instance, if a worker accidentally stores an item in the wrong place. Given that RFID offers details about the issue's cause, warehouse managers may find it easier to take preventative measures.

5. **Enhances the availability of products** – Customers of today want everything to be available at all times, and suppliers may guarantee their products will be in stock when needed by merging RFID product tracking with consumer demand information. RFID allows manufacturers, suppliers, and retailers to track products across the supply chain, giving them constant visibility into the locations of their products. These teams can then coordinate the quantity of products in a certain area to make sure they have enough to fulfill sales targets and projections. When combined with consumer demand data, RFID has the potential to enhance the customer experience by increasing product availability.

6. **Facilitates automated product delivery, storage, and receipt** – Automation is a common tool used in modern warehouses to try and expedite picking, distributing, and receiving items. RFID allows robotics and other technologies to recognize, handle, and route products. Product tags enable automated technologies to choose the best package types for certain things, while packaging tags help robots sense products and store them in or retrieve them from a given area. Equipment tags facilitate the movement of goods by robots that use specific picking and packing technologies. Automation technology has the potential to lower a company's overall costs by eliminating the need for human labor.

7. **Facilitates in optimizing the production process** – RFID can help reduce production costs and improve productivity while upholding quality standards. RFID tags allow suppliers

to track parts and raw materials inside their facilities, which may eliminate the requirement for reordering in the event that a part that was thought to be lost turns out to be located. RFID can also be used by manufacturing equipment to recognize and pick components and assemble them into things that are ready for consumers.

15.3 SMART MANUFACTURING SYSTEMS FOR INDUSTRY 4.0

Industry 4.0 smart manufacturing systems, encompassing a variety of subjects such industrial implementation, smart design, smart machining, smart monitoring, smart control, and smart scheduling (Fig. 15.3) are discussed as follow.

1. **Customized smart wearable device with smart design based on user experience** – There are two common developing trends in the product development stage of Industry 4.0 environments, and they are:

- The manufacturing paradigm of mass customization involves customers participating more actively in the product design process to co-create personalized products that improve user experience (UX) and satisfaction;
- Products themselves become smart, able to communicate with other things throughout their lifecycle, as defined by the term Internet of Things (IoTs).

The physical layer, cyber layer, and user experience layer make up the three levels that make up the conceptual framework of the product development process. The physical layer refers to tangible goods and services (such as wristbands and app subscriptions); the cyber layer refers to web-based virtual co-design tools (such as CAD models and product configuration systems); and the user experience layer refers to the cognitive and affective behaviors (such as feedback and emotions) of the user throughout the product development process.

Modern design approaches, such as adaptive design and innovative design thinking, are incorporated into smart design to direct the user-interactive conceptual design process. In order to facilitate co-creation, a graphical user interface system for product configuration is also being created. 3D scanners are used to record the unique features of the user in order to prototype the customized items. The geometric parameters are then optimized in the CAD program for subsequent 3D printing.

Fig. 15.3 A conceptual model for an Industry 4.0 intelligent production system

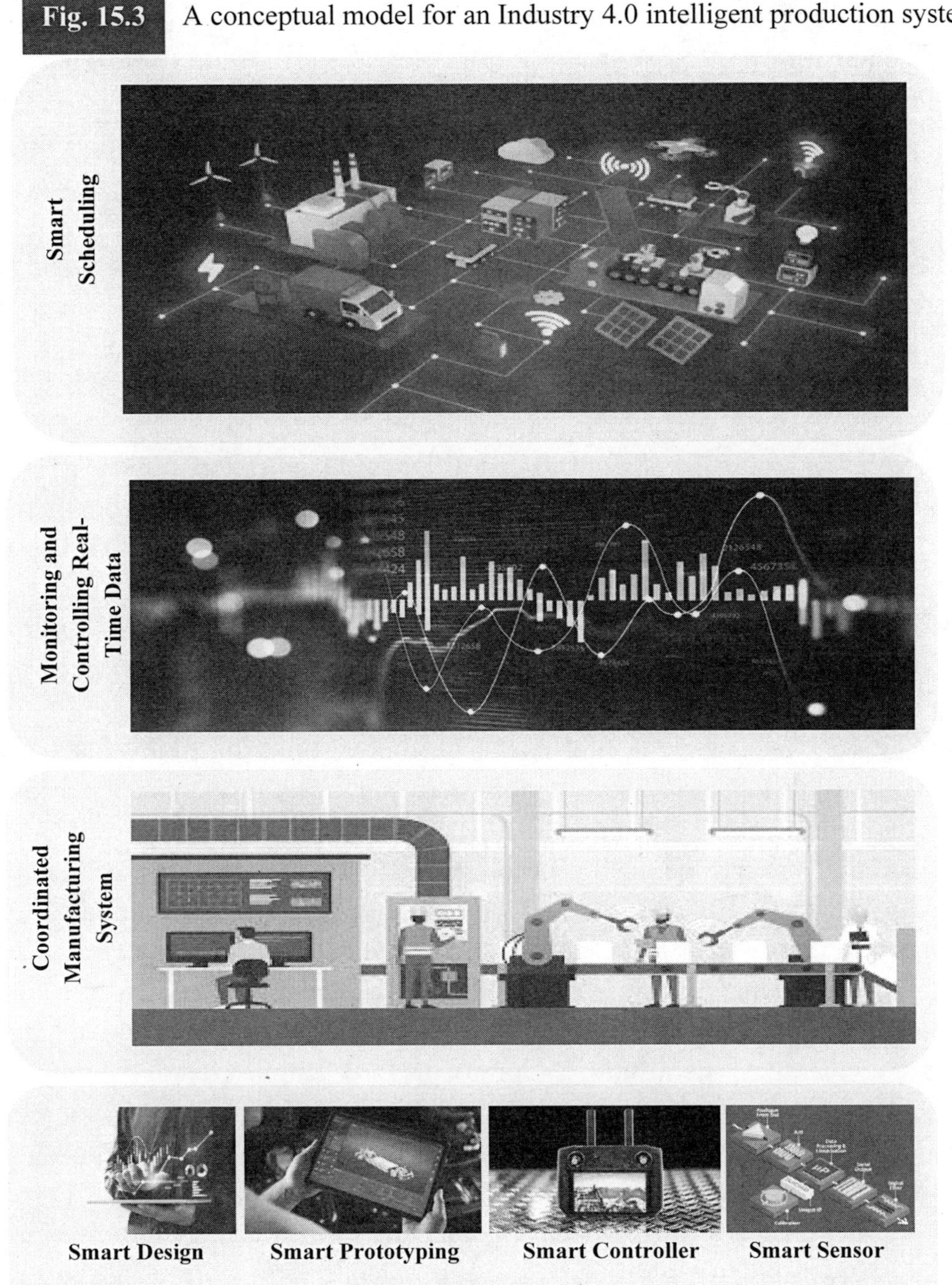

The prototype product uses a smart sensor platform to test its smart features (such as heart rate and breathing frequency) using apps on smart mobile devices. The IoT platform then

analyses the sensor data for additional data analytics and product status tracking (e.g., location, usage time, etc.). Concurrently, during the stages of prototype product testing and product development, the user experience is recorded. Users' opinions of the co-design process are gathered through the use of digital tools like eye trackers and video cameras, as well as marketing techniques like questionnaires and focus groups. Digital tools (such eye trackers and virtual reality headsets) and marketing tactics record their experiences.

2. **CPS-based Smart Machine Tools for Smart Machining** – Physical items are manufactured using smart machine tools that are enabled by CPS. CPS can bridge the gap between the real and virtual worlds to establish a fully networked environment where intelligent items may communicate and engage with one another. Production systems are transformed into CPPS (continuous production and process systems) in the framework of Industry 4.0. These systems include digitally generated smart equipment, warehousing systems, and production facilities with end-to-end ICT-based integration.

As illustrated in Fig. 15.4, smart machine tools can be thought of as combinations of several CPS. Critical parts like spindles, bearings, and cutting tools have RFID tags affixed to them so that the actual things can be uniquely identified. Various cameras, data gathering devices, and sensors (dynamometers, accelerometers, AE sensors, etc.) are installed in machine tools to gather real-time machining data of each crucial component and the machining operations.

The integration, management, and exchange of real-time machining data gathered from intelligent machine tools are the domains of communication services. Various data formats originating from various machine controllers and sensors pose significant challenges for the data integration and management process, even though different data communication technologies (e.g., Ethernet, RS 232, 5G network, Bluetooth, etc.) can be used to transmit real-time data depending on different data acquisition devices. After all the data has been collected, each crucial component must also have a digital twin created in order to fully capture both its current state and its physical characteristics. Information modeling techniques and standardized data transfer protocols are employed to overcome these problems. With the goal of improving device and application data gathering capabilities and facilitating a plug-and-play environment to lower data integration costs, MTConnect is an open, royalty-free communication standard. It can convert the data gathered from various devices into the XML data format, which is compatible with the majority of software programs. ISO 10303, commonly referred to as STEP (Standard for the Exchange of Product model data), is an ISO (International Organization for Standardization) standard that may describe product data independently of any specific system at any point in a product's life cycle. The communication service builds digital twins of the essential components based on these standards and uses the internet to deliver well-formatted real-time data to a range of applications.

Fig. 15.4 Smart manufacturing enabled by CPS

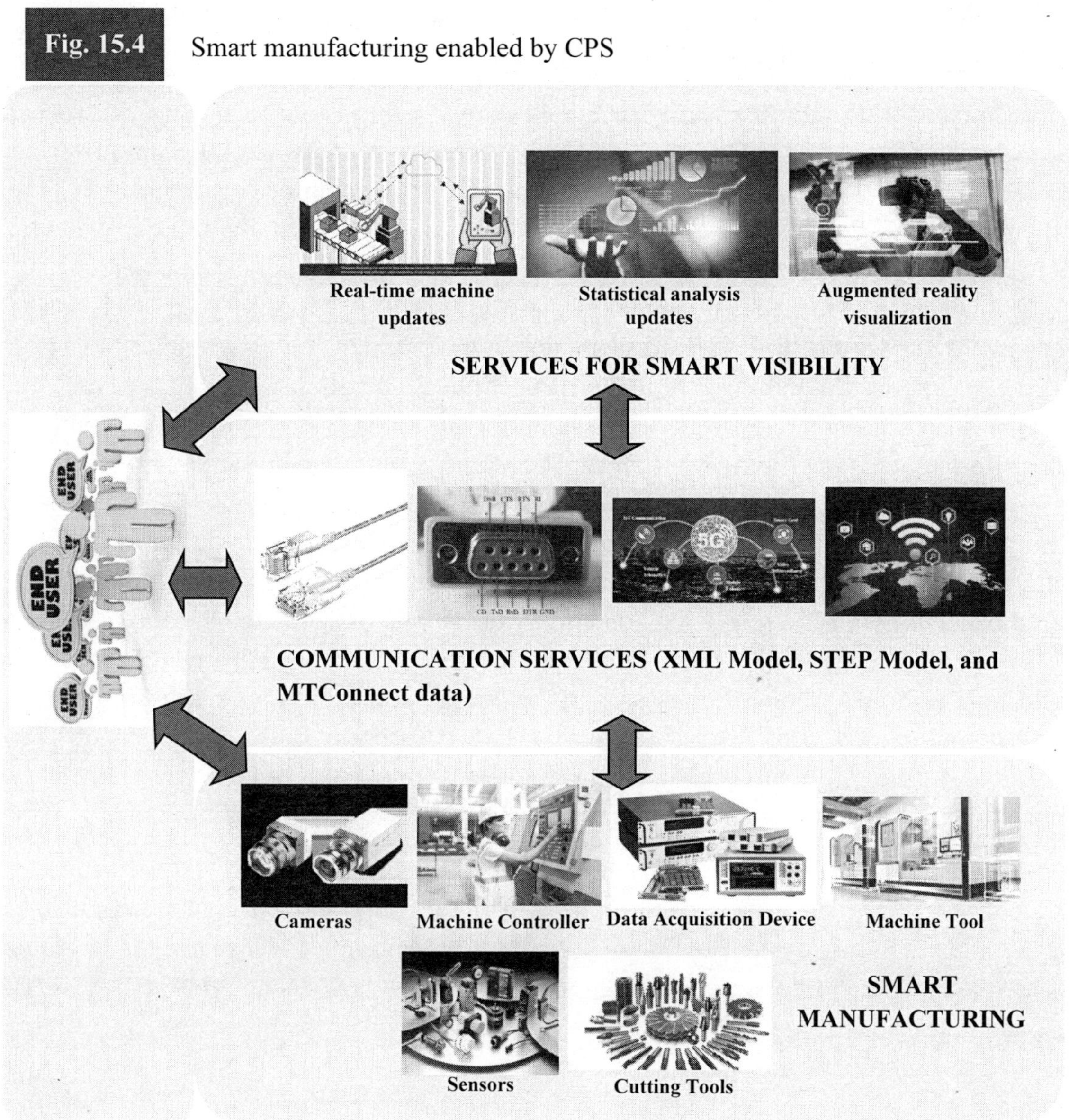

The communication service's real-time data is utilized by several applications, including the smart visibility service. Since the real-time data from field-level devices is accessible online, mobile devices like tablets and smartphones may be used to remotely visualize the current state of every vital component of the smart machine tools. ERP and other business management systems can immediately access machine tool status statistics reports, allowing for smooth communication between field-level manufacturing equipment, and sophisticated decision-making systems. Comprehensive history data is retained locally and in the cloud by logging the real-time information supplied by the communication service.

3. **Energy Consumption Monitoring with Smart Monitoring** – Many industrial firms are concerned about energy efficient production in the context of Industry 4.0 manufacturing systems. A workshop is filled with numerous pieces of machining equipment. At the moment, energy costs are rising, and many nations are very concerned about environmental protection. Generally, every piece of machining equipment has a defined characteristic of energy consumption. Certain energy-demanding procedures are typically fixed, such as the power needed to start a machine tool, idle, spindle start, cut, and power machine functions (tool change, work piece handling) throughout machining operations. Formulas cannot be used to express certain parts. Complex expressions for the spindle start power, for example, can make it more challenging to determine the energy requirement and carry out the necessary optimization. In addition, power fluctuations occur in a workshop, which makes it challenging to develop the energy consumption model. Real-time monitoring of the machining energy consumption is required to accomplish energy-efficient production.

In the context of industry 4.0, data on energy usage may be gathered because different types of sensors have been widely deployed. The obtained data can be subjected to machine learning techniques to determine the features of the energy consumption. A type of machine learning technique called deep neural networks (DNNs) focuses on the processing of big datasets. Based on the information gathered from energy consumption monitoring, it can be utilized to extract the energy consumption traits or trends of manufacturing equipment.

4. **Cloud-based numerical control for smart control** – The increasing sophistication of machine tools and their control systems underscores the importance of smart control in Industry 4.0 manufacturing systems. With an existing CNC system, for instance, an operator can manage the machine to do a machining task using the Human Machine Interface (HMI), switches, and buttons. There is an "information isolated island" problem since each machine tool's control system functions separately. Control System as a Service (CSaaS), a novel and cutting-edge form, will be made available in a cloud manufacturing setting. To meet the evolving needs of the new business models, the CSaaS users include not only machine operators but also machine supervisory vendors and even the product's end users. Fig. 15.5 shows a cloud-based smart control system that uses CNC control as an example to highlight the main ideas. Every non-real-time job will run on the cloud. In order to allocate and

schedule machining jobs among linked machine tools, which are regarded as local manufacturing resources, consideration is given to their availability and capability.

Fig. 15.5 Smart Control System over the Cloud

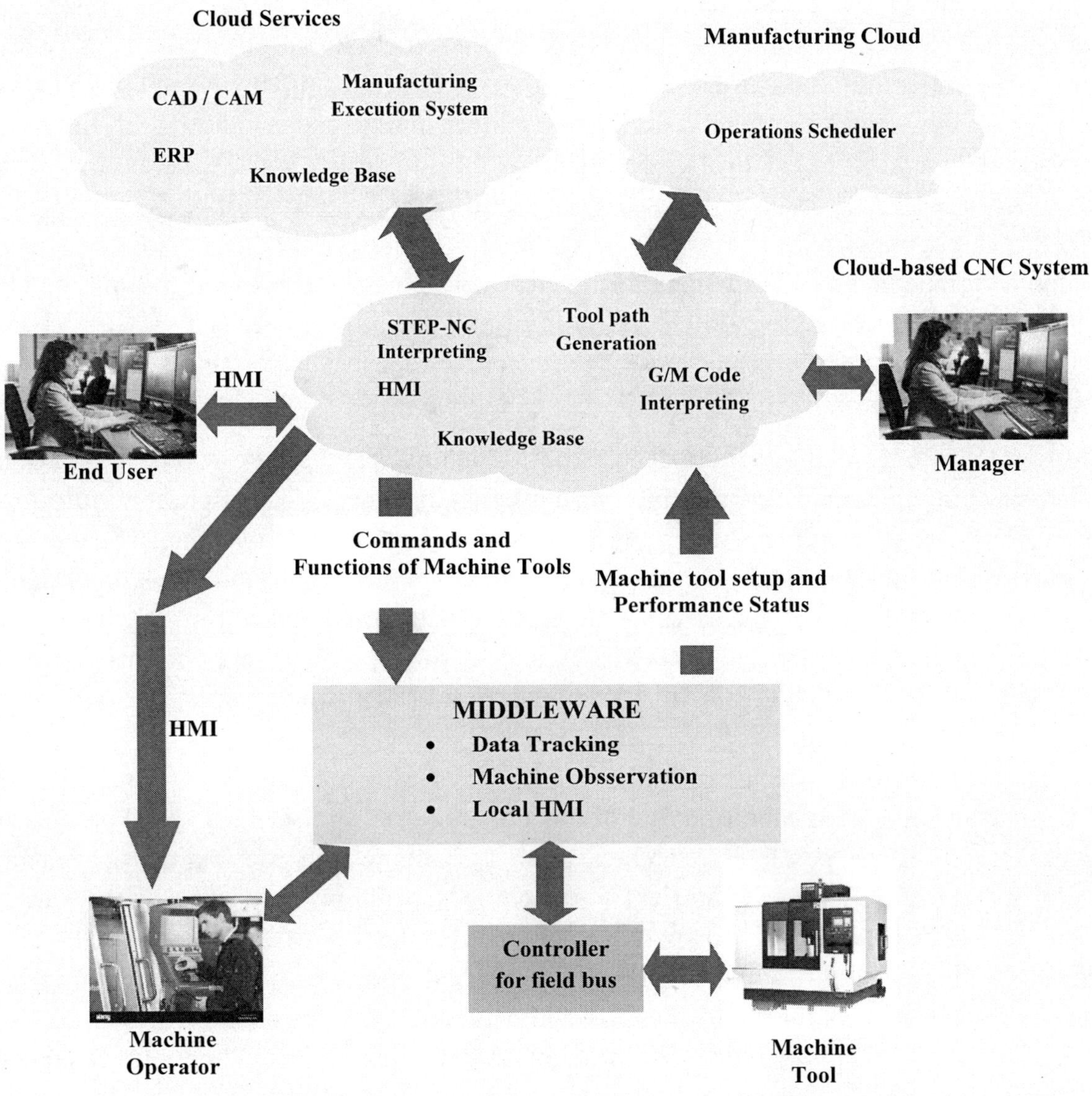

By logging a part programme, a local operator can also initiate a machining process. Whether the application is in STEP-NC or G/M code, the cloud can understand it. The toolpath for a

STEP-NC program will be generated by the cloud if one exists. With the use of a knowledge base or other optimization services, offline optimization tasks can be completed throughout the tool-path generation process, such as the optimization of the cutter selection, resequencing the working stages, and the cutting parameter.

The connection management function of the local control system is in charge of overseeing the Internet connection between the local and cloud. The data monitoring is in charge of keeping an eye on the data that is received and handling any transmission faults. The drives will receive the correct set-points and process them into a pulse command, which is then sent over fieldbus and carried out by the motors. The machine monitoring module will make use of the encoder's feedback. The machine monitoring module will offer the machining and machine tool status by combining data from various sensors. Even though the cloud provides the HMI, the local control system still has a basic HMI that shows essential data so that the operator may operate the machine tool in the event that the cloud service is unavailable. A machine tool sends data to the cloud, which is used to build tool paths. This data includes the cutter statues, setup, and current axis locations. The local control system will communicate to the cloud the status of the machine tool (e.g., operating status, warning information) and the progress of the machining operations.

Machine scheduling in smart factories – Smart machine scheduling can be accomplished by smart machine intelligence, smart monitoring (such as energy consumption monitoring), and smart cloud-based control systems. As illustrated in Figure 15.6, machine scheduling in the context of Industry 4.0 requires a variety of attributes. Machines in Industry 4.0 possess a certain level of intelligence and are able to interact with one another through the use of wireless communication devices (like RFID) and a variety of sensors. In this instance, machines are transparent to a great extent since data about each component of the system can be easily gathered in real time.

The best machine scheduling can be achieved by taking meaningful information (such energy usage and operating condition) out of the gathered data. In the Industry 4.0 production environment, it will be possible to predict when a machine will break down or become unavailable, which will remove barriers to machine scheduling and bring about various benefits. The fact that products (or parts) are intelligent and can communicate with other machines is another significant distinction between Industry 4.0 machine scheduling and traditional machine scheduling. This presents both new opportunities and difficulties.

Every machine in the Industry 4.0 production environment is a CPS entity, capable of interacting with other machines both in the real and virtual worlds (Fig. 15.6). The scheduling of collaborative CPS is the fundamental component of machine scheduling in Industry 4.0. The typical features of CPS, such as autonomous (e.g., selfaware, self-predict, self-compare), decentralized, and real-time, are what give machine scheduling in Industry 4.0 its complexity.

Fig. 15.6 Machine scheduling in Industry 4.0

Efficient, flexible, distributed, and multi-objective scheduling techniques (or algorithms)

Scheduling Prerequisites and Attributes

Data Collection on the Working Condition, Workload and Energy Consumption of Machines and Products in Real Time.

Reconfigurable and Adaptable Machine Architecture

Multi-objective (quality, cost, and time)

Decentralized, Autonomous Devices Operating in Real Time

Small-Scale, Highly Customized Batches

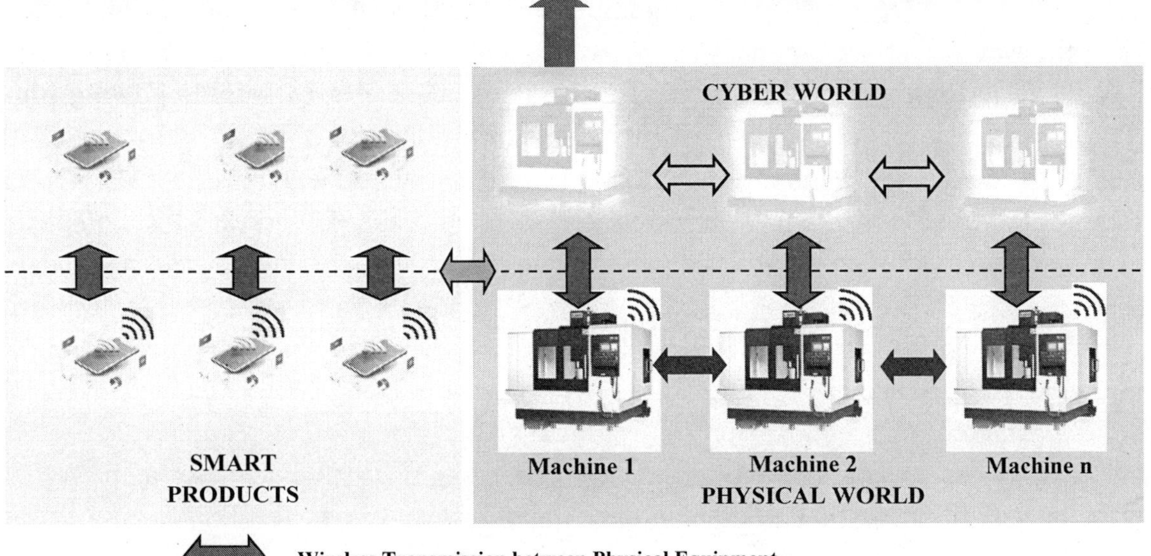

Wireless Transmission between Physical Equipment

Transmission between the physial world and the cyber

Transmission between cyber twins of machines

Wireless connectivity between machines and smart products

Thus, Industry 4.0 machine scheduling demands decentralized, flexible, and effective scheduling techniques. In actuality, Industry 4.0 machine scheduling will be well-supported

Industry 4.0 machine scheduling will be well-supported by turning a machine into a CPS with full perception. In an Industry 4.0 smart factory, artificial intelligence offers a useful tool for scheduling machines. Scheduling models and algorithms are implemented in the CPS's cyberspace (such as the cloud) in Industry 4.0 manufacturing systems. These elements communicate with the actual machinery and work together to drive output.

15.4 ADDITIVE MANUFACTURING

Additive manufacturing (AM), also referred to as 3D printing, is an advanced fabrication technique that produces three-dimensional things by layering material on top of one another thinly. Typically, the 3D printing process starts with a three-dimensional computer-aided design (CAD) model of the component. A polyhedral representation of the part, typically in the STL, OBJ, or AMF file type, is created from the solid CAD model. This 3D file is fed into a program known as a "slicer," which divides the file into multiple levels after receiving user-supplied settings. The 3D printer's microcontroller can then read the numerical instructions that the slicer creates for building each layer in sequential sequence and stores them in a file type known as G-code. The material is added to the part by the 3D printer layer by layer while it constructs it in accordance with the G-code instructions. Following print completion, the user can carry out post-processing procedures like curing, cleaning, heat treatment, and removing the support material. One way to categorize 3D printers is based on how they work. Table 15.1 provides a summary of several popular 3D printing technologies.

In essence, additive manufacturing (AM) processes involve adding materials to the prior surface using various deposition methods, which produce parts with varying densities, geometric accuracy, and quality. Typically, subtractive procedures or a combination of multiple processes are used in traditional operations when dealing with complex parts. The main disadvantage of conventional processes is their high material loss rate and absence of control mechanisms to continuously adjust the processes according to the situation. AM increases the benefit-cost ratio by reducing the amount of control over various manufacturing processes and enabling fabrication in fewer steps with reduced time and material waste.

Table 15.1 Some common 3D printing technology's working principles.

Process	Description
Fused Deposition Modeling (FDM) or Fused Filament Fabrication (FFF)	Layers are created by fusing together lines of melted thermoplastic filament. To cut down on material expenses, certain FDM printers can utilize polymer pellets in place of filament. Because of its inexpensive cost of materials and machines, as well as its ease of use, FDM printing is the most popular type of AM.
Stereolithography (SLA)	An ultraviolet laser scanning system with numerical control is used to selectively solidify a thin layer of liquid photopolymer resin. SLA is the earliest method for 3D printing and provides extremely high resolution.
Digital light processing (DLP)	Through a shaped light projection, an extremely thin layer of liquid photopolymer resin is selectively hardened. Although DLP equipment is far less expensive than SLA equipment, it does not give as great of a resolution as SLA equipment.
Selective laser sintering (SLS)	A laser numerically controlled laser scanning system melts a layer of powder selectively. Depending on the laser's power, metal or polymer powders can be used with SLS printers.
Material Jetting (MJ)	UV-cure photopolymer resin droplets are expelled from the printhead and instantaneously cure under a UV light after landing on a build plate or in a layer of powder.

Advantages of Additive Manufacturing over Traditional Manufacturing Processes

Various additive manufacturing (AM) techniques have been created, not to completely replace existing manufacturing methods, but to increase the choice of processes that producers and customers can choose from. Every procedure has benefits and drawbacks of its own, and the best one to choose depends on the particular application. It is necessary to describe the main characteristics of AM processes in order to go over their benefits. The three main characteristics of AM – time, money, and flexibility – are the foundation upon which its benefits can be assessed. Some of the advantages of additive manufacturing are outlined as:

- Accelerating output and reducing manufacturing time are two of AM's primary goals. This will shorten the time it takes to produce replacement and spare parts and speed up prototyping.

- The performance of the supply chain for spare parts can be enhanced by moving production facilities and decentralizing production to several regional locations near key markets.
- Reduced downtime, cheaper total costs, lower capacity utilization, less need for inventory management, increased resilience, and increased adaptability to supply chain fluctuations are some advantages of distributed production with regard to spare parts.
- By reducing the time and expense of item shipping, on-site manufacturing technologies allow for the quick creation of customized parts.
- AM utilizes resources skillfully by reusing the leftover materials for producing the next section, in contrast to traditional production, where massive amounts of materials must be eliminated.
- AM products may be more cost-effective when labor costs are reduced and expensive warehousing is avoided.
- Additionally, fixtures, cutting tools, jigs, and coolants are not needed while using additive manufacturing. Moreover, since there are no unsold finished goods, manufacturing to order lowers inventory risk.
- Designers can more readily change the process settings to suit their demands and are free to create complicated parts.
- AM allows for the fabrication of parts with complicated geometries and does not impose any limitations on part functionality due to the lack of tooling constraints.
- A single part can be constructed with different qualities in different places, such as greater ductility in one place and greater strength in another.
- Output can precisely match customer demand because operator skills have no bearing on part quality, which is determined by the process.

Additive manufacturing (AM) has become a viable and quick distribution option for personal protective equipment (PPE) and medical devices during COVID-19. The reader can scan the QR code to get more information about additive manufacturing's role in COVID 19.

SCAN ME
for
AM in COVID 19

15.5 BLOCKCHAIN TECHNOLOGY

In 2008, Satoshi Nakamoto initially created blockchain as a cryptocurrency known as "Bitcoin." It is suggested to be used as a peer-to-peer (P2P) distributed network's public ledger. Blockchain is regarded as a fantastic invention that records and stores data on a distributed ledger with an efficient protection mechanism, despite the concept that it should replace the current currency. A distributed database of records, or shared public/private ledgers, of all digital events that have been carried out and shared among blockchain participating agents is what blockchain technology is all about. One can trace its history back to distributed ledger technology. Five essential characteristics of blockchain technology set it apart from the majority of current information systems designs: decentralized database, security, transparency of information, immutability of data and information, and smart contracts (Fig. 15.7).

An agent in the blockchain initiates a new transaction to be appended to the blockchain. The network is notified of this new transaction so that it can be audited and verified. A new block is added to the chain as soon as this transaction is authorized by the majority of nodes in the chain in accordance with pre-established acceptable rules. For security purposes, the transaction record is stored among multiple distributed nodes. In the meantime, legitimate transactions can be carried out without the assistance of third parties thanks to the smart contract, a crucial component of blockchain technology.

One of the main distinctions between blockchain technology and the current state of the Internet is that the latter was created to transfer copies of items rather than original information, and information (not value). Value in blockchains is represented by transactions that are entered into a shared ledger and secured by offering an auditable, verifiable record of transactions that is time-stamped. These transactions show up after being verified in accordance with the guidelines of the network consensus. Upon verification and addition to the blockchain, several copies are generated in a decentralized fashion to establish a chain of trust.

Characteristics of Blockchain

1. **Decentralized database** – One of the key components of blockchain technology is decentralization. Blockchains usually do not involve a central database, organization, or authority in the transaction process. Peer-to-peer networks provide direct communication between network users thanks to decentralized record databases. Every network member has an identical copy of the ledgers, which are updated in a decentralized way with new information or modifications to the recorded data.

The network partners must agree on every modification to a ledger. The fundamental principle of blockchain is decentralized consensus, which verifies the validity of recorded transactions using a variety of algorithms, including proof of stake and proof of labor. To ensure the legitimacy of transactions, decentralized consensus typically involves the validation of the majority of network participants through votes. Consensus algorithms are heavily used in public blockchains and need a lot of power and energy. This trait undermines sustainability principles and include to environmental deterioration. The consensus requirement in a private or permissioned blockchain refers to a set of guidelines established by network users for adding and amending transactions to ledgers. In a private network, consensus rules offer flexibility and make the deployment of laborious consensus methods easier.

2. **Security** – Blockchain technology maintains information as blocks. Every block on the chain has a timestamp and a hash value that points to earlier blocks. The distinct cryptographic architectures of hash values guard against tampering and changing the data on the blockchain. The use of cryptography logic enhances the trust and security of the system by making it easier for anonymous parties to authenticate and transact on public, permissionless blockchains.

A key component of a private or permissioned blockchain is the participants' ability to rely on the validator, who grants them authorization to record and trace data. The blockchain's decentralized architecture enhances security. Decentralization leads to network members evaluating the veracity of information according to the consensus rules. This feature restricts network manipulation and data exploitation. Additionally, decentralization makes the network less susceptible to crashes and hacking. A common security issue with centralized databases is the single point of failure, which has been mitigated with blockchain technology. With regards to lead time, delivery, and perishability concerns, among other time-based competitive difficulties, the timestamp is essential to the supply chain. Traceability and information transparency also depend on the timestamp.

3. **Transparency of information** – The ledger, which is a list of transactions, is kept up to date by authorized participants in the blockchain network. The most recent approved transactions are updated in the ledgers. Network participants have access to the full transaction history, facilitating auditability and traceability. Fairness and ease of access to data inside a network are improved by the blockchain's level of openness. Reduced risks, increased efficiency, and elimination of middlemen are all benefits of transparent information.

Supply chain procedures using blockchain technology are driven by growing customer demands for transparency. Tracing the origin and flow of goods and processes, the participants to transactions and transportation data are all made possible by a high degree of transparency. Records can be tracked and audited by supply chain partners, ranging from upstream to downstream. Data modification and fraudulent activities can be identified and tracked on the blockchain due to its time-stamped and secure records. For supply chain partners, this fosters confidence and reliability. Smart gadgets, the Internet of Things, and radio frequency identification (RFID) are examples of tracking technologies that create inputs for blockchain technology that are kept on transparent ledgers by connecting the physical product to its corresponding electronic record.

4. **Immutability of Data and Information** – Information and data on blockchains are unchangeable. Records that are immutable cannot be altered or amended without the agreement of all network users. Participants can feel secure knowing that the records' history is trustworthy and untainted. The append-only principle of the blockchain, which states that entries may only be added to ledgers and cannot be changed or erased, is theoretically the source of this capability. On the other hand, collusion is conceivable if a majority of miners choose to change or remove a transaction on a public or permissionless blockchain, where miners vote for transactions and govern the system. On the other hand, altering or deleting data on a private or permissioned blockchain necessitates following specific guidelines and agreements as well as alerting all network participants.

5. **Smart contracts** – Smart contracts are computer programs and scripts that hold business policies and contractual conditions. Smart contracts carry out agreements' terms automatically. Smart contracts verify predefined terms, such as guidelines and penalties that have been agreed upon by parties and initiate the appropriate response.

Network members validate contracts' terms and conditions. These computer programs operate autonomously in an effort to do away with human involvement in contracts. Smart contracts do not require confidence between parties, in contrast to traditional contracts where trust is crucial. Contract terms are digitally encoded as computer programs and kept on the blockchain network, along with the associated legal processes. Transactions involving digital contracts are free from human judgment. The adoption of smart contracts can reduce the role of middlemen, such as financial advisors and attorneys, who are involved in traditional contracts. The disintermediation that follows lowers expenses associated with conducting business and increases efficiency.

The distinct features of blockchain technology have encouraged its further application across several industries and even for non-financial commercial endeavors. Among the successful use cases include supply chains, real estate, government, healthcare, and the energy sector. The reader can access additional information about blockchain's real-world applications in the healthcare industry by scanning the QR code.

SCAN ME
for
Blockchain application
in healthcare

Fig. 15.7 Blockchain information and transaction process

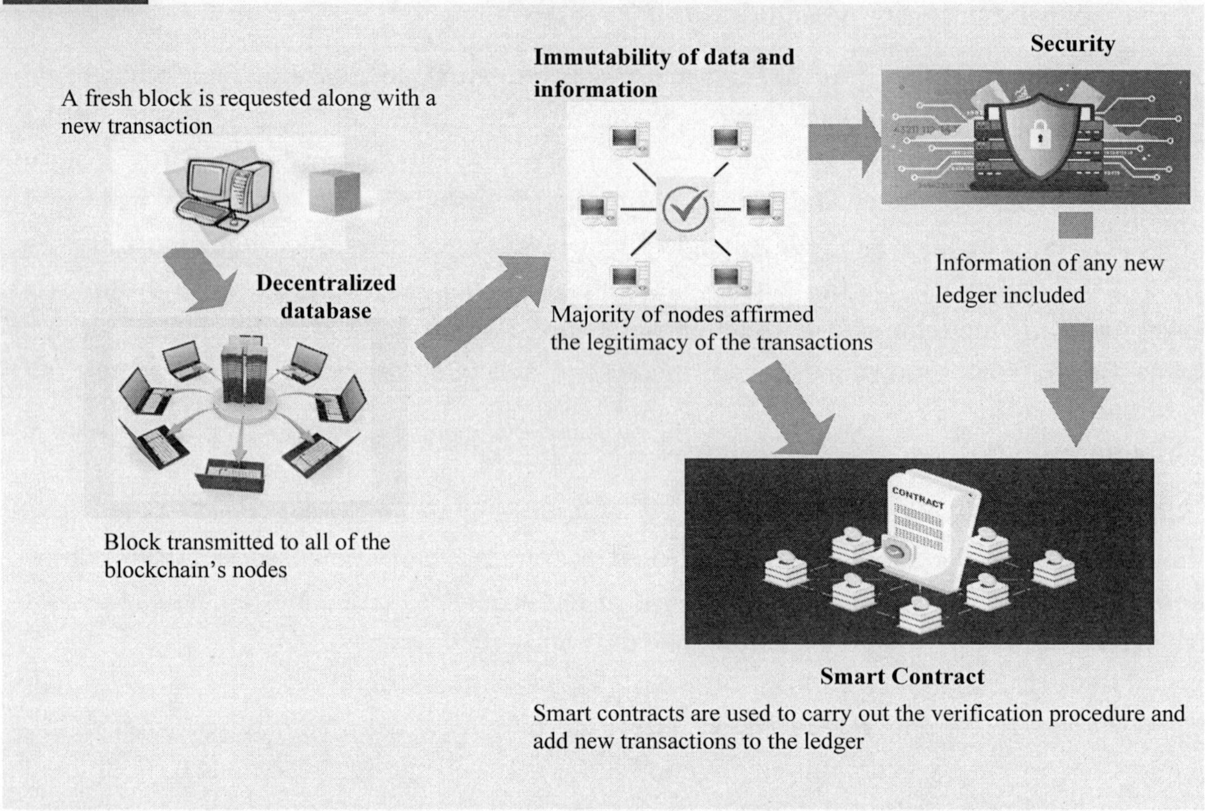

A fresh block is requested along with a new transaction

Decentralized database

Block transmitted to all of the blockchain's nodes

Immutability of data and information

Majority of nodes affirmed the legitimacy of the transactions

Security

Information of any new ledger included

Smart Contract

Smart contracts are used to carry out the verification procedure and add new transactions to the ledger

15.6 ARTIFICIAL INTELLIGENCE IN OPERATIONS MANAGEMENT

Artificial intelligence (AI) is a strategic strategy that companies use to design and implement procedures that maximize productivity and efficiency. Every operation is more optimized and efficient when artificial intelligence (AI) is used in operations management. To stay up to date with the rapidly evolving world of today, it is imperative to understand the benefits of artificial intelligence in operations management. By enabling machines and systems to learn from data, make intelligent decisions, and automate difficult processes, artificial intelligence adds a new level of complexity to operations management. Operations management can benefit greatly from AI in the following important areas:

(a) **Automation of Processes** – Artificial intelligence (AI) may automate repetitive and routine processes, freeing up human resources to concentrate on higher-value jobs. Robotic process automation (RPA) can expedite data input procedures, virtual assistants can automate administrative jobs, and AI-powered chatbots can answer consumer inquiries.

(b) **Predictive analytics** – AI systems are able to forecast future trends, demand patterns, and performance measures by analyzing enormous volumes of data. Making well-informed decisions about resource allocation, inventory control, and capacity planning is aided by this. AI can also optimize maintenance schedules based on past patterns and real-time data through predictive maintenance, which minimizes equipment downtime.

(c) **Supply chain optimization** – AI has the potential to completely transform supply chain management by improving inventory control, demand forecasting, and logistics. It is capable of analyzing a variety of data sources, such as supplier performance, market trends, and consumer behavior, to offer real-time insights and suggestions on sourcing, production, and distribution tactics. AI can improve resource allocation in a few areas, including task assignment and workforce scheduling. Operating expenses can be considerably decreased with an efficient schedule.

(d) **Risk management and quality control** – Algorithms driven by artificial intelligence can examine sensor data and carry out real-time quality control inspections to find flaws or irregularities in the manufacturing process. Artificial intelligence has the potential to improve risk management through its ability to detect fraudulent activity patterns, identify cybersecurity threats, and improve regulatory compliance.

Organizations have never-before-seen opportunity to improve decision-making, reduced expenses, and streamline processes when AI is integrated into operations management. Businesses may increase quality control, foresee trends, streamline supply chains, and automate repetitive processes by utilizing AI capabilities. Careful planning, data management, change management, and ethical considerations are necessary for a successful implementation, though.

Utilizing AI for Asset Optimization

1. **Predictive maintenance** – It is essential to undertake maintenance tasks proactively as this reduces downtime. AI uses predictive analytics, machine learning (ML) algorithms, and data to foresee and stop equipment faults. Businesses can use the models to identify anomalies or departures from standard operating procedures. By using predictive maintenance, a business can minimize unplanned downtime by preventing unforeseen malfunctions. By just carrying out maintenance when required, an organization can also reduce the cost of repairs and replacements. These steps prolong the equipment's lifespan by promptly resolving problems. Lastly, by lowering the chance of equipment failures, predictive maintenance raises workplace safety.

2. **Inventory management** – Companies that want to control their inventory must be able to forecast the demand for their goods or services. AI is able to forecast how companies will handle supply chain operations, production scheduling, and inventory management by analyzing previous data and extracting insights. Real-time inventory tracking is possible for a business with AI. In the event that inventory or demand fluctuates, it can also design AI systems to issue purchase orders. It serves to lower the possibility of overstock or out-of-stock circumstances. To put it briefly, artificial intelligence uses variables like transporting, holding, and stockout costs to determine cost-effective thresholds.

Using AI to Optimize Processes

1. **Automation of workflow** – A company uses AI to automate tedious jobs and incorporates automation into current processes to handle routine duties. It improves operations management efficiency by lowering errors and freeing up staff members for more difficult jobs. AI utilization also lowers human error rates, which is essential for increasing operations management efficiency. Making decisions based on accurate real-time information can be aided by this. AI algorithms can also spot differences in quality control, where accuracy is crucial, and detect them.

2. **Using Data Analytics to Make Decisions** – AI systems are capable of processing massive amounts of data quickly, yielding insightful results and patterns. In summary, AI is able to discover areas for improvement and predict trends more quickly than humans. Based on real-time insights, businesses need to make well-informed decisions. Operations managers can react swiftly and precisely to shifting market trends or operational difficulties thanks to the application of AI. AI is crucial for organizations because it helps to drastically reduce errors as well.

15.6.1 MACHINE LEARNING

The amount of data being collected and stored, as well as the availability of faster computing power, algorithms for identifying trends or patterns in data has significantly improved in recent years. The field of machine learning (ML) was born out of this. The topic of operations management (OM) is only one of several academic disciplines that have benefited greatly from machine learning, which has a wide range of applications from business to engineering. To be sure, machine learning has made operations managers' lives easier when it comes to estimating issues in operations design and optimization. However, it has forced OM managers to reconsider OM issues because, in addition to utilizing mathematical models to gain insights, ML algorithms and data may be combined to enable precise forecasts, identify diagnoses, and directly solve problems.

Machine learning is divided into three categories: *supervised learning*, *unsupervised learning*, and *reinforcement learning*. To learn a function mapping from inputs, also known as features, and outputs, also known as labels, ML models are trained with labeled data in supervised learning. This is done by using example input-output pairs as examples.

The objective of supervised learning algorithms is to "learn by example," or infer a function from a set of labeled training samples. These training cases serve as "supervisors" to ensure that the model generated by the algorithm can generate a high-quality forecast of these labels. Formally speaking, the expression for each training sample is (x_i, y_i), where y_i is the observed label (which may be discrete or continuous), and x_i is the observed feature vector. Generally, we consider (x_i, y_i) to be an independent and identically distributed variable with an uncertain distribution. For instance, x_i might indicate a client's age, gender, location, and even the brand of the mobile device they are using when they visit a website; y_i would be 1 in the event that the customer clicks an advertisement and 0 in the other case. From a class of functions, let's say F, a supervised learning algorithm would select a function f such that $y_i \approx f(x_i)$. Typically, the difference between the predicted labels and the actual label in the data – also known as a loss function and often represented by the popular mean squared error (MSE) – is used to assess the quality of learning. The training loss of any function $f \in F$ in this situation can be expressed as follows:

$$\sum (y_i - f(x_i))^2$$

The next step in the training process is to identify $\hat{f} \in F$ that minimizes the selected error metric, or as close to it as possible. Applying the function $\hat{f}$ to a new testing sample with feature vector x and predicting its label as $f(x)$ is typically simple once it has been trained.

The simplest type of supervised learning models can be thought of as those based on linear regression. In its simplest form, $f(x)$ is represented as a linear function of x, or $\beta \times x$, where β is an estimate that is obtained from data by minimizing the training error. There are other types of linear regression models that are optimized for high-dimensional issues, such as logistic regression models that are appropriate for classification tasks or regression models with regularization (e.g., LASSO or ridge regressions) that control model complexity.

A crude model is the k-nearest-neighbor model (KNN), which finds a few training instances that are the most close to the testing data in terms of feature vectors given any testing data. More effective models are more widely used in practice because this model requires a lot of memory and compute to discover neighbors. Tree-based models, in particular, go beyond these local models by efficiently storing local information in a tree-like structure. They are simple to apply, have strong empirical performance, and lend themselves well to interpretation and visualization. As such, they are frequently thought of as an "off-the-shelf ML method."

It is commonly acknowledged that *deep learning* is most likely the most effective supervised learning technique yet created. It simulates intricate functional forms by utilizing *artificial neural networks*, a model ensemble architecture derived from the human brain. The word "deep" refers to the fact that deep layers in a network are typically effective in solving complex machine learning tasks. Because of its exceptional capacity to handle vast amounts of data, its ability to model intricate functional forms, and its unmatched prediction accuracy when backed by sufficient training data, deep learning has emerged as the most widely used machine learning technique in recent times.

In unsupervised learning, the machine learning algorithm searches a data set without any pre-existing labels for patterns. The daily operations of an online advertising platform that assists in managing the campaigns of the advertisers, for instance, could be taken into consideration. The platform gathers a vast amount of information about people who visit websites and click on advertisements. The software uses supervised learning to forecast which user will click on a certain advertisement. Here, the label is the focal user's response to an advertisement, like a click or conversion, and the features are the focal users' past behaviors, demographics, and advertisement attributes. Unsupervised learning can also be used in this same environment to find trends in past consumer behavior, group customers into distinct groups, and modify ad exposure in response. The customer categories in this example are learned from the characteristics rather than the labels, which is an example of unsupervised learning.

Reinforcement learning is the third category of ML problems, and it is connected to the substantial dynamic optimization in operations management. It is applicable to scenarios where an agent engages with the surroundings, makes decisions, and gains knowledge from the outcome. Reinforcement learning uses longer-term rewards since actions can dynamically change the state, in contrast to supervised learning where rewards are established instantly (depending on whether the label is true). For instance, in online advertising platforms, businesses might use reinforcement learning to adjust advertising techniques in real-time during customer interactions in order to reduce the long-term negative effects of advertisement on user experience and maximize long-term cumulative income. Scan the provided QR code to learn more about machine learning.

SCAN ME
for
Machine Learning

UNIT SUMMARY

- ***Introduction to Digitalization & Industry 4.0***: (i) Examines the shift from traditional to digital manufacturing, and (ii) Discusses Cyber-Physical Systems (CPS) and Internet of Things (IoT) integration.
- ***Smart Manufacturing Systems***: (i) Wearable smart devices for monitoring workers' health and productivity, (ii) Energy consumption monitoring to optimize factory operations, and (iii) Cloud-based numerical control (CNC) for real-time machine scheduling.
- ***Additive Manufacturing*** (3D Printing): (i) Explores FDM, SLA, SLS, and Material Jetting for prototyping and production, and (ii) Highlights reduced material waste and enhanced design flexibility.
- ***Blockchain in Manufacturing***: (i) Enhances supply chain transparency, security, and traceability, and (ii) Uses smart contracts for automated transactions and quality verification.
- ***Artificial Intelligence & Machine Learning***: (i) Predictive maintenance reduces downtime and optimizes asset use, and (ii) AI-driven process automation improves quality control and decision-making.

EXERCISES

MULTIPLE CHOICE QUESTIONS

15.1 What is a key characteristic of an advanced factory system in the context of digitalization?

(a) Reliance solely on manual labor	(b) Absence of data collection and analytics
(c) Use of traditional machinery without digital controls	(d) Integration of Internet of Things (IoT) technologies for real-time monitoring

15.2 What does IIoT stand for, and what is its primary function in advanced factory systems?

(a) Industrial Internet of Things; it connects machines and devices for real-time data exchange and analytics	(b) Industrial Internet of Technology; it focuses on upgrading computer systems only
(c) Industrial Integration of Operations Technology; it replaces manual labor	(d) Internet of Integrated Operations; it solely manages supply chain logistics

15.3 How do CPPS contribute to the efficiency and flexibility of manufacturing operations?

(a) By allowing for the complete replacement of physical machines with virtual simulations	(b) By enabling dynamic adjustments to production processes based on real-time data and conditions
(c) By removing the need for any form of data collection or analysis	(d) By focusing only on traditional manufacturing methods without any digital integration

15.4 What is a key benefit of using Artificial Intelligence (AI) in advanced manufacturing?

(a) It limits data collection to manual inputs only	(b) It completely removes human oversight from manufacturing processes
(c) It enhances decision-making and process optimization by analyzing large volumes of data	(d) It focuses solely on the aesthetics of factory design

15.5 Which of the following is a key characteristic of Industry 4.0?

(a) Exclusive use of analog data collection	(b) Implementation of smart factories with interconnected machines and systems

(c) Focus solely on manual labor and traditional processes	(d) Restriction of data sharing and real-time monitoring

15.6 In Industry 4.0, what is the purpose of using real-time data analytics?

(a) To create physical copies of data reports	(b) To manually adjust production schedules without data input
(c) To limit data collection to quarterly reports	(d) To optimize production processes, improve efficiency, and enable predictive maintenance

15.7 What is the primary role of RFID in product lifecycle management?

(a) To track the geographic location of products in real-time	(b) To monitor environmental conditions around the product
(c) To automatically identify and track tags attached to products	(d) To facilitate real-time communication between product components

15.8 In which phase of the product lifecycle is RFID technology most beneficial for inventory management?

(a) Distribution and Logistics	(b) Disposal and Recycling
(c) Design and Development	(d) Manufacturing

15.9 What advantage does integrating GPS with RFID offer in product lifecycle management?

(a) Improved product design capabilities	(b) Enhanced tracking of product location across global supply chains
(c) Reduction in the need for environmental monitoring	(d) Increased efficiency in production processes

15.10 Which IoT capability is essential for enabling predictive analytics in operations?

(a) Device connectivity	(b) Data encryption
(c) Manual data entry	(d) Scheduled system reboots

15.11 How does IoT contribute to predictive maintenance in industrial settings?

(a) By reducing the amount of data collected from sensors	(b) By providing historical data without real-time updates
(c) By analyzing real-time sensor data to predict equipment failures	(d) By eliminating the need for regular maintenance schedules

15.12 What is a Digital Twin primarily used for?

(a) To create a virtual replica of a physical asset for real-time monitoring and simulation	(b) To replace physical assets with virtual models completely
(c) To manage financial transactions in real time	(d) To store and archive historical data only

15.13 In which industry is the use of Digital Twins most prevalent for optimizing the design and operation of complex systems?

(a) Agriculture	(b) Manufacturing and industrial processes
(c) Retail	(d) Hospitality

15.14 What is the primary function of Cyber-Physical Systems (CPS) in smart manufacturing?

(a) To replace traditional manufacturing processes with manual labor	(b) To integrate computational algorithms with physical processes for real-time monitoring and control
(c) To solely focus on data storage without real-time interaction	(d) To limit the interaction between physical machines and computational systems

15.15 Which of the following is a key feature of Cloud-based CNC systems in smart manufacturing?

(a) Manual programming of CNC machines	(b) Limited access to real-time data
(c) Increased reliance on physical control panels	(d) Centralized data storage and processing in the cloud, facilitating collaboration and scalability

15.16 Which technology is commonly used to improve machine scheduling and coordination in smart factories?

(a) Manual scheduling spreadsheets	(b) Basic mechanical timers
(c) Cloud-based scheduling systems and advanced algorithms	(d) Traditional paper-based scheduling systems

15.17 What is the fundamental principle of additive manufacturing?

(a) Adding material layer by layer to build a 3D object	(b) Subtracting material from a solid block
(c) Joining materials together through welding	(d) Compressing materials into molds

15.18 How does Stereolithography (SLA) achieve the solidification of the liquid resin in additive manufacturing?

(a) By heating the resin to a high temperature	(b) By using a laser or ultraviolet light to cure and solidify the resin layer by layer
(c) By injecting a hardening agent into the resin	(d) By cooling the resin to solidify it

15.19 Which of the following is a fundamental characteristic of blockchain technology?

(a) Centralized data storage	(b) Single point of control
(c) Decentralized and distributed ledger	(d) Manual record-keeping

15.20 Which of the following best describes the immutability characteristic of blockchain?

(a) Transactions can be modified after being recorded	(b) Transactions are temporary and can be deleted
(c) Once recorded, transactions cannot be altered or deleted	(d) Data is frequently updated without tracking changes

15.21 In which area of operations management can AI improve decision-making?

(a) By relying on manual data analysis and human intuition	(b) By focusing only on short-term goals without long-term planning
(c) By restricting access to data and insights	(d) By providing real-time data insights and advanced analytics to support informed decision-making and strategic planning

15.22 Which type of machine learning involves training a model on labeled data to predict outcomes for new, unseen data?

(a) Supervised Machine Learning	(b) Unsupervised Machine Learning
(c) Reinforcement Machine Learning	(d) Semi-supervised Machine Learning

Answers of Multiple Choice Questions

15.1 (d), 15.2 (a), 15.3 (b), 15.4 (c), 15.5 (b), 15.6 (d), 15.7 (c), 15.8 (a), 15.9 (b), 15.10 (a), 15.11 (c), 15.12 (a), 15.13 (b), 15.14 (b), 15.15 (d), 15.16 (c), 15.17 (a), 15.18 (b), 15.19 (c), 15.20 (c), 15.21 (d), 15.22 (a)

SHORT AND LONG ANSWER TYPE QUESTIONS

Category I

15.1 What role does Industrial Internet of Things (IIoT) play in advanced factory systems?

15.2 What is Industry 4.0, and how does it differ from previous industrial revolutions?

15.3 How does the concept of smart factories relate to Industry 4.0?

15.4 What role does big data play in Industry 4.0?

15.5 How does the use of cyber-physical systems contribute to the goals of Industry 4.0?

15.6 How does the integration of real-time data with predictive analytics impact decision-making in Industry 4.0 environments?

15.7 How does the integration of RFID with other Industry 4.0 technologies, such as IoT, benefit manufacturing operations?

15.8 How can digital twins improve product development and innovation?

15.9 What role does cloud-based smart manufacturing play in integrating IoT devices?

15.10 How does additive manufacturing integrate with digital twins in Industry 4.0?

15.11 What are some limitations of Fused Deposition Modeling (FDM) technology?

15.12 What is a key feature of blockchain technology that ensures data integrity?

15.13 How does AI improve supply chain optimization and decision-making?

15.14 How does machine learning contribute to demand forecasting in operations management?

Category II

15.15 How does the concept of smart factories embody the principles of Industry 4.0, and what are its practical implications in an industrial setting? Provide a detailed real-life industrial example to illustrate how smart factories operate and the benefits they offer.

15.16 How does the Industrial Internet of Things (IIoT) contribute to the transformation of traditional factories into smart factories, and what are the specific benefits observed in real-world industrial applications? Provide a detailed example from a leading company in the manufacturing sector.

15.17 How does the integration of RFID with other Industry 4.0 technologies, such as IoT, Cyber-Physical Systems (CPS), cloud services, and augmented reality, benefit manufacturing operations? Provide a detailed real-life industrial example to illustrate the impact of this integration on manufacturing efficiency, visibility, and flexibility.

15.18 How do digital twins contribute to the goals of Industry 4.0, and what are their practical applications in industrial settings? Provide a detailed real-life industrial example to illustrate how digital twins enhance operational efficiency, maintenance, and decision-making.

15.19 How does artificial intelligence (AI) contribute to operations management in modern industries, and what are its practical applications and benefits? Provide a detailed real-life industrial example to illustrate how AI enhances operational efficiency, decision-making, and overall performance.

REFERENCES AND SUGGESTED READINGS

1. Brettel, M., Friederichsen, N., Keller, M., and Rosenberg, M. *How Virtualization and Digitalization Are Changing the Manufacturing Industry*. Springer, 2014.

2. Brettel, M., Friederichsen, N., Keller, M., and Rosenberg, M. How Virtualization and Digitalization Are Changing the Manufacturing Industry. *International Journal of Information and Management Sciences*, Vol. 25(1), 73-94, 2014.

3. Dev, N. K. Shankar, R., and Swami, S. Diffusion of green products in industry 4.0: Reverse logistics issues during design of inventory and production planning system. *International Journal of Production Economics*, Vol. 223, 107519, 2020.

4. Dev, N. K., Shankar, R., Gupta, R., and Dong, J. Multi-criteria evaluation of real-time key performance indicators of supply chain with consideration of big data architecture. *Computers and Industrial Engineering*, Vol. 128, 1076-1087, 2019.

5. Dev, N. K., Shankar, R., Zakharia, Z. G., and Swami, S. Supply chain resilience for managing the ripple effect in Industry 4.0 for green product diffusion. *International Journal of Physical Distribution & Logistics Management*, Vol. 51(8), 897-930, 2021.

6. Harmon, R. R. *Additive Manufacturing: Materials, Processes, Quantifications, and Applications*. Elsevier, 2020.

7. Kagermann, H., et al. Recommendations for Implementing the Strategic Initiative INDUSTRIE 4.0. *Journal of the European Federation of National Engineering Associations*, Vol. 1(2), 17-22, 2013.

8. Kagermann, H., Wahlster, W., and Helbig, J. *Recommendations for Implementing the Strategic Initiative INDUSTRIE 4.0: Final Report of the Industrie 4.0 Working Group*. Springer Vieweg, 2013.

9. Lee, J., and Yang, S. *Smart Manufacturing Systems: Internet of Things and Industry 4.0 Applications*. Springer, 2017.

10. Liu, Y., and Wu, D. Machine Learning Applications in Industrial Manufacturing: A Survey. *Journal of Manufacturing Science and Engineering*, Vol. 142(9), 1-17, 2020.

11. Negi, S., and Hossain, M. *Digital Transformation in Smart Manufacturing: Technologies and Applications*. Wiley-IEEE Press, 2020.

12. Russell, R. S., and Taylor, B. W. *Operations Management: Creating Value Along the Supply Chain*, 10th Edition, Pearson, 2020.

13. Serrano, A., and Restrepo, J. *Machine Learning in Manufacturing: Applications and Techniques for Efficiency and Innovation*. Wiley, 2019.

14. Srinivasan, S., and Jain, M. Applications of Artificial Intelligence in Operations Management. *International Journal of Operations & Production Management*, Vol. 38(5), 3-21, 2018.

15. Sung, T. K., and Hwang, H. S. Smart Manufacturing Systems for Industry 4.0. *International Journal of Advanced Manufacturing Technology*, Vol. 100(9-12), 1-16, 2019.

16. Xu, L. D., He, W., and Li, S. Internet of Things in Industries of Future: The Cyber-Physical Systems Approach. *IEEE Access*, Vol. 2, 1-9, 2014.

17. Xu, X., Xu, C., and Li, L. *Industry 4.0: Smart Manufacturing and IoT for Improved Productivity and Performance*. Elsevier, 2019.

18. Zhang, Y., and Qiu, X. *Artificial Intelligence in Industry 4.0: Applications, Challenges, and Opportunities*. Springer, 2021.

UNIT **16**

HUMAN RESOURCE MANAGEMENT & SAFETY NORMS

UNIT SPECIFICS

This unit elaborately discusses the following topics:

- Introduction to Human Resource Management (HRM)
- Job training
- Cross training
- Employment prospects
- Teams
- Adjustable working schedules
- Alternate work environments and remote work
- Overseeing diversity in the workplace
- The Indian Factories Act, 1948 (Health and Safety provisions)

The unit's topics foster increased curiosity and inventiveness. In addition to several multiple-choice and short/long answer questions, the unit also has a list of references, recommended readings, and projects that are categorized into two groups based on Bloom's taxonomy's lower and higher orders. One can gain experience by completing these. The unit was thoughtfully created with the reader in mind. The use of QR codes, which may be scanned to provide relevant additional information on a range of fascinating topics, is one noteworthy feature.

RATIONALE

This unit serves as a comprehensive introduction to Human Resource Management (HRM), emphasizing its critical role in fostering a productive workforce. It explores essential topics of recent trends in HRM such as job training and cross training, which are vital for enhancing employee skills and adaptability. The unit also addresses employment prospects and the importance of teamwork in driving organizational success. Additionally, it examines adjustable working schedules and alternate work environments, including remote work, which cater to the evolving needs of today's workforce. A focus on overseeing diversity in the workplace highlights the importance of inclusivity, while the inclusion of the Indian Factories Act, 1948, underscores the necessity of health and safety provisions in maintaining a secure work environment. Collectively, these elements illustrate the multifaceted nature of HRM and its impact on organizational effectiveness and employee well-being.

UNIT OUTCOMES

List of outcomes of this unit is as follows:

U16-UO1: Understanding HRM Principles

U16-UO2: Skill Development through Training

U16-UO3: Navigating Employment Prospects

U16-UO4: Team Dynamics and Collaboration

U16-UO5: Flexible Work Arrangements

U16-UO6: Diversity and Legal Compliance

UNIT-16 Outcomes	EXPECTED MAPPING WITH COURSE OUTCOMES (1-Weak Correlation; 2-Medium Correlation; 3-Strong Correlation)					
	CO-1	CO-2	CO-3	CO-4	CO-5	CO-6
U16-UO1	1	2	1	2	2	-
U16-UO2	2	3	3	3	3	2
U16-UO3	1	1	1	1	2	1
U16-UO4	2	2	2	2	2	1
U16-UO5	1	1	1	1	1	-
U16-UO6	1	1	1	2	1	-

16. 1 INTRODUCTION

Operations management in the first half of the 20th century was dominated by the scientific management theories created by F. W. Taylor in the 1880s and 1890s. Taylor's strategy involved breaking down jobs into their most basic functions and streamlining job designs such that learning a job required only a restricted set of abilities, hence cutting down on the amount of time needed for learning. This method separated the tasks requiring less expertise from the more skilled operations needed to set up and maintain machinery. According to Taylor's concept, a task is an individual activity made up of pieces that include multiple job motions or fundamental bodily movements. A job is the collection of all the tasks that an employee completes. The work of F. W. Taylor was not adopted or approved right away. In order to make the enormous number of workers required for the increasing number of occupations cost-effective, this system required tremendous volumes of output. Henry Ford and the assembly line production of autos combined the concepts of scientific management with mass production.

In the latter half of the 20th century, American businesses reassessed their management techniques in comparison to those of the Japanese due to the competitive edge that numerous Japanese companies had in the global market, particularly in the automotive sector. Japanese and American methods and outcomes differed noticeably in the field of Human Resource Management (HRM), for example. As an illustration, a Japanese automaker in the 1980s was able to manufacture a car in roughly 14 hours in Japan as opposed to 25 hours in the US using half the blue-collar labor of a comparable U.S. automaker. Traditional Western methods of working have not been adopted by Japan. Instead, Japanese labor allowed for higher worker skill levels, group work and interaction, more individual worker responsibility and less supervision, and training across a range of skills and jobs. Americans had a predisposition at first to believe that these traits were exclusive to Japanese culture. But the success of American businesses like Ford and Motorola in putting quality-management programs into place, as well as the achievements of Japanese businesses doing business in the US like Nissan and Honda, demonstrated that management techniques were more crucial than cultural considerations. Thus, for successful businesses both domestically and internationally, a few modern HRM trends have become standard.

16. 2 PRESENT TRENDS IN HUMAN RESOURCE MANAGEMENT

Any organization's most valuable resource is its human capital. The employees of the company are its human resources. Humans are essential to any business's efficient running. Managers must recognize the potential of human resources and then recruit, develop, and retain these personnel in order to face the difficulties and competitive nature of today's business environment. This is the cornerstone of HRM, or human resource management. The "people" aspect of management is the focus of HRM. People make up every organization; in order to obtain their services, improve their talents, inspire them to provide high levels of performance, and make sure they stay committed to the organization's goals, HRM is essential to its operation. HRM involves many different tasks, but some of the most important ones are identifying your staffing needs and determining whether to hire employees or use independent contractors to meet them, as well as finding and developing the best candidates and developing them into high performers, handling performance concerns, and making sure you're hiring and management procedures comply with regulations. It's the department inside an organization that is generally responsible for hiring, managing, and giving instructions to its employees.

16.2.1 JOB TRAINING

Job training is comprehensive and varied in organizations that prioritize quality. Both the management and the individual typically have high expectations for performance and advancement. Usually, a wide range of courses are offered for training in various positions and duties. Along with cross-training and work rotation, job training is seen as a component of an organized system for career development. The previously mentioned production process's flexibility is increased by this training and job rotation mechanism. It builds talent pools that can be tapped into when labor is scarce or needs to be adjusted due to changes in procedures, goods, or workforce.

NEED FOR TRAINING

The following factors make training necessary:

1. **Job requirements**: To familiarize new hires with the position and the company, orientation training is required.
2. **Technological developments**: With the usage of rapidly evolving techniques growing, knowledge of new technologies is necessary.

3. **Organizational viability**: An organization must constantly adapt to the changing environment in order to endure and expand. In the era of globalization, businesses need to improve their capacities to compete globally. Refresher training is necessary to keep current staff informed about new developments. Employee initiative and innovation are encouraged via training programs, which also serve to keep skills current.
4. **Internal mobility**: When an employee transfers or gets promoted, training becomes necessary for the new position. Employees need training in order to be prepared for higher level positions.

ASSESSING TRAINING REQUIREMENTS

Each and every training session needs to be tailored to the unique requirements of the company and each employee. The gap between the current and necessary levels of performance, aptitudes, knowledge, and abilities should be defined in order to determine the need for training, as well as the problem areas that need to be addressed. The analysis of organization is typically performed to determine the needs for training:

(a) Task analysis
(b) Worker analysis, and
(c) Organization environment analysis

Task analysis – Task analysis establishes the best way to do each task and how they all work together to create a job. It entails outlining each activity and figuring out the best order for it, how long it will take, how it relates to other tasks, and how often it will happen. The task analysis should yield a step-by-step approach for the job with enough information. In certain activities, the steps must be completed in a logical order. For instance, cutting the material wedges needed to make a baseball cap is a necessary step before they can be sewed together, and the cap bill cannot be attached until the steps are completed. The amount of time needed to finish a work, the precision with which it must be completed in accordance with the standards, the productivity yield or output level, or the quality of performance can all be considered performance criteria. Certain jobs require information to be completed, such measuring furniture pieces, processing food at a certain temperature, filling fertilizer bags with weight, or doing a litmus test for a chemical process.

Worker analysis – Worker analysis establishes the qualities an individual must have in order to fulfill the requirements of the position, the duties they will perform, and the manner in which they will be compensated. While some careers need physical strength and hard labor, others don't. In addition to ensuring that the proper person is assigned to a task, physical requirements are evaluated to see if they are excessive and call for change. When it comes to mental stress, the same kind of design queries need to be answered.

Environmental analysis – The physical placement of the task within the manufacturing or service facility, as well as the necessary environmental conditions, are referred to as environmental analysis. Proper lighting, ventilation, noise levels, and temperature are a few examples of these conditions. The manufacturing of microchips necessitates a sterile, climate-controlled, enclosed space. Appropriate illumination is necessary for detail work like sewing or engraving, and ventilation is necessary for certain occupations that produce dust, like handling lint in textile processes. There are some jobs that need a lot of room surrounding the work area.

16.2.2 CROSS TRAINING

An employee learns multiple jobs inside the organization through cross-training. There are several appealing aspects of cross-training that benefit both the employer and the employee. It offers greater job coverage as a safety precaution for the organization in the event of staff resignations, absenteeism, or unexpected growth in a certain job activity. More information and variety are provided to employees in order to reduce their susceptibility to boredom, boost their sense of worth in their work, and raise their level of interest in the organization. With their newfound expertise, they will be able to advance to other positions without having to quit the organization. Given their increased familiarity with one another's jobs, employees will respect one another. The organization must be dedicated to implementing cross-training and confident in the advantages it expects to reap as it necessitates a substantial financial and temporal commitment.

Cross-training and job rotation is not exactly the same thing. An employee with cross-training can transition between roles as needed. In addition to requiring cross-training, work rotation also refers to moving horizontally between two or more positions in accordance with a schedule or plan. This decreases monotony and raises employee engagement in addition to making the worker more adaptable.

16.2.3 EMPLOYMENT PROSPECTS

Increasing job variety, responsibility, and accountability will increase opportunities for individual accomplishment and recognition. This is the goal of employment prospects. Improved direct interaction with coworkers, increased task identification, and increased worker autonomy can all result from this. Frederick Herzberg created the following guidelines for potential employees:

- Vertical job enlargement is the practice of maintaining accountability while giving workers authority over their own work and a portion of supervisory responsibilities.
- Assign each employee a comprehensive work unit that comprises all the duties required to finish a process or product, with well-defined beginning and ending points, to help them feel a feeling of closure and accomplishment. We also refer to this as horizontal job enlargement.
- Give your employees more power and autonomy.
- Employees should have access to periodic reports rather than simply managers.
- Add more challenging and novel tasks to the work.
- Encourage the growth of competence by putting people in charge of specific tasks.

16.2.4 TEAMS

Teams or work groups are regularly used to achieve employee involvement. One well-known example of a team method is quality circles, in which a group of eight to ten workers plus their supervisor work on issues in their immediate work area. Teams can vary in terms of their tenure, level of responsibility, and purpose. Certain teams are formed to focus on a particular issue and then dissolve, while others have a longer term and are designed to keep an eye on a work area or process in order to continuously improve it. In general, teams need to be able to work effectively together, have the knowledge and expertise required to accomplish their goals, understand their responsibilities, and purpose in relation to the company's objectives, and be able to cooperate well.

Self-directed teams typically have the authority to make decisions and modifications to the procedures within their particular work area, even if they are not completely autonomous. This level of accountability is predicated on management's conviction that those who are walled off to the work process are best suited to optimize it.

The advantages of self-directed teams include less managerial control (and fewer managers), faster problem identification and resolution, increased job satisfaction, positive peer pressure, and the common feeling of "not wanting to let the team down" shared by military and sports teams. On the other hand, self-directed teams typically require more training to function as a team. However, there may be certain drawbacks to such a team. It could be challenging for managers and supervisors to get used to their new position, which now involves monitoring and supervising rather than directing work. Additionally, disagreements among team members might make a team less productive.

16.2.5 ADJUSTABLE WORKING SCHEDULES

Workplace formats that allow for flexible work hours, or flextime, are becoming more and more significant. It describes a spectrum of schedules where "core" or fixed time and flexible time are combined to replace set arrival and departure hours. Core time is the set time, such as 9:00 AM to 2:30 PM, when every employee is expected to be present. Employees can select their own arrival and leave times during flexible time, which is a component of the daily work schedule. In certain instances, a worker may "bank" or "credit" hours – that is, put in more time at work one day and use that time to take a later, shorter workday. Other times, a worker might switch up their workdays during the week. For instance, they might put in four 10-hour days and then take a three-day weekend off. Flextime can make it challenging to make up for unforeseen changes in workload or issues that may develop and call for prompt resolution, even while it helps the business recruit, retain, and enhance job satisfaction.

16.2.6 ALTERNATIVE WORK ENVIRONMENTS AND REMOTE WORK

A hybrid of non-traditional work environments, settings, and procedures that complements or replaces the standard office is known as an alternative workplace. A home office, a satellite office, a shared office, a shared desk, or an open workspace with numerous people working side by side can all be considered alternative workplaces. Telecommuting is another alternate workplace model where employees work remotely from any location of their choice using electronic devices.

Businesses that use alternative workspaces typically combine a variety of forms and customize the workspace to meet unique business requirements. Establishing alternate work environments can also come with costs, albeit they are typically lower than the steadily rising costs of real estate. The expenditures include training, networks, phone bills, hardware and software, and equipment. Some businesses, including manufacturing firms, on the other hand, cannot afford alternative workspaces since their workers must report to designated workstations, facilities, or fixed equipment, or they must operate under close management supervision.

One of the more popular new alternative work environments is telecommuting, sometimes known as "telework," or a "virtual workplace," when employees work remotely using electronic devices. An estimated 3% of American workers work from home at least half the time, while approximately 40% of American businesses allow their employees to telecommute in some capacity. Benefits of telecommuting include lower real estate expenses, decreased employee turnover, lower absenteeism and leave utilization, more productivity, and easier compliance with federal workplace rules like the Americans with Disabilities Act for businesses.

There are drawbacks to telecommuting as well. It could have a bad effect on the rapport between workers and their direct managers. It could be unsettling for managers and supervisors to not be able to see their staff members directly. If they are not physically there, they could also believe that they lack authority and control over their staff. In actuality, some workers might not be good telecommuters since they lack drive and could need more in-person guidance and outside encouragement.

16.2.7 OVERSEEING DIVERSITY IN THE WORKPLACE

For many years, diversity has been a crucial management concern for American businesses. But as more businesses enter the international market, diversity is becoming an increasingly more important consideration in human resource management globally. Companies now have a more varied workforce than ever before thanks to the growth of global commerce and employee mobility. American corporations outsource their business operations and run facilities and operations abroad with a combination of foreign and American management teams and workers, whereas foreign businesses run plants and operations within the United States with comparable personnel. Considered varied workers in the United States are those who, in terms of race, gender, age, ethnicity, or other characteristics, differ from the majority of workers by almost 40%. Hispanic workers already make about 17% of the workforce, but by 2050, that percentage is predicted to rise to almost 30%. Nearly half of American workers are women.

Companies that want to succeed with a diverse workforce must create an environment where all workers can perform their duties, feel valued by the company, and believe they are being treated fairly. However, discrimination against workers due to factors such as age, gender, color, religion, cultural origin, and physical or mental disabilities occurs far too frequently. It is impossible for upper management to enforce or control the eradication of racism, sexism, cultural apathy, and religious intolerance through financial incentives. To face the challenges posed by a diverse workforce, companies as a whole – starting with senior management – need to establish a comprehensive approach to managing diversity.

Nowadays, human resource management heavily relies on artificial intelligence (AI) for talent acquisition. Scan the provided QR code to learn more about this topic.

SCAN ME
for
AI in Talent Aquisition

16. 3 THE INDIAN FACTORIES ACT, 1948

The interests of workers employed in industries are protected by this Act. The Act is currently in effect throughout India. It was first put into effect on April 1st, 1949, and was later expanded to include the States of Jammu and Kashmir in 1970, as well as the Union Territories of Goa, Daman, and Diu in 1963.

1. Before a factory can begin operations, the Act stipulates that:
   (a) The Chief Inspector must grant prior permission for the factory's construction or extension;
   (b) The Factory Inspector must approve the plans and specifications; and
   (c) The factory must be registered and license fees must be paid.
2. If an application for permission referred to in item (a) above is sent by registered mail to the State Government or the Chief Inspector, along with the plans and specifications required by the rules referred to in item (b) above, and no order is received by the applicant within three months of the date of the application, the permission applied for the said application will be deemed to have been granted.
3. If a State Government or Chief Inspector declines to authorize a factory's location, construction, or expansion, or to register and license a factory, the applicant may appeal to the Central Government within 30 days of the date of the refusal if the State Government made the decision.

16.3.1 HEALTH PROVISION

The following measures are offered by this Act to protect employees' health and lower the likelihood of physical harm to them:

1. **Cleanliness**

Every factory must be maintained tidy and clear of any gases coming from drains or other annoyances. The actions listed below in particular should be done for this purpose:

(a) Every day, sweeping is required to clear the trash and dust from the floors, workroom benches, stairwells, and hallways.

(b) Every workroom's floor must be washed at least once a week, and disinfectant must be used as needed.

(c) It is necessary to provide and maintain efficient drainage methods.

(d) Everywhere inside the room and hallway ceilings, walls, and partitions.

2. **Ventilation and Temperature**

(a) Effective and appropriate measures must be used to:

(i) Ensure proper ventilation by circulating fresh air throughout the workspace.

(ii) Ensure reasonable comfort levels and prevent worker health injuries.

(b) Roofs and walls should be constructed with a material and design that prevents temperature increases and keeps it as low as is practical. It is imperative to devise efficient measures to safeguard laborers against operations that generate excessively elevated temperatures. The machinery's hot sections need to be insulated.

3. **Artificial Humidification**

(a) In the event that artificial humidification is used, it must adhere to specified standards and be produced using specified techniques.

(b) The water utilized for this type of humidification needs to be pure and dirt-free.

4. **Overcrowding**

No space in a factory may be overcrowded; in factories that existed prior to the Act's start, at least 350 cu.ft., or 9.9 m^3, of space is required for each worker, and in factories constructed after the Act's start, at least 500 cu.ft., or 14.2 m^3, of space must be provided for each worker. Any area that is higher than 14 feet, or 4.2 meters, above the room's floor level will not be taken into consideration for this reason; that is, heights higher than 4 feet, or 4.2 meters, above the floor will not be taken into consideration.

5. **Lighting**

(a) Enough appropriate illumination, either artificial or natural, or both, must be kept up in the workspace and hallways.

(b) The interior and exterior surfaces of all glass windows and skylights must be maintained spotless.

(c) To reduce eye strain and accident risk, glare and shadow creation should be avoided.

6. **Drinking water**

All employees should have access to drinking water throughout working hours, and it should be maintained and supplied at strategic locations. Each of these locations must have the word "Drinking Water" written on it in a language that most employees can understand. These locations cannot be found 20 feet to 6.0 meters from urinals, washing machines, or other sources of pollution.

16.3.2 SAFETY PROVISIONS

The Act contains the crucial safety provisions listed below:

1. **Machinery Fencing**

The following items need to be fenced in every factory:

(a) Every flywheel and moving part of a prime mover;

(b) Every water turbine's head and tail races;

(c) Every component of an electric generator, motor, or rotary convertor;

(d) Every piece of transmission machinery and other machine parts need to be adequately protected.

2. **Operate on or close to moving machinery**

A suitably attired adult male worker with specialized training must perform any task on or near moving machinery. It is forbidden for anybody to service, lubricate, or alter any component of a primary mover or transmission machinery while it is operating.

3. There must be tools available to turn off the electricity to operating machinery in an emergency.

4. **Machinery casing**

All power-operated machinery installed in factories after the effective date of this Act must have all set screws, bolts, and keys on rotating shafts, spindles, wheels, and pinions completely encased, sunk, or otherwise effectively guarded to prevent hazards.

5. **Lifts and hoists**

Every factory must have:

(a) Lifts and hoists with sturdy mechanical construction and sufficient strength. They must be routinely and properly inspected and maintained. The maximum safe operating load must be marked on it.

(b) An enclosure with gates must provide adequate protection for each hoistway and liftway.

(c) Hoists and lifts that are used to carry people must have at least two ropes or chains attached to them, and each rope or chain must be able to support the cage's weight plus the maximum load.

6. **Hoisting tackles, chains, and machinery for lifting**

Every component, including the lifting machines, chains, ropes, and lifting tackles, as well as the working gears, must be strong enough, well-constructed, and subjected to routine maintenance and inspections at least annually. A lifting machine is something like a winch, pulley block, crane, or crab.

7. **Revolving devices**

Every grinder must have a notice attached that states the maximum safe operating peripheral speed of each grind stone or abrasive wheel, as well as the speed of the shaft or spindle that the wheel is installed on.

8. **Excessive weights**

Nobody working in a workplace is allowed to lift, transport, or move any weight that would be dangerous for them to handle. Regulations dictating the maximum weight that adult men and women may lift or carry may be issued by the state government.

9. **Protection of eyes**

It is required that anyone involved in the following production operations wear screen protectors to safeguard their eyes:

(a) Welding or cutting metal with an electric or oxyacetylene flame, or any similar technique.

(b) Any procedure that involves the possibility of eye injuries from flying debris throughout the process, such as fettling, rivet cutting, scale removal, dressing metal, or stone work.

10. **Precaution from dangerous fumes**

(a) No person shall enter or be allowed to enter any chamber, tank, pit, pipe, flue, or other confined place in a factory where hazardous gasses are expected to be present to a degree that poses a risk to human health unless such a space has an appropriate manhole.

(b) No portable electric light that runs on more than 24 volts is allowed in such a small area.

(c) Any person entering a confined space must first ensure that all fumes have been removed, obtain a written certificate from a qualified individual based on their own testing, and wear appropriate breathing equipment and a belt securely fastened to a rope, the free end of which is held by someone standing outside the confined space.

11. **Precaution against fire**
   (a) Every factory must have an escape route in place in case of fire, per any applicable regulations.
   (b) Doors that provide access to an exit from any room must not be secured or locked in a way that makes it difficult for someone inside the room to quickly and easily open the door from the inside.
   (c) All windows, doors, and other escape routes that provide a way out in the event of a fire, aside from the regular routes, must be labeled in a language that the majority of employees can understand.
   (d) There should be effective ways to alert everyone in the event of a fire. There must always be a clear path for people to evacuate in the event of a fire.

ALONG THE HUMAN RESOURCE MANAGEMENT

The reader can study an interesting article on "How can leader improve employee engagement in the office" published by Forbes. Scan the given QR code.

SCAN ME
for
Forbes article

UNIT SUMMARY

- ***Introduction to HRM*** – Discusses the evolution of HRM, highlighting scientific management by F.W. Taylor and the influence of Japanese vs. American HR practices in modern businesses.
- ***Current Trends in HRM*** – Explores: (i) Job Training & Cross-Training – Developing skills for workforce flexibility and efficiency, (ii) Employment Prospects – Career growth opportunities, job enrichment, and employee recognition, (iii) Team Dynamics – Formation and management of work teams, including self-directed teams, (iv) Flexible Work Arrangements – Adjustable work schedules, flextime, and remote work models, and (v) Workplace Diversity – Managing inclusivity and equity in global workforces.

- ***Indian Factories Act, 1948*** – Covers essential health and safety provisions, including: (i) Cleanliness, ventilation, lighting, and drinking water requirements, (ii) Machinery fencing, emergency shut-off mechanisms, and worker safety in hazardous conditions, and (iii) Fire prevention, protection from dangerous fumes, and safe handling of materials.

EXERCISES

MULTIPLE CHOICE QUESTIONS

16.1 Which of the following is a key trend in HR management for improving employee experience?

(a) Increased use of traditional performance reviews	(b) Focus on employee well-being and mental health
(c) Reduction in remote working opportunities	(d) Emphasis on rigid work hours

16.2 What is a significant shift in training and development trends in HR?

(a) Adoption of personalized and on-demand learning platforms	(b) Focus solely on in-person training sessions
(c) Decreased investment in employee development	(d) Exclusive use of printed materials for training

16.3 Which of the following is a common method used in job training to enhance skills and knowledge?

(a) Classroom-based lectures without hands-on practice	(b) Prohibiting feedback from supervisors
(c) Sole reliance on written manuals	(d) Job rotation and cross-training

16.4 What is the main purpose of conducting a job analysis when assessing training requirements?

(a) To evaluate employee work hours	(b) To identify the skills, knowledge, and abilities required for a specific job role
(c) To determine employee compensation packages	(d) To review company financial statements

16.5 What is the role of employee feedback in the process of assessing training requirements?

(a) It provides insights into employees' perceived skill gaps and training needs	(b) It is used to determine organizational budget allocations
(c) It serves as a final step before training implementation	(d) It focuses on employee attendance records only

16.6 What is the primary goal of conducting a work analysis in the context of assessing training requirements?

(a) To determine employee compensation levels	(b) To evaluate employee job satisfaction
(c) To identify the specific tasks, skills, and competencies needed for each job role	(d) To assess the overall organizational performance

16.7 What is the primary benefit of cross-training employees within an organization?

(a) Limiting the number of job roles employees can perform	(b) To evaluate employee job satisfaction
(c) Enhancing employees' skills in multiple areas and increasing organizational flexibility	(d) To access the overall organizational performance

16.8 In the context of cross-training, what is a key factor for ensuring the effectiveness of the program?

(a) Offering cross-training only to senior management	(b) Limiting feedback and evaluation of the training process
(c) Randomly assigning employees to different roles	(d) Clearly defining the goals and objectives of the cross-training program

16.9 In Herzberg's view, which approach is most effective for improving employment prospects and ensuring long-term employee satisfaction?

(a) Offering high salaries as the primary solution	(b) Enhancing job enrichment and providing opportunities for advancement
(c) Minimizing training and development programs	(d) Limiting employee recognition and feedback

16.10 What is one of the main benefits of cross-functional teams in HRM?

(a) They bring together diverse expertise and perspectives to address complex issues	(b) They discourage collaboration among different departments

(c) They focus solely on short-term tasks	(d) They operate with minimal communication

16.11 What is a common type of adjustable working schedule where employees have the freedom to choose their start and end times within a set range?

(a) Compressed workweek	(b) Job sharing
(c) Telecommuting	(d) Flextime

16.12 How can adjustable working schedules impact organizational productivity?

(a) They lead to increased absenteeism	(b) They eliminate the need for team meetings and collaboration
(c) They generally decrease productivity due to lack of structure	(d) They can enhance productivity by allowing employees to work during their most productive hours

16.13 Which of the following best describes a "hybrid work environment"?

(a) Employees work exclusively from a central office	(b) Employees work from multiple locations without a consistent schedule
(c) Employees alternate between working remotely and working in the office	(d) Employees work only part-time hours

16.14 What is a potential benefit of a diverse workforce in terms of organizational performance?

(a) Enhanced creativity and a broader range of perspectives	(b) Reduced creativity and innovation
(c) Increased groupthink and decreased problem-solving abilities	(d) Greater likclihood of workplace conflicts

16.15 In the context of AI and talent acquisition, what is the role of predictive analytics?

(a) To manually assess each candidate's qualifications	(b) To predict future hiring needs and identify potential high-performing candidates based on historical data
(c) To randomly select candidates for interviews	(d) To only focus on current job openings without forecasting future needs

16.16 Which provision under the Indian Factory Act focuses on the prevention of occupational diseases and the health of workers?

(a) Prohibition of employment of children under 14 years of age	(b) Requirement for regular rest breaks during work shifts
(c) Medical examinations and the provision of protective measures for workers exposed to hazardous substances	(d) Provision of recreational facilities

16.17 Under the Indian Factory Act, which of the following is a mandatory safety requirement for machinery to protect workers?

(a) Machinery must be painted in bright colors	(b) Machinery must have proper safety guards to prevent accidental contact
(c) Machinery must be operated by automated systems only	(d) Machinery must be cleaned daily by workers

Answers of Multiple Choice Questions
16.1 (b), 16.2 (a), 16.3 (d), 16.4 (b), 16.5 (a), 16.6 (c), 16.7 (c), 16.8 (d), 16.9 (b), 16.10 (a), 16.11 (d), 16.12 (d), 16.13 (c), 16.14 (a), 16.15 (b), 16.16 (c), 16.17 (b)

SHORT AND LONG ANSWER TYPE QUESTIONS

Category I

16.1 What are some effective strategies for reducing workplace stress and preventing burnout?

16.2 What are the primary benefits of adopting personalized learning platforms for employee training?

16.3 What strategies can HR use to successfully implement a job rotation or cross-training program?

16.4 What methods can HR use to gather information about the skills and abilities required for a job role from current employees?

16.5 What role does a learning management system (LMS) play in developing employees' skills across multiple areas?

16.6 How can HR measure the effectiveness of bringing together diverse perspectives in solving complex issues?

16.7 How can HR measure the success of a flextime program in terms of employee satisfaction and organizational performance?

16.8 How can HR ensure that remote and in-office employees are equally engaged and have access to the same opportunities?

16.9 How can diverse teams contribute to enhanced creativity within an organization?

16.10 How can predictive analytics be used to improve the accuracy of hiring forecasts?

16.11 What does the Indian Factory Act require regarding safety guards on machinery?

Category II

16.12 Consider a large multinational corporation, ABC Industries, which operates in the competitive field of technology development. The company has recently experienced high levels of workplace stress among its employees, leading to increased turnover rates and reduced productivity. To address these issues, ABC Industries decided to implement a training program designed to build personalized learning platforms for their employees.

Describe the steps taken by ABC Industries to develop and implement these personalized learning platforms. Include an analysis of how these platforms addressed specific stressors faced by employees and evaluate the effectiveness of this strategy in reducing workplace stress.

16.13 Imagine a large manufacturing company, XYZ Corp, which has been experiencing challenges with employee engagement and skill gaps across various departments. To address these issues, the HR department at XYZ Corp decided to implement a job rotation and cross-training program.

Detail the strategies employed by XYZ Corp's HR department to successfully implement this program. Include an analysis of how these strategies facilitated skill development, improved employee engagement, and enhanced operational efficiency. Additionally, discuss the challenges faced during the implementation and the measures taken to overcome them.

16.14 Consider a mid-sized tech company, InnovateTech Inc., which has recently implemented a flexible working hours policy to improve employee satisfaction and productivity. Under this policy, employees are given the freedom to choose their start and end times within a specified range, while ensuring they meet their contractual work hours.

Describe the steps InnovateTech Inc. took to implement this flexible working-hours policy. Analyze how this adjustment impacted employee satisfaction, productivity, and operational efficiency. Additionally, discuss the challenges the company faced during the implementation and the strategies used to overcome them.

16.15 GlobalTech Solutions, a leading multinational technology firm, recognized the importance of managing workplace diversity to foster innovation and create an inclusive work environment. The company has diverse employees from various backgrounds, including different ethnicities, genders, ages, and abilities.

Describe the strategies implemented by GlobalTech Solutions' HR department to manage diversity in the workplace effectively. Analyze how these strategies contributed to creating an inclusive work environment, improving employee satisfaction, and enhancing organizational performance. Additionally, discuss the challenges faced during the implementation of these strategies and the solutions employed to address them.

16.16 SteelWorks Ltd., a large steel manufacturing company in India, operates several factories across the country. In light of the Indian Factory Act's provisions focused on worker health and mandatory safety requirements, the company undertook a comprehensive review and enhancement of its health and safety practices.

Detail the steps SteelWorks Ltd. took to comply with the health and safety provisions under the Indian Factory Act. Analyze how these measures impacted worker health, safety, and overall operational efficiency. Additionally, discuss the challenges faced during implementation and the strategies employed to overcome them.

REFERENCES AND SUGGESTED READINGS

1. Armstrong, M. *Armstrong's Handbook of Human Resource Management Practice*, 15th Edition, Kogan Page, 2020.
2. Becker, B. E., and Huselid, M. A. Strategic Human Resources Management: Where Do We Go from Here? *Journal of Management*, Vol. 32(6), 898-925, 2006.
3. Chakraborty, A. *Labor and Industrial Laws in India*. Tata McGraw-Hill, 2016.
4. Day, D. V. Training and Development Programs for Cross-Functional Teams. *Journal of Applied Psychology*, Vol. 85(5), 680-686, 2000.
5. Dessler, G. *Human Resource Management*, 15th Edition, Pearson Education, 2020.

6. Jackson, P. R. *Developing Cross-functional Teams*. Palgrave Macmillan, 2003.
7. Jackson, S. E., and Schuler, R. S. Understanding Human Resource Management in the Context of Organizations and Their Environments. *International Journal of Human Resource Management*, Vol. 6(2), 237-264, 1995.
8. Kothari, M., and Singh, M. The Indian Factories Act, 1948 and Occupational Health: A Critical Analysis. *International Journal of Labor Studies*, Vol. 8(2), 60-79, 2011.
9. Kumar, R. *The Indian Factories Act: An Insight into Health, Safety, and Welfare Provisions*. Eastern Book Company, 2003.
10. Mathis, R. L., and Jackson, J. H. *Human Resource Management*, 15th Edition, Cengage Learning, 2020.
11. Noe, R. A. *Fundamentals of Human Resource Management*, 8th Edition, McGraw-Hill, 2017.
12. Ramaswamy, R. *Industrial Relations and Labour Laws*, 3rd Edition, Macmillan India, 2012.
13. Robbins, S. P., and Judge, T. A. *Organizational Behavior*, 18th Edition, Pearson Education, 2019.
14. Roberson, Q. M. *The Oxford Handbook of Diversity and Work*. Oxford University Press, 2019.
15. Schuler, R. S., and Jackson, S. E. *Strategic Human Resource Management*, 2nd Edition, Wiley, 2019.
16. Schuler, R. S., and Jackson, S. E. Strategic Human Resource Management: A Critical Review of the Literature. *International Journal of Human Resource Management*, Vol. 19(7), 1181-1198, 2008.
17. Shore, L. M., Cleveland, J. N., and Sanchez, D. Inclusive Workplace Climate: A Review of the Literature and Future Directions. *Journal of Management*, Vol. 44(6), 2021-2057, 2018.
18. Swanson, R. A. *The Handbook of Human Resource Development*. Wiley, 2001.
19. Swanson, R. A., and Holton, E. F. *Foundations of Human Resource Development*, 2nd Edition, Berrett-Koehler, 2009.
20. Tannenbaum, S. I. *Human Resource Management: A Critical Approach*. Palgrave Macmillan, 2017.

UNIT **17**

LINEAR PROGRAMMING

UNIT SPECIFICS

This unit elaborately discusses the following topics:

- Introduction and scope of applications of Linear Programming (LP) models
- Model Formulation
- Graphical solution method (Sensitivity analysis, multiple solutions, infeasible solutions, unbounded problem)
- Simplex method to solve LPP
- Dual model and its interpretations

In order to foster increased creativity and curiosity as well as improve problem-solving abilities, the topics' practical applications are investigated. Along with several multiple-choice questions and questions with short and long-answer types categorized into two groups based on lower and higher order of Bloom's taxonomy, the unit also includes a list of references, recommended readings, and assignments through a number of numerical problems. One noteworthy feature of some of the interesting topics is the usage of QR codes, which can be scanned to provide relevant supplementary information.

RATIONALE

This unit provides a foundational understanding of Linear Programming (LP) models, highlighting their significance and broad applications across various fields such as operations research, economics, and logistics. It begins with model formulation, guiding readers through the essential steps of translating real-world problems into mathematical representations. The unit further explores the graphical solution method, delving into critical concepts such as sensitivity analysis, multiple solutions, infeasible solutions, and unbounded problems. Building on this, the simplex method is introduced as a powerful technique for solving

Linear Programming Problems (LPP), offering readers a systematic approach to optimization. Lastly, the unit examines the dual model and its interpretations, fostering a deeper comprehension of the relationships between primal and dual solutions. Together, these components equip learners with the skills needed to effectively apply LP models to complex decision-making scenarios.

UNIT OUTCOMES

List of outcomes of this unit is as follows:

U17-UO1: Understanding LP Applications

U17-UO2: Model Formulation Skills

U17-UO3: Graphical Solution Techniques

U17-UO4: Proficiency in the Simplex Method

U17-UO5: Understanding Duality in LP

U17-UO6: Analytical Skills for LP Problems

UNIT-17 Outcomes	EXPECTED MAPPING WITH COURSE OUTCOMES (1-Weak Correlation; 2-Medium Correlation; 3-Strong Correlation)					
	CO-1	CO-2	CO-3	CO-4	CO-5	CO-6
U17-UO1	2	3	2	2	2	3
U17-UO2	2	2	3	2	2	3
U17-UO3	1	2	1	2	1	3
U17-UO4	2	2	2	2	1	3
U17-UO5	1	2	2	2	1	3
U17-UO6	2	3	2	2	2	3

17.1 INTRODUCTION

A mathematical modeling method known as "linear programming" (LP) is used to establish the operational activity level necessary to accomplish a goal while adhering to limitations. An operations manager makes a lot of decisions that are based on how to effectively accomplish the company's goals within the limitations of the operational environment. These limitations can be constrained rules, like a recipe for cereal, engineering specifications, or a blend for gasoline, or they can be limited resources, like time, labor, energy, materials, or money. While cost reduction is frequently the goal of specific operational divisions within a company (like the production or packaging department), the primary goal of business firms is typically profit maximization.

Determining the quantity of units to create to maximize profit (or reduce cost) while taking labor and material constraints into account is a frequent linear programming problem. The manner in which the choices, goals, and limitations of the decision-making scenario are represented as mathematically linear connections that come together to form a model.

Table 17.1 Types of linear programming models and applications

Linear Programming Model Type	Operations management application
Aggregate Production planning	Decides how many units are produced, how many people are employed and fired, and how much inventory is needed in order to meet demand over the short term (see unit 5).
Transportation	The movement of commodities or services logistically from one place to another; truckloads of goods from factories to warehouses are one example of this.
Product mix	Mix of goods to be produced in order to optimize profit or reduce expenses considering limitations on labor, materials, money, and other resources.
Assignment	Assigns tasks to available resources, a process known as "loading." For instance, jobs or workers may be assigned to various machines (see unit 4).
Transshipment	Movement of goods from sources to destinations and between locations, such as when goods are shipped from a facility to a distribution center and subsequently to retail locations.
Multiperiod scheduling	Establishes a production schedule that includes overtime and normal output, along with reserves for future need.
Blend	Establishes the "recipe" requirements, such as the ratios at which different petroleum components should be blended to create various grades of gasoline and other petroleum products.

Diet	Menu items that satisfy certain dietary needs or other criteria, such as those found in hospital or school cafeterias.
Investment/Capital Budgeting	Financial model that calculates how much to invest in various options given return goals and restrictions for risk, diversity, and other factors; for instance, how much to invest in a new facility, piece of machinery, or plant.
Data Envelopment Analysis (DEA)	Examines the resources and outputs of similar service units, such as banks, hospitals, and colleges, to determine which are less effective or productive.
Shortest Route	The shortest highway truck route from coast to coast is one example of the routes that are the shortest for sources to destinations.
Maximal Flow	Optimize the quantity of flow from sources to destinations; in an assembly operation, for instance, maximize the flow of work-in-process.
Sheet Metal Working	Determines the best ways to cut sheet materials, such as wood, film, fabric, glass, and so on, in order to reduce waste.
Facility Location	Determines the placement of facilities in accordance with limitations such production capacity, fixed, operational, and transportation costs, and so on.
Last Mile Distribution	The process of choosing a facility that can provide services to another facility, such as choosing distribution hubs capable of distributing products to a group of customers via a last-mile delivery system.

The increasing use of linear programming problem (LPP) across various industries can be attributed to the availability of comprehensive operating information and the drive for process optimization to minimize expenses. Options for optimization are available from many software providers for use with enterprise resource planning systems. These are referred to by certain businesses as process optimization, synchronized planning, and advanced planning options.

For linear programming to be applicable in a problem scenario, there are five prerequisites. In order for there to be an issue, there must first be restricted resources (such as a limited number of personnel, equipment, cash, and material). Secondly, there needs to be a clearly defined goal (such increasing profit or reducing expenses). Third, linearity is required (two is twice as much as one; for example, if a part takes three hours to create, two parts would take six hours and three parts, nine hours). Fourth, there needs to be homogeneity (either all of a worker's available hours are equally productive, or all of the items produced on a machine are same). Fifth, it needs to be divisible: It is a standard assumption in linear programming that resources and products can be divided into fractions. An alternative kind of linear programming known as integer programming can be utilized if this subdivision is not feasible (e.g., operating half of an aircraft or employing one fourth of a person).

We can utilize linear programming when we have a single target that needs to be maximized (like profit) or minimized (like costs). Goal programming is utilized when there are several objectives. Dynamic programming is used when a problem is best tackled gradually or within a specific time limit. Other limitations on the nature of the problem can necessitate using different approaches, like nonlinear programming or quadratic programming, to solve it.

17.2 MODEL FORMULATION

Decision variables, an objective function, and model constraints make up a linear programming model. The degree of activity of an operation is represented by mathematical symbols called **decision variables**. A company that manufactures electrical devices, for instance, wants to make juicers, food processors, and electric irons. The symbols x_1, x_2, and x_3 indicate the quantity of each item to be produced. Consequently, x_1 represents the quantity of electric irons, x_2 denotes food processors, and x_3 denotes juicers. A decision is defined by the final values of x_1, x_2, and x_3, as decided by the firm (e.g., $x_1 = 10$ is a decision by the firm to create 10 electric irons).

A linear mathematical relationship known as the **objective function** expresses the operation's objective in terms of the decision variables. A value is always maximized or minimized by the objective function (e.g., maximizing the profit or minimizing the cost of making electric irons). $Z = \$6x_1 + \$4x_2 + \$2x_3$ is the total profit, for instance, if the profit from an electric iron is \$6, the profit from a food processor is \$4, and the profit from a juicer is \$2.

The operating environment's constraints on the decision scenario are represented by the model **constraints**, which are likewise linear relationships between the decision variables. The constraints may take the shape of stringent policies or scarce resources. For instance, if producing an electric iron takes two hours, producing a food processor takes four hours, and producing a juicer takes three hours, and there are only forty hours of labor available, then the constraint that reflects this is $2x_1 + 4x_2 + 3x_3 \leq 40$.

The following represents the general structure of the linear programming model:

$$\text{Optimize (Minimize or maximize) objective function } Z = \sum_{j=1}^{n} C_j x_j$$

subject to the constraints:

$$\sum_{j=1}^{n} a_{ij} x_j \ (\leq, =, \geq) b_i \quad \text{for all } i = 1,2, \dots \text{m}$$

$x_j \geq 0; j = 1,2, \ldots, n$ (non-negativity constraints)

where

$x_j = j^{th}$ decision variable about which the decision maker is interested.

C_j = Unit contribution to the jth decision variable in the objective function.

a_{ij} = constraint coefficients.

b_i = Requirement or availability of ith constraint.

i = Constraint number; $i = 1, 2, \ldots, m$.

j = Decision variable number; $j = 1, 2, \ldots, n$.

$(\leq, =, \geq)$ means that any of the three notations is required.

Example 17.1

Formulation of Linear Programming Model

The Techno Craft Store is a small crafts business that uses skilled labor and special pottery clay to create earthenwares, including cookers and curd pots. Given these limited resources, the business needs to know how many cookers and curd pots to produce daily in order to maximize profit.

The following resources are needed to create the two items at the selling price per unit produced (i.e., the model parameters):

	Resource Requirements		
Product	Labor (hr/unit)	Clay (lb/unit)	Revenue ($/unit)
Clay Cooker	1	4	40
Curd Pot	2	3	50

Every day, 120 pounds of clay are available and 40 hours of labor are needed. Create a linear programming model for this issue.

Solution

The following decision variables describe the management's choice on the number of cookers and curd pots to produce:

$$x_1 = \text{number of cookers to produce}$$

$$x_2 = \text{number of curd pots to produce}$$

The company's objective is to increase total revenue, which is calculated as the total of the individual earnings made from each curd pot and cooker:

$$\text{Maximize } Z = \$40x_1 + 50x_2$$

The labor and clay constraints are included in the model and are as follows:

$$x_1 + 2x_2 \leq 40 \text{ hr.}$$

$$4x_1 + 3x_2 \leq 120 \text{ pound}$$

The equality operator (=) is replaced with the less than or equal to inequality (≤) since the maximum quantity – 40 hours of labor or 120 pounds of clay – *that can be utilized* is 40 or 120, not that *must be used*. Nevertheless, limitations may take the form of equalities (=), larger than or equal to inequality (≥), or less than or equal to inequality (≤).

At this point, the entire linear programming model for this issue can be summed up as follows:

$$\text{Maximize } Z = \$40x_1 + \$50x_2$$

subject to

$$1x_1 + 2x_2 \leq 40$$

$$4x_1 + 3x_2 \leq 120$$

$$x_1, x_2 \geq 0$$

The model's solution will provide x_1 and x_2 numerical values that maximize overall profit, Z, while abiding by the constraints. $x_1 = 24$ cookers and $x_2 = 8$ curd pots, with a corresponding revenue of \$1360, are the solutions that accomplish this objective. Next, we will look into how we arrive at these values.

17.3 GRAPHICAL SOLUTION METHOD

All linear programming models share some characteristics with the model described in the previous section. The various variables are continuous (not limited to integers), the interactions are linear, the model parameters are presumed to be known with certainty, and the mathematical relationships are additive. Models with two choice variables, or two dimensions, can be graphically solved due to linearity. A graphical solution is helpful since it shows how a solution is produced, albeit it is a complex.

The fundamental stages of the graphical solution approach involve plotting the model constraints on a plane's coordinate system and locating the region of the graph that simultaneously meets each constraint. The solution is the point on this space's boundary that maximizes (or minimizes) the objective function. These procedures are shown in Example 17.2.

Example 17.2

Graphical Solution

Determine the solution for Techno Craft Store in Example 17.1:

$$\text{Maximize } Z = \$40x_1 + \$50x_2$$
$$\text{subject to}$$
$$x_1 + 2x_2 \leq 40$$
$$4x_1 + 3x_2 \leq 120$$
$$x_1, x_2 \geq 0$$

Solution

The following figure of the possible solution space displays the graph of the model constraints. Given that both decision variables must be positive or zero, that is, $x_1, x_2 \geq 0$, the graph is generated in the positive quadrant.

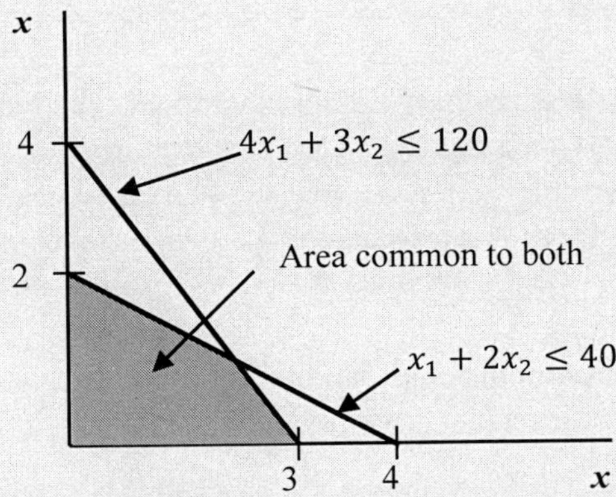

Plotting the constraints on the graph is the initial step. Plotting each line on the graph and treating both constraints as equations or straight lines is how this is accomplished. Finding the locations on a line where the horizontal and vertical axes intersect and drawing a straight line to connect them is a basic method of plotting a line. The region shared by both model constraints is indicated by the darkened area in the preceding figure. As a result, the only region of the graph with points (i.e., values for x_1 and x_2) that will concurrently satisfy both criteria is this one. Since it is the sole region with values for the variables that are either feasible or do not violate the constraints, this region is known as the feasible solution space.

Finding the point that reflects the largest total income in the feasible solution region is the second step in the graphical solution approach. For a randomly chosen revenue level, we shall plot the objective function line. For instance, if Z, the income, is \$800, then the objective function is:

$$\$800 = 40x_1 + 50x_2$$

Plotting this line in the same manner as we plotted the constraint lines yields the graph that appears in the following figure, which indicates the optimal position. Every combination of x_1 and x_2 on this line will provide a

Z value of \$800, meaning that every point on the line is in the feasible solution region and will generate revenue of \$800. The objective function line extends from the origin through the feasible solution space as Z increases. It does so until it reaches the final feasible point on the solution space's boundary, at which point it exits the solution space.

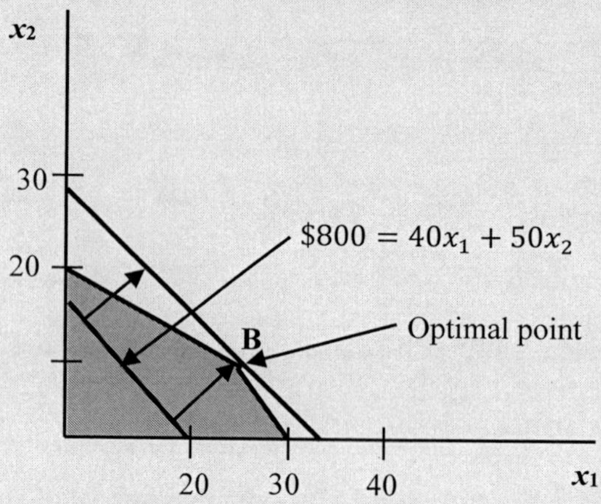

Since the boundary includes the points that are furthest from the origin (i.e., the points that correspond to the largest profit), the solution point is always on this boundary. Furthermore, the solution point will be at one of the boundary's corners, where two constraint lines connect, in addition to being on the edge of the possible solution area. Extreme points are protrusions that are denoted A, B, and C in the following picture. The optimal solution in a linear programming model will always arise at an extreme point, as demonstrated by mathematical proof. As a result, in our example problem, the three **extreme points** A, B, and C are the only potential solution points. Since B is the **solution point** the objective function touches before leaving the feasible solution area, it is the **optimal**, or "one best," solution point.

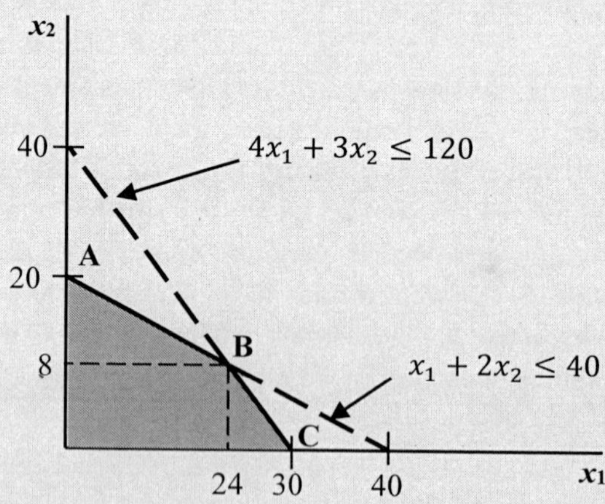

Two constraint lines intersect at point B; hence these two lines are equal at that location. Thus, by resolving the two simultaneous equations, the values of x_1 and x_2 at that intersection can be determined.

$$x_1 + 2x_2 = 40 \qquad \text{... (17.1)}$$

$$4x_1 + 3x_2 = 120 \qquad \text{... (17.2)}$$

Multiply Equation 17.1 by 4 and then subtract Equation 17.2 from the resultant equation, we get

$$5x_2 = 40$$

$$x_2 = 8$$

Thus, putting value of x_2 in equation 17.1, we get

$$x_1 + 2(8) = 40$$

$$x_1 = 24$$

At point B in the previous picture, $x_1 = 24$ clay-cookers and $x_2 = 8$ curd pots represent the optimal solutions. The highest revenue is obtained by changing these variables in the objective function.

$$Z = \$40(24) + \$50(8) = \$1360$$

Rather than graphing the objective function and seeing which point it last touches as it moves out of the feasible solution area, you can find the solution by testing each of the three extreme corner points (A, B, or C) to see which yields the greatest revenue. The solution values for points A, B, and C as well as the total income, Z, at each point are displayed in the figure that follows.

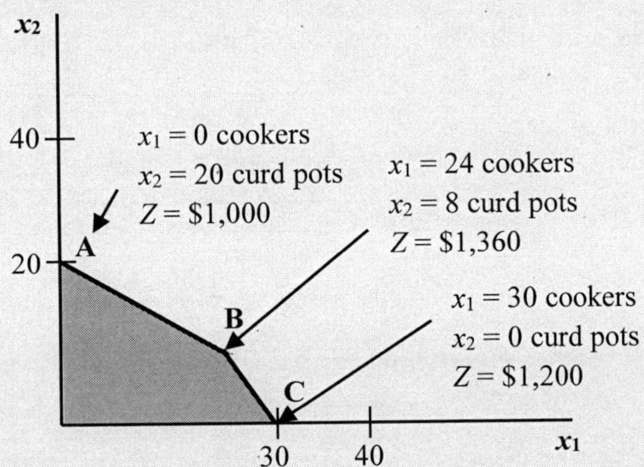

Since the objective function specifies the revenue that will be earned from every combination of x_1 and x_2 values at the extreme points, it is able to identify which extreme point is optimal. One of the extreme locations other than B would have been optimal if the objective function had other coefficients, or different x_1 and x_2 profit values.

For the sake of argument, let's say that the sales of a curd pot are \$20 instead of \$50 and the sales of a clay cooker are \$70 instead of \$40. $Z = \$70x_1 + \$20x_2$ is the new objective function that is produced by these values.

The possible solution area stays the same if neither the labor nor the clay model limitations are altered, as seen in the following figure. The objective function's location in this figure differs from the original objective function's placement in the preceding image, though, because the linear objective function now has a new slope due to the new profit coefficients. At $Z = \$2100$, point C becomes the ideal position. This illustrates sensitivity analysis, a helpful feature of both linear programming and model analysis in general. Sensitivity analysis refers to the capacity to evaluate variations in model parameters that represent various operating conditions and assess the effect on the solution.

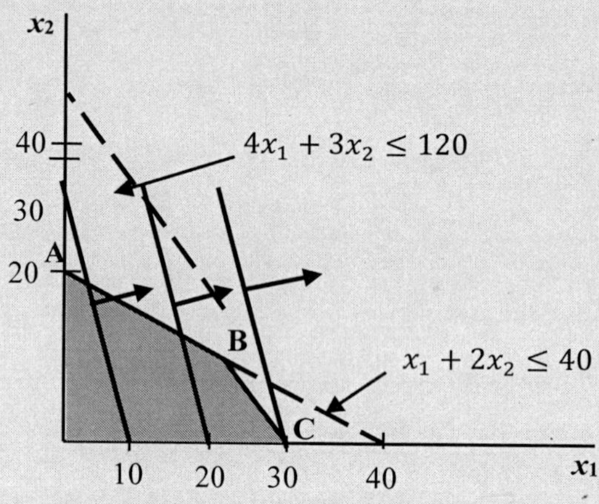

How to convert a Maximization problem into a Minimization problem?

With a changed sign, the maximizing objective function is identical to the minimization objective function.

Thus,

$$\text{Maximize } Z = \sum_{j=1}^{n} C_j x_j$$

is equivalent to

$$\text{Minimize } Z = \sum_{j=1}^{n} -C_j x_j$$

Similar to this, by altering the decision coefficients' sign, a minimization problem can be changed into a maximization problem.

Thus,

$$\text{Minimize } Z = \sum_{j=1}^{n} C_j x_j$$

is equivalent to

$$\text{Maximize } Z = \sum_{j=1}^{n} -C_j x_j$$

Example 17.3

Precision Products Company has a daily manufacturing capacity of 9 units and makes two items, A and B. A and B needing an equal amount of production capacity. The business has a long-term agreement with another business to provide it with 2 units of A and 3 units or more of B every day. 20 machine hours are needed to produce each unit of A, while 50 machine hours are needed to produce each unit of B. 360 machine hours is the maximum that can be completed in a single day. What product mix would you recommend if the objective is to minimize the total manufacturing cost and the total cost of production for component A is \$250 per unit and component B is \$520 per unit?

Solution

$$\text{Minimize } Z = 250x_1 + 500x_2$$

Subject to

$$x_1 + x_2 \leq 9 \text{ Production constraint}$$

$$x_1 \geq 2 \text{ supply constraint}$$

$$x_2 \geq 3 \text{ supply constraint}$$

$$20x_1 + 50x_2 \leq 360 \text{ Machine hour constraints}$$

$$x_1 \geq 0 \quad \text{Non} - \text{negativity constraint}$$

$$x_2 \geq 0 \quad \text{Non} - \text{negativity constraint}$$

The following values of the objective function are obtained from the feasible region's corner points:

Point (x_1, x_2)	Objective function $Z = 250x_1 + 500x_2$
A (3, 6)	$250 \times 3 + 500 \times 6 = 3750$
B (6, 3)	$250 \times 6 + 500 \times 3 = 3000$
C (2, 3)	$250 \times 2 + 500 \times 3 = 2000$
D (2, 6.4)	$250 \times 2 + 500 \times 6.4 = 3700$

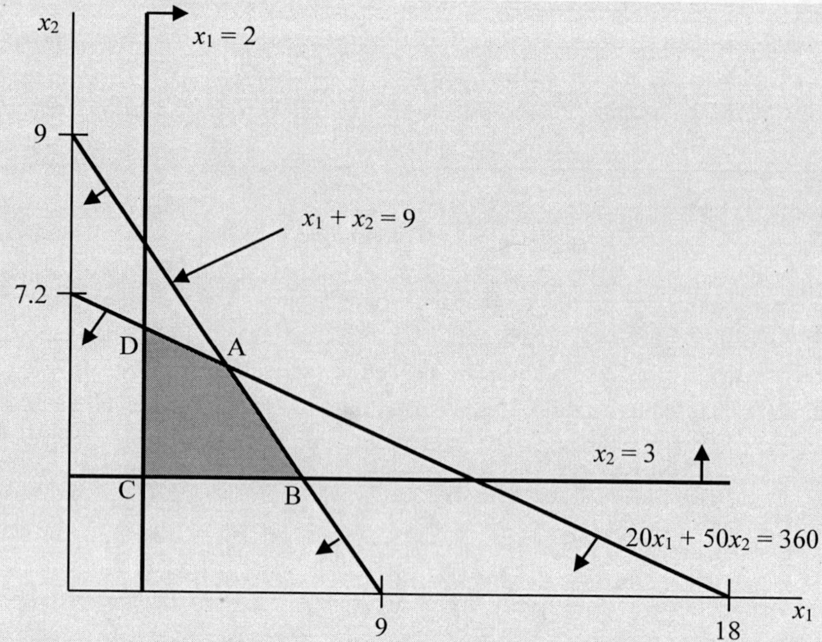

Point C gives minimum value of the objective function which is $2,000. Therefore, produce 6 units of A and 3 units of B.

17.3.1 SENSITIVITY ANALYSIS IN GRAPHICAL SOLUTION

Occasionally, our focus lies in how the optimum solution reacts to minor modifications in the constraints and additional estimated values. The estimations of expenses, earnings, processing time, and machine capacity might also be inaccurate. These deterministic estimates come into play while modeling an LP problem. For analyzing little variations in these estimations, sensitivity analysis could be helpful.

Example 17.4

Let's look at a profit maximization situation where the two constraints are manpower and machining capacity:

$$\text{Objective function } Z \text{ (Maximize)} = x + y$$

subject to

$$x + 2y \leq 400 \text{ (Machine capacity)}$$

$$3x + y \leq 600 \quad (Manpower\ capacity)$$

$$x, y \geq 0.$$

Solution

Expressing constraints as:

$$x + 2y + M = 400$$

$$3x + y + N = 600$$

or,

$$x = 400 - 2y - M$$

and,

$$x = \frac{1}{3}(600 - y - N) = 200 - 0.33y - 0.33N$$

Hence, $400 - M - 200 + 0.33N = 2y - 0.33y$

or,

$$y = \frac{1}{1.67}(200 - M + 0.33N)$$

$$= 119.76 - 0.6M + 0.197N$$

Similarly,

$$x = 400 - 2(119.76 - 0.67M + 0.197N) - M$$

$$= 160.33 - 0.20M - 0.4N$$

Putting these values of x and y in the objective function, we get:

$$Z = 160.33 - 0.2M - 0.4N + 119.76 - 0.6M + 0.197N$$

$$= 280 - 0.04M - 0.20N$$

Let's examine the aforementioned expression.

CONCEPT OF SLACK VARIABLE

The profit is impacted by \$0.04, the coefficient of M; in the profit statement above if one unit of machine capacity is left unutilized. Similarly, there is a \$0.20 loss in profit margin for every unit of labor that is not employed. We refer to these ideal capacity variables (M and N) as **slack variables.**

CONCEPT OF SHADOW PRICE

Examine the coefficients of the slack variables, M and N, in the final Z equation. The coefficient of M, or \$0.04, would be the profit margin contribution if one unit of more machine capacity was available. In a similar vein, an additional manpower capacity unit contributes \$0.20 units to profit. We refer to these factors as the "**shadow price.**" The explanation of the shadow price of a constraint is that a minor alteration in the constraint results in a marginal gain or loss in the objective function.

Decision-makers may find the shadow price to be significant in a variety of ways. It is frequently the case that a small increase or decrease in an estimate is not difficult to achieve in real life. The model's budget limit, for instance, is $2000. They might want to know how it might impact their earnings first, though, before making that move. The answer might lie in the shadow price. The capacity of a machine, facility, supplier, etc., can also be slightly changed by a manager with minimal work. An understanding of the shadow price could help determine how the objective function will represent it. Increased capacity (or utilizing the flexibility) of those restrictions, which have a higher shadow price, should generally be the focus of attention. Therefore, management may focus on examining the shadow price of constraints in order to increase profit (or decrease cost).

Software addressing LP problems is widely accessible; examples include LINDO, LINGO, and others. These programs offer a shadow price for every restriction. These programs may be able to tackle more complex issues with plenty of variables and restrictions.

17.3.2 MULTIPLE OPTIMUM SOLUTIONS

There may be situations when an LPP gives multiple solutions. Consider the following problem.

Example 17.5

$$\text{Maximize } Z = 40x + 30y$$

Subject to

$$x + 2y \leq 40$$
$$4x + 3y \leq 120$$
$$x, y \geq 0$$

Solution

By solving this problem graphically, we obtained the following graph with their coordinates.

Putting the values of coordinates of A, B, and C in the equation of Z, we get

A (0,20) = $40 \times 0 + 30 \times 20 = 600$

B (24,8) = $40 \times 24 + 30 \times 8 = 1200$

C (30,0) = $40 \times 30 + 30 \times 0 = 1200$

Thus, this is the case of multiple optimum solutions.

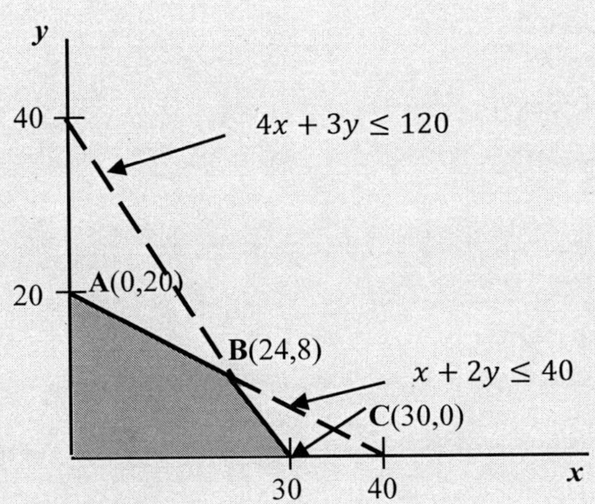

17.3.3 INFEASIBLE SOLUTIONS

When two constraints are inconsistent, an LPP cannot provide a feasible solution. Now let's look at the following problem.

Example 17.6

$$\text{Maximize } Z = 1.5x + y$$

Subject to

$$5x + 4y \geq 20$$
$$3x + 2y \leq 6$$
$$x, y \geq 0$$

From the above two constraint equations, we obtain the graph shown below.

With two constraints, the graphical solution shown below does not contain a feasible region. As a result, there will never be an optimal solution for these problems.

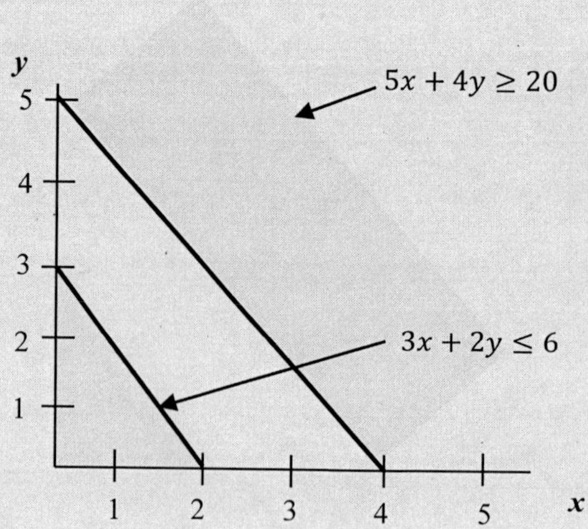

17.3.4 UNBOUNDED PROBLEM

Typically, the collection of constraints provides a specific region. The objective function always has an upper (or lower) constraint, making it a bounded problem. Nonetheless, the feasible region in some LPP is unbounded or open-ended. Let's look at the next problem.

Example 17.7

$$\text{Maximize } Z = 1.5x + y$$

Subject to

$$x \leq 3$$
$$4x + 5y \geq 20$$
$$x, y \geq 0$$

From the above two constraint equations, we obtain the graph shown below

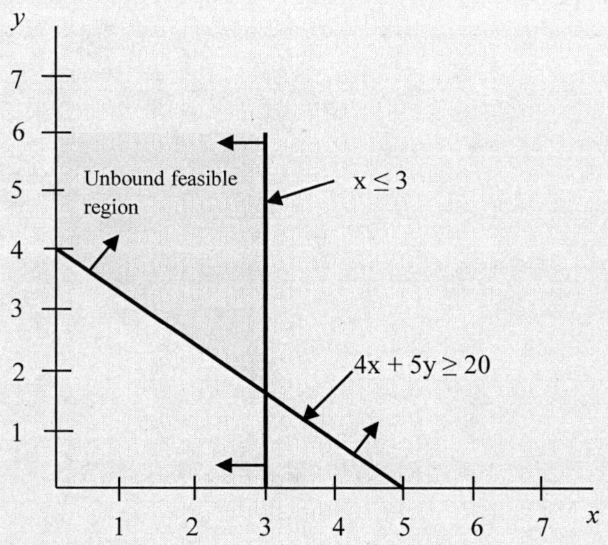

A wrong formulation of an LPP is the cause of an unbound problem. An unbound problem has no single feasible solution.

17.4 SIMPLEX METHOD TO SOLVE LPP

By using the simplex approach, linear programming problems (LPPs) are solved. The graphical method is inadequate when there are more than two choice variables. It was created in 1947 by George Dantzig for a US Air Force assignment. The foundation of the simplex technique is the fact that, in the event that an LPP has an optimal solution, it can always be found in one of the basic feasible solutions.

The constraints need to be slightly altered before applying the simplex approach in order to obtain a standard form of the problem. To turn the LPP into an equation, each constraint is expanded with one or more additional variables; for example, the ≥ and ≤ signs must be changed to an equal to (=) sign.

Example 17.8

Constraint

$$5x + 4y \leq 50$$

becomes

$$5x + 4y + S_1 = 50$$

As an extra variable in this case, S_1 is referred to as the **Slack Variable**. What makes $(5x + 4y)$ less than 50 is this difference.

Example 17.9

Constraint

$$20x + 30y \geq 600$$

becomes

$$20x + 30y - S_2 = 600$$

In this case, the **Surplus Variable**, S_2, is subtracted in order to use the excess of (20x + 30y) over 600.

But it is necessary to include an additional variable, also known as an **Artificial Variable**. Consequently, a surplus variable and an artificial (slack) variable with an equality sign should be added to the constraints of "greater than type," i.e., with a ≥ sign. Consequently, the restriction 20x + 30y ≥ 600 would turn into

$$20x + 30y - S_2 + A_2 = 600$$

What is the purpose of adding the artificial variable? We do not want to go against the non-negativity requirements, which is the rationale. The initial solution used by the simplex approach assumes that all of the rel variables are equal to zero. What happens if we take $20x + 30y - S_2 = 600$ into account? When we set both x and y to zero, we have $S_2 = -600$, which is against the non-negativity criterion.

The improved constraint $20x + 30y - S_2 + A_2 = 600$ is now apparent. S_2 is zero and A_2 is 600 by setting x and y to zero. Consequently, the condition for variables to have non-negativity may be preserved.

17.4.1 AUGMENTATION OF OBJECTIVE FUNCTION

Every variable that appears in the constraints needs to be present in the objective function. Thus, the objective function is expanded to include slack, surplus, and artificial variables in the following manner:

Constraint type	Add following	
	In the constraint	**In objective function**
≤	$+S$	$0.S$
≥	$-S + A$	Max $0.S - MA$
		Min $0.S - MA$
=	$+A$	For Maximization $- MA$ or for Minimization $+ MA$

M is an extremely big number in this case. We will use the example that follows to show this.

Example 17.10

The Precision Products Company is manufacturing two different types of products, A and B. Two resources are used to produce these products: Labor hours and raw material. The linear programming was originally formulated as:

Objective function Maximize $Z = 40x + 50y$

Subject to

$$x + 2y \leq 40 \text{ (labor hours)}$$
$$4x + 3y \leq 120 \text{ (raw material in pounds)}$$
$$x, y \geq 0$$

Remember that we added slack variables to each constraint in order to put this model into standard form.

Revised objective function is Maximize $Z = 40x + 50y + 0S_1 + 0S_2$

subject to

$$x + 2y + 1S_1 = 40$$
$$4x + 3y + 1S_2 = 120$$
$$x, y, S_1, S_2 \geq 0$$

You will recall that the amount of underutilized labor and raw material are represented by the slack variables, S_1 and S_2, respectively. For instance, if $x = 0$ and $y = 0$ and no products A and B are formed, then the problem's solution is

$$x + 2y + 1S_1 = 40$$
$$0 + 2(0) + 1S_1 = 40$$
$$S_1 = 40 \text{ hours of labor}$$

and

$$4x + 3y + 1S_2 = 120$$
$$4(0) + 3(0) + 1S_2 = 120$$
$$S_2 = 120 \text{ (lb of raw material)}$$

Put another way, all the resources are unused when we first start solving a problem and nothing is being used. The profit is zero because there is no benefit from unused resources.

$$Z = 40x + 50y + 0S_1 + 0S_2$$
$$= 40(0) + 50(0) + 0(40) + 0(120)$$
$$Z = 0$$

This is the point where the simplex approach is applied. The model is in the necessary format, and the simplex method may be used to solve the inequality constraints by converting them into equations.

After both model constraints have been converted into equations, it is necessary to solve the equations concurrently in order to ascertain the values of the variables at each potential solution point. But take note of the fact that our example problem involves four unknowns (two slack variables and two decision variables) in addition to two equations, which prevents direct simultaneous solution. This issue is resolved by the simplex approach, which sets some of the variables to zero. The number of variables assigned values of zero are $n - m$, where n is the number of variables and m is the number of constraints (apart from the non-negative constraints). Since there are two constraints and four variables in this model, two of the variables are given a value of zero (4 – 2 = 2).

For example, letting $x = 0$ and $s_1 = 0$ results in the following set of equations.

$$x + 2y + s_1 = 40$$
$$4x + 3y + s_2 = 120$$

and

$$0 + 2y + 0 = 40$$
$$0 + 3y + s_2 = 120$$

First, solve for y in the first equation:

$$2y = 40$$
$$y = 20$$

Then, solve for s_2 in the second equation:

$$3y + s_2 = 120$$
$$3(20) + s_2 = 120$$
$$s_2 = 60$$

By resolving the simultaneous equations, we have arrived at the precise solution. We call this approach a **basic feasible solution**. Any solution that meets the constraints is considered feasible. As long as there are m variables with nonnegative values and $n - m$ values set equal to zero, the basic feasible solution satisfies the constraints and includes as many variables with nonnegative values as there are model constraints. The basic feasible solution is said to be degenerate when one of the m variables equals zero, but normally the m variables have positive nonzero solution values. A later section of this unit will cover the subject of degeneracy.

But the finding of these solutions poses two specific questions.

(a) How did the determination of which variables to set to zero come about?

(b) What is the process for identifying the optimal solution?

The simplex approach can be used to find the answers to both of these problems. The simplex technique is a series of mathematical procedures that establishes when an ideal solution has been obtained and which variables should equal zero at each stage.

17.4.2 STEPS IN SIMPLEX METHOD

The simplex method's steps are completed within the structure of a tableau, or table. The model is arranged by the tableau in a way that facilitates applying the mathematical processes. To illustrate the simplex tableau and approach, we shall refer back to the earlier example.

$$\text{Maximize } Z = 40x + 50y + 0S_1 + 0S_2$$

Subject to

$$x + 2y + 1S_1 = 40$$
$$4x + 3y + 1S_2 = 120$$
$$x, y, S_1, S_2 \geq 0$$

Below is the original tableau (Table 17.2 for this model, complete with different column and row headings.

Table 17.2 The Simplex Tableau

c_j	**Basic variables**	**Quantity**	x	y	s_1	s_2
	z_j					
	$c_j - z_j$					

Initially, the model variables should be entered along the second row from the top of the tableau. First, the two decision variables are stated according to their subscript magnitude, followed by the slack variables, which are also listed in the same manner. In the tableau, this step creates the row containing x, y, s_1, and s_2.

Finding the most basic feasible solution is the next step. That is, which two variables will be set to zero and which two will constitute the basic feasible solution? The simplex technique chooses the origin as the first basic feasible solution rather than picking a random location because, in any linear programming problem, the values of the decision variables at the origin are always known. As $x = 0$ and $y = 0$ at this moment, s_1 and s_2 are the variables in the basic feasible solution.

$$x + 2y + S_1 = 40$$
$$0 + 2(0) + S_1 = 40$$
$$S_1 = 40 \text{ hours}$$

and

$$4x + 3y + S_2 = 120$$
$$4(0) + 3(0) + S_2 = 120$$
$$S_2 = 120 \text{ lb}$$

To put it another way, at the origin, where there is no production, all resources are slack, or unused. Two variables, s_1 and s_2, which are listed in the table 15.2 under the column "Basic Variables," make up the basic viable solution. The corresponding values, 40 and 120, are indicated in the "Quantity" column (Table 17.3).

Table 17.3 The basic feasible solution

c_j	Basic variables	Quantity	x	y	s_1	s_2
	s_1	40				
	s_2	120				
	z_j					
	$c_j - z_j$					

Whenever the solution starts at the origin, where x and y equal zero, that is the initial simplex tableau. The slack variables, s_1 and s_2, are therefore the basic variables at the origin. These quantity values can be read straight from the original constraint equations because they are always represented as the values on the right hand side of the constraint equations in the original solution.

All tableaus must have the same top and bottom two rows; the number of intermediate rows, however, corresponds to the number of constraints in the model. For instance, this problem includes two center rows, corresponding to s_1 and s_2, because it has two constraints. (Remember that the number of variables in the problem having values of zero is equal to n variables minus m constraints). This suggests that there will be m constraints equal to the number of basic variables with values different than zero.

Comparably, the remaining columns in the tableau correspond to the number of variables, whereas the three columns on the left are standard. Four columns – corresponding to x, y, s_1, and s_2 – are located on the right side of the tableau, reflecting the four variables in this model.

The objective function coefficients, or c_j values, must then be filled in, each of which represents the contribution to profit (or cost) for each of the variable x_j or s_j in the objective function. For every variable in the model, the corresponding values 40, 50, 0, and 0 are put across the top row, as the table 17.4 illustrates.

Table 17.4 The Simplex Tableau with c_j values

			40	50	0	0
c_j	**Basic variables**	**Quantity**	x	y	s_1	s_2
0	s_1	40				
0	s_2	120				
	z_j					
	$c_j - z_j$					

The variables that contribute to profit in the basic feasible solution – in this case, s_1 and s_2 – are represented by the values for c_j on the left side of the tableau. It is possible to compute the values in the z_j row by using these values, which are introduced at this point in the tableau.

The coefficients of the slack and decision variables in the model constraint equations are entered into the columns under each variable (x, y, s_1, and s_2). Because the first model constraint is represented by the s_1 row, the coefficients for x and s_1 are 1, the coefficient of y is 2, and the coefficient of s_2 is 0. The second constraint equation coefficients, 4, 3, 0, and 1, are the values in the s_2 row, as indicated in the table 17.5.

Filling in the first simplex tableau is now finished. Simplex formulas are used to perform a mathematical computation of the values that remain in the rows z_j and $c_j - z_j$, as well as next tableau values.

Table 17.5 The Simplex Tableau with model constraint coefficients

			40	50	0	0
c_j	**Basic variables**	**Quantity**	x	y	s_1	s_2
0	s_1	40	1	2	1	0
0	s_2	120	4	3	0	1
	z_j					
	$c_j - z_j$					

The following list lists the phases in the simplex approach (for a maximizing model).

1. Add slack variables to all of the inequalities to convert them into equations.
2. Create a simplex tableau where the number of rows is equal to the number of constraints plus four, and the number of columns is equal to the number of variables plus three.
3. Establish table headers with a list of the slack and decision variables in the model.
4. Enter the slack variables and their quantity values, which provide the first basic workable solution.
5. Give the model variables in the upper row and the basic variables of the feasible solution on the left of their respective c_j values.
6. Place the model constraint coefficients in the table's body.

Thus far, values directly extracted from the model have been used to construct up the simplex tableau. The values are now ascertained through computation. Prior to summing each of these sets of values, the values in the z_j row are calculated by multiplying each c_j column value (on the left side) by each column value under Quantity, x, y, s_1, and s_2. The following table 17.6 displays the z_j values.

Table 17.6 The Simplex Tableau with z_j row values

			40	50	0	0
c_j	**Basic variables**	**Quantity**	x	y	s_1	s_2
0	s_1	40	1	2	1	0
0	s_2	120	4	3	0	1
	z_j	0	0	0	0	0
	$c_j - z_j$					

For example, the value in the z_j row under the quantity column is found as follows.

c_j	**Quantity**	
0	40	$0 \times 40 = 0 \ldots$ (i)
0	120	$0 \times 120 = 0 \ldots$ (ii)
	z_j	(i) + (ii) = 0

In a similar manner, the value under the x column in the z_j row is located.

c_j	x	
0	1	$0 \times 1 = 0 \ldots$ (i)
0	4	$0 \times 4 = 0 \ldots$ (ii)
	z_j	(i) + (ii) = 0

When the other z_j row values for this tableau are calculated with this formula, they will all equal zero.

Subtracting the values of the z_j row from the values of the c_j (top) row yields the $c_j - z_j$ row. For instance, the row value of $c_j - z_j$ in the x column is calculated as 40 – 0 = 40. The table 17.7 displays this value along with other $c_j - z_j$ values. This is the whole initial simplex tableau with all values filled in. The solution at the origin, where $x = 0$, $y = 0$, $s_1 = 40$, and $s_2 = 120$, is shown in this tableau. The Z value, or profit represented by this solution, is indicated in the z_j row under the quantity column – 0 in the table that follows. Since no profit is being made, this solution is definitely not the optimal one. As a result, we wish to proceed to a solution point that offers a superior resolution. Stated differently, our objective is to generate a certain number of units of either product A or product B. A nonbasic variable – that is, a variable not included in the current basic viable solution – will make an appearance in the solution and turn into a basic variable.

Table 17.7 The Complete Initial Simplex Tableau

			40	50	0	0
c_j	**Basic variables**	**Quantity**	x	y	s_1	s_2
0	s_1	40	1	2	1	0
0	s_2	120	4	3	0	1
	z_j	0	0	0	0	0
	$c_j - z_j$		40	50	0	0

The Entering Nonbasic Variable

Let's take an example where the Precision Products Company chooses to manufacture certain items of A. This choice will turn x into a basic variable. Because that is the profit contribution of product A, profit will increase by \$40 for each unit of x (i.e., each product A) produced. However, some of the previously unutilized resources will be used during the production of product A (x). For instance, in the event that

$$x = 1$$

then

$$x + 2y + S_1 = 40$$
$$1 + 2(0) + S_1 = 40$$
$$S_1 = 39 \text{ hours of labor}$$

and

$$4x + 3y + S_2 = 120$$
$$4(1) + 3(0) + S_2 = 120$$
$$S_2 = 116 \text{ lb of raw material}$$

The labor constraint shows that the quantity of slack, or unused, labor is reduced by one hour with the production of one piece of product A. There is a 4 pound reduction in slack in the raw material constraint. These increases (for x) and decreases (for slack) when substituted into the objective function result in

$$Z \quad \overbrace{= 40(1) + 50(0) +}^{c_j} \quad \overbrace{0(-1) + 0(-4)}^{z_j} = \$40$$

The values in the c_j row are represented by the first portion of this objective function relationship, and the values in the z_j row by the second part. The function articulates the necessity of forfeiting a portion of the profits from the things they substitute in order to manufacture certain items of product A. In this instance, no profit was lost because the manufacture of item x just replaced slack. The values in the $c_j - z_j$ row typically indicate the next increment per unit when a nonbasic variable is entered into the basic solution. Since the goal is to maximize profit, it makes sense that we would want to generate as much money as we can. The variable that will result in the largest net increase in profit per unit is therefore entered. We choose variable x as the entering fundamental variable from the table 17.8 because it has the largest net increase in profit per unit, \$50, which is the highest positive value in the $c_j - z_j$ row.

Table 17.8 Selection of the Entering Basic Variable

			40	50	0	0
c_j	**Basic variables**	**Quantity**	x	y	s_1	s_2
0	s_1	40	1	2	1	0
0	s_2	120	4	3	0	1
	z_j	0	0	0	0	0
	$c_j - z_j$		40	50	0	0

The pivot column is the y column, which is highlighted in the table above. (In mathematical terminology, pivot operations are frequently used to describe the procedures employed to solve simultaneous equations.)

One of the two basic variables – s_1 or s_2 – must exit the solution and become zero since any basic feasible solution only has two variables with nonzero values. We wish to manufacture as many of item B (y) as we can because we have decided to do so, or as many as our resources will allow. First, as there is no way of making item A, $x = 0$; also, since we will spend all available labor hours and s_1 = unused labor resources, $s_1 = 0$ as well, we will use all available labor hours to create item B in the labor constraint.

$$1x + 2y + S_1 = 40 \text{ hr}$$
$$1(0) + 2y + 0 = 40$$
$$y = 20 \text{ units of product B}$$

Put another way, there is sufficient labor to create 20 units of product B. Proceed to apply the same approach to the raw material constraint.

$$4x + 3y + S_2 = 120 \text{ lb of raw material}$$
$$4(0) + 3y + 0 = 120$$
$$y = 40 \text{ items of product B}$$

This suggests that there is sufficient raw material to make 40 units of product B. However, enough labor is available to make just 20 units of product B. Because we lack the labor to create more than 20 units of product B, we are limited to producing only that number.

By dividing the quantity values of the basic solution variables by the pivot values, this analysis is carried out using the simplex approach. Regarding this tableau,

Basic variables	Quantity	y
s_1	40	÷ 2 = 20, the leaving variable
s_2	120	÷ 3 = 40

In this example, the least nonnegative quotient, 20, is the variable corresponding to the exiting basic variable. (Take note that the value zero would be the option for the departing variable and would be considered the minimum quotient.) Consequently, the leaving variable is s_1. Another name for s_1 row is the pivot row, which is indicated in the table 17.9.

Table 17.9 Pivot column, Pivot Row, and Pivot Number

			40	50	0	0
c_j	**Basic variables**	**Quantity**	x	y	s_1	s_2
0	s_1	40	1	2	1	0
0	s_2	120	4	3	0	1
	z_j	0	0	0	0	0
	$c_j - z_j$		40	50	0	0

The pivot number is the value of 2 at the point where the pivot row and pivot column intersect. The row, column, and pivot number are all crucial for creating the following tableau. Now that we have the second simplex tableau and a better solution, we may proceed. The following table 17.10 displays the subsequent simplex tableau using the new basic variables of y and s_2 and their associated c_j values for a feasible solution.

Table 17.10 The Basic Variables and c_j Values for the Second Simplex Tableau

			40	50	0	0
c_j	**Basic variables**	**Quantity**	x	y	s_1	s_2
50	y					
0	s_2					
	z_j					
	$c_j - z_j$					

The following tableau's (Table 17.11) different row values are calculated using multiple simplex formulas. The y row, also known as the pivot row of the new tableau, is first calculated by dividing each value in the pivot row of the old tableau by the pivot number. For these calculations, the formula is

$$\text{new tableau pivot row values} = \frac{\text{old tableau pivot row values}}{\text{pivot number}}$$

The table 17.11 below displays the updated row values.

Table 17.11 Computation of the New Pivot Row Values

			40	50	0	0
c_j	**Basic variables**	**Quantity**	x	y	s_1	s_2
50	y	20	1/2	1	1/2	0
0	s_2					
	z_j					
	$c_j - z_j$					

Another formula is used to calculate the values of all remaining rows (in this example, there is only one remaining row).

new tableau row values = old tableau row values − (corresponding coefficients in pivot column × correwsponding new tableau pivot row value)

As a result, this formula necessitates using both the old and new tableaus. Table 17.12 below computes the s_2 row values.

Table 17.12 Computation of the New y Row Values

Column	Old tableau Row value –	(Corresponding coefficients in pivot column × new tableau pivot row value)	= New tableau row value
Quantity	120 –	(3 × 20)	= 60
x	4 –	(3 × 1/2)	= 5/2
y	3 –	(3 × 1)	= 0
s_1	0 –	(3 × 1/2)	= – 3/2
s_2	1 –	(3 × 0)	= 1

The simplex tableau 17.13 below now has these values added to it. At this point, $x = 0$, $y = 20$, $s_1 = 0$, $s_2 = 60$ is the solution. Stated differently, 60 pounds of raw material remain unused after the production of 20 units of product B. No labor hour is unused, and no units of product A are produced.

Table 17.13 The Second Simplex Tableau and Row Values

			40	50	0	0
c_j	**Basic variables**	**Quantity**	x	y	s_1	s_2
50	y	20	1/2	1	1/2	0
0	s_2	60	5/2	0	– 3/2	1
	z_j					
	$c_j - z_j$					

The z_j and $c_j - z_j$ row values are calculated in the same manner as in the first simplex tableau to complete the second one. Summing the products of the values in the c_j column and every other column yields the z_j row.

Column	
Quantity	$z_j = (50)(20) + (0)(60) = 1000$
x	$z_j = (50)(1/2) + (0)(5/2) = 25$
y	$z_j = (50)(1) + (0)(0) = 50$
s_1	$z_j = (50)(1/2) + (0)(-3/2) = 25$
s_2	$z_j = (50)(0) + (0)(1) = 0$

The completed second simplex tableau, which is displayed in the table 17.14, is created by adding the z_j row values and the $c_j - z_j$ row values to the tableau. The objective function (profit) for this basic feasible solution has a value of 1,000 in the z_j row.

Table 17.14 The Completed Second Simplex Tableau

			40	50	0	0
c_j	**Basic variables**	**Quantity**	x	y	s_1	s_2
50	y	20	1/2	1	1/2	0
0	s_2	60	5/2	0	– 3/2	1
	z_j	1000	25	50	25	0
	$c_j - z_j$		15	0	– 25	0

Row operations in the solution of simultaneous equations are effectively achieved by the computational processes we took to create the second tableau. Every succeeding tableau – referred to as iteration – is derived using the same procedures.

The third tableau is created by repeating the processes that we used to obtain the second simplex tableau. First, the basic variable to be entered, or pivot column, is identified. Since the largest positive net increase in profit is represented by number 15 in the $c_j - z_j$ row, x is the entering nonbasic variable. The pivot row and the leaving bsic variable, s_2, are found by dividing the values in the pivot column by the values in the quantity column. The following table displays the pivot row, pivot column, and pivot number.

Table 17.15 The Pivot Row, Pivot Column, and Pivot Number

			40	50	0	0
c_j	**Basic variables**	**Quantity**	x	y	s_1	s_2
50	y	20	**1/2**	1	1/2	0
0	s_2	**60**	**5/2**	**0**	**– 3/2**	**1**
	z_j	1000	**25**	50	25	0
	$c_j - z_j$		**15**	0	– 25	0

You may be wondering why, instead of the initial profit of $40, the net gain in profit per product A (x) is $15 at this time. The reason for this is that some of the resources that were previously used to make product B (y) alone will now be used to produce product A (x). We are giving up some of the profit from manufacturing product B in order to gain even more by producing product A, since producing some of product A entails producing less of product B. The net increase of $15 represents this disparity.

Using the same formula as before, the new tableau pivot row (x) in the third simplex tableau is calculated. The pivot number, 5/2, is then divided by all previous pivot row values. Table 17.17 displays these numbers. Table 17.16 displays the values that were computed for the other row (y).

Table 17.16 Computation of the y Row for the Third Simplex Tableau

Column	Old tableau Row value –	(Corresponding coefficients in pivot column × new tableau pivot row value)	= New tableau row value
Quantity	120 –	(1/2 × 24)	= 8
x	1/2 –	(1/2 × 1)	= 0
y	1 –	(1/2 × 0)	= 1
s_1	1/2 –	(1/2 × – 3/5)	= 4/5
s_2	0 –	(1/2 × 2/5)	= – 1/5

Table 17.17 The Pivot Row, Pivot Column, and Pivot Number

			40	50	0	0
c_j	**Basic variables**	**Quantity**	x	y	s_1	s_2
50	y	8	0	1	4/5	–1/5
0	x	24	1	0	–3/5	2/5
	z_j	1,360	40	50	16	6
	$c_j - z_j$		0	0	–16	–6

Since all of the values in the $c_j - z_j$ row are zero or negative, it is evident that a nonbasic variable would not produce a positive net increase in profit when examining the $c_j - z_j$ row to identify the entering variable. This indicates that the optimal solution has been found. The answer is as follows:

$x = 24$ unit of product A
$y = 8$ units of product B
$Z = \$1,360$ profit

There is something more to say about simplex solutions in general. It is possible to obtain a fractional solution for decision variables even when the variables represent objects that should be integers, such as cars, electrical devices, etc., even though this solution produced integer values for the variables (i.e., 24 and 8). One needs to acknowledge this restriction in order to use the simplex approach. An approach that guarantees integer solutions can be used to solve linear programming models.

A minimization problem requires a few changes in the normal simplex process, which can be studied by scanning the given QR code.

SCAN ME
for
Simplex solution of a Minimization problem

17.4.3 THE DUAL

We covered dual values, or shadow prices, and the subject of sensitivity analysis in section 17.3.1. These subjects were covered in relation to the graphical examination of linear programming models. We described how to calculate sensitivity ranges for several model parameters, such as the constraint quantity (i.e., values on the right side) and the objective function coefficients. We also discussed how resource decisions could be made using dual values. Though we have demonstrated where the sensitivity ranges originated through graphical analysis, we have not yet provided an explanation for how they were mathematically formed. We will also demonstrate the mathematical derivation of dual values and sensitivity ranges using the simplex method.

There are two forms for each linear programming model: **primal** and **dual**. The primal is the original version of a linear programming model. Every example we have covered thus far is a primal model. The dual is helpful because it gives the decision-maker a different perspective on a situation. The dual provides information on the value of the limited resources used to achieve that profit, whereas the primal gives solution results in terms of the amount of profit made from creating things.

The next example will show you how to derive and interpret a model's dual form. Every day, the Precision Products Company manufactured goods A and B. Profits from the manufacturing of one unit of product A total \$160, while profits from the production of one unit of product B total \$200. The availability of labor, raw materials, and storage space are restricted resources that are necessary for the creation of items A and B. The following lists the total resources available as well as the resources needed to produce products A and B.

	Resource Requirements		
Resource	Product A	Product B	Total available per day
Labor (hr)	2	4	40
Raw material (pounds)	18	18	216
Storage (ft^2)	24	12	240

In order to optimize profit, the company would like to know how many units of product A and product B should be produced each day. The following is the formulation of the problem model.

$$\text{Maximize } Z = \$160x + 200y$$

Subject to

$$2x + 4y \leq 40 \text{ hr of labor}$$
$$18x + 18y \leq 216 \text{ pounds of raw material}$$
$$24x + 12y \leq 240 \text{ ft}^2 \text{ of storage space}$$
$$x, y \geq 0$$

where

x = number of product A
y = number of product B

The primal form is represented by this model. The dual form of a primal maximization model is a minimization model. This example's dual form is:

$$\text{Minimize } Z = 40x_1 + 216x_2 + 240x_3$$

Subject to

$$2x_1 + 18x_2 + 24x_3 \geq 160$$
$$4x_1 + 18x_2 + 12x_3 \geq 200$$
$$x_1, x_2, x_3 \geq 0$$

The particular connections between the primal and the dual that this example illustrates are as follows.

1. The model constraints in the primal are corresponding to the dual variables, x_1, x_2, and x_3. There will be a variable in the dual for each constraint in the primal. For instance, the dual in this instance has three decision variables as the primal has three constraints.

2. The objective function coefficients in the dual are represented by the quantity values on the right side of the primal inequality constraints. The dual objective function, $Z = 40x_1 + 216x_2 + 240x_3$, is formed by the constraint quantity values in the primal, 40, 216, and 240.

3. Decision variable coefficients in the dual are the model constraint coefficients in the primal. Coefficients 2 and 4, for instance, are present in the fundamental constraint. In the dual model constraints, these numbers represent the x_1 variable coefficients; $2x_1$ and $4x_1$.

4. The dual model constraint requirements (quantity values on the right side of the constraint) are represented by the objective function coefficients in the primal, 160 and 200.
5. The minimization dual model features ≥ constraints in contrast to ≤ constraints in the maximization primal model.

The two model forms can be compared to observe the primal-dual relations are shown with similar font colors below.

Primal	Dual
Maximize $Z = \$160x + 200y$	Minimize $Z_d = 40x_1 + 216x_2 + 240x_3$
Subject to	Subject to
$2x + 4y \leq 40$	$2x_1 + 18x_2 + 24x_3 \geq 160$
$18x + 18y \leq 216$	$4x_1 + 18x_2 + 12x_3 \geq 200$
$24x + 12y \leq 240$	$x_1, x_2, x_3 \geq 0$
$x, y \geq 0$	

Determining the meaning of the dual comes next after developing the model's dual form. Put otherwise, what are the meanings of the decision variables x_1, x_2, and x_3, what are the constraints of the ≥ model, and what is being minimized in the dual objective function?

Interpreting the Dual Model

By looking at the simplex solution to the model's primal form, one can understand the dual model. Table 17.18 displays the primal model's simplex solution.
Understanding this primal solution, we have

$x = 4$ units of product A
$y = 8$ units of product B
$s_3 = 48$ ft^2 of storage space
$Z = \$2{,}240$ profit

Table 17.18 The Optimal Simplex Solution for the Primal Model

			160	200	0	0	0
c_j	Basic variables	Quantity	x	y	s_1	s_2	s_3
200	y	8	0	1	1/2	–1/18	0

160	x	4	1	0	–1/2	1/9	0
0	s_3	48	0	0	6	–2	1
	z_j	2,240	160	200	20	20/3	0
	$c_j - z_j$		0	0	–20	–20/3	0

Information about the dual is also contained in this optimal primal tableau. The negative values of –20 and –20/3 under the s_1 and s_2 columns in the $c_j - z_j$ row of Table 17.18 show that profit would decrease by $20 or $6.67 (i.e., 20/3), respectively, if one unit of either s_1 or s_2 were entered to the solution.

Remember that unused labor is represented by s_1, and unused raw material is represented by s_2. Since s_1 and s_2 are not basic variables in the current solution, they are both equal to zero. This indicates that there are no extra (slack) labor hours or raw materials remaining after all the material and labor are used to create products A and B. Consequently, adding s_1 or s_2 to the solution would cause s_1 or s_2 to no longer equal zero, reducing the need for labor or raw materials. For instance, if one unit of s_1 is added to the solution, one unit of previously employed labor is not used, and the profit is $20 less.

Let's assume that the answer contains one unit of s_1, meaning that we have one hour of labor that is not being used ($s_1 = 1$). To ensure that all labor is once more being employed, let's now eliminate this wasted hour of labor from the solution. As we previously saw, adding an hour of unused labor reduced profit by $20. Therefore, it is reasonable to assume that adding this hour back (and using it again) will improve profit by $20. This is like stating we could make $20 more profit if we could just acquire an extra hour of labor. As a result, we would be ready to pay up to $20 for an hour of labor if we could buy it, as it is the amount that would improve profit.

The marginal values of labor (s_1) and raw materials (s_2) are $20 and $6.67(20/3), respectively, in the negative $c_j - z_j$ row values. Since they represent the highest "price" one would be willing to pay to gain one additional unit of resource, these dual values are also frequently referred to as shadow prices.

And what about storage space, the third resource? Table 17.18 provides the answer. It's important to note that the value of the $c_j - z_j$ row for s_3, which denotes vacant storage space, is zero. Since we wouldn't pay anything for an additional foot of storage space, storage space has a marginal value of zero.

Because storage space was not a constraint on the creation of product A and product B, greater storage space has no marginal value. Table 17.18 demonstrates that following the production of 4 units of product A and 8 units of product B, 48 square feet of storage space were left unutilized (i.e., $s_3 = 48$). An additional square foot would not add value to the company's 48 square feet of remaining storage space, as the company is currently unable to utilize all of its existing storage space.

There's one more thing about these marginal values that we should think about. The greatest amount that would be paid for extra resources is known as the marginal value, or shadow price, as we have seen in our examination of the marginal value of these resources. The Precision Product Company would not necessarily pay \$60 for an hour of labor, which is the marginal value of the labor. This is contingent upon the definition of the objective function. We are presuming that the 40 hours of labor, 216 pounds of raw material, and 240 square feet of storage space that are available in this scenario have all previously been paid for. The business is still responsible for paying for the resources even if it does not use them completely. Those expenses are sunk. Stated differently, the coefficients of the objective function include the expenses of any additional resources that are secured. Therefore, the profit is independent of the resources utilized; that is, the profit values in the objective function for each product are unaffected by the actual amount of a resource used. Securing more resources would lower the marginal value if the cost of the resources is not taken into account by the profit function.

As we proceed with our study, we see that the primal model's profit was \$2,240. The resources required to create products A and B must be valued by the Precision Product Company in terms of this profit. Stated differently, the labor and raw material resources' worth is established by how much each contributes to the \$2,240 profit. As a result, the corporation was unable to place a value on the resources it employed that was higher than the profit those resources generated. Conversely, according to the same reasoning, the resources' entire worth must likewise equal or exceed the profit they generate. The profit made by the optimal solution must therefore precisely equal the value of all the resources.

Now let us look again at the dual form of the model.

$$\text{Minimize } Z_d = 40x_1 + 216x_2 + 240x_3$$

Subject to

$$\begin{gathered} 2x_1 + 18x_2 + 24x_3 \geq 160 \\ 4x_1 + 18x_2 + 12x_3 \geq 200 \\ x_1, x_2, x_3 \geq 0 \end{gathered}$$

Now that the value of the model resources has been discussed, we may define the dual decision variables, x_1, x_2, and x_3, to reflect the marginal values of the resources:

x_1 = marginal value of 1 hour of labor = \$20

x_2 = marginal value of 1 pound of raw material = \$6.67
x_3 = marginal value of 1 ft^2 of storage space = \$0

Use of the Dual

The decision maker finds value in the dual because of the information it offers regarding the model resources. Because they often have greater control over resource utilization than profit accumulation, managers are typically more concerned with resource use than profit. When determining whether to obtain more resources and how much to pay for them, the management can make informed decisions based on the worth of the resources, which is provided by the dual solution.

UNIT SUMMARY

- ***Introduction to Linear Programming*** (LP): (i) Defines LP as a method for optimizing a linear objective function subject to constraints (e.g., labor, materials, cost), and (ii) Common applications include production planning, transportation, scheduling, and investment decisions.
- ***Model Formulation***: (i) Introduces key components of LP models, including decision variables, objective functions, and constraints, and (ii) Demonstrates real-world problem formulation, such as maximizing profit or minimizing costs.
- ***Graphical Solution Method***: (i) Explains feasible regions, optimal points, and how to plot constraints and objective functions on a graph, and (ii) Covers special cases like multiple solutions, infeasibility, and unbounded problems.
- ***Simplex Method***: (i) A step-by-step approach to solving LP problems with more than two variables, and (ii) Introduces tableau representation and pivoting operations for iterative optimization.
- ***Dual Model and Its Interpretations***: (i) Defines primal vs. dual relationships and their significance in resource allocation, and (ii) Introduces shadow prices, which indicate the value of an additional unit of a constrained resource.
- ***Sensitivity Analysis***: (i) Examines how changes in constraints and objective function coefficients impact the optimal solution, and (ii) Includes slack variables and shadow pricing for effective decision-making.

EXERCISES

MULTIPLE CHOICE QUESTIONS

17.1 What is the primary goal of linear programming?

(a) Maximize costs
(b) Minimize resources
(c) Optimize a linear objective function subject to constraints
(d) Decrease waste

17.2 In a linear programming model, what is a constraint?

(a) A function to be optimized
(b) A limitation or requirement that must be satisfied
(c) A decision variable
(d) A method of solution

17.3 In a linear programming problem, the feasible region is defined by:

(a) The objective function only
(b) The constraints
(c) The decision variables
(d) The shadow prices

17.4 Which of the following is a characteristic of a linear programming model?

(a) Non-linear relationships among variables
(b) Integer constraints only
(c) Dynamic objectives
(d) Proportionality and additivity

17.5 Which method is commonly used for solving linear programming problems with two variables?

(a) Graphical method
(b) Monte Carlo simulation
(c) Heuristic method
(d) Mixed-integer programming

17.6 What is a "basic feasible solution" in the context of linear programming?

(a) A solution that violates one or more constraints
(b) A solution that is the same as the optimal solution
(c) A solution that satisfies all constraints with as few non-zero variables as possible
(d) A solution that cannot be improved

17.7 Which of the following statements about slack variables is true?

(a) They are used to convert equality constraints to inequalities
(b) They represent unused resources in a constraint
(c) They must always be positive
(d) Both B and C

17.8 What does the term "unbounded" mean in linear programming?

(a) The feasible region has no solution	(b) The objective function can increase indefinitely
(c) The problem is infeasible	(d) The solution is not optimal

17.9 In the Simplex method, what is meant by "pivoting"?

(a) Adjusting the objective function	(b) Calculating the shadow price
(c) Finding a feasible solution	(d) Selecting a new basic variable and adjusting the tableau

17.10 If the feasible region of a linear programming problem is empty, the problem is said to be:

(a) Bounded	(b) Unbounded
(c) Infeasible	(d) Degenerate

17.11 What does the term "shadow price" refer to in linear programming?

(a) The cost of an additional resource	(b) The maximum profit achievable
(c) The slope of the objective function	(d) The total cost of the constraints

17.12 In a maximization problem, if the optimal solution occurs at a vertex of the feasible region, this is known as:

(a) Degeneracy	(b) Corner solution
(c) Optimality condition	(d) Interior solution

17.13 When formulating a linear programming problem, which of the following is considered an objective function?

(a) Maximize profit	(b) Subject to labor hours
(c) $x + y \leq 10$	(d) Both A and B

17.14 In linear programming, what is the purpose of introducing artificial variables?

(a) To find the optimal solution	(b) To simplify constraints
(c) To replace decision variables	(d) To help find an initial basic feasible solution in the Simplex method

17.15 What does the term "objective function coefficient" refer to in a linear programming model?

(a) The limit set by constraints	(b) The total resources available
(c) The value that weighs the decision variable in the objective function	(d) The solution to the problem

17.16 If the primal problem has n variables and m constraints, how many variables and constraints does the dual problem have?

(a) m variables and n constraints	(b) n variables and m constraints
(c) Both n variables and n constraints	(d) Both m variables and m constraints

Answers of Multiple Choice Questions

17.1 (c), 17.2 (b), 17.3 (b), 17.4 (d), 17.5 (a), 17.6 (c), 17.7 (d), 17.8 (b), 17.9 (d), 17.10 (c), 17.11 (a), 17.12 (b), 17.13 (a), 17.14 (d), 17.15 (c), 17.16 (a)

SHORT AND LONG ANSWER TYPE QUESTIONS

Category I

17.1 What is the objective function in linear programming?

17.2 What are the components of a linear programming model?

17.3 What are decision variables?

17.4 What is a constraint in linear programming?

17.5 What is the feasible region in linear programming?

17.6 What is meant by "optimal solution"?

17.7 What is the graphical method in linear programming?

17.8 What is the Simplex method?

17.9 What is duality in linear programming?

17.10 What is sensitivity analysis in linear programming?

17.11 What is a shadow price?

17.12 What types of problems can be solved using linear programming?

Category II

Formulation of Linear Programming Problem

17.13 A car manufacturer produces sedans, SUVs, and trucks. Each sedan requires 2 hours of labor and 3 units of materials, each SUV requires 4 hours of labor and 5 units of materials, and each truck requires 3 hours of labor and 4 units of materials. The total available labor is 100 hours and materials are limited to 120 units. The profit for each sedan is \$5, for each SUV is \$8, and for each truck is \$6. Formulate the linear programming model to maximize profit.

17.14 A meal service has three food items: chicken (cost \$3, 300 calories, 25g protein), rice (cost \$1, 200 calories, 5g protein), and vegetables (cost \$2, 100 calories, 2g protein). The target is to create a meal plan of at least 800 calories and 40g of protein. Formulate the linear programming model to minimize costs.

17.15 A factory produces two types of products, P1 and P2. Each P1 requires 1 hour of machine time and 2 units of material, while each P2 requires 2 hours of machine time and 1 unit of material. The factory has a maximum of 40 hours of machine time and 30 units of material. The profit for each product P1 is \$10 and for P2 is \$15. Formulate the linear programming model to maximize profit.

17.16 A construction firm has three projects that require labor and materials: Project A (5 labor hours, 10 units), Project B (8 labor hours, 4 units), and Project C (4 labor hours, 8 units). The firm has a total of 40 labor hours and 30 material units available. The profits for projects A, B, and C are \$200, \$300, and \$150, respectively. Formulate a linear programming model to maximize profit.

17.17 Explain the concept of duality in Linear programming by an example. What are the implications of the three duality theorems?

NUMERICAL PROBLEMS

17.18 Solve the following problem graphically

$$Maximize\ Z = 3x + y$$

Subject to

$$12x + 14y \leq 84$$
$$3x + 2y \leq 18$$
$$y \leq 4$$
$$x, y \geq 0$$

17.19 Solve the following problem using the graphical method of linear programming.

$$Minimize\ Z = 2x + 4y$$

Subject to

$$4x + 6y \geq 120$$
$$2x + 6y \geq 72$$
$$y \geq 10$$

$$x, y \geq 0$$

17.20 Solve the following problem graphically

$$Minimize\ Z = 12x + 9y$$

Subject to

$$x \leq 10$$
$$3 \leq y \leq 8$$
$$2.5x + y \geq 10$$
$$4x + 3y \geq 18$$
$$x, y \geq 0$$

17.21 An animal feed company must produce 200 kgs of a mixture consisting of ingredients X_1 and X_2 daily. X_1 costs \$3 per kg and X_2 costs \$8 per kg. No more than 80 kgs of X_1 can be used, and atleast 60 kgs of X_2 must be used. Find how much of each ingredient should be used if the company wants to minimize cost.

17.22 An unprofitable product line has been phased out of production by a manufacturer. As a result, a sizable excess of production capacity was generated. The management is thinking about using this extra capacity for one or more of the following three products: X, Y, and Z. The necessary machine hours per unit are:

	Product		
Machine type	X	Y	Z
Milling machine	8	2	3
Lathe	4	3	0
Griinder	2	0	1

The weekly machine hours available are 800, 480, and 320 for milling machine, lathes, and grinding machines, respectively. The salespeople project that they will be able to sell every unit of X and Y that is produced. However, Z can only sell a maximum of 80 units per week. The unit profits for X, Y, and Z are \$20, \$6, and \$8, respectively.

(a) Create the equations that can be solved in order to increase weekly profit.
(b) Use the simplex method to solve these equations.
(c) What is the optimal solution? What should the profit margin be after producing each product, and how many each product should be produced?

(d) What is the current state of affairs concerning the machine groups? Would they be operating at full capacity or would some time be left over? Will Z be selling as much as possible?

17.23 Solve the following linear programming problem by simplex method.

$$Maximize\ Z = 5x_1 + 2x_2 + 10x_3$$

Subject to

$$x_1 - x_3 \leq 10$$
$$x_2 - x_3 \geq 10$$
$$x_1 + x_2 + x_3 \leq 10$$
$$x_1, x_2, x_3 \geq 0$$

17.24 A bicycle manufacturer makes two models – a sports cycle and a racer. In order to make a sports model, 6 man-hours are needed, while a racing model requires 10 man-hours. The manufacturer can employ no more than 15 men and these men work 8 hours per day for 6 days each week. The cost of materials amounts to $50 per cycle and the manufacturer's weekly quota of such materials may not exceed $4000. The firm has a contract to supply at least 30 sports models and 20 racer models per week. How many cycles of each type should be made in order to obtain the maximum possible profit, if the profit on each sports cycle is $10 and on each racing cycle model is $30?

17.25 Obtain the dual of:

$$Maximize\ Z = 5x_1 + 3x_2$$

Subject to

$$x_1 + x_2 \leq 2$$
$$5x_1 + 2x_2 \leq 10$$
$$3x_1 + 8x_2 \leq 12$$
$$x_1, x_2 \geq 0$$

REFERENCES AND SUGGESTED READINGS

1. Dantzig, G. B. Linear Programming and Extensions. Princeton University Press, 1951.
2. Dantzig, G. B. Linear Programming Models and Their Formulation. *Mathematical Programming Studies*, Vol. 40(3), 213-223, 2008.

3. Gass, S. I. The Simplex Algorithm: A History. *Mathematical Programming*, Vol. 106(1), 257-274, 2006.
4. Goldstein, R. L., and Williams, C. A. Applications of Linear Programming in Supply Chain Management. *International Journal of Operations and Production Management*, Vol. 27(3), 256-268, 2007.
5. Hillier, F. S., and Lieberman, G. J. *Introduction to Operations Research*, 10th Edition, McGraw-Hill, 2015.
6. Ravindran, A. *Operations Research: Principles and Practice*, 2nd Edition, Wiley, 2017.
7. Roussy, R., and Krejci, S. Graphical Solutions for Linear Programming with Multiple Solutions. *Journal of Applied Operations Research*, Vol. 5(3), 43-54, 2011.
8. Taha, H. A. *Operations Research: An Introduction*, 10th Edition, Pearson, 2017.
9. Taylor, A., and Lee, S. Graphical Methods for Solving Linear Programming Problems. *European Journal of Operational Research*, Vol. 224(1), 24-32, 2012.
10. Turing, A. A Method for Solving Linear Programming Problems. *Computational Mathematics Journal*, Vol. 40(2), 55-68, 1952.
11. Valliant, R. *Linear Programming and Network Flows*. Wiley, 2005.
12. Vázquez, D. F., and De Oliveira, M. S. The Application of Linear Programming in Real Life Decision Making. *Journal of Industrial Engineering and Management*, Vol. 7(1), 221-235, 2014.
13. Vohra, N. *Quantitative Techniques in Management*, 5th Edition, Tata McGraw-Hill, 2017.
14. Williams, H. P. Duality Theory and Its Applications in Linear Programming. *Journal of Operations Research*, Vol. 45(2), 44-60, 2012.
15. Williams, H. P. *Model Building in Mathematical Programming*, 5th Edition, Wiley, 2013.
16. Winston, W. L. *Operations Research: Applications and Algorithms*, 4th Edition, Thomson Brooks/Cole, 2004.

UNIT 18

TRANSPORTATION AND ASSIGNMENT PROBLEMS

UNIT SPECIFICS

This unit elaborately discusses the following topics:

- The Transportation model and its solution
- Northwest corner method
- Minimum cell cost method
- Vogel's approximation method
- Stepping stone optimization method
- Modified distribution (MODI) optimization method
- Unbalanced and Degeneracy problems
- The Assignment model
- Traveling salesman problem

The topics' practical applications are examined in order to promote greater creativity and curiosity as well as enhance problem-solving skills. The unit contains a list of references, suggested readings, and assignments through a variety of numerical problems in addition to a number of multiple-choice questions and questions with short and long-answer types divided into two groups according to lower and higher order of Bloom's taxonomy. Using QR codes, which may be scanned to yield pertinent additional information, is a notable aspect of some of the interesting topics.

RATIONALE

This unit delves into the intricacies of transportation and assignment problems, highlighting various methods to optimize resource allocation efficiently. It begins with an exploration of the Transportation Model and its solutions, emphasizing practical techniques such as the Northwest Corner Method, Minimum Cell Cost Method, and Vogel's Approximation Method for initial feasible solutions. The unit further examines optimization strategies, including the Stepping Stone and Modified Distribution (MODI) methods (using QR codes), which enhance the efficiency of transportation networks. Additionally, it addresses complexities such as unbalanced and degeneracy issues that can arise in these models. The Assignment Model is also discussed, showcasing its application in resource allocation scenarios, while the Traveling Salesman Problem is introduced to illustrate the challenges of route optimization in logistics. Collectively, these topics provide a comprehensive framework for understanding and solving critical problems in operations research.

UNIT OUTCOMES

List of outcomes of this unit is as follows:

U18-UO1: Understanding Transportation Models

U18-UO2: Applying Solution Methods

U18-UO3: Optimizing Transportation Solutions

U18-UO4: Identifying and Addressing Complexities

U18-UO5: Implementing the Assignment Model

U18-UO6: Analyzing the Traveling Salesman Problem

UNIT-18 Outcomes	EXPECTED MAPPING WITH COURSE OUTCOMES (1-Weak Correlation; 2-Medium Correlation; 3-Strong Correlation)					
	CO-1	CO-2	CO-3	CO-4	CO-5	CO-6
U18-UO1	2	2	2	2	2	3
U18-UO2	2	3	2	2	2	3
U18-UO3	2	2	3	2	2	3
U18-UO4	1	1	2	2	1	3
U18-UO5	2	2	2	2	1	3
U18-UO6	1	1	2	1	2	3

18.1 INTRODUCTION

This unit will look at two specific kinds of linear programming problems, namely transportation problems and assignment problems that can be resolved using techniques other than the simplex method. The simplex approach could be used to solve either of these issue types, but it would require a lot of simplex iterations and very big simplex tableaus. Nevertheless, because every problem is different, there are other approaches to solving it that require a lot less mathematical work than the simplex method. In this unit, these solutions will be explained and shown.

18.2 THE TRANSPORTATION MODEL

The transportation model is designed for a class of problems that have the following special features: (i) a product is transported at the lowest feasible cost from a number of sources to a number of destinations; (ii) each source can supply a fixed number of units of the product, and each destination has a fixed demand for the product. While there are many different applications for the general transportation model, the problem gets its name from its most well-known use in the delivery of products.

The way the transportation model is formulated will be shown in the example below. In warehouses located in several cities, including New York, Washington, and Florida, Precision Product Company kept its semi-finished products. San Francisco, Las Vegas, and New Jersey are the three assembly plants that receive the products. Railroad containers are utilized for the shipment of semi-finished products. Semi-finished goods are supplied to the assembly plants in the following quantities measured in tons:

Warehouses	Supply
1. New York	150
2. Washington	175
3. Florida	275
Total	600 tons

The following is the monthly requirement for tons of semi-finished products for each plant.

Plants	Demand
1. San Francisco	200
2. Las Vegas	100
3. New Jersey	300
Total	600 tons

Depending on the distance and rail system, the cost of moving one ton of merchandise from each warehouse (the source) to each facility (the destination) varies. These expenses are displayed in the table that follows. For instance, it costs $7 to ship one ton of goods from the Washington warehouse to the San Francisco plant.

	Plants		
Warehouse	**A. San Francisco**	**B. Las Vegas**	**C. New Jersey**
1. New York	$6	8	10
2. Washington	7	11	11
3. Florida	4	5	12

In order to reduce the overall cost of transportation, the problem is figuring out how many tons of products to move each month from each warehouse to each plant.

The linear programming model for this problem is formulated in the equations that follow.

$$\text{Minimize } Z = \$6x_{1A} + 8x_{1B} + 10x_{1C} + 7x_{2A} + 11x_{2B} + 11x_{2C} + 4x_{3A} + 5x_{3B} + 12x_{3C}$$

subject to

$$\begin{aligned} x_{1A} + x_{1B} + x_{1C} &= 150 \\ x_{2A} + x_{2B} + x_{2C} &= 175 \\ x_{3A} + x_{3B} + x_{3C} &= 275 \\ x_{1A} + x_{2A} + x_{3A} &= 200 \\ x_{1B} + x_{2B} + x_{3B} &= 100 \\ x_{1C} + x_{2C} + x_{3C} &= 300 \end{aligned}$$

The amount of tons of goods delivered from each warehouse, i (where i = 1, 2, 3), to each factory, j (where j = A, B, C), is represented by the decision variables, x_{ij}, in this model. The overall cost of transportation for any route is represented by the objective function. The cost of the tonnage transported for a single route is reflected in each term of the objective function. In the event that 20 tons are carried, for instance, from warehouse 1 to plant A, the $6 cost is multiplied by x_{1A} (= 20), resulting in $120.

The supply at each warehouse is represented by the first three constraints in the linear programming model, while the demand at each plant is represented by the final three constraints. Take the first supply limitation, $x_{1A} + x_{1B} + x_{1C} = 150$, as an illustration. The tons of goods shipped from New York to the three plants – San Francisco (x_{1A}), Las Vegas (x_{1B}), and New Jersey (x_{1C}) – are represented by this limitation. The 150 tons that can be moved from New York is the maximum quantity that can be done. To meet the 600 tons of total demand, all of the product tons available will be required, therefore note that this restriction (along with all others) is an equation (=) rather than a ≤ inequality. In other words, the combined requirement of the three plants is 600 tons, which is precisely what the three warehouses can provide. Thus, in order to meet demand, all that may be supplied will be. We call this kind of model – where supply and demand are exactly equal – a *balanced transportation* model. We'll utilize the balanced model to show how to solve a transportation problem.

18.2.1 SOLUTION OF THE TRANSPORTATION MODEL

Although these models can also be solved using an Excel sheet, we limited our manual solution of the transportation model to the context of a tableau. Table 18.1 displays the tableau for our section 18.2 problem.

Table 18.1 The transportation Tableau

From \ To	A	B	C	Supply
1	6	8	10	150
2	7	11	11	175
3	4	5	12	275
Demand	200	100	300	600

In the tableau, the quantity transferred from one source to one destination is shown in each cell. As a result, the value of a choice variable for each cell is represented by the amount entered there. For instance, the decision variable x_{1A} is represented by the cell at the intersection of row 1 and column A. Each cell's smaller box holds the unit transportation cost for that particular route. For instance, the value of $6 in celll 1A represents the cost of shipping one ton of goods from New York to San Francisco. The supply and demand constraint quantity values, also known as boundary requirements, are located along the outside boundary of the tableau.

The stepping-stone method and the modified distribution method, or MODI, are the two approaches used to solve a transportation model. Remember that the first simplex tableau required the establishment of an initial solution before the simplex method could be applied. While solving a transportation model, the same requirement needs to be fulfilled. But take note that Table 18.1 does not contain artificial variables – the starting solution variables for a problem with = constraints. Because of this, the initial solution in a transportation model is not at the origin, where the artificial variables would assume all possible quantity values. Several other methods, such as Vogel's Approximation Method, the Northwest Corner Method, and the Minimum Cell Cost Method, can be used to find an initial feasible solution in a transportation model.

THE NORTHWEST CORNER METHOD

The cell in the upper left-hand corner of the tableau – also referred to as the "northwest corner" – is initially allocated using the northwest (NW) corner method. The amount allotted is the maximum that can be given the limits of supply and demand for that particular cell. In our case, we start by giving cell 1A (the northwest corner) as much as we can. This is 150 tons since that is the most that warehouse 1 in New York can provide, even if plant A in San Francisco is demanding 200 tons. Table 18.2 displays this initial allocation.

Table 18.2 The initial NW Corner Solution

From \ To	A	B	C	Supply
1	[6] 150	[8]	[10]	150
2	[7] 50	[11] 100	[11] 25	175
3	[4]	[5]	[12] 275	275
Demand	200	100	300	600

Next, we distribute to a cell that is next to cell 1A, in our example, either cell 2A or cell 1B. Cell 1B, however, is no longer a viable allocation because the 150 tons of product available at source 1 have already been allotted in full. Cell 2A is therefore the sole practical option, and it receives the greatest amount of attention. The quantity allotted at 2A may be either 50 tons, which is the current amount required at destination A, or 175 tons, which is the supply available from source 2 (Washington). Remember that 150 tons of the 200 tons required at point A have already been provided. Table 18.2 shows that 50 tons, the most constrained amount, is assigned to cell 2A.

The second allocation and the third allocation are made in the same manner. Cell 2B is the only viable cell that is next to cell 2A. The maximum quantity that can be allotted is either 125 tons (175 tons less the 50 tons allotted to cell 2A) or 100 tons, which is the quantity, required at plant B. Table 18.2 displays that cell 2B has been assigned 100 tons, which is the smaller (most constrained) amount.

Table 18.2 displays the fourth allocation, which is 25 tons to cell 2C, and the fifth allocation, which is 275 tons to cell 3C. You'll see that the total row and column allotment meets the necessary boundary requirements.

The transportation cost of this solution is computed by substituting the cell allocation (i.e., the amounts transported),

$x_{1A} = 150$

$x_{2A} = 50$

$x_{2B} = 100$

$x_{2C} = 25$

$x_{3C} = 275$

into the objective function

$$Z = \$6x_{1A} + 8x_{1B} + 10x_{1C} + 7x_{2A} + 11x_{2B} + 11x_{2C} + 4x_{3A} + 5x_{3B} + 12x_{3C}$$

$$= 6(150) + 8(0) + 10(0) + 7(50) + 11(100) + 11(25) + 4(0) + 5(0) + 12(275)$$

$$= \$5{,}925$$

This is a summary of the northwest corner method's steps.

1. Give the cell in the upper left corner as much as you can, keeping in mind the constraints on supply and demand.
2. Give as much as you can to the next feasible cell that is adjacent.
3. Until all boundary requirements are satisfied, repeat step 2 again.

THE MINIMUM CELL COST METHOD

Allocating to the cells with the lowest costs is the fundamental rationale behind the minimum cell cost approach. The tableau cell with the lowest cost receives the first allocation. Cell 3A in our example problem's transportation tableau has a minimum cost of $4. This cell receives the maximum allocation; 200 tons or 275 tons are the options. Since only 200 tons are required, we can only allot a maximum of 200 tons, even if 275 tons might be delivered to cell 3A. This distribution is displayed in Table 18.3.

Table 18.3 The initial Minimum Cell Cost Allocation

From \ To	A	B	C	Supply
1	6	8	10	150
2	7	11	11	175
3	4 200	5	12	275
Demand	200	100	300	600

As you can see, source 3, Florida, is now the source of the entire product that was demanded at destination A, San Francisco, and has eliminated all of the remaining cells in column A. The cell that is both feasible and has the lowest cost receives the next allocation. This is cell 3B, which is $5 in cost. (275 tons less the 200 tons previously delivered) is the maximum that can be allotted. Table 18.4 displays this allocation. At a minimum cost of $8, the third allocation is given to cell 1B.

Table 18.4 The Second Minimum Cell Cost Allocation

From \ To	A	B	C	Supply
1	6	8	10	150
2	7	11	11	175
3	4 200	5 75	12	275
Demand	200	100	300	600

It should be noted that cells with lesser prices, like 1A and 2A, are not taken into account because they were previously determined to be infeasible. A total of 25 tons are allotted. Cell 1C receives the fourth allotment, totaling 125 tons, while cell 2C receives the last allocation, totaling 175. Table 18.5, which presents these allocations, completes the initial minimum cell cost solution.

Table 18.5 The Initial Solution

From \ To	A	B	C	Supply
1	6	8 25	10 125	150
2	7	11	11 175	175
3	4 200	5 75	12	275
Demand	200	100	300	600

The initial northwest corner solution cost $5,925 in total, but this initial solution only costs $4,550. The logical outcome of employing the minimum cell cost method is to get a reduced overall cost; this is not an accident. The minimum cell cost approach takes cost into account while allocating resources; the northwest corner method does not. Thus, it makes sense that the latter approach will result in a cheaper initial cost. Because it is closer to the optimal solution due to its lower cost, the initial solution obtained by the least cell cost technique is typically preferable; less iteration will be needed to reach the optimal solution.

Below is a summary of the particular procedures involved in the minimum cell cost method.

1. Modify the boundary criteria and allocate as much as possible to the feasible cell with the lowest transportation cost.
2. Continue from step 1 until all boundary conditions are satisfied.

VOGEL'S APPROXIMATION METHOD

Vogel's Approximation Method (VAM) is the third approach to finding an initial answer; it is predicated on the idea of regret or penalty cost. A wrong selection may result in a penalty (and the decision maker may come to regret the choice they made) if there are multiple options to consider. Allocating to a cell that does not contain the lowest cost is a bad decision when it comes to a transportation challenge; the other routes are the courses of action.

To commence using the VAM approach, a penalty cost needs to be created for every source and destination. Take column A in Table 18.6, for instance. Washington, Florida, and New York can supply San Francisco, the first destination. Given that cell 3A has a minimum cost of $4, it would be better to feed San Francisco from source 3. A $2 per ton penalty would be incurred if the next higher cost of $6 were chosen at cell 1A due to a incorrect decision (i.e., $6 – 4 = $2). This shows how the penalty cost is calculated for every tableau row and column. In order to calculate a penalty cost, one generally deducts the lowest cell cost from the subsequent higher cell cost in each row and column. In Table 18.6, the penalty costs for our scenario are displayed at the bottom and on the right.

Table 18.6 The VAM Penalty Costs

From \ To	A	B	C	Supply	
1	**6**	**8** 25	**10** 125	150	2
2	**7**	**11**	**11** 175	175	4
3	**4** 200	**5** 75	**12**	275	1
Demand	200	100	300	600	
	2	3	1		

In the VAM approach, the row or column with the largest penalty cost receives the first allocation. At $4, row 2 in Table 18.6 has the highest penalty cost. We distribute as much as we can to the row's feasible cell that has the lowest cost. Cell 2A in row 2 has the lowest cost of $7 and the maximum amount that may be assigned to it is 175 tons. Since the optimum course of action has been chosen, this allocation has avoided the largest penalty cost of $4. The distribution is displayed in Table 18.7.

Table 18.7 The Initial VAM Allocation

From \ To	A	B	C	Supply	
1	6	8	10	150	2
2	7 175	11	11	175	
3	4	5	12	275	1
Demand	200	100	300	600	
	2	3	2		

All penalty costs need to be recalculated after the initial allocation is completed. The penalty costs may vary in certain situations while being unchanged in others. For example, the penalty cost in row 2 was deleted completely (since no more allocations are feasible for that row) and the penalty cost for column C in Table 18.7 changed from $1 to $2 (because cell 2C is no longer considered in determining penalty cost).

Table 18.8 The Second VAM Allocation

From \ To	A	B	C	Supply	
1	6	8	10	150	4
2	7 175	11	11	175	
3	4	5 100	12	275	8
Demand	200	100	300	600	
	2		2		

We next go back to the previous step and assign to the row or column that has the largest penalty cost (see Table 18.7), in this case, column B, with a penalty cost of $3. We allot 100 tons, the maximum amount, to cell 3B, which has the lowest cost among the cells in column B. Table 18.8 displays this allocation.

Take note that Table 18.8 now shows the updated total of all penalty fees. We allot 25 tons to cell 3A because it has a minimum cost of $4 and row 3 now has the highest penalty cost of $8, as Table 18.9 illustrates.

Table 18.9 The Third VAM Allocation

From \ To	A	B	C	Supply
1	6	8	10	150
2	7 175	11	11	175
3	4 25	5 100	12	275
Demand	200	100	300	600
			2	

The recalculated penalty costs following the third allocation are also displayed in Table 18.9. Currently, the only column with a penalty cost is column C. As there is just one viable cell in rows 1 and 3, there is no penalty for these rows. Column C receives the final two allocations as a result. Since cell 1C has the lowest cell cost, 150 tons are allotted to it first. Only cell 3C remains a viable option, hence 150 tons are allotted to this cell. Table 18.10 displays the allocations for both of them.

Compared to the initial solution from the northwest corner, which cost $5,925, this initial VAM solution is less expensive at $5,125 total. Furthermore, it is not as low as the $4,550 minimum cell cost option. VAM usually yields a lower initial solution cost than the northwest corner approach, similar to the minimum cell cost method.

The following list provides a summary of the VAM steps.

1. Take the lowest cell cost in a row or column and subtract it from the next lowest cell cost in the same row or column to find the penalty cost for each row and column.
2. Decide which row or column has the highest penalty cost (either by picking the cell with the lowest cost or by randomly breaking ties).

3. In the row or column with the highest penalty cost, assign as much as you can to the viable cell with the lowest transportation cost.
4. Continue with steps 1, 2, and 3 until all boundary conditions are satisfied.

Table 18.10 The Initial VAM Solution

From \ To	A	B	C	Supply
1	6	8	10 150	150
2	7 175	11	11	175
3	4 25	5 100	12 150	275
Demand	200	100	300	600
			2	

After identifying an initial basic feasible solution using any of the three previously mentioned methods, the next step is to solve the model to find the optimal solution, which is the lowest possible total cost. The *modified distribution* (MODI) and the *stepping-stone* solution method are the two fundamental approaches to solving problems. Scan the provided QR code to learn more about the two approaches.

SCAN ME for Stepping-stone solution and MODI method

We have discussed the transportation problems so far under the assumption that the total destination requirement equals the total source capacity. In actual practice, the manufacturing company has more orders that it can fulfill or its available inventory exceeds the demand. Such type of transportation problems is called unbalanced transportation problems. To find out more about how to handle issues with unbalanced transportation problems, scan the QR code that is provided.

SCAN ME for Unbalanced Transportation Problem

In above discussion we established that an initial basic feasible solution from an '*m*' source to '*n*' destination transportation problem consists of at most *m*+*n*-1 positive (non-zero) basic variables (occupied cells). If a feasible solution occurs with less than $m+n-1$ occupied cells, the transportation problem is said to be *degenerate*. To study how to handle issues with degeneracy in transportation problems, scan the QR code that is provided.

SCAN ME
for
Degeneracy case
in
Transportation
Problem

18.3 THE ASSIGNMENT MODEL

To determine which task to assign to a person or which job to allocate to a machine, a particular linear programming solution approach called the Assignment method is used. Based on a table including tasks and resources, the process generates an opportunity cost matrix and determines the optimal assignment by weighing the trade-offs between possibilities. A single task can be allocated to every employee or device using this method. Below is an outline of how to approach a minimization problem:

1. To do row reductions, take each row's minimum value and subtract it from all other row values.
2. To perform column reductions, take each column's minimum value and subtract it from all other column values.
3. An opportunity cost matrix is the table that results from this. In the matrix, cross out every zero by using the fewest possible horizontal or vertical lines.
4. The optimal solution has been found and the zeros can be assigned where they occur if the number of lines in the matrix equals the number of rows. In the event that this is not the case, adjust the matrix by deducting the least uncrossed value from each and every other uncrossed value, then adding this amount to each cell in which two lines meet. The other values in the matrix don't change at all.
5. Continue steps 3 and 4 until the optimal solution is found.

Hands-on solutions are typically used for smaller assignment issues, like Example 18.1. Excel Solver and other softwares such as LINDO/LINGO, CPLEX, etc. can be used to answer larger problems. Profit maximization and customer satisfaction are two other possible assignment problems. Any element in the first matrix should be deducted from the greatest matrix value when addressing maximizing problems by hand. This should be done before moving on to a minimization issue.

Example 18.1

AccuPrec Company has four projects to finish and four engineers with different levels of industrial machine erection experience. The processing times (in hours) that each engineer estimates will take for each project is displayed below. An hour of erection time costs $100 on average. Assign every engineer to a project in order to minimize cost.

Initial Matrix	Project 1	Project 2	Project 3	Project 4
Sam	10	5	6	10
Tom	6	2	4	6
David	7	6	5	6
John	9	5	4	10

Solution

1. Row reduction – Sort each row's assignments into the best one. Each row's smallest value is subtracted from all other row values. The opportunity cost of sending an engineer to work on that project is the resulting number. Project 2, for instance, would be Sam's ideal assignment. Its value in the ensuing matrix is therefore zero. That would take an additional (10 – 5) = 5 hours for Sam to finish projects 1 or 4, and an additional hour for project 3.

Row Reduction	Project 1	Project 2	Project 3	Project 4
Sam	5	0	1	5
Tom	4	0	2	4
David	2	1	0	1
John	5	1	0	6

2. Column reduction – In each column, identify the optimal assignment. Take the least number in each column and subtract it from all the other values in the column. With David as the project engineer, for instance, project 1 can be finished the quickest and has zero opportunity cost. Sam's assignment to project 1 has an opportunity cost of three since it would take three more hours of processing.

Column Reduction	Project 1	Project 2	Project 3	Project 4
Sam	3	0	1	4
Tom	2	0	2	3
David	0	1	0	0
John	3	1	0	5

3. Search for distinctive assignments – Cover all zeros in the matrix as you examine it. Keep in mind that each individual can only be allocated to one project, and there can only be one leader for each project. When project

2 works best for Sam and Tom while project 3 works best for David and John, there is a dilemma. The rows or columns in the following matrix that have optimal asignments are highlighted in red. "Covering all zeros" is the term for this. The matrix must be modified if there are fewer highlighted lines than there are assignments to complete (four in this example).

Initial Assignment	Project 1	Project 2	Project 3	Project 4
Sam	3	0	1	4
Tom	2	0	2	3
David	0	1	0	0
John	3	1	0	5

4. Adjust the marix – For each entry that is not highlighted, find its lowest value. To the entries where the lines intersect, add that value and subtract it from all other non-highlighted entries. At the intersection points (i.e., David's project 2 and project 3 values), we have subtracted 2 (the least non-highlighted entry) from the other non-highlighted entries as shown below.

Adjusted Matrix	Project 1	Project 2	Project 3	Project 4
Sam	1	0	1	2
Tom	0	0	2	1
David	0	3	2	0
John	1	1	0	3

5. Search for distinctive assignments – Repeat Step 3 of covering all zeros and check if number of highlighted lines are equal to the number of required assignments. We observe that there are four highlighted lines which are equal to the required assignments. Thus, we obtained the optimal solution of assignments. Sam is assigned to project 2. Tom can be assigned to project 1 since project 2 is already assigned to Sam. Similarly, David is assigned to project 4 and project 3 is assigned to John.

Optimal Matrix	Project 1	Project 2	Project 3	Project 4
Sam	1	0	1	2
Tom	0	0	2	1
David	0	3	2	0
John	1	1	0	3

6. **Compute performance** – To determine how long it will take the allocated engineer to complete each project, see the original assignment matrix. The project will cost $(5+6+6+4) \times \$100 = \$2100$ to accomplish at an hourly rate of $100. The project assignments to each engineeer are highlighted as shown below.

Final Matrix	Project 1	Project 2	Project 3	Project 4
Sam	1	0	1	2
Tom	0	0	2	1
David	0	3	2	0
John	1	1	0	3

The reader may scan the provided QR code to examine the maximization case in the assignment problem.

SCAN ME
for
Maximization case in Assignment problem

The solution procedure discussed in Example 18.1 requires that the number of rows in the matrix equal the number of columns. Quite often, however, the number of objects or persons to be assigned does not equal the number of jobs or clients or machines listed in the columns. When this is the case and we have more rows than columns, we simply add a *dummy colum*. If the number of jobs exceeds the number of persons available, we add a *dummy row*.

SCAN ME
for
Unbalanced Assignment Problem

Creating a dummy row or column will give us a matrix of equal dimensions and allow us to solve the problem as before. Since the dummy job or person does not exist, it is reasonable to enter zeros in its row or column as the cost or time estimates. Such a case is considered as an unbalanced assignment problem. The reader may scan the provided QR code to examine the unbalanced case in the assignment problem.

The **Traveling Salesman Problem** (TSP) could be a special case of assignment problem and is fundamentally about finding the shortest possible route that visits a set of cities and returns to the starting point. In contrast, the Assignment Problem (AP) focuses on assigning tasks to agents in a way that minimizes the total cost. Although they address different scenarios, TSP can be viewed through the lens of the assignment problem, especially when formulated in specific contexts. The reader may scan the provided QR code to examine the traveling salesman problem as a special case of assignment problem.

SCAN ME
for
Traveling Salesman Problem

UNIT SUMMARY

- ***The Transportation Model***: (i) Used to minimize the cost of transporting goods from multiple sources to multiple destinations, and (ii) Requires balancing supply and demand constraints for an optimal solution.
- ***Solution Methods for Transportation Problems***: (i) Northwest Corner Method – A simple but inefficient approach for an initial feasible solution, (ii) Minimum Cell Cost Method – Allocates based on the lowest transportation costs, (iii) Vogel's Approximation Method (VAM) – Uses penalty cost logic to improve the initial allocation, (iv) Stepping Stone & Modified Distribution (MODI) Methods – Advanced techniques for optimization, and (v) Handling Unbalanced & Degeneracy Problems – Adjustments for cases where supply is not equal to demand.
- ***The Assignment Model***: (i) Used for optimally assigning tasks to workers or machines while minimizing costs, and (ii) Solved using the Hungarian Method which reduces an opportunity cost matrix iteratively.
- ***The Traveling Salesman Problem*** (TSP): (i) A special case of the Assignment Problem, where a salesman must visit multiple locations with minimal travel distance, and (ii) Involves route optimization techniques.

EXERCISES

MULTIPLE CHOICE QUESTIONS

18.1 In a transportation problem, what do the supply and demand constraints represent?

(a) The cost of transportation	(b) The maximum capacity and required amounts at destinations
(c) The time taken for transportation	(d) The types of goods transported

18.2 Which method is commonly used to find an initial feasible solution for the transportation problem?

(a) Least-Cost method	(b) Simplex method
(c) Branch and Bound method	(d) Dynamic Programming

18.3 In a balanced transportation problem, what must be true?

(a) Total supply equals total demand	(b) Total supply is greater than total demand
(c) Total demand is greater than total supply	(d) All costs are equal

18.4 If a transportation tableau has more supply than demand, how is it typically adjusted?

(a) Reduce supply	(b) Add a dummy column
(c) Increase costs	(d) Ignore excess supply

18.5 What does a "dummy" source or destination represent in a transportation problem?

(a) A location with no supply or demand	(b) An alternative transportation route
(c) A way to balance supply and demand	(d) A non-existent cost

18.6 The stepping-stone method is used for what purpose in the transportation problem?

(a) To compute costs	(b) To find the initial feasible solution
(c) To balance the tableau	(d) To check for optimality

18.7 In the context of a transportation problem, what does "feasibility" refer to?

(a) Reducing costs to zero	(b) The possibility of achieving maximum profit
(c) Simplifying calculations	(d) Meeting supply and demand constraints

18.8 When using the MODI method, what is the significance of the 'u' and 'v' variables?

(a) They represent supply and demand constraints	(b) They help in determining the opportunity cost
(c) They indicate the total transportation costs	(d) They are decision variables for shipping quantities

18.9 In the context of transportation problems, what does "degeneracy" mean?

(a) There are multiple optimal solutions	(b) The total cost cannot be minimized
(c) Fewer routes are used than available	(d) All routes are fully utilized

18.10 When calculating opportunity costs in the MODI method, what does a positive opportunity cost imply?

(a) The corresponding route should be included in the solution	(b) The corresponding route should not be used
(c) The solution is optimal	(d) There is excess supply at that node

18.11 In the context of Vogel's Approximation Method, if two routes have the same penalty value, which criterion is typically used to make an allocation decision?

(a) Choose the route with the higher transportation cost.	(b) Allocate to the route that has the higher remaining supply.
(c) Randomly select between the routes	(d) Choose the route with the lower cost

18.12 Which method is commonly used to find an optimal solution for the assignment problem?

(a) Hungarian method	(b) Simplex method
(c) Branch and bound	(d) Transportation method

18.13 Which of the following is NOT a characteristic of the assignment problem?

(a) Each task must be assigned to exactly one agent	(b) The objective is typically to minimize costs or maximize profits
(c) Each agent can be assigned to multiple tasks	(d) The problem can be represented by a cost matrix

18.14 When applying the Hungarian method, what does "covering a zero" in the cost matrix involve?

(a) Marking the zero to ensure it's part of the solution	(b) Counting the number of zeros in each row and column
(c) Identifying the cost associated with that assignment	(d) Drawing lines or highlighting to indicate potential assignments

18.15 In which scenario would you prefer the assignment problem over the transportation problem?

(a) When dealing with resource distribution	(b) When tasks are independent and uniquely assigned to agents
(c) When maximizing profits is the goal	(d) When there are more tasks than agents available

18.16 When should you stop the Hungarian method iterations?

(a) When all agents are assigned to tasks	(b) When there are no more zeros in the cost matrix
(c) When a predetermined cost limit is reached	(d) When number of lines covering all zeros is equal to the number of assignments to be made

18.17 When applying the Hungarian method, if a zero appears in multiple locations within a row, how should the assignment be made?

(a) Assign to the first zero encountered	(b) Randomly choose one of the zeros
(c) Evaluate which zero minimizes the overall cost	(d) Assign based on the row with the highest remaining capacity

18.18 Why do we subtract all entries from the maximum value in the profit matrix?

(a) To create a new problem formulation	(b) To ensure all values are positive
(c) To simplify the assignment problem	(d) To apply minimization algorithms effectively

18.19 When using an assignment problem approach for Traveling Salesman Problem, what transformation is often required for the cost matrix?

(a) Make the cost symmetric if not already	(b) Convert all values to their absolute differences
(c) Create a complete graph with zero-cost edges	(d) Include a penalty for unvisited cities

18.20 What is a significant limitation of using the assignment problem approach to solve Traveling Salesman Problem?

(a) It cannot guarantee an optimal solution	(b) It only works for small datasets
(c) It does not handle time windows effectively	(d) It requires all distance metrics to be symmetric

Answers of Multiple Choice Questions

18.1 (b), 18.2 (a), 18.3 (a), 18.4 (b), 18.5 (c), 18.6 (d), 18.7 (d), 18.8 (b), 18.9 (c), 18.10 (b), 18.11 (d), 18.12 (a), 18.13 (c), 18.14 (d), 18.15 (b), 18.16 (d), 18.17 (c), 18.18 (d), 18.19 (a), 18.20 (c)

SHORT AND LONG ANSWER TYPE QUESTIONS

Category I

18.1 What is the transportation cost matrix?

18.2 Describe the term "optimal solution" in a transportation context.

18.3 What methods can be used to find an initial feasible solution of transportation problem?

18.4 What is the purpose of the stepping-stone method?

18.5 Define the MODI method in transportation problems.

18.6 What is the Vogel's Approximation method in transportation problems?

18.7 What are unbalanced transportation problems?

18.8 What are the limitations of the transportation model?

18.9 What are the typical components of an assignment problem?

18.10 How can an assignment problem be formulated mathematically?

18.11 What are the steps involved in the Hungarian Method?

18.12 What is an unbalanced assignment problem?

18.13 How is the Traveling Salesman Problem related to assignment problems?

18.14 Explain the difference between the symmetric and asymmetric Traveling Salesman Problem.

18.15 What are the common exact algorithm method, heuristics, and metaheuristics methods used to solve the Traveling Salesman Problem?

18.16 What are some real-world applications of the Traveling Salesman Problem?

Category II

18.17 In the event that the transportation problem's solution is not optimal:

a. How do you choose which unoccupied cell to move units into?

b. How do you choose which cells to use in the operation of shifting?

c. How do you determine the number of units to move?

18.18 Why is the North-West Corner approach inferior than the minimal cell cost method and Vogel's Approximation method for figuring out an initial solution to a transportation problem?

18.19 Describe how the transportation problem with profit maximization can be transformed into a transportation problem with cost minimization similar to it.

18.20 Explain how to formulate a basic transportation model in operations research. What are the key components, such as decision variables, objective function, and constraints? Provide a simple example of a transportation problem involving factories and warehouses, detailing how to set up the model, including supply and demand constraints.

18.21 Explain how to formulate a basic assignment model in operations research. What are the key components, such as decision variables, objective function, and constraints?

Provide a simple example of an assignment problem involving workers and tasks, detailing how to set up the model, including the costs associated with each assignment.

18.23 Describe the traveling salesman problem's characteristics and provide a mathematical solution.

NUMERICAL PROBLEMS

18.1 Obtain the initial basic feasible solution to the following transportation problem using the north-west corner rule:

	P	Q	R	S	Supply
A	11	13	17	14	250
B	16	18	14	10	300
C	21	24	13	10	400
Demand	200	225	275	250	

18.2 Obtain an initial basic feasible solution to the following transportation using the least-cost method:

	D_1	D_2	D_3	D_4	Supply
O_1	1	2	3	4	6
O_2	4	3	2	0	8
O_3	0	2	2	1	10
Demand	4	6	8	6	

where O_i and D_j denote i^{th} origin and j^{th} destination respectively.

18.3 To come up with a basic feasible solution to the transportation issue, use Vogel's Approximation Method.

	P	Q	R	S	Supply
A	11	13	17	14	250
B	16	18	14	10	300
C	21	24	13	10	400
Demand	200	225	275	250	

18.4 W1, W2, and W3 warehouses are supplied by a company's plants located in F1, F2, and F3. The plant can produce 200, 160, and 90 units each week, accordingly. Weekly warehouses requirements are 180, 120, and 150 units respectively. Unit shipping costs (in $) are as follows:

Factory	Warehouses			
	W_1	W_2	W_3	Supply
F_1	16	20	12	200
F_2	14	8	18	160
F_3	26	24	16	90
Demand	180	120	150	

Determine the optimum distribution for this company to minimize shipping costs using Vogel's Approximation method for feasible solution and Stepping Stone method for optimality.

18.5 Find the feasible solution in the following transportation problem by Vogel's Approximation method. Also obtain the optimum solution by MODI method:

	D_1	D_2	D_3	D_4	Supply
S_1	3	7	6	4	5
S_2	2	4	3	2	2
S_3	4	3	8	5	3
Demand	3	3	2	2	

18.6 Consider the following transportation problem:

Factory	Warehouses						Stock Available
	1	**2**	**3**	**4**	**5**	**6**	
A	7	5	7	7	5	3	60
B	9	11	6	11	–	5	20
C	11	10	6	2	2	8	90
D	9	10	9	6	9	12	50
Demand	60	20	40	20	40	40	

No quantity can be transported from factory B to Warehouse 5.

Determine:

(a) Initial solution by Vogel's Approximation method.

(b) Optimum Basic Feasible Solution.

(c) Is the optimum solution unique? If not, find an alternative optimum basic feasible solution.

Hint: *This problem has degeneracy*

18.7 A department head is responsible for four duties and four subordinates. Both the tasks' inherent difficulty and the efficiency of the subordinates vary. The following matrix shows his estimate of how long each man would take to complete each task:

Tasks	Men			
	E	F	G	H
A	18	26	17	11
B	13	28	14	26
C	38	19	18	15
D	19	26	24	10

18.8 A department head has three subordinates with varying levels of efficiency and four duties that need to be completed. The matrix below provides an estimate of how long each subordinate would take to complete a task. In order to reduce the overall number of man-hours, how should he assign each work to a different man?

Tasks	Men		
	1	2	3
A	9	26	15
B	13	27	6
C	35	20	15
D	18	30	20

18.9 Four zones (A, B, C, and D) and four sales engineers (P, Q, R, and S) are available for assignment in a manufacturing organization. The engineers' abilities as sales person varied. By placing the best engineer in the richest zone, the next best in the second richest zone, and so on, the maximum predicted total sales criteria will be satisfied. The following table (matrix) shows the sales (in thousands) for each of the four zones. Determine the maximum sales and optimum assignment.

		Zones			
		A	B	C	D
Sales engineer	P	140	112	98	154
	Q	90	72	63	99
	R	110	88	77	121
	S	80	64	56	88

18.10 Starting from his home city of A, a salesperson intends to tour cities B, C, D, and E. The following table displays the distances between cities:

	A	B	C	D	E
A	∞	103	188	136	38
B	103	∞	262	176	52
C	188	262	∞	85	275
D	136	176	85	∞	162
E	38	52	275	162	∞

How can he arrange his tour to ensure that he (i) only goes to each city once and (ii) covers the least amount of distance?

REFERENCES AND SUGGESTED READINGS

1. Barker, J. R. *Operations Research: An Introduction*. Pearson Education, 2012.
2. Dantzig, G. B. The Transportation Problem. *Econometrica*, Vol. 19(3), 195-208, 1951.
3. Gillett, B. E. *Operations Research: A Practical Introduction*. McGraw-Hill, 1989.
4. Hillier, F. S., and Lieberman, G. J. *Introduction to Operations Research*, 10th Edition, McGraw-Hill, 2021.
5. Kuhn, H. W. The Hungarian Method for the Assignment Problem. *Naval Research Logistics Quarterly*, Vol. 2(1–2), 83-97, 1955.
6. Minkov, A., and Rachev, P. An Optimization Algorithm for Solving Transportation Problems with Unbalanced Supply and Demand. *European Journal of Operational Research*, Vol. 218(1), 186-192, 2012.
7. Rai, R. K., and Tiwari, M. K. Solving Unbalanced Transportation Problems Using Modified Distribution Method. *International Journal of Operations and Quantitative Management*, Vol. 19(1), 43-55, 2013.
8. Taha, H. A. *Operations Research: An Introduction*, 10th Edition, Pearson Education, 2017.
9. Toth, P., and Vigo, D. The Vehicle Routing Problem. *Society for Industrial and Applied Mathematics*, 2014.
10. Vasiliu, L., and Vasiliu, C. On the Stepping Stone Method for Solving the Transportation Problem. *Computers & Industrial Engineering*, Vol. 61(3), 667-674, 2011.
11. Vora, J. S. *Quantitative Techniques in Management*. McGraw-Hill, 2010.
12. Winston, W. L. *Operations Research: Applications and Algorithms*, 4th Edition, Thomson Brooks/Cole, 2004.
13. Zimmerman, A. *Introduction to Operations Research and Management Science*. McGraw-Hill, 2013.

UNIT 19

QUEUING ANALYSIS

UNIT SPECIFICS

This unit elaborately discusses the following topics:

- Components of waiting line analysis
- The single-server waiting line system (discipline of queues, calling population, arrival rate, and service rate)
- The single-server model (M/M/1):(∞/FIFO)
- The single-server model (M/M/1):(N/FIFO)
- Multiple channel queuing model (M/M/C):(∞/FIFO)

In order to foster increased creativity and curiosity and improve problem-solving abilities, the topics' real-world applications are investigated. A list of references, recommended readings, and assignments including a range of numerical problems are included in the course along with several multiple-choice questions and questions with short and long answers categorized into two groups based on Bloom's taxonomy's lower and higher order. Among the intriguing subjects is the use of QR codes, which can be scanned to provide relevant further information.

RATIONALE

This unit focuses on the fundamental principles of waiting line analysis, which is essential for optimizing service efficiency in various contexts. It begins by outlining the key components of waiting line systems, including queue discipline, calling population, arrival rates, and service rates. The exploration of the single-server waiting line system, specifically the M/M/1 model, provides a framework for understanding how to manage queues effectively, with variations such as (∞/FIFO) and (N/FIFO) illustrating different scenarios involving infinite or limited population sizes. The chapter also introduces multiple channel queuing models, like the M/M/C model, which demonstrate the dynamics of service systems with multiple servers. By examining these models, students gain critical insights into managing wait times and improving customer satisfaction in service-oriented environments.

UNIT OUTCOMES

List of outcomes of this unit is as follows:

U19-UO1: Identifying Components

U19-UO2: Understanding Single-Server Systems

U19-UO3: Applying the M/M/1 Model (∞/FIFO)

U19-UO4: Utilizing the M/M/1 Model (N/FIFO)

U19-UO5: Analyzing Multiple Channel (M/M/C) Model (∞/FIFO)

U19-UO6: Evaluating Performance Metrics

UNIT-19 Outcomes	EXPECTED MAPPING WITH COURSE OUTCOMES (1-Weak Correlation; 2-Medium Correlation; 3-Strong Correlation)					
	CO-1	CO-2	CO-3	CO-4	CO-5	CO-6
U19-UO1	2	3	2	3	2	3
U19-UO2	1	2	2	2	2	3
U19-UO3	1	2	1	2	1	3
U19-UO4	1	2	1	2	1	3
U19-UO5	2	2	2	2	1	3
U19-UO6	1	2	2	2	1	3

19.1 INTRODUCTION

Everyone has experienced waiting in lines or qucucs at some point in their lives. Anyone who has ever gone for shopping at mall has probably encountered the annoyance of having to wait in line to pay or make purchases. Not only do people spend a large amount of time in lines, but production factories have items lined up, machinery needs to be repaired, planes need to take off and land, and so on. Since waiting time is a scarce resource, it is crucial to analyze ways to cut down on it.

Recent years have seen a greater emphasis on quality, particularly in operations related to services, which has made waiting time improvements even more crucial. Consumers increasingly associate speedy service with quality when they visit a bank to obtain a loan, cash a check, or make a deposit, take their automobile to a dealer for maintenance, or buy at the grocery store. Because of this, an increasing number of businesses view cutting down on waiting times as a crucial aspect of their operations. Increasing service capacity, which typically entails hiring more employees, such as tellers at banks, mechanics at auto dealerships, or checkout clerks at grocery stores, allows businesses to generally cut down on wait times and offer speedier service. The cornerstone of waiting line analysis, which weighs the trade-off between the cost of better service and the cost of making consumers wait, is the financial cost associated with expanding service capacity in this way.

To handle various queuing systems, there are numerous queuing models available. Many of these queuing variations will eventually be covered, but for now, we will focus on the two most popular system types: single-server and multiple-server systems.

19.2 COMPONENTS OF WAITING LINE ANALYSIS

There is a waiting line because more persons or items come at the server or serving function than can be served in a timely manner. This does not, however, imply that the customer inflow can't be handled by the service operation because of a lack of workers or resources. In actuality, the majority of companies and organizations have enough serving capacity on hand to accommodate their clientele over the long term. Customers do not arrive at a steady, uniform pace or are served in an equal period of time, which leads to waiting lineups. Customers show in at different times, and serving each one of them takes a different amount of time. In the end, this means that a waiting line approaches an average rate of customer arrivals and an average time to serve the customer, and it is always growing and shrinking in length (and occasionally empty). At a grocery shop, for instance, the checkout counters may have enough employees to handle an average of 100 clients per hour, but only 60 people may come in any given hour. Waiting lines, however, could occur at particular times during the hour if more customers than usual arrive and make more purchases than usual.

These wait periods for customer arrivals and service hours are the basis for decisions regarding waiting lines and their management. In order to calculate operating parameters like the average number of customers waiting in line and the average amount of time a customer must wait in line, they are utilized in queuing formulas. The type of waiting line system under investigation determines which set of formulas is employed. A single line of clients in cars at a bank drive-in teller window, for instance, is not the same as a single line of passengers at an airport ticket counter attended to by three or four airline agents. Before looking at queuing formulas in the next sections, we will first discuss the many parts and components that make up waiting lines in the next section.

19.3 THE SINGLE-SERVER WAITING LINE SYSTEM

The most basic type of queuing system consists of a single server and a single waiting line. It will therefore be utilized to illustrate the principles of a queuing system. Take the Mall Shopping system as an illustration of this type of arrangement.

One employee runs the cash register at the checkout counter in the mall shopping system, which has one checkout counter. In this queuing system, the cash register and operator work together as the server, or service facility; consumers who wait in line to pay for their purchases constitute the queue. Fig. 19.1 depicts the setup of this sample queuing system.

Fig. 19.1 The Mall Shopping system

The following are the most important factors to take into account when examining a queuing system like the one in Fig. 19.1:

1. The discipline of the queue (the sequence in which clients are serviced).
2. The composition of the calling population (the origins of customers).
3. The arrival rate or the frequency with which clients join the line.
4. The service rate or how quickly clients are attended to.

Each of these topics will be covered in relation to our scenario.

THE DISCIPLINE OF QUEUES

The order in which customers who are waiting are served is known as the queue discipline. The "first-come, first-served" policy governs customer service at the mall shopping system. Meaning that at the checkout counter, service is given to the first person in line. Queue discipline of this kind is the most prevalent. It is feasible to pursue alternative disciplines. In order to determine which component will be chosen first, a machine operator may, for instance, stack parts that are still in progress next to a machine. We would call this kind of queue discipline "last-in, first-out." Alternately, the machine operator may just reach into a box containing several parts and choose one at random. The queue discipline in this instance is arbitrary. Customers visiting places like dentists or doctors' offices, or patrons of restaurants that require reservations, are frequently scheduled for service in accordance with a prearranged appointment. In this instance, regardless of the customers' arrival time to the facility, they are handled in accordance with a predetermined schedule. When consumers are arranged alphabetically by last name at events like job interviews or school registration, it is an example of one of the various forms of queuing disciplines.

THE CALLING POPULATION

The market's source of customers, which is considered to be infinite in this instance, is the calling population. Put another way, the number of potential customers is considered to be infinite because there are so many potential customers in the area where the store is located. There are finite calling populations in certain queuing systems. For instance, there are 20 cars in the finite calling population of the repair garage that are waiting to be serviced. On the other hand, queuing systems with an underlying infinite calling population are more common.

THE ARRIVAL RATE

The frequency of consumers arriving at the service facility during a given time frame is known as the arrival rate. The empirical data obtained from researching the system or one comparable to it can be used to estimate this rate, or the empirical data can be averaged. In the event where 100 consumers visit the store's checkout counter in a 10-hour day, for instance, we may state that the arrival rate is 10 customers per hour on average. While measuring the number of paying customers at the market over the course of a 10-hour day could allow us to calculate an arrival rate, it would be impossible to predict with certainty when these customers would actually show up on the premises. In other words, it is possible that one hour may see no consumers arrive, while the next hour may see 20 customers arrive. These arrivals are often taken to be independent of one another and to fluctuate randomly over time.

It is further assumed that arrivals to a service facility follow a certain probability distribution in light of these presumptions. The number of arrivals per unit of time at a service facility can often be defined by a Poisson distribution, despite the fact that arrivals could be represented by any distribution. This conclusion has been reached after years of research and the practical experience of those working in the queuing field.

THE SERVICE RATE

The average number of customers that can be handled in a given amount of time is known as the service rate. Thirty customers can be checked out (serviced) in an hour using our example of mall shopping. Because it is a random variable, a service rate and an arrival rate are comparable. Stated differently, the number of people who can be serviced varies over time depending on several aspects such the quantity of the client purchases, the amount of change the cashier needs to count out, and the types of payments accepted. Once more, it is feasible that 40 customers will be checked out in the hour that follows and just 10 customers will be checked out in the first hour.

In queuing theory, it has become customary to describe arrivals in terms of a rate and services in terms of time. Service time is taken to be determined by a probability distribution, just like arrival rate. Queuing researchers have shown that an exponential probability distribution can often be used to characterize service times. However, arrivals and service must be in units of measure that are compatible in order to study a queuing system. In order to match an arrival rate, service time must be expressed as a service rate.

19.3.1 THE SINGLE-SERVER MODEL (M / M / 1): (∞ / FIFO)

One example of a single-server queuing system with the following features is the checkout counter at the mall shopping.

1. An infinite calling population

2. A first-in-first-out queue discipline
3. Poisson arrival rate
4. Exponential service times

A single-server queuing system model has been created using these assumptions. In this queuing model notation, M is traditionally indicative of exponential distribution. Therefore, (M/M/1): (∞/FIFO) indicates a queuing model when the inter-arrival time and service time are distributed exponential with distribution (equivalent to this: M stands for Poisson arrivals and departures). There is one server, the permissible number of customers in the system is infinite, and the server discipline is First-in-first-out (FIFO). Even yet, the mathematical derivation of this most basic queuing model is quite involved and time-consuming. Consequently, we will ignore the detailed derivation of the model and focus just on the resulting queuing formulas. It is important for the reader to remember that these formulas are limited to queuing systems that meet the previously mentioned requirements.

Given that

λ = the arrival rate (average number of arrivals per time period)

μ = the service rate (average number served per time period)

Assuming that the operating characteristics of a single-server model are given by the following formulas: $\lambda < \mu$ (customers are serviced faster than they arrive).

The probability that there are no customers using the queuing system – that is, neither in the line nor receiving service – is

$$P_0 = \left(1 - \frac{\lambda}{\mu}\right)$$

In the queuing system, the probability that *n* customers are

$$P_n = \left(\frac{\lambda}{\mu}\right)^n \times P_0 = \left(\frac{\lambda}{\mu}\right)^n \left(1 - \frac{\lambda}{\mu}\right)$$

The average number of customers within the queuing system, meaning both those receiving service and those in the queue, is

$$L = \frac{\lambda}{\mu - \lambda}$$

The average number of customers in the waiting line is

$$L_q = \frac{\lambda^2}{\mu(\mu - \lambda)}$$

The average amount of time a customer spends waiting and receiving service over the whole queuing system is

$$W = \frac{1}{\mu - \lambda} = \frac{L}{\lambda}$$

The average time of a customer's wait in the queue for service is

$$W_q = \frac{\lambda}{\mu(\mu - \lambda)}$$

The *utilization factor*, which measures the probability that the customer will have to wait because the server is busy, is

$$U = \frac{\lambda}{\mu}$$

The probability that a customer can be serviced, or the probability that the server is idle, is

$$I = 1 - U = 1 - \frac{\lambda}{\mu}$$

The last term, 1 – (λ/μ) is likewise equivalent to P_0. The probability that there are no customers in the queueing system is equal to the likelihood that the server is not in use.

By simply replacing the average arrival and service rates in the previous calculations, these different operating parameters for the Mall Shopping system may be derived. In instance, if

λ = 24 customers per hour arrive at checkout counter

μ = 30 customers per hour can be checked out

then

$$P_0 = \left(1 - \frac{\lambda}{\mu}\right)$$

$$= \left(1 - \frac{24}{30}\right) = 0.20 \text{ probability of no customers in the system}$$

$$L = \frac{\lambda}{\mu - \lambda}$$

$$= \frac{24}{30 - 24} = 4, \text{the average number of customers in the queuing system}$$

$$L_q = \frac{\lambda^2}{\mu(\mu - \lambda)}$$

$$= \frac{(24)^2}{30(30-24)} = 3.2, \text{the average number of customers in the waiting line}$$

$$W = \frac{1}{\mu - \lambda}$$

$$= \frac{1}{30-24} = 0.167 \text{ hr (10 min), the average customer's time in the system}$$

$$W_q = \frac{\lambda}{\mu(\mu - \lambda)}$$

$$= \frac{24}{30(30-24)} = 0.133 \text{ hr (8 min), average waiting time per customer in the line}$$

$$U = \frac{\lambda}{\mu}$$

$$= \frac{24}{30} = 0.80, \text{probability that the customer will have to wait because the server is busy}$$

$$I = 1 - U$$

$$= 1 - 0.80 = 0.20, \text{probability that a customer can be served when the server is idle.}$$

19.3.2 THE SINGLE-SERVER MODEL (M / M / 1): (N / FIFO)

In this model, the capacity of the queue is limited to N rather than infinity as in earlier model. For this model,

$$P_0 = \begin{cases} \dfrac{1-\rho}{1-\rho^{N+1}} & for\ \lambda \neq \mu \\ \dfrac{1}{N+1} & for\ \lambda = \mu \end{cases}$$

where

$$\rho = \frac{\lambda}{\mu} = \text{traffic density}$$

$$P(n > 0) = 1 - P_0$$

$$P_n = P_0 \rho^n \quad for\ n \leq N$$

$$L = \begin{cases} \dfrac{\rho}{1-\rho} - \dfrac{(N+1)\rho^{N+1}}{1-\rho^{N+1}} & for\ \lambda \neq \mu \\ \dfrac{N}{2} & for\ \lambda = \mu \end{cases}$$

$$L_q = L - (1 - P_0)$$

The average number of units in queue for busy system is

$$L_b = \frac{L_q}{1 - P_0}$$

The average waiting time or expected time in the system

$$W = \frac{L_q}{\lambda(1 - P_N)} + \frac{1}{\mu}$$

The average waiting time or expected time in the queue

$$W_q = W_s - \frac{1}{\mu}$$

Expected time in queue for busy system is

$$W_b = \frac{W_q}{1 - P_0}$$

19.4 MULTIPLE CHANNEL QUEUING MODEL (M / M / C): (∞ / FIFO)

In this model, more than one server is assumed to provide service. Each service station is assumed to provide same type of service and is equipped with similar facility for service. The waiting line breaks into shorter lines, one each for each service station as shown in Fig. 19.2. There will be two situations:

(a) Number of parallel service stations (C) is greater than or equal to number of customers in the system (n):
i.e., $C \geq n$
For this situation, there will be no queue and thus the mean service rate will be equal to ($n\mu$).

Fig. 19.2 The Multiple channel queuing system

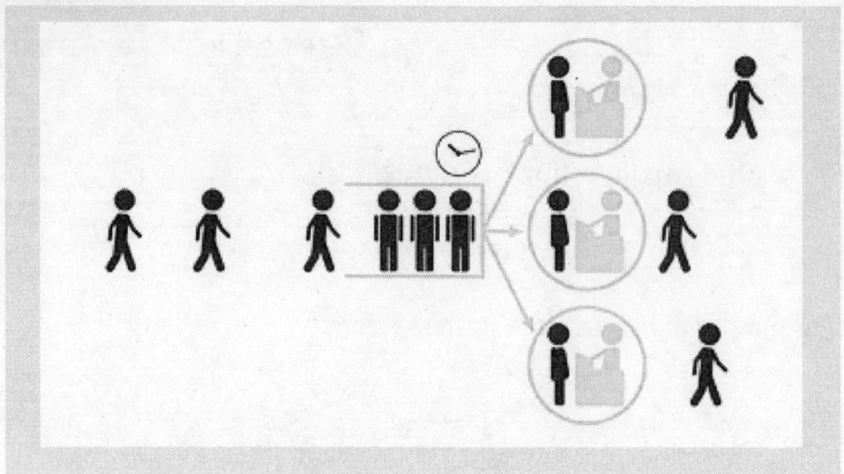

(b) Case when $C < n$, queue will be formed. For this situation, the utilization factor is given by the probability that a service channel is being used (ρ_c). This is the ratio of average arrival rate (λ) and maximum service rate of all the C channels, which is C time μ. Thus,

$$\rho_C = \frac{\lambda}{\mu C}$$

Probability of n units in the multichannel system (for $n < C$),

$$P_n = \frac{1}{n!}\left(\frac{\lambda}{\mu}\right)^n P_0 \qquad 0 \le n \le (C-1)$$

Probability of n units in the multichannel system (for $n > C$),

$$P_n = \frac{1}{C!\,C^{(n-c)}}\left(\frac{\lambda}{\mu}\right)^n P_0$$

Probability that a service station is idle or waiting for customer = Probability that at least C customers are present in the system,

$$P(n \le C) = \frac{\mu\left(\frac{\lambda}{\mu}\right)^C}{(C-1)!\,(\mu C - \lambda)} \times P_0$$

Probability of no customer in the system

$$P_0 = \frac{1}{\left[\sum_{n=0}^{C-1} \frac{1}{n!}\left(\frac{\lambda}{\mu}\right)^n\right] + \left[\frac{1}{C!}\left(\frac{\lambda}{\mu}\right)^C \frac{\mu C}{\mu C - \lambda}\right]}$$

$$L = \left\{\frac{\lambda\mu\left(\frac{\lambda}{\mu}\right)^C}{(C-1)!\,(\mu C - \lambda)^2} P_0\right\} + \frac{\lambda}{\mu}$$

$$L_q = \frac{\lambda\mu\left(\frac{\lambda}{\mu}\right)^C}{(C-1)!\,(\mu C - \lambda)^2} P_0,$$

$$W = \frac{L}{\lambda}$$

$$W_q = \frac{L_q}{\lambda}$$

Formulas for calculating the operating characteristics of single and multi-channel waiting lines with Poisson arrivals and exponential service times were discussed above. John D. C. Little demonstrated that the characteristics – L_q, L, W_q, and W – have several interactions with each other that are applicable to a range of waiting line systems. The reader can use the provided QR code to learn more about Little's Law for generalized model as it relates to queueing theory.

SCAN ME
for
Little's Law for generalized model in queueing theory

Example 19.1

A commercial bank has four tellers counter for its customers. The services at these tellers are exponentially distributed with mean of 5 minutes per customer. With a mean arrival rate of 36 per hour, customer arrivals are Poisson distributed. Analyze the system.

Solution

$\lambda = 36$ per hour; $\mu = 60/5 = 12$ per hour

$= \lambda/\mu = 36/12 = 3$

C = 4 tellers

$$P_0 = \frac{1}{\left[\sum_{n=0}^{C-1} \frac{1}{n!}\left(\frac{\lambda}{\mu}\right)^n\right] + \left[\frac{1}{C!}\left(\frac{\lambda}{\mu}\right)^C \frac{\mu C}{\mu C - \lambda}\right]}$$

$$= \frac{1}{\left[1 + \left(\frac{\lambda}{\mu}\right) + \frac{1}{2}\left(\frac{\lambda}{\mu}\right)^2 + \frac{1}{6}\left(\frac{\lambda}{\mu}\right)^3\right] + \left[\frac{1}{4!}\left(\frac{\lambda}{\mu}\right)^4 \frac{\mu C}{\mu C - \lambda}\right]}$$

$$= \frac{1}{\left[1 + 3 + \frac{1}{2}(3)^2 + \frac{1}{6}(3)^3\right] + \left[\frac{1}{24}(3)^4 \frac{12 \times 4}{12 \times 4 - 36}\right]}$$

$$= \frac{1}{1 + 3 + 4.5 + 4.5 + 4.5 + 13.5} = 0.0377$$

(ii) Average number of customers in the queue

$$L_q = \frac{\lambda\mu\left(\frac{\lambda}{\mu}\right)^C}{(C-1)!\,(\mu C - \lambda)^2} P_0$$

$$= \frac{(36)(12)\left(\frac{36}{12}\right)^4}{(4-1)!\,[(12)4 - 36]^2} \times 0.0377 = 1.53$$

(iii) Average number of customers in the system,

$$L = L_q + \frac{\lambda}{\mu} = 1.530 + 3 = 4.53$$

(iv) Average time, which a customer waits in a queue,

$$W_q = \frac{L_q}{\lambda}$$

$$= \frac{1.53}{36} = 0.0424 \text{ hour} = 2.54 \text{ minutes}$$

(v) Average time a customer spends in system

$$W = W_q + \frac{1}{\mu}$$

$$= 0.0424 + \frac{1}{12} = 0.1257 \text{ hour} = 7.54 \text{ minutes}$$

(vi) Number of hours the tellers are busy during the 6-day week,

Utilization factor, $\rho c = \lambda/\mu C = 36/12 \times 4 = 0.75$

Hence if the bank works for 6 days on 6 hours daily basis, the teller is busy for 75% of time, i.e., 0.75 × 6 × 6 = 27 hours per week.

(vii) Expected number of tellers idle at any point of time.

For this, let us find the probability of no customer (P_0), probability of one customer (P_1), probability of two customers (P_2) and probability of three customers (P_3):

We already found that $P_0 = 0.0377$.

as

$$P_n = \frac{1}{n!}\left(\frac{\lambda}{\mu}\right)^n P_0$$

$$P_1 = \frac{1}{1!}\left(\frac{36}{12}\right) 0.0377 = 0.1131$$

$$P_2 = \frac{1}{2!}\left(\frac{36}{12}\right)^2 0.0377 = 0.1696$$

$$P_3 = \frac{1}{3!}\left(\frac{36}{12}\right)^3 0.0377 = 0.1696$$

Now, all four of the tellers are idle as there isn't a single customer. Three teller positions are vacant when there is just one customer. In a similar vein, one teller is idle for every three customers, whereas two tellers are inactive for every two customers.

Thus, expected number of idle tellers

$= P_0(4) + P_1(3) + P_2(2) + P_3(1)$

$= 0.0377(4) + 0.1131(3) + 0.1696(2) + 0.1696(1) = 0.9989.$

Thus, on an average 0.9989 or one teller will remain idle at any point of time.

UNIT SUMMARY

- ***Components of Waiting Line Analysis***: (i) Queue discipline (order of service: FIFO, LIFO, priority-based), (ii) Calling population (finite vs. infinite sources), and (iii) Arrival & service rates (Poisson arrival and exponential service time distributions).
- ***Single-Server Waiting Line System***: (i) M/M/1 Model (∞/FIFO) – Single-server system with an infinite queue, (ii) M/M/1 Model (N/FIFO) – Single-server system with a limited queue, and (iii) Formulas for calculating waiting times, queue lengths, and server utilization.

- ***Multiple-Server Queuing Model***: (i) M/M/C Model (∞/FIFO) – Multiple servers providing the same service, and (ii) Analysis of queue length, probability of idle servers, and efficiency.
- ***Performance Metrics & Little's Law***: (i) Average queue length and waiting time relationships, and (ii) Utilization factor and service efficiency calculations.
- ***Real-World Applications & Case Studies***: Bank tellers, supermarket checkout lines, hospital emergency rooms, and manufacturing plants.

EXERCISES

MULTIPLE CHOICE QUESTIONS

19.1 Queues only start to build when:

(e) Arrivals surpass the capacity of the service	(f) Arrivals and service capacity are equal.
(g) The service facility can handle every arrival at once	(h) There are multiple places to provide service

19.2 Multiple servers could be:

(a) In parallel	(b) In series
(c) In combination of parallel and series	(d) All of the above

19.3 What does the notation *M*/*M*/1 represent in queueing theory?

(a) A single server with deterministic arrivals and exponential service times	(b) A system with multiple servers and Poisson arrivals
(c) A single server with Poisson arrivals and exponential service times	(d) A system with infinite servers and deterministic arrivals

19.4 In an *M*/*M*/*c* queue, what does '*c*' represent?

(a) The number of servers	(b) The service rate
(c) The queue length	(d) The arrival rate

19.5 Regarding a queueing model that is "Poisson exponential, single server and infinite population":

(a) There is only one servicing facility in the system	(b) The arrivals take place in a Poisson manner

(c) The exponential distribution describes the service rate	(d) All of the above

19.6 It is assumed that the calling population is infinite when:

(a) The order of arrivals depends on one another	(b) Arrivals happen independently from one another
(c) The system has infinite capacity	(d) The rate of service exceeds the rate of arrival

19.7 In the framework of deterministic queueing model:

(a) Both the arrival rate and the service time are known	(b) The relationship between service time and rate is reciprocal
(c) The service rate cannot be higher than the arrival rate	(d) The inter-arrival periods would be exponentially distributed if the arrivals follow a Poisson distribution

19.8 Which of the following does NOT constitute a crucial component of a queueing system's operation?

(a) Average amount of time a customer waited in the queue and system	(b) Utilization factor
(c) Percent idle time	(d) None of the above

19.9 Which of the following measures the utilization factor in a queueing system?

(a) $\boldsymbol{\rho = \lambda/\mu}$	(b) $\boldsymbol{\rho = \mu/\lambda}$
(c) $\boldsymbol{\rho = c/\lambda}$	(d) $\rho = \lambda/(c.\mu)$

19.10 What does the term 'queue discipline' refer to?

(a) The average waiting time in the queue	(b) The order in which customers are served
(c) The maximum queue length	(d) The server efficiency

19.11 If a system operates under an *M*/*M*/1 queue and the arrival rate is double the service rate, what will happen?

(a) The system remains stable	(b) The queue will grow indefinitely
(c) The average waiting time decreases	(d) The utilization factor will be 1

19.12 Given an *M*/*M*/4 queue where the arrival rate λ is 20 customers per hour and the service rate μ per server is 6 customers per hour, what is the traffic intensity ρ for the system?

(a) 0.5	(b) 0.67
(c) 1.0	(d) 0.83

19.13 In an *M/M/c*, if the system is stable, what condition must hold true?

(a) $\lambda > c\mu$	(b) $\lambda < c\mu$
(c) $\lambda = c\mu$	(d) $\lambda = 0$

Answers of Multiple Choice Questions

19.1 (a), 19.2 (d), 19.3 (c), 19.4 (a), 19.5 (d), 19.6 (b), 19.7 (c), 19.8 (d), 19.9 (a), 19.10 (b), 19.11 (b), 19.12 (d), 19.13 (b)

SHORT AND LONG ANSWER TYPE QUESTIONS

Category I

19.1 What is queueing theory?

19.2 Explain what is meant by "utilization" in a queueing system.

19.3 Name and briefly describe one common queueing model.

19.4 What are the differences between a single-server and a multi-server queue?

19.5 Explain the significance of the "M/M/1" queueing model.

19.6 What is meant by "steady state" in queueing theory?

19.7 What is a "balking" customer in a queue?

19.8 What is the difference between an "open" and a "closed" queueing network?

19.9 How does the arrival process affect the performance of a queue?

19.10 What factors can influence the average waiting time in a queue?

19.11 How can queueing theory be applied in real-world scenarios? Provide one example.

19.12 What are the potential limitations of using queueing theory for performance analysis?

Category II

19.13 Analyze a busy fast-food restaurant during peak hours. How can queueing theory be applied to understand customer wait times? Discuss the arrival and service rates, queue disciplines, and potential improvements to reduce wait times.

19.14 Consider a hospital emergency department (ED) facing high patient volumes. How can queueing theory assist in optimizing patient flow? Discuss different service strategies and how they affect wait times and patient outcomes.

19.15 Examine the workflow in a manufacturing plant where products go through various stages of assembly. How can queueing theory be used to optimize production lines and reduce bottlenecks? Discuss the role of machine service rates and worker allocation in this context.

19.16 Describe the M/M/1 queueing model in detail, including assumptions, mathematical formulations, and performance measures. Extend the discussion to variations of the M/M/1 model, such as M/M/c, and explain how they differ in terms of complexity and application.

19.17 Discuss the importance of system utilization in queueing theory. Explain how high utilization affects performance metrics such as wait times and service efficiency. Use mathematical models to support your discussion, and provide strategies to manage utilization effectively.

19.18 Critically evaluate the limitations of queueing theory as a tool for performance analysis. Discuss scenarios where queueing models may fail to accurately predict system behavior, and suggest alternative approaches or models that could be used to overcome these limitations.

NUMERICAL PROBLEMS

19.1 A Poisson distribution with an average rate of 7 arrivals per hour is used to describe the distribution of machinists at a tool crib. With a mean of 4 minutes, the service time at the tool crib is distributed exponentially.

(a) What is the probability that a machinist arriving at the tool crib will have to wait?

(b) What is the average number of machinists at the tool crib?

(c) The company made a policy decision that it will install a second crib if a machinist has to wait at least five minutes before being served. What should be additional flow of machinist to the tool crib to justify a second tool crib?

19.2 At a telephone booth, arrivals are assumed to follow Poisson distribution with average time of 10 minutes between two calls. Four minutes is the average length of a phone call, and it is believed to be exponentially distributed. Find:

(a) Average number of calls (customers) within the system.
(b) Average number of calls that are awaiting service.
(c) The average time of a call within the system.
(d) Percentage of time that a booth is vacant.
(e) Probability of having a minimum of one customer at the booth.
(f) The probability of the system receiving more than three calls.

19.3 Assume that the goods trains are coming in a yard at the rate of 30 trains per day and suppose that the inter-arrival times follow an exponential distribution. Each train's service time is taken to be exponential, averaging 36 minutes. If the yard can admit 9 trains at a time, calculate the probability that the yard is empty and find the average queue length.

19.4 Two girls serve the counters in a supermarket. At a rate of 12 per hour, the consumers arrive in a Poisson fashion. Every consumer receives exponential service, with a mean of six minutes. Determine (i) the probability that a new customer will have to wait for service, (ii) the typical number of customers in the system, and (iii) the typical amount of time a user spends in the super-market.

19.5 In its manufacturing sector, a company now has two tool cribs with one clerk per crib. Only the tools needed for the large machines are stored in one tool crib; all other tools are stored in the second. The distribution of arrivals for each tool crib is found to be Poisson, with an average of 20 per hour, and the distribution of service times is negative exponential, with an average of 2 minutes.

The tool manager believes that combining tool cribs so that any clerk can handle any kind of tool when needed would increase efficiency and somewhat alleviate the waiting issue. The service time is expected to be the same, but the mean arrival rate at the two tool cribs is anticipated to be 40 per hour.

Examine the current queue situation and the proposal in relation to the anticipated total number of mechanics at the tool crib or cribs, the anticipated waiting period that accounts for each mechanic's service time, and the probability that the mechanic will have to wait more than five minutes.

REFERENCES AND SUGGESTED READINGS

1. Chakrabarty, S. *Operations Research*: *Optimization Models*. PHI Learning, 2010.
2. Cooper, R. B. Introduction to Queueing Theory and Stochastic Teletraffic Models. *IEEE Transactions on Communications*, Vol. 20(5), 660-673, 1972.
3. Graham, R. L., and Knuth, D. E. Analysis of Queuing Systems with Infinite Buffers. *Mathematical Operations Research*, Vol. 1(4), 287-303, 1973.
4. Gross, D., and Harris, C. M. *Fundamentals of Queuing Theory*, 4th Edition, Wiley, 1998.
5. Hillier, F. S., and Lieberman, G. J. *Introduction to Operations Research*, 10th Edition, McGraw-Hill, 2021.
6. Jackson, J. R. *Queueing Networks*, 1st Edition, Wiley, 2006.
7. Kingman, J. F. C. The Single Server Queue in the Steady State. *Mathematical Reviews*, Vol. 28(3), 17-41, 1961.
8. Kleinrock, L. *Queueing Systems, Volume 1*: *Theory*, 2nd Edition, Wiley-Interscience, 1975.
9. Mandelbaum, A., and Zeltyn, S. The Impact of Multi-Server Queuing Systems on Customer Behavior. *Operations Research Letters*, Vol. 34(5), 621-626, 2006.
10. Miller, H. L., and Miller, E. H. *An Introduction to Queueing Theory*, 3rd Edition, Springer, 2015.
11. Taha, H. A. *Operations Research: An Introduction*, 10th Edition, Pearson Education, 2017.
12. Takagi, H. Analysis of Waiting Times in Multi-Channel Queues. *ACM Computing Surveys*, Vol. 25(2), 155-171, 1993.

UNIT **20**

NETWORK FLOW MODELS

UNIT SPECIFICS

This unit elaborately discusses the following topics:

- Introduction to Networks
- Network components
- The shortest route problem
- The minimal spanning tree problem
- The maximal flow problem

The topics' practical applications are examined in order to promote greater creativity and curiosity as well as enhance problem-solving skills. Along with a number of multiple-choice questions and questions with short and long answers divided into two groups according to Bloom's taxonomy's lower and higher order, the course also includes a list of references, suggested readings, and assignments that cover a variety of numerical problems.

RATIONALE

In this unit, we introduce the foundational concepts of networks, which are essential for understanding complex systems in various fields, including computer science, logistics, and transportation. We explore key network components such as nodes, edges, and weights, which serve as the building blocks for analyzing network structures. The discussion then delves into critical problems faced in network theory, including the shortest route problem, which optimizes paths for efficiency; the minimal spanning tree problem, which ensures connectivity with minimal cost; and the maximal flow problem, which addresses capacity and flow in network systems. These topics collectively highlight the significance of network analysis in solving real-world challenges and optimizing resource allocation.

UNIT OUTCOMES

List of outcomes of this unit is as follows:

U20-UO1: Overview of Networks

U20-UO2: Identify Network Components

U20-UO3: Solve the Shortest Route Problem

U20-UO4: Analyze Minimal Spanning Trees

U20-UO5: Evaluate Maximal Flow Scenarios

U20-UO6: Apply Network Theory to Real

UNIT-20 Outcomes	EXPECTED MAPPING WITH COURSE OUTCOMES *(1-Weak Correlation; 2-Medium Correlation; 3-Strong Correlation)*					
	CO-1	**CO-2**	**CO-3**	**CO-4**	**CO-5**	**CO-6**
U20-UO1	1	2	2	2	2	3
U20-UO2	1	2	3	2	2	3
U20-UO3	1	2	2	2	2	3
U20-UO4	-	1	2	1	1	3
U20-UO5	1	2	2	1	2	3
U20-UO6	1	2	3	2	2	3

20.1 INTRODUCTION

The image of Königsberg, Prussia (now Kaliningrad, Russia) dates back to about 1650 AD and was found in a book written by M. Zeiller. Situated near the banks of the Pregolya River, the city encompasses two large islands. The image showed that the river encircling the islands was split into two branches, or mainlands. Seven bridges connected (crossed) these branches, as seen in the image. A popular pastime in the city involved charting a path that began anywhere in the city, crossed each bridge exactly once, and ended up back where you started. Not single one of these routes could be found by anyone.

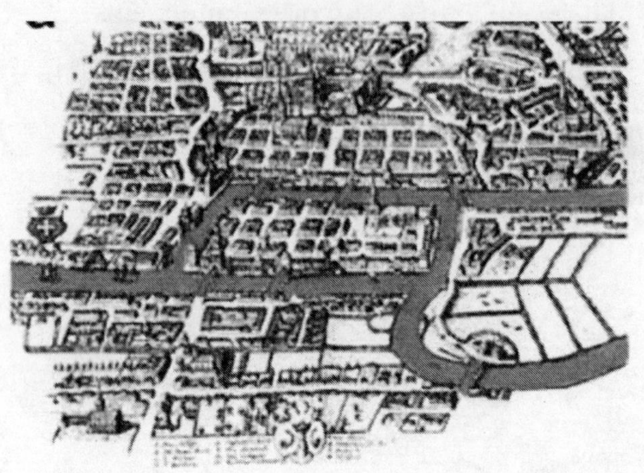

The renowned mathematician Euler established the nonexistence of such a path in 1736. He defined a network flow problem for the first time in his study. Here is how he phrased the overarching issue: "No matter how the river is arranged and split into branches, or how many bridges there are, is it feasible to figure out if you may cross each one precisely once?" According to Euler's proof, in order for such a route to exist, the network must be connected (that is, each region must be reachable from every other region via bridges) and there must be an even number of bridges contacting each land. This was undoubtedly not the case with the Königsberg bridges.

A network is a configuration of interconnected paths that allows one or more objects to move from one location to another. Networks like telephone, railroad, television, and transportation systems are all well-known to everyone. A railroad network, for instance, is made up of numerous fixed rail routes, or tracks, that are connected by terminals located at various rail route intersections.

For a few very significant reasons, network models have gained a lot of popularity in management science in recent years. A network is first represented as a diagram, which offers a visual representation of the system being studied. This improves a manager's comprehension of the system by allowing them to visually comprehend it.

We will look at various kinds of network models in the present lesson. We will introduce a class of network models focused on the movement of objects through a system in the current lesson. Consequently, the term "network flow models" is applied to these models. Three different problem types – the shortest route problem, the minimal spanning tree problem, and the maximal flow problem – will be examined in relation to the use of network flow models.

20.2 NETWORK COMPONENTS

Diagrams of networks usually show nodes and branches as their two primary constituents. Junction points, like a crossroads of multiple roadways, are represented by nodes. Representing the flow from one node to another in the network, branches link the nodes. In a network diagram, nodes are represented by circles, and the lines that connect the nodes are called branches. Whereas branches are all the paths that connect the nodes, such roads connecting cities and intersections and train tracks or air routes connecting terminals, nodes usually represent locations, like cities, intersections, or air or railroad terminals. Figure 20.1 illustrates the various railroad routes that connect four cities.

There are four nodes and four branches in the network seen in Fig. 20.1. Depending on what we are attempting to ascertain from the network, the origin, which is the node that represents city A, could be any of the three remaining nodes. Observe that every node has been given a number. A more practical way to distinguish the nodes and branches is with numbers. For instance, we can now designate the branch that goes from A to B as branch 1 – 2, and the origin (A) as node 1.

Fig. 20.1 Network of railroad routes

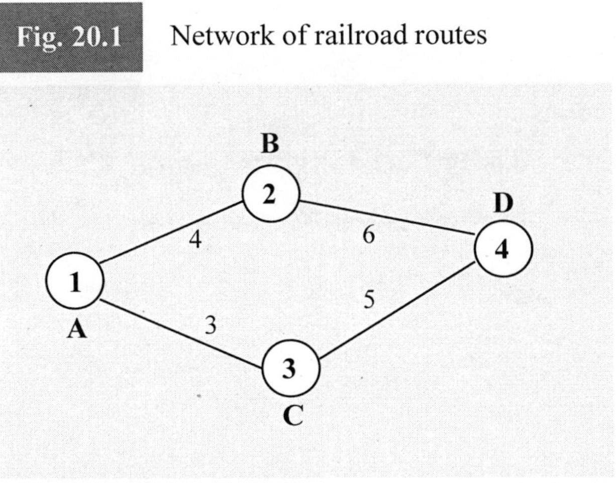

Generally, each branch is given a value that corresponds to a cost, a distance, or duration. Therefore, the network's goal is to ascertain the least amount of time, least amount of distance, or least amount of cost needed to go between any two sites in the network. The times in hours between the linked nodes are represented by the values 4, 6, 3, and 5 in Fig. 20.1, which correspond to the four branches. As a result, a traveler can see that it takes 10 hours to get from point A to destination D through B, and 8 hours to get from point A to destination D through C.

20.3 THE SHORTEST ROUTE PROBLEM

The shortest path algorithm that is most frequently employed is Dijkstra's shortest path algorithm. Finding the shortest path between an origin and multiple destinations is known as the shortest route problem. For instance, the shipping company Perfect Logistics uses six trucks to deliver apples from location A to six locations. Fig. 20.2 shows the various routes from location A to the destination locations along with the number of hours a truck needs to travel each route.

The management of the shipping company wants to know which routes will allow the trucks to arrive at their destinations with the least amount of travel time. Using the shortest route solution technique, this problem can be resolved. It is convenient to portray the truck route system as depicted in Fig. 20.2 when using this technique.

We want to find the shortest routes from the origin (node 1) to the six destinations (nodes 2 through 7) in Fig. 20.2, to reiterate our goal.

Fig. 20.2 Network of shipping routes

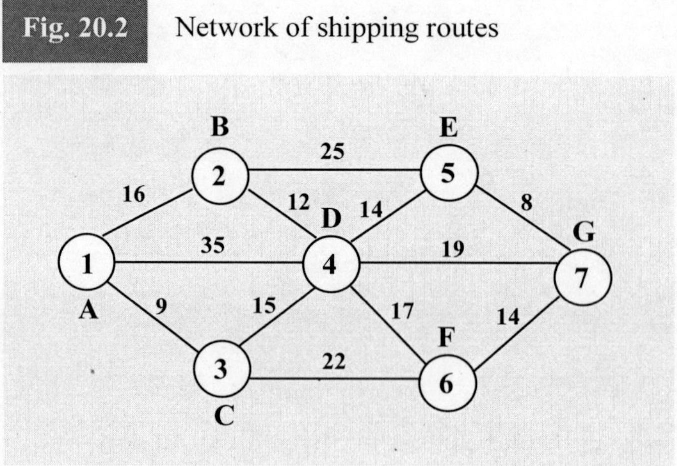

Starting at node 1, or the origin, we apply the shortest route solution technique to find the shortest time needed to travel to a node that is immediately related, or nearby. As seen in Fig. 20.3, there are three nodes that are directly connected to node 1: 2, 3, and 4. The shortest duration between these three nodes is nine hours for node 3. As a result, we have identified the initial shortest path from terminal A to terminal C, or node 1 to node 3. Now that we have discovered the shortest path to nodes 1 and 3, we will refer to them as the permanent set. (Node 1 is automatically in the permanent set because it lacks a route to it.)

Fig. 20.3 Node 1 in the permanent set of the network

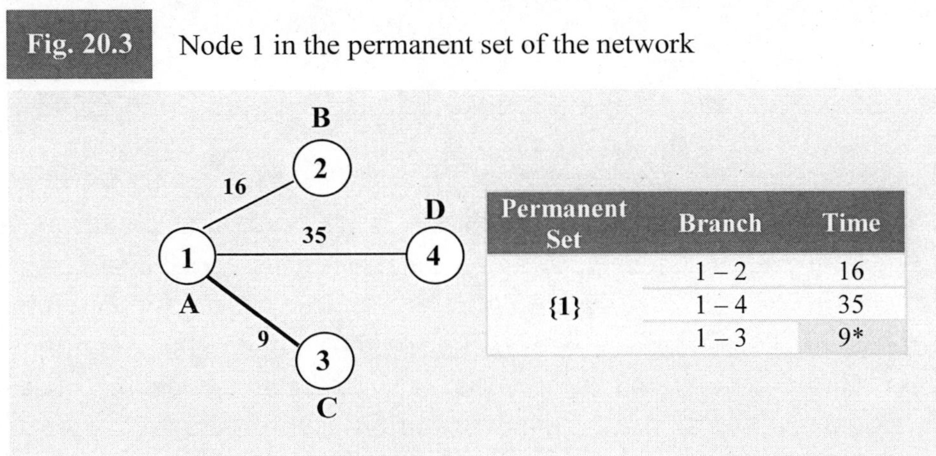

Permanent Set	Branch	Time
{1}	1 – 2	16
	1 – 4	35
	1 – 3	9*

The shortest path to node 3 is indicated in Fig. 20.3 by a thick line. The procedure for choosing the shortest route is explained in the table that goes with Fig. 20.3. It is proved that there is only one node in the permanent set. There are three branches originating from node 1, namely 1 – 2, 1 – 4, and 1 – 3. The last branch requires a minimum of 9 hours to complete. To find the shortest path to node 3, we will then go through the previous procedures again. First things first, we need to figure out every node that is directly linked to nodes 1 and 3 in the permanent set. According to Fig. 20.4, nodes 2, 4, and 6 are all directly connected to nodes 1 and 3. Finding the shortest path to the three nodes (2, 4, and 6) that are directly connected to the permanent set nodes is the next stage. These are the two branches that originate at node 1 (1–2 and 1–4) and the two branches that originate at node 3 (3 – 4 and 3 – 6). At 16 hours, the branch to node 2 takes the least amount of time. Node 2 therefore joins the permanent set. The time to node 6 (branch 3 – 6) is 31 hours, as you can see in the calculations that go with Fig. 20.4. This time was calculated by adding the time of branch 3 – 6 of 22 hours to the shortest route time of 9 hours at node 3.

Fig. 20.4 Nodes 1 and 3 in the permanent set of the network

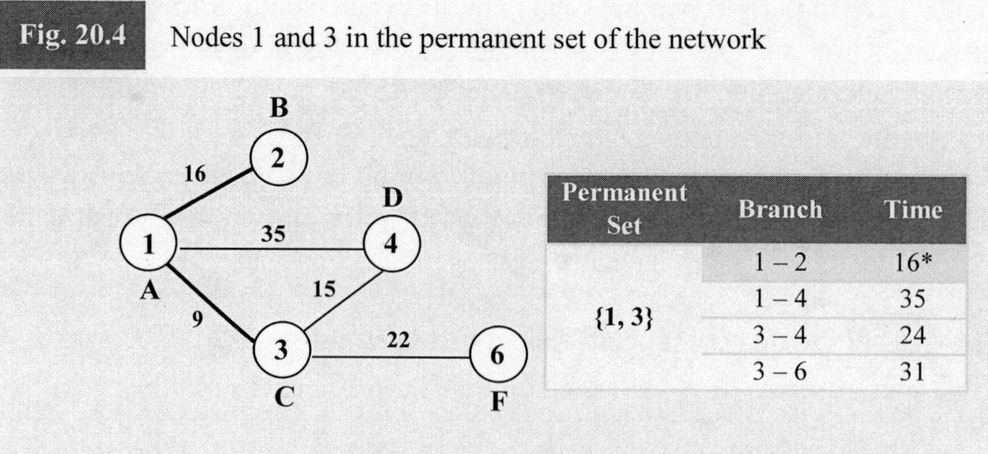

Permanent Set	Branch	Time
{1, 3}	1 – 2	16*
	1 – 4	35
	3 – 4	24
	3 – 6	31

Nodes 1, 2, and 3 make up the permanent set as we proceed to the next stage. This shows that the shortest path to nodes 1, 2, and 3 has been discovered. The nodes that are directly connected to the permanent set nodes are what we need to identify presently. Node 5 is directly connected to Node 2 since it is the sole neighboring node that is not now part of the permanent set. Furthermore, because node 2 has entered the permanent set, node 4 is now directly connected to node 2. In figure 20.5, these additions are displayed.

Fig. 20.5 Network with nodes 1, 2, and 3 in the permanent set

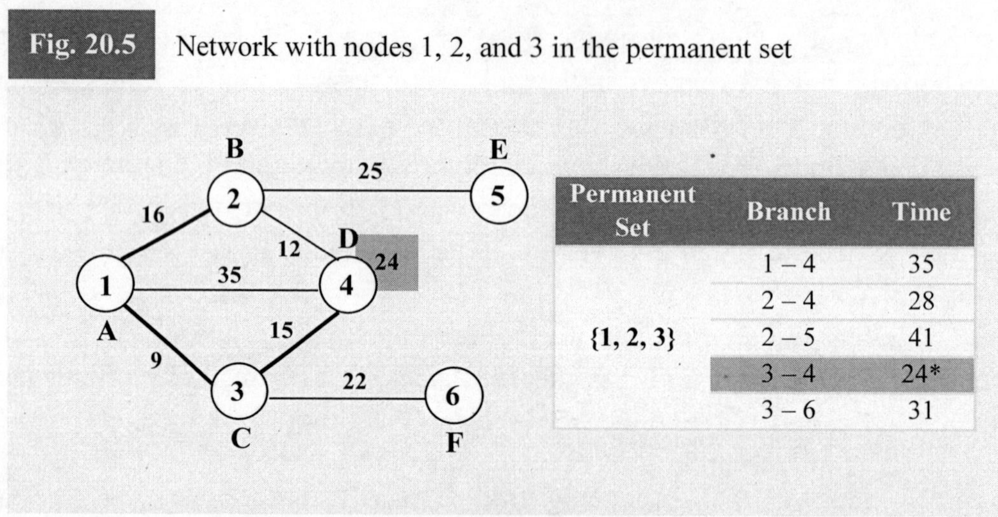

Permanent Set	Branch	Time
{1, 2, 3}	1 – 4	35
	2 – 4	28
	2 – 5	41
	3 – 4	24*
	3 – 6	31

As illustrated in the table that goes with Fig. 20.5, there are five branches that connect the permanent set nodes (1, 2, and 3) to their directly associated nodes. With duration of 24 hours, the branch that represents the path with the shortest time is 3 – 4. Node 4 now joins the permanent set after we have found the shortest path there. Observe that the path from node 1 through node 3 has the least travel time to node 4 (24 hours). Since the other routes from node 1 to node 2 to node 4 are longer, we won't be considering them as viable routes going forward.

In conclusion, nodes 1, 2, 3, and 4 now comprise the permanent set since the shortest paths to them have all been found. The procedure of identifying the nodes that are directly related to the permanent set nodes is then repeated. In Fig. 20.6, these are the nodes 5, 6, and 7 that are directly connected. As you can see in Fig. 20.6, we have removed the branches that lead from nodes 1 and 2 to node 4, as the path that takes the least amount of time to reach node 4 does not pass through these branches.

The branch that leads to nodes 5, 6, and 7 has the smallest cumulative time of 31 hours, as shown in the table that goes with Fig. 20.6. Node 6 is now a part of our permanent set. This indicates that the shortest paths to nodes 1, 2, 3, 4, and 6 have now been found.

After we go through the process again, we find that nodes 5 and 7 are the ones that are directly connected to (adjacent) our permanent set, as Fig. 20.7 describes. The reason for eliminating branch 4 – 6 is that the optimal path to node 6 is via node 3, not node 4.

Fig. 20.6 Network with nodes 1, 2, 3, and 4 in the permanent set

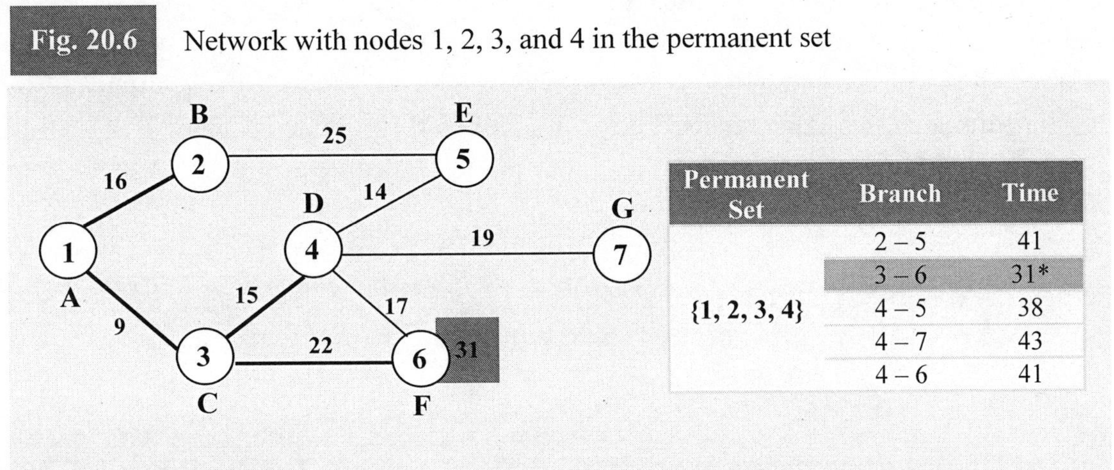

Permanent Set	Branch	Time
{1, 2, 3, 4}	2 – 5	41
	3 – 6	31*
	4 – 5	38
	4 – 7	43
	4 – 6	41

Fig. 20.7 Network with nodes 1, 2, 3, 4, and 6 in the permanent set

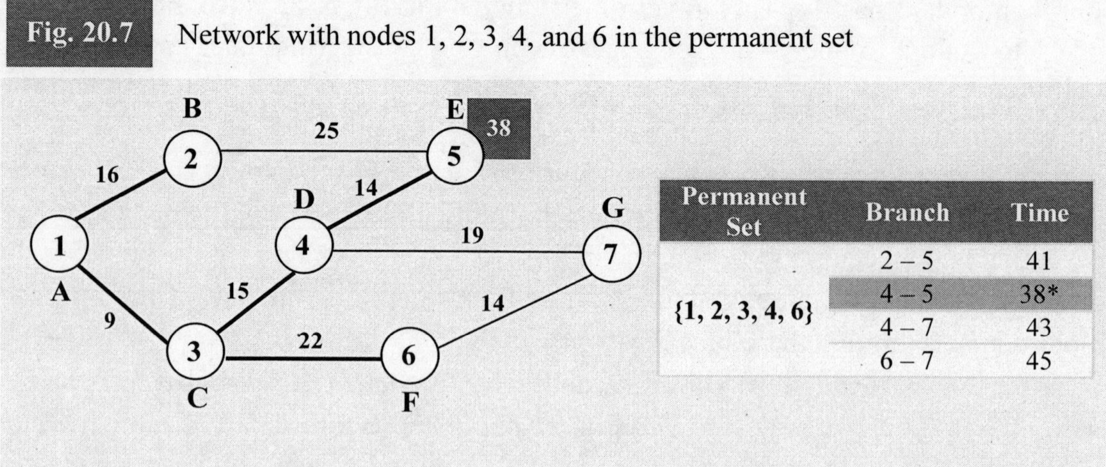

Permanent Set	Branch	Time
{1, 2, 3, 4, 6}	2 – 5	41
	4 – 5	38*
	4 – 7	43
	6 – 7	45

Branch 4 – 5 has the least total time of 38 hours among the branches that connect the permanent set nodes to nodes 5 and 7. Thus, node 5 becomes a part of the set that is permanent. Now, as indicated by the heavy branches in Fig. 20.7, we have identified the paths that take the least amount of time to reach nodes 1, 2, 3, 4, 5, and 6. Node 7, as illustrated in Fig. 20.8, is the only node that is still directly connected to the permanent set. With duration of 43 hours, branch 4 – 7 is the shortest of the three branches that connect node 7 to the permanent set. As a result, node 7 is added to the permanent set.

Fig. 20.8 Network with nodes 1, 2, 3, 4, 5, and 6 in the permanent set

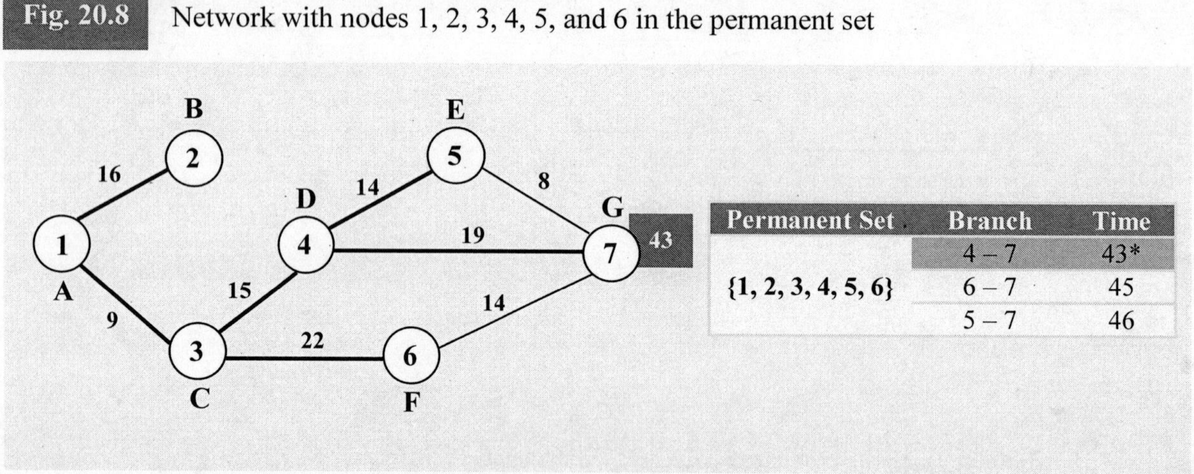

Permanent Set	Branch	Time
{1, 2, 3, 4, 5, 6}	4 – 7	43*
	6 – 7	45
	5 – 7	46

A summary of the shortest paths from the origin (node 1) to each of the other six nodes and the corresponding travel durations can be found in Fig. 20.9 and Table 20.1.

Fig. 20.9 Network with optimal routes from origin A to all destinations

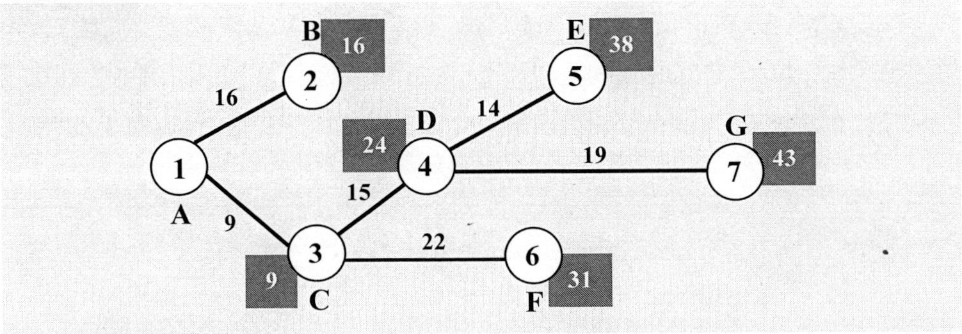

Table 20.1 Shortest travel time from origin to each destination

Route	Total hours
1 – 2	16
1 – 3	9
1 – 3 – 4	24
1 – 3 – 4 – 5	38
1 – 3 – 6	31
1 – 3 – 4 – 7	43

20.4 THE MINIMAL SPANNING TREE PROBLEM

The goal of the shortest route problem discussed in the preceding section was to ascertain the shortest paths in the network between the origin and destination nodes. For each of the six destinations in our example, we found the shortest path from the origin. Similar to the shortest route problem, the *minimal spanning tree problem* aims to connect every node in the network while minimizing the overall branch lengths. The network that is created spans (connects) every point in the network at the smallest possible total distance (or length).

We will look at the following example to illustrate the least spanning tree problem. A neighborhood made up of seven suburbs will have an internet cable system installed by the Perfect Cables Company. The main server must be connected to each of the suburbs in a manner that minimizes the overall amount of wire that needs to be deployed. Fig. 20.10 shows the alternative paths that the cable firm may use (with the town council's approval) and the number of feet of cable (measured in thousands of feet) needed for each path.

The available cable path between suburbs 1 and 2 is shown by the branch in Fig. 20.10 that runs from node 1 to node 2. It takes 16,000 feet of cable to reach the branch. As you can see, the network in Fig. 20.10 is the same as the network in Fig. 20.2, which we utilized to illustrate the shortest path issue. To show how the two kinds of network models' outcomes differ from one another, the networks were purposefully created identical.

Fig. 20.10 Network of internet cable paths

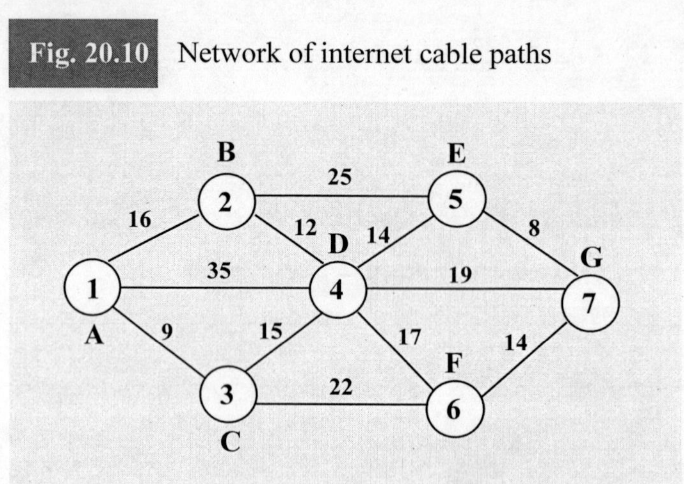

In actuality, the minimal spanning tree problem's solution methodology is simpler than the shortest path solution technique. We can begin at any network node when using the minimal spanning tree solution technique. Nonetheless, the standard method begins at node 1. We choose the nearest node, or the shortest branch, to join our spanning tree starting at node 1. At 9 thousand feet, the shortest branch from node 1 to node 3 is found. In Fig. 20.11, this branch is indicated by a bold line. As of right now, there are two nodes in our spanning tree: 1 and 3. Finding the nearest node that isn't already in the spanning tree is the next step. With a branch length of 15 thousand feet, node 4 is the node that is closest to either node 1 or node 3 (the nodes in our current spanning tree). Fig. 20.12 illustrates the addition of node 4 to our spanning tree.

Fig. 20.11 Spanning tree with nodes 1 and 3

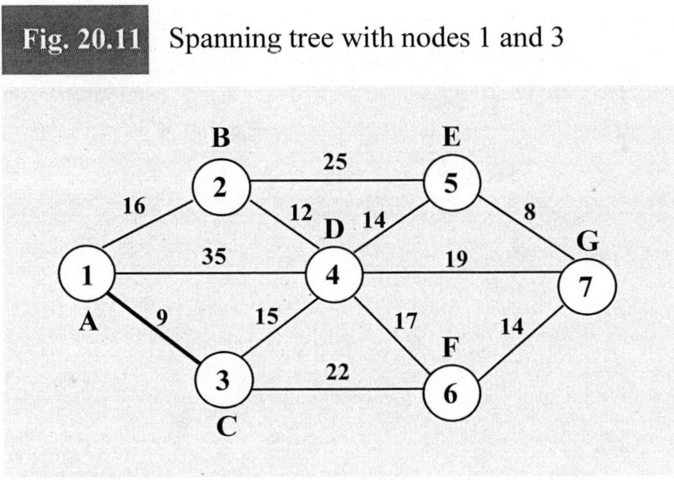

Fig. 20.12 Spanning tree with nodes 1, 3, and 4

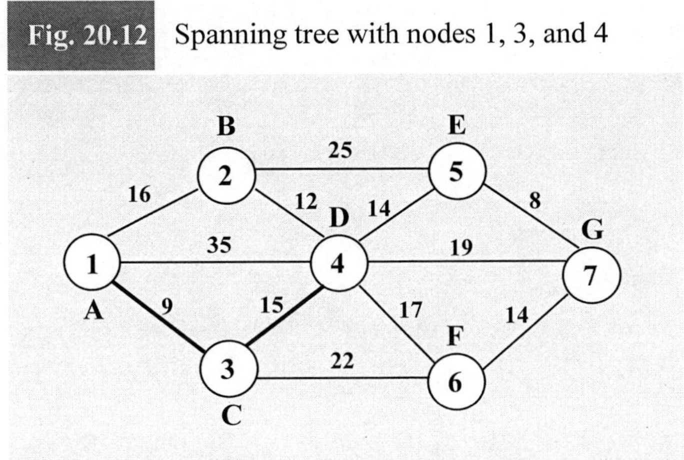

The procedure of choosing the node that is closest to our current spanning tree (nodes 1, 3, and 4) is then repeated. Node 2 is the nearest node that isn't currently connected to the nodes in our spanning tree. The branch spans 12 thousand feet from node 4 to node 2. Fig. 20.13 illustrates the addition of node 2 to the spanning tree.

Fig. 20.13 Spanning tree with nodes 1, 2, 3, and 4

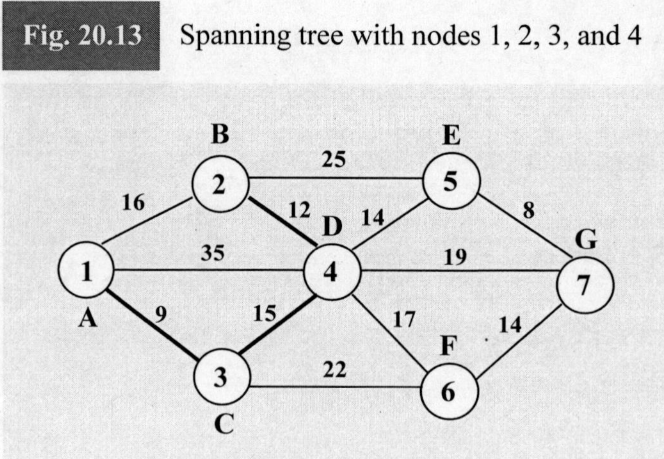

At this point, nodes 1, 2, 3, and 4 make up our spanning tree. With a branch length of 14 thousand feet to node 5, node 5 is the node that is closest to this spanning tree. Node 5 thus joins our spanning tree, as Fig. 20.14 illustrates.

Fig. 20.14 Spanning tree with nodes 1, 2, 3, 4, and 5

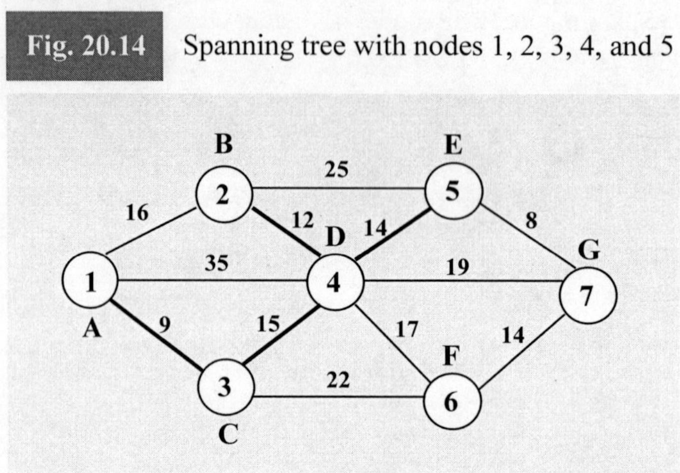

Nodes 1, 2, 3, 4, and 5 are now present in the spanning tree. Node 7 is the nearest node that isn't linked to the spanning tree right now. Eight thousand feet is the length of the branch that goes from node 5 to node 7. Node 7 has been added to the spanning tree, as shown in Fig. 20.15.

Fig. 20.15 Spanning tree with nodes 1, 2, 3, 4, 5, and 7

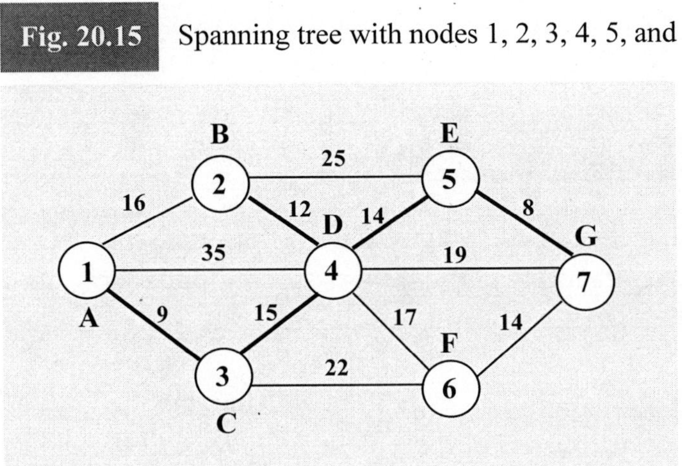

There are now nodes 1, 2, 3, 4, 5, and 7 in our spanning tree. Node 6 is the only node that is still disconnected from the spanning tree. With a branch length of 14 thousand feet, node 7 is the node in the spanning tree that is closest to node 6. Fig. 20.16 displays the whole spanning tree, which now has all seven nodes.

Fig. 20.16 Spanning tree with nodes 1, 2, 3, 4, 5, 6, and 7

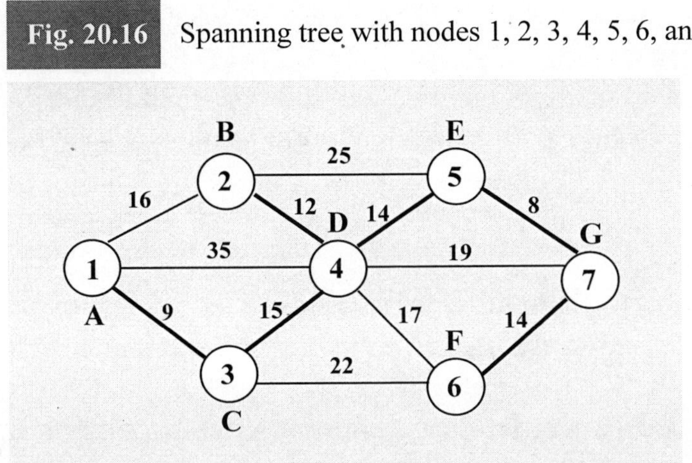

The spanning tree in Figure 20.16 uses the bare minimum of 72,000 feet of cable to link the seven suburbs. Starting at any of the six nodes except node 1 would have yielded the same minimal spanning tree.

Take note of the variations among the minimal spanning tree networks depicted in Fig. 20.9. The six distinct routes that are the shortest paths between each destination node and the origin are represented by the shortest route network. The minimal spanning tree network, on the other hand, demonstrates how to link each of the seven nodes to reduce the overall distance (length).

20.5 THE MAXIMAL FLOW PROBLEM

We found the shortest path between the origin and six destinations in the shortest route problem. We discovered the internet cables' shortest connected network by solving a minimal spanning tree problem. The capacity of a branch was not constrained to a certain number of items in any of these two issues. Nonetheless, there exist network issues where the network's branches have constrained flow capabilities. Maximizing the total quantity of flow from an origin to a destination is the aim of these networks. We call these issues "maximum flow problems." The maximal flow network problem approach was established by Ford and Fulkerson and originated from the study of transportation problems.

A network of pipelines carrying water, gas, or oil; a paper processing system (like one used by a government agency); traffic on a road network; or a manufacturing line system processing forms are examples of situations where maximum flow problems can arise. The network branches in all of these cases have restricted and frequently varying flow capacity. Determining the maximum flow achievable via the system is what the decision maker wants to know under these circumstances.

The network of a railway system between origin A and final destination F, as shown in Fig. 20.17, provides an example of a maximal flow problem. The Perfect Products Company uses the railroad to transport product parts from origin A to destination F. The quantity of railroad cars the business is able to secure on each branch in a given week is however restricted by a contract.

The company is trying to find out how many train cars full of product parts can be shipped in a week from origin A to destination F in light of these constraints. The number on the branch immediately to the right of each node (a rail junction) indicates the number of railroad cars accessible to the Perfect Product Company on each rail branch. Six cars are available, for instance, from node 1 to node 2, eight cars from node 2 to node 5, five cars from node 4 to destination node 6, and so on. The number of automobiles that can be shipped in the other direction is indicated by the number on each branch directly to the left of each junction. For instance, there are no cars available from node 2 to node 1. Because flow may only occur in one direction – from node 1 to node 2, not from 2 to 1 – the branch that connects nodes 1 and 2 is known as a directed branch. Observe that on the branches connecting nodes 2 and 4 as well as nodes 3 and 4, flow is allowed in both directions. The term "undirected branches" describes these.

Fig. 20.17 Network of a railway system

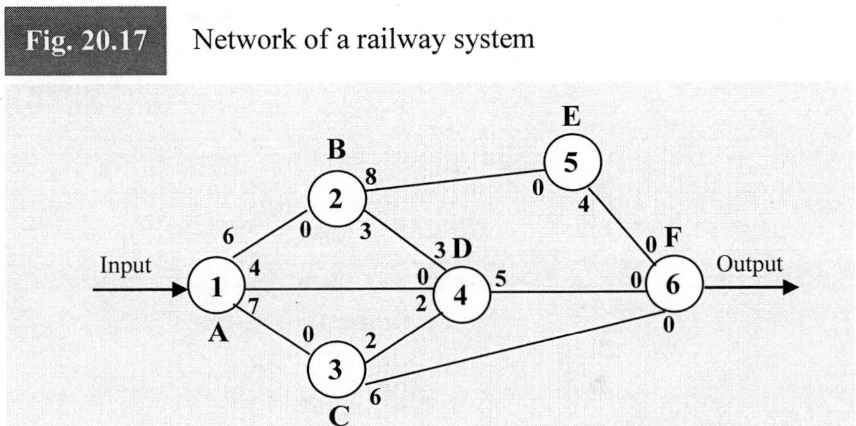

The first stage in figuring out the maximum number of railroad cars that can pass through the rail system is to choose any path from origin to destination at random and ship as much of the cargo along that path. We shall choose the paths 1 – 2 – 5 – 6 at random in Fig. 20.18. Four railroad cars are the most that can be sent along this route at a time. Since there is only room for four cars on the branch between nodes 5 and 6, it is the maximum number we can have. Fig. 20.18 depicts this path.

It is evident that the branches from node 1 to node 2 and node 2 to node 5 have two and four cars left in their capacity, respectively, and that no cars are accessible from node 5 to node 6. These figures were calculated by deducting the four cars' flow from the total number of cars available. Shown enclosed in a box is the real four-car flow along each branch. It's important to note that nodes 1 and 6 have allocated input and output for four cars each.

The last modification to this path is to add the four-car specified flow to the values immediately to the left of each of the path's nodes, 1 through 6. These are the flows that are going the other way. Consequently, at nodes 2, 5, and 6, the value of 4 is added to the zeros. Designating flow in a direction that is not achievable may appear contradictory, but this solution strategy uses it as a way to calculate the net flow down a branch. (The net flow in the right direction would be calculated by deducting the one flow in the incorrect direction from the 4 that flows in the correct direction from the previous iteration, for instance, if a later iteration revealed a flow of one car from node 5 to node 2. A net flow of three in the right direction would be the outcome.)

Fig. 20.18 Maximal flow for path 1 – 2 – 5 – 6

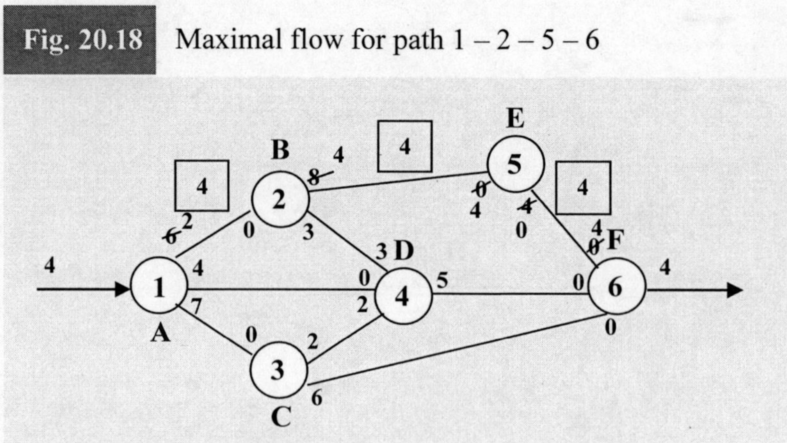

After completing one iteration of the solution procedure, all earlier steps must be carried out again. Once again, we choose a path at random. This time, as seen in Fig. 20.19, we will choose paths 1 – 4 – 6. This path has a maximum flow of four cars, which is deducted at each node. Due to the addition of the four flows along paths 1 – 4 – 6 to the flow previously calculated in Fig. 20.18, the total flow through the network now stands at eight cars.

Fig. 20.19 Maximal flow for path 1 – 4 – 6

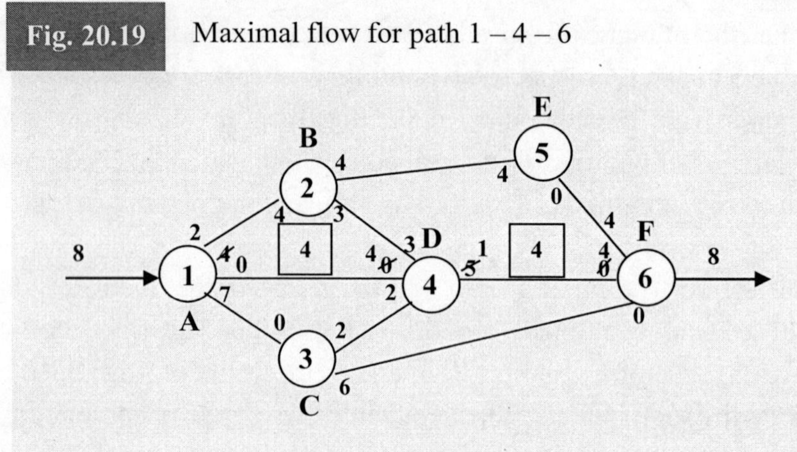

As a final step, the flow of four cars is added to the flow along the path in the opposite direction at nodes 4 and 6. We now select a different route at random. This time, we'll go with paths 1 – 3 – 6 with a maximum cars flow of 6. As illustrated in Fig. 20.20, this flow of six is added to the branches in the opposite direction and deducted from the branches along path 1 – 3 – 6. There are a total of 14 railroad cars flowing when the flow of 6 from this path is joined to the flow of 8 from the preceding path.

Fig. 20.20 Maximal flow for path 1 – 3 – 6

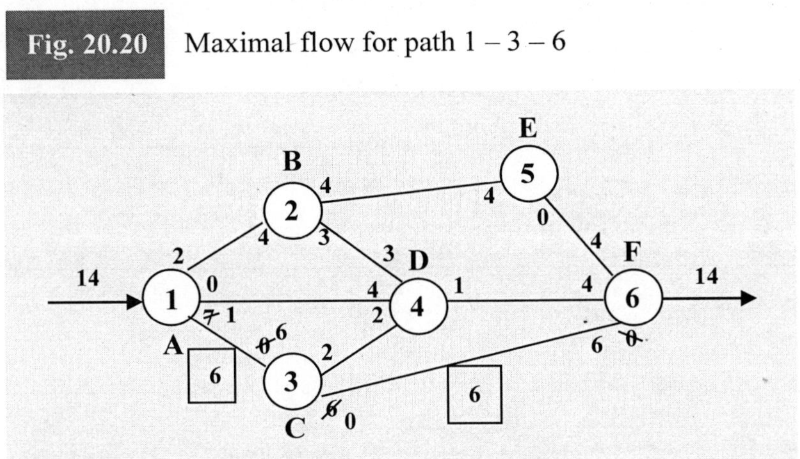

We'll choose 1 – 3 – 4 – 6 as the next path. Observe that we are now limited in the number of possible routes that we can follow. For instance, there is zero flow capacity available; therefore we are unable to take the branch from node 3 to node 6. In the same way, it is not possible to find a path that goes from node 1 to node 4.

Fig. 20.21 Maximal flow for path 1 – 3 – 4 – 6

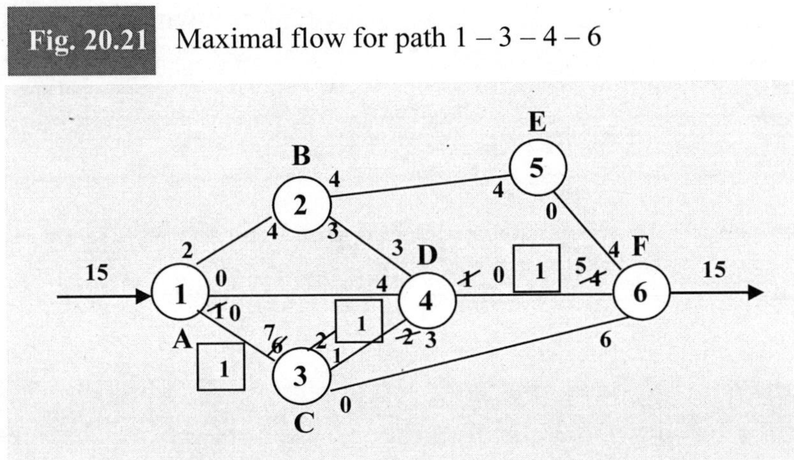

As seen in Fig. 20.21, the available flow capacity along paths 1 – 3 – 4 – 6 is one car. As a result, there are now 15 cars in total rather than just 14. The network that is produced is displayed in Fig. 20.22. A detailed examination of the network in Fig. 20.22 reveals that all pathways with available flow capacity have been used. There is no more capacity available for any channel leaving nodes 3, 4, or 5, which prevents them from connecting to any other node in the network.

displayed in Fig. 20.22. A detailed examination of the network in Fig. 20.22 reveals that all pathways with available flow capacity have been used. There is no more capacity available for any channel leaving nodes 3, 4, or 5, which prevents them from connecting to any other node in the network.

Fig. 20.22 Maximal flow for railroad network

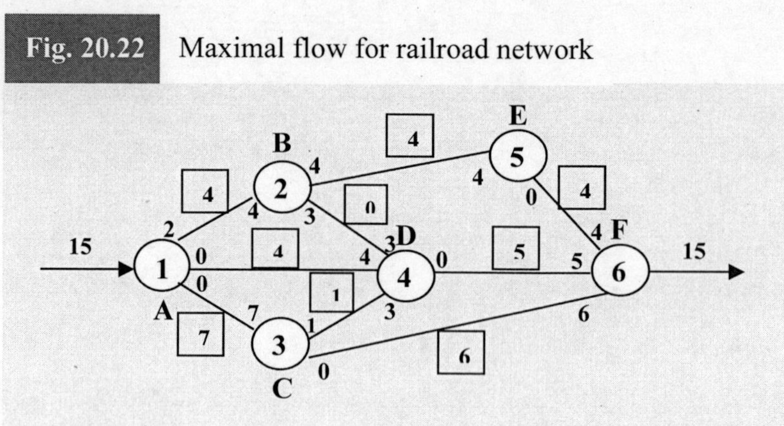

The maximal flow solution for our example case is now complete. Fifteen train cars are the maximum flow. In Fig. 20.22, the flows along each branch are shown as boxes.

UNIT SUMMARY

- ***Introduction to Networks***: Networks consist of nodes (locations) and edges (connections), representing transportation systems, supply chains, and communication networks.
- ***Network Components***: (i) Nodes represent junction points, while branches (edges) define paths between them, and (ii) Weights on edges signify costs, distances, or time constraints.
- ***The Shortest Route Problem***: (i) Focuses on finding the shortest path between two nodes, and (ii) Dijkstra's Algorithm is commonly used for solving this problem.
- ***The Minimal Spanning Tree Problem***: (i) Ensures all nodes in a network are connected with minimal total cost, and (ii) Prim's and Kruskal's Algorithms are used to find the optimal spanning tree.

- ***The Maximal Flow Problem***: (i) Determines the maximum possible flow from a source to a destination in a network with capacity constraints, and (ii) Ford-Fulkerson Algorithm is used to optimize flow distribution.
- ***Practical Applications***: (i) Supply Chain Optimization – Reducing transportation costs, (ii) Telecommunications – Efficient data routing, and (iii) Project Planning – Resource allocation in large projects.

EXERCISES

MULTIPLE CHOICE QUESTIONS

20.1 In a network flow model, what do nodes typically represent?

(a) Resources	(b) Decision variables
(c) Locations or points of supply and demand	(d) Constraints

20.2 Out of all the operations research problems, which one cannot formulate as a network flow problem?

(i) An assignment problem	(j) A transportation problem
(k) A replacement problem	(l) A queueing problem

20.3 Which of the following scenarios does not fit within the definition of a network flow problem?

(a) Figuring out the shortest path between two cities	(b) Determining the pipe lines' maximum water flow capacity
(c) Choosing the optimal stock to maintain for cattle	(d) Determining the weekend's most picturesque driving route

20.4 What type of graph structure is used in the shortest route problem?

(a) Linear	(b) Non-linear
(c) Directed or undirected graphs	(d) Circular

20.5 Which statement about the shortest path tree is true?

(a) It includes all possible paths in the graph	(b) It represents the shortest paths from a single source to all other nodes

(c) It only includes paths to the sink node	(d) It cannot be constructed for directed graphs

20.6 Which of the following is a limitation of Dijkstra's shortest route algorithm?

(a) It cannot handle negative edge weights	(b) It cannot handle undirected graphs
(c) It is only applicable to tree structures	(d) It does not guarantee an optimal solution

20.7 Which of the following is NOT a typical application of the shortest path problem?

(a) Route planning in GPS systems	(b) Network design for telecommunications
(c) Scheduling tasks in manufacturing	(d) Urban traffic management

20.8 What is a characteristic of a Minimal Spanning Tree?

(a) It may contain cycles	(b) It includes all edges of the graph
(c) It can have disconnected components	(d) It connects all vertices with the least total edge weight

20.9 Which of the following conditions must be met for a graph to have a Minimal Spanning Tree?

(a) The graph must be directed	(b) The graph must be connected and undirected
(c) The graph must contain at least one cycle	(d) The graph must have distinct weights on all edges

20.10 In the context of the Maximal Flow problem, what is the "residual graph"?

(a) A graph that includes only the source and sink nodes	(b) A graph that shows the remaining capacity of the edges after flow has been assigned
(c) A graph with no edges	(d) A graph that represents the original network without flow capacities

20.11 In a flow network, if the capacity of an edge is set to zero, what does that mean for flow?

(a) No flow can pass through that edge	(b) The edge is not part of the network
(c) The flow will automatically increase	(d) The edge becomes a source.

20.12 What type of network does the Maximal Flow problem apply to?

(a) Only directed graphs	(b) Only undirected graphs
(c) Both directed and undirected graphs	(d) Only weighted graphs

Answers of Multiple Choice Questions

20.1 (c), 20.2 (d), 20.3 (c), 20.4 (c), 20.5 (b), 20.6 (a), 20.7 (c), 20.8 (d), 20.9 (b), 20.10 (b), 20.11 (a), 20.12 (a)

SHORT AND LONG ANSWER TYPE QUESTIONS

Category I

20.1 By the terms listed below, what do you mean?

(a) A node (b) A link (c) Flow (d) A potential link

20.2 Describe the following:

(a) A tree (b) A spanning tree (c) minimal spanning tree (d) A cycle

20.3 What is the main difference between the shortest path problem and the traveling salesman problem?

20.4 What distinguishes an undirected flow from a directed one through a link?

20.5 What type of graph is commonly used in the shortest route problem?

20.6 What is a real-world example of the shortest route problem?

20.7 What is a minimal spanning tree?

20.8 How can minimal spanning tree be applied in network design?

20.9 What is the difference between a spanning tree and a minimal spanning tree?

20.10 What is the maximal flow problem?

20.11 In the context of a maximal flow problem explain the following terms:

(a) A source (b) A sink (c) Transshipment nodes (d) Link capacity

20.12 How can the maximal flow problem be applied in transportation networks?

20.13 What are some real-world applications of the maximal flow problem?

Category II

20.14 Give a brief explanation of the "Shortest Path Problem" algorithm.

20.15 What are some practical applications of the shortest path problem in real-world scenarios? Discuss at least three different fields and how shortest path algorithms are implemented in each.

20.16 Discuss the applications of minimal spanning trees in various fields. Provide examples of at least three different domains and explain how minimal spanning tree contribute to solving real-world problems in each.

20.17 What is the maximum flow problem, and how is it formulated in the context of network flow theory? Discuss the key components of a flow network and the significance of flow conservation and capacity constraints.

20.18 Discuss the practical applications of the maximum flow problem in various industries. Provide examples from at least three different fields and explain how maximum flow algorithms are used to solve real-world problems.

NUMERICAL PROBLEMS

20.1 Find the shortest path from A to C for the following network:

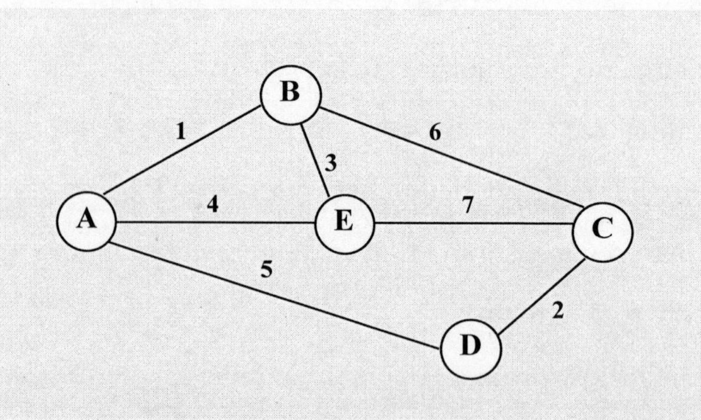

20.2 Find the shortest route from station 1 to station 8. The distance (in miles) between different stations is shown on each link in the network shown below.

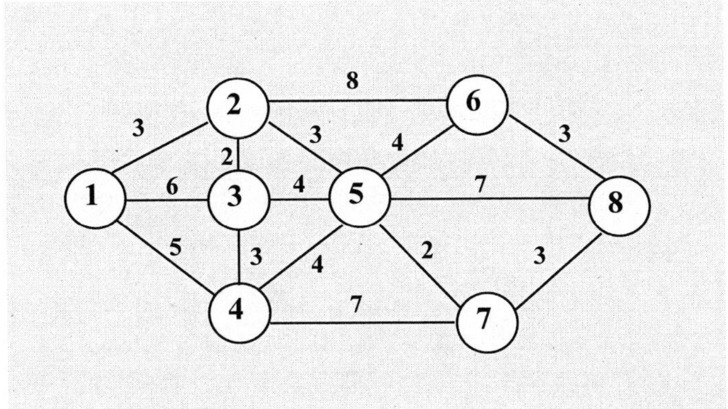

20.3 Five new housing development sites are currently undergoing the process of receiving cable services from Sky Television Cable Company. The figure below depicts the potential T.V. linkages among the five areas. The cable miles are shown on each branch.

Determine the most economical cable network for the Sky Company. Furthermore, ascertain the network's minimal spanning tree when:

(a) Nodes 2 and 5 connot be linked.

(b) Nodes 5 and 6 are linked by a 2-mile cable.

(c) Nodes 6 and 2 are linked by a 4-mile cable

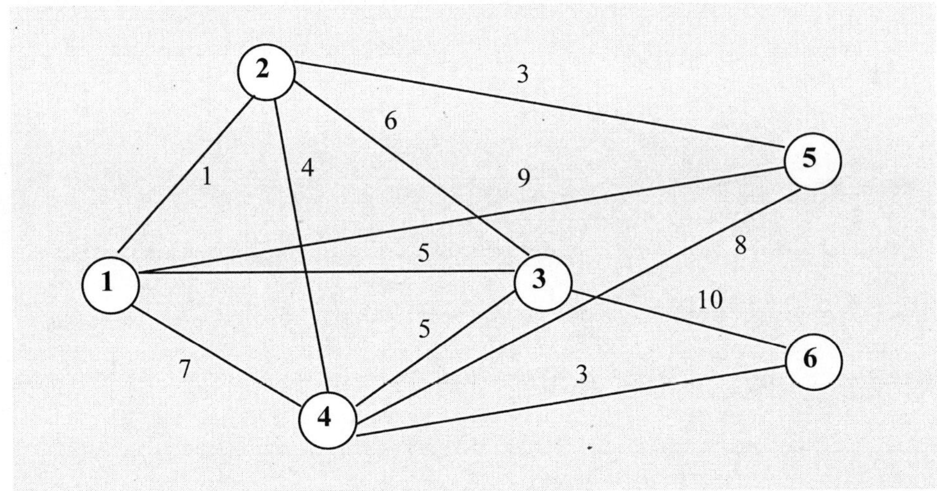

20.4 A sales representative for Medicure Pharmaceutical Company leaves his Mumbai, India office once a week to travel to one of five North Indian locations where he has clients. The following network shows the amount of time (in hours) it takes to travel between cities using interstate highways along each branch.

(a) Find the shortest path between Mumbai and each of the other five network cities.

(b) Assume that the network now comprises six distinct communities inside a city, and that the goal of the local transportation authority is to create a rail system that uses the least amount of track possible to connect all six areas. Each branch indicates the distance in miles between each community. Create a simple spanning tree to solve this problem.

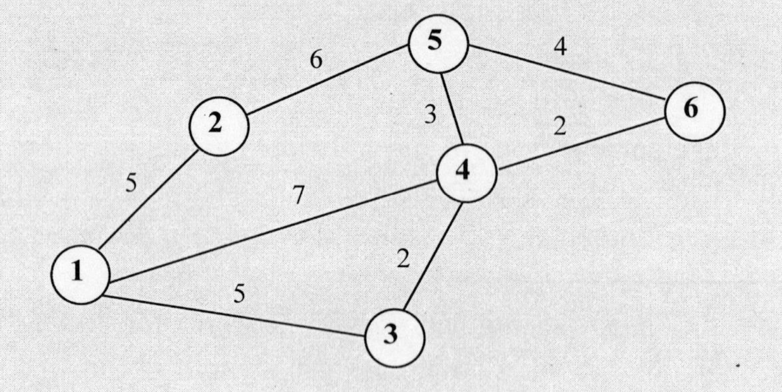

20.5 Given that the number nearest node *i* along the link between these nodes is the link capacity from node *i* to node *j*, identify the flow pattern for the network below that provides the maximum flow from the source to the sink. Node 'O' is the Source and Node 'S' is the Sink.

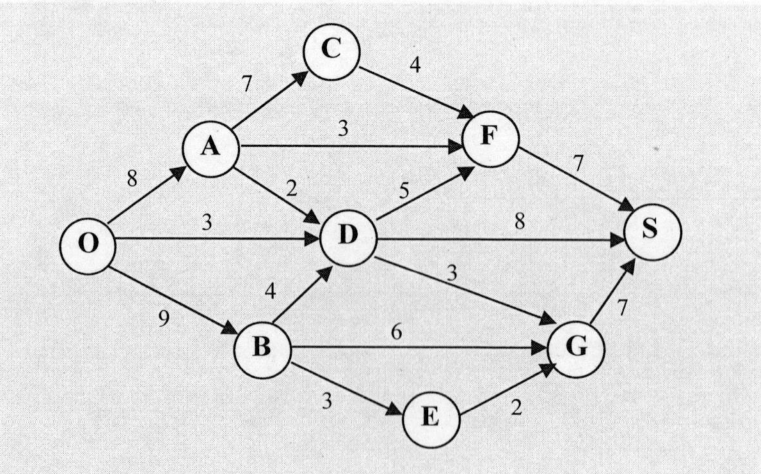

REFERENCES AND SUGGESTED READINGS

1. Ahuja, R. K., Magnanti, T. L., and Orlin, J. B. *Network Flows: Theory, Algorithms, and Applications*. Prentice Hall, 1993.
2. Ahuja, R. K., Magnanti, T. L., and Orlin, J. B. Network Flows: Theory, Algorithms, and Applications. *Mathematical Programming*, Vol. 42(1), 175-200, 1988.
3. Chang, L., and Satyam, K. Applications of the Shortest Path Algorithm in Network Optimization. *Operations Research Proceedings*, 214-220, 1992.
4. Dijkstra, E. W. A Note on Two Problems in Connexion with Graphs. *Numerische Mathematik*, Vol. 1(1), 269-271, 1959.
5. Dorfman, R., Samuelson, P. A., and Solow, R. M. *Linear Programming and Economic Analysis*. McGraw-Hill, 1958.
6. Goldberg, A. V., and Tarjan, R. E. A New Approach to the Maximum Flow Problem. *Journal of the ACM*, Vol. 35(4), 921-940, 1988.
7. Jain, S. *Introduction to Network Optimization*. McGraw-Hill, 2003.
8. Kruskal, J. B. On the Shortest Spanning Subtree of a Graph and the Traveling Salesman Problem. *Proceedings of the American Mathemati*
9.
10. *cal Society*, Vol. 7(1), 48-50, 1956.
11. Snyder, L. V. *Introduction to Operations Research Models and Methods*. Wiley, 2012.
12. Taha, H. A. *Operations Research: An Introduction*, 10th Edition, Pearson Education, 2017.
13. Winston, W. L. *Operations Research: Applications and Algorithms*, 4th Edition, Thomson Brooks/Cole, 2004.

CO AND PO ATTAINMENT TABLE

Course outcomes (COs) for this course can be mapped with the programme outcomes (POs) after the completion of the course and a correlation can be made for the attainment of POs to analyze the gap. After proper analysis of the gap in the attainment of POs necessary measures can be taken to overcome the gaps.

Course Outcomes	Attainment of Programme Outcomes *(1- Weak Correlation; 2- Medium correlation; 3- Strong Correlation)*											
	PO -1	PO -2	PO -3	PO -4	PO -5	PO -6	PO -7	PO -8	PO -9	PO -10	PO -11	PO -12
CO-1												
CO-2												
CO-3												
CO-4												
CO-5												
CO-6												

The data filled in the above table can be used for gap analysis.

INDEX